FRITZ LANG

PATRICK McGILLIGAN

FRITZ LANG

THE NATURE OF THE BEAST

ST. MARTIN'S PRESS ≈ NEW YORK

for
Bertrand

FRONTISPIECE: an early self-portrait—one of Lang's few youthful drawings to survive and be reproduced widely—in the tormented mode of one of his artistic heroes, Egon Schiele.

Design by Pei Koay

Library of Congress Cataloging-in-Publication Data

McGilligan, Patrick.
    Fritz Lang : the nature of the beast / by Patrick McGilligan.
       p.   cm.
    ISBN 0-312-13247-6
    1. Lang, Fritz, 1890–1976. 2. Motion picture producers and directors—United States—Biography.   I. Title.
PN1998.3.L36M38   1997
791.43'0233'092—dc20   96-30622
[B]   CIP

First Edition: June 1997

10 9 8 7 6 5 4 3 2 1

C O N T E N T S

My private life has nothing to do with my films.

— FRITZ LANG

A C K N O W L E D G M E N T S

GRATEFUL ACKNOWLEDGMENT IS MADE TO THE FOLLOWING
PUBLISHERS FOR REPRINTED MATERIAL:

Bertolt Brecht Journals 1934–1935 quoted with permission of the publisher, Routledge, Chapman & Hall.

Mathew Bernstein's *Walter Wanger: Hollywood Independent* quoted courtesy of the University of California Press.

Jonathan Rosenbaum's *Placing Movies: The Practice of Film Criticism* quoted courtesy of the University of California Press.

GRATEFUL ACKNOWLEDGMENT IS MADE TO THE FOLLOWING INDIVIDUALS
AND ORGANIZATIONS FOR PREVIOUSLY UNPUBLISHED MATERIAL:

Erich Kettelhut's *Memoirs*, an unpublished manuscript, quoted courtesy of the Stiftung Deutsche Kinemathek, Berlin.

Curt Siodmak's reminiscences quoted with permission from his unpublished *Ruminations*.

Marlene Dietrich's correspondence quoted courtesy of the Marlene Dietrich Collection at the Stiftung Deutsche Kinemathek, Berlin.

Kay Francis's diaries quoted with permission of Wesleyan Cinema Archive, Wesleyan University.

The Joan Bennett, Jackie Cooper, Joan Fontaine, Gene and Marjorie Fowler, Anna Lee, Viveca Lindfors, and Joseph Ruttenberg oral histories quoted courtesy of the Oral History Project, DeGolyes Library, Southern Methodist University.

The Martha Feuchtwanger and Albert Maltz oral histories quoted courtesy of the University of California at Los Angeles.

The Gene and Marjorie Fowler and Hans Salter oral history interviews from the Academy of Motion Picture Arts and Sciences quoted with permission of Barbara Hall; Oral History Program.

Paul Kuttner's reminiscence of Lang quoted with his permission.

Leo Laitin's interview with Marlene Dietrich quoted with his permission.

SPECIAL ACKNOWLEDGMENT IS MADE TO THE FOLLOWING INDIVIDUALS
AND ORGANIZATIONS FOR THE USE OR LOAN OF ILLUSTRATIONS:

Academy of Motion Picture Arts and Sciences, Archive Photos, John Baxter, Steven Bach, Eddie Brandt's Saturday Matinee, British Film Institute Collector's Bookstore, Collector's Originals, Alan Dein, Gene Fowler Jr., Kurt Weill Foundation for Music, London Museum of Jewish Life, Photofest, John Pommer, Silvia Richards, Dr. Friedrich Steinbach, Stiftung Deutsche Kinemathek, Kevin Thomas, USC Cinema-Television Library and Archives of the Performing Arts, Howard Vernon, and the Wisconsin Center for Film and Theater Research.

The photograph of Fritz Lang's grave is by Alison Morley.

P R O L O G U E

The end of genius is sometimes spectacular: a bomb's explosion, a madman's gibbering, an orgasmic suicide before a sell-out audience. Sometimes—more often, to be sure—it is lonely and poignant, as with most ordinary human beings.

Fritz Lang, who had lived a long, colorful, and combative life, was nearing the end. He knew it. The Last Dinosaur spent more and more time in bed as his health waned. His weight continued to slip away, though his journal recorded the same persistent diet that had sustained him for most of his time on earth—pills, martinis, eggs for breakfast, steak, or a Viennese specialty for supper, with something rich and chocolaty for dessert.

Call girls visited, but few peers or friends. Few of his contemporaries were left. He never had many real, close friends anyway. And *no* peers, he might add with a laugh.

Irony of ironies, the man with the monocle was virtually blind. He was one of the cinema's greatest visionaries, this director who conjured a mythic world in *Die Nibelungen* and created a fantastical future in *Metropolis*. His Dr. Mabuse was the emblematic madman of Hitler's Germany. In *M* he explored the depths of human depravity. After rejecting a Faustian pact with Joseph Goebbels—if it really happened that way—he came to Hollywood, where he found a second life exploring the depths of America, and his own inner demons, in masterly films like *Fury, You Only Live Once, The Woman in the Window, Scarlet Street,* and *The Big Heat.*

On good days the retired film director got up and moved about, making his way around the house by his fingertips. Youthful acolytes who came calling, bearing their tape recorders, might not even realize the old man could barely see, for he met them at the door with a firm handshake and escorted them into the invariably darkened living room. Lang maintained his pride and theatricality for visitors. He was "elegant" and "courtly," people said afterward—genteel words used by many to describe the film director in his twilight years. Elegant and courtly, though the director's behavior on the set had reminded many who worked with him in his prime of Adolf Hitler himself. Though he had a history—long, and well known—of sadistic behavior. Though he had been party, perhaps, to the deaths of one or two people, years ago.

Eisenstein, Buñuel, Hitchcock, and others, the new filmmaking generation of Truffaut and Godard—all lionized him, emulated him, stole from him. The director's career spanned fifty years, from the early silent era to the French nouvelle vague. A handful of his titles had become acknowledged as classics, their prints held in museum collections. But Fritz Lang guided his last motion picture in 1960, and for the last sixteen years he had lived like a ghost in his Summit Ridge house, on a hill high above Hollywood.

Lang liked to sit in the living room of his home in his favorite chair, an inch or two away from the television set, holding up to the screen a enlarging magnifying glass—a parody of the famous monocle. One eye was black-patched at the end; the other, though almost worthless, peered through the enlarging lens at the screen. In the early 1970s, Lang was watching the same thing on television as everybody else in the United States. He watched Watergate unfold, cursing Nixon. He liked to pass the time watching the situation comedies, the cornpone "Green Acres" or, later on in time, the saucier "The Mary Tyler Moore Show." Born in Vienna, a German citizen at his professional height, in the end Lang wanted nothing more than to be an American.

Lang always kept his journal close at hand; his beloved wooden monkey sitting next to him. A clock ticked somewhere in the house. The only other regular presence in the house was an enigmatic woman who might or might not be the director's wife. Whenever Lang heard her, scraping a pan in the kitchen, he shrieked that she was interrupting his concentration. When he felt like it, he carried on a conversation with the monkey. He kept meticulous notes about his daily life in his journal, though no longer did he write down ideas, as once he had done obsessively, for his next project: Ein Film von Fritz Lang.

Retirement had rewarded him with ample time to reflect. The director had time to reflect on the roller-coaster ups and downs of his life and career, to ponder his errors, to repent for his sins. Lang was, above all, a perfectionist, ruthless toward himself as well as his films. Musing on his mistakes, he, a lapsed Catholic, couldn't exclude the possibility that there might be a heaven and a God after all. That for him, as for Liliom—a character in one of his lesser-known movies—there might come a reckoning.

At rest in his favorite chair, his pencil poised, with the monkey observing silently, Fritz Lang's mind would drift. He might doze off, then suddenly be aroused by a tremor from the wellspring of memory: an image from long ago that could bring an almost involuntary half-smile to features carved like a monument. An incident of great importance—or perhaps of no importance—might be dredged up from memory, producing an insight so unexpected and crystal-clear that the Meister would blink momentarily in astonishment and forget to write down what he had just remembered.

VIENNA

Fritz Lang lived his life—and cultivated his legend—with the glinted eyes of a maniac.

He was determined to carry his secrets to the grave. The true story of his life, he believed, was nobody's business. It was irrelevant, according to his point of view. Irrelevant to his vast audience of moviegoers, though they might be fascinated by the bigger-than-life figure who directed with such mesmerizing force some fifty motion pictures over the span of forty-five years. It was irrelevant to a behind-the-scenes chronicle of the great and near-great films, and especially to those that were not all that great.

Though he might offer up tidbits of his life story, and enhance biographical interviews with personal detail, it was all part of his conscious myth-making. Understanding early that cunning publicity could nurture his career, Lang cultivated and controlled—literally blue-penciled—his own self-mythology. One thing the director feared was genuine reportage, or biography. It would turn him into a hunted man—the fated victim, as in one of his suspense stories. Biography would kill the mystique.

Journalists or acquaintances who inquired into the film director's life, into the twists of fate that dictated the wandering path of his career, into the tales of famous and obscure women who figured in dramatic interludes in his life, or into the machinations of a particularly troubled production, might receive clever fiction or convenient lies, a stony look or a brusque invitation to leave. They might even receive a helping of truth. It depended.

Lang could be liberal with his favorite anecdotes, tirelessly repeated, polished to a glow. The story of how he fled Goebbels and Nazi Germany in 1933 is famous because the director told it so many times. It was his crowning concoction, replete with details a novelist would relish: an office with swastika decor, the hands of an enormous clock ticking toward a fateful hour, the director's pockets sewn with escape money. Lang dodged the Nazi taint in much the same way he would later evade a Communist one in America, with a well-knit story that could not easily be dissected or disproved.

Usually, though, he was stingy with the facts of his life. It was Lang himself who dictated and edited the brief autobiographical essay (some 2,600 words— six pages of text, as set against more than four hundred pages of appreciative gloss) in what has been widely regarded as the definitive book about the director, Lotte Eisner's *Fritz Lang*, first published in 1976. Lang emphatically told his old friend Eisner, with whom he had been acquainted since the late 1920s, "My private life has nothing to do with my films." He uttered the same sentiment in interviews more than once.

Did Herr Lang realize that mountains of contradictory records and sources would survive him: journals, home movies, immigration papers and interrogation files, studio and government archives, even the memories of trustworthy friends and acquaintances? That not all of his associates could be trusted to disremember, or remain discreet?

Did Herr Lang realize—was it a private joke?—that his films themselves offered a kind of autobiography, revealing perhaps more than he intended of his own life story? That, in fact, his films had a great deal to do with his private life?

Or was the subconscious—that inner cacophony of voices that in his best-known films always cried out to be heard, triggering crime and entreating punishment—working a dark magic on Fritz Lang all along?

Certainly life began auspiciously for Fritz Lang, born to favorable circumstances in the Golden Autumn of Vienna, Austria—the last decade before the nineteenth century was rolled away to make way for the new.

Austria, under the benevolent and seemingly interminable reign of "der alte Herr," Franz Josef, emperor from 1848 to 1916, was enjoying an era of unprecedented confidence and revitalization; tolerance and liberalism in politics; a renaissance of the arts and sciences that established the names of Klimt, Schnitzler, Mahler, and Freud.

Vienna, the pulse and soul of the nation, grew and prospered. The capital, in Lang's memory, was like "a confectionery city in a fairy-tale time," whose lucky citizens lived untroubled by what was happening in the world beyond its limits. In 1890, it was one of the world's five largest cities, with a mushrooming population that included not only native Austrians but immigrants and intellectuals from all over eastern Europe and the rest of the world. No city was more cosmopolitan. No city offered greater cultural riches, or was more splendid to behold.

The architecture of the city towered in Lang's psychology. The director's unique visual style, especially in his epic silent films, was nurtured by his boyhood experience of dwelling in the shadow of gargantuan statues and massive stairwells, steepled churches and huge public buildings. The baroque of the old Kaiserstadt, with its exaggeration of detail, insinuated itself into many Lang films. The characteristic shots from high places, the extreme upward-slanting low angles, the lingering emphasis on the size and structure of massive buildings, the people dwarfed by walls or doors—these were a legacy that was distinctly Viennese.

The dome and spire of the St. Stephansdom, the magnificent imperial palace known as the Hofburg, the imposing cluster that included the Opernhaus, the Rathaus, the Burgtheater, the Universität, and the Parlament—these and other civic edifices were within walking distance of the house where the future film director, Friedrich Christian Anton Lang, was born on December 5, 1890.

His parents, Anton and Paula Schlesinger Lang, at that time lived on the narrow lane of Schönlaterngasse in the Innere Stadt, or First District, inside the Ringstrasse, the wide beltway around the inner city.

The shadow cast by Vienna's architecture is rendered all the more germane to Fritz Lang's life story by that of his father. Anton Lang was thirty years old when his son was born, and city records attest that he was a Baumeister and part owner of Honus and Lang, a prominent construction enterprise located in a three-story building along the east side of the imperial park, the Augarten.

In latter-day books and articles about his world-famous son, Anton Lang is usually described as an architect. In fact, *Baumeister,* a German word often confused and translated as "architect" in English and French, means more precisely that Lang's father was a builder or executor of architectural plans. He had the additional honorific, in city archives, of *Stadtbaumeister,* which simply meant that he was licensed to appear as a project manager before Vienna municipal boards.

Architects were college-educated; they were designers, not merely contractors. They moved in higher social circles. Fritz Lang always described his father as an architect in interviews; once, drafting a press release eventually published under his byline in the United States, he even tried "famous architect." The fancier word put a gloss on his father's occupation, just as Lang would also stretch the truth when it came to his own fleeting studies in architecture, claiming, for publicity's sake, to have studied for "several years in the best architectural schools."*

Perhaps "architect" was convenient terminology, the natural choice of a son proud of his father's profession and innocently overstating his expertise. Or perhaps it was better for a director to boast the genes of an architect than a builder—even if Lang, like his father, was only occasionally, to his eternal frustration, the supreme architect, and more often the master builder orchestrating the plans of others.

Honus and Lang had previously been known as Endl and Honus. Adolf Endl and Josef Honus had made a fortune during the time of optimism and construction known as the Gründerzeit, when Vienna was expanded and reorganized, and the Ringstrasse was inaugurated. Endl and Honus did not construct any of the more renowned buildings; they were builders of lesser distinction, and in general restricted to the lucrative trade of erecting the offices and residences for the well-to-do that proliferated around the Ring. These were typically four-to-six-story block dwellings, with offices and management on the first floor, residences and tenants occupying the floors above. Their palatial faces and interior courts proclaimed their grandeur.

The bustling company had several sidelines, including, in the late 1880s, the construction and operation of the Wiener Centralbad, or Vienna Central Baths. The luxurious Wiener Centralbad was situated on valuable real estate close to the St. Stephansdom and the Stadtpark, behind the baroque facade

---

*Both exaggerations are quoted from versions of publicity releases on deposit among Lang's papers at the University of Southern California–Los Angeles. In the final published draft of the article in question ("Famed Director Fritz Lang Poses the Question: Ambitious to Direct?"), "famous" was changed to "well-known," and the "several years in the best architectural schools" became "a year in the best architectural school." That was less of a gloss, if still a convenient exaggeration.

of an everyday apartment block which Endl and Honus had constructed in 1880. The only public baths in the center of town, the Wiener Centralbad catered to the business community, with cold-water pools inside pillared halls for both men and women, a steam room, mud baths, hydrotherapy, electro-therapy, and massages.

The design offered rooms and halls "as Islamic as Meister Endl could build them," according to a 1976 article in the magazine *Wien Aktuell.* "Pompeian" murals, a marble staircase, changing rooms decorated in the Moorish style, walls covered with Majolica tiles: The Oriental influence manifest in Fritz Lang's films was not only common in Austro-Hungarian architecture, but rooted in his family's personal history.

Anton Lang appears to have begun an apprenticeship with Endl and Honus in his late teens, learning to trace architectural plans. He worked his way up in the firm and was already married, in 1887, when he visited En-gland to select the ceramic tiles for the interior of the Wiener Centralbad. While touring British potteries and bathhouses, he learned that Adolf Endl had died suddenly at age forty; cutting his trip short, Anton Lang returned to Vienna.

Endl's untimely death precipitated a dramatic change in professional status for Fritz Lang's father. The year of Fritz Lang's birth, 1890, also saw Anton Lang's ascendancy; in that year, Endl and Honus was reincorporated as Honus and Lang. How a mere employee, a one-time draftsman, came so suddenly to share equal ownership in this substantial firm, however, is a central piece of the family jigsaw puzzle. Only one person knew for sure how this came to be; only one person could have supplied the whole explanation—Anton's mother, Johanna Lang. She inherited half the business, and turned it over to her only son.

How did Johanna Lang, who hailed from a humble background, come into this inheritance? Like many of the women central to a Lang film, Anton Lang's mother was a beautiful woman, mysterious, almost ruthlessly determined to accomplish her goals in life—a trait, relatives always said, Fritz Lang inherited from her.

Johanna Lang was born in 1839 in Sichelbach, a village in southern Moravia, then a Habsburg province approximately ninety miles northwest of Vienna near the Austrian border. Today this area is part of the Czech Republic.

Lotte Eisner wrote that Lang told her his paternal grandmother grew up in the country, came to Vienna as a young girl, and became housekeeper of a patrician Viennese family. There Johanna Lang fell in love with the son of the house, and found herself pregnant. Born and raised a Catholic (the first inkling of the Catholicism deeply ingrained in Lang's life), she had landed in a sinful, scandalous predicament. "Class barriers in those days were as rigid as castes in India," explained Eisner. But things worked out in the end: "She married an honest man who gave her child his name," Eisner wrote.

This synopsized account, retold by Eisner, made a good story, and Lang himself must have relished the India touch (doubtless he suggested it). How-ever, no records survive to prove Lang's case, none that give any indication of Johanna Lang's lineage, nor point to the identity of the patrician family—

which didn't have to be very patrician really, since many middle-class house-holds could afford the modest expense of servants.

There is, in fact, no documented evidence of the true identity of Anton Lang's natural father. Only this can be substantiated from Viennese archives: the child of Johanna Lang was born August 1, 1860, in the maternity ward of a foundling's home in what was then the western suburb Alservorstadt (today located more or less downtown). Georges Sturm, a European specialist on Fritz Lang, has performed exhaustive detective work on the family tree, and his research confirms that on the day of the birth the nuns crossed the Alserstrasse and had the infant baptized by a parish priest. The godfather was the sacristan, the father's name unspecified. The birth register plainly listed Anton Lang as an "illegitimate child."

Johanna Lang never named the father, and it appears that Anton himself did not know his identity—a theme repeated almost by chance in Fritz Lang's 1955 film *Moonfleet*, in which a wistful boy searches for his mother's long-lost "friend," while never quite realizing that the gentleman-smuggler watching over him is his wayward father. People familiar with the director's work will recognize the illicit love affair, illegitimacy, and the "doubling" of identity as recurrent plot situations that would become almost obsessional in his films. Lang liked to glamorize his own illegitimate family history right down to the happy ending in which an "honest man" comes to the rescue as father to the child.

Obviously a resourceful figure, Johanna Lang did set out to marry and le-gitimize her child. According to Dr. Friedrich Steinbach, a cousin of Lang's who visited the family at intervals as a young boy in the early 1900s, Johanna Lang's first marriage was to a member of the Endl family associated with the building firm. He may have been the "honest man" referred to by Lang; he may even have been the young man who impregnated Johanna Lang. One thing is certain: he did *not* give his name to the child.

Nor is there any documented proof of a Lang-Endl marriage. Yet Steinbach insisted on this point in an interview, as he equally insisted that Anton Lang did not like or respect his first "stepfather"—a pattern destined to be repeated by his own son. The first marriage ended in Endl's death when Anton Lang was still a youth, according to Steinbach, and Johanna set out to marry a second time. The second marriage, Johanna Lang's only documented marriage, was to a schoolteacher named Karl Schott, from the Alsergrund, or Ninth District, of Vienna. This occurred when Anton Lang was already sixteen, in 1876.

It can be hypothesized, from these tangled circumstances, that when Jo-hanna Lang's first husband, an Endl, died, she inherited a partnership in Endl and Honus. Perhaps she withheld her claim during the lifetime of Adolf Endl; or, necessarily, until Anton came of age. Upon Adolf Endl's death, the mother of Anton Lang signed that inheritance over to her only child, in exchange for which Anton Lang agreed to pay her a periodic stipend for living expenses.

Anton never became an Endl or Schott in any case, and Johanna Lang conferred her own surname on the child. The "Lang," therefore, comes directly from Fritz Lang's paternal grandmother—her name and Catholicism being the first strong, lasting imprints on his identity.

Mothers are evanescent in Fritz Lang films; fathers, on the other hand, command an inordinate presence. *Metropolis*, early in the director's career, depicted a dictatorial overlord who fostered rebellion in his workers and alienation in his own son; a wise and courageous professor is a heroic father in *Hangmen Also Die*; later comes the anti-heroic swashbuckler of *Moonfleet*. When it came to father figures in his oeuvre, Lang swung from pitiless characterization to idealized sentiment, reflecting his own inability on some subconscious level to come to satisfactory terms with his own father, the "architect" Anton Lang.

In real life, Lang's father was commercially astute and fantastically hardworking, and under his aegis the construction business flourished. A tall man, the elder Lang was always impeccably dressed, usually sporting a mustache or goatee. He was aloof and strict with his children, however, and showed little interest in anything other than his work—certainly not in art or politics. Growing up, the more aesthetically minded son grew to disapprove of his father, for whom money was all-important. The disapproval grew into rebellion, settled into a cold-hearted dislike.

Fritz Lang's mind was made up on the subject of his father for a long time. It is ironic that his father's elusive connection to Honus and Endl provided the son with a solid footing in the world, considering that, later in life, the director made a point of discouraging anyone with family ties from trying to use him to get on the inside track in motion pictures. It is especially interesting considering the scorn the director heaped on the producers with powerful relatives whom he encountered in both Berlin and Hollywood.

Lang, owing in large part to his hostility to Anton Lang, was left without much feeling for family. And because of his father's apparent illegitimacy, he could easily discount Anton's influence while emphasizing, in loving tones, the roles of his mother and grandmother. These were the only two family members whom Lang professed to adore.

Toward the close of his richly eventful life, however, when Lang's brooding grew morose, he had to admit that there must have been something good, strong, and capable in Anton Lang, for things to have turned out so well for his son.

Children, education, and religion were a mother's business. Lang's mother, Paula Schlesinger Lang, was the woman who nurtured and shaped the boy. Conversing with friends, Lang always placed his mother on a pedestal. The undying reverence he felt for her colored his attitude toward the women in his private life—they could never mother him enough—as well as toward the actresses and female characters who populated his films.

Paula was born Pauline Schlesinger on July 26, 1864, on the outskirts of Brno, the provincial capital of Moravia, a grim industrial city near where Napoleon had won the battle of Austerlitz. Brno was known for its textiles, metallurgical industries, and close commercial ties to Vienna. Part of the Habsburg Empire, the city was directly linked by rail to Vienna. Today it is in the Czech Republic.

Visiting Paris for the premiere of *Die Nibelungen* in 1925, Lang gave an interview in which he referred to himself as the grandson of a modest landowner "who worked the land himself" in a valley along the river Kamp. This appears to be more romanticization, salt-of-the-earth variety. In fact, Paula's father was a Fabrikant, or factory owner, most likely of a mill for spinning and weaving wool. Her family was Jewish.

Pauline, by early 1883, was residing in Vienna in the Leopoldstadt, or Second District, a section of Vienna overwhelmingly comprised of Jewish immigrants and families, especially those with connections to the thriving garment and textile industry. Attracted, like generations before her, by the excitement and opportunity of the city, Pauline was part of an influx of Jews during the latter half of the nineteenth century that changed the balance of Vienna's population and played a key role in the rise of the middle class. Persecuted in previous generations, cyclically ostracized, Vienna's Jews had proved stubborn adherents of the city, and had recently prospered under an era of emancipation and reform.

Pauline lived in an apartment building that was listed in municipal files as the property of her father, Jakob Schlesinger, and she worked at a clothing store in the Mariahilf, or Sixth District, which her father owned and operated as well. It seems likely that Pauline's father had real estate dealings with Endl and Honus that brought her into contact with Anton Lang. From 1880 on, Anton lived near Pauline Schlesinger at Obere Augartenstrasse 64, on the southern edge of the Augarten in the Leopoldstadt. Josef Honus, Anton Lang's employer, lived in the same building.

Pauline Schlesinger, not quite nineteen and Anton Lang, her senior by nearly five years, were married in Vienna on May 22, 1883. Indications are that Pauline received a substantial dowry, and was not only financially independent, but perhaps wealthier than her new husband. After Anton Lang was accepted into the firm as a partner in 1890, Paula Lang—changed from Pauline, part of her social integration—acquired greater-than-equal status. She was actually listed as "Owner," with Anton Lang as "Manager," once Josef Honus had retired in 1900. The concern was renamed A. Lang & Co.

Curiously, the Lang-Schlesinger marriage was formalized by a civil ceremony. Although "mixed" marriages between Catholics and Jews were forbidden by law, the common custom was for Vienna's Jews to convert to Catholicism, or for non-Jews to declare themselves without religious faith. Yet Anton Lang, though himself baptized and raised a Catholic, declared himself without religious denomination, while Paula Schlesinger was listed in the records—meticulous city records the Nazis would later peruse—as mosaisch, or Jewish.

Anti-Semitism was on the rise in Vienna. Assimilation was important, and it may be that Paula Schlesinger felt socially obliged to convert. Vienna's long-standing preoccupation with Catholicism as well as "Germanness" would dramatically mark the Lang family.

This was a family that displayed obvious equivocation about religion. Before their marriage, Pauline Schlesinger and Anton Lang made a special request for dispensation for the religious ceremony, a request rejected by authorities. Seventeen years elapsed before Lang's parents arranged a "double conversion" to Catholicism and a second, religious ceremony in August of 1900, embracing Catholic precepts. This occasion, which necessitated a special license, was orchestrated not in Vienna, but over one hundred miles to the west, at Ort am Traunsee, near Salzburg, where the Langs had a vacation villa. Church records show that Lang's mother was baptized, while Anton Lang was formally readmitted "to the breast of the Holy Catholic Church."

Fritz Lang was almost ten years old by 1900, and up to that time had been diligently raised a Catholic by his Jewish mother. He himself had been baptized on a Sunday less than a month after birth, in the baptismal font of the parish Schottenkirche, or the Scots Monastery, in the Innere Stadt. The Langs had set up house around the corner from the Schottenkirche on Schenkenstrasse, the road that leads to the Burgtheater.

The two witnesses were Christian Cabos, Fritz Lang's godfather, a KuK Hoflieferant,* or purveyor to the royal court, associated with a biscuit company that supplied the imperial household; and Johanna Lang's then-husband Karl Schott. While it was unusual that the parents of the baptized child were not Catholics in good standing, this irregularity was addressed by a clause added to the baptismal affidavit to the effect that the non-Catholic mother and father pledged to raise the boy in the Catholic faith. So they did—"Catholic and very puritanical," in Lang's words.

Ironically, according to Friedrich Steinbach, it was Lang's mother, the convert, who took responsibility for indoctrinating her son in the catechism and rituals, while Lang's father, busy with work and more ambivalent about religion, skipped Mass on Sundays and acted almost heretically upon occasion. Steinbach told this anecdote: As a young boy, Steinbach was standing on the balcony of the Lang summer home in Gars am Kamp with Anton Lang, who was his godfather as well as his uncle. A storm was brewing. Thunder rang out, lightning flashed across the sky. Suddenly, Anton Lang opened his arms to the heavens, and, to his horror, cried out, "Hit me! Hit me now! Send a bolt for me!" Then, turning to the boy, who cowered before such blasphemy, Anton Lang asked with a malicious grin, "Do you really believe everything they tell you?"

Young Fritz Lang was probably present at the "double conversion" in 1900, and likely blocked it out of his memory. Georges Sturm made an interesting comparison between that family incident and a scene in *Secret Beyond the Door*, a film Lang directed in America in 1947. In the film, an heiress recollects her marriage to an architect. A flashback shows the wedding taking place amid the twinkling gloom of a Mexican cathedral, four centuries old. The occasion is photographed from extreme low-to-the-ground angles, "which isn't justified in the continuity of the other shots in the sequence, unless it is seen, for example, by a child," in Sturm's words.

Fritz Lang's older brother, more intriguingly, would have been present for the occasion—the brother Lang never acknowledged in public. Adolf Lang (named in honor of Adolf Endl?) was born on March 19, 1884, less than a year after the marriage of Paula and Anton Lang. A full six years older than Fritz, Dolf (as he was called) was a few inches shorter than his brother, who grew to five feet eleven. With his dark-blond hair, Dolf resembled his father,

---

*KuK, meaning *kaiserlich und königlich* (imperial and royal), referred to the dual monarchy of Austro-Hungary.

while Fritz Lang, with his deep-brown hair, gray eyes, long face, straight nose and pointed chin, took after Paula. Dolf's character and personality were more like his father's, too. He took no interest in artistic pursuits, and in time became a staid businessman like his father—a bank manager; in fact, utterly middle class.

Dolf, the oldest boy carrying the family surname, ought to have been the favored son, but the opposite was true. Dolf was disadvantaged within the family, treated almost as a leper. The reason, as Steinbach remembered—and Austrian military records confirm—must have carried with it a devastating personal humiliation. Adolf Lang had a rampant psoriasis that resulted in scabs and rashes all over his body. When guests came to call, Dolf was actually hidden away in the Lang household, like the boy whose father cannot abide him, who is closeted in one of the mansion's many rooms in *Secret Beyond the Door*. The ugly, embarrassing Dolf was hidden away, while the handsome Fritz—with his intelligent face, his shock of tawny hair, his creamy complexion—was paraded in front of visitors, his ego petted and pampered.

The brothers, as a result, had a terrible relationship, a lifelong violent antipathy to each other. It wounded their mother, Paula Lang, even though she helped spur their lopsided rivalry. Fritz Lang learned superiority and domination, even over his older brother, from adolescence. Throughout adulthood the brothers communicated with each other only when absolutely necessary. Not once, when expounding on his past in the dozens upon dozens of published interviews he gave, did the film director ever mention his older brother. Even Lotte Eisner, in her authorized book about Lang, presents the man she knew as well as anyone as an "only child."

There is a surprising number of brothers represented in Lang's films. To name but a few, the outlaw brothers James in *The Return of Frank James*; the dichotomous brothers of *Western Union* (their blood bond a secret until the end); the mildly sparring upper-crust brothers of *Man Hunt*; the hateful and complicit brothers of *House by the River*; the cutthroat siblings of *Der Tiger von Eschnapur* and *Das indische Grabmal*.

The brother-characters were sometimes Lang's contribution to a scenario, more often not. But he could seize on such characters in a film's story line and make them vivid. In life as in imagination, he understood weak and bothersome brothers.

The Lang family lived a "thoroughly bourgeois" existence, according to the director, whose childhood (if not his brother Dolf's) was blessed by comfort and indulgence. Vienna might be a cold and drab, not to mention inhospitable, place to some, but Fritz Lang led a boyhood of modest privilege, and his earliest memories of the place would be almost paradisical.

The Langs moved several times before settling down, in November of 1900, in a stone fortress at Zeltgasse 1, in the Josefstadt, or Eighth District. The family occupied the first floor of a massive five-story, U-shaped building, which was surrounded on three sides by narrow streets and opened onto a cramped square. It was situated near the Piaristen Church, short blocks from the Josefstadt-Theater and a place that must have loomed in the psyche of a boy destined to make his mark as a crime-story filmmaker—the Landesgericht, or Criminal Court Building.

Lang remembered this as a period of "great, decisive change" in Vienna. Miraculous twentieth-century technology, beginning to transform daily life, exerted a profound effect on the future director. The fantastical was made real before his very eyes. The marvels Lang would predict in his career—the television devices, criminal, police, and spy gadgets, rocket-ship flight—were a logical outgrowth of the fact that his boyhood was a time of unprecedented scientific and technical revolution.

The Fiaker were typically Viennese, and Lang fondly remembered these two-horse open carriages on springs, their wheels covered with India rubber. The name applied to the drivers too, famous for their facility with whip and tongue, as well as the vehicle. The Fiaker were drawn by two well-fed horses trotting in harness. Only the "very rich," in Lang's words, could afford to ride in the luxurious carriages, yet he was able to ride the Fiaker often enough to learn to recite the Fiakerlieder, the rollicking folk songs sung by the coachmen and popularized by Alexander Girardi, an irreverent Viennese actor of the turn of the century.

The Fiaker gave way to electric rails and horseless vehicles. Lang remembered, from his boyhood, the city streetcars pulled by two horses. When he was old enough to go to Volksschule on Josefstädterstrasse, several blocks away, he had to ride the city transport up a hill, and a third horse had to be harnessed to the streetcar in front of the other two. The little boy was sometimes permitted to sit up front on the coach box.

Lang remembered how the lantern igniters disappeared as the gas lanterns were replaced by electric ones. He remembered his father's phonograph "as his most modern acquisition," and a time when all the music was recorded and played on metal cylinders. He remembered when his father took him out to the suburb of Breitenfurt to see a wagon that moved without horses—the first automobile; and how the proud Fiaker were forced gradually to defer to automobiles on the chestnut-tree-lined boulevards of the city.

The family enjoyed distinctly Viennese activities, such as the promenade past elegant shop windows in the late afternoon. Lang remembered the men in their frock coats and toppers, the military clicking of heels, the corseted women with furs and boatlike hats. Idly gazing into shop windows—kicking one in, in *Rancho Notorious*—became ritual behavior in Lang's films. Two of his finest Hollywood dramas, *The Woman in the Window* and *Scarlet Street*, begin, with deceptive innocence, with window-shopping.

There were annual parades and pageants tied to the changing calendar, and regular trips to the scenic parks and formal gardens; best of all were the family outings to the Prater, the huge amusement park on the east fringe of the city. Naturally the Prater was the boy's favorite haunt, his adventure through the looking glass. The park boasted the famous giant Prater wheel, a carousel, amusement booths, a penny arcade, a shooting gallery, test-your-strength machines, a freak show, the Wiener Watschenmann ("a big leather mannequin" that looked "like a cross between a gorilla and an antediluvian Cro-Magnon man," according to Lang's sometimes uncanny memory, "dolled up in silken knee breeches and a green hunting jacket"); and simple open-air restaurants with female orchestras.

Unlike many of the places the boy visited with his family, the Prater was a democratic crossroads, egalitarian in its appeal. The gentry mixed with servants and factory workers, the privates of the Viennese house regiment, swells, hustlers, and peasant girls. ("Their faces are fresh and radiant and their breasts full and inviting under embroidered blouses," Lang wrote of the peasant girls in one of his unproduced scripts. "They all carry the indispensable fat umbrella and wear gaudy-colored, wide-skirted native costumes, hair tucked in under big fringed kerchiefs.") When Ferenc Molnár's *Liliom* was translated from Hungarian into German, the setting was shifted from Budapest's amusement park to Vienna's Prater. Later on, when Lang fled to Paris and was handed the screen adaptation of *Liliom*, some people thought it was a case of "director miscasting," yet he was quite at home commemorating the Prater.

Viennese theater was at a historical peak of creativity. The Hofburgtheater was probably the leading playhouse in the German-speaking world, while the Theater in der Josefstadt, near Lang's home, was run by a gifted impresario from Budapest, Josef Jarno, who alternated French farces, for audience appeal, with productions of two forerunners of modern expressionism, Strindberg and Wedekind. (In the 1920s, this theater would be taken over by Max Reinhardt and his celebrated ensemble.)

It must have been Paula Lang who prompted regular excursions to these and other legitimate theaters. "My parents went twice a month to see a play, and then they discussed it with friends," Lang once recalled. "It was an event." Sometimes the boy was permitted to accompany his parents; later in time, Lang attended many plays on his own and with school friends. He remembered frequenting the Volkstheater, where the plays of Anzengruber and Grillparzer were performed, and especially the Raimund-Theater, which specialized in fairy tales by leading dramatists.

He would never forget Girardi in Ferdinand Raimund's *Der Bauer als Millionär (The Farmer As Millionaire)*, in a scene where Youth takes its leave of him. The character of Youth was played by a "full-breasted soubrette," in Lang's words, and Girardi, without benefit of makeup or special effects, made a magical metamorphosis into an old man in full view of the audience. The persistent refrain of many typically Viennese plays was death and destiny. From his earliest films, notably in 1921's *Der müde Tod*, with Bernhard Goetzke impersonating a somber, weary Death, the director explored kindred terrain.

Perhaps the theater that gave him the most pleasure also exerted the greatest influence—the fantastical Kratky-Baschik Zaubertheater in the Prater. Hardly Vienna's most eminent, it was Lang's favorite as a boy. Ghosts, goblins, witches, gnomes, and fairies pranced across the stage of this little theater in the park, which specialized in pyrotechnics, optical illusions, smoke, and mirrors. Lang made sure that Lotte Eisner took note of the Zaubertheater, and that she mentioned it in her book about him.

Although the Lang family patronized Vienna's theaters, they may have visited museums and attended classical concerts less religiously. Lang admitted, in one interview, an obliviousness to the Sezession, the artists' movement that broke with tradition and swept Vienna in the late 1890s and early 1900s. Although he visited museums elsewhere in Europe during his Wanderjahre, he rarely mentioned Vienna's galleries in his reminiscences, and as a youth appears to have spent little time exploring them.

He was not infatuated with still art. Although he amassed a modest private gallery in Berlin, he would leave collecting—and museum-going—behind in Hollywood. In his spare moments, according to friends and associates, it was more the director's wont to head to the Los Angeles planetarium or to Sea World. "He was an intelligent and artistic man, but he didn't collect art," said Sam Jaffe, Lang's longtime agent in Hollywood and a noted art patron of the screen colony. "I didn't see [much] art in his house, unlike [the director Josef] von Sternberg, for example, who collected pictures and paintings. I never got the idea Lang went to concerts. I never got the feeling he went to a museum."

Lang said on more than one occasion that he was also left uninspired by classical music, growing up in this city that had succored Haydn, Mozart, Beethoven, and her native Schubert. The director made a point of telling friends that he was a musical ignoramus; Lang liked to boast that as a boy he was thrown out of Realschule music class because he couldn't carry a melody and always hit the wrong notes.

One day, many years after Realschule, the director and his friend, actor Howard Vernon, were visiting London together. Lang rang for Vernon in his hotel room, but the actor did not answer right away because he was listening to a Mozart composition on the radio. Later, Vernon apologized to Lang, explaining that he was held spellbound by the music. The director reacted surprisingly, confessing, somewhat shamefacedly, that he envied Vernon's love of Mozart's music, which left him cold. "I like folk songs, but ten horses couldn't bring me to a concert or an opera," he liked to say.

Lang did love traditional folk music, the colorful, sometimes bawdy, often sentimental songs of Vienna's streets and cabarets. This was an affection he transferred to the United States, where he fervently embraced American folk songs and cowboy tunes. He couldn't recognize many pieces by Mozart, but with tremendous zest he could and would sing, at the drop of a hat, the Fiakerlieder, Heurigenlieder (wine songs), or American cowboy verses—word-perfect, even in advanced old age.

"Music is the same to me as it was to Goethe—a pleasant noise," Lang said in one interview. "I am an eye man, not an ear man." His films had to take this deficiency into account. Where the sound track, or musical accompaniment, was concerned, Lang was forced—more than was characteristic—to rely on the ideas of others. Perhaps as a consequence the director preferred sparseness, the absence of music. "Having a musical background for a love scene, for example, has always seemed like cheating to me," Lang said in one interview. This element of his sensibility added an unusual quality to his work; of his weakness, he made a strength.

The "eye man" was certainly a wide-ranging reader from early boyhood. The family owned the collected works of Jules Verne, whose books became well-thumbed—natural nourishment for the future director of *Metropolis* and *Die Frau im Mond*. Lang admitted once that he preferred the Germans who emulated Verne: Willi Gail, Kurd Lasswitz (pseudonym: Velatus), and espe-

cially Hans Dominik, whose cliché-laden works employed the Langian strategy
of impressing readers with scientific know-how within imaginary settings. As
he grew, Lang graduated to occult books and a species of literature known as
Schundliteratur, or "trash literature," one branch of which dealt with the love
life of the insane King Ludwig II of Bavaria; another of which related lurid
tales of robbers and criminals.

Lang had discovered the existence of this titillating genre one day when he
furtively visited the maid's quarters in his parent's apartment ("probably
driven by some youthful sex urge"). That visit resulted in two disappointments: ". . . that this very good-looking girl wasn't in and the heap of installments of *The Phantom Robber*, which I found on her nightstand, was a
miserable substitute for what I had hoped to find . . . and, secondly, when my
father found me reading the penny dreadfuls, he not only took them away,
but slapped my face with them several times, forehand and backhand."

This particular weekly magazine carried a regular cover illustration, often a
crude depiction of a murder or rape. Minor and major characters in Lang's
films, from *Fury* to *While the City Sleeps*, are similarly held in thrall by lowbrow
crime magazines. More than once, in his American interviews, the director
boasted that he kept up with "ze pulp." "I find much of it very dull, yes,"
Lang told a columnist in 1945, "but I find much of it interesting too."

American Westerns also captivated him. Many he read were dime novels
in crude translation, including one, Lang recalled years later, that chronicled
the exploits of the outlaw James brothers. (When Lang filmed *The Return of
Frank James*, he reportedly told Henry Fonda, "I thought the James boys were
the greatest heroes since Robin Hood—I used to cry over Jesse's death.")
Others were homegrown, from the fertile imagination of the German novelist
Karl May, author of over sixty published works.

Beloved among a generation of Germans, May did not leave his provincial
hometown in Germany to visit the faraway places he wrote about until he'd
finished some thirty novels, but his descriptive sagas of the Middle East, the
American frontier, and other distant lands made those places seem authentic
and inviting. Lang's enthusiasm for Karl May was something he claimed in
common with his wife and scenarist Thea von Harbou. Regardless of their
intellectual orientation, German-speaking people, from Adolf Hitler to Albert
Einstein, found in the author a shared touchstone. Even Einstein declared,
"My whole adolescence stood under his sign."

Karl May was Lang's ticket to the Wild West—in a sense his first escape
from Vienna. A love of the American frontier was deeply rooted in his boyhood,
and never lost its purity, or naïveté. Later on, in Hollywood, the director's
Western films would prove labors of love, even tainted as they were by the
simplistic perspective of dime novels and Karl May.

The boy's infatuation with American frontier mythology must have reached
euphoria when Buffalo Bill and his Wild West Show arrived in Vienna, during
the troupe's farewell European tour, in 1905. It was a high point, and an end
point, of Lang's childhood. Though he was nearly fifteen, he always remembered his brief glimpse of Buffalo Bill, one of his towering Western heroes,
with the awed eyes of youth.

Lang would write only two screenplays about Vienna, one being the 1951 unproduced "Scandal in Vienna," which featured a recreation of Buffalo Bill's Wild West Show. Mixing vivid recall and fancy, Lang depicted the opening of the show: the tall rider in uniform heading the colorful parade, carrying a streaming American flag, the cavalry, the Indian scouts and bareback braves, the chiefs in regalia, the trumpeter, the cowboys and cowgirls in picturesque costumes, the dancing and prancing horses, which evoked "mythical centaurs," the procession of covered wagons and prairie schooners, the remuda of horses, the settlers driving cattle.

Lang brought two of his heroes together in this 1951 scenario. *Der alte Herr* himself sits in the stands, keenly observing the show. (Perhaps Lang, as a boy, saw him there from afar.) The emperor observes the cavalcade rounding the arena. The American national anthem is struck up. Buffalo Bill enters the arena, riding a hero's white horse, "with his long white hair falling to his shoulders," wearing buckskin attire and embroidered gauntlets, carrying his Kentucky long rifle. He gallops to the center of the arena, his horse rears on hind legs, then Buffalo Bill gallantly raises his hat to greet the grandstand.

The company sings out:

> *Buffalo Bill, Buffalo Bill,*
> *Never missed and never will;*
> *Always aims and shoots to kill,*
> *And the comp'ny pays his buffalo bill.*

Another boyhood folk song Lang could recite, word for word.

There were times of his life that Lang felt wistful about, among them his boyhood years, before entering secondary school. There were seasons of the year when Lang felt the pangs of the past most strongly, the times of his favorite holidays in Vienna—especially Christmas, which in his youth was a prolonged event.

The Christmas season would coincide with his birthday, with Advent usually falling around the fifth or sixth of December. Just as his birthday celebrations concluded, the good man Nikolaus would appear with his long white beard, trailed by Grampus, the horned devil who carried a sack in which he put the bad children and carried them off to hell if they hadn't said their prayers. They were costumed friends of his father's, rewarding good behavior with bonbons, or sweets.

Christmas in Vienna, above all, meant *Christkindlmarkt*—literally, the Market of Little Jesus, a seasonal market Lang always missed in his Hollywood years as much as he missed snow. The Christkindlmarkt, in those days, took place around a beautiful square called Am Hof. Lang could rhapsodize about the rows of wooden huts featuring Christmas articles. Between the huts were passages, canopied and lit by candle and oil, "even in the worst snowstorm." There you could find all the basic Christmas provisions and household goods, unique presents, rare delicacies and precious ornaments. Lang wrote about his *Christkindlmarkt* memories, upon request once, for publication: "There were the most lovely things there: many colored ornaments, balls and stars and silver festoons and baked apples and yellow-gold oranges and dates and dried Málaga grapes and gingerbread, toys and play horses and Punch and Judy shows. Tin soldiers and dragons and the Vienna military band and the candy house from *Hänsel and Gretel*, with the witch of course flying out of the chimney in all her ugliness.

"There were thousands of things to see there, and it was worth the box on the ears I'd get (when instead of coming home at seven, as told, I'd get in at ten)."

Christmas at home was always celebrated before Midnight Mass on Christmas Eve a custom Lang adhered to in America. There was always a candlelit tree that stretched to the ceiling, with presents piled underneath. Lang recalled once that the presents of his boyhood became more and more practical over the years, especially those from his father, while his mother gave him the beribboned treasures a boy wished for, such as ice skates and picture books.

Lang felt a deep ambivalence about Vienna, the place he left behind in 1918, but could not leave behind in his emotions. The Golden Autumn of Vienna was over too soon. He existed half in a dream-state, too young to understand and appreciate the experience; the director lived with memories too rich for the boy to have absorbed.

Fritz Lang was displaced twice; he lived through the Golden Decade of Berlin and the Golden Age of Hollywood. He thought of himself, at different times, as a Berliner and an American. Sometimes he didn't mind being identified with Vienna and things "typically Viennese": personality traits, ideas and influences, ingrained experiences, favorite foods. More often, Lang hated the association, resisted being yoked to Vienna and experiences in the remote past. He resisted any sort of categorization.

It was a double blow when he was grouped in people's minds with other figures in cinema who also happened to be born in Vienna. He recoiled at the fact that Otto Preminger, another director from Vienna who had an American career, shared his birthday (though Preminger was sixteen years his junior). Lang's lifelong disregard for colleague Josef von Sternberg was exacerbated by the fact that von Sternberg, too, was Viennese. ("He always thought he was greater than he was, don't you think?" Lang would ask.)

Sentimental in his heart, Lang resisted sentimentality in others. He disliked conversations that began, "Do you still remember . . . ?" Although it was not quite true, as he liked to aver, that almost forty years passed between his departure for Germany and his eventual return to Austria, he did not hurry back to Vienna after emigrating to the United States. Warily, he evaded gold-star invitations on his seventieth and seventy-fifth birthdays. He admitted to friends in Hollywood a worry that his "dream-Vienna, the Vienna of my youth," probably no longer existed. "I have lost a long list of things in my life that I held dear," Lang would say, "and I don't want to add the Vienna of my youth to them."

The director had the habit of professing a longing for Vienna out of one side of his mouth, while from the other side he found fault with his roots. Only in retrospect did certain criticisms of his boyhood there occur to him. Only in retrospect did Lang become, for example, socially conscious—analyzing, with 20-20 hindsight, the political currents that had swirled around him and his family during the Golden Autumn.

It was true, Lang conceded years later, that when he was in fourth or fifth grade, there occurred a sharp rise in anti-Semitism in Vienna, signaled by a series of public anti-Semitic remarks by Vienna mayor Karl Lueger. Indeed, there was a student club at Lang's Realschule that accepted no Jews as members, and whose members loudly proclaimed Germany as their fatherland. "I went about my business in those days without paying much attention to nor understanding these things," he said in an interview.

When the crown prince committed suicide under mysterious circumstances in 1889—he and his mistress found dead at the prince's hunting lodge at Mayerling—Lang was not yet born. But the film director remembered growing up aware of the suicide as part of the national folklore, and feeling sympathy with his countrymen for the crown prince's grief-stricken father.

The crown prince's death was the first, and perhaps most psychologically significant, of the suicides in Lang's lifetime. Otto Weininger, the influential Austrian philosopher, killed himself in 1903. The Viennese painter Richard Gerstl, a stark visionary, committed suicide in 1908, shooting himself after an unhappy affair with Arnold Schoenberg's wife. These were widely reported events. Suicide would become as customary as moonrise in the director's films, often, as in the case of the crown prince, involving an unhappy love affair. One of the most sensational episodes in Fritz Lang's own love life would also involve a woman's apparent suicide . . . under unclear circumstances.

The emperor was a popular symbol of lost Danubian unity, considered a charitable, almost democratic "old gentleman," though he believed in the divine right of the monarchy. Only with the passage of time did Lang learn about the reactionary court tendencies and intrigues of Franz Josef's reign. Though in many ways Lang always seemed one step ahead of history, in others he was doomed to lag behind.

When Lang wrote the emperor and Buffalo Bill into his never-produced "Scandal in Vienna," he made a political manifesto of the past. Franz Drexler, the Viennese rival to the American cowboy, is described as "by no means a stiff person . . . Being of middle-class origin and having an eye for the needs of the people, he has become liberal and is strongly opposed to regimentation and the reactionary suppression of the working class in the absolute monarchy of Austria in 1890." The director usually had at least one character in his films who was his stand-in, or alter ego; in this case, it was Franz Drexler.

When in the story Buffalo Bill encounters the emperor at a reception, they have a preposterous discussion about free will and democratic principles. The script happened to be written by Lang after the harsh lessons of the Third Reich, and during the anti-Communist crusade of U.S. Senator Joseph McCarthy. The director was flaunting political lessons learned. Nonetheless, even in looking back, he was no political braveheart; an equivocal note appended to his script warned that the "political material in the story [is] to be treated lightly, more tongue-in-cheek than it now sounds."

Only with the advantage of hindsight did unhappy incidents intrude upon Lang's rose-colored memories. Only thinking back would Lang remember that his father complained all the time, at the supper table, about the pressures of business. Only as an adult would Lang decide that his mother and father had a bad marriage; that he was born perhaps because they had "a good hour" one day. "I loved my mother very much and that is the only nice memory of my youth," the director wrote to one friend. Growing older, as Lang himself would admit, he preferred to remember "the bad things better."

His first real disaffection set in at K. und K. Staatsrealschule, the secondary school Lang attended in the Neubau, or Seventh District.

The Realschule entailed a seven-year course of study and focused on technical and scientific subjects, mainly physics, chemistry, mathematics, and the natural sciences, as a preparation for more specialized technical studies. A *humanistisches Gymnasium* education, alternatively, took eight or nine years, and focused more on humanistic studies—philosophy, Greek and Latin, classic literature—as a preparation for a university education. *Realschule* trained middle-class boys for high-level jobs in civil service, the trades, or technical professions. This course of study would advance Lang pragmatically toward a career as a *Baumeister*, a dismayingly mundane prospect for a youth whose spare time was by now eagerly given over to drawing and painting.

The K. und K. Staatsrealschule, which had just celebrated its fiftieth anniversary when Lang entered, was one of Vienna's best, dating from the period of Austrian educational reform in the mid-1800s. Students had to take an entrance exam to qualify to enter. The student body was drawn overwhelmingly from well-to-do families; contributions were pooled for the fifty Kronen annual tuition dispersed to a handful of needy students admitted each year. When Lang started his first class, at the age of ten in September of 1901, he was one of the precocious youngest in a class that included students as old as thirteen.

At K. und K., Lang was mandatorily drilled in English (as well as in French), with Italian an elective. Seven hours of classes per week were divided among the sciences and natural history; four hours went to geometry; three hours to geography and history; six hours to drawing and sketching; two hours to handwriting.

School opened with a church service, at which attendance was obligatory for Catholic students. Two hours a week were devoted to religious classes. The school strove for an atmosphere of tolerance, however, and rabbis and Protestant ministers visited the school at intervals. There was a minority of Jewish students, and partly as a consequence classes were usually divided into "a" and "b" groups. It was an implicit circumstance that the "a" groups were all Catholic, while up to half of the members of the "b" groups were Protestant and Jewish. Interestingly, Lang was placed in the "a" group for the first four years; then, at the time when anti-Semitism flared up in Viennese society (especially 1905–1906), he was switched to the mixed "b" group.

A student for the Matura, or final exam, had to write essays on topics ranging from ethical issues ("Law and Order") to the meaning of Gotthold Ephraim Lessing's "Hamburg Dramaturgy," to similarities and differences between industry and agriculture. The exam called for three hours of literary translation from German into French (from Ploetz, *Exercises on Syntax*), and another three hours from English into German (from *Seeliger's English Reader*). Five hours were allotted to three questions on geometry.

Lang liked to grumble that he was informed in advance by a certain professor what the essay topics for his Matura were going to be. But the topics were switched on him, with the result that he failed "miserably." This was the first of many real or imagined treacheries he would experience in his life, attributed by Lang to the fact that it was considered good policy to fail a certain percentage of students. The youth went out and got drunk for "the first time in my life," his first overt act of rebellion. It was early summer of 1907, with Vienna in the grip of a punishing heat wave, and Lang was just seventeen.

Realschule failure did not augur well for a career as a businessman; indeed, Lang would always be a failure as a businessman. But the teenager did not really care. Lang was already budding as an artist, and determined—as rigorously determined as Johanna Lang, his grandmother—to pursue his own high-minded aspirations.

Lang's love of beauty and artistry, his penchant for aesthetics, was certainly a trait inherited from his mother. The Lang family owned not only a spacious home in Vienna, but villas in the Salzkammergut and the valley of the river Kamp in Lower Austria—a vacation retreat, northwest of Vienna, for the affluent merchant and industrialist class—where the family could hike and ride horses. (The latter residence was affectionately referred to, inside the family, as the "Villa Lang.") It was Paula Lang who supervised the decoration of these various Lang dwellings with furniture, art, wall hangings, and elegant appointments—all that money could buy.

There were chandeliers, Persian rugs, wood carvings, and porcelain vases everywhere. There were, at one point (as documented in Paula Lang's will), some twenty-one paintings in the parlor, another twenty-four watercolors in the study (which also contained a billiard table), and twenty-three oils in the living room, as well as numerous ivory and Japanese statuettes.

Lang's mother also organized the family social life and hosted a salon in their Vienna home, as was the custom among the new bourgeois (particularly the Jewish bourgeois). The at-homes were attended by musicians, artists, and writers of modest stature. Here Lang as a boy caught his first glimpse of the artistic life, and his insistence on pursuing similar goals was at once a glorification of his mother and a condemnation of his thrifty, practical-minded father.

Starting in Realschule, Lang was reading more adventurously—Schopenhauer, Kierkegaard, Nietzsche, Schiller, Goethe, Shakespeare, Heinrich Heine, and Hans Sachs (not so well known outside Germany, but a serious Meistersinger who wrote poems on moral and religious subjects, medieval dramatic tragedies, and moral comedies). The Lang family owned deluxe editions of these authors as well as all the classic plays and books.

Then Lang discovered, at the Richard Liany Bookstore on Kärntnerstrasse, vulgar works—"a secret selection of censored books," in his words, including the works of the Marquis de Sade, which Lang said he "devoured but somewhat without appetite." One series he enjoyed were the comically erotic tales sometimes referred to as Mutzenbacher, after the candid memoirs of a prostitute named Josephine Mutzenbacher—so widely read when originally published in Vienna in 1906 that the author's name entered the vernacular.*

Outside influences began taking over. Cafés and cabarets became Lang's, as well as many other young people's, home away from home. Anton Lang had invested in a café at one point; Lang's father's regular spot was the Landtmann, a landmark even then, where stuffy types and government officials collected. His son's was the Café Dobner, on a busy corner where the Getreidemarkt cuts the Linke Wienzeile. With its billiard tables and cabaret performances, the Dobner was well-known as a meeting place for theater artists, opera stars, journalists, and beautiful prostitutes.

Every Viennese had two or three such favorite cafés. Lang liked to say he knew a man who had his business hours printed on stationery in the following fashion:

> From 2 to 4 o'clock—Café Landtmann
> From 4 to 5 o'clock—Café Rebhuhn
> From 5 to 6 o'clock—Café Herrenhof

Cafés were for loneliness, commiseration, misanthropy, deep thought, loud argument, and creativity. Cabarets supplied cheap entertainment, but, more than that, they were the underground of nonconformity. The cabarets in Vienna, as well as elsewhere in Europe, provided food and drink accompanied by satirical and topically charged songs and sketches. Some of the foremost writers, artists, and musicians of the day—such as the playwright Frank Wedekind, Expressionist artist Oskar Kokoschka, and the writer Peter Altenberg—enlivened Vienna's cabaret scene with presentations of their work.

One of the most lustrous cabarets was Die Fledermaus (The Bat), which was run by Egon Friedell, "a strange mixture of journalist, humorist, scholar, and actor," in Egon Erwin Kisch's words. There, amid Jugendstil decor, Kokoschka mounted his Indian fairy tale "Das getüpfte Ei" ("The Dotted Egg") on slides, writer Alfred Polgar—the future translator of *Liliom*—read his short prose and caustic commentary, and Friedell and other authors of rising repute presented their sketches and short plays. (After Lang directed *Der müde Tod* in 1921, Friedell would perform a sketch entitled "Müdes Obst," or "Weary Fruit," satirizing the film's portentousness, and remembered by all who saw it as a high point of his parodic skills.)

These and other cabarets hosted the godsends and gadflies of Vienna. Lang claimed that Friedell personally taught him the art of drinking Pommard, a fine Burgundy wine. The future director became friends with cabarettist Dr. Fritz Beda-Löhner, who was writing under the name Beda Chanson. Beda-Löhner, an early pacifist and Zionist, was a sometime librettist for Franz Lehár, and he also wrote the *Wienerlieder* (including "Ausgerechnet Bananen," or "Yes, We Have No Bananas") that Lang liked so much. Lang also met and admired the mustachioed Peter Altenberg, one of the most brilliant of the *Feuilletonisten*—writers of biting prose vignettes.

A self-proclaimed pauper, bohemian, and apostle of nature, Altenberg gave

*Some scholars believe the book was actually ghost-written by Felix Salten, who later wrote *Bambi*.

the Café Central as his address in one literary handbook, though he actually lived in a tiny hotel on a side street next to a graveyard. His relationships with women were as controversial as his prose. An avowed worshiper of prostitutes, Altenberg also had a proclivity for underage girls. The writer's "exalting of women," in Lang's words—for Lang saw things Altenberg's way—must have exerted an effect on the future film director. It became a philosophy Lang was to espouse in his own private life.

Foremost among the teenager's icons was Karl Kraus, dubbed "the Pied Piper of Vienna" by author Gina Kaus, for the spell he cast over Vienna's youth and cognoscenti. This satirist, polemicist, social critic, master dramatist, and all-around diatribist ("the scourge of the Viennese conscience," in Kokoschka's words) not only made cabaret appearances but gave public lectures which Lang enthusiastically attended. And for a long time Lang collected the paperback editions of Kraus's scarlet-bound *Die Fackel*, containing his discourses, of which there were some 922 numbers over thirty-seven years.

Six months after failing his Matura, Lang wound up taking the Realschule exam a second time. Then, in October of 1909, compromising with his father, he registered for the 1909–1910 academic year at the *technische Hochschule*—not a university, but a technical college for advanced studies in the sciences. Although Lang often claimed this stint of higher education on his résumé, he did not in fact attend enough classes to merit any marks. The charade he later carried on with his publicity he first carried on with his parents.

Unbeknownst to them, while he continued to live at home, he began working in two cabarets, the Femina Revue Bühne (Femina Music Hall) and Theaterkabarett Hölle (Cabaret Hell). Accordingly, as he once explained to the Viennese periodical *Mein Film*, Lang learned to carry on a double life. He created some posters for these cabarets, and occasionally took the stage himself for impromptu performances, according to *Mein Film*. "While his parents thought he was asleep," the Viennese publication reported, "he was appearing at a cabaret where he gave 'modern' poetry readings."

Since he made little money, legitimate theater was now an expense to be weighed, and so Lang found himself more often in standing-room or gallery seats. He began to spend time watching movies in the many theaters clustered in the Innere Stadt, showing predominantly German productions. There were also cheap circuses, magic shows, and all-dog vaudeville.

He might have taken in the oddity known as "Peter the Human Ape," opening at the Ronacher in December of 1908. This Peter, very much like the monkey named Peter who would figure as a curious sidelight to Lang's life years later, was advertised as a sensation. He acted "just like a human being, has better table manners than most people, and behaves so well that even more highly evolved creatures would do well to model themselves on him." Peter smoked, drank, ate on stage, pedaled a bicycle, rode a horse.

When, eventually, it became clear that Lang was neglecting his studies at the technische Hochschule, he had to drop out of the program. Nor did he reenroll for the 1910–1911 academic year. He bickered with his father, then tried to mollify Anton by telling him he was earnest about his goals and intended to become more diligent about pursuing the study of painting. It is unclear how much studying he did—even how much painting—or whether this was simply a pose.

Friedrich Steinbach told this anecdote: Lang, in his teens, made a big show of presenting one of his oil paintings to his mother for her birthday. Paula Lang cooed over the painting, while the youth gloated over Anton's stern-faced reaction. Only a few days passed before a shop owner came by to reclaim the work of art. It turned out that Lang had not painted it himself but had bought it on consignment, then found himself unable to pay up.

Lang's artwork consisted mostly of cabaret posters, sketches, even postcards, for which there was a long Viennese tradition. The young man's first sale may well have been a line drawing of Karl Kraus which he sold to the bookstore on Kärtnerstrasse where they hawked Kraus's *Fackel*s. It was duly reproduced as a postcard. "Karl Kraus never forgave me for that," recollected the director on one occasion.

Oblivious though he may have been to the Sezession, the youth's artistic paragons were polar opposites spawned by that artistic revolt: Gustav Klimt and Egon Schiele. Klimt, with a glittering, ornamental style, portrayed alluring models and bourgeois society ladies, emphasizing their sensuality as well as arrogance and vanity. Schiele, with more of a proletarian bent, depicted ordinary people contorted by hatred, hunger, tragedy.

His reverence for Klimt, Lang liked to say, might have influenced the excessive stylization of *Die Nibelungen*. But Schiele, who died very young (a victim of the 1918 influenza epidemic) was his true idol, "whom I never surpassed." He was the only artist the director ever really collected. A youthful self-portrait by Lang, which has been reproduced in several books, self-consciously emulated Schiele's tortured approach.

Cabarets and cafés were also for romantic assignations and conversations à deux. "Viennese women were the most beautiful and generous in the world," Lang said on one occasion. "They were wonderfully dressed, and you met secretly in a café. You set up an evening rendezvous during the intermission of a play, or met 'coincidentally' after eleven o'clock."

Lang had learned about love and sex from Catholicism, and his outlook remained intrinsically Catholic throughout his life. There were Madonnas, like his own mother, pure and saintly (Kriemhild before the vengeful transformation; one-half of Brigitte Helm/Maria in *Metropolis*). And there were whores, who possessed the tempting inducements of sin. Sins could always be forgiven, and like Mary Magdalene, prostitutes could be uplifted. Prostitutes in the end were for Lang, as for Peter Altenberg, a shrine at which to prostrate himself and worship.

The religion teacher at the Realschule had been a priest who also heard the pupils' confessions. Lang always remembered that this particular clergyman would force one student, who had been held back in his matriculation, to recite the Ten Commandments, then, after the Sixth Commandment, interrupt him each time with "Thou shalt not be unchaste! Not true, my dear boy?" This student was the most sexually mature of them all and one time invited "the boldest of us," including Lang, to visit three of the most notorious spots on Spittelberg, regarded as an immoral part of town.

"Spittelberg," as Lang put it, "was not a Berg [mountain] at all, it's just that one of the streets was called that. This was where girls with exposed breasts lay in street-level windows and invited passersby to a visit with the most obvious gestures."

This was Lang's first "Scarlet Street." The film director claimed that even before he left high school he already had notched "a few affairs," that he was an "early bloomer" sexually. "Women have always been my best friends," he liked to add with equal measures of disingenuousness and truth.

Some of these early affairs were no doubt platonic. Even as an old man Lang was bothered by the memory of a cabaret performer named Trude whom he could never quite succeed in seducing. No doubt there were also encounters with prostitutes, the first of many such experiences. The call girls in the director's life may not have been among his best friends exactly, yet some of the regulars in Hollywood were known to stay in touch—phone him, after many years, to hit him for money or just to say hello.

The youthful Lang spent too much time in the cabarets, from his father's point of view, and not always for the entertainment. "He pretended to be studying painting," the ex-Berlin newspaperman Curt Riess reported in one of his books. "When his father found out they had a fight, mostly about a young lady—who wasn't really a lady—an actress at a cabaret called Fledermaus."

Lang resented the fact that he was financially dependent on his father's goodwill. "About halfway through every month there was a fight at home," the director said in a interview later on. "My source of money dried up and I had to try to find thirty Kreuzer, which was the subsistence level per day in Vienna back then. One had little success walking head down, hoping to find money in the street. That was usually a bad bet. It was better to stride proudly into a café house and mention casually that you were getting money the next day and oh, by the way, could I borrow thirty Kreuzer till then?"

The squabbling escalated until Lang decided to leave home—in fact, to leave Vienna. His Meldezettel, or police registration, shows that he officially lived at home as late as January 15, 1909. The technische Hochschule registration came in October of that year. The young man appears to have attended some art classes and launched his café life in earnest in 1910.

Lang likely departed either late in 1910 or early the following year. Saying his good-byes, he tucked away the "splendid fortune" of forty Kronen in his pack—in those days about the price of a winter overcoat and a pair of shoes.

The film director, in his interviews, liked to urge young people to prove their mettle by running away from home, "something every decent human being should do." But Fritz Lang himself—gently cushioned in his youth—waited until he was on the precipice of his twenty-first year.

Fritz Lang began his Wanderjahre by visiting galleries and museums in Nuremberg, Munich, and Frankfurt, before journeying down the Rhine to Belgium and landing at his destination of Brussels.

Arriving with twenty-five francs in his pocket, Lang began to sketch postcards, caricatures, watercolors, and easel art, selling them to tourists for coffee and bread. Years later he liked to relate how he lived by his wits in those pre-World War I salad days. He learned, for example, to sell a postcard for the price of a martini, then stretch that martini into two martinis by ordering the first in a café and drinking it very slowly, contemplatively, until the martini was two-thirds gone—when, with a sudden display of irritation, he would summon the waiter and complain that it wasn't properly made. Then he would receive a second martini free of charge.

Martinis were already, as they would always remain, his favorite any-time-of-day drink. A martini tasted good, even for breakfast. A properly made martini, in Lang's opinion, was made with Tanqueray gin—exceptionally dry, perfectly chilled, with just a small olive. Lang set great store by martinis, and enjoyed expounding on the subject. One of the virtues of Gloria Grahame's character Debby, in the director's 1953 film _The Big Heat_, is that she can mix a first-class martini.

Brussels proved both stimulating and educational, according to the director's interviews and publicity. Vienna's _Mein Film_ carried an article in 1926 wherein Lang claimed to have joined a Belgian circus during his residency there. That is how he picked up the "clown routines" he occasionally dredged up to amuse his friends, according to the magazine. The magazine also reported that circus folk taught Lang how to throw lassos and knives, and that for a time he earned money as a sharpshooter—a regular Buffalo Bill.

"Then I fell in love with a woman. Her mother was from Indochina; her father was an officer in the French Army."

What happened to this first sweetheart Lang never revealed. Romance is more plausible than the lasso-throwing and circus-clown bit on his résumé, however. Lang fell in love easily, earnestly, and often. His head was stuffed with romantic notions, especially in this youthful period, even if invariably he woke up the next morning to embark on a quest for a new and different bed partner.

His infallible seduction technique, he told author Charlotte Chandler many years later, was to flaunt his own special brand of martini. He would invite the girl he was "in love with at the moment" up to his place and offer her an unheard-of "blue martini." "She would be mystified, intrigued, enchanted, and fall into my arms." The secret of the blue martini, which Lang swore he had never told anyone before? "Blue food coloring."

Perhaps the exigencies of love drove him to Munich, where Lang claimed to have enrolled in the Staatliche Kunstgewerbeschule (which became the Academy of Art and Design, now part of the University of Munich). There, the film director said in later interviews, he attended the master class of Julius Diez, an illustrator and painter of the period, who was influenced by symbolist painter Franz von Stuck. Lang essayists, trying to trace his artistic forebears, have extracted some mileage out of the director's connection with Diez, who drew fairy-tale books, worked in ceramics and mosaics, designed noteworthy public murals and triptychs. Perhaps Lang did audit some of Professor Diez's classes—although, already back in Vienna, he showed a tendency to pad his education. And the files of the Kunstgewerbeschule for that era do not show that anyone by the name of Fritz Lang registered as a student or attended any classes.

Supposedly to pay for these undocumented classes, Lang again cashed in on his artistic ability. "I even painted a fresco for a bordello," he often claimed. Newspapers and fashion magazines, Lang said in interviews, purchased his cartoons, as well as advertising, fashion, and travel sketches. Probably Lang did sell a few such items to periodicals. No doubt he had a degree of familiarity with the world of publishing; he returned to the milieu often in films, and gravitated to former newspaper reporters as scenarists. His rate of success, however, must have been less than phenomenal. Lang researchers in Europe have yet to turn up any authenticated examples of this self-declared copious early output of piece-art.

The future director's stay in Munich lasted an unverifiable period of time; it was probably less than a year (Lang didn't deem Munich worth much mention in Lotte Eisner's book). He claimed that thereafter "my wanderings took me over half the world, to North Africa, Turkey, Asia Minor, and even as far as Bali." Other times he added Japan and an assortment of Mediterranean nations to his elastic itinerary.

This is the period when, according to the standard narrative of his life, Lang developed his passion for Oriental and folk culture, and began to collect primitive art, particularly skulls and masks. (They abound in his films, both in close-ups and as background decoration on the walls of sets and scenes.) Again, according to interviews, Lang took up the hawking of paintings, postcards, and newspaper sketches to cover his cost-of-living expenses. At one point, visiting Bali, he found himself so bereft of resources, so down on his luck, that he passed time as a beachcomber.

Could he really afford such constant travel, and did he in fact journey to these far-flung places? As the course of his life would prove, Lang liked to play tricks with his passport as well as his vitae. Curt Riess wrote in one of his books that "Fritz Lang never told me how he paid for this [time of global travel], not even later, when we were close friends." Even the Parisian cineast and press attaché Pierre Rissient, one of Lang's confidants in his twilight years and among his staunchest defenders, doubts the director traveled as far and wide as claimed.

No matter. By April 1913, Lang was registered with authorities in Paris, a resident of 42 rue de Maistre in the Eighteenth Arrondissement, living in a small, shuttered atelier "overlooking the marble bust of Heinrich Heine, Germany's tragic lyricist, in the cemetery of Montmartre," according to Frederick Ott in his book about Lang. "Manger de la vache enragée" was a venerable artistic credo,* and Montmartre, a cobblestone district presided over by the famed Sacre Coeur, was home at one time or another to Picasso, Braque, Raoul Dufy, Maurice Utrillo, and other luminaries, as well as many bread-and-butter artists.

Lang's talent fell into a humble category. Otto Hunte, one of the top production designers for Germany's famed Ufa film company, once remarked that Herr Director had sketching ability, but lacked the perspective that came from formal training. Lang himself realized his limitations, or grew to realize them, probably during these years spent "finding himself" as an artist. In Lang's 1945 film *Scarlet Street*, he makes a passing joke of his abilities, when a character praises the work of the cashier-turned-painter played by Edward G. Robinson, saying the paintings have originality, masculine force, "a certain peculiar something—but no perspective."

Lang's interviews state once again that he sold cartoons and sketches to newspapers in order to stay afloat. He attended the Maurice Denis École de Peinture in Montparnasse by day, while at the same time taking evening instruction at the long-established Académie Julien on the rue du Dragon, where aspiring American artists congregated and where it was a tradition to study nudes. There were also classes for illustration, design, and layout for periodicals, publicity, and posters.

Paris proved "particularly fertile," in Lang's words, more fertile than Munich. If Lang evinced little feeling for Munich as time went by, Paris would shine in his memory. After his initial, youthful sojourn there, he had dramatic occasion to return; then, at the end of his life, when he felt terminally alienated from Germany and unappreciated in Hollywood, the director came to view Paris as his second home, perhaps the home of his broken heart. There, at the Cinémathèque Française, he chose to deposit the bulk of his valued and sought-after professional papers, and there, again and again, he met his most fervent and knowledgeable fans.

Dreaming the impractical dream of becoming a painter, Lang roamed Paris. He dined at the Moulin de la Galette, an elegant restaurant in Sannois, where artists used to come and spend time on the hills overlooking Argenteuil, making sketches. He toured the worthwhile museums: the Guimet in the Sixteenth Arrondissement—where he nurtured his appreciation for Oriental, especially Japanese, art—and of course the peerless collections of the Louvre. He frequented the Moulin Rouge dance hall, where he filled his sketchbook with costumed showgirls à la Toulouse-Lautrec. More than once he took the train

---

*"To eat the wild cow" means to have endured things nobody should have to endure.

to Chartres, and is reputed to have executed a series of paintings of the soaring Gothic cathedral, whose somber interior and brilliant stained-glass windows might have given him, the future master of shadow and light, early inspiration.

One of his classmates at the École de Peinture was Vienna-born Julius Singer, a painter who later became a professor and respected art dealer in London specializing in Old Masters. They shared youthful adventures and stayed in touch, intermittently, for most of Lang's life. One of the director's venerable anecdotes was of the time he and Singer, lacking enough money for two ballet tickets, were forced to share one—changing places at intermission— for the Russian Ballet in the Paris Opera.

Despite his stories of living hand-to-mouth, the young postcard artist may not have been crushingly poor. It appears that he journeyed by train back to Vienna several times during his European interlude; his military status form shows that he registered with the army annually, in Vienna, from 1911 on. Despite protests to the contrary, he stayed in close touch with his parents, on whom he likely called for financial assistance. Lang, during this bohemian phase, seems to have traveled at ease, and lived and dined well on occasion.

It is difficult to say how much genuine progress Lang was making in his instruction. Published sources indicate he was preparing "a public exhibition of his work, together with a collection of Oriental and oceanic objets d'art acquired on his trip to the Far East," when newspaper headlines intervened to force his departure from Paris, but this, without any proof, must be considered suspicious exaggeration.

His friend Julius Singer liked to joke that Lang was more interested in women than in painting. A diary-like 1914 letter to Singer, the earliest known letter by Lang in any archive, is dotted with references to a young woman named Suzanne, a "sweet and plump" model working at a fashion house. Lang toyed with Suzzy, was amused at her expense, and after their dates, Lang boasted, she always disappeared back to her Mama's.

The signs of approaching war cast a convenient cloud over the relationship between him and Suzzy. Lang remembered posters stuck up all over the city, in mid-summer 1914, declaring that banks and restaurants could not change fifty-franc notes because the Bank of France had suspended exchange and reimbursements. Gold and silver currency was disappearing, and on every street corner citizens gathered and spoke in angry voices, "Maudite soit la guerre—je m'en moque de la Serbie."*

Archduke Franz Ferdinand, nephew of Emperor Franz Josef and heir presumptive to the Austrian throne, and his wife, Sophie, were assassinated in Sarajevo on June 28, during a tour of Bosnia and Herzegovina. The Austrians used the act as a pretext to crush Serbian nationalism. The Austro-Hungarian ultimatum to Serbia came on July 23, and a declaration of war followed on July 28. General mobilization ensued on July 30.

Austria's historical ally was Germany; Serbia's, Russia. Germany's historical enemies were Russia and France, who had a mutual defense pact. Therefore, after June 28 in Sarajevo, France was in prospect Austria's and Germany's foe.

"We did think of war occasionally," wrote Vienna-born writer Stefan Zweig,

---

*"To hell with the war. I don't give a hoot about Serbia."

who was enjoying life in Paris at the same time as Fritz Lang. "But no more than we did of death—as a possibility, yet probably a distant one. And Paris was too beautiful in those days, and we were too young and too happy . . ."

The aforementioned events were in the news as Lang and his girlfriend Suzzy dined at one of their favorite Italian restaurants on Thursday, July 30, 1914. "She wanted to stay with me," wrote Lang to Singer afterward. "I had a hard time getting rid of her. I promised her a small gift in the event that I would have to leave to Austria—but at heart, no one considered that eventuality."

A rendezvous with Suzzy to work out their differences was negotiated with all good intentions for the following evening. "She was a little devil, but kind and pleasant enough to pass time with," Lang informed Singer. But he never saw Suzzy again.

One of the last barriers to a French declaration of war was Jean Jaurès, the socialist leader, apostle of peace, and champion of Franco-German rapprochement. But on July 31, Jaurès was shot down, murdered, by a young, fanatical patriot. Lang heard the shocking news even as he was contemplating the evening's prospects with Suzzy. Lang told Julius Singer what happened that fateful Friday:

"Faire l'amour was not on the agenda. I walked slowly toward the Champs-Elysées. It was the calm before the storm. I entered a bar—heard a few men—Germans—saying that the possibility of war was greater than one thought. Suddenly the door was wrenched open: 'Jaurès assassiné!'

"We turned pale suddenly. An augury of great events. He had been assassinated by a Camelot du Roi [a member of a militant right-wing, anti-Semitic faction], and suddenly the atmosphere on the boulevard changed completely. 'À bas les Prussiens! À bas les Autrichiens! À Berlin, à Berlin!' I saw to it that I hurried back home."

The next day was Saturday, August 1. The young artist woke up lazily in bed, momentarily deceived into thinking everything looked better in the light of sunshine. That was before he read the daily newspapers, which reported rumors that there were no longer any railroad connections to Germany and Austria, and that key bridges had been blown up. "Now, you could smell trouble . . ."

Without bothering to wash, Lang quickly dressed. He hurried to the post office, sent emergency telegrams. Then he rushed to the Austrian consulate. No one knew anything for certain. The only advice was to flee quickly, by any route available.

According to Lang's letter to Singer, he was lucky to secure a ticket to Liège, Belgium, about fifty miles southeast of Brussels, with a connection to Germany. People were massed in front of the police station trying to arrange their passports (foreigners in France required, as well as the usual visa, a Visa de Préfecture, without which one couldn't leave the country). There was not enough time to fix Lang's visa—there would be passport shenanigans and suspenseful train schedules in more than one Lang anecdote—so he made the decision to try to cross the border without duly stamped papers.

His train was scheduled to leave at 9:30 P.M. He returned home and finished packing before lunch. "My servant helped me, otherwise it would have been impossible." Burdened with his luggage, Lang took a carriage to the station. The Gare de l'Est was flooded with panicked people. There were no porters to be found. The ticket counters were mobbed. Newspaper extras brought a fresh disclosure: "Caillaux killed by a bullet. The assassin is a son of Calmette."*

"The train whistled and I left Paris."

It was "the last train from Paris," Lang declared on more than one occasion. What he had seen in the train station was unfortunate, Lang wrote Singer, but what he saw on the train was even worse. "Everywhere people were crying and complaining about what was lost."

The passengers were forced to leave the train at the Belgian border. It was a pitch-black night. Sneering railway employees gathered along the tracks, surrounded by "the drunken army rabble that escorted us in Belgium." The passengers, Lang among them, fretted. Rumors circulated that they would not be allowed to cross the German border. Yet they were only ten minutes from the checkpoint. What would happen to them?

"A few gentlemen conferred: 'Does anyone have any arms on them?' "

Well, Lang did; it turns out that he had a gun in his possession, a weapon familiar enough to friends like Julius Singer that it could be referred to casually, in his 1914 letter: "The Browning, so often scoffed at, [here] came to honor."

"Ten to fifteen men, including me, marched forward, the Browning ready to fire, followed by the women and children with baggage, then the other men. Suddenly a ray of light—I thought the shooting was about to start, and here we were near Valkenswaard, at the Belgian border station, and no one was preventing us from crossing the border. The rumors were all false. But thank God the ordeal was over and done with. My nerves were ready to crack."

The journey was then continued until they entered the safety of the fatherland. After six days, "without any sleep, almost without any food," Lang made it to Vienna. "I traveled first class but always for free." His luggage also arrived intact. "We were the last people to leave Paris. At five o'clock they already started arresting people and deporting them to Spain."

It would be tempting to proclaim that Fritz Lang left innocence behind in Paris, and that would be true enough, if a little tidy. He did leave painting behind, in favor of a new, destined to be more enduring, passion—motion pictures.

One of the first motion pictures Lang recalled seeing was, of course, an American Western. *The Great Train Robbery*, the Thomas Edison ten-minute silent film directed by Edwin S. Porter—one of the first with a dramatic story line—played Vienna in 1904, when he was almost 14. When the film's bandits tried to break into a telegraph station, Lang remembered, he and his friends,

---

*This false report was only indirectly related to the war fever. Calmette was Gaston Calmette, editor of *Le Figaro*. He had written articles denouncing Joseph Caillaux, a radical French politician, as a Germanophile. It was Calmette who was shot dead; the killer was Madame Caillaux, whose love letters, purportedly from Caillaux, dating from the time when she had been his mistress, were published in *Le Figaro*. Her subsequent trial—in which she was acquitted—captivated the French public.

with that Langian ingenuity that later would create so many wondrous effects, applied a sound track with their feet—bang! bang!

The aspiring painter did not pay any serious attention to the upstart medium of photoplays until after he left Vienna. Film first grabbed hold of him in Belgium—in Brussels, where he was struck by a film he chanced to see in a garden restaurant; the non-paying customers like him were allowed to watch from the reverse side of the draped cloth that served as a screen. In the medieval city of Bruges, the cradle of Flemish art, another film Lang happened upon also "captivated" him, and for the first time he began to feel an unusual "presentiment of new possibilities" about the medium. Lang was "amazed," wrote Curt Riess, as he realized "you could also paint using a camera!"

Paris, later on, afforded regular filmgoing experiences. Lang acquired the habit of seeing a film per day, sometimes two or more. He did not recall seeing many American movies, mainly French ones. One day in Montparnasse he watched a film about a peasant revolt and was thrilled at seeing horses in motion. He recalled attending films featuring the gentleman thief Arsène Lupin, as well as the popular comedies of Max Linder. He saw the *Rocambole* series of crime melodramas directed by Georges Denola ("I looked at these things with great pleasure, it was a time-killing, and maybe they were an influence on me, I don't know"), and the crime and detective stories of director Louis Feuillade.

Feuillade, especially, was the prolific genuine original—"a forerunner of German expressionism and the prime mover in the thriller and suspense film genres," in the words of Ephraim Katz in his *Film Encyclopedia*. One should not underrate Lang's debt to Feuillade. Their films, in their fondness for secret societies, gambling clubs, trapdoors, peepholes, and mysterious avengers, are kindred.

Lang was already susceptible to crime stories. The Vienna newspapers, when he was growing up, positively shrieked with tabloid-style accounts of brutal robberies, prostitute and pauper killings, sex murders; and the French tradition of lurid faits divers, and crime reports, could only have reinforced his hobbyist interest in the brief news items from the daily papers. These would serve as inspiration for many of his films.

The train from Paris to Vienna took him away from painting then and toward a future in film. But Lang was still young and changeable, and far from cemented in his mind.

Arriving back in Vienna on the fifth of August, 1914, Lang felt like a stranger. The Cabaret Femina had changed hands. The owner of his favorite café was dead. Mobilization fever gripped the city. Trains were filling up with recruits; everywhere there were banners flying, parades in the street.

He wrote to Julius Singer from the villa in Gars am Kamp. The twenty-three-year-old then moved in temporarily with his parents (his military papers give the Zeltgasse address). But he kept himself aloof from his father and mother. He would rarely mention them in any context after his first departure from Vienna; it was as if they had ceased to exist.

He rented a studio for a brief time. But he spent little time painting. His thoughts "wandered around the new medium that occupied me more and more, namely film. I often visited the cinemas, often seeing two or three films a day, but everything was still confused and unclear."

Slowly Lang adjusted, rediscovering Vienna's sights and pleasures. He visited museums and the Habsburg summer palace. Some excursions were almost talismanic. He joined other pilgrims at the two-towered Maria Taferl Church high above the Danube, across the river from the burial site of the archduke and his wife, at another church in Arstetten. He touched the iron tree stump at Stock-im-Eisen Square for good luck.

Vienna's glorious nightlife and culture beckoned, in spite of the mounting war fever. The stage play *Liliom* had ended its German-language premiere at the Theater in der Josefstadt (Lang probably saw it for the first time in Berlin in 1922). But there were many other noteworthy productions on tap, including one of Friedrich Hebbel's *Kriemhilds Rache* (*Kriemhild's Revenge*) at the Burgtheater. The cabaret circuit was relatively intact, and other pleasures were there for his sampling.

"The Viennese women and girls were even more elegant and beautiful than before, and merrier and more devoted, too," Lang reminisced on one occasion.

However, the "sudden rapture of patriotism," in Stefan Zweig's words, the "mass psychosis" was pervasive in Vienna. Few could resist it. Ernst Lissauer's "Hymn of Hate," a scathing song denouncing the British, was on everybody's lips. Lang still went to Karl Kraus's pacificist lectures, "but not as often as before," and current audiences sometimes laughed at Kraus when he put together his newspaper headlines "to show how war-crazy and superfluous the newspaper reports were . . ." The newspapers, printing only what was permitted, were oblivious to any opposition point of view, and "made it look like war would be a walk in the park," Lang recalled. "And so the Viennese went to war, I would almost say, 'comfortably' "

Austria's declaration of war on Serbia, on July 28, had unleashed a Pandora's box of treaties and alliances that dragged in the border nations as well as distant flags. Germany declared war on France on August 3. Within a few short months, Austria-Hungary and Germany were pitted against the combined Allied Powers of Serbia, Russia, Belgium, Montenegro, France, Great Britain, and Japan.

The fighting had begun in August—Lang's brother Dolf was already a lieutenant in the reserves—but still Lang stalled his action. There is no doubting Lang's own patriotic fervor or, as subsequent military records attest, his physical bravery. Perhaps he was trying for the cavalry, the more dashing job, or waiting until his call-up was imminent. In romance, Lang was impulsive. In all else, he was inclined to weigh his options.

Lang had been declared unfit for officer training since 1911 because of a hernia. Now the hernia required surgery and stretched out the delay, but "instead of enjoying myself, I suddenly suffered a rash of patriotism and felt it my duty to go."

He spent his twenty-fourth birthday, Christmas 1914, and the holiday season that followed, at home. His hernia was repaired. After languishing for five months, Lang was newly determined to prove himself as patriotic as the rest, even if he missed the irony that one of Austria's enemies was the country of his former residence—beloved France. The young man was admittedly a po-

litical naïf, hazy on the subtleties of the world situation. "My social and political thinking first began many years later with the appearance of Hitler,"
Lang would explain years later.

Austrian military archives attest that Friedrich Christian Anton Lang enlisted
on January 12, 1915. Volunteering, combined with his Realschule diploma,
more or less guaranteed him an officer's rank within one year.

Bank clerks and office workers swelled the army, but Lang was not the only
Austrian artist or intellectual to be swept up in the chauvinist frenzy. The
eminent poet and dramatist Hugo von Hofmannsthal was one reluctant con-
script, while Oskar Kokoschka and composer Arnold Schoenberg were among
other cultural volunteers caught up in momentary delusions of heroism. "I
saw the war as an adventure, at least in the beginning," Lang himself remembered.

His occupation, in the records of the Imperial Landwehr Field Gun Division
number 13, is listed as "artist." Initially, Lang was attached to a battery in
Rennweg, in Austria's Alps, from which recruits were assigned and dispersed
to the field as needed. For the first few months of 1915, he had to undergo
basic drills and preparation. Even while undergoing military training, however,
Lang managed to find time to pursue his emerging ambitions.

According to the curator of a gallery of modern art in Ljubljana, Jure Mikuz,
who investigated Lang's military interval, the future film director lived for
some months, probably spring through fall of 1915, in Ljutomer, a small town
famous for its wine, in the Mura valley in Slovenia. While attending instruction for officer candidates, Lang was billeted at the home of Karol Grossman,
a Slovenian lawyer.

An educated man, Grossman boasted an extensive library, including numerous travel books for Lang to peruse. Grossman dabbled at writing, staged
amateur plays, and experimented with photography and motion pictures. He
also held occasional screenings at his villa. Apart from some photoplays that
Grossman managed to bring back from Vienna, he showed amateur films that
he had photographed himself, including *Aufbruch nach der Sonntagsmesse (After the Sunday Mass)*, *Markt-und Messetag in Ljutomer (Market in Ljutomer)*
and *Im heimischen Garten (In Our Garden)*.

Lang and Grossman became fast friends, according to Mikuz. Since Lang
wasn't particularly busy with military duties at first, he was able to make time
for his own artistic projects at the local pottery, working with clay. Lang fashioned several figures during his Ljutomer stay, leaving behind, as gifts to his
host, four terra-cotta sculptures, two life-sized busts of Bacchus, and two tall,
oddly-shaped flower vases.

The Bacchus motif, Mikuz wrote, was closely connected to Ljutomer and
its tradition of wine-making, although it was also popular in fin de siècle art.
As Mikuz pointed out, Lang used groupings of mythological and allegorical
figures in a number of his films, notably in *Die Nibelungen*. Huge vases and
statuary became common decorations in his interiors. Pieces similar to the
Ljutomer pottery can be glimpsed in the background of several of his films,
the fireplace scene of the killing in *The Woman In the Window* among them.

"The mask of a man with protruding eyes and elongated nose on the han-

dles of the four-sided vase reminds one of the Moloch monster in *Metropolis*,"
wrote Mikuz.

Another writer assessing Mikuz's findings for a 1989 article in a Vienna
magazine, Neva Skapin Slibar, saw in these same sculptures—with their wide
faces, swollen lips, fleshy noses, low wrinkled foreheads, and prominent eye-
balls—portents of Fritz Lang's future, evoking the similarly over-expressive
features of two of his favorite actors, Peter Lorre and Edward G. Robinson.

These vases and sculptures were packed away for years in the attic of a villa
in Ljutomer, until Mikuz discovered them in the early 1980s and placed them
on exhibit. Some Lang enthusiasts doubt their provenance (the proof is an-
ecdotal), but the chronology and circumstances fit. Indeed, witnesses placed
Lang at the Grossman home on Christmas Eve of 1915; in an interview, Grossman's surviving daughter remembered the "affable lieutenant."

Slibar theorized in his essay that Lang never bothered to mention the pottery interlude in articles and interviews in later years for the same reason that
the film director rarely discussed other violent and haunting experiences of
his lifetime.

"Lang," wrote Slibar, "managed to appear open about his life story by telling the same anecdotes and stories over and over again and so managed to
distract people from the actual facts of a very stormy life. He applied this self-
censorship to the time he spent in the Austro-Hungarian Army during the
First World War—when he made the clay sculptures—too, because it didn't
tally with the outspoken apolitical and pacifist attitudes he later espoused."

The volunteer cadet's advance up the ranks was swift but not extraordinary.
Starting as a cannoneer, Lang was promoted by degrees first to gunner, then
corporal, platoon leader, cadet sergeant, and finally to second lieutenant during
action on the Galician front. Assigned to an artillery battery in October, 1915,
Lang led a horseback patrol whose specialty was reconnaissance. His small
team operated behind the infantry, scouting the temporary fronts and advising
brigade headquarters, by messenger or telephone, where to concentrate forces
or to lob shells.

The German High Command would have preferred to concentrate on
crushing France, while Austria-Hungary engaged Russia. The French had persuaded the Russians to undertake a simultaneous two-pronged offensive
against the Germans in East Prussia and the Austrians in Austrian Poland
(Galicia). The Germans therefore had to join with the Austrian Army in its
offensive on the Eastern front. Throughout much of 1915, the Austrian forces
challenged Russian might, thrusting northeastward into what was then Russian
Poland, waging a fluid strategy over vast distances bounded by East Prussia to
the north, by German Poland and Silesia to the west, and by Galicia to the
south.

Austrian troops, with German reinforcements, occupied most of Poland by
the fall of 1915. The Russians proved stubborn, however, launching a fierce
counterattack on the Eastern front in the spring of 1916, which met with
determined Austro-Hungarian resistance. Archduke Josef Ferdinand's army
hunkered down under conditions of extreme cold, fighting to hold positions
against a relentless barrage of air and gas attacks, and the continuous thunder

of Russian cannons. Lang was among the predominantly Austrian troops fighting to hold east Galicia and the Volyn region (today in southeast Poland and west Ukraine).

His particular unit—Fourth Army, Tenth Corps, Thirteenth Landwehr Feldkanonen-Division—was spread out in the area surrounding Lutsk. There, on this terrain of endless primeval forests and marshy woodlands, with only a few rough roads connecting the main railways to inner Russia, Lang first distinguished himself.

His quick-sketch ability and superior horsemanship came in handy. According to Austrian military archives, on March 27, 1916, Lang placed himself alone, six hundred meters in front of his own outpost, under enemy fire, returning with a sketch of Russian fortifications not previously surveyed. This intrepid act enabled an effective bombardment of the Russian lines and the destruction of an especially troublesome enemy machine gun.

Lang was awarded the Silver Medallion, and a salary bonus, for "bravery second class." According to his citation, "Many times infantry commanders took the opportunity to have him take part in their reconnaissance missions due to this successful action."

This citation was swiftly followed by another "special recognition." "He [Lang] played an exceptionally significant role at the battle at the bridgehead at Teremno [near Lutsk], again due to his reconnaissance work. He successfully detected and therefore foiled a strong three-part enemy attack, by observation in an exposed position."

The relentless cold stalled the Russian offensive until June, when the Russians resumed their thrust west toward Brest-Litovsk, and south toward Kovel, L'vov and Chernovtsy. In early summer the swollen rivers flooded the land for miles around, making the area even more impenetrable. The Austrians were largely positioned in deep trenches.

Before the furious Russian counteroffensive began on June 6, Lang was on the front lines, exhibiting "exceptionally conscientious and courageous" behavior while commanding reconnaissance at Chromiakova, a small town near Lutsk. According to records, he repeatedly repaired malfunctioning equipment while under heavy artillery attack.

The Austrian Army was pushed back, after two days of costly fighting. Abandoning their ruined trenches and supplies, the Austrians took up new positions west of the river Styr. Many soldiers drowned in the chaotic retreat. Now the battles involving Lang's unit shifted to the west of Lutsk, along the road to Vladimir-Volynski. The Russian cavalry made repeated assaults on Austrian fortifications. The Austrians more or less kept up a measured retreat, being attacked from behind all the time. The Russian drive resulted in tremendous casualties, while the Austrians in their flight gave up thousands of prisoners as well as munitions and other inventory.

Lang was hurt for the first time at the battle at Cholopieczy on June 17, according to his military file. "It was mainly due to his exemplary reports that a strong enemy did not gain ground." During the twelve hours of heavy fire Lang was wounded slightly in the shoulder.

No sooner did one front die down than another would flare up nearby. The then-platoon sergeant was wounded again on June 25, at Zaturcy, another town on the Vladimir-Volynski road where the fighting had moved. The records attest that during the Vladimir-Volynski stalemate, Lang proved "outstanding . . . consistently at the very front of the line of battle," so much so that he was awarded a second Silver Medallion on August 4, 1916, and promoted to the highest rank he would achieve: lieutenant.

This time the wounds were serious; he would have to spend time in a hospital. He was dispatched to Vienna for a protracted convalescence. The records are vague on this point, but the June 1916 injury could be the eye wound that necessitated the director's famous—some might say notorious—monocle. More than once in his life Lang mentioned that his horse had been shot out from under him in World War I when a mortar shell exploded nearby, and that the shrapnel damaged his eyesight, rendering him "momentarily blind."

It was at this juncture that the temporarily blinded Lang, lying in bed in a Vienna hospital staffed by volunteer ladies of the aristocracy by day and Catholic nuns at night, began to envision a future and profession for himself in motion pictures.

Lang began to keep a meticulous journal. The habit of keeping a journal would, later in the director's lifetime, become a compulsion, but this first one—at least the earliest known example to survive—recorded his daily activities, thoughts and ideas, and first cinematic impulses. The journal became a sketchpad of plots, scenes, and stories.

Lang was still in the hospital recuperating when der alte Herr, Emperor Franz Josef, died in November of 1916, after a life of eighty-six years and a reign of sixty-eight. The lieutenant must have witnessed the slow funeral cortege on a foggy day, moving along the Ring until it halted at Capuchin Vault. The emperor's death was, for Lang, the beginning of the end of his ties with Vienna and Austria. He already disliked his own father; for him *der alte Herr* had been the one and only father figure.

"With the death of the old Kaiser, a strange emptiness began in me and the other officers in the Austrian Army. Of course we swore another oath to his successor, but that strange love we didn't really have for Kaiser Karl [Charles I, grandnephew of the Emperor, who ascended to the throne] as we did for the old Herr. This love was unendurable."

While on leave from the hospital, Lang met a "bank employee" in a cabaret where he was moonlighting, doing his customary posters. Sometimes, in interviews, the director dated his relationship with this man to his time in Vienna prior to enlistment. On other occasions, he said it was during this hospital stay that they began writing together. Probably it was both, an acquaintance Lang met before the war with whom he had stayed in touch.

The bank employee was also a songwriter. Lang needed a partner where writing was concerned. His embryonic story ideas were promising, yet their bare bones needed flesh. The bank employee was interested in motion pictures. Why shouldn't they collaborate?

Four or five short treatments, maybe more, were concocted during what turned out to be a fruitful ten-month respite from war. However, according to Lang, the bank employee did not pull his weight. "As it turned out, I had the ideas and he was rather dry. So I said, 'Look, I'll do the writing, you try to sell them.' "

This man, who happens to have been in the same profession as Lang's brother Dolf, was never identified by the director—curiously—though he often referred to him in interviews. Nor is any writer other than Lang credited on the first films with which he was associated. This man ceased being his collaborator, according to Lang's interviews, and in effect became his agent, peddling the scenarios to prospective producers.

Lang himself, as time went on, had only the dimmest memory of these earliest stories. One of them may have been *Die Peitsche* (*The Whip*). "No one now knows if it was ever made into a film nor what it was about," wrote Lotte Eisner in her book. Some sources report that *Die Peitsche* was directed by Adolf Gartner in 1916 or 1917 for the Stuart Webbs-Film Co. in Berlin, but it remains one of Lang's several "lost" films of the silent era.

Another scenario was a detective story. Another, which never sold, was a "werewolf story," Lang recalled in one interview.

A third was *Die Hochzeit im Exzentrikklub* (*The Wedding in the Eccentric Club*).

A fourth: *Hilde Warren und der Tod* (*Hilde Warren and Death*).

The bank employee-cum-songwriter initially tried to sell Lang's scenarios to the Austrian firm Sascha-Messter—the company which later proved the springboard for producer Alexander Korda—without luck. Then Lang's silent partner managed to swing a deal with Joe May, a Vienna-born film editor, director, and producer who had his own established motion picture production company, May-Film GmbH. This transaction seems to have been arranged entirely through the intermediary; in later interviews, Lang never gave the slightest indication of having met May, personally, at the time.

Born in 1880, May was a resourceful, imaginative producer and director, a moviemaking veteran whose films, produced with his own family fortune, often starred his wife, the "stunningly beautiful" (Billy Wilder's words) actress Mia May. Headquartered in Berlin, he had returned to Vienna, like Lang, at the outbreak of World War I, then managed to wangle an extended leave of absence from the hostilities, permitting him to work on behalf of military film auspices while continuing to churn out a popular derring-do "Detektivfilm" series featuring a character named Joe Deebs.

Making trips between Berlin and Vienna during 1916 and 1917 on behalf of military operations, May kept an eye out for people and properties that might fit into the program of his production company. Almost immediately after purchasing *Exzentrikklub* and *Hilde Warren*, he launched *Hilde Warren* into production.

Mia May starred as the actress Hilde Warren, who makes the mistake of marrying a murderer. The murderer is slain by police, but a son inherits his father's evil genes. Hilde Warren discerns the truth, and must act to seal her son's fate. This first Lang scenario already had some elements that would become familiar to the mold, including superimpositions that introduced the figure of Death into everyday scenes of the heroine's life, foreshadowing her eventual fate—surrender to Death's embrace.

Some published sources report Lang's oft-made claim that he acted in *Hilde*

Warren, but the lieutenant had no knowledge of or involvement in the actual filming. In fact, Joe May shot *Hilde Warren* in Berlin, while in Vienna Lang was preparing to reenter combat.

Fritz Lang was eager for more war. Friedrich Steinbach, his cousin, remembered that it was a family joke that horses kept getting shot out from under the reconnaissance officer. Since the Austrian Army was running out of everything—armaments, supplies, horses—Anton Lang personally had to put up the money to buy another horse for his son, according to Steinbach.

The lieutenant was transferred with his regiment to the Romanian border, near Focşani, about one hundred miles northeast of Bucharest, in May of 1917. The line of Russian retreat had stalled there. His unit would be involved in a number of skirmishes around Precistanul, at Prisaca, north of Odobeşti, but the worst of this war was behind Lang in Galicia. His time with the Thirteenth Feldkanonen-Division for the remainder of the war was divided between the Romanian and the less volatile Italian front.

Probably in late August or early September of 1917, Lang's division was sent to the Isonzo battleground in Italy, joining hostilities there in the Hotenya Valley near Tribusa, and later supporting the Austro-Hungarian offensive on the lower Piave River, near Montello. Greatly outnumbered by the Italians in this theater, the Austrian infantry made occasional charges across bridges and up the mountainsides, while, entrenched above them, Italian long-range guns tried to bombard their positions.

Field Artillery Headquarters, on August 24, applied for another medal for Lang, and he was granted "highest recognition" on October 15, for deeds that go unspecified in the archives.

The fighting crisscrossed the Tagliamento and Piave rivers, resulting in heavy Austro-Hungarian losses. Lang, in January of 1918, again proved himself—again the details are cloudy—and was awarded the Karl Truppenkreuz, one of the highest possible honors, a commemorative medallion unrelated to specific action. A fresh injury must have occurred, because the lieutenant was returned to Vienna for a projected two-month recuperation at the beginning of 1918. No documentation exists as to whether the new wounds were serious, or if previous injuries had been aggravated. The military records show Lang diagnosed with rheumatoid arthritis, a dilated heart, eye problems, and a "nervous disorder" contracted at the front.

No one can dispute Lang's stellar military performance: two Silver Medallions and other recognitions, at least three injuries, courageous action on several different fronts (Russia, Galicia, Romania, Italy). At this stage of the war, however, "nervous disorders" were epidemic among Austria's disenchanted veterans. Lang may have been among those claiming a common battle-fatigue syndrome. He first made his application to be declared unfit for duty in the spring of 1918, but his application was met with extensions of leave and final-decision delays for months, until his files could be reviewed, indicating that a superior officer may have called his deferment into question.

War had shown him "life stripped to its rawest, hunger and desperation and death," as Lang once put it, "scenes that neither fiction nor the screen can ever picture." Death, so prevalent in his later motion pictures, became an old acquaintance, a sobering reality, not an abstraction. Everywhere Lang went on the Eastern front, suspected traitors dangled from trees. Stumps of bodies jutted out of frozen mud. Soldiers near to him bled to death from bullet wounds, or from shells that blew away pieces of their flesh. There was a surfeit of amputees and worse, in the hospitals.

Not for the last time had Lang been swept up by historical forces. A catastrophic loss was looming for Austria. Undoubtedly Lang was strengthened by his training, hardened by his experience, and matured by his leadership role, while at the same time he felt dazed and exhausted by everything that he had witnessed and undergone.

War had taught him something important—defeat. And defeat taught him resilience.

The film director almost never discussed his wartime experiences in interviews and conversations with friends, except in the most general possible terms. Surprisingly, Lang also avoided direct depiction of war in scripts and motion pictures, though it was one subject in which he had unquestionable expertise. Although there are fierce, pitched battles between rival armies in some of his motion pictures (notably, the second half of *Die Nibelungen*, which is a long, sustained bloody combat), and skirmishes and guerrilla action in others (the church assault at the film's climax is one of the most effective scenes in the otherwise tepid *American Guerrilla in the Philippines*), by and large Lang chose to bury the memories that recalled an ugly episode in his life.

The war was nearly over for the wounded lieutenant. And his injuries were not really serious, so that, after a short while, Lang was able to leave the hospital during the daytime, as long as he checked back in at night.

Things were grim on the home front. There were shortages of food and coal. A deadly influenza epidemic gripped Vienna.

Lang, for the first few months of 1918, moved about as if coming out of a trance—slow, mechanical, uncertain.

He had few friends. "In spite of my relations with women, I was still a very shy person," the director conceded in one interview. "I made new acquaintances only with great difficulty, was always a loner, and was therefore seen as arrogant. In reality I was probably just trying to find myself, as perhaps film, which later occupied my entire life, was also just an adventure in the beginning."

One of those friends was a certain young woman. Lang may have met her earlier in his Vienna period, perhaps just before enlistment. But sometime between 1917 and 1918, Lang's World War I journal—which only a few people can claim ever to have seen—introduced references to a young lady he identified only by the initial "L." The journal makes clear that Lang found himself falling in love with "L," who after the war would figure in the most mysterious and closely guarded chapter in the director's life.

All along Lang had been looking forward to seeing one of the films Joe May had crafted from his scenarios. *Die Hochzeit im Exzentrikklub* was playing at

the Rotenturm theater, and Lang attended with "L" and other friends, receiving "the first shock of my professional life."* This early effort, which is
lost today, had become, in Joe May's hands, just another routine episode of
his Joe Deebs series.

Lang felt insulted, even disdainful. "As the film rolled, I saw that my name
was not the name listed as the author's (although my script was filmed scene
for scene as I had written it), but rather Joe May's, who had directed it.

"The production didn't impress me. I had seen a lot in my imagination
much differently and I believe that I, even if completely unconscious of the
fact, had already decided to become a director. This decision, which would be
the deciding factor in my life, didn't happen after a lot of reflection, but rather
through a strange type of certainty that has accompanied me through all of
my film productions . . ."

Lang, in another interview, told what happened next: "The owner of the
theater must have thought that I was an idiot or crazy, or something, because
I went to see him and said, 'Look, there are two scenes that aren't in continuity, and if you let me in, I could change them around.' He was very polite,
but he had a certain look in his eyes—I think he was very happy when I left.
Naturally, the film was never changed."

Perhaps Lang's disillusionment prompted him to enroll in the Hochschule
für bildende Kunst (College of Fine Art) at the end of April 1918, where he
signed up for the spring session of classes in nudes, composition, landscape,
and animals. It was a half-gesture toward his previously declared avocation.
Lang paid his tuition, but attended only a few classes before his enthusiasm
waned.

His ambitions remained muddled. He felt "completely unconscious" of any
stirrings toward film. Then, in the summer of 1918, two decisive encounters
changed Fritz Lang's life.

The first occurred one day in late June. The lieutenant had been lolling
around at his favorite café, the Dobner. He had been "racking his brains"
about his finances. ("I had a sweetheart and no money. Including sickness and
hospital compensation, I got exactly one hundred twenty Kronen, which would
equal maybe thirty dollars a month.") Nevertheless, he must have looked impressive, sitting there "in his field-gray tunic and breeches, boots glistening, a
monocle stylishly planted in his right eye," as Frederick Ott described Lang.

Actually, it was his *left* eye. This reference, from June 1918, is the first
glimpse in the historical record of Lang's monocle—that ribbonless single lens
inserted directly in the eye socket which more than anything symbolized the
enigma of the man. Some Viennese cognoscenti, even then, would have made
fun of such a Prussian affectation, and it is a mystery just why and when,
precisely, Lang adopted the monocle. Friedrich Steinbach, for one, insisted in
an interview that Lang began to sport a monocle earlier than World War I,
shortly after Realschule, in fact.

If true, that would contradict Lang's story that the monocle was forced on

*Contemporary sources indicate that *Exzentrikklub* premiered in Vienna on November 30,
1917, but likely it was still playing in some theaters by the time Lang returned to the city to
recuperate.

him by World War I injuries. Or the anecdote the director sometimes told about a filming accident in Berlin, in the 1920s, that worsened the initial injury and further mandated the monocle. "According to what he told me," said his Hollywood friend, editor Gene Fowler, "a mercury klieg light blew up and he got a wound in his eye. Then it was further aggravated by the time he was examining some light tests close to his face, and he touched a cigar to a light test. The film was nitrate, which is very explosive and flammable—and it blew up in his face. It kicked the hell out of his retina."*

That afternoon at the Dobner a passerby, observing Lang in uniform, paused, struck by the man, the monocle, the Prussian bearing. The passerby was Peter Ostermayr, or his brother Ottmar Ostermayr—Lang told the story both ways. Peter, the older brother, was a charter member of the Vienna-Berlin film axis. He would already have been made aware of this Austrian officer who doubled as the scenarist of *Hilde Warren* and *Exzentrikklub*. Originally a portrait photographer, Peter Ostermayr had begun to cultivate a reputation for his nature films when World War I intervened. During his lengthy career, he would serve as cameraman, screenwriter, director, or producer of several hundred motion pictures, and in time would be considered "the grand old man of the Heimatfilm," or the genre known as "mountain films." Ottmar Ostermayr was a scenarist and producer, often working hand in hand with his brother.

Like Joe May, Peter Ostermayr was then engaged in wartime morale-building projects, directing the war play *Der Hias* by Heinrich Girlardone, in conjunction with the Red Cross. *Der Hias* was being staged in Vienna for the general public and soldiers on leave. Ostermayr asked Lang if he would consider taking a major role in the production, playing a Prussian officer. The compensation would amount to eight hundred Kronen monthly.

Lang was overjoyed. "I sometimes have bright spots in my life," he once remembered, "and this was one of them." But, according to the director, his poker face gave nothing away as he declared he couldn't possibly agree to such a measly salary. He recalled the scene, with precise dialogue, for one reminiscence:

"'Eight hundred crowns,'" Lang told Ostermayr ("as haughty as haughty can be"), "'that's not very much.'"

"'We cannot pay more than one thousand, that would be the limit,'" Ostermayr countered. "'The Red Cross can also see to it that you are temporarily relieved of your military duties.'"

The play was about an Austrian lieutenant who is wounded on the French front and taken prisoner in a castle, where he falls in love with a French maid. His loyal friend, a Bavarian named Hias, follows him voluntarily into captivity, but flees as the lieutenant is about to be dragged in front of a French military court. Hias notifies a Bavarian reserve battalion which, led by a Prussian captain, storms the castle and rescues the lieutenant in the nick of time.

Ostermayr, whose family was native to Bavaria, couldn't help but realize during rehearsals that although Lang *looked* Prussian, the accent he affected

---

*Film editor Rudi Fehr confirmed in an interview that his uncle, Oskar Fehr, a renowned eye surgeon, operated on Lang in Berlin in the late 1920s.

was faulty. The people in Hollywood who, years later, remarked on Lang's stubborn Germanic accent missed those soft consonants that any German would always spot as subtly Viennese. "With the best will and the best coach they were able to give me, nobody with my Viennese accent could portray a Prussian officer."

"Something which only happens in fairy tales [next] took place; since I had a contract, he had to give me, not the subsidiary role I couldn't play, but the main part, that of a wounded Viennese lieutenant who is captured by the French."

The show, with Lang in the lead, was presented at the Ronacher, one of Vienna's premiere variety theaters, from May 3 through July 18, 1918, before moving over to the Konzerthaus. The second act was written around a series of skits allowing popular entertainers to step into the show as artists for a good cause. The evening included an interlude of film clips (war footage), folk music, and comedy routines. "Every member [of the cast] had to make collections for the Red Cross during the intermission," Lang recollected, "and at the end I would read the latest war news to the audience."

Members of the Austrian aristocracy, generals from the Ministry of War, and Red Cross officials were among the audience at performances, which principally benefited tuberculosis victims, the poor, and "artists who have been severely wounded in the war."

"It is a harmless bit of fun, a simple, unsentimental and effective play," wrote the *Wiener Allgemeine Zeitung*, "It cannot claim to be highbrow—it is a lively, modern Volksstück . . ."

This was the first—perhaps only—acting stint under Lang's belt. Acting would become, perhaps, his area of least expertise. His iron-fisted tactics with actors did not always have the desired result. But perhaps his exacting methods were a kind of psychological revenge on the profession, for acting was one thing on a motion picture set which, the director had to realize—even if he would never admit it—he couldn't do better himself.

Events indicated a man still at loose ends. The lieutenant's aspirations remained divided. Motion pictures—or painting? The future was still up in the air.

Military records show, in fact, that Lang applied for a leave from the army, on July 26, 1918, for the purpose of traveling to Saint Petersburg, Russia, to pursue his artistic studies. The lieutenant identified himself in his application as a "painter by profession," whose Saint Petersburg sojourn "would further his knowledge of the subject he is specializing in, primitive Russian folk art. A study of Russian painting and religious art would enable him to establish himself in his future profession."

Although Lang did have an interest in folk art, this request is certainly a curious one. Some Lang researchers have interpreted it as an excuse for Lang to visit the homeland of his girlfriend "L," preparatory, perhaps, to making wedding arrangements. More curious still is that permission was granted. Yet Lang did not go to Russia. He might well have pursued this course of action if the second, more propitious, encounter of the summer of 1918 had not transpired.

*   *   *

Erich Pommer was twenty-nine, only one year older than Fritz Lang. He was the same height as Lang, of medium build, with curly black hair and sensitive light-blue eyes.

Not yet an august figure, Pommer was still some years away from proving himself "the real genius behind the great years of the German cinema," in the words of Paul Rotha. Nonetheless, compared to Lang, Pommer was already a veteran in the field, advanced in knowledge, accomplishment, and authority.

Pommer's self-made career dated from 1907. First employed by French Gaumont in Berlin, he had worked his way up from a job as traveling salesman of projection equipment to general manager for Central Europe of the new French Éclair production company. Before the onset of World War I, he had co-founded Wiener-Autoren-Film and supervised several Franco-Austrian co-productions. Inducted into the German Army during the first week of hostilities, Pommer was wounded seriously twice during two years of service on the front lines.

After recovering from his second set of injuries, he was assigned, a sergeant but in civvies, to the Bild-und-Film-Amt (Bufa), the army department for the production of educational, propaganda, and entertainment films for Germany's front line, reserve forces, and occupied territories. Bufa was to be absorbed after the war into the newly formed Universum Film Aktiengesellschaft (Ufa), which started out with one-third of its assets held by the government of Germany.

Because of his knowledge of the Balkans, Pommer operated out of a special unit headquartered in Bucharest. Until mid-November 1918, he oversaw Bufa activities, not only regulating production and distribution, but exercising final authority over what plays and motion pictures appeared in theaters in the capital and the occupied zone.

Pommer had founded his own production company, Decla (Deutsche Éclair), in Berlin, officially, in February 1915, but Decla was managed by others, including Pommer's brother, his wife, and director Otto Rippert, in his absence. Decla managed, however, to produce some eighty films during World War I. Because of Decla as much as his military obligations, Pommer was a frequent traveler back and forth to Berlin. He was on his way back to Bucharest, in August of 1918, when he got off the train to spend the night in Vienna.

A friend—probably Peter Ostermayr, who would have known Pommer well through film and military circles—persuaded him to attend a performance of *Der Hias* in order to meet a budding show business recruit. That night Pommer watched the show with some trepidation, as he later recalled. He was not impressed by the actor, nor by his acting, and he disapproved of the "especially irritating" monocle the man wore.

It had been prearranged that afterward Pommer would meet the young actor, Fritz Lang, for drinks and conversation at a bar in the Kärntnerstrasse. Pommer debated making an excuse and skipping out, but out of politeness he gave in to the urging of his friend and kept the appointment.

"I expected a personal talk to be a waste of time. I was all the more pleasantly surprised to meet a sensitive human being who was trying to hide his manifold talents and honest aspirations behind the arrogant mask.

"Lang explained his thinking to me. He was searching for a new path that would not follow the tried-and-true footsteps of stagecraft. With the instinct of a painter he sensed that film in the future could no longer content itself with a simple photographic rendition of plots and things, as was customary until then. With the eyes of a painter Lang saw that the photographic lens, that is, the eye of the camera, must serve, by using light-and-shadow effects, to fuse performance, plot, and background into a unified entity, to somehow create a film composition.

"That evening all this sounded pretty half-baked and not necessarily obtainable in practice. There also was the danger that, with primary emphasis on visual aspects, a film easily could neglect story and actors. But one thing was clear to me: I was sitting with a true talent who was making a serious attempt to develop a new style of motion picture narrative."

They talked into the wee hours—the born promoter with visionary good taste and the artistic would-be director—two members of Germany's future screen pantheon.

Pommer praised Lang's ideas but explained that first he needed to learn "the ABCs of filmmaking." Lang never forgot his exhortation: "You must learn to know the camera. It is with the camera that you write the film!" When they parted, Pommer invited Lang to come and study filmmaking at Decla, offering him a job as a *Dramaturg*—which combined the positions of reader, story editor, and remedial writer—for his Berlin company.

This was the turning point, the moment without which Lang's yearnings might never have crystallized.

The film director never forgot his gratitude. Pommer, who produced films by F. W. Murnau, E. A. Dupont, Robert Wiene, Josef von Sternberg, Max Ophüls, and Alfred Hitchcock, as well as Lang, always remained an exalted figure in Lang's life. Although they were never close friends, neither, in spite of rocky times, did they ever become enemies. That was saying a lot for Lang where a producer was concerned.

Lang felt he never had a more understanding boss than Pommer. In fact, Pommer's sterling example ultimately became a chink in Lang's psychology, an obstacle to his acceptance of any other, lesser, figure in that position.

It now became an easy matter to arrange Lang's discharge, with Pommer's military connections and the imminent conclusion of the war. Lang was finally given permanent leave on November 1, 1918.

Actually, he was already gone from Vienna. In September, he had left for Berlin, the El Dorado of the German-speaking world. The twenty-seven-year-old took only "two sets of civvies" while he scouted out the new job and found a place to live, making train trips back and forth until matters were settled and Vienna was left behind almost as thoroughly as folk art in Russia.

By December 1, Lang had permanently relocated, a move verified by his registration at the Population Department as a new resident of the city of Berlin.

Lang never made a film about Vienna, or directed any production set in his native city, yet he may have left one Vienna story behind.

Lang's script of *Lilith und Ly* was researched in 1965, and written about, first, in an Austrian film periodical by Walter Fritz, today the director of the Austrian Film Archives. Piecing together press and publicity accounts, Fritz undertook to reconstruct the script of "Fritz Lang's Forgotten Film," offering the most complete known example of Lang's pre-1920 storytelling.

Perhaps it was his very first script. Although Fritz placed the film in 1919, it seems possible, nevertheless, that *Lilith und Ly* was one of Lang's earliest hospital scenarios (the one he once vaguely recalled as a "werewolf story"), and that it was filmed in Austria without his knowledge or participation shortly before he left Vienna in late 1918.

The film's director was the founder of the Fiat Film company in Vienna, Erich Kober ("a director apparently unknown outside Austria," in Lotte Eisner's words), whose short-lived company made several silent pictures. The leads of the film were Elga Beck and Hans Marschall, the latter quite well-known, both as an actor and director, in Austria.

Contemporary newspaper notices claimed the *Lilith und Ly* script was inspired by an original Sanskrit manuscript ("parchment strips"), which Lang acquired during his "extensive" travels in Asia. But the film's main idea, of an artificial creature brought to life with a slip of parchment, is clearly pinched from the Jewish legend of golem, a monster of clay which can only be brought to life by placing a sacred text into its mouth.

The main character, Frank Landov (played by Marschall), was a type that would recur in several of Lang's early scenarios. A kind of wish-fulfillment figure for Lang, Landov was an upper-class scientist-hero embroiled in fantastical, macabre adventures.

"Every modern woman's ideal man; a young gent, a scholar, a globe-trotter, inventor, and sportsman," according to Walter Fritz's plot synopsis, this brilliant researcher lives a life of isolation in his laboratory, consumed by his quest to develop one of Lang's typical leaps of technology, a "telescopic mirror." Landov suffers from insomnia and relaxes from work by riding horseback— more of Lang writing himself into the part.

Landov's old friend Mudarra, a sculptor, falls in love with Ly (Elga Beck), the daughter of a powerful civil servant, Delinaros, who is also an executive at a company interested in investing in Landov's inventions. When the daughter spurns his love, Mudarra decides to commit suicide. Landov argues him out of it, telling Mudarra he, too, is searching for the woman "that we are all searching for and never find." Landov's advice: Mudarra should pour his love and pain into a masterpiece of sculpture—a likeness of Ly. The sculptor does so, and makes a gift of the statue to Landov.

While traveling through India, Landov discovers a ruby at a shaman's grave and some strips of parchment adorned with Sanskrit. Back home, the scientist-hero translates the text and discovers a formula for bringing objects to life. Using the ruby, he transforms Mudarra's statue into a creature "as beautiful and lissome as a gazelle," with whom he falls deeply in love. The revivified statue is named Lilith.

Dr. Worman, an old friend of Landov's, returns from India, bringing more parchment strips and a protective amulet with him. The missing Sanskrit fragments explain that if the statue-creature discovers the true nature of its origin, it will metamorphose into a vampire.

When Landov meets Ly, he realizes that she is the living embodiment of the statue. Things change. Landov grows alienated from Lilith. "All he can think of is Ly and when he is with Lilith he feels only disgust."

Landov sets up a demonstration at Delinaros's company of his new "telescopic mirror"—two huge concave mirrors projecting images across a distance, a kind of television prototype. The telescopic mirror illuminates Dr. Worman, studying the Sanskrit parchment, and Lilith, now a vampire. She attacks Dr. Worman, feeds on Landov's friend's corpse, tears up the parchment, and escapes.

Stricken with typhoid, Landov is nursed back to health by Ly, and asks her to marry him. Lilith uses her ghostly powers to ruin their engagement party. Landov is frightened, mistakes Lilith for Ly, and gives her the amulet for protection. Back home, he drinks a bottle of champagne. Through the telescopic mirror he spots his fiancée sitting on a divan, with Lilith hovering outside her window. Landov attacks the accursed invention with a Tibetan sword, and destroys the statue of Lilith.

Now Ly comes down with typhoid. Landov begs to see her but the doctor will not allow him. At the end of the film, according to the scenario pieced together by Dr. Fritz, Landov stands on a bridge with the ruby in his hand which he used to bring the statue to life. The ruby was found next to Ly, as she lay unconscious, after Landov destroyed the Lilith statue. "It is the heart of the vampire . . . the stone falls into the water."

"This singular idea, and a brilliant direction combined with accomplished actors, add up to a sensational film," wrote *Die Filmwelt* in July of 1919.

The film, today, is lost. According to Walter Fritz, *Lilith und Ly* was meant to launch a series of Frank Landov films, but there is no evidence that further installments were written or filmed. Lang was done with Frank Landov. Having discarded that first alter ego, he was already working on more auspicious projects in Berlin.

Yet the synopsis will resonate with fans familiar with Fritz Lang's work. The well-bred expert who is the film's hero; the doppelgänger, or double personality, who tortures the hero with conflicting impulses of love and lust; the speculative science and Oriental mysticism—these were conceits that would attract the director again and again. As early as *Lilith und Ly*, a Fritz Lang film could be counted on to weave together pulp clichés with story components that aimed for a higher meaning. This blend of lowbrow trappings and lofty truths, when it worked, was—along with a certain visual intensity, somber atmosphere, and unhurried rhythm—a unique combination. A signature tone. And there would come to be a word for it: Langian.

BERLIN

1918
1921

The Allies broke through German defenses in France and Belgium. General Ludendorff of the high command demanded that peace be proposed to the Allies. There were rumors, in spite of strict censorship, of a naval revolt in Kiel, cabinet disarray in Munich, a revolutionary government in Bavaria. News went around of a pending general strike. Workers and police clashed everywhere, troops deserted, soldiers joined the newly established people's councils.

Terrible food and fuel shortages crippled the country. The population virtually lived on cabbage, potatoes, and turnips.

Austria-Hungary surrendered on November 3. The Kaiser considered a fight to the bitter end, but on November 9 he abdicated. The same day, upheaval shook Berlin. Crowds streamed toward the Reichstag—workers, women, and children—carrying posters appealing to police and soldiers. A republic was proclaimed. A coalition government was declared, under the stewardship of the Socialist Friedrich Ebert.

Fritz Lang was in Berlin for these historic events. He was there for the Armistice of November 11, 1918; for the collapse of the monarchy; for the dismal conclusion of the World War and the commencement of the 1920s, a decade of rampant unemployment, malnutrition, crime, black marketeering, profiteering, inflation, and political turmoil.

Germany was a sea of strife, but the film world was a fantasy island. Lang would thrive there, insulated and immune from outside forces. The disturbing events of those years must have affected his thinking and influenced his filmmaking. Yet it was as though—as he sometimes liked to put it—he were "sleepwalking consciously" through history.

Ironically, Germany's film industry survived the war in healthy condition. The size and number of movie theaters, the average attendance, the number of films, and production companies—all dramatically boomed after World War I.

People were starved for food, but also hungry for titillation. The gambling clubs and decadent nightspots were thriving; but the cinemas, more than anything else, offered the universal escape from beggars, riots, social ills. "At night," wrote Herman G. Weinberg, a New Yorker who would become one of

Lang's champions among the American cognoscenti, "everybody flocked to the movies, at least those who couldn't afford seats for *Die Fledermaus* or the classical theater of Reinhardt."

The years 1918–1919 were undoubtedly among the most crammed and hectic of Lang's long, prodigious career. In that time he managed to write seven full-length features, and was credited for the first time as full-fledged director of two films.

Erich Pommer had opened offices on Friedrichstrasse, a broad boulevard that ran north to south through the center of Berlin. The true heart of the city, Friedrichstrasse was crowded with government buildings, embassies, shops, banks, offices, theaters, cafés, and cabarets. More than one hundred film companies operated along the Friedrichstrasse by 1919, including Joe May's as well as Pommer's.

Pommer, at first, stayed in the background of Decla, continuing to supervise the company's foreign distribution. Only gradually, after his release from the military, did he assume production reins. Because Decla owned only a small studio in Weissensee, Lang's first films were often photographed in space rented from other Berlin producers, including the main studio of the newly constituted Ufa in Tempelhof. A large studio in Babelsberg (on the way to Potsdam) was operated by Deutsche Bioscop AG, which also owned a theater chain. Not until 1920 did Decla merge with Bioscop into Decla-Bioscop AG, giving Pommer his own stages and theaters. The property then dubbed Neubabelsberg became one of the incentives for the subsequent merger of Decla into Ufa.

Lang, at first, seesawed between jobs for Pommer and May. Though toiling for Pommer as a Dramaturg, advising on the merits of other people's scenarios, within weeks Lang was writing his own screen stories. This brief period from 1918 to 1920 was the only time in Fritz Lang's career when in fact he was credited with writing scenarios without a collaborator, and it may be that, as in Vienna, he was not really working alone. A secretary, friend, or silent partner might have been sharing the work—without credit.

But the scripts were short, a dozen pages or so, and the former lieutenant seemed able to knock one out over several nights with the help of a bottle of good red wine. The scenes were numbered separately, and the pages could be shuffled to allow for changes and improvisation. His initial scenarios were for horror, detective, and historical films directed by two of the era's forgotten figures, directors Alwin Neuss and Otto Rippert.

A native of Cologne, Neuss had made his debut in film in 1906, and after a spell in the infantry made his reputation as the star and director of his own Sherlock Holmes series for Decla. Rippert, another ex-actor with a long theater career behind him, was well-known as a prolific director—among whose many titles was 1916's ornate serial *Homunculus*. Lotte Eisner admired Rippert's epic, and in her book *The Haunted Screen* pointed out that *Homunculus* exerted a definite influence on Lang—especially obvious in the Expressionist acting, the lighting effects, and the staging of crowd scenes, with the rabble arranged in triangular patterns—later echoed in *Metropolis*.

Lang's first Decla film was directed by Neuss—1918's *Die Rache ist mein* (*Revenge Is Mine*). In quick succession Lang also wrote scenarios for *Die Bet-*

tler-GmbH (Beggars Ltd.) and *Wolkenbau und Flimmerstern (Castles in the Sky and Rhinestones)*. *Die Bettler,* also directed by Neuss, was one of a Decla series featuring actress Ressel Orla, whom Lotte Eisner ungenerously described as "a mediocre and rather plump actress." It was "filled with humor and spirit," according to the reviewer for *Der Film* in May of 1919, whereas *Wolkenbau* was cited by state censors as "forbidden to children."

Then Lang wrote an Otto Rippert melodrama called *Die Frau mit den Orchideen (The Woman With Orchids)*. This may be the 1919 film (Lang was never clear about which one) where he claimed to have acted more than one role. "In order to earn a few more marks," the director said in an interview, "I appeared in a film of mine which Otto Rippert directed, as an actor in three roles: as a German mounted telegraph messenger, as an old priest, and as Death. The Viennese touch!" *Die Frau mit den Orchideen* has been sketchily reported as the story of an orchid-wearing femme fatale who wreaks havoc among men. But did the film truly exist? Scholars can't be sure.

Lang followed with another similarly themed script for Rippert. Tales that taught the pitfalls of love and sex—featuring respectable men ruined by lusty temptresses—would predominate throughout Fritz Lang's career; *Totentanz (Dance of Death)* was just such a cautionary tale, set in the house of a crippled doctor (Werner Krauss), who psychically controls a dancer (Sascha Gura). Contemporary synopses indicate plot points that were quintessentially Langian: psychic phenomena, rape and other violence, an underground labyrinth that figures in a climactic chase, a wild dance to the death.

Lang's final scenario for Rippert boasted a lavish budget. *Die Pest in Florenz (Plague in Florence)*, which was produced by Pommer for Decla, recreated Renaissance-era Florence on the Arno. Berlin journalists were chauffeured to the Decla studio in Weissensee to experience the filming in September 1919. "They came in carriages and rented cars which Decla generously paid for," wrote German film historian Michael Hanisch. "The gentlemen of the press were overwhelmed and dutifully praised it [the film] to the skies."

The plot of *Pest* revolved around another woman of sin, a courtesan who transforms the town of Florence into a place of debauchery and death. A father and son compete bitterly for her favors. "The son then kills the father, [and] the churches are turned into places of lust," according to a synopsis in *Der Film*. The Plague descends on the town, death spreads, and "all perish miserably." The publicity outlay and gala premiere, in October 1919, helped ensure glowing reviews for a film whose ambitious scope was heralded in its day.

A blend of eroticism, violent crime, and the supernatural had already begun to emerge as Fritz Lang's forte. It was certainly not unique to him; Germany's screens would overflow, in the heyday of the 1920s, with nightmarish tyrants, somnambulant monsters, fantastic arch-criminals, and devouring vamps. But this director was destined to epitomize, as well as reflect, the tortured soul of the national cinema.

After *Pest,* Lang went to work for Joe May, collaborating for the first time directly with the producer-director who had given him his toehold in motion pictures. Before Lang developed his reputation for arrogance, May had his own for extravagance and high-handed behavior. Acrimony crackled between the two. Lang often said so, and May's wife Mia May confirmed, in one late-in-life interview, that her husband "respected him [Lang] as an artist, but I do not believe that he liked Lang personally, ever."

Apart from her loveliness—Mia May possessed "a sweet dumpling face ringed by blond curls," in the words of one film historian—Joe May's wife was a good-hearted person who often sat in on the editing of her husband's motion pictures, chipping in with suggestions. Lang had begun to frequent the cutting rooms too, looking to the future and broadening his expertise. It would have been just like him to set himself against the husband in the marriage, while cultivating an affinity with the wife.

Lang got along better with Pommer. Especially during the early days in Berlin, the producer acted as "more of a friend to me than a boss," said Lang in one interview. "I earned little but was happy to be making films." Pommer could be a consuming personality too, but he was always permissive with Lang, tactful and respectful, while drawing the lines between his responsibility and Lang's. May, on the other hand, was not only the producer, but also the director. One couldn't escape his preeminence, and Lang resented it.

Now, for May, Lang wrote the final segment of *Die Herrin der Welt (Mistress of the World)*, a sprawling eight-part, forty-eight-reel serial filmed largely at May's hilly one-hundred-acre complex on the shore of Woltersdorf Lake. Mia May starred as a Danish student-adventuress who learns of the existence of a hermit in a Chinese temple. The hermit possesses a jewel with a secret diagram revealing the whereabouts of an ancient treasure. The story whirls around the globe, from China to Africa to the site of a lost city, before climaxing with an earthquake.

The part that Lang wrote—*Die Rache der Maud Ferguson (The Revenge of Maud Fergusson)*—might be considered a rough draft of subsequent work. Frederick Ott wrote that one chapter, set in Africa, featured a towering citadel that evokes both the stylized medievalism of the cathedral in *Die Nibelungen* and the expressionist modernity of the Tower of Babel in *Metropolis*. European film critics who have seen a recently restored version of Joe May's eight-part serial argue that it is mature in scope and style, in many ways a harbinger of Lang's later epics. That would put the director deeper in May's debt, and could be another reason for Lang to discount this particular mentor.

It must be said, however, that too many of these pre-1920 films scripted by Lang are lost or exist in dubious condition, or have been squirreled away in motion picture archives restricted to scholars. Ordinary film students interested in assessing Lang's primitive work are forced to rely on the synopses of contemporary reviewers—"the clumsy and sentimental plot descriptions of third-rate critics," in the words of Lotte Eisner.

"Lang had already begun his practice of giving very detailed indications of the action," reported Lotte Eisner in her book. "He recalls how he tried in one of these early [Otto] Rippert scripts to confine himself to a single sentence: 'Here an orgy takes place,' without going into details. Rippert came to him and asked, 'But what shall I do here?' so from then on Lang made a habit of describing every sequence in great detail."

That wasn't enough. Now, Lang, in talks with Pommer, strongly criticized

Rippert's directing. He thought he could do just as well himself, and Pommer promised to give him a chance. When Lang wrote a new, "particularly pleasing" script called *Halbblut (Half-Breed)*, he made it a condition of sale that he be allowed to direct the film himself.

Events were moving swiftly, in Lang's life, and in Germany's realignment. A general strike on January 6, 1919, had brought Berlin to a standstill. Communist leaders Rosa Luxemburg and Karl Liebknecht were executed by army units suppressing the uprising on January 15, and on January 19 came the first election of the national assembly of the Weimar Republic.

Lang said more than once in interviews that the Spartacists—Liebknecht's organization of left-wing militants—were rioting as he drove his car to work for the first time as a director. "My car was repeatedly stopped on the way to the studio by armed rebels, but it would have taken more than a revolution to stop me directing for the first time." If that colorful story emphasizing his bravery is true that would date the filming of *Halbblut* to January of 1919, when the Spartakisten uprising provoked street fights, strikes, and martial law to disrupt the newly elected National Assembly.

Halbblut is the story of a daughter of a mixed-race liaison, a former whore from an opium den who ruins two men, one of whom dies in an asylum, the other in a penitentiary. According to a summary in *Der Film*, "Only a *mestizo*, a kindred spirit, finds happiness with her. Together with him she engages in cardsharping in their own establishment until their game is up. Before they succeed in fleeing from Europe, intending to escape to Mexico with all their spoil, fate catches up with her in the shape of a bullet from the revolver of a man whom she has cheated."

The film was another to star the Decla actress Ressel Orla. The excellent cameraman was Carl Hoffmann. Nobody on a Fritz Lang set would be more important to the "eye man" than his cameraman, who was always chosen with deliberation and then pushed to extremes. The director would work on a number of his early films with Hoffmann "because he had a Decla contract," as the director put it—in contrast to "my beloved Fritz Arno Wagner," who photographed several of Lang's later and better-known works for Ufa.

A former still photographer from Freiburg, Hoffmann had worked his way up in the industry, becoming chief cameraman for Pommer's productions. His all-around proficiency could not be questioned; in his long career, Hoffmann even authored screenplays. But Lang clashed with cameramen who had their own stubborn ideas, and he and Hoffmann, both vain perfectionists, had a stormy relationship.

Still, Hoffmann was like Lang in another respect: The director insisted on technical experimentation, and Hoffmann was a tireless innovator. With the same boyish zest that had led him to devour mechanical science magazines and feast on future fiction, Lang set out to attack the accepted limits of lighting, camera movement, and technological engineering. The director was never happier than when rigging some new device for creating atmosphere or sparking the drama. His appetite for camera stunts was an essential part of his directorial persona, though it tended to exasperate as well as inspire people who worked alongside him.

Lang wanted one scene in *Halbblut* to be filmed only with the flickering light of candles, for example. Hoffmann, half-grudging, was badgered into attempting the setup—and accomplished the impossible. The scene amazed everyone. Darkness and shadows would henceforth become crucial to the mystique of a Fritz Lang film, and for many who study the director's work, an incessant, visual metaphor for the dark soul of the human race.

Ressel Orla was popular in her day, and Lang's first film as director was well-received when it premiered at the prestigious Marmorhaus on Berlin's main artery, the Kurfürstendamm. "Fritz Lang's direction shows taste, expert knowledge, and a rare instinct," exclaimed the *Der Film* reviewer. "Top quality," agreed the motion picture trade paper *Licht-Bild-Bühne*.

Halbblut was exhibited in April. *Totentanz* showed in June. Lang was already entrenched in the business; advertisements had begun to proclaim him one of the "big names in modern film" in Germany. And already he was at work on his second film as director.

Der Herr der Liebe (*The Master of Love*) was made for the smaller Helios Film Studios. Lang acted as producer as well as director, but did not write the scenario, which was contributed by Leo Koffler. This feature, which was not released until the autumn, recounted another love story about "unhappy love in the mode of a society drama," according to press accounts. The dashing Carl de Vogt, who was to become one of the director's recurring actors, and Gilda Langer, who had appeared in *Halbblut*, took the starring roles. The cameraman was Emil Schünemann, who photographed a number of Lang's pre-Ufa films.

Years later, Erich Pommer would say that with *Halbblut* and *Der Herr der Liebe*—two films unavailable today—"Fritz brilliantly proved himself." The director himself was not sure how exceptional they really were. He made *Halbblut* in just five days, Lang recalled in a 1967 interview. "Do you think it can be good?"

The year 1919 was also, probably, the year the film director married "L." Perhaps the marriage took place during the summer, when Lang requested official forms from Austrian authorities to certify, for some unstated purpose, his birth and citizenship. Public records were searched in several countries, but "L" 's real name shows up only once: in family archives at Vienna's Rathaus, or City Hall. There the first wife of Fritz Lang was added to files as "Lisa Rosenthal." It is impossible to know who placed the name there; unclear (and unlikely) that Lang's mother and father were at the Lang-Rosenthal nuptials; unclear where, when, even *if*, such a wedding took place.

Lisa Rosenthal may have been a pseudonym, after all—like "Patti Grey," whose stage name misleads police in *Beyond a Reasonable Doubt*, the director's last American film. Or Lisa may have been a shortened form of Elisabeth or Elise. Lang researchers have tried without success to verify her identity. Frederick Ott claimed Lang's first wife was a "Russian from Vilna." Georges Sturm, quoting various sources, thought she might be the daughter of a minister from the Baltics. Professor Cornelius Schnauber, who explored the subject of the first wife in guarded terms with the director (and then, like Lotte Eisner, withheld discussion of her from his books about Lang), believed she may have been Jewish.

It is possible she was a nurse in the hospital in Vienna, one of the aristo-cratic volunteers, and that it was there Lang first met her during World War I. More likely, as Lang hinted on more than one occasion, Lisa Rosenthal performed as a dancer in Vienna's cabarets. Lang (like certain characters in his films) had a penchant for chorus girls, dancers, actresses, and fashion mod-els, while he showed little interest, in life or films, in housewives or ungla-morous women.

It seems reasonable to infer that Lang brought Lisa Rosenthal to Berlin when he left Vienna, and installed her in his apartment. The *Todesfalls-Aufnahme,* or protocol taken in Gars am Kamp at the time of Lang's mother's death in August of 1920, clearly states that the director was married and living in Berlin at Tharandterstrasse 1, a side street in the solid middle-class area of Wilmersdorf. This is the only public document referring to a marriage that must have taken place before Lang's career really blossomed.

The director rarely spoke about the first Frau Lang, never gave her name for the public record. Only on rare occasions, always to the most intimate friends, would he confess that she had existed. And "confess" is the right word, for her tragic fate was the result of one of his worst transgressions. Her story was one legend he would never trumpet.

The second half of 1919 was devoted to Lang's third film as director, the first in the filmography that can be said to hint at a budding master.

Die Spinnen (The Spiders) was an elaborate adventure epic composed of two parts: *Der goldene See (The Golden Lake)* and *Das Brillantenschiff (The Diamond Ship).* *Der goldene See* was produced first, while the second part, *Das Brillantenschiff,* was actually filmed some months later.

The film had a long subtitle, roughly translated as "The Adventures of Kay Hoog in Worlds Known and Unknown." Lang's script for the film, the last in his career for which he would take solo credit, was one of those recipes for which he had a soft spot—*The Perils of Pauline*–type cliffhangers whose pop-ularity was then sweeping the globe.

The main character, Kay Hoog, is a sportsman-explorer with a vast library, loyal servants, and the finest wines at his disposal. Lost treasure beckons him. Incredible dangers litter his path. And a secret, conspiratorial organization, dubbed the Spiders for their habit of leaving tarantulas behind as calling cards, is determined to make trouble for him.

The story begins at a high-society club in San Francisco, where Kay Hoog tells of a message found in a barnacle-encrusted bottle, relating to a missing Harvard professor and an ancient cache of valuables lying under the sea at seventy-five degrees west longitude. A cross-continent race ensues between Hoog and the Spiders, led by the evil temptress Lio Sha. The film offers a parade of hypnosis and clairvoyance; secret conclaves of top-hatted gentlemen; descending platforms and crystal-gazing mirrors; train, balloon, and boat chases; cowboy and Peruvian Inca sequences; giant snakes; and the first, though hardly the last, climactic flooding of underground chambers in a Fritz Lang film.

Although the treasure is lost forever beneath the sea, Hoog manages to rescue Naela, the Priestess of the Sun, who falls in love with the heroic playboy, then forgoes her ancient ways, and returns with him to San Francisco. The jealous Lio Sha, who craves Hoog, then takes revenge, and the good-hearted Priestess is murdered. A tarantula reveals the culprit. The first part of *Die Spinnen* ends with Hoog grieving and vowing retribution.

It was (as the synopsis indicates) a chock-a-block production, the director's most expensive to date. Lang was not alone, especially in the silent era—in Germany, and elsewhere—in equating budget and running length with importance. Starting with *Die Spinnen* and for a long time after, the director would make a credo out of bigness.

Some of *Die Spinnen* was photographed outdoors in picturesque locations. The Incan sets were constructed on the grounds of Hamburg's well-known Hagenbeck Zoological Garden, a private zoo arranged partly in a Chinese style. The arrangements were made by Heinrich Umlauff, curator of an ethnographic museum and an acquaintance of the director, who inaugurated the tradition of having an "expert" brought in to consult on a Fritz Lang film.

Publicity extolled the authenticity of costumes and decor supplied by the museum. The director claimed the *Die Spinnen* settings had been inspired by the "memories of my travels" (in her book, Lotte Eisner would praise the "documentary instinct" of the replicated locales). Today, the cowboys and Incas look more playful than documentary-like, though no more nor less ersatz than similar attempts in other films of the period. Authenticity was part of the psychology of Lang's creativity, and also made good publicity for him.

Die Spinnen, more importantly, marked the first time Lang worked with the ingenious art directors Hermann Warm and Otto Hunte. Hunte, particularly, served the director long and well. Beginning his career as an experimental artist in Munich, Hunte would become the outstanding architect of Lang's visual ideas in *Dr. Mabuse, Der Spieler, Die Nibelungen, Metropolis, Spione,* and *Die Frau im Mond*—usually working so closely with his colleague, the master builder Karl Vollbrecht, that their teamwork was inseparable.

Lang had come of age in World War I as an officer, and being in command was fundamental to his personality. He needed to spearhead a corps of skilled subordinates and preside over a veritable army of cast and crew. On a film set he acted very much the general, and this, *Die Spinnen*, would prove his first outstanding campaign.

His troops encompassed, for the first time, literally hundreds of actors, extras, and technical personnel. Kay Hoog was portrayed by Carl de Vogt. Lio Sha, the Spider Lady, was acted by Ressel Orla. Georg John, Edgar Pauly, Paul Biensfeldt, and Paul Morgan played featured roles, and would recur in noteworthy character parts in future Fritz Lang productions. They and others were in the process of becoming an informal stock company for the director. Comfortable with character actors—who needed minimal guidance for their colorful parts—Lang adopted them and made them his friends.

The crucial role of Priestess of the Sun was given to Lil Dagover. Destined to become one of Germany's great silent screen heroines—in films such as *Das Kabinett des Dr. Caligari* (*The Cabinet of Dr. Caligari*) for Robert Wiene and F. W. Murnau's version of *Tartuffe*—here she took her first major part. Lang, from the very outset of his career, made a point of eschewing the established "star system," rejecting faces already well-known to the public. Better to mold newcomers, especially actresses, who were not yet ego-mad narcissists. It was an added benefit that these "virgin stars" felt more susceptible and beholden to the director who had launched them.

Dagover's memoirs relate how, starting out, she met some of Germany's most illustrious figures, among them Fritz Lang. In her memory the director was tall and superbly conditioned, a masculine man. His presence was at once magnetic and intimidating. He hypnotized people with his air of supreme confidence, and terrified them with his barking orders. Men and women alike found him exciting.

One trademark was his elegant, form-fitting suits (sky-blue a favorite color), furnished by Vienna's finest tailors. His hair was always impeccably groomed. The monocle was an undeniable facet of his image, alternately attractive and repellent; it never failed to draw people in, giving him the air of a Cyclops with weltschmerz in the eye.

Dagover met directors Robert Wiene and Alwin Neuss around the same time as Lang. These personalities were similarly omnipotent, she recalled, but also alike in their nervousness and volatility; they were touchy and easily offended. "Everybody thought of himself as the greatest and they were entitled to do so too, as I quickly found out." Each of the Decla-Bioscop directors, upon meeting her, commended her beauty, rhapsodized over her lovely skin, perfectly shaped face, exquisite eyes. Startling metamorphoses would follow these soft-spoken compliments. Suddenly they would turn away and begin to rampage through the studio, screaming at their assistants. "The next minute they would be gentle again—especially when the executives came into the studio."

This was Lang to a T—if he was imperious with his foot soldiers, he was slippery with other generals and deferential to the higher-ups. And he was not always gentle and ingratiating with the stars, not even in Lil Dagover's case. He could behave unkindly to actresses as well as actors; more unkindly to actresses, some people thought, because the men had a tendency to bark back. The scenes in Lang's films were generally weighted toward women, and actresses were urged by the director to explore a broader range of behavior and emotion. The stakes were always higher for them.

Technical problems were easier for Lang to handle, and *Die Spinnen* abounded in the showy moves that were becoming a defining characteristic of his work. Superimpositions, wipes, fade-outs, and split-screen vignettes gave verve and energy to Lang's serial. Amazingly, everyone was working with cumbersome arc lights, immovable, hand-cranked equipment, and film stock that today would be considered shockingly primitive.

The director took only a short time off before he put Lil Dagover back in exotic costume, amid Japanese scenery, for *Harakiri*.

Harakiri was based on the American play *Madame Butterfly* by David Belasco, adapted in this instance not by the director but by the prominent German scenarist Max Jungk. The story, set in Asia, revolved around a young Japanese woman's tragic romance with a European naval officer, an affair that produces an illegitimate child. She is a geisha in the play, a noblewoman in *Harakiri*—all the worse for her shame. Her disgraced father commits ritual disembowelment, and inevitably his daughter's suicide must follow. "It's better to die with honor than live with shame!" she proclaims before killing herself.

More than one critic commented, when the picture was released in December of 1919, on the breathtaking ("beautiful to cry for") footage of O-Take-San (Lil Dagover) vainly waiting on the seacoast for her loved one to return. Actually, it was Joe May's property on Woltersdorf Lake that provided the stunning backdrop; most of the production actually consisted of interior sequences, and most interiors, in a Lang film, were likely to be suffocating enclosures. The director's characters were always escaping flooded rooms, mental wards, jail cells, bourgeois marriages . . . or caves.

Caves, which were important emblems for Lang, crop up in his earliest extant work—*Die Spinnen* and *Harakiri*. Lotte Eisner discounted any psychological explanation for this proclivity, suggesting that Lang's love for caves was "no more than a love of the mysterious, atmospheric, and unusual, a curiosity about the mysteries that lurk beneath the surface of the earth" as well as an excuse for "chiaroscuro effects." A simpler explanation may be that Lower Austria was well-known for its caves, and Gars am Kamp, where Lang's family retreated every summer during his boyhood, had castles and ruins and several caves large enough to figure in area travel guides.

For many years *Harakiri* was considered another one of the director's lost works, until, in the mid-1980s, a Dutch version was discovered moldering in the Netherlands Film Museum in Amsterdam. When the film was restored and presented to modern audiences, it was seen as a delicate and mannered work by Lang's later measure.

The release of *Harakiri* was preceded in October by distribution of *Der goldene See*, the first half of *Die Spinnen*.

Advertisements for *Die Spinnen* boasted that Decla had achieved parity with the U.S. motion picture industry ("which makes mainly Westerns"), as evidenced by this first-class Fritz Lang achievement ("which may also attract attention abroad").

The plot was a hastily stitched patchwork. Pacing was uneven. Action parts whizzed by, and dialogue scenes seemed to take forever. Even Lotte Eisner in her book celebrating Lang wrote that "Fritz Lang has yet to discover the accelerating power of ellipsis." But if *Der goldene See* was unabashedly light-weight—its intellectual content "nonexistent," in the words of Paul M. Jensen, author of *The Cinema of Fritz Lang*—it was also rousing entertainment, its youthful bravura impressive nearly eighty years later.

Contemporary critics rated it highly, a crowd-pleaser as unpretentious as it was likable. "A thrilling well-made plot without any literary ambitions," exclaimed *Der Film*, "the first German film deliberately to use the technique of the penny dreadful." Throughout Germany and the consortium of German-language nations, audiences flocked to see *Die Spinnen*, helping to consolidate the future of Lang, Pommer, and Decla.

In mid-1919, Lang had been approached by Erich Pommer with a script about the head of a lunatic asylum who manipulates a somnambulist in order to commit murder. The Decla-Bioscop staff of art directors—Hermann Warm,

Walter Reimann, and Walter Röhrig—had prepared sketches of the Expressionist-style sets. Would Lang be interested in making *Das Kabinett des Dr. Caligari* (*The Cabinet of Dr. Caligari*) his next project?

The script was a collaboration by two friends: a Czech poet, Hans Janowitz, and writer Carl Mayer, from the Austrian city of Graz. Janowitz was inspired by a strange incident from his youth, and Mayer embroidered his story with scenes from his own experience and imagination. A Dramaturg for a small theater on the Blumenstrasse, Mayer wrote a starring role for actress Gilda Langer, with whom he was in love. The untimely death of Langer had nominated Lil Dagover as the film's next-likely leading lady, which was one more reason Lang seemed the obvious candidate as director.

Lang, in script discussions, made at least one significant suggestion: that the scenario be framed by a *Rahmenhandlung*, or conventional flashback—with prologue and epilogue, in a realistic mode—better to convey the point of view of the main character, a madman. "Lang argued that the Rahmenhandlung would intensify the terror of the Expressionist sequences," wrote Frederick Ott in his book about Lang. "Pommer adopted this proposal by adding a scene in the garden of the asylum to open and close *Caligari*."

Now, however, the extraordinary success of *Die Spinnen* forced Lang to drop any further involvement in *Dr. Caligari* and focus on putting together Part Two of the Kay Hoog serial. And *Dr. Caligari* was handed over to another director born in Austria, Robert Wiene.

Wiene went along with Lang's idea wholeheartedly. Janowitz and Mayer vehemently protested on the principle that, in the words of Siegfried Kracauer, the Rahmenhandlung "perverted, if not reversed, their intrinsic intentions. While the original story exposed the madness inherent in authority, Wiene's *Caligari* glorified authority and convicted its antagonist of madness. A revolutionary film was thus turned into a conformist one." In the event, the Rahmenhandlung became Lang's crucial contribution to a production later to be considered one of the all-time silent-era classics.

Lang did nothing on *Das Brillantenschiff* to tamper with the mold that had proved successful with the first part of *Die Spinnen*. His script was another marvel of nonstop implausibility, involving mental telepathy, a secret Chinese city guarded by tigers, classified documents coveted by foreign powers, a kidnapping, a sea race to find a Buddha-headed diamond linked to an ancient prophecy, explosions and underground flooding in the faraway Falkland Islands off the coast of Argentina.

Das Brillantenschiff was significant as the first Fritz Lang film photographed by Karl Freund, undoubtedly "the most important German cameraman" of the silent age, in the words of Hans Michael Bock. A native Bohemian, Freund had been a newsreel photographer, then a projectionist at Gaumont, where he and Pommer met and became lifelong friends. He had started his career as a cameraman for Sascha Film in Vienna prior to the war. Like Lang, Freund had served in the Austrian Army. After the war, he swiftly became known as a pioneer of camera movement, lighting, high-speed film, and early color processing.

The cameraman was also an inventor, known to have a share in several valuable patents. Freund would become so pre-eminent at Ufa that, at his height, later in the 1920s, the studio placed a servant and luxury limousine at his round-the-clock disposal. Enormous in size and equal to Lang in autocratic style, Freund did not endear himself to Lang; he was another photographer with whom the director fought. But at Pommer's urging Lang would work with Freund, masterfully, not only on *Die Spinnen*, but again on the epic *Metropolis*.

Nowadays, people can see *Der goldene See* and *Das Brillantenschiff*, the two parts of *Die Spinnen*, in video or revival, as a single, exhilarating entity. But the first half is the better-constructed film, tighter, faster-paced, the freshness and freedom of creativity reflected on the screen. Lang knew, even at the time, that Part Two was an inferior product.

There were understandable reasons. *Das Brillantenschiff* had to be rushed into production. *Der goldene See* had been spiced with Mexican and Incan vistas, but this time, weather prematurely forced the company from the Hagenbeck grounds into the studio. Much of *Das Brillantenschiff* ended up taking place in rooms and buildings, the plot remained murky, and the sea chase and Falkland Islands scenes amounted to a stingy spectacle. Matters were not helped that the Priestess of the Sun had been killed off in the first half; Lil Dagover was not only ravishing to behold, but her character had provided emotional ballast.

When released in February of 1920, *Das Brillantenschiff* proved popular enough, but the director remained "angry" about the circumstances of production, according to Lotte Eisner. Acting accordingly, he severed his Decla contract, signing up again with Joe May and May-Film GmbH. It was May then who introduced Lang to a woman whose close affinity with the director would make her his most important—and controversial—collaborator.

Thea von Harbou was blond and blue-eyed, a stately German type. People remember her as "tall" because of her commanding air, although she was only five feet six. Her hair in those days was usually smoothed down, pageboy style. She dressed simply but with individuality—silk or lace dresses, fur coat, cloche hat.

"Her photographs show her as the handsome 'Germanic' type and suggest an Ibsen character, oscillating between Hedda Gabler, Hilde Wangel, and Solveig," wrote Reinhold Keiner in his book *Thea von Harbou und der deutsche Film bis 1933*. "Feminine and emancipated at the same time; domestic and maternal and yet sophisticated; sensitive and psychologically oriented."

Her lineage was more Prussian than Lang's monocle. The von Harbou family tree was stocked with minor nobility, government officials, and military officers. The family lived for a time in southern Saxony, in rolling countryside south of Dresden, on the border of Czechoslovakia. Her father, a former Prussian officer, was a senior forester. Her brother, the firstborn, was Horst von Harbou, who grew up with an interest in photography and in due time also went to work for Ufa, becoming the still photographer for Fritz Lang and Thea von Harbou's most famous productions.

Educated in a convent and by private tutors, von Harbou learned several languages, possessed an ear for music (a complement to Lang in that category), and played both violin and piano. Indeed, according to relatives, she was something of a child prodigy. At eleven, she could recite from Goethe's *Faust*; at twelve, Schiller's *Don Carlos*. As a young girl von Harbou sold her first short story to a magazine, and on her thirteenth birthday had a volume of poems privately published—"not love poems, which would be normal at her age, but poems which impressed adults with an understanding of art," according to her cousin, Dr. Anne-Marie Durand-Wever, who first met her in the winter of 1904–1905.

A child of privilege, von Harbou nonetheless understood that her future lay in going out and earning a living. Her decision to become an actress led to a family crisis. Her father was horrified and forbade her to use the name of von Harbou, but she was supported by her mother, who accompanied her early tours along with her grandmother, a French marquise.

Von Harbou made her theater debut in the Düsseldorfer Schauspielhaus in 1906, and thereafter acted in Weimar, Chemnitz, and Aachen before World War I. It was in Aachen that she came under the direction of her future husband, Rudolf Klein-Rogge, a cultivated and good-humored man with profuse blond hair and a beak of a nose.

She had effortlessly dashed off her first novel as a teenager; now, while touring as an actress, she began to publish short stories, animal tales, fairy tales, and full-length novels. Drawn to epic subjects, myths and legends, her writing took a nationalistic turn with the onset of the war. Her novels became patriotic and morale-boosting, urging women to sacrifice and duty while promoting the eternal glory of the fatherland.

Von Harbou married Klein-Rogge during the war, and switched to full-time writing. They moved to Berlin in 1917, where she launched a series of popular novels, while he looked for work as an actor, on the screen. Late in 1918 or early in 1919, von Harbou met Joe May—and through May, a brief time later, Fritz Lang. Two years older than the director, she was already well-established as an author in her own right.

According to her own account of things, von Harbou happened to read a brief newspaper item announcing that one of her stories had been bought by May-Film GmbH. She phoned her publisher right away, asking for an explanation. He put her in contact with Joe May, who was preparing to direct *Die heilige Simplizia* (*St. Simplicia*), the first of several features the producer-director would adapt from von Harbou's work.

Up to this time von Harbou had not given much thought to motion pictures, but now she plunged into writing scenarios for Joe May. One job swiftly led to another. Her fiction output slowed down. In short order she would become one of Germany's most celebrated film writers, not only because of her partnership with Fritz Lang, but also for writing scripts for F. W. Murnau, Carl Dreyer, E. A. Dupont, and other German luminaries.

Lang and Thea von Harbou discovered an instant kinship.

Von Harbou, as a young girl, had been raised on a country estate, which gave her a love of nature and animals that she shared with Lang. Horses and riding were a mutual passion. Like Lang, von Harbou also enjoyed popular fiction; she worshiped Karl May and in her twenties could regale visitors by reciting May's translation of parts of the Koran. On one occasion, Hans Feld, an editor of the *Film-Kurier,* Berlin's answer to *Variety,* tracked down a set of rare first editions of Karl May books, and sent them off as a gift to Lang and von Harbou. "Several days after that," Feld recalled in a published interview, "I received a letter that didn't say anything besides: 'Volume four, page seventeen, line seven.' I went to get the book and read: 'Of course those two went into raptures.'"

Among their common interests was a restless curiosity about foreign cultures. Von Harbou was, like Lang, fascinated with India, where she hoped to journey one day. And according to her publicity (though publicity could stretch the truth as imaginatively as fiction), von Harbou had visited Africa as a young woman, climbed the peak of Kilimanjaro and "nearly lost her life amid the snow and ice." Her first scenario in collaboration with Lang would exploit their mutual fixation with India. The second would be set in the dangerous vastness of mountains, amid snow and ice.

Von Harbou was busy with the adaptation of her 1917 novel *Das indische Grabmal (The Indian Tomb),* when Joe May assigned Lang to help her with the writing and plan the details of production. Her novel was about a German architect who falls in love with a temple dancer in India. The scenario would be divided, as in the case of *Die Spinnen,* into two parts: Part One, called *Die Sendung des Yoghi (The Mission of the Yogi),* would be followed by Part Two, *Das indische Grabmal.*

At the same time, von Harbou and Lang began to develop a second, project, an original story that could not have been more dissimilar from the Indian epic. This scenario was drenched in melodrama and Christian mythology. The plot involved a woman and an out-of-wedlock child fathered by an author-philosopher who espouses free love. The illegitimate mother marries the man's twin brother. The author fakes his own suicide and goes off to live as a hermit in the mountains, where he is pursued by the distraught woman. The story ends with a miracle amid a spectacular snowstorm and avalanche, with a statue of the Virgin Mary that appears to come alive and walk on the snow. Hence the working title: "Madonna im Schnee."

Joe May praised the script of *Das indische Grabmal* but unaccountably delayed the two-part Indian film. Instead he gave a priority go-ahead to *Das wandernde Bild (The Wandering Image),* as "Madonna im Schnee" was eventually retitled. The director had little choice but to acquiesce. "He [Lang] was probably not quite as motivated as he was for *Das indische Grabmal,*" conceded production designer Erich Kettelhut.

Kettelhut, who hooked up with Lang on *Das wandernde Bild,* was a key addition to the director's army. A native Berliner, Kettelhut was a former theater-set artist whose friendship with Otto Hunte had led him into motion pictures. One of Kettelhut's specialties was the building of scaled-down or "miniaturized" sets. His unpublished memoirs, on deposit at the Stiftung Deutsche Kinemathek in Berlin, provide a vivid reminiscence of working with Lang.

"Everybody in Berlin was talking about him [Lang]," Kettelhut recalled in his memoirs. "He had joined the ranks of the biggest directors overnight because of the films he had made recently, which everyone admired for their striking images. Insiders told real horror stories about his fanatical devotion to work and the huge demands he made on his crew."

The mountain scenes of *Das wandernde Bild* were scheduled to be photographed in the Bavarian Alps in July 1920. Mia May was cast as the victimized mother. Rudolf Klein-Rogge, acting his first role for Fritz Lang, played not one of the leads but a featured role as a cousin of the twin brothers.

According to Kettelhut, Lang was slow to realize that all along Joe May had been maneuvering to take over the directorial reins of *Das indische Grabmal*. It was von Harbou who brought Lang the bad news, up in the Alps. May, according to Lang, used as his excuse the argument that the costly production, in the hands of a relatively novice director, alarmed bank investors. "It was a lie. In truth, Joe May was convinced the film would be a huge success and he wanted to make it himself."

Perhaps Lang associated location work, ever after, with that signal disappointment. He would basically retreat inside the studio—even for exteriors—for the rest of his career. Filming *Das wandernde Bild* took a psychological as well as physical toll, and the physical challenges were considerable. The director struggled with the mountain terrain, the arduous weather, and especially the avalanche climax, which he had hoped to accomplish with explosions. Try as he might, he could not capture that vital shot of the Madonna statue gliding miraculously downhill. He finally decided to solve the problem in Berlin, with special effects, later on. A miniaturized shot would have to be devised, and that is when Erich Kettelhut was introduced to Lang.

"I would have recognized him right away without an introduction, since his picture was in the papers a lot," recalled Kettelhut. "He gave me a detailed and clear description of what the scene should look like, which way the Madonna statue should glide, and showed me the photos of the failed attempts. It was an expert speaking; someone who knew about technical things, who knew his stuff right down to the smallest detail, who knew what he wanted to do and how to do it and who got more and more enthused in the course of our meeting. And he asked me, sounding extremely doubtful, whether I could really scale down a section of the cliff face and still retain the proportions that were in the photos."

A week later, Lang checked back with Kettelhut. The director looked over "the lousy job we had done critically, but quite indulgently, hardly paid any attention to my short explanations and called out for a camera right away," remembered Kettelhut. "Lang peered through the lens for a long time, altered the specifications by a few millimeters several times, then nodded curtly. 'We can use it.'

"Suddenly a different Lang was in the studio; no longer the cautious skeptic, but an enthusiastic member of the team. We tried out the scene all day long. Fritz Lang pitched in, too, and never flagged. Finally, at ten P.M., he declared himself satisfied: we could film it the next day.

"He was so obsessed, so uncompromising and so driven to capture the image he had visualized on film, without taking his needs or those of others into consideration—just for a miniature shot. What could it be like when Fritz Lang shot an important scene with actors and extras? I would find out later. The next day the little Madonna moved up and down the hillside at least twenty times before Fritz Lang was satisfied."

At the time of the film's release in December 1920, the prestigious *Film-Kurier* would hail Lang's newest work as "outstanding." Described as "another lost film" in authoritative texts as late as 1981, *Das wandernde Bild* was located in the Cinematica Brasiliera in São Paulo in 1986, and carefully reconstructed by archivists. Some scenes are missing in the restored version, and therefore the plot doesn't add up. But the atmosphere is evocative, and the outdoor photography—by another pioneering cameraman, Guido Seeber, with whom Lang worked only this once—is spectacular.

Das wandernde Bild was successful enough, yet it gnawed at Lang that *Das indische Grabmal* had been stolen away. The two-part Indian epic was being built up in the press because of its grandiose scope and mammoth budget. It must have gnawed further when *Das indische Grabmal* was released, more than a year later, and *Der Film* extolled Joe May's achievement as "the world's greatest film," thrillingly directed, yet unfortunately saddled with "a script that is logically and psychologically weak."

The loss of *Das indische Grabmal* was a betrayal, one of those setbacks the director never forgot. That was one film he always wanted back. Fritz Lang would have made "the world's greatest film" even better. After finishing *Das wandernde Bild*, a furious Lang quit May-Film GmbH, and vowed never again to work under the auspices of Joe May.

Now Lang returned to Erich Pommer and Decla-Bioscop, bringing Thea von Harbou with him. Pommer handled Lang more shrewdly, genuinely admiring the director while at the same time always careful to stroke his ego. He was canny and strategic about applying directorial restraints. One of Pommer's policies was to appoint an assistant to Lang, diplomatic but without any real power, to serve as a foil, a go-between for production crises.

Alfred Zeisler, Pommer's erstwhile location manager, would take all the heat from Lang and insulate Pommer. Yet whenever Lang tried to do something behind Pommer's back, Zeisler would be obliged to report secretly to the producer. Confronted by Pommer, Lang could fault Zeisler's treachery. Lang claimed to suffer watchdogs in Hollywood later on, more than once complaining about producer's spies and traitors in published interviews, but his paranoia was deeply rooted in his career, back in Berlin.

Lang had certain bad habits, Pommer warned his location manager. The director would tinker with the set and lighting and procrastinate forever with a shot if allowed. "Listen," Pommer warned Zeisler, "Lang starts shooting at two o'clock in the afternoon. It's costing a fortune—you can't [let him] do that. And before that he plays around with girls." Zeisler, thinking to win Lang over, made the mistake of taking him aside and repeating Pommer's true views in confidence. "After that, Lang hated me," recalled Zeisler.

Lang was already notorious for his multiple takes, a constant source of aggravation to his producers. The perfectionist director was known to shoot twenty or thirty versions of a scene, sometimes printing only two or three of the takes. This time-consuming practice annoyed Pommer all the more because he noticed little difference between the takes. Lang chose one of the

1918-1921   **67**

first and one of the last takes automatically, Pommer believed, regardless of
their quality.

On one of their films, Pommer asked the editor to switch the identifying
slates on the printed takes. The producer kept up the deception for a week. Lang
of course continued to choose randomly from among the first and last takes,
although in reality the slate numbers had been switched around. When, at last,
Pommer told him what he had done, Lang was brought up short. His reaction
was good-humored, but for a while the director was forced to improve his behavior, shooting only a few takes of each setup, saving time and footage. Later,
when Pommer wasn't watching so closely, Lang would drift back to his old ways.

No doubt the disappointment of losing *Das indische Grabmal* was entwined
in Lang's mind with the untimely death of "my adored mother." The two
events wounded him almost simultaneously.

The director was up in the mountains filming *Das wandernde Bild*—near
Mount Watzman in the Bavarian Alps, at an altitude of over six thousand
feet—when word came that Paula Schlesinger Lang had passed away. She died
in Gars am Kamp on July 11, 1920, at age fifty-five. The cause is listed on the
death certificate as "Rotlauf," also known as erysipelas, or Saint Anthony's
fire—an acute skin disease, coupled with pneumonia. But these may have been
complications from breast cancer, which is what Lang often told acquaintances
was his mother's fate.*

Lang was advised of funeral plans but made the decision to keep working. In
the course of his life he had more professional regrets than personal ones; still, in
candid moments, the director would confess to friends his heartache that he had
declared himself too busy to interrupt a film to attend his mother's funeral.

The firm of A. Lang & Co., under Paula Lang's co-stewardship, had expanded its activities, buying and selling real estate and dealing in construction
supplies. Though it prospered before World War I, the company faltered and
ceased operation a few years after the war. In 1920, the family estate was
valued roughly at 102,400 Kronen.** The inventory listed the villa in Gars am
Kamp, the contents of the house in Zeltgasse, along with savings, bonds, jewelry, and furniture. The Lang family also owned a piece of land in Vienna's
Second district, as well as four plots of farmland in Lower Austria.

Curiously, Paula Lang's last will and testament took seven years to finalize.
The case went all the way up to the Vienna Supreme Court as the Langs
fought among themselves over disposition. According to court papers, Lang
sided with his father Anton Lang against his brother Dolf, who was physically

---

*Paula Lang preceded Lang's grandmother, Johanna Lang—mother of Anton Lang and the doy-
enne of the family—in death. Johanna Lang did not die until 1922, at age eighty-three, and
she was buried in the Endl family plot in Vienna. Lang's mother, on the other hand, was laid
to rest at Gars am Kamp in the Catholic parish cemetery.

**It is extremely difficult to calculate the estate's actual value in today's terms. Roughly, the sum
might be converted to $8,931 in U.S.-1996 dollars, which doesn't sound like very much, for the
good reason that nothing was worth much in Austria in August 1920, due to the big devaluation
and post–World War I shake-up. The same total of 102,400 Kronen before World War I would
amount roughly to more than half a million dollars, converted to 1996 terms. Suffice to say
that, by the time of Paula Schlesinger Lang's death, the family estate had depreciated considerably and was worth well under ten thousand dollars.

barred by Anton at the door from entering Zeltgasse for an inventory of the fixtures and belongings.

Eventually, Dolf was worn down. Declaring himself a "poor bank clerk" without resources, he yielded to his brother and father, dropped all claims and reached a truce. Under the terms of a 1927 agreement, Dolf relinquished all inheritance claims. The estate was then allocated equally between Fritz Lang and his father; by then, though, because of catastrophic devaluation, its value had been reduced drastically. The settlement was virtually symbolic.

Though he had allied himself with Anton Lang, Lang grew to believe that his father had withheld certain precious objects, jewelry, and mementos that had belonged to his mother, in order to sell them during hard times later on. The director discovered a letter from his mother in a linen closet indicating that some items had been set aside expressly for him. When Lang passed through Vienna, later on in the 1920s, he made a point of visiting the house— from which he, unlike Dolf, was not barred—where he rummaged around in drawers, looking for these promised personal effects. They could never be found.

After *Das wandernde Bild*, Lang and von Harbou rushed into a picture for Decla called *Kämpfende Herzen (Fighting Hearts)*, but also known as *Die Vier um die Frau (Four Around a Woman)*. Shown in February of 1921, this film has generally been overlooked in Lang's canon, not least because for a long time it too was thought to have vanished and only recently became a rediscovery. On the evidence available today, *Kämpfende Herzen* turns out first-rate, showing the progress and development of Lang's filmmaking.

Again, one of the stars was Rudolf Klein-Rogge, who was still married to Thea von Harbou. Others in the ensemble included Carola Tölle, Hermann Böttcher, Ludwig Hartau, and Anton Edthofer. Otto Kanturek, who would also work with Lang on 1929's *Die Frau im Mond*, served as cameraman. Lang and von Harbou were jointly credited with the scenario, adapted from a pre-existing script by Ralph E. Vanloo.

The plot was, even for Lang, labyrinthine: A businessman purchases a stolen gem as a gift for his wife. Counterfeit money causes complications. A doppelgänger creates further confusion, with assumptions of mistaken identity. Marital infidelity is wrongly suspected. One night all the mysteries are resolved—masks fall, scores are settled—when all the main characters wind up together in a Tiergarten villa.

Contemporary film reviewers were "disconcerted by the plot," according to Lotte Eisner, "finding the relationships between characters unclear" and the idea of the look-alikes preposterous. Even after the "lost" work was restored and presented in 1987, a critic for the *Neue Züricher Zeitung* complained that "the plot is hard to follow and gets even more complicated because of Lang's obvious love of mystery characters."

Von Harbou's over-elaborate storytelling techniques sometimes compounded Lang's: Both liked to use Rahmenhandlungen (framing devices), flashbacks within flashbacks, digressive asides, jarring transitions, and symbolistic cutaways. Usually several subplots vied with each other before weaving into resolution.

Scenes like the one in *Kämpfende Herzen*, in which a man gazes at stolen jewels—while an image flashes on the screen of the woman from whom the jewels were stolen, precipitating a long, parenthetical backstory—were narrative devices that Lang often indulged. These could be clumsy, especially early on, although over time the director's touch would grow increasingly sophisticated.

But it is the verisimilitude and gritty realism of *Kämpfende Herzen* that astonishes nowadays. Indications are that Lang was working on an abbreviated schedule. This is the first of his "tabloid" films, focusing on the streets and society of Berlin, and Lang was always more stimulated by urban life than by nature's splendor.

Kämpfende Herzen can be seen now as an obvious transition to *Dr. Mabuse*. Here was a Lang equally at home in posh hotel rooms and sleazy dives. The layers of society were peeled away, the director wryly dissecting the contrast between private clubs of rich, top-hatted gamblers and Berlin's teeming underworld. Here, for the first time, Lang began to show an appetite for dizzying montage: intercut close-ups of street signs, sidewalk activity, telephones ringing, people gulping food, wafted cigarette smoke, grimacing faces. It was as if Lang had just discovered the "insert"—the inert close-up, speaking volumes about a character, or scene, which is spliced into the action. Other directors usually delegated their inserts to an assistant, not Lang. "An insert," he liked to say, "is just as important as a big close-up of your star." For him it was, and the insert became one of Fritz Lang's acknowledged masteries.

Kämpfende Herzen made for raucous enjoyment, and was a leap forward for the increasingly proficient director. But Lang was over with it swiftly and on to the next project, which many consider the director's first true masterpiece.

Der müde Tod (*The Weary Death*, a.k.a. *Destiny*) was the first original script Fritz Lang and Thea von Harbou worked on from beginning to end without a hovering producer, and with the sure knowledge that Lang would direct. This film, which came on the heels of his mother's death, would be the director's most thoughtful and compassionate meditation on mortality.

The director said once that the film was inspired by "the childhood dream which most influenced my life and work"—which came to him "on the threshold of boyhood and adolescence" as Lang lay in bed fighting a fever. He recalled envisioning the approach of "the dark stranger" in a wide-brimmed hat, illumined by the moonlight streaming in through a half-open window. "I slept and dreamed—or was I awake?" He glimpsed "the tear-stained face of my adored mother," as she slipped from view. He raised himself up weakly, to be led away by Death. Helping hands grabbed him, pushed him down, saved him.

The horror of the dream-experience combined with "a kind of mystical ecstasy which gave me, boy though I still was, the complete understanding of the ecstasy which made martyrs and saints embrace Death." Lang recovered, "but the love of Death, compounded of horror and affection," he said, "stayed with me and became a part of my films."

A fount of such anecdotes, usually with himself as sole witness, served the director well throughout his career, but Death in *Der müde Tod* would resemble that dark stranger he described, and indeed would be treated with a unique commingling of horror and affection.

Lang and von Harbou divided their scenario into three main sections, or parables—with the lead actors playing equivalent roles in each—framed by a Rahmenhandlung. It is the story of a young woman desperately trying to dissuade Death from claiming the life of her betrothed. The drama is played out between the final strokes of the hands of a tower clock approaching midnight.

It begins with the two young lovers in a horse-drawn coach, whose path is crossed by a forbidding cloaked figure. Joined by the cloaked traveler, they approach a small town adrift in the past. Here, stopping in the public inn, Lang has some fun depicting, in colorful strokes, the local citizenry: a notary, a schoolteacher, a self-important burgher, the town's gravedigger. The young man disappears after supping with the cloaked figure, whom the audience recognizes as Death.

A flashback explains that Death has settled in this timeless town and purchased a plot of land next to the cemetery, walling it off. Local officials are disturbed by the mysterious stranger and his impenetrable garden, but gold has sealed the bargain.

Wandering in the moonlight, the young woman, distraught over her beau's disappearance, encounters Death outside his oppressive wall. She has a vision of an army of the doomed marching into the Garden of Death, faints, and is rescued by the local druggist, out collecting herbs in the moonlight. Awakening later in his pharmacy, she despairingly seizes a vial of poison and swigs it down, then, in a dream-state, is transported inside the mysterious garden, where she communes with Death.

Death explains himself, in a room of tall candles, each symbolizing the fleeting life of a human being—an image from one of Grimm's fairy tales, as Lotte Eisner has pointed out. "His hour had come," Death explains about the young woman's vanished lover. By way of demonstration, a candle is snuffed out, and a baby materializes in Death's arms. A mother is glimpsed, sobbing brokenheartedly over the body of her deceased child.

"Believe me, my task is a hard one," explains Death, "I am weary of seeing the sufferings of men and hate my duty though I obey . . ."

"Is there no way to relight one of these? Is there no way to overcome you, Death?" the young woman pleads. "We are taught that love is stronger than Death."

Death points to three flickering lights and tells the young woman that if she can save even one of those fated souls, he will return her lover to her. Then follow three costumed episodes, all involving tragic, outlawed romance.

First the audience visits ninth-century Baghdad during the fast of the Ramadan, to be entertained by an Arabian Nights tale of forbidden love between a caliph's sister and a shunned infidel. This episode abounds in sword fights and Islamic ornamentation, but overall is the shortest, simplest, and least spectacular of the three.

The second film-within-a-film focuses on ill-destined lovers in fourteenth-century Venice during the carnival season. It is a tale that features secret love letters that backfire on the heroine, and a cockfight filmed with vivid lighting and composition. Even Siegfried Kracauer, in his book that sometimes disapproves of Lang, calls the Venetian episode worthy of Stendhal.

The third episode—"The Story of the Third Light"—is the most fantastical. Set in ancient China, it features a despot who commands the foremost magician of the empire to regale him with astounding magical tricks—or be beheaded. Two young lovers serve as the magician's helpers. The emperor cannot help but notice the pretty female assistant and, though satisfied with the sensational magic, announces that he will take the young woman into his household as one of his concubines.

A flying carpet, a phantasmal miniature army, a winged steed, fire demons, and a magic wand that grows smaller each time the doomed heroine is forced to use it, are among the story's distinctive touches. Pursued by the emperor's minions, the young woman, at the end of the story, uses the last spell of the magic wand to transform herself into a bodhisattva statue and her lover into a tiger. Death, however, cannot be cheated. The tiger is killed by a stalking archer, and the statue is seen to weep as the tale ends.

The conclusion of the Rahmenhandlung is the most gripping. After the heroine has been worn down by the irresistible arguments of Death, she is offered one last opportunity to trade someone else's life for that of her lover. All she has to do, within the time alloted by Death, is find someone who is willing to switch places with him. The young woman beseeches the elderly herbalist, a destitute beggar, a suffering infirmary patient, all with little left to live for. But will any of them choose to sacrifice themselves before their time? No.

Accidentally, she sparks a fire in the infirmary, which is enveloped in flames. The premises are evacuated, while on the sidelines a woman screams, "My baby!" Somewhere inside the fire-enveloped building an innocent is being readied for Death. The young woman rushes inside, dashing from room to room and finally scoops the baby up in her arms. Death appears, and she almost hands the baby over, but her conscience wins out in the last instant; she wrenches away and rescues the baby by lowering him in a swaddled curtain from a burning window.

The building explodes and collapses—a thrilling moment. Death sorrowfully leads the heroine off, reuniting her with her lover behind the walls of his garden.

The cast featured Lil Dagover and Walter Janssen as the two lovers (who recur in each of the segments), Rudolf Klein-Rogge (in the Oriental and Venetian episodes), and an actor who would work auspiciously for Lang on several occasions, Bernhard Goetzke, as a gaunt and anguished Death. A familiar figure to Berlin theatergoers, Goetzke, born in Danzig, would also serve the director as chief Detective von Wenk in *Dr. Mabuse* and as the minstrel of the Burgundians in *Die Nibelungen*.

Actors such as Klein-Rogge and Goetzke were professionals who little needed, or heeded, torrential directorial advice. The two young leads, Lil Dagover and Walter Janssen, were relative newcomers, and Lang boxed himself in with their limitations and the pallid characters they were forced to play. His leading men could be tedious under the best circumstances—whether pummeled by overbearing direction, or left to their own devices. But Lang's heroines, especially in the 1920s, could be sublime.

About Lil Dagover the director had mixed feelings. He cherished her beauty. She would act in two of his greatest films. She gave her utmost in rehearsals and before the camera. But Lang was doomed to be disappointed by his leading ladies. Two or three films were his limit with an actress; after that, his feelings wore thin. The face he had romanticized let him down, became too familiar. He could turn instantly abusive with an actress when she came up short, in his estimation, and, though he effectively launched her career, he never showed a real appreciation for Lil Dagover.

The actress took verbal blows, maintained her equilibrium, and made strides in *Der müde Tod*. Von Harbou was always nearby, encouraging and defusing, a constant presence on the set, famously knitting sweaters for cast and crew. Not only could she solve script emergencies on the spot, but in whispered tones she was able to soothe everybody during crises. Being an actress of some experience, she was deeply involved with casting, and always there to counsel—or console—Fritz Lang's actors.

The acting, in Lang's earliest silent films, could be stagy. Expressionism was carried over to exaggerated visualizing of emotion. Germans were in love with exaggeration and pantomime, and this histrionic style, which undoubtedly played well in theaters at the time, makes some of his early works difficult to credit today. But the director was increasingly raiding the theater and, especially, Max Reinhardt's ensemble—from which sprang many of the mainstays of German film. And the acting in his films—even that of the novices— would over time grow more restrained and natural.

Lang threw down the gauntlet to Decla's design team of Robert Herlth, Walter Röhrig, and Hermann Warm: For *Der müde Tod*, they had to visualize Death, fashion an allegorical small town, create a slew of magical effects, and top everything off with a blazing inferno at the climax. The director always worked closely on the design and production challenges, and was known to propose solutions that bettered the team's.

"I shall never forget," wrote Robert Herlth in his memoirs, "how Lang, who always did everything himself, worked the trick with the letter sent by the magician . . .

" 'The letter,' the script stipulates, 'bows to the emperor.' Because in those days there was no such thing as an optical bank or back projection, Lang produced this trick "directly" or "in the original" on a nine-by-twelve-foot black velvet-covered wall, where the letter measuring about fifteen by twelve feet was pinned up in the desired position and moved between every frame. Shooting thus, in stop-motion, each frame separately exposed, the letter had to be rearranged some eight hundred times to produce fifty seconds of film.

"Every time, Lang himself jumped up and changed the pins supporting the giant letter. He worked incessantly, the sweat pouring down his face, becoming so involved that he forgot time and place. After this, the exposed negative had to be rewound and kept in the camera in order to allow the main action to appear on the same strip [of film].

"The scene had to be fitted in accordingly. The action had to be played with the letter remaining imaginary. Only Lang seemed able to imagine the result, and that is why his behavior seemed to us like magic-making. But how astonished we all were, we who had been in on every phase of the work, when we watched the film re-run, with the superimposition. The letter really unrolled itself and bowed to the emperor . . . "

Importantly, *Der müde Tod* was Lang's first experience with cameraman Fritz Arno Wagner, who is officially credited with the Venetian and Chinese episodes. Wagner shared a Paris background with Lang. He had attended the Academy of Fine Arts there and launched his career as a photographer with Pathé, joining Decla-Bioscop after the war. Wagner proved himself energetic and imaginative, willing to undercrank the camera or use negative film for Expressionist effects; in time he became internationally recognized, working for Lubitsch, Wiene, Murnau, and Pabst as well as Lang. Cinematography was as prickly a profession as directing, but Wagner was one of the congenial ones. He truly liked Lang, and stuck by the director when others bolted.

With Wagner at his side, Lang reached new heights in *Der müde Tod*. The daring interplay of shadow and light (including nighttime and low-lit scenes that defied all known standards), the images reflected in water and mirrors, the smoke and flames of the final conflagration—all were highlights of a film that was a triumph of atmosphere and mood.

The final scene was one of the hellfires Lang doled out periodically throughout his career. He was the cinema's most dedicated pyromaniac. It was almost a boyish impulse—he loved fireworks and a big-bang climax. Nobody devised an explosion, or stoked a bonfire, with more relish.

Sometimes, the exciting effects were obtained almost by accident. "For the fire in the old people's home [in *Der müde Tod*] I shot the scene where the water buckets are handed along a chain of people late in the afternoon," explained Lang in one interview. "Since the house could only burn down once, and I had to shoot the fire willy-nilly, I went on shooting into the dark. The effect of bright flames clearly picked out against the dark sky was excellent and easy to discern (we had lit up the house with floodlights). But how astonished we were when the scene which we had shot in late afternoon, with the human chain passing the buckets, also turned out to be a night scene."

Yet such accidents happened often with Lang, who recklessly pushed the limits. On the set, tellingly, it was always the director who lit the fuse, shot the bullets, or put the first match to the fire. He didn't mind thrusting himself—or others—in harm's way. The danger was intoxicating. His cameraman had to be willing to accept personal, as well as professional, risks.

Others were forced to take risks on the director's behalf too. One who did during the filming of *Der müde Tod* was Gustav Püttcher. A former circus artist, Püttcher was an extra on the set one day when Lang, "passionately caught up in directing, had taken a false step and fallen off a high platform," according to Erich Kettelhut. Waiting for his scene, Püttcher dashed forward and functioned "quasi as a living mattress, throwing himself at Lang" and there by saving the director. From that day forward, Püttcher had a full-time job with Lang.

The director was accumulating a retinue: secretaries and assistants, household and studio staff, friends and personnel who followed him from production to production. A German film director was all-powerful. Though in 1921 he had not yet reached his zenith, Lang—who liked to refer to himself in the third person, a trait not uncommon among egoists—could be forgiven for thinking himself one of the supreme lords of the earth.

Der müde Tod had its premiere on October 7, 1921, simultaneously at the U.T. on the Kurfürstendamm and at the Mozartsaal on Nollendorfplatz, two of Berlin's luxury theaters.

Initially, German critics were underwhelmed. The film's fusion of the religious and allegorical, travelogue and swashbuckling, seemed, to many, excessive and pretentious. A reviewer for the *Berliner Zeitung* made a famous quip,

"A tiresome death . . ." The reaction was not much better elsewhere in the German-speaking world.

Lang's film played only two weeks in Berlin; then *Der müde Tod* was exported to other countries, where it was as though critics were watching a different film. *Der müde Tod* was greeted in London as "one of the most original and impressive films that have ever been made," while in Paris, where Lang found a receptive environment more than once in his life, reviewers reacted ecstatically. One French critic wrote about the film (known there as *Les Trois Lumières*, or *The Three Lights*), "This is the Germany we love, the world of Dürer and Grünewald, that speaks to us in this film."

Der müde Tod was the first work of Lang's to gain a wide European reputation and it would become a famous example of a German motion picture rejected in Germany itself that was given a second chance at home on the strength of rhapsodic foreign notices.

The second time around, Lang's film had a long run in Berlin. Now *Film-Kurier* reappraised *Der müde Tod* as a work which "reflects the German soul more than any film until now . . . it diverges from everyday life, shaped as it is by the hand of a poet and given form by the finest directorial touch." The *Berliner Börsenzeitung* chimed in, hailing Lang's latest as "a mood painting which never succeeded better in film." The *Licht-Bild-Bühne* said whoever believed in the future of cinema should rush to see it.

The film director would forever after be skeptical about critics and reviews, whether they lined up for or against him. "When my writer, architect, cameraman, and so on," Lang liked to say, "give up their lives for months for the preparation of a film, and then again months working on the editing, then the night of the premiere comes and a critic, immediately after seeing the film, sits down to write a critique as quick as possible in order to get it in tomorrow morning's newspaper, and this critique of their long months of work is bad, I cannot accept it.

"But if I don't accept a bad critique, then I can't accept a good one, either."

"In a general sense," Lang wrote in a 1968 letter to Lotte Eisner, referring to *Der müde Tod*, "my first real success was only after my collaboration with von Harbou."

Der müde Tod was released on the eve of Decla's merger with Ufa, which had just been reconstituted as a private company. At the time, the cream of Germany's internationally reputable directors and acting stars were under contract to Ufa. Ufa owned stages and laboratories in the suburb of Tempelhof, where Berlin's main airport was located, and with the merger took over proprietorship and began to expand and renovate the Decla studio at Babelsberg, southwest of Berlin.

Neubabelsberg (as it was dubbed) swiftly became the most modern and best-equipped facility in Europe. It was a small city unto itself, with twenty-two administration buildings and departments, a film-processing lab, two immense interior stages—one of them, the older, dubbed the "small glasshouse," the other the "big glasshouse."* The adjacent locations included riv-

---

*Glass houses—immense glass buildings designed to utilize daylight for filming rather than flooders, parks, woodlands, and a zoo. Its remoteness and fenced-in grounds made it an enclave, another island of make-believe. Indeed, every film set, for Fritz Lang, was an opportunity to create and revel in his own blinkered world.

Ufa also operated ten of Berlin's finest movie palaces (including the country's largest, the Ufa-Palast am Zoo, just outside Berlin's Zoological Gardens and a block from the end of the Kurfürstendamm), and one hundred regional theaters. Additionally, the company controlled cinemas in Spain, Holland, Switzerland, and Scandinavia, as well as maintaining assets in Danish and Viennese film production companies.

It was no monopoly, but it was the biggest and most important film studio in the world outside Hollywood, and no German company could rival Ufa's national predominance. Now, after *Der müde Tod*, Pommer was placed in charge of Ufa's production and distribution, and Lang, at age thirty-one, became the studio's leading light—"one of the best directors in the world," in the words of Erich Pommer.

It was no secret that Lang and Thea von Harbou had fallen in love almost immediately.

Von Harbou and her husband, Rudolf Klein-Rogge, were living, in 1919, at Siemensstrasse 52–53 in Lankwitz; Lang continued to live on Tharandterstrasse, at least until August 1920. That fall, Lang moved to a western residential neighborhood of the city—apartment number 3 at Hohenzollerndamm 52— and was listed in the city registry as "Regisseur und Schriftsteller" (director and writer). Then Von Harbou and Klein-Rogge separated, and von Harbou took up residence in a separate apartment in the same building as Lang.

Frau Lang—the shadowy "L," Lisa Rosenthal—must have been distraught, but what could she do? The director dictated the order of things in his personal life as on the set. The only morality was his. This bold young man, growing ever more imperious, had grown accustomed to waving around his Browning.

Lang was seen around town with each of them alone, wife and scenarist— and sometimes with all of them together. Publicly humiliated, Lisa Rosenthal pleaded with her husband. But Lang met her remonstrations with fury and derision—that his behavior would even be questioned! Producer Hermann Millkowski's wife, one of Frau Lang's best friends, was witness to one violent episode in a Paris hotel, while the director was holed up doing publicity there.** A nasty argument developed between the director and his wife, Mrs. Millkowski implied to one confidante, and Lang took out his Browning and flourished it for effect.

Sometime, probably late in 1920, came the climax. Erich Kettelhut, in his memoirs, hinted that it occurred during the production of *Das wandernde Bild*, likely during the postproduction and just before its release. Karl Freund placed the incident roughly in the midwinter of 1920–1921, during the preparation of *Der müde Tod*, the director's meditative film on the inevitability of fate.

---

lights—were the architectural fashion. "Apparently weightless structures glittering in the sunlight and designed to bring daylight indoors, plainly constructed yet as inspiring as spaceships, they stood out among the stolid Wilhelmine buildings and signaled a new age," according to Klaus Kreimeier's *The Ufa Story*.
**In America, later, the producer modified his name to Herman Millakowsky.

That day Frau Lang discovered her husband and Thea von Harbou, supposedly in script conference, in a state of obvious undress. Lang's wife flew into a rage, or plunged into a depression. What followed is far from certain, and must be pieced together from the accounts of persons who, on rare occasion, told the story secondhand. There were "no eyewitnesses, no direct testimony . . . only circumstantial evidence," to lift a line from Lang's film *Beyond a Reasonable Doubt*. Only one thing is beyond doubt: Lisa Rosenthal was killed that day, of a bullet wound through her chest, fired from the Browning revolver owned by Fritz Lang.

Hans Feld, the *Film-Kurier* editor, was the source of one version that would be repeated by others—including Lotte Eisner—over the years. Feld had hired Eisner in the 1920s; he later became her good friend after the two had fled Hitler, she to Paris and he to London. Feld discussed Frau Lang's death with Eisner a number of times; he was clearly biased against Lang—he thought the director a "nasty customer"—and when Eisner recorded Feld's version of events she softened the account, casting few aspersions on Lang.

In her memoirs, *Ich hatte einst ein schönes Vaterland*, published only in Germany well after Lang's own death, Eisner held simply that Lisa Rosenthal surprised the film director in the act of making love to his scenarist on their apartment sofa. "Then she went into the bedroom and shot herself." Eisner made no explicit mention of foul play, but noted that "there were two strange things about the story. Because she was so proud of her perfect breasts, the young woman did not put the gun to her left breast but in the middle [of her breasts], but she died anyway. . . . The second unusual thing was that Lang and von Harbou had to answer before a court for denial of assistance, since too much time had elapsed between the suicide and their calling the police."

But Hans Feld, from whom Eisner had heard the story, believed something worse: He thought Lang capable of manslaughter, or even murder. And another contemporary account, that of Karl Freund, seconded Feld's convictions. Spreading the story as he knew it—in Berlin film circles, and later in Hollywood—Freund professed a hatred for Fritz Lang based in part on what had transpired between the director and his first wife. According to Freund's version of the story, repeated in a taped interview with Alfred Zeisler on deposit at the Kinemathek in Berlin, it was not a clear case of suicide. Freund suspected Lang of a killing, intentional or otherwise, for which the director refused to accept any blame.

That fateful night, Freund told people, he had received an urgent phone call summoning him to Lang's residence on Hohenzollerndamm. A snowstorm had engulfed Berlin, the streetcars weren't running, and Freund had to walk a great distance, whipped by snow and gale-force winds. Arriving at Lang's place, the Ufa cameraman was met by a mass of people gathered outside. Erich Pommer and Fritz Arno Wagner, who were already there, greeted him. Escorted inside, Freund briefly glimpsed the draped corpse in a room, and Lang and Thea von Harbou, framed in the doorway, as they were being grilled by police.

Lang insisted it was a suicide. Von Harbou backed him up.

According to this account, Lang told the Berlin police he had discovered his wife in the bathtub, dead from a bullet wound, with his own revolver strewn outside the tub, where it had fallen out of her hand. But there was one trouble with Lang's story, Zeisler noted: Shortly before her death, Frau Lang had called a girlfriend—the wife of a well-known Ufa set designer—from the apartment. They had made plans to go on a shopping expedition after Frau Lang took a short bath.

What sort of woman plans a shopping trip before committing suicide? Hans Feld, Karl Freund, Alfred Zeisler, and others believed that the simple suicide story was a lie. And the police must have wondered, too, for even Lotte Eisner admitted that a formal inquiry had to be convened. "Thea von Harbou said under oath—perjury, of course—that Lang was with her the whole time and so the police couldn't do anything," said Zeissler.

How did the scandal get contained so effectively? If it hadn't been for Erich Pommer, the whole thing might have turned out otherwise. Coming to Lang's defense, Pommer brought his prestige and enormous persuasive skills to bear. Behind-the-scenes pressure was exerted. Lang was an important director, an honorable man, a man who could be trusted. So the case was ultimately waived. In the end, it appears, the Berlin police expunged the incident from official records. No record of an inquest—no record, even, of Lisa Rosenthal's death—could be found in the course of research for this book.

One additional detail: The director made certain that the burial was held immediately, before his wife's father could journey to Berlin and stir up any fuss. It was a move always held against Fritz Lang, not only by Karl Freund but by Fritz Arno Wagner, the director's otherwise agreeable compatriot, who felt that the only reason for rushing the funeral was Lang's own convenience.

Everyone in the film industry heard about Frau Lang's death—instantly. Berlin was electric with the news. Gilbert Mandelik, later Lang's assistant director and loyal friend, was only about twenty and living at home with his parents. His stepfather was Alfred Weiner, owner and publisher of the *Film-Kurier*, which had a close association with the director; the trade paper published advertisements for Fritz Lang films and also issued autographed programs, complimentary and well-written, for each new production. Mandelik, like many other Berliners, first heard about Lisa Rosenthal's death at the supper table.

"I knew about the first wife," said Mandelik in an interview. "When she died, Thea was practically around the corner, waiting. I think Fritz wanted to leave her [Lisa Rosenthal], then she committed suicide. At dinner one night, I overheard my mother and father talking about it. They said something about Fritz and Thea being in the apartment when she died. They thought if they had called for help [sooner], maybe something could have been done. It was common knowledge in Berlin circles, but one didn't talk about it."

It was common knowledge later in Hollywood émigré circles, but one still didn't talk about it.

One of the people with direct knowledge of the incident was Mrs. Hermann Millkowski. Lang had phoned her from his apartment immediately after his wife's death, knowing that Mrs. Millkowski was not only Lisa Rosenthal's dear friend but witness to the previous incriminating incident in Paris. The director assured her that his wife's death was a domestic mishap. The Millkowskis were among those who later fled Germany during Hitler's reign and came to live in Hollywood during Lang's tenure there. Occasionally they and others who had known the director's first wife socialized with Lang, but the subject was taboo. Mrs. Millkowski confirmed some details in conversation with Cornelius Schnauber of the University of Southern California.

"He [Lang] knew that Mrs. Millkowski was the close friend of his wife," said Schnauber. "He talked to her right away, in his shock. This is how she told it to me."

In Hollywood Lang maintained few friendships from the Berlin years (fewer still that dated back before 1921); and the existence of a predecessor to Thea von Harbou was unknown to most of his American acquaintances, who in general had scant knowledge of what had transpired in Germany. Friends like editor Gene Fowler Jr., actor Dan Seymour, producer David Bradley, and journalist Kevin Thomas—among the people closest to the director in his twilight years—heard no inkling from Lang of a first wife.

Never—not once—did Lang mention his first wife in a published interview; Lisa Rosenthal was as much a "nonperson" as the director's brother Dolf. Given the chance to talk about women or marriage, or (for instance) Lang's first meeting and subsequent marriage to Thea von Harbou, the director smoothly dropped his first wife from the narrative.

Therefore it was all the more surprising when one day out of the blue Lang himself brought up the subject, speaking to actor Howard Vernon, one of his closest friends—who was neither German nor American—when they were alone together in Paris.

"One day in Berlin," Lang told Howard Vernon, "I was sitting in my house with Thea von Harbou. We had fallen more or less in love. We were sitting on the couch, petting rather violently, and in comes the girl to whom I was married at the time. She saw us, went upstairs, and we heard a shot. She had killed herself on the spot, right away. Of course there was a big inquest. Naturally I had a very hard time explaining the situation and the circumstances, because she had shot herself with my gun, which I kept from the war days."

From the first film to the last, guilt, complicity, false accusation, irredeemable crime, inadvertent killings, and suicide haunt Lang's work. On the evidence of recent restorations, it can be seen that murder and self-destruction were part of Lang's work even from the earliest phase—before the death of Lisa Rosenthal—with *Lilith und Ly* and *Hilde Warren* written in his Vienna days, as well as 1919's *Harakiri*. But these plot twists and ideological motifs were elevated to ceremonial status afterward by the director some believed killed his first wife.

After the death of Lisa Rosenthal, the litany is compelling:

The suicide of Brunhild in *Die Nibelungen*.

The clown who shoots himself on stage in *Spione*.

The astronomer who chooses to die by staying on the moon with her true love in *Frau im Mond*.

Eddie and Joan, their flight from the law in *You Only Live Once*, a form of self-destruction.

Liliom, turning the knife on himself.

The false justice of a mob lynching the wrong man in *Fury*.

Jerry's "suicide," a murder faked by the Nazis in *Man Hunt*.

The killer who makes a mess of his suicide, and is pursued to the end of his days by the ghost of his beloved, in *Scarlet Street*.

The suicide that triggers the plot of *The Big Heat*. The faked suicide of a witness which is in fact a murder in the same film.

The murder of a burlesque dancer, who turns out to have been the wife in a clandestine marriage, in *Beyond a Reasonable Doubt*.

These and more—the untoward demises of major and minor characters in the best-and least-known Fritz Lang films compromising tossed-off moments as well as emphatic, unmistakable thematic statements.

Perhaps suicide was such a familiar condition in his mind that it leapted to Fritz Lang's tongue unbidden when police arrived at his apartment on that fatal day, asking him to explain the inexplicable. There is no question that Lisa Rosenthal died under murky circumstances. But can it ever be known whether she killed herself? If the director killed her accidentally, during a struggle? Or if something worse, more intentional, occurred?

The director stated in interviews that after *Der müde Tod* he began to visit insane asylums as part of the research for his next project. Georges Sturm's research led him to suggest a more tantalizing possibility: that the director was institutionalized, however briefly, following his wife's death. Whether such confinement might have been intended as a sop to authorities—or perhaps, as is true, poignantly, of Chris Cross in *Scarlet Street*, guilt had driven Fritz Lang over the edge, such an event does not seem unlikely.

"He [Lang] could be pretty rude and mean, even the way he talked to people," observed Cornelius Schnauber, "but deep inside he was a very tender and soft person. I'm pretty sure that the death of his wife, whether or not it was a suicide, was a shock for him, influenced his whole life and became part of his films."

Fritz Lang's long, brilliant career would be repeatedly stimulated by unhappiness, obstacles, setbacks, disasters.

Now, in the wake of this personal scandal, Lang and Thea von Harbou embarked on a new professional project: a film based on a contemporary novel about a lunatic crime lord sowing fear and disorder in an out-of-control society. It would take their work out of the realm of the allegorical. Modern Germany—torn and reeling after its war defeat, presided over by crime and corruption—would be personified under their vision.

Berlin in 1922 was a city of such affluent decadence and everyday rot and desperation that people had to reach way back to the Old Testament to come up with a suitable analogy. The future film director Jean Renoir, visiting Berlin after World War I, remarked, "Sodom and Gomorrah were reborn there." Thomas Mann's son Klaus, who frequented the city as a student, called it "the Babylon of Europe." Stefan Zweig, going further, said it was "the Babylon of the world."

The poor scrounged for bread crusts, while private sex clubs proliferated for the privileged class, indulging every whim and predilection. Drugs flooded the streets and were marketed openly in cabarets and nightclubs. Vice bosses and speculators reigned as the new royalty of a city frantically seeking new and ever more gaudy thrills.

Lang knew well the milieu he would depict in his next film: the floor shows of the posh hangouts, the deviant sex clubs, the *Spielklubs* (card-playing dens) for jaded women and rich gambling addicts, the hangouts for prostitutes, séances, or cocaine. These addresses were part of his nightly routine. Lang himself was addicted to sex and not a little fond of drugs.

The director never mentioned drugs in any interview; nor did any interviewer see fit to bring up the subject with him. Yet Lang devoured pep pills on the sets of his films, which helps explain his phenomenal energy, his willingness to skip lunch and dinner, to work past midnight—everybody else be damned. Off the set, Lang was open to marijuana, cocaine, opium—whatever was being handed around at private parties.

At the same time, though, Lang liked to distance himself objectively from the milieu of his films. He thought of himself as a sort of newspaper reporter. He enjoyed the pose. Seeking documentation for what he depicted, he would tour actual sites, meet real people, collect data to support his pet theories. He had begun his habit of reading newspapers with a pair of scissors at hand to clip items to file into categories in folders. This became a mania in his career— a proof of fact, a validation of his approach. But it was also true that this self-styled reporter usually needed a professional with newspaper experience close by, to give his scripts the ring of authenticity he desired.

Norbert Jacques was not the last, but certainly the first, important ex-newspaperman to fill this function for the director.

Jacques, from Luxembourg, had worked briefly in the Berlin office of the *Frankfurter Zeitung* before taking up independent work as an essayist, travel writer, and novelist. A war reporter from 1914 to 1918, Jacques had supplied dispatches from the various fronts that were serialized in German newspapers. Although Jacques would write many historical and biographical novels in his career, his fame would rest on his 1921 novel *Doktor Mabuse, Der Spieler* (*Dr. Mabuse, the Gambler*), about a master criminal with "psychic eyes" bidding for riches and unbridled power.

Dr. Mabuse will stop at nothing. With his gang of tyrannized confederates, he orchestrates the theft of state secrets in order to manipulate the stock market. Roving at will among the layers of high society, he hypnotizes millionaire victims into betting at cards until they are crushingly indebted to him. Every crime is elaborately contrived and regulated by clockwork (a Langian touch actually drawn from Jacques's novel, where Mabuse is petty about punctuality). His own supremacy is the only thing Dr. Mabuse believes in.

A policeman inspector, von Wenk, emerges as the only man who might be able to stop Dr. Mabuse. The book—and film—are a deadly cat-and-mouse game between these two masterminds on opposite sides of the law. They share a longing for the same woman—the ennui-stricken Countess Told.

The film would be divided into two parts: *Der grosse Spieler—Ein Bild der Zeit* (*The Great Gambler—A Picture of Our Time*) and *Inferno: Ein Spiel von Menschen unserer Zeit* (*Inferno: A Play About People of Our Time*). Overlong, overblown productions continued to be the fashion of the era, and at this stage of his career Lang helped lead the fashion by choosing to direct only so-called monumental films—"super-films."

In general Lang treated writers much better than he treated other people, and he and von Harbou were faithful, with caveats, in bringing the Norbert Jacques novel to the screen. The story, curiously, was set in Munich and towns along the German-Swiss border (near where Jacques lived, on the German side of Lake Constance), with only the climactic scenes taking place in Berlin. The setting of the film is certainly Berlin, recognizably so to natives, though it is never named. By changing the novel's locale and then blanking out precise identification, Lang and von Harbou gave their film a more sinister universality.

The novel served as a solid blueprint. The director liked to claim in interviews that the script was influenced enormously by a book about the Chicago bootlegger Al Capone sent to him by "a producer friend in Hollywood." But Dr. Mabuse and the other main characters did not vary from fiction to film. Norbert Jacques is the one who gave Mabuse the Langian trait of "psychic eyes"—although it no doubt struck a nerve with the director, for mind control was a persistent feature of his work, dating from his boyhood devotion to penny dreadfuls, magic tricks, and Oriental culture. Telekinesis likewise intrigued Thea von Harbou, and *Das indische Grabmal*, the film based on her novel, had its own mind-bending character in Rahmigani the yogi.

Not only mental telepathy, but inflation (and profiteering), sex and gaming clubs, séances and drug addiction—these were all story points carried over from book to film. If anything, Mabuse is *more* of an Al Capone-style gangster in the book. Killings abound in the novel, whereas in the film it is suicides that seem to proliferate. Three are especially significant: one by poison, one by razor blade, one by the character's hanging himself by a necktie.

Jacques's novel ended with Dr. Mabuse and the countess up in an airplane, with Detective von Wenk clinging to the side of the careening craft. The countess strikes Mabuse from behind with a heavy wrench, and the kingpin of evil topples over the side into oblivion. This ending was changed for the screen, and here may be where Al Capone figured into the equation: Lang's film made it a Chicago-style ending, with police and military laying siege to Mabuse's hideout, with the gang, barricaded inside, battling back.

Countess Told is rescued, but through the smoke, fire, and explosions, Mabuse somehow manages to elude von Wenk. The crime lord descends through a trapdoor and wades through a tunnel of sewage, emerging into a room where a slave force of blinded old men are busy counterfeiting his money. The way out is barred, however. Mabuse is trapped. The blind counterfeiters encircle him. The ghosts of his victims taunt him. Monsters bulge from the walls. The genius of crime has been reduced to dementia by the time the police finally locate him and lead him off to an asylum.

The director cast a Viennese contemporary, Paul Richter—who had become well-known after starring in *Das indische Grabmal*—as Edgar Hull, a rich industrialist's heir "with much money and little to do." Aud Egede Nissen, the Norwegian actress who was married to Richter for a time (and who had appeared, notably, in *Homunculus*) would play Cara Carezza, the nightclub dancer in love with Mabuse; she serves as Mabuse's pawn and, when imprisoned, is ordered to commit suicide to protect his identity. Gertrude Welcker would act the bored but beautiful Countess Told.

Count Told, whom Mabuse forces against his will to cheat at cards and then to commit suicide, would be portrayed by Alfred Abel, an unusually economical actor trained by Max Reinhardt. Specializing in playing aristocratic gentlemen, Abel would also make a notable appearance for Lang in *Metropolis*. Bernhard Goetzke from *Der müde Tod* played Detective von Wenk, and Rudolf Klein-Rogge would have his prototypical role in a Lang film, portraying Mabuse in his numerous guises.

Once again, Carl Hoffmann served as cameraman, with Günther Rittau helping out on a number of scenes. Carl Stahl-Urach and Otto Hunte led the art direction, assisted by Karl Vollbrecht and Erich Kettelhut. Hunte had been working exclusively for Joe May, but they had engaged in a nasty fistfight, and May got the worst of the altercation. Lang persuaded Erich Pommer to take advantage of the situation by hiring Hunte away from his nemesis.

Filming started in late 1921 at the Neubabelsberg studio, which was big enough to accommodate some of the simulated street scenes. The budget rose alarmingly. Lang and Pommer engaged in spirited arguments, but Pommer, trusting in the director, "gave in to all of Lang's demands," said Kettelhut. Ever the perfectionist, Lang held up production at will as he worked on important scenes, refined moments, added subtleties, and captured signal effects.

Rudolf Arnheim, Siegfried Kracauer, and Lotte Eisner all remarked on one memorable vignette, which transpires in a gambling scene where Mabuse tries (and fails) to overpower von Wenk mentally. "A small bright spot, Mabuse's face gleams out of the jet-black screen, then, with frightening speed, rushes to the foreground and fills the whole frame, his cruel, strong-willed eyes fastened upon the audience," in Kracauer's words. The effect thrilled contemporary audiences.

An elevated train which roared by on the screen was simply a toy train, photographed in the studio, then superimposed on background footage. Titles with animated movement were devised from letters cut out of a piece of wood-grained paper, then lit from underneath. The nonsense syllables "TSI NAN FU," and the recurring word "MELIOR," which races ahead of von Wenk's car, luring him toward the Melior cliffs, were accomplished by gradually enlarging the cryptic animated titles until they flooded the screen. These flourishes, devised and accomplished with the limited means at hand, were extraordinary at the time.

For one sequence, the director wanted the camera to take the point of view of a passenger in a car pursuing another car full of criminals, guns blazing back and forth. As the guns fire, the windshield explodes with holes. To add to the excitement, Lang insisted on the scene taking place outside in the dark of night.

How to do it? It was a problem that, in the end, the director solved himself. He sat on a makeshift stand behind one driver, holding a pistol, with Günther Rittau and his camera perched behind him. August-Bebel-Strasse outside the Ufa studio had been cordoned off by police, lit up by red spotlights. "The car zoomed down the street with Lang in it and he shot the holes in the wind-screen," recalled Erich Kettelhut. "The light was dim, the car was shaking, and he shot right over the driver's head. They did this three times . . ."

Shoot-outs, car chases, bomb explosions, gruesome deaths—*Mabuse* teemed with the story components that made directing a rapturous adventure for Fritz Lang. The all-out police attack on Dr. Mabuse and his gang, which takes place at the end of the story, had to be the most spectacular. The director felt he had to top everything that had come before.

People had already worked long hours when the time came to film that scene. Beer was handed around as day became night. Lang kept insisting on extra takes. The mood on the set began to turn ugly. Erich Kettelhut passed Otto Hunte, standing near a stage door and looking peevish, and asked him if people were growing "hot under the collar." "Yes," Hunte replied. "Literally and metaphorically. Take a look inside, you could cut the air with a knife. We've been working on the shoot-out scene since four. Lang has been re-hearsing for hours. We just filmed the same thing three times—Lang still isn't satisfied. He already shot three doors to pieces, and we didn't make more than three. Now Karl [Vollbrecht] is trying to repair the holes. As soon as the first door is back in place, we're starting again."

Inside on the stage, the atmosphere was "suffocatingly hot and smelly, despite the open door and ventilators in the windows," in Kettelhut's words. They returned to work; the raid had already been filmed three times, then was shot once more, then a fifth and sixth time. "Lang stood next to Hoffmann's camera on the riser, called out 'Group one,' then 'Group two,' and so on. They ran up to the house and pretended to shoot, while Lang stood up on the riser, and—right over their heads, using real bullets—shot the door to pieces. He carried out his job as a marksman without a touch of excitement and with an admirable perfection."

The siege is one of the memorable high points of the film. But sometimes the details that preoccupied Lang were doomed to be all but invisible to the average spectator. When an idea captured his fancy, the audience was almost beside the point. Such details became like the documentary facts or newspaper clippings he collected—nothing more than ammunition for his imagination. First and foremost, he was trying to satisfy himself.

Lang needed a pubescent beauty for one of the floor shows in the film, to emerge in the nude from a half-shell à la Botticelli's *Birth of Venus*. The scene would be risqué by American standards, if staid by Berlin's. Lang himself, of course, volunteered to comb "all the appropriate nightspots for a Venus that would fit the bill," according to Kettelhut, and he was not satisfied until he had thoroughly scoured the territory. At the last possible moment, the director selected a suitable young lady and made an appointment with her club man-ager for her to come to the studio the very next day.

Arriving at Neubabelsberg early the next morning, Lang went straight to the set and was upset to learn the designated showgirl had not yet material-ized. "Lang got progressively more tense until finally he was actually hopping nervously from one foot to the other and peering over through the studio door toward the porter's lodge, where the lovely lady was to arrive," remembered

Kettelhut. "Everyone in the studio stood around smoking cigarettes and making silly jokes to keep him company."

When, just before 10 A.M., a taxi pulled up, the stupid jokes dried up and everyone gawked as Lang made a show of gallantry, opening the taxi door for the lady of the day. Although onlookers were dutifully impressed by her "dazzling beauty," in Kettelhut's words, the lady herself seemed indifferent to Fritz Lang or the transcendent importance of her surroundings. The director asked her courteously why she was tardy. She waved her hand dismissively and said, "Oh, who cares about two hours. If my date stays at the joint till eight, I can't be here earlier, can I? After all, I have to fix myself up a little. I took a taxi. Getting out here wasn't exactly cheap. You're paying, right?"

"I never saw Lang's face look so thunderstruck as at that moment," wrote Kettelhut in his unpublished memoirs. Forthwith, the nightclub beauty was handed over to the wardrobe mistress, then to chief makeup artist Otto Genath, who spent some time fashioning her gold-blond hair in the Venus mode. Patiently, Lang waited.

Kettelhut took up the story in his memoirs: "She positioned herself on the shell in the raw; the extras and the lighting crew reacted with a loud 'aaah' of admiration. Her perfectly proportioned but not quite fully developed figure and her graceful movements were a lovely sight.

"Lang was the only one who was not quite satisfied. Her thick blond pubic hair bothered him and he demanded that it be shaved off. But the blond Venus didn't agree with him. 'No dice, not with me you don't,' the sweet thing said categorically, 'not with me! What would the audience think if I were to hop around onstage like a sparrow that's molting? If you don't like my hair, I'm off.' Lang talked about art, about aesthetics, but it didn't work; she stood her ground.

"Finally, they decided to cover it with a skin-colored piece of material. And so a nervous, sensitive artist, Genath, had to get down on his knees in front of the stubborn goddess and try his best to fix the triangle of fabric onto the relevant area with adhesive, and to color it with makeup to fit her skin tone. It was not at all easy to work on the soft surface, and Genath's job was only made more difficult because he was nervous, and because the victim kept making tiny, seemingly unintentional movements. The whole thing almost turned into a disaster . . . But during the shooting she stood there amazingly still without a complaint until the late evening."

The scene is very brief, and the showgirl's nudity is scarcely lingered on in the director's choice of shots. Whatever happened in his private life, whatever transpired off the screen—where sex was concerned, Lang's films were only fleetingly prurient.

Afterward, when all the filming was done, the director disappeared into the cutting room, day and night, to work alongside the editor. Erich Pommer often supervised the editing of his productions, but knowing Lang was capable of improving his films in the cutting room, he made another exception, and let the director proceed more or less independently.

Fritz Lang found both joy and frustration at the editing table. As the film took shape, editing offered an unlimited number of second chances. Still, Lang's mind perpetually buzzed with things he could have—should have—done better on the set.

The director could still change scenes around again and again. He would finish, then start all over again. When he was finally obliged to hand one of his films over, just before the premiere, he was always "heavy-hearted," Kettelhut recalled. The director hated to finish the job. That was part of his perfectionism.

Ufa not only boasted the greatest directors and stars in the German film industry, it had the best advertising and publicity departments. The serialization of Norbert Jacques's novel was timed to appear in the *Berliner Illustrierte Zeitung* along with the first production stills for Lang's film, following the multimedia marketing strategy Pommer had pioneered at Decla. The screenplays were brought out in time for the premiere by one of the publishers affiliated with Ufa, decorated with stills, signed, bound in silk, and presented to the priviliged guests.

The highly publicized premiere of *Doktor Mabuse, der Spieler* came on April 27, 1922, at the Ufa-Palast-am-Zoo. The two parts of Lang's film, which added up to almost four and a half hours of screen time, had to be scheduled for viewing on two consecutive evenings.

The pace was slow: German films of the time were characteristically long and languorous. Especially when Mabuse, or Detective von Wenk—described in the program as Mabuse's Gegenspieler, or "opponent-in-play"—disappeared from the narrative, the story lost momentum. But the sheer advancement of technique was stunning. That first audience witnessed scenes of spellbinding action, spectacle, and montage. And *Doktor Mabuse, der Spieler* was held together by its fervent belief in a top-rotting society threatened by a dark, fantastical conspiracy, with one of the cinema's most mesmeric figures at its core: Rudolf Klein-Rogge as Dr. Mabuse.

"A mirror of the age," declared *Das Tagebuch*.

"An archive of its time," agreed *Vorwärts*, the leading Social Democratic Party organ.

"A document of our time," echoed *Die Welt am Montag*.

About two months after *Doktor Mabuse, der Spicler* was released, Walther Rathenau, Germany's widely respected Minister of Foreign Affairs, a democrat, a statesman, and a Jew, was murdered by right-wing fanatics on his way to work. Historians have cited Rathenau's June 24, 1922, assassination as one of the crucial events facilitating the rise of the Third Reich, while film historians, noting that *Doktor Mabuse* begins with a similar assassination—that of a ministerial courier—have described Lang's film as "one of those deep-rooted premonitions which spread over the German postwar screen," in the words of Siegfried Kracauer.

The ending of the film—with Mabuse being captured and led off to a mental asylum—was intercut with another prescient scene. Georg, Mabuse's chief henchman, languishes in a prison cell where, before hanging himself, he scribbles something on the wall. In Norbert Jacques's book, it is one word, "the word that one of Napoleon's generals had made renowned after he had lost the battle of Waterloo."* In the film it is the name "Götz von Berlich-ingen," the title character from a play by Goethe about a medieval nobleman who sides with the peasants in an abortive revolt. (This was tantamount to saying, "Kiss my ass.")

Later, looking back, some would see that flourish as a political statement and another cinematic augury of Adolf Hitler, who, after the abortive Beer Hall Putsch—the year after *Doktor Mabuse, der Spieler* was released—began, while imprisoned at Landsberg, the writing of *Mein Kampf*.

Erich Pommer, commenting years later, identified the demonic Dr. Mabuse as a sort of Spartacist in the ongoing war, in early 1920s Germany, between Spartacists and political liberals.

The actor playing the part, Rudolf Klein-Rogge, was articulate and philo-sophical about his roles in interviews; he explained that he viewed Mabuse as "a symptom of a Europe that was falling apart . . . a guiding force, a creator, if only in destruction . . ."

Lang described "the great unknown" at the center of the film differently at various times. Sometimes he offered the comparison to Al Capone. More often the director defined Mabuse as an abstract force of evil, or, in Nietz-schean terms, an *Übermensch* ("Dr. Mabuse was a Superman . . . a Nietzschean superman, in a bad sense of the term"). "I had in mind a monster that controls people," Lang told Curt Riess. "A monster that hypnotizes people and forces them to do things that they don't want to do at all, to commit monstrous crimes. And afterward they have no idea of what they did."

It is also true, however, that some of Mabuse's gnomic utterances would have been at home in Lang's mouth. The director invested himself—person-ality, character, values and beliefs—in his best films; and his most memorable characters, such as Dr. Mabuse, revealed his inner self, sometimes to a chilling degree.

In one scene, for example, Dr. Mabuse espoused a Langian philosophy about romance, "There is no such thing as love—there is only desire, and the will to possess what you most desire," Mabuse states.

In another, Dr. Mabuse tells the bored Countess Told, "Nothing is inter-esting in the long run—except one thing. Playing with human beings and human fates." That could be a film director's credo, a few words that encap-sulated Fritz Lang.

The period of hard work, the crisis of his wife's death, the pressures of making *Doktor Mabuse, der Spieler*—all had passed by the mid-summer of 1922. Per-haps, then, it was merely to keep up appearances that Fritz Lang and Thea von Harbou decided to be married, on August 26, 1922, in Berlin-Schmargendorf at 8:30 A.M. They formally celebrated the success of the film, and cemented their husband-and-wife partnership.

---

*At Waterloo, Comte Pierre Jacques Etienne Cambronne, General of the Imperial Guard, asked to surrender, always claimed to have told the English, "The Guard dies but never surrenders." What he actually said was, "Merde!" This became known as "le mot de Cambronne," and that phrase a famous circumlocution.

In the marriage papers, Lang, following his father's example, declared his religion as agnostic ("without confession"), while von Harbou named herself a Protestant. Shortly after the wedding, according to her World War II interrogation papers, she stopped practicing any religion, "for private reasons."

Marriage was not the only realignment for the film director. Shortly after the ceremony, the Vienna-born Lang took out citizenship papers and pledged his patriotism to Germany. Such a move was "fashionable" at the time, he would have to explain, defensively, years later.

The extraordinary achievements of *Der müde Tod* and *Doktor Mabuse, der Spieler* would have been enough to ensure Fritz Lang's lasting position among the greatest German directors, even if he had never worked again. One who equaled Lang in stature, Ernst Lubitsch—a proven master of both Jewish comedy and grandiose epics—had left Berlin for Hollywood in December of 1922, armed with a contract from America's sweetheart, actress Mary Pickford. Another filmmaker raised in Vienna, G. W. Pabst, who arguably matched Lang in his uneven career, was just emerging in 1923. Only F. W. Murnau rivaled Lang's pre-eminence.

In the United States, by contrast, Lang was virtually unknown. German theaters were heavily dependent on Hollywood features for the home market, and in fact, by 1923, the number of U.S. releases had reached a rough parity with German films. But despite Herculean business and legal maneuvers, the U.S. market refused to reciprocate. Especially after 1924, the marriage was one-sided. "Hollywood bit deeply into the domestic market, fairly or otherwise limited German markets abroad, and deprived the native industry of its best personnel," wrote Thomas J. Saunders in *Hollywood in Berlin*. The history of German efforts to penetrate the American market would be tangled and bitter.

The German-language intelligentsia in the United States had heard of Fritz Lang, surely, but average American filmgoers had not been exposed to his work. So far films had been relegated to small houses and brief runs in German enclaves of the big cities. And when one of his titles did receive distribution, it was usually slashed by several reels by Americans dismayed by the slow pacing.

Der müde Tod was reportedly licensed for exhibition by Douglas Fairbanks, Sr., through his United Artists partnership with his wife, Mary Pickford, Charles Chaplin, and director D. W. Griffith. After expropriating camera tricks from the Baghdad episode for his 1924 version of *The Thief of Baghdad*—among them the flying-carpet sequence—Fairbanks ultimately declined to release Lang's first masterpiece in U.S. theaters. Lang, in interviews, always expressed magnanimity about the disappointment. "Naturally, because he had more money and greater technical facilities at his disposal, he [Fairbanks] improved on the tricks," said the director. Which was true enough.

A smaller distribution company picked up *Der müde Tod* and booked it into New York City theaters, drastically shortened and re-edited, as *Between Worlds*, for summer filler in July of 1924. It was virtually unrecognizable, and incoherent. *Doktor Mabuse, der Spieler*, was whittled down to ninety minutes for U.S. theaters, but that 1922 film, Lang's second great achievement, wasn't shown in America until August of 1928.

Not only was Fritz Lang one of the most critically acclaimed directors of Germany's film world, but he and Thea von Harbou were one of its most glamorous couples.

They worked hard at achieving public recognition. Lang cultivated relationships with the best and brightest of Germany's press corps, and would include in his circle of close acquaintances a number of top-ranked critics. These included Kurt Pinthus, who wrote mainly for the left-wing, political-cultural weekly *Das Tagebuch*, and was esteemed as much for his association with literary Expressionism as for his opinions about the screen; and two journalists destined to write influential books about German film history—Siegfried Kracauer and Lotte Eisner. Kracauer worked on the *Frankfurter Zeitung*, a newspaper of national stature, and Lotte Eisner, beginning in 1927, toiled on Berlin's *Film-Kurier*, the leading screen paper for the public and film specialists.

Press exposure was important to Lang, both as an adjunct to marketing and also because the attention gratified him. He and his wife were trailed avidly by reporters and society columnists as they moved about in public. Arm in arm, the couple attended opening nights at Max Reinhardt's theaters. They were staples of the annual motion picture ball, where Berlin's screen elite mingled to promote their upcoming projects, held at one of the expensive hotels near the Ufa-Palast am Zoo. They were seen at the best restaurants, such as the elegant Horcher's, well-known for its tender venison and baked potatoes with caviar; the Förster, a restaurant with Russian specialties; and the bar and grill at the Hotel Adlon on Unter den Linden, the preferred accommodation of diplomats, politicians, and visiting U.S. screen stars.

They were also conspicuous at sporting events, especially boxing matches—boxing, once verboten under the emperor, now was all the rage—and the Sechstagerennen, or "Six-Day Races," a bicycle marathon at the Sport-Palast on Potsdamer Strasse, which lasted some 144 hours and attracted not only factory and office workers, but also Berlin's upper crust.

The spacious apartment where they lived and worked was a showcase for their partnership. A correspondent for the magazine *Innendekoration* visited the place to write an article about its interior splendor. Erich Kettelhut, in his memoirs, also left a detailed portrait of the Lang–von Harbou residence at the time of *Die Nibelungen*, when production meetings were held there. One of its rooms was so studded with works of art, according to Kettelhut, that it could have doubled as a small gallery in a museum.

Indeed, Hohenzollerndamm 52 was dotted with exotic masks, folk art, paintings, woodcuts, and watercolors. Lang, by the early 1920s, owned several works by Egon Schiele, but also a collection of Johann Ridinger prints and animal etchings, and several works by Viennese secessionist Oskar Laske—in particular a Saint Francis of Assisi and a Noah's Ark.

The library walls were dark purple, contrasting with the black, white, and red of the South Seas sculptures and the multicolored book bindings, lithographs, and drawings. Colors in the conference room were an elegant gray sprinkled with gold, while the living room, which showcased masks and temple flags, was done up in ocher.

Von Harbou's office, covered the whole length by a Chinese dragon carpet, contained a massive dark-brown collector's cabinet that was dubbed "the cabinet of the thousand delights." It included some of Lang's most cherished possessions—small, imaginative Japanese netsuke, carved toggles of wood and ivory—as well as Ming bronzes and Chinese porcelain. An enormous wooden bust of Buddha perched on top of the case.

"I was never able to bring myself to store the objects I love in boxes and cupboards, while waiting for the day when I found a perfect place to keep them in the house with the old big garden that I dream of," Lang told *Innendekoration*, "and so I resign myself to the fact that the South Seas, Africa, and Mexico are next to each other on my bookshelves, or that Japanese No masks, Siamese temple flags, and Chinese sacred vessels simply have to get along with total strangers—with European-style chairs, sofas, an Ibach piano, and the bookcase in the living room."

Lang, in this interview, added a peculiar detail, which others, recollecting the Berlin home he shared with von Harbou, also remembered: "Innocent visitors who enter our apartment for the first time find themselves confronted with human scalps, petrified but creepily real, with tiny silvers of mother-of-pearl, the last tears of the victim, gleaming in the eyeholes. But once I tell them the story behind these grotesque and beautifully painted human heads, they are no longer horrified but are transformed into a similar but completely different state; for, as Goethe would have put it, 'Schaudern ist der Menschheit bester Teil.'*

"They feel horror not at the sight of the decapitated heads, but for the people who practice these mystical religions, which are limited to fear and lack of freedom and, precisely because of these, to a permanently unfulfilled longing; and then they understand why they are ushered from the library with its twisted grimaces and winged monsters of the South Seas into the room where a bust of the all-knowing Buddha on 'the cabinet of the thousand delights' greets them—he, the incarnation of fearlessness, of freedom, of peace."

If Lang presided over the stage set, the memories of visitors to their home suggest that von Harbou ruled the roost, assuming all social as well as domestic responsibilities. It was she who organized the couple's busy itineraries and hosted their dinner parties. A conscientious homemaker, von Harbou not only perfected the preparation of all of Lang's favorite home-cooked dishes from boyhood, but made the serving of a hot meal ("a simple but delicious dinner," in Kettelhut's words) a mid-evening intermezzo and highlight of the long, sometimes acrimonious, production meetings.

Kettelhut, in his memoirs, painted a vivid portrait of a woman comfortable

---

*Translation: "The chill of dread is mankind's best quality."

at meetings, with dachshunds and Angora cats roaming underfoot—as well as pet parrots and squirrels in the house. She was not only well-liked by her colleagues, but also as much a creative force, as highly motivated and smoothly efficient, as her husband. Her loving personality was crucial to the professional teamwork. Von Harbou's ability to reach out to people and find compromise in the worst situations was a vital resource.

"I was especially impressed by her ability to concentrate," recalled Kettelhut. "She could sit amid the chaos of the studio during a shoot, knit, dictate a new novel to her secretary, and meanwhile watch her husband direct and offer him her advice. She chatted with two women visitors in French and English while she replaced the piano player, accompanying the filming with music."

The marriage, from the outside looking in, appeared perfect, perfectly blended. Lang and von Harbou seemed unthinkable without each other. "The marriage was, in a way, a very happy one," said Hilde Guttmann, von Harbou's personal secretary from 1929 to 1939. "On the other hand, they had differences, and were humanly mountains apart."

Von Harbou, for one thing, was inclined to be privately extravagant with money—and generous with friends—while Lang was thrifty. Von Harbou preferred to host guests at home, or spend a quiet evening of reading; she often liked to be early to bed. Lang, who yearned to go out on the town, stayed up late and had trouble sleeping.

The director also made a sport of arguing and debate. Von Harbou matched Lang's strong will, and though she did not enjoy argumentation she was willing to be drawn in when he provoked disagreement. When they did argue, everything was fair game—film, art, politics. Talk was ceaseless with Lang. Von Harbou was capable of staying pleasant, even in demurral. Most people thought their constant verbal fencing was another perfect part of the marriage.

If it was no secret when Lang first fell in love with von Harbou; it was also no secret that he didn't stay devoted very long, and was hardly a faithful husband.

The sexual ardor they felt for each other, which had precipitated the death of Lisa Rosenthal, was soon relegated to the past after their wedding. It was always that way for Lang, who fell in and out of love with ease. And the well-known director wasn't secretive about his liaisons, either. Being a ladies' man was part of his public cachet.

Just a short time after marrying von Harbou, the director began to seek out the company of other young ladies. He could be sweet and shy about his approach; like the characters in his films, he was always introducing himself with formal politeness, nurturing his extramarital affairs with flowers and chocolates. But Lang also flaunted his mistresses, making a point of escorting them to the bars and soirees and the so-called "beauty dances" in private apartments where he knew he would be spotted. These were known as places to meet and recruit attractive women who might be promised small parts or work as extras in a Fritz Lang film; more than one would-be actress started out with the advantage of a love affair and screen test conducted by the Meister.

The director's companions were sometimes familiar to the public; one was a well-known Berlin opera star of the time. Sometimes they were only short-term girlfriends. And sometimes they were prostitutes, whose paid ministrations Lang periodically preferred.

Von Harbou did not share her husband's sexual restlessness, according to Hilde Guttmann, and contented herself with her role as the dutiful wife and invaluable scenarist. To her it would have seemed bourgeois to begrudge Lang his crushes, flings, and affairs. She and the director remained friends and kept busy professionally.

"We were married eleven years," Thea von Harbou told her secretary many years later, "because for ten years we didn't have time to get divorced."

During this tranquil domestic period, instability and unrest wracked Germany. Even the motion picture industry was affected. Liquidations, bankruptcies, and a flurry of mergers took place among producers attempting to consolidate their resources. The number of film releases dropped off. Hollywood companies made further inroads into the German-language market.

To celebrate his citizenship and to bolster Germany's sagging pride, the newly naturalized director proposed to make a film of *Das Nibelungenlied*, a time-honored epic poem in four-line stanzas dating back to the twelfth or thirteenth century, whose many stage and literary interpretations had proved its enduring appeal to national patriotism.

Erich Pommer accepted his proposal, and Thea von Harbou went to work on a script that would draw on the original epic while borrowing and blending ideas from other versions, notably Richard Wagner's famous opera and Friedrich Hebbel's mid-nineteenth-century play, *Die Nibelungen*. Von Harbou knew the Hebbel text well, having appeared on the stage in that version; she had in fact performed the role of the Burgundian beauty Kriemhild, who enters into an ill-destined wedding contract with the hero of the tale, the noble Siegfried. The couple set out to mount a new version that would combine the epic poem, Wagner, Hebbel, and other influences in such a way as to "fit with our modern feeling," as von Harbou explained in a prepared publicity statement.

According to the saga (partly derived from Scandinavian legends), Siegfried is a pure-hearted warrior who journeys through an accursed mistland to woo the proud, aloof Kriemhild, sister of King Gunther of Burgundy. Siegfried vanquishes a dragon and slays a dwarf-king, taking the dwarf's cloak of invisibility and shape-shifting, along with his treasure of gold and jewels. Bathing in the dragon's blood makes Siegfried invincible, except for a patch of vulnerability on his shoulder where a lime leaf falls and covers his flesh.

Arriving in Burgundy, Siegfried is greeted warily by the court, especially by Lord Hagen, uncle and loyal vassal of King Gunther. Siegfried vows to help the king woo the warrior-woman Brunhild, Queen of Iceland, in exchange for Kriemhild's hand in marriage. Brunhild is won over in contests of strength with the help of Siegfried's invisibility magic. However, on their wedding night, Brunhild shuns Gunther, and it is Siegfried, disguised as Gunther, who must break Brunhild's iron resistance in bed.

When Brunhild learns the truth from a jealous Kriemhild, she angrily denounces Siegfried to the weak-willed Gunther (whose idea the charade was in the first place). A trusting Kriemhild reveals Siegfried's vulnerability to Lord Hagen, who conspires against Siegfried. Gunther and Kriemhild's other brothers plot Siegfried's murder during a festive hunt. Hagen spears him in the shoulder, and Siegfried dies. Stricken with guilt, Brunhild kills herself on his bier, and a grief-crazed Kriemhild vows to exact revenge.

In the second half of the story, Lord Hagen steals Siegfried's treasure, and Kriemhild makes a marriage alliance with King Etzel (aka Attila) of the Huns, in order to facilitate her vengeance. When the Nibelung family is invited to celebrate the birth of her firstborn, Kriemhild's scheming is exposed, and Hagen slays her infant son. The Nibelungs barricade themselves inside Etzel's castle. An all-out Götterdämmerung ensues, a bloodbath that leaves only a handful—including Hagen, the murderer—alive.

"For a long time the mistress Kriemhild stood unmoved," von Harbou wrote at the end of her novelized adaptation of *Das Nibelungenlied*. "She stood all by herself, buried in her robe. She glowed like a female in the late evening light. She let her eyes wander across the courts and over the large, terrifying royal hall, the walls of which were covered with traces of blood. It looked at once like a temple and a cruel god. Crushed bodies lay at its feet. The sand around it was moist from hot blood. Bodies lay horribly silent in the sun, their faces buried in the sand or grinning toward the sky. Human bodies hung from the balcony's parapet like rugs during festivities. And those swallowed by the hall could not be counted. There it was, silent and malicious, with pitiless gates. And the Whitsuntide sun rested like a helmet on the roof."

Von Harbou's script divided the epic into two films: *Siegfried* and *Kriemhilds Rache (Kriemhild's Revenge)*. The writing was finished shortly after the exchange of marriage vows, by the autumn of 1922. Then came several months of production planning. This would be Lang's most lavish film to date, making demands on his team and indeed on Ufa's company resources.

Daily meetings convened at the Lang–von Harbou apartment, so recently the setting of a dramatic demise not unlike Kriemhild's. The meetings usually did not begin until about 4 P.M., often ended well after midnight, and sometimes dragged on till 3 A.M. With only one dinner break at about 8 P.M., the members of the group had better learn to grab a snack at a nearby café beforehand to tide themselves over.

The team consisted mostly of veterans of previous Fritz Lang films. They were studio personnel foremost, assembled by Pommer as much as Lang, and used, in shifting constellations, on many classic German silent films. Usually present, besides the director and his wife, were the cameramen Carl Hoffmann and Günther Rittau, who complemented each other by encouraging different facets of Lang. Hoffmann, Lang once said, "knows the secret of how to photograph a woman. He can capture her face in such a way that not only the woman herself but all the physical content of a scene is revealed—thanks to a glint in the corner of her eye, a shadow that passes over her forehead, or a highlight of her temple." Rittau, on the other hand, was the happy experimentalist. "He Rittau attacks the *plastique* of the film through mathematics. Every third sentence he uttered began, 'What will happen if . . . ?'"

A third cameraman introduced to the operation was Walter Ruttmann, who would photograph Siegfried's famous animated "Dream of the Falcon" sequence. A fourth was Eugen Schüfftan, who had started out as a painter, sculptor, and architect, studying under Bauhaus architect (and art director for theater and film) Hans Poelzig. As much inventor as cameraman, Schüfftan was beginning to develop his reputation in realistic miniatures and blended animation.

Other participants included art directors Otto Hunte, Karl Vollbrecht, and Erich Kettelhut, makeup artist Otto Genath, and composer Gottfried Huppertz. Paul Gerd Guderian, in charge of costume design, was excused periodically because he suffered from tuberculosis. The museum curator Heinrich Umlauff—who had contributed design touches to *Die Spinnen* and *Der müde Tod*—made the trip from the Ethnographical Museum in Hamburg to consult on the armor, costumes, and weapons of the barbaric Huns.

"Every set and every detail, every position in every one of an actor's movements, was discussed in detail and the pros and cons of every opinion thoroughly analyzed," recalled Kettelhut. "Lang didn't give the okay to carry out the designs and the technical drawings until nobody had any objections." After sketches had been executed, everyone met again. "Then they were checked and assessed by all present and finally Lang either accepted, changed, or rejected them. In the latter case, the whole procedure started all over again. Otherwise it was time to start nitpicking about the next set in the same way. No wonder the production meetings took almost three months . . ."

Lang was sometimes accused by critics of being an Expressionist. "What do you think of Expressionism, Herr Doktor?" Countess Told asks Mabuse in *Dr. Mabuse, der Spieler*. And Mabuse replies, "Expressionism is nothing but a game, but nowadays in life everything is just a game." Expressionism was definitely on the director's chain of borrowings, but Lang resisted categorization as an Expressionist—forcing Lotte Eisner, for one, to declare it was too much of an "arbitrary label for such an eclectic director."

Now, for *Die Nibelungen*, Lang transformed a series of celebrated paintings into cinematic imagery. Kriemhild would be costumed and made up to suggest the work of both Wilhelm von Kaulbach (a painter noted for his grandly heroic historical murals) and Franz von Stuck (an allegorical artist of sensuous nudes); in close-up, she looked not unlike a glittery Klimt subject. Siegfried would resemble one of the folk characters of Hans Thoma. Siegfried's homeland was partly inspired by the works of Caspar David Friedrich, one of Germany's masters of the allegorical landscape, known for woodland scenes almost religious in their romantic quality. In places, Lang strove to evoke Arnold Böcklin's haunting *Island of the Dead* and, specifically for Siegfried's journey through the misty forest, *The Silence of the Forest*. The Jugendstil idylls of Heinrich Vogeler would figure in the staging of Siegfried's death.

The Huns would be dressed in rags and fur and equipped with native African and Asiatic weapons. To replace the fading Guderian (in fact, Guderian would die during the long course of the production), Pommer came through with his knack for discovering unknown talent. Plucked from a fashion house, Aenne Willkomm, young and obscure, took over as costumer, choosing to incorporate "medieval, folkloristic, and modern elements" in her design. She made good overnight, with her boundless energy, and after *Die Nibelungen* would be promoted to head of Ufa's costume department.

These influences and more—a mingling of German romanticism, symbolism, and Jugendstil—were brought to the table by the collective. Set designer Robert Herlth was reminded of "a medieval builders' guild (Baühutte)" when speaking of Ufa teamwork. Cameraman Karl Freund, speaking of the camaraderie on the set of *Metropolis*, coined the term *"geistiger Konzern"* ("intellectual partnership") for the unusual team spirit. Lang operated at his best drawing on the imagination of others, absorbing and compiling ideas, with himself the absolute arbiter. This was an advantage in Germany that he never accrued in the United States: the continuity and loyalty of such a united team.

"This 'drawing together,' this mysterious communication among talents, this 'alchemy' of minds, makes it difficult for us today to determine what the key factor in any given film was," wrote Klaus Kreimeier in *The Ufa Story*. "Was it the director's planning, the practicability of the set, the lighting design, the mobility of the camera, or (more rarely) the ability of certain performers to incorporate their body language into the filmic reality?"

Casting went forward. Paul Richter, Edgar Hull in *Mabuse*, would play Siegfried. Margarethe Schön would portray Kriemhild. Theodor Loos was King Gunther. Hanna Ralph would play Brunhild. Hans Adalbert von Schlettow would make an intimidating Hagen Tronje. Georg John had multiple roles: Mime, the Smith, and Alberich, the dwarf king, in Part One; and Blaodel, Etzel's underling, in Part Two. Rudolf Klein-Rogge, who was still working with Fritz Lang despite ceding his wife to him, had another key part as Etzel, King of the Huns.

Principal photography began in the late fall. The production schedule was extraordinary: Filming would eventually consume nine months. The prolonged schedule, as Kettelhut recalled in his memoirs, allowed the design staff to take advantage of Mother Nature. Vollbrecht planted seeds in the fall, so that in the spring, when they were scheduled to photograph the meadow scene in which Siegfried is pierced by Hagen's spear, real flowers would blanket the ground.

There were daily crises and chaos in the real world—empty bellies, crime waves, political protests, and strikes. "While demonstrations, riots, and looting were daily occurrences all over the country, while hunger and poverty were becoming alarmingly more frequent, while the police force was hardly bothering to deal with crime and theft anymore, we worked on in Babelsberg for the Ufa as if we were on an island," recollected Kettelhut.

The production had to scrounge essential goods from the black market, just like everyone else in Berlin. Nails especially were in short supply, and at one point, in order for set construction to continue, a ragtag army of elderly retirees and wounded war veterans was hired to roam the Neubabelsberg grounds with gunnysacks, collecting stray nails left over from abandoned sets.

It was characteristic of Lang—and of the entire silent-film period, before the consolidation of unions—to demand the utmost of everyone in his crew. There was no overtime in that era. Cast and crew worked ten-, twelve-, fourteen-hour days, sometimes without break. People were forced to work such long hours during the shooting of *Die Nibelungen* that they couldn't always get to the stores in time to purchase their daily bread, which in any case was a scarcity among the general population. Food prices kept climbing, so the studio took it upon itself to buy groceries at the beginning of every week and sell them to employees, on payday, at beginning-of-the-week prices.

Realizing that desperate conditions were mounting, von Harbou offered to prepare regular hearty meals for everybody. She had a curious habit of choosing a favorite dress for each production, and wearing it throughout filming; the outfit she donned for *Die Nibelungen* was an elegant light-purple-gray dress with a lace neckline, which she displayed now, even while supervising all the cooking for cast and crew.

Von Harbou set up a makeshift shed next to the canteen with two huge cauldrons, a washing-up basin, and a big table. The canteen staff was organized to prepare food for the actors, employees, and extras with the help of additional women she hired. "She was even able to talk the Ufa into carrying the costs so the crew could get their meals for free," Kettelhut said. "I admired Frau von Harbou for that. She stood there on the rough floor of that drafty shed for hours and didn't mind peeling potatoes or cleaning vegetables with the other women." Such was the spirit of sacrifice.

Much of the photography took place after midnight in the studio—to ensure an evenness of light in artificially illuminated scenes. (Even so, strips of film had to be retouched later by hand to accent the tones.) Siegfried's journey through the magical stone forest was filmed partly on a soundstage. Stagehands cast wagonloads of salt over the studio floor to create the impression of a vast frozen forest; the tree trunks were straight plaster coated with cement, real soil and moss piled about their roots.

Many of the marvelous effects were obtained by deviously simple means. The dense mist in the sequence where Alberich, made invisible by the Tarnkappe (cloak of invisibility), tries to strangle the hero, was produced by the spray of fire extinguishers. A sword so sharp it could split a feather was illustrated, in reality, by two feathers dropped and photographed in reverse. The rainbow in the film—one of Günther Rittau's inspirations—was "a superimposition of the mountain, made in the studio, and a curved arc made with chalk on a black piece of cardboard," in the director's words.

Many regarded one particular effect, the petrification of the dwarfs holding up a giant platter of treasure in Alberich's cave, as cameraman Rittau's highest accomplishment. The dwarfs slowly turn to stone, their faces gradually becoming immobilized, as the spell completes its grip. The resourceful Rittau accomplished this by step-by-step superimposition. "All, it must be remembered," reminded Eisner, "done directly inside the camera by a footage and frame count."

Lang and Karl Vollbrecht had endless difficulty with the crucial scene in which Siegfried slays the dragon. The dummy dragon was about seventy feet long and "inconceivably heavy," in the words of Frederick Wynne Jones, the managing director of Ufa's interests in America. Its skin was plaster covered with vulcanized hard rubber. The breathing effect was obtained with bellows, and a powerful water pump spewed out "blood" when the dragon was finally slain by Siegfried's sword. "Ten men were concealed in the body while several more were placed in a pit under the dragon to give it a forward crawling motion," explained Jones in publicity remarks. "Some of these men received their instructions by telephone so as to get simultaneous action."

Under Lang's prodding, the dragon men practiced walking, crawling, and dying for weeks. When photographing the dragon fight, the "conscientious and obsessed" director, in Kettelhut's words, asked for repeated takes. The flicking tail of the beast moved amazingly fast, and at one point "either the men working the tail-lever had gotten overenthusiastic, or Paul Richter, who was very tired, didn't jump at the right time or high enough," according to Kettelhut. "The hard end of the tail hit him full force on his upper leg. Fortunately the doctor, who was called immediately, didn't diagnose a broken bone but a very severe contusion, yet the invulnerable Siegfried was put out of action for a while."

The dragon had to be rebuilt, the sequence refilmed. It is one scene that is really dated; invariably the dragon-slaying—a highlight in 1924—provokes laughter from contemporary audiences accustomed to more sophisticated action.

Lang wished the actors, too, had buttons and dials and mechanical parts. He went to extreme lengths to dictate their slightest nuances of movement and gesture, demonstrating himself what they should do in every instance. Some directors, like Lubitsch, got away with that; unlike Lubitsch, though, Lang was no role model as an actor. He tried to compensate with elaborate script annotations for camera placement, and equally detailed instructions for the actors to follow. These were methods the director would refine and alter from film to film as his career progressed.

Erich Kettelhut recalled Lang's directive to the *Die Nibelungen* cast members. "It sounded like this: 'Listen, on one-two-three you bend your upper body slightly forward—turn your head toward me; four-five-six-seven, you raise your left arm slowly. You open your clenched fist, hold it as high as your head. An astounded expression comes over your face, your mouth opens slightly; ten, you fling both your arms forward and spread out your fingers, you fling your body backward, you scream.'

"The numbers could go up to fifty, depending on the scene and how varied the movements were," explained Kettelhut. "Several actors could be given different movements for the same numbers. Also, sometimes whole groups, sometimes all of the extras, had to move according to the series of numbers."

The sometimes arrogant and overly precise manner in which Lang dictated their behavior often inhibited actors; trying to follow his guidance as closely as possible, they inevitably stiffened up on screen. The humanity of the characters sometimes suffered, one of the reasons why some critics were led to accuse his films of "coldness."

Lang would even stay at work after everyone had long gone home, pacing the set, making his little diagrams and specifications. During the making of *Die Nibelungen*, he spent hours every morning before first call marking with colored chalk the movements and positions for his actors on the floor of the studio stage. These techniques amounted to a rehearsal in his mind, but right up to the final take there was always the possibility that he might switch gears, and pursue a sudden inspiration. "There were no fixed dates for shooting time and order of shooting [in those days]," recalled Kettelhut. "Improvisation was in fashion. Many people seriously believed that working according to fixed plans would not leave enough space for artistic intuition."

Pommer was on the set as often as possible, eyeing the budget and trying to nudge ahead the schedule without stepping on Lang's toes. Everyone knew that when the producer was in a bad or nervous mood his cigarette dangled loosely. Filming dragged on, with costs elevating, and Pommer's cigarette dangled a lot.

The producer got cold feet shortly before the shooting of the scene involving the Huns sitting in bare branches, spying out the arrival of Kriemhild, and then riding off on their horses on a wild chase. The location was the Rehbergen, an uninhabited area of wooded hills. Lang had asked for several hundred extras and horses. Pommer questioned whether the added expense was really essential, and the two argued furiously.

The next day, Lang was conciliatory. "I think that we do not need the scene," the director told Pommer. "Thea and I will cook up something else." The producer's response was characteristic; after thinking it over, he surrendered to Lang's vision. "I've done some thinking too," said Pommer, "I think we should shoot the scene as it was originally planned." The extras stayed in.

"I remember the Huns, led by Etzel, galloping down a wooded draw," said John Pommer, who visited his father's sets as a young boy. "I remember a camera set up in the middle of the draw, with horses galloping to its left and to its right. The Huns did not ride in formation; only one or two horses were on each side of that camera at the same time. Based on a lifetime of experience, I could make that scene look very exciting with less than a hundred extras. The same applies to the shots of the Huns sitting in the branches. I judge that Lang had no more than a hundred extras, one hundred fifty at most. 'Several hundred' seems a Lang exaggeration, but he was wont to exaggerate."

Lang, himself on horseback and wearing jodhpurs, directed the outdoor scenes with a megaphone. Lang's cousin Friedrich Steinbach was passing through Berlin on his first European *Wanderjahr*. He recalled visiting the director at the Rehbergen location, and glimpsing Lang astride a splendid white horse, supervising crowds of extras. How proud the director seemed, how ebullient!* But the wild bareback rides caused several accidents, and a tent hospital had to be set up to care for the casualties.

The director planned, for the final scene, an apocalyptic inferno that would outdo the ending of *Der müde Tod*. This was the attack on the Burgundians, barricaded inside Etzel's great hall, which culminates in the Huns' setting fire to the place. An abandoned factory site in Spandau was renovated at considerable expense, just so it could be reduced to rubble in a scene that would be photographed simultaneously by some sixteen cameras. Of course Lang chose to ignite the final explosion himself.

---

*Lang further demonstrated his ebullient mood when he stuffed Steinbach's backpack with millions of marks before sending him on his way. Because of inflation, however, the money wasn't worth that much. Toward the end of the inflationary period, bank notes were in multiples of billions.

"It was starting to get light in the east," wrote Erich Kettelhut. "The wind conditions were especially good—a light wind was blowing from west to east, so the smoke wouldn't blow over to the cameras trained on Etzel's palace. There was a quiet air of expectancy among the many people who were involved and the guests.

"Fritz Lang, standing off camera, drew his bow and let loose an arrow with magnesium powder on its head. It flew in a high arc over one corner of the roof. The flames spread like the ripples from a stone thrown into water. A huge fire flamed incredibly quickly over the building. The mushroom of smoke grew higher and higher, and spread into the sky. The roof collapsed. It became hotter and hotter. The outer walls of the Etzel building, soaked in water beforehand to prevent them catching fire, started to smoke. Lang signaled that the shot was over. The whole thing had taken about ten minutes. The people standing around had been completely quiet, deeply touched."

Every scene, every highlight, was documented behind the scenes by Horst von Harbou, the director's brother-in-law. Lurking perpetually in the background with his heavy camera, tripod, and accessories, he vividly documented the production for posterity.

Pommer was in an upbeat mood, his cigarette once again jutting horizontally from his lips during the last days of filming in January of 1924. The producer sidled up to Erich Kettelhut and told the set builder to count on working on Fritz Lang's next production too. "It is going to have just as many interesting challenges as the Nibelungen," Pommer informed Kettelhut. "In fact, it's going to go it one better . . ."

A few days before the *Die Nibelungen* premiere on February 24, 1924, Lang decided to take the editing apart and start over again. He was working around the clock, but "the nearer the deadline got, the harder time he had editing," recalled Kettelhut.

Come noon of the opening day, Lang still wasn't finished. It became apparent that the film wouldn't be ready for the much-publicized premiere, whose audience included scores of prominent guests and dignitaries. In fact, the finished reels had to be driven from the editing room in Neubabelsberg to Ufa-Palast am Zoo in Berlin, a forty-minute drive away, in sections. Lang, as nervous as a new daddy, could hardly be persuaded to let the reels go out into the world. Cars were spaced along the road to the theater in case one broke down.

Finally, the moment arrived. The cream of Berlin society, including journalists, government officials, stage and opera stars, and motion picture personalities, sat expectantly in the audience. Those in the know watched in "mortal fear of the dreaded sign 'technical breakdown' lighting up at any moment—it would interrupt the flow of the film," in Kettelhut's words.

Fears of a breakdown materialized as the first sign went up. The film was stopped for a few minutes, then resumed after a brief interruption. Then the sign lit up again, and this time the film didn't resume quite so quickly. The audience became restless. The houselights went up. The director of the Ufa-Palast got up on stage and explained that they were trying to solve the problem. The Hungarian-American music director with Ufa, Ernö Rapée, was conducting for the occasion a sixty-piece symphonic orchestra, which did its best to distract the audience with impromptu entertainment.

Future director Edgar G. Ulmer and editor Rudi Fehr were among those in the audience at the disastrous premiere. "When the second reel was being shown, he [Lang] was cutting the third," recalled Ulmer, a Viennese just entering the German film industry. Rudi Fehr had tickets because his father was an official of Deutsche Bank, one of the Ufa directorate. A musician and aficionado, Fehr noticed right away that the cues were off. The lights went on, again and again, as Ernö Rapée's orchestra struggled to match the director's last-minute changes. Finally the manager came out and announced, "Ladies and gentlemen, anybody who has paid can get their money back . . ."

"It was a long time before the lights went down again [for the last reel]," recalled Erich Kettelhut, "and the audience, which seemed to find the whole thing quite amusing, slowly stopped chatting and settled down to watch the last reel. Of course after this they were not so attentive as before, so there was not so much applause at the end."

The premiere, held hostage to the director's perfectionism, was one of Germany's all-time fiascos. "That's Fritz Lang for you," remembered Rudi Fehr. "He didn't give a damn. If the picture wasn't right, he wanted to get it right."

Seen today, *Die Nibelungen* remains one of the breathtaking wonders of the silent screen.

The spectator is swept along on a journey to a mythic time of dwarfs, ogres, giants, and dragons; a place of spectacular landscapes and grandiose settings; a world of primal images and emotions. Lang was never more in command of his flair for drama and sensation on a panoramic scale. Scene after scene is richly imagined. The costumes and design are magnificent. The camerawork is beautifully composed. Every scene is inventively dappled with sparkle and haze, smoke and fire, gusts of wind, reflection in water and mirrors, and the constant interplay of shadow and light.

Some scenes are pageantry, others staged with admirable simplicity. Lang's bold use of close-ups forces an intimacy with the kaleidoscopic array of characters, the beautiful and the grotesque, who have in common only that their actions are legislated by fate. The director's characterizations are surprising: He gazes coldly on Kriemhild and finds Siegfried more naive than innocent; he loathes the impotent, arrogant Burgundians, and perceives courtliness and élan in the King of the Huns.

The finale is still harrowing. The Huns stream out of their hive to deliver the harsh justice of Kriemhild, who is consumed by the devil of her own hatred. The Burgundians, most loyal of Teutonic clans, fight to the death, yet prove nothing except the hollowness of their vaunted honor. Hundreds die in battle, but Lord Hagen is left alive and Kriemhild's wickedness is thwarted. Hagen is led out of the ruined castle; Kriemhild eagerly grabs a sword and hurries to slay him herself. Then, in her warped ecstasy, she suffers a heart attack and dies.

After all these years the film still conveys with tremendous power the inbred stench of nobility, the suffocating embrace of family, the impossibility of love and marriage, and, perhaps most important, "the inexorability," in the words of Thea von Harbou, "with which the first guilt entails the last atonement."

Seventy years after it was made, Lang's 1924 film continues to be shown in revival and on video, provoking awe from viewers and lively discussion among film critics.

The director said repeatedly in interviews that he had turned to *Die Nibelungen* after coming to a conscious decision to make a film to give Germany a lift after years of economic and political turmoil. Not everyone in his adopted country was as convinced of the film's nationalistic spirit, however.

The *New York Times* took an unusual interest in Lang's new film, and *Die Nibelungen* became the first of the director's works to receive any genuine attention in the United States. The newspaper published an April 29, 1924, article about the Berlin premiere, in which correspondent T. R. Ybarra related how disgruntled some Germans were that Ufa advertisements for *Die Nibelungen* referred to the characters of Lang's film as "a pack of false-hearted murderers and other highly uncomplimentary names, and in the final scene Kriemhild, of whom the epic makes a heroine, was shown committing murder under the most treacherous circumstances." The advertisements caused "a howl of protest," according to the *New York Times*, and after early showings "the producers of the film rushed wildly into print with feverish explanations that the objectionable text of the advertisement was due to careless rearrangement of the text as originally written." The revised text was supplied, "showing that the ancient Germans of the Nibelung days, though occasionally violent and temperamental, were, after all, a splendid lot whose virtues all present-day Germans should emulate."

The uncompromising attitude toward Siegfried, Kriemhild, and the Burgundians disturbed certain German critics. A reviewer for the mainstream cultural journal *Der Kunstwart* said the ugly excesses of the protagonists made him long for the innocence of Jackie Coogan films. Others griped about falsification of a "gem in the German cultural crown." The socialistic *Kulturwille* meanwhile noted that the film's jingoism was only partial, and "gave little opportunity for nationalistic demonstrations, unlike the truly German film *Fridericus Rex . . .*"*

When the Nazis came to rule, Lang's film seemed to rise up in patriotic esteem, even taking on a hint of dark political meaning. In 1929 the National Socialist paper *Der Angriff* praised *Die Nibelungen* as a "film of German loyalty." It is true that, as Lotte Eisner wrote, "this German film was the favorite viewing of Hitler and Goebbels, dark-complexioned men who saw themselves as blond heroes of a heroic race." In his speech of March 28, 1933, at the Kaiserhof, Goebbels would praise Fritz Lang's film; that same year, the Nazis would authorize a re-release of *Siegfrieds Tod*, with a voice-over by Theodor Loos, one of Lang's recurrent actors, who had played King Gunther.

---

*Siegfried Kracauer in *From Caligari to Hitler* writes extensively about *Fridericus Rex*, a nationalistic 1922 film directed by Arzén von Cserépy, which was about the life of Frederick the Great and was widely regarded as "pure propaganda for a restoration of the monarchy."

Siegfried Kracauer, in his highly influential book *From Caligari to Hitler*—one of the first authoritative post–World War II cultural histories of Germany—went further. He branded Lang's film an incipient Nazi document which "somewhat anticipated the Goebbels propaganda" of the Third Reich. Hagen, Gunther's loyal vassal, obviously foreshadowed "a well-known type of Nazi leader," according to Kracauer. Lang's spatial compositions of massive edifices, and cliffs towering over human figures in the foreground reduced people "to accessories of primeval landscapes or vast buildings." Worse, according to Kracauer, Nazi propaganda pieces like *Triumph of the Will* drew their inspiration from *Die Nibelungen*: "In Nuremberg, the ornamental pattern of Nibelungen appeared on a gigantic scale: an ocean of flags and people artistically arranged."

Lang's visual strategy was "the complete triumph of the ornamental over the human," Kracauer theorized. "Absolute authority asserts itself by arranging people under its domination in pleasing designs. This can also be seen with the Nazi regime, which manifested strong ornamental inclinations in organizing masses."

Kracauer was not the only one to point out the racial implications of certain characters. This was noticed by critics in 1924, when the film was first released. According to Frank Aschau in the widely read Berlin weekly *Die Weltbühne*, "The evil dwarf Alberich, who represents obscure powers, is, and it can't be mistaken, depicted as a Jew. Not as a handsome Jew, naturally, but as a vile Jew." Lotte Eisner, coming to the director's rescue, argued in her book that if anyone exaggerated the racial implications, it was not the fault of Lang or Pommer. She insisted that makeup artist Otto Genath was "simply influenced" by the "grotesque character makeup" of the Russo-Jewish Habimah ensemble visiting Berlin at the time. Also in her book Eisner quoted Friedrich Engels, the socialist collaborator of Karl Marx, on the moving subtext of the Siegfried legend. She extolled Lang's "realistic view" of the characters, which precluded any racism.

The fact is that Lang's *Die Nibelungen* was never universally popular in Germany. The first half was considered too long, and during the Nazi era the second part was not made available to the public, because its all-out nihilism conformed even less to Nazi ideology—though the first half, without the payoff, was essentially meaningless. Lang detested all the bastardized versions, especially the shortened one released in America with music from Richard Wagner's opera; he detested Wagner with even more passion than his usual dislike of classical music, and said he had resisted suggestions to use the archetypal (and notoriously anti-Semitic) Wagner as background orchestral music for the film's original release in Germany.

The inklings may have been there, but Lang the patriot was more an artist than a practical man, largely unaware of the nascent Nazi movement in 1923–24. He was still sleepwalking through history. How many in Germany were not? The accusations of Kracauer, whom he had befriended, haunted the director to the end of his days. In interview after interview, people brought up the film and its Nazi coloration, citing *From Caligari to Hitler* and other reputable sources. Though he tried very hard, Lang could never quite dispel the doubts and speculation.

In what was billed as "Fritz Lang Gives His Last Interview" in New York City's *Village Voice* (August 16, 1976), published the month of his death, the director was still trying to explain away the implications.* Questioned by Gene D. Phillips about *Die Nibelungen*, Lang patiently explained, "When I made my films, I always followed my imagination. By making the Siegfried legend into a film, I wanted to show that Germany was searching for an ideal in her past, even during the horrible time after the First World War in which the picture was made. To counteract the pessimistic spirit of the time, I wanted to film the great legend of Siegfried so that Germany could draw inspiration from her epic past, and not, as Mr. Kracauer suggests, as a looking-forward to the rise of a political figure like Hitler or something stupid of that sort. I was dealing with Germany's legendary heritage—just as in *Metropolis*, I was looking at Germany in the future."

Lang, Erich Pommer, and Pommer's wife Gertrud sailed from Hamburg on October 2, 1924, aboard the S.S. *Deutschland* for the American premiere of *Die Nibelungen*. While in the United States for the first time, the director and producer planned to visit the Ufa branch offices in New York City and afterward travel to Los Angeles to meet film personalities and observe Hollywood studio methods.

When the *Deutschland* docked in New York, Lang and Pommer were obliged to spend a night on board as "enemy aliens" until their permission to land was authorized. Lang's first glimpse of the New York skyline was from the deck of the ship. "There," Lang would declare to Peter Bogdanovich, "I conceived *Metropolis*." It was a proclamation echoed in dozens of the director's other interviews.

"I saw a street lit as if in full daylight by neon lights," Lang said on another occasion, "and topping them oversized luminous advertisements, moving, turning, flashing on and off, spiraling . . . something which was completely new and nearly fairy-tale-like for a European in those days . . ."

"The buildings seemed to be a vertical veil, shimmering, almost weightless, a luxurious cloth hung from the dark sky to dazzle, distract, and hypnotize. At night the city did not give the impression of being alive; it lived as illusions lived. I knew then that I had to make a film about all of these sensations."

Walking around the city with Pommer the next day, Lang was again awestruck. The weather was "dreadfully hot," the city seemed "a crater of blind, confused human forces—pushing together and grinding upon each other, motivated by greed."

"I remarked to Pommer," recalled Lang, "that under different labels, most humans are really slaves. He said Hollywood would never make a film about this because they live inside of it. So *we* [author's emphasis] said, 'Let us make a film about it.' I said, 'Let's call it *Metropolis*.' "*

---

*This interview is actually a condensed excerpt from a longer transcript published in the Spring, 1975 issue of England's *Focus on Film*.

*Note the "we." The earliest published versions of this anecdote gave the credit more to Lang and Erich Pommer both, according to Pommer's son John, who added, "Eventually Lang took it over as his sole inspiration."

nn had arrived before them. Traveling with
Jones, the firm's American representative,
n trip to the West Coast. First they stopped
corted by "a very stylish and charming young
reets of the Windy City ("incidentally, perhaps
world").

or the first time, Europeans were inevitably struck
f the country, but too, they projected their own
d they had read and dreamed about. The German
er Carl Zuckmayer, who made the trip by automo-
ensational landscape intoxicated me; every look and
very." Bertolt Brecht, ever the vinegary observer, looked
thought "Arizona and Texas remind you very much of

Siberia, ... the train. The gray two-story wooden farms and the people
look very poor."

Lang, closer to Carl Zuckmayer in spirit, experienced America as the land
of Karl May and Buffalo Bill. He saw the Mississippi rolling beneath him for
the first time through train windows as his train chuffed across those mighty
waters dividing East from West. The fast-vanishing frontier unfolded mes-
merically before his eyes. The yellow plains, the parched desert, the rocky
peaks—all captivated him. America was a new and strange place—yet familiar
to Lang, in his heart, from a childhood of yearning and imagining.

Arriving in Hollywood, the Ufa contingent went to see *The Thief of Baghdad*, "going directly from the railroad station to the Egyptian theater," according to the *New York Times*. Lang and the dignitaries launched a busy
month-long schedule of meetings and get-togethers, exploiting contacts in
Hollywood's German émigré community to forge future business relationships.
Among others, they met with motion picture executives Samuel Goldwyn,
Joseph Schenck, and Marcus Loew (who took Lang on a tour of his MGM
plant, shortly to relocate in Culver City); producer-director Thomas Ince (who
would die of mysterious causes shortly afterward, in November); French director Maurice Tourneur; America's big stars Douglas Fairbanks, Mary Pickford, and Charles Chaplin; and the fellow Berliner lately transplanted to
Hollywood, Ernst Lubitsch.

Lang visited the First National facilities of Warner Brothers, where Lubitsch
was employed, and watched special effects for the adaptation of Arthur Conan
Doyle's *The Lost World*. "They saw brontosauri which were a foot high and
towered above miniature forests," reported the *New York Times*. "Twelve cameras were employed in taking one frame at a time of this picture, and often
the director only made a few feet a week, each slightest movement of the
animal miniatures having to receive the most careful technical attention. Mr.
Lang referred to this production as a technical masterpiece."

Impressed, Lang declared the First National facilities far superior to any-
thing available in Germany. Universal Pictures was another stop, where Lang
toured a familiar setting, the Paris opera house. *Phantom of the Opera* with
Lon Chaney in the starring role, was being filmed, Carl Laemmle, another
German émigré, presided over the Universal operations. Lang and the
Laemmle family would enjoy a long acquaintance based on this early associ-

ation. The director declared the semi-rural studio site, on the outskirts of Hollywood, "one of the most wonderful lots imaginable."

Lang's appointment with Douglas Fairbanks and Mary Pickford was especially congenial, for Hollywood's dream couple were knowledgeable about Lang's status in the film world. Fairbanks was of Austrian heritage, a Germanophile who spoke excellent German and was even known to sport a monocle himself. The director of Pickford's latest picture (1923's *Rosita*) was Lubitsch; her next was slated to be directed by Josef von Sternberg. Pickford "told Mr. Lang that she admired the courage of foreign directors, who risked everything to obtain originality," according to the *New York Times*, asserting that "often she and American directors were afraid to carry out ideas which were attacked with enthusiasm by foreigners like Lubitsch."

The American who had borrowed the special effects of *Der müde Tod* for *The Thief of Bagdad* now took the foreign visitor on a tour of the *Bagdad* sets on the back lot of the Goldwyn studios, at Santa Monica Boulevard and Formosa. There William Cameron Menzies's fabulous minarets and towers were still standing ("gleaming and glittering in the sunlight," in Lang's words).

Lang and Fairbanks discussed the differences between American and German motion picture production. According to Wolfgang Jacobsen in his book about Erich Pommer, Lang explained to Fairbanks that in Germany the quality of the film was the main object, and players deferred to a director's vision. "For example, in *Siegfried*, six or seven of the most important German actors had participated." Fairbanks replied that American films were dependent on individual stars, or personalities, to create excitement at the box office and guarantee a profit. In Hollywood, Fairbanks told him, "the star was the most important person." It was a prophetic exchange, considering the problems the director would have later on adjusting to the American film industry.

Lang respected Fairbanks, whose costume adventure pictures were kindred to *Die Spinnen.* "With Fairbanks," Lang said later, "each set is like a child and we have the same feeling in our studios. It is a pity that he has got to devote so much of his energy to conferences, as I thought that his forehead was furrowed with distribution troubles. He ought to concentrate, without bothering about such things, on his glorious pictures."

The director also met with Chaplin, an equal partner with Fairbanks, Pickford, and D. W. Griffith in their production and distribution venture, United Artists. "Charlie Chaplin was evidently in love when we saw him," Lang told the *New York Times.* "He is married now and therefore we know that he must have been in love. He was very gracious on the evening of the dinner at the Los Angeles Biltmore; very happy, too, but he did not seem to be thinking much about films. I understand that his next picture [Chaplin was finishing *The Gold Rush*] is wonderful, but he is not satisfied with it yet, as he is going to rewrite and retake the last two reels. When he works, he works, but he can also play like a boy. He is a big artist, and in Germany we say that he has a twinkle in one eye and a tear in the other. We love Charlie because there is a touch of tragedy in his comedies—laughter with underlying pathos."

Lubitsch's house with swimming pool at 616 Beverly Drive was a magnet for the German-American crowd in Hollywood, a group dubbed the Foreign Legion. Lang and Pommer (who knew Lubitsch better) spent Sundays there mingling with other show-business people with thick accents. Lang looks al-most paunchy next to Lubitsch, a sleek seal, in vintage photographs of both men in their swimming suits. Frolicking at poolside, impishly brandishing a monocle, Lubitsch mimicked Lang for a publicity photograph. "Meeting Lu-bitsch," said Lang afterward, "was like greeting a brother. I was indeed glad to see him."

Lang's visit to the motion picture capital was capped by a luncheon hosted by Samuel Goldwyn at a luxury hotel, where Pommer gave a speech exhorting international cooperation between film artists. Returning east, Lang and Pom-mer made a side trip to Montclair, New Jersey, to call on the last of the four United Artists partners. The pioneering director of American silent film, D. W. Griffith, greeted them cordially, screening his newly completed feature. *Isn't Life Wonderful?*—in a remarkable twist of irony—was a film about family life in post-war Germany; much of it had been photographed in the fatherland during its worst phase of unrest.

Precious little is known about the face-to-face meeting between these two titans of the silent era. Frederick Ott consulted the *New York Times* report of the visit and wrote that the realism of Griffith's picture made an abiding impression on Lang. "He [Lang] found *Isn't Life Wonderful* to be as remark-able for its touches of human interest as *Lost World* was for its technical achievements." Wolfgang Jacobsen consulted other sources, and noted that Lang appeared a bit irritated to realize the film took place on his home ter-ritory.

Lang traveled back to Germany in the company of Ufa executive Felix Kallmann at the end of November, while Erich Pommer followed a week later.

Not long after, the director bylined a rhapsodic paean to America in the German magazine *Filmland*, for its January 1925 issue. In the essay Lang ex-tolled the miles and miles of roads, the vistas of oil derricks and palm trees he encountered. He praised the wide open spaces and palatial homes. "They build things big in America," the director concluded. "There's enough space. And Paradise has been created."

CHAPTER 6

1925
1927

The director's account of how *Metropolis* came into existence—his awe-inspired brainstorm after gazing on New York City from the deck of the *Deutschland* ("his first premonition of a city of the future," in Frederick Ott's words)—was one of those anecdotes Lang didn't mind repeating, with minor variations, in interview after interview.

But it couldn't have happened quite that way. Erich Pommer was already telling people about this next Fritz Lang project during the final days of filming *Die Nibelungen*, months before the American trip. Erich Kettelhut said he first read a version of the *Metropolis* script at Hohenzollerndamm right after the premiere. "What [Lang and von Harbou] wanted could only be carried out on a utopian-scale budget," he recalled. "It took me a long time to read the screenplay."

Further proof that Lang's version of the genesis of *Metropolis* was simply one of his carefully cultivated myths comes in a May 1924 report of the director's publicity jaunt to Vienna. Accompanied by Thea von Harbou, Lang visited the city of his birth as a guest speaker at a conference on the cinema, as well as to promote the Austrian premiere of *Die Nibelungen*. A reception was held at the Hotel Österreichischer Hof, where the people who gathered in the director's honor urged him, among other things, to make a film commemorating Vienna.

This was not, however, a trip soaked in the romance of nostalgia. Lang was still litigating over his mother's will, and the conference organizers annoyed him with their patronizing and censorious attitude toward the cinematic medium. He wrote a letter afterward denouncing "the pure hatred of these ladies and gentlemen for film and the film industry," and then assigned his speaker's fee to a society for war-blinded veterans.

Some fortuitous encounters brightened his stay. A Viennese actress brought her fourteen-year-old daughter to meet Lang. Lien Deyers was half-Dutch, a blossoming young girl, like Lil Dagover, "very beautiful and very blond," with "an interesting face." Having practiced a few German phrases, Deyers walked up to the film director, stuck out her hand and asked, "Don't you want to discover me for one of your films?"

"A calm stern glance through his monocle," recalled Deyers, "and Fritz

Lang wrote on the paper I gave to him, 'Come to Berlin.' " Several weeks later Deyers arrived there with her mother, was granted a screen test, and assured of a role in some future Fritz Lang production.

Also importantly, Vienna in May of 1924 is where the director made the acquaintance of Gerda Maurus, another blue-eyed blonde, from the suburb of Breitenfurt. Her father was an engineer and inventor, and like Lang she had been raised a Catholic.

Maurus had started acting when she was fifteen years old, and had built a reputation in Vienna as a stylish presence in cabarets, plays, and operettas. Lang couldn't help but notice the sensuous twenty-one-year-old beauty when he made the rounds of Vienna's theaters, as he usually did on such home-comings. "She handled a small part very well," recalled the director. "I was impressed by the fact that she had worked out every facet of her characteri-zation—even down to a hole in her stocking."

Her ethnic background was Croatian. "Gerda Maurus had an indescribably beautiful face," in the words of Curt Riess, "an almost classically beautiful face, but note the 'almost.' She had very high cheekbones, eyes set wide apart. This gave her face something foreign, something strange, something tremen-dously riveting and exciting."

Everybody except Gerda Maurus wondered whether the famous director sitting in the front row of the Kammerspiele would pay a backstage visit. Maurus herself had no burning ambition to appear in motion pictures. As it happened, though, Lang did not materialize; he arrowed one of his compli-mentary notes backstage, urging the actress to come to Berlin for a screen test. The theater manager insisted she was vital to the Vienna stage scene, and her note back to Lang ("I am indispensable here") made an impression. Maurus was encouraged to stay in touch.

The Vienna newspapers covered the native son's every movement. Most interesting of all, a July 4, 1924, item in the Austrian newspaper *Illustriertes Wiener Extrablatt* noted that after leaving the city Lang and von Harbou were embarking on their summer vacation in the Salzkammergut (the Alps outside Salzburg), where the director and his scenarist-wife would labor "to finish the screenplay for their new film *Metropolis . . .*"

July was three months before Lang went to America, and five months before he returned in December, supposedly inspired by those glittering skyscrapers. By then, Christmas of 1924, his hardworking wife had certainly completed the *Metropolis* scenario.

There were times when Thea von Harbou worked her screenplays into novels for publication to coincide with a film's release. Other times she wrote her stories first as novels, then adapted them into scripts. This appears to have been the case with *Metropolis*, where the screen credits make the point that the script is "based on a novel by Thea von Harbou."

The story envisions a futuristic city built on the shoulders of slave labor. High above the city dwells a leisure class presided over by its supreme master, Joh Fredersen, who is at odds with his pampered son, Freder. A strange in-ventor, Rotwang, subservient to the overlord, lives in a medieval house in the center of the city. Deep below, on subterranean levels, workers toil under terrible conditions, tyrannized by monstrous machines. Farther down, in ancient caves and catacombs, discontent and rebellion brew.

A "daughter of the people," Maria, seeks to uplift the workers. Her character was pure von Harbou—and in sync with the side of Lang that idealized women. She is Christ the Redeemer and Madonna the Virgin rolled into one (a reference made explicitly in the novel, where von Harbou speaks of her "Madonna voice"). The creed she espouses to the workers—glassy-eyed zombies leading undead lives—sounds like biblical phraseology half the time and Marxist dogma the rest.

In the story, Freder, the overlord's son, takes notice of the downtrodden masses and experiences a vision of the great energy-machine which sustains the city: in his mind it takes the shape of Moloch, the god of fire. Smitten with Maria, Freder finds himself siding with the workers. His father is alarmed, and authorizes Rotwang to create a robot facsimile of Maria to confuse the workers and incite a false uprising. The replication is successful; Maria's "dupe" stirs anarchy. The underground workers rise up and attack the heart-machine that dominates their desperate lives. The revolt ends in wholesale destruction, a flood tide, and a kind of surreal crucifixion scene where the workers turn on the robot-Maria—thinking her the human-Maria—and burn her at a stake in the Cathedral Square.

Von Harbou described the stake-burning scene in her novel:

"The pyre flamed up in long flames. The men, the women, seized hands and tore around the bonfire, faster, faster, and faster, in rings growing ever wider and wider, laughing, screaming with stamping feet, 'Witch—! Witch!'

"Freder's bonds broke. He fell over on his face among the feet of the dancers.

"And the last he saw of the girl, while her gown and hair stood blazing around her as a mantle of fire, was the loving smile and the wonder of her eyes—and her mouth of deadly sin, which lured among the flames:

" 'Dance with me, my dearest! Dance with me—!' "

Lang envisioned *Metropolis* as the "costliest and most ambitious picture ever" made in Europe, according to the *New York Times*, with thousands of extras, huge sets, special effects that would outshine anything previously attempted. The projected budget was unprecedented. Even from the beginning, Ufa never expected to turn a profit on the production; it was hoped that the colossal motion picture would recoup its investment and create an opening for future German films in America, where Lang and Pommer had returned from making inroads.

Once again, at the regular late-afternoon time of day, the Ufa team gathered at the Lang and von Harbou residence. The team comprised mostly the same people, with some noteworthy substitutions. Carl Hoffmann was gone; Karl Freund sat in his chair, partnered with Günther Rittau. Freund still bore animosity toward Lang as a result of the Lisa Rosenthal tragedy, but Erich Pommer had coaxed him into working with the director one more time—reputedly by promising him a special assistant as intermediary. Like Freund, Aenne Willkomm would have preferred to forgo the pleasure of working again with Lang, but Pommer was persuasive; and she returned to the job—a formidable task, for *Metropolis*—of designing and supplying literally thousands of costumes.

Eugen Schüfftan was back. The ingenious photographic specialist had invented an optical trick shot dubbed the "Schüfftan process," which, originally intended for an Ufa version of *Gulliver's Travels*, would be employed for the first time on *Metropolis*. The Schüfftan process made possible the composite of live action in the foreground and miniature scenery in the background. This revolutionary illusory effect was accomplished by scraping off a portion of a mirror and reflecting miniature sets in the untouched remainder, then photographing the live action through the clear part of the mirror at a prescribed forty-five-degree angle to the lens of the camera, thereby reflecting the image onto the visual field. This reduced the expense of large-scale set construction.

Erich Kettelhut—who was back working with Otto Hunte and Karl Vollbrecht—decided from the earliest meetings that Thea von Harbou was consciously setting a different style for this modernistic production. Her severely parted pageboy had been altered to a short bob. Gone was *Die Nibelungen*'s elegant dress; "for the first time she showed off her shapely legs in a modern suit with a hemline at the knee," recalled Kettelhut. High-heeled shoes completed the scenarist's fashionable ensemble.

Once again the pre-production meetings, which began in the winter of 1924, seemed to proceed eternally. The animation meetings were "especially time-consuming," and the "merciless schedule" didn't even allow Sundays off, remembered Kettelhut.

The layout of the futuristic cityscape was the first order of business. Writing in the *Film-Kurier* of December 1924, Lang had described the sights of Manhattan "full of turning, twisting, circling light, like a paean to human happiness," with sky-high towers "picked out of the darkness of night by floodlights." Von Harbou in her novel lushly described the skyline in similar terms: "The houses, dissected into cones and cubes by the moving scythes of the searchlights gleamed, towering up, hoveringly, light flowing down their flanks like rain. The streets licked up the shining radiance, themselves shining, and the things gliding upon them, an incessant stream, threw cones of light before them. Only the cathedral, with the star-crowned Virgin on the top of its tower, lay stretched out, massively, down in the city, like a black giant lying in an enchanted sleep."

Von Harbou's writing, however, was impressionistic. And Lang's ideas always needed testing and tinkering. It fell to the keen minds at the pre-production meetings to come up with the concrete specifications and blueprints that would give the place a convincing reality.

People threw out diverse and contrasting suggestions. More than one essay has been published tracing the polyglot antecedents of the film's design, which reflected in all its violent diversity the artistic ferment in 1920s Germany. The director, though his own career as a painter had reached its pinnacle with postcard sketches, evinced a wide-ranging appreciation for contemporary schools and trends—be they Dada, Surrealist, Bauhaus, or Expressionist. *Metropolis* would be as avant-garde as *Die Nibelungen* was classically stylized. A confident, up-to-date knowledge of the society in which he was immersed would be crucially absent, later on, from many of Lang's Hollywood films, no matter how much the director strove to absorb and reflect American culture.

The influences of Bauhaus teachers Lyonel Feininger and Oskar Schlemmer, architects Bruno Taut and Hans Poelzig, sculptor Rudolf Belling—whose figurative style fused Cubist and Futurist principles—and even the Swiss free fantasist Paul Klee—would crop up in *Metropolis*. "In the twenties the Expressionist imagery of technology as a nightmare existed side by side with the Constructivist fascination with technology—both found their place in avant garde art," wrote Heide Schönemann in her monograph *Filmbilder—Vorbilder*. "In *Metropolis*, too, this is not an element to be underestimated. The beauty and the horror of the machine world excited many artists."

Similarities have been pointed out between the scenes of panicked worker-slaves and early sketches of the emotionally powerful artist Käthe Kollwitz—"a similar mass of people pushing upward in a spiral," wrote Schönemann. "The contrast between 'below' and 'above' had philosophical significance, from both a psycho-erotic and a political point of view." Rotwang's medieval house, in the city center, would evoke paintings by Bauhaus director Otto Bartning, and might even be compared to *Der Hagestolz*, a well-known sketch by Lang's onetime professor from Munich, Julius Diez.

Lang, as usual, steered the choices. The director was the arbiter of the grand design, mixing bravura strokes with personal grace notes. If the skyline of Metropolis was an exaggerated Manhattan, the streamlined office of Joh Fredersen evolved to resemble "in its sober simplicity Lang's own study in the twenties," as Lotte Eisner's book pointed out.

Erich Kettelhut recalled in his memoirs how the final rendering of the Tower of Babel was negotiated. Otto Hunte's initial presentation "alluded to familiar designs by the Old Masters," while Kettelhut had drawn "a round tower that narrowed sharply toward the top, with a wide path winding up to the flat top." Günther Rittau and Karl Freund preferred Kettelhut's version, which was more "primitive and foreign," and also because Hunte's overlooked a discrepancy "between the method of moving the big stone and the tools used to build the technically advanced tower." Lang, who himself had sketched one "quite similar" to Otto Hunte's, sided with Hunte. The director didn't want to be handicapped by logic or petty reasoning. "His justification," wrote Kettelhut, "was that the audience should not be unnecessarily taxed, and one should express oneself so that it was as universally understood as possible." Others were split down the middle, and tempers flared.

"The discussion turned into psychological hair-splitting; it became unobjective and even aggressive." The upshot was always the same. "Finally the Thea von Harbou–Fritz Lang faction settled things their own way. And so every scene, every shot, and frequently even the settings of the very instruments was talked over and decided upon beforehand."

Once the Tower of Babel (a blend of Hunte and Kettelhut) and other plans were approved, Erich Pommer put pressure on Lang to finalize casting and launch rehearsals. As the rehearsals proceeded, construction began on the extensive outdoor sets as well as the interior mock-ups. Meanwhile the miniatures would be constructed in the glassed-in studio, where Schüfftan and

Freund, under Lang's fussy supervision, would photograph the all-important establishing scenes.

The signs on the Metropolis buildings were to be lettered in a futuristic, abstract language. On the mock streets, the crew positioned tiny cars—advance-design Berlin taxis and the earliest Opels. The toy cars were moved about an inch at a time, then photographed, exposing one frame of film with a stop-motion camera. The toy airplanes that buzzed overhead were pulled on wires and photographed the same way. Elevated trains on wires were tugged along by someone out of camera range.

The lower stories of tall buildings were the only parts to be photographed, while the upper stories would be images reflected in mirrors. (Also "mirrored in" was a vast stadium of the rich, and a gigantic bust of Hel, Freder's mother.) Although the establishing shots of the cityscape would last only seconds on the screen, they took literally months to prepare, then several full days to shoot satisfactorily.

The miniaturized photography went well at first, but the techniques were so novel that the laboratory bungled the processing. "The cameraman told the technicians to process the exposed film in the normal manner, but the head of the lab, knowing the enormous amount of time taken in shooting the short scene, decided to develop the footage himself," recalled Lang on one occasion. "No one had thought it necessary to explain to him that for perspective reasons the cameraman had shot the background rather dimly, so as to give the impression of great distance. The lab head then proceeded to develop the exposed film in relation to the background instead of the foreground! The footage was, of course, spoiled. I tried to be calm. 'These things happen, children,' I said. 'Let's do it again.' And we did."

The acting team, as much Ufa's as Lang's, also carried over from film to film. Alfred Abel would portray Joh Fredersen, the master of Metropolis. Heinrich George, a well-known actor, massive and eccentric, would play Grot, the foreman. The rake-thin Fritz Rasp, another Max Reinhardt alumnus, who played a range of sly roles over his long career, would act the part of Slim, Fredersen's executive assistant. Rudolf Klein-Rogge was the obvious choice for Rotwang, the flamboyant inventor.

Gustav Fröhlich, who took the role of Freder Fredersen, was a von Harbou "find." Another young actor had been designated to play the role and indeed acted the pivotal part during the first few weeks of production. Fröhlich, a former journalist, vaudevillian, and Volksbühne actor, was on the set, relatively inconspicuous as one of the worker-slaves. But von Harbou noted his good looks and youthful earnestness, and when the original Freder proved unexceptional, she convinced the director to make the switch.

The leading lady was the sole province of the director. There are differing versions as to how Lang's own "find," Brigitte Helm, happened to make her screen debut in *Metropolis*. Born Eva Gisela Schnittenhelm in 1906, she came from Berlin, and like Lien Deyers she was saddled with a stage mother who pushed her into show business. The mother sent photographs of her daughter to Lang and von Harbou, according to one account, and was awarded with an invitation to bring the girl onto the set of *Die Nibelungen*. It was instantly apparent to everyone that she had the makings of a blond goddess, with her drooping lids and soulful orbs.

Asked if she wanted to be an actress, young Eva, not yet seventeen and still in boarding school at the time, declared, "Never in my life!" "Lang was actually amused," wrote Peter Herzog and Gene Vazzana in their biography of Helm, "and did not take Eva's words seriously. She also complained that she thought it was immoral to be an actress. Her mother stood there, chalk-white, not knowing what to do. She told Lang that her daughter was young and innocent. Lang laughed so hard that he cried, and in fact no one cared about Helm's protestations."

Another version, Lang's, pooh-poohed this anecdote. Helm not only aspired to be an actress, according to the director, but she told him she even dreamed of starring in Schiller's well-known play *Maria Stuart (Mary Stuart)*—"about the poor queen who is locked up by the wicked Elizabeth and killed." The director asked the schoolgirl which of the two characters, the imprisoned Queen of Scots or the dark-hearted Queen of England, she expected to play. "I thought I knew what her answer would be (the sympathetic part, of course)," recalled Lang. "But she surprised me by saying: 'Elizabeth!' So I thought, here was genuine talent."

An impromptu screen test was arranged. Willing or not, young Eva was heavily made up and escorted under bright lights, where she had "the strange sensation of feeling undressed," according to her biographers. Lang shouted for her to do something. The nervous young woman couldn't even remember her name. An assistant handed her a prop letter. All she could think was, why am I being handed this letter?

"Don't you see your father coming?" Lang's voice boomed. All of a sudden a stranger, an actor, materialized in front of the girl. "What have you got in your hands?" the man shouted at her. She instinctively hid the letter behind her back. "Why are you hiding it behind your back?" Slowly, Helm began to react, weaving a clever, fabrication. "Well, a friend wrote this letter to me, and it says Nixe . . . my friend's dog . . . has had twelve pups . . ." People roared with laughter. Lang thanked her, and the stage went dark.

She heard nothing for more than a year; then Helm was brought back for another audition in front of Lang and Erich Pommer. She decided to imitate one of Margarethe Schön's demonstrative scenes as Kriemhild in *Die Nibelungen*. "This 'test' was a sensational success," wrote Herzog and Vazzana. "She was better than Schön, with real tears and pathos. It stunned Pommer and Lang, and Eva was immediately taken to another room to sign a contract."

Lang and Pommer would rename the young unknown Brigitte Helm. Destined to become the greatest of the director's "virgin stars" (the actress's inexperience made it a double joke, for her nickname around Ufa was "the Virgin of Babelsberg"), Helm was taken under wing by Lang, who tried to enhance her sophistication—teaching her dancing and horseback riding.

"He [Lang] had a weakness for the female sex, and he was capable of going into boundless rapture about the most inexperienced female," wrote Lotte Eisner (in her memoirs, naturally, not her Fritz Lang book). The director's leading ladies were guaranteed overnight stature; it hardly mattered that this newly minted actress had every intention of settling down one day to marry a doting husband, become a housewife, live quietly, and raise a family. ("Later," added Eisner, "she did that.")

Though Brigitte Helm had never appeared before a camera, "the virgin of Babelsberg" would carry the heaviest burden of all the *Metropolis* cast, playing the Janus-faced roles of Maria and robot-Maria, as Lang's most costly and adventurous film to date went into production.

Shooting started on May 22, 1925. Apart from the eight principals, there were 750 actors engaged to play small roles, 26,000 male extras, 11,000 female ones, and 750 children, "100 Negroes and 25 Chinese." Lang was proud of the "size" of *Metropolis*, even if, years later, he would voice misgivings about certain elements of the film. To the end of his life, the director, a devoted reader of his own publicity, could proudly reel off these dubious Ufa statistics.

Lang's method of guiding the actors underwent revision. He had insisted on large, expressive movements and pathos for *Die Nibelungen*, calling out numbers to indicate the desired intensity of emotion. "Acting by numbers had imposed an even rhythm," in Erich Kettelhut's words, but now for *Metropolis* "there were [to be] no more numbers," and instead the director dictated "hectic gestures and a nervous play of changing expressions."

His "virgin stars" had all the more responsibility to their mentor, and the director was especially rough on the novice Brigitte Helm. "He acted out a scene himself, corrected her untiringly, tried to calm her nerves, but sometimes laid into her," wrote Kettelhut.

One seemingly simple scene, with Rotwang chasing Maria through the catacombs, was one of Lang's visual set pieces—the darkness lit by a single beam alighting on skeletal bones and skulls, intercut with shots of Maria's wildly darting eyes. Just the rehearsal, with camera, lighting, and blocking of movement, seemed to take forever, and yet the director remained unsatisfied. Kettelhut passed by the stage at one point and ventured to ask members of the lighting crew if anything had yet been captured on film. "Naw," was the answer he received, "he [Lang] is rehearsing with the girl 'bis zum Weissbluten'."* That might have been the director's motto.

One of Helm's key scenes required her to do virtually nothing; yet this particular scene, showing the creation of the robot-Maria—which takes place amid bubbling liquids, flashes of electricity, smoke and steam in Rotwang's laboratory—consumed weeks of trial and error, and, for Helm, agony. The scene involved a unique preparation. The actress was encased in an armor of "liquid wood," which had to fit skintight; on screen, the robot-creation, superimposed over the image of a somnolent Maria, would tremble to life. The wooden material was added to a plaster mold. "The plasterers had trouble with a living body," recalled Kettelhut, "and because they wanted to proceed especially cautiously, the separate fittings took especially long." A doctor was constantly present on the set to monitor Brigitte Helm, who already had fragile health.

The fittings went on for weeks. Helm's young body was still growing, and the uncomfortable armor required constant adjustment. Moreover, according

---

*Literally: "Until she is bled white."

to Kettelhut, the plaster mold was taken for the actress's erect form; then Lang decided the metamorphosis would take place, on camera, while she was *seated*, a position for which the wood casing turned out to be unduly tight and painful. The designers tried to minimize the pain by smoothing down "the most torturous points," but spending long hours for days "in such a stiff narrow position in a hot studio was really a kind of torture," said Kettelhut.

It was cameraman Günther Rittau who masterminded some of the film's best-known visual effects—including the on-camera transformation of the robot-Maria, in Rotwang's laboratory, from a creature of cubistic metal parts to a being of flesh and blood.

Concentric rings of light encircle the robot and whirl luminously around the figure, until a slow, spectacular dissolve reveals an evolving circulatory system. Rittau achieved this effect by photographing a small, rapidly whirling silver ball against a backdrop of black velvet. The impression of expanding and contracting rings, ascending and descending, was obtained by raising and lowering the camera on this single silver ball. This scene—which involved such pain for Brigitte Helm—culminated in a shot superimposed in the laboratory over the previously photographed seated form of the robot-Maria.

"It is unquestionably one of the great moments in the history of the science fiction film," wrote Frederick Ott in *The Great German Films*.

The director seemed equally intent on bleeding all his actors. He took particular delight in inflicting his demands on the "virgin" male star, Gustav Fröhlich. The director demonstrated what he wanted Fröhlich to do in his catacombs scene with Brigitte Helm by falling to his knees himself, whispering to and caressing an imaginary woman. "Spellbound, Brigitte and I followed his movements," the actor recalled. They rehearsed and rehearsed, Fröhlich gesturing tenderly as Brigitte Helm stroked his hair. The director corrected him, again and again. "No good . . . You must look at her with deeper feeling." Fröhlich spent hours falling to increasingly battered knees.

The rehearsal went on and on until, fatigued from the effort, Fröhlich felt overtaken by a kind of trance, transformed by his character's ardor for Brigitte Helm. It was only then that Lang shouted, "Achtung! Lights! Action!" Still Lang demanded take after take, insisting their embrace wasn't "deeply felt enough," the kiss was "too short," or the camera angle was wrong. Fröhlich estimated he was on his knees, from morning until midnight, for two days running. When they were finished, he could barely stand.

Another scene called for the lead actor to bang on a heavy wooden door with his bare fists. Lang didn't stop the multiple takes until Fröhlich crumpled, blood running down his arms. A scene in which Fröhlich scuffled violently with a group of workers was likewise halted by Lang only after the actor's thumb became dislocated. Fröhlich had to be narcotized and the thumb rejoined. Lang graciously permitted a half-hour break ("coffee and cigarettes") before sending once more for the actor to resume shooting.

Fröhlich admired the director, but stubbornly argued with him throughout the filming. He was convinced that his insubordinate behavior explained why another young dreamboat, Willy Fritsch, would replace him in the next couple of Fritz Lang films. "Nothing was allowed to seem fake, everything had to look real [in *Metropolis*]," wrote Fröhlich in his autobiography. "In scenes of physical suffering, he [Lang] tormented the actors until they really did suffer."

Not only the actors, but the crew; Lang believed in his own superhuman willpower, and tried to use that Mabusian belief to hypnotize everybody, pushing them to their limits. One person the director fixated on throughout the filming was costume designer Aenne Willkomm, who was working on several Ufa productions at once, against the director's wishes. Lang wanted her services exclusively. He stepped up his demands on her time in an effort to "put her on the spot," in Erich Kettelhut's words.

One day, according to Kettelhut, Lang suddenly asked to see Brigitte Helm in a dress for which she had been fitted nine months earlier—certain that the dress would come up a little too snug. Willkomm had anticipated Lang, however, and had already had the dress altered, a bit of foresight that did nothing to improve the director's disposition.

Another day, things reached a genuine crisis. Arguing with Willkomm, Lang deliberately knocked a case of costume jewelry out of the designer's hand, causing her to break down and flee the set. The director gloated openly. Erich Pommer had to step in, insisting that Lang apologize. "He [Pommer] said Aenne Willkomm rated high with him," recalled Kettelhut. Willkomm came back, and the war of wills continued.

"Lang could be winning and polite," recollected Kettelhut, "could pass the time of day charmingly, but also [he could be] tough, full of biting humor, a master of thinking up small and not-so-small jabs that he used to prod his victims to despair. If you got in his line of fire, be you guilty or not guilty, you had to be just as much of a thick-skinned clever old fox to hold your own against him."

Between Lang and the equally contentious Otto Hunte it was a stand-off. Poor Kettelhut had to mediate between them so often that the crew made a joke of it. The last scene of the film envisioned a handshake of peace between the workers and the master of Metropolis, with a title card that declared, "Between the mind and the hands, the heart must mediate." The crew had their own version: "Mittler zwischen Lang und Hunte muss der Kettel sein."*

Lang and Hunte nearly came to blows over one trivial scene that was filmed on a staircase, part of a more ambitious sequence that would be intercut with the explosion of the heart-machine. It was an inconsequential scene, but costs were mounting, and Hunte's sketches—which "often cost too much money," in Kettelhut's words—had begun to alarm Ufa executives. "The bosses decided the set had to be simplified and built in the small glasshouse studio," recounted Kettelhut. Hunte went along with management, scaling down his plans.

Everyone assumed the director had been notified of the revised specifications. Extra cast members had been engaged for the day's shoot. Lang arrived on the dot for the morning call and flew into a rage when he spied the scaled-down setting, demanding to see Hunte at once. His face flushed, the set designer arrived, the sketches hastily bundled under his arm.

"Lang refused to film anything that did not correspond to what had been

---

*"Between Lang and Hunte, Kettel must mediate."

planned in the sessions," said Kettelhut. "Hunte said Lang had had enough time and opportunity to complain to the bosses and that his carryings-on were pure sadism. The two men screamed at each other. Both of them knew how senseless and embarassing this behavior was, the upshot being that neither spoke to the other for months. Lang gave the extras the day off. Finally, under a lot of pressure from the bosses, Lang filmed the scene, with a small cast and with absolutely no enthusiasm."

The director's tendency was to flatter the powerful, while picking on the weak and vulnerable, not only the crew, but the lowly extras. The flooding of the workers' underground city was one of the truly astounding scenes in the film. It was accomplished on one of the large roofed-in areas especially built for filming outdoors, where a pool was dug (the famous Metropolis-Becken, or Metropolis basin). Nearly five hundred small children were rounded up from north Berlin slums—among them many "skinny, malnourished creatures," Kettelhut recalled, whose deprivation was in keeping with the story line. Water was forced through pipes and directed at the buildings from above. Pipes at street level ejected water in a geyser-like effect. Along with Brigitte Helm, the extras and little tykes had to swim for their lives.

A special raft was built to hold cameraman Karl Freund, his assistants, and the mercury lamps. Riding with Freund, or on his own floating pontoon, Lang would steer around between the actors and the children, shouting his instructions. "With his megaphone he encouraged us, again and again, to be sure and move toward the biggest jets of water," Theodor Loos, who played one of the workers, recalled.

When this scene was photographed, in the fall of 1925, the rainy gray weather blocked out sunlight. Therefore the water became steadily more chilly and unpleasant. The children had to be mothered between takes by von Harbou. They received warm meals and, because the scene took almost two weeks to film, cocoa and cake at regular intervals to keep them going. With food and toys as rewards, their number kept multiplying as word spread about the studio's largesse. But Lang, who used children regularly in his films, gave them no special treatment, and indeed there were people who thought—here as during other times in his career—that he took particular umbrage at their presence.

Meanwhile, the hundreds of extras playing the workers may as well have been actual slaves, for all the humanity with which Lang treated them. Who would dare stick up for them?

To film Freder's vision of Moloch, the director decided he needed an entire army of nude men to march into the mouth of the belching energy-machine. "The fact that unemployment was getting higher each month was actually a blessing for Lang," recalled Kettelhut. Extras were cheap, with work so scarce, and several hundred hungry-looking men turned up for filming that scene in a former zeppelin hanger turned fully-equipped studio in Staaken.

But the cavernous hangar was unheated and bitterly cold in the winter of 1925. The minions donned hats, scarves and coats to cover their shivering naked bodies while, for hours, the crew set up and tinkered with the camera and lights. The crews were working eight to twelve hours a day next to huge coke furnaces spewing out smoke. Clinging to catwalks overhead, lighting assistants with half-frozen hands operated huge equipment with a total capacity of fifteen-to-twenty-thousand amps.

Even Lang acted more tense than usual. "He was always finding fault with something and made the poor guys line up over and over again," said Kettelhut. "They were standing there on the cold floor, freezing, being sprayed from above with icy water—they could hardly feel it on their bare heads and naked bodies—swearing and waiting impatiently for the signal to start and jump at long last into the brightly lit steam of the mouth of the Moloch. What was happening was no longer the result of logical thought—it was a state of trance, though no one realized that."

Lang, naturally, demanded take after take after take of the extras trudging into Moloch's maw. The extras grew rebellious, muttering oaths and threats. So did the crew. And even Gustav Püttcher, Lang's hardworking assistant, who knew how to cheer people up by clowning around—he was the butt of many of the director's practical jokes for general amusement—was hard-pressed to lighten the mood.

An article appearing in *Berliner Zeitung* at the time of the *Metropolis* premiere quoted cameraman Karl Freund's description of the unbearable circumstances. "We spent fourteen to sixteen hours a day working in there. Every day members of the lighting crew showed symptoms of poisoning, even though they wore gas masks over their faces; every day people called in sick. But we kept on working with only half the crew. We were told to bite the bullet, to just mop our foreheads with a damp sponge and to keep going, so we could get the damned scene done with."

The stage was only slightly less inhospitable on the rare sunny day. "The floodlights and the fanlights were on almost all the time but they hardly helped at all," recalled Freund. "The warmth just disappeared in the huge, high-ceilinged room." The naked extras took advantage of breaks to line up next to the huge boilers, which at least heated the floor directly next to them. "Steam condensed and dripped down all over everything continuously like a light drizzle," said Freund.

The combination of electric lights, overworked boilers, drizzle, and steam became so extreme that finally there was danger of real disaster on the set. One afternoon, according to Kettelhut, Erich Pommer was alerted to the crisis in the making and abruptly materialized on the set, quickly diagnosing the situation. "He used his diplomatic talents to intervene and convince Lang that he [Pommer] had been assured by Freund and Rittau there was enough material for him so that he could dispense with any more takes," said Kettelhut.

With Christmas nearing, the director scheduled a cathartic scene: the explosion of the heart-machine. It loomed as one of those special eruptions that stimulated Lang and served as big moments in his films. No matter if the visual preparations were usually more exhaustive than the human precautions.

The bodies of scores of workers were supposed to fly through the air, hurled by the concussive power of the blast. And despite the danger, the director insisted on using real bodies suspended from thin wires attached to hidden belts, because dummies might look stiff and comical on the screen. As the scene was organized, and Lang's intentions became clear, apprehension spread throughout the set.

To relax people during the setup, according to Gustav Fröhlich, Lang ordered the omnipresent Püttcher, "a.k.a. clown Tünnes, to test out the belt apparatus on himself, to demonstrate that it was tight enough and fitted correctly. When Tünnes had put on the harness and the thin wire cables were attached, the director gave a secret signal and the poor guy, to the merriment of all present, was whipped high up under the roof of the hangar." ("To crown the fun and games," Fröhlich added, "Lang had a bottle of beer and a sausage sent up to him on another wire, but only high enough that Tünnes couldn't quite reach them, twist and turn as he might.")

This incident broke the nerve-racking atmosphere, and Lang was able to proceed. Filming his endless series of takes, the master puppeteer finally found himself able literally to dangle actors on strings, pulling them through smoke, steam, and fire in the service of his vision. "He even demanded that these men show pain and shock during the whirling," recalled Fröhlich—just in case they needed reminding.

If the extras froze in Staaken in the winter, in the spring they sweated in the Rehbergen, where they enacted Maria's parable about the building of the Tower of Babel—which compared the lives of the workers to those of the slaves of ancient Babylon. Lang demanded at least four thousand slaves with shaved heads to drag huge stone blocks through desert sand for the sequence. The director had to settle for the one thousand Pommer was able to scrounge up who were willing to be completely shorn. "The hundred barbers who did the shaving could have taken the 'wool' from the Rehbergen, where we did our shooting, into Berlin and sold it to a mattress factory," recalled Karl Freund.

The extras had to march in a crowded formation at a controlled speed while dragging their huge carved rocks. The rocks were actually lightweight props, but the huge tree trunks the extras had to shoulder were real. The sun was out, and it grew extremely hot. During preparations, the men "lay around on the sand, many got sunburned, some even got blisters on their unprotected heads," according to Kettelhut. Then, of course, Lang wasn't satisfied the first time out; the extras were forced to drag the stones and tree trunks back and forth several more times.

One way or another, it seemed, the director always got his way: Though he mustered only a thousand extras up in the Rehbergen, they were photographed, then optically multiplied, so that in the negative they would meet Lang's original arithmetic.

Gustav Fröhlich was not the only person on the set of *Metropolis* who wondered if the director's methods had crossed the line into "the abnormal." Whether or not people knew the scuttlebutt about the fate of Lang's first wife, some members of the cast and crew saw the director as the embodiment of murderous evil. "Malicious tongues whispered that if he could have, Lang would only too gladly, and without any scruples, have someone really shot, stabbed, or strangled—for say, an execution scene, murder, or suicide. Then he would have been able to film—guaranteed for real—the death throes of a human being before his life was blotted out," wrote Fröhlich.

*   *   *

Nineteen hundred twenty-six dawned, winter passed, and after almost a year *Metropolis* was still filming.

Bad weather delayed outdoor scenes, while the director's perfectionism prolonged indoor ones. The production was far from finished. Major crowd scenes were yet to be filmed. *Metropolis* continued to drain Ufa's production capacity, precipitating a boardroom crisis. In January, the executive board members had convened to debate shutting down the all-consuming production. That might mean ditching everything; only Fritz Lang knew what needed to be done in order to finish.

The immediate consequence was that producer Erich Pommer was officially held responsible, and was dismissed from duties as director of Ufa production as of January 22, 1926. "Unfairly, Pommer alone was declared guilty for the whole debacle," wrote Kettelhut in his memoirs. "He was only rarely on the set."

Pommer continued to act as liaison with *Metropolis* for a short time before leaving on April 1 for the United States, where he had a standing offer as a staff producer from Famous Players–Lasky. The newly-appointed chief of production, Major Alexander Grau, had little personal relationship—good or bad—with Lang. He almost never imposed himself the set, leaving Karl Freund and Otto Hunte without any listening ear for their increasing complaints about Lang and his methods.

One upcoming scene, in which Rotwang chases Maria across the top of the cathedral roof, had them both terrified. Though it actually occurs at the end of the story, it was due to be filmed out of sequence in the spring of 1926.

Lang's blocking warranted extraordinary physical daring. The two principals had to scale a ladder behind the standing set, then scramble on planks and walkways roughly twenty-five feet above the ground while performing a kind of tussling match. Hunte, upon hearing of the plans, turned apoplectic. "What Lang is doing to Helm is just too much! It's pure slavery!" the art director complained.

Cornered in the story, Maria must make a last desperate leap for the bellpull in order to escape Rotwang's clutches. Erich Kettelhut watched the dangerous choreography grimly: "There was a chance that Fräulein Helm would miss it, which would have meant a twelve-foot fall. There were mattresses carefully spread out on the ground, but a fall from that height is not harmless. She jumped and the bell cord started to swing to the side and the bell did the same because of the weight of the girl swinging. She was hanging from the cord, completely at the mercy of its irregular movements. And the poor girl slid slowly down the rope as it swung wildly. She was thrown from one wall to the other. She was covered in bruises, abrasions, contusions, and her clothes were ripped. That was it. Brigitte Helm was physically and emotionally completely finished, and she ran from the set in tears . . ."

All along, the press and important visitors had made spot excursions to Neubabelsberg, glimpsing the busy director, cast and crew, touring the remarkable *Metropolis* sets.

On nearby stages, early in the filming, Erich Pommer had also been co-producing a Gainsborough-Ufa production, *The Blackguard*. Its writer, assistant director, and set designer was a Londoner passing through Berlin for the first time. The future "master of suspense," Alfred Hitchcock—only a few months away from making his own directing debut—made a point of strolling by to gaze at the *Metropolis* set and observe the illustrious Fritz Lang at work.

In the future, film critics would often compare the two directors. Yet Hitchcock would express little enthusiasm for Lang's work in interviews over the years; and Lang himself detested the comparisons, feeling that in the category of thrillers and suspense the critics tended to favor the upstart Englishman—who, after all, borrowed shamelessly from him.

A more eminent visitor than the still-unknown Hitchcock was Sergei Eisenstein, the Russian film director, theoretician, and proponent of montage. Eisenstein had been one of the people who re-edited the director's *Dr. Mabuse* (which the Soviets retitled *Gilded Putrefaction*) for distribution in the Soviet Union. Lotte Eisner insisted in her book that when Eisenstein tackled the Mabuse film, he found Lang's mise-en-scéne impossible to improve. Eisenstein "rearranged the scenes, putting them in new order, only to arrive back at fitting them together in their original form," wrote Eisner.

However unlikely that may seem, the visiting Soviet director did express a desire to meet his noted German colleague. Eisenstein arrived at Neubabelsberg around the time Lang was photographing a vignette on a stairwell where Freder and Maria are knocked off their feet by the reservoirs' erupting under the future-city. Lang wanted the audience to experience the bomb blast subjectively—"to give the impression of what the two actors would feel under the impact of a pressure wave." To achieve this, he had attached a camera to a kind of children's swing; sent careening toward the actors on the set, then back again, the camera replicated the sensation of a concussion.

In her biography of Eisenstein, Marie Seton wrote that Eisenstein was greatly intrigued by the methods the Ufa director was employing to liberate the camera from static angles. He and his German counterpart engaged in a brief dialogue. "The conversation regarding the pros and cons of static or moving cameras was cut short by the shooting schedule," wrote Seton, "He [Lang] planned to meet Eisenstein again, but never did, as Sergei Mikhailovich left Berlin in a few days."

Now came the last intricate sequences on the calendar and the climactic ones for *Metropolis*: the Yoshiwara sequence and the burning of the witch-robot. Again, the sequences called for laborious preparations, and again, in spite of all the pressures to rush the filming, Lang insisted on modifications and improvements.

The Yoshiwara scene took place in an elite nightclub where the robot-Maria performs an erotic dance before a crowd of thrill-seekers, crying out, "Let's watch the world going to the devil!" This statement clearly echoed a poster, with a line from poet Walter Mehring, that Lang said he remembered seeing plastered around Berlin in the 1920s: "Berlin, dein Tänzer ist der Tod!" ("Berlin, your dancing partner is Death!").*

The sequence included an incident in which two sons of the rich, aroused to an orgasmic pitch over the robot-woman, pull out guns and fire point-blank at each other. The crowd of revelers then spills out into the city streets, dancing wildly along a high overpass until they encounter the upsurging mass of rioting workers.

Half of 1926 had elapsed before the time came to mount this scene. Summer was turning to fall. Despite daytime warmth, the cold was fearsome when the mercury plunged, and the exteriors had to be filmed, according to Lang's custom—the mood was more auspicious, lighting possibilities more intriguing—at night.

The crew's preparations for the scene were tricky. The exodus of the night-club revelers involved a complicated synchronization of movement, lights, and camerawork. After a double door was pushed open, the revelers would stream out and down a twelve-foot-high stairway, most of the ladies perched on their escorts' shoulders. The scene called for the extras to carry festive Japanese lanterns that burned atop long poles. Electric cables had to be strung as inconspicuously as possible along the poles, over the shoulders and backs of the ladies, through the tuxedos of the gentlemen, and down through their pants to the floor, where they were hooked up to a power source.

Past midnight, everybody's breathing made frosty puffs. The crowd of extras had to rehearse again and again. "After each attempt there was a pile of totally tangled cable, poles and lanterns lying on the floor," recalled Kettelhut. After each take came the untangling, the replacing of lightbulbs. Lang sat up on a platform near the camera, wearing a snug leather jacket and his favorite white scarf ("an indispensable object for me"), his voice booming through the megaphone. "Attention! Rehearsal! More lights! Look happier, everybody!"

Not everybody was so warmly dressed; not everybody could look happy. The chilly temperature was taking its toll. The wind came up, cutting into bare skin like needles. Freezing cast, crew, and extras huddled in front of coal fires Kettelhut had set up out of the wind. The Yoshiwara dancers, wearing scanty costumes, cowered beneath what blankets and coats they could beg. Several of the extras were deputized to approach Lang. They complained of the cold and asked for alcoholic refreshment to warm up their blood.

"So I called to my assistant," recalled Lang, " 'Püttcher, put a flask of cognac on my bill!' and the assistant said, 'One flask of cognac for ten shivering people?' 'Halt!' I shouted, 'Ten flasks of cognac!' A jubilant cry ran through Metropolis. Everyone clapped. "Hurrah! Prost, Fritz Lang! Prost, girls!' 'Quiet on the set!' I called."

The way Kettelhut remembered it, Lang had little choice; he had to comply with people's wishes if he wanted to buoy their spirits, and soon the liquor flowed freely. "As the extras got more and more cheerful," Kettelhut said, "they also got more and more affectionate. Some couples didn't seem to feel

---

*This was also one of the left-wing signals of the film. Mehring, closely associated with Bertolt Brecht, became well-known later on for his anti-Nazi songs, poetry, and writing. He fled Berlin for Vienna in 1933, and later became a U.S. citizen.

the cold anymore while they found a secluded corner and showed just how attached they were to each other."

The numerous takes continued, each time creating the same puddle of cables and burned-out lightbulbs—but no acceptable shot. Lang always remembered a chivalric gesture he observed, during one delay, that may even have shamed the director. He overheard one of the girls crying, "Please, somebody, give me a coat, I can't stand up anymore, I'm wearing hardly anything and the cognac's all drunk up!" Then one of the film's stars, Alfred Abel, took off his own coat and handed it to the shivering young woman.

At last one shot worked to the director's satisfaction. Lang wanted another, just to be sure. The repeat shot worked out fine, too. Then it was on to the robot-Maria's auto-da-fé.

The director insisted, for the stake-burning scene, that Brigitte Helm must submit to real, life-threatening flames. Everyone felt this was going too far, and his scheme was fiercely debated. But Pommer was long gone, and nobody else dared to overrule Lang.

Thea von Harbou was on the set that night, as she was virtually every moment of the protracted filming. When Lang filmed that scene, which is unforgettable to everyone who has ever seen *Metropolis*, the director's wife dictated a piece of reportage to her secretary describing the atmosphere and conditions on the set. Though it was used for publicity purposes, her article had the ring of a bulletin from the front:

"Two hours till midnight. But at the same time, spooky brightness. Above the fantastic, wide Cathedral Square of Metropolis, about twenty yards up, are the six-tube mercury lamps, at least several dozen of them. You can see neither the strings nor wires that support them. They seem to be attached to the blackness of the moonless sky, motionless green glowworms. Trestles everywhere. Megaphones scream like the horns of Jericho: 'Everything!!!'

" 'Everything!' means: 'Everybody in his position! Everything!'

"Suddenly the square is crowded with people.

"At improvised tables, the last makeup is put on, hair is brushed once more real quick. Among many men, one single female actor, she appears very young, almost like a child. The actress of the Janus-character—Maria in Metropolis.

"Fritz Lang climbs up the platform where the equipment is; next to him, Karl Freund, who always appears like the sun. He's wearing a winter coat and it is summer in Europe. Underneath the coat you can see a white smock—without it shooting would be incomplete.

"The director says: 'Listen, everybody! The scene we're going to practice is simple: You caught the girl that is responsible for the decline of your city, and you are going to build a stake around the lamp pole there in order to burn her. Understood?'

"An unequivocal 'Yes!' is the answer. Indeed: Very simple. The people pretend to understand: No big deal . . .

"Then it actually starts—where? how?—from four corners at the same time . . .

" 'Build the stake—! How do you do that? Easy! Somewhere during the outbreak of the rebellion, when the chaotic darkness broke in, the cars stopped running. The ideal material for a stake! Let's get it!'

"The crowd throws itself against the wheels, lifts, pushes, pants. The small cars, animal-like, whose still-burning headlights stare, start to move, roll—bang!—into each other, and are added to the rubbish which is brought by howling women. Even a piano is among the rubbish. As well as desks—books, tons of books—window frames, doors! The stake grows . . .

" 'Stop,' Lang cries.

"Everyone freezes.

" 'Once again—!'

"For a fifth and sixth time the stake is taken apart again. Everybody takes his piece of the stake back.

"Now it's getting serious. Now the blond, tender witch is going to get it.

"With the leather belt of the director, they tie her arms together on her back. They push her around—the crowd is going wild—laughing like crazy: 'There—there—you will burn, damned witch!'

"They push her up to the top of one of the cars where four, six, eight brutal fists are waiting for her . . .

"Once—? Twenty times! And still it is not wild enough, not fantastic enough.

"Poor little Brigitte Helm! The next day her whole body will be covered with bruises.

"This simple run-through lasts about three hours and thirty minutes. Then all the participants are in a state of trance. And ready to film.

"Last banality, last empty play-acting, last habitual gestures are banned, destroyed. Mercy on that actor who moves both his hands in front of him the old-fashioned way! A very short break before the great moment.

" 'If everything goes right, we'll take a break after the shooting!'—Hurrah! The anger of the crowd will be real.

"All the men responsible for lighting put more coal in. There is a very intensive smell of gasoline, spirit, and kerosene.

"Bales of wood shavings soaked with everything that burns and smokes are being pushed between parts of the rubbish on the stake. Five men have hoses ready—you can never be too careful . . .

"You can sense that everybody's nerves are vibrating . . . A thought comes to my head. Weird that there hasn't been a painter yet who has been attracted by the great expressionism of such a night shooting . . .

"The clash of the different light sources, the strange colors of the faces of the actors, the strange atmosphere . . .

"A while later. Two-fifty A.M. In the east you can already sense some red light. A bird sings, sweet and fearless. In the curve of the stone lions' tails by the cathedral, two thrushes nest. They don't care about thousands of people, the ocean of light, the screams, the permanent disturbance. They are used to it.

"Fritz Lang has pulled out his inner face—which he doesn't even know himself. The face of a boy who is going on an adventure into the wide blue world. And believe me: Every film shooting, let it be short or long, is an

adventure. A fight with the dragon called chance, an expedition into the unknown, a venture onto new ground. Lang has a torch in his hand to light up
the stake. One last look around.

" 'Ready! Action!—Go!'

"The torch is tossed into the rubbish. The flames reach high. The crowd
howls like crazy. The cameras buzz and I count the turns of the cranks spon-
taneously. As if they were the beatings of my heart.

"Tomorrow we will see the long hours of work as a quintessential ten seconds."

Author Curt Siodmak corroborated this account, while providing terrifying
details about Brigitte Helm's ordeal. Siodmak was making an unauthorized
visit to the *Metropolis* set. The filming of this crucial scene, the burning of
the robot-Maria, had been declared off limits to the press, but he and his
girlfriend (later his wife) Henrietta had managed to get hired as extras. Siodmak, a cub reporter working undercover for a Berlin evening newspaper, would
be paid fifty marks as an extra—a tremendous sum, three times what he would
earn for his article.

"The atmosphere on the gigantic *Metropolis* stage was tense," remembered
Siodmak. "A strike was brewing among the hired extras. Lang had kept them
for more than fifteen hours, but refused to pay for the overtime. I knew I was
witnessing an important story for my portable typewriter, and pushed my way
to the stake where the girl robot, dressed in a shiny material which clung to
her body, was to be burned alive."

Lang directed "hypnotically," said Siodmak. "I don't how good an actress
she [Brigitte Helm] was at the time, but here was Svengali and Trilby, and
Lang coaxed her into a state of near hysteria.

"In the darkened stage, flames shot up at the stake where the robot was to
be burned to cinders. But sparks caught Brigittte's dress, setting her afire.
Standing as close as possible to the fiercely burning stake, I took advantage of
this unexpected opportunity and jumped across the flames, but Fritz Lang
and the fire department were even quicker than I and beat out the flames.
Brigitte collapsed in Lang's arms, but the cameras had recorded her agony.
She was not hurt.

"In the tradition of a good reporter," recalled Siodmak, he cornered Helm
and tried to interview her, "stupidly revealing that I was a reporter. A minute
later I found myself outside the stage. Lang had me thrown out instantly."

The very last scene in *Metropolis* would not be the stake-burning, or Rotwang
chasing Maria across the rooftops. After all the horror and ruination, the film
offered a brief, surprisingly sweet coda—which indicated Fritz Lang's (and
Thea von Harbou's) romantic politics at a time when left-and right-wingers
were shedding blood over the future of Germany.

Freder, trying to make peace, grasps the hand of the foreman and forces it
into a handshake with his father; not only is the breach between the workers
and the master of Metropolis repaired, but so is the alienation between father
and son. "Mittler zwischen Hirn und Händen muss das Herz sein," states the
intertitle. ("Between the mind and the hands, the heart must mediate.")

How different from the savage ending of *Die Nibelungen*! Critics then and later would seize on the handshake as one of the silly, or "Kitsch," elements of a film that failed to achieve intellectual depth. "Kitsch" was one of the words often wielded by German sophisticates to damn Lang; even Lotte Eisner in her book about Lang cannot help but mention the "kitschiness" of parts of *Metropolis*. Quoting Lang, however, Eisner attributed the "old-fashioned emotionalism" of the ending (which "even at the time, when people were still close to the ecstatic mood of the previous years . . . was not received uncritically") to the director's wife, Thea von Harbou.

Lang labored over his endings, devoting the same excessive attention to the final moments that he gave to the opening shots. He often said in interviews that he had agonized over this particular ending, which, he always emphasized, was principally von Harbou's contribution. Indeed, it does appear to have been von Harbou's; it was there in the novel—providing a symmetry in the story line. If harks back to a moment, earlier in the story, where the Madonna-Maria, preaching to the downtrodden workers, intones an identical moral.

Years later, Lang claimed that he briefly considered—and rejected—a different, more Langian, ending, with Freder and Maria escaping together by spaceship to another, unknown world in a kind of prelude to *Die Frau im Mond*. Yet at the time Lang deferred to von Harbou on this key point—a concession that says something important about their relationship.

In retrospect, the ending became symbolic for Lang of *Metropolis*'s shortcomings. "I have often said that I didn't like *Metropolis*," Lang was quoted in the prestigious French film magazine *Cahiers du Cinéma* in 1965, "and that is because I cannot accept today the leitmotif of the message of the film. It is absurd to say that the heart is the mediator between the hands and the head, that is to say, of course, between employee and employer. The problem is social, not moral."

And he declared in 1967, "I was not so politically minded in those days as I am now."

It is true that Lang's politics were changeable, and that amity between labor and capital was not always practicable—or fashionable. The problem with the ending wasn't simply political, however, it was also emotional, and pointed up another directorial shortcoming. The American director Frank Capra, for example, could have carried off "the kind of sentimentality," in Lotte Eisner's words, that the handshake-ending warranted. Such a scene, in which an alienated son made peace with his father, called not just for sentimentality, but a humanism—and open feeling—that Lang as a director simply could not muster.

For a long time, the director was adamant about *Metropolis*, almost "childishly defending himself," in the words of Pierre Rissient, even while the film became a beloved classic to many. Late in life, as he softened, the director began to equivocate. Maybe the "kitschy" message was valid, after all. Maybe a little dose of humanity was not such a bad thing for a film. The handshake-ending was a sore subject, brought up in interview after interview. The director, at the end of his life, was still mulling it over, making up his mind.

"I didn't think in those days a social question could be solved with something as simple as the line: 'The mediator between brain (capital) and hand (working class) must be the heart,' " Lang was quoted in 1976, the last year of his life. "Yet today, when you speak with young people about what they miss in the computer-guided establishment, the answer is always, 'The heart!' So, probably the scenarist, Mrs. Thea von Harbou, had foresight, and therefore was right and I was wrong."

Filming was completed. The photography, which officially ended October 30, 1926, had consumed 310 days and 60 nights. The costs had exceeded five million marks.*

Lang had a ritual he observed with his assistant, Gustav Püttcher, at the end of the filming—the assistant who "would have gone to the ends of the earth for Lang," according to Gustav Fröhlich. At the outset of each production, the Meister always ordered "a durable gabardine suit," in Fröhlich's words, made to fit by Knize's, the crème-de-la-crème tailor shop of Vienna, which had a branch on Wilhelmstrasse in Berlin. "This suit was only for work," said Fröhlich. "Lang put it on every morning in his private room in the studio and took it off every evening. In the meantime the expensive object was brushed and kept clean. After the very last day of shooting Püttcher was given this wonderful suit in thanks for all the small services, the unvarying doglike loyalty, but also for his occasional spy reports on employees' private conversations."

Erich Kettelhut was among those strained to the limit, and by the end of the shoot he was fairly certain he would never work with Lang again. He'd exchange "entirely amicable and kindly" good-byes with the director and Thea von Harbou in the cutting room, but once outside the door, he'd wonder if he had just experienced genuine gratitude and affection, or "a subconscious expression of relief at knowing they had gotten rid of me."

The premiere of *Metropolis* took place on January 10, 1927. The audience of distinguished guests included Chancellor Wilhelm Marx, several cabinet officers, members of the diplomatic corps, and "the foremost figures of Berlin in society, art, and literature," according to a contemporary report in the *New York Times*. A live orchestra accompanied the film with a score composed by Gottfried Huppertz.

What people experienced was a visual symphony whose formal clarity and aesthetic power remains exhilarating today. Metropolis itself was magnificently realized—not only the needletop buildings (the New York skyline, "multiplied a thousandfold and divested of all reality," in Siegfried Kracauer's words), but the subterranean settings—the inhuman factory and workers' warren.

The crowd scenes were boldly crafted. The director had been in his element, pitilessly gazing from a great height on the spoiled, pleasuring rich, the shaven-headed drones, the flood-endangered children. The tireless thought and effort he put into the major set pieces—the Tower of Babel sequence, the flooding of the underground, the sacrifice of the robot-Maria—had contributed to a monumental achievement.

---

*This is over one million U.S. dollars, at the time, but it is a deceptive figure. Most film historians agree that some of Ufa's overhead was charged to the production and that the total was further inflated by Germany's weak economy.

The film offered these spectacular moments, yet there were also highlights forged by simple means: the opening montage of piston, dial, wheel, and siren inserts auguring the "day shift"; taut scenes in tunnels and caves, with feverish pursuit and minimal lighting; actors arranged in profile against velvety backdrops, facing each other and squaring off, the camera cutting back and forth like a spinning coin.

The timepieces that so often cropped up in Lang's films are glimpsed everywhere, presiding over the action: wristwatches in close-up, office and factory monitors, a giant clock·face in a tower overseeing the city. One of the film's enduring images is that of Freder Frederson struggling to avoid being impaled on a giant clock mechanism after he steps in to pull levers for an exhausted worker. (His anguished cry echoes the Crucifixion: "Father, father, why have you forsaken me?")

Not all of the acting was virtuosic. Rudolf Klein-Rogge did his customarily audacious job, but Gustav Fröhlich plays at a strained fever pitch and receives an overly generous allotment of screen time. The chance Lang took on Brigitte Helm, on the other hand, was validated; her Virgin Mary reborn as a Frankenstein monster ranks as one of the immortal performances of the silent screen.

Erich Kettelhut made it to the first-night, and here, too, he proved an attentive chronicler. "At some points they [the audience] even applauded over the music. At the end they broke into spontaneous applause, needed absolutely no prompting, and clapped for a long time. There were a lot of flowers in addition to those the company had ordered. The ensemble, especially Brigitte Helm and Fritz Lang, took curtain calls again and again."*

Under such circumstances, the *Metropolis* company was in a mood to celebrate, and afterward, at the requisite first-night party, they all congratulated and praised each other, "although every one of them was completely convinced that their own work was significantly better—in short, the kind of euphoria there always is at a party after a premiere that went off well," in Kettelhut's words. Lang and Otto Hunte buried the hatchet; they would persevere as collaborators. The director gave Aenne Willkomm a public hug; they would never work together again.

"A spirit of brotherhood reigned supreme," said Kettelhut. It was a real-life ending as kitschy as that of the film.

Germany's film critics had no such spirit of brotherhood. *Metropolis*'s allusions—the borrowings, woven dissonantly together, from H. G. Wells and Jules Verne, Karl Marx and the Bible—provided highly charged grist for the national press. In general, the reviews were "not chary with praise," according to Klaus Kreimeier's *The Ufa Story*, "but there were negative and undecided voices as well, which—disregarding the pans from the leftist intellectual press that Ufa regarded as marginal anyhow—seem to have occasioned panic in the firm."

The critic for *Die Filmwoche* called Lang's future-film lifeless, dehumaniz-

---

*Even at the height of her fame, Brigitte Helm gave few interviews. One of the times she did, speaking to the Italian *Cinema Illustrazione* in 1933, she stated, "*Metropolis* was the worst experience I ever had."

ing, and unrealistic, while Berlin's cultural journal *Die literarische Welt* characterized *Metropolis* as technically and artistically monumental, but intellectually empty. "What is this?" asked a horrified Hans Siemsen in *Die Weltbühne*, the influential left-wing weekly. "This is not just *Metropolis*; it is not just German film. It is . . . all of official Germany as we know it and experience it every day on our own hides."

One of the spiritual godfathers of the film, H. G. Wells, was quoted in the *Frankfurter Zeitung* of May 3, 1927 as saying, "I have recently seen the silliest film. I do not believe it would be possible to make one sillier." Wells went on to denounce *Metropolis* as comprised of "almost every possible foolishness, cliché, platitude, and muddlement about mechanical progress and progress in general, served up with a sauce of sentimentality." Because Lang had been weaned on Wells, he was especially wounded by this published essay, widely reprinted in other German newspapers and around the world, including the *New York Times.**

But the film's running time in the end, appears to have hurt *Metropolis* as much as the critical brouhaha. Without Erich Pommer around to exert some control and force a compromise over the length, Lang had settled on an impractical final cut of two-and-a-half-hours. The German film industry was in a difficult period, and theaters needed a faster turnover. The overlong film couldn't possibly attract large audiences quickly enough to meet the studio's expectations.

Almost immediately after the film's opening, Ufa began to backpedal. In March 1927, Ludwig Klitzsch, the lieutenant of industrial and communications magnate Alfred Hugenberg, joined Ufa. He remained boss of Hugenberg's Scherl Publishing (publisher of Thea von Harbou's books) and the all-important news agencies, while taking over management and restructuring of the film company. Uniform production regulations were instituted. Labor was put on notice. Cuts were levied. All operations were be called to account.

In April, Hugenberg himself assumed obligations as the company's leading investor. Under Hugenberg, an ultra-nationalist who later became a minister in the Third Reich, and the energetic Klitzsch, the company would gradually transform itself politically as well as culturally, becoming an arch-conservative entity. For the moment, however, the new bosses' priorities included modernizing facilities and converting to sound.

Ufa had signed an initial sound licensing agreement, in 1925, with Tri-Ergon AG, a Swiss-financed company which controlled patents for a sound-on-film system. This deal allowed Ufa to set up a department to institute talking pictures. The vast resources consumed by *Metropolis*, as well as the sheer daily noise of ongoing production, had cut into research progress, and the licensing agreement had lapsed.

Neubabelsberg once had been Europe's foremost production facility, but now more up-to-date studios challenged its superiority. A new, artificially lit

---

*Wells never let up on *Metropolis*. In a memo he circulated to Alexander Korda and others working on the 1936 British film *Things to Come*, he wrote, "All the balderdash one finds in such a film as Fritz Lang's *Metropolis* about 'robot workers' and ultra-skyscrapers, et cetera, et cetera, should be cleared out of your minds before you work on this film. As a general rule you may take it that whatever Lang did in *Metropolis* is the exact opposite of what we want done here."

stage that the company had built during the filming of *Metropolis* was already obsolete, and plans had to be hastily drawn up to hollow it out to accommodate sound. Eventually the Metropolis-Becken and other sections of the studio Lang had commandeered for filming would be torn down, and Ufa's Tonkreuz, a complex of four bunkerlike studios grouped around an inner courtyard, would be constructed on the remains of the standing sets. Ufa's massive overhaul would require adrenaline, leadership, and sacrifice.

One of the first items to be sacrificed was *Metropolis*. Already the smell of failure was in the air, according to *The Ufa Story*, when the board met in the spring of 1927. The film's message, as well as its length, fell under suspicion. The Ufa management debated, on April 7 and 8, removing "those insert titles with Communist tendencies in the American version; furthermore, to continue showing the film in about ten or twelve of the larger provincial cities and to reopen in Berlin in the fall—if the weather is bad, in the late summer." Shortly after the board met again, this time to reconsider the heretical religiosity of the picture.

It wasn't long before the board voted to yank *Metropolis* from theaters. Desperate to lure audiences, the Ufa management would condense the original two-and-a-half-hour *Metropolis* to two hours, before re-releasing the film widely throughout Germany in August, eight months after its January premiere. When censors sat down to judge the film a second time, on August 5, 1927, it had been reduced from its original 4189 meters to 3241 meters, according to surviving records. No doubt Lang was consulted about this diminution, which nonetheless was forced upon him.

"*Metropolis*, the 'world's greatest film,' which was going to beat the Americans at their own game, had been a disaster for Ufa," according to *The Ufa Story*, "A second disaster of comparable proportions had to be avoided at all costs."

Meanwhile, an agreement had been reached between Paramount and Ufa in December 1925 to form a mutual distribution organization called Parufamet. It gave Paramount and MGM wide distribution rights for American films in Germany in exchange for a massive loan to the then-beleaguered Ufa company. This agreement, all accounts agree, was precipitated in part by the *Metropolis* financial crisis, and was regarded in Germany as Ufa's capitulation to Hollywood. Although the United States pledged to facilitate reciprocal exhibitions, in practice, serious limitations were placed on the choice, length, and acceptability of German films that could be distributed in America.

Parufamet was permitted to distribute its own edited version of *Metropolis* in European markets, where the box office proved modest and the critical reaction generally favorable. In London, *The Times* exclaimed upon the film's "remarkable pictorial power," while Iris Barry wrote in *The Spectator* that "there are moments when it touches real greatness."

Luis Buñuel, in Paris—then an acolyte, one year away from directing his first film, *Un Chien Andalou*, and beginning his climb to the highest ranks of filmmakers—added his name to the list of people impressed by Lang's artistry. Writing for the *Gaceta literaria*, Buñuel was among those who complained that the narrative was "trivial, bombastic, pedantic"; but "from the photographic angle, [the film's] emotive force, its unheard-of and overwhelming beauty, is unequaled. It is of such a technical perfection that it can stand a prolonged analysis."

Of necessity the film had to recoup its costs in English-language countries, and all along Ufa had looked for redemption from America, where Lang and Erich Pommer had done their ambassadorial work. The premiere showings, in March of 1927, were widely anticipated in the United States, and preceded by a *New York Times* report from Berlin by Herman G. Sheffauer, hailing *Metropolis* as "a wonderful film, in many ways one of the most remarkable achievements in the history of the 'light play' . . . [which] will bid fair to become one of the master-films of all times."

But Paramount, which controlled distribution in America, also fretted about the film's length. Dramatist Channing Pollock was employed by the company at a thousand dollars a day to reduce *Metropolis* from sixteen reels to nine for the New York City opening. One of the people Pollock—best known for his play *The Fool*, a hit of the 1922 season—answered to at Paramount was a rising executive by the name of Walter Wanger, who supervised the bookings for the company's nationwide theater chain.

After viewing *Metropolis* half a dozen times, Pollock sat down to write "a quite different story that, I believed, could be told with the available 'shots.' " His new story, as summarized in his autobiography, altered the original scenario into something virtually unrecognizable: "A greedy employer hoped to grow rich by hiring the inventor to create hundreds of steel workmen. These proved to be perfect, except that they could not be endowed with souls, and the result was catastrophic."

The film went from two and a half hours in Berlin to one hour and forty-seven minutes in Pollock's American edition. Characters' names were changed (Freder became Eric), subplots and flashbacks disappeared, subtitles were shifted. "The note of pathos prevailing in the original German titles" was altered to "prosaic declarative sentences in English," according to film historian David L. Parker, who analyzed the American *Metropolis* for the *Library of Congress Newsletter*. Among the eliminated material were scenes spotlighting the character of Freder's assistant, played by Fritz Rasp; an elaborate opening sequence, in which a buoyant Freder is seen running a race in a modern coliseum; and all reference to the character Hel, Joh's wife, who—though she has died before the film opens—figured importantly in the story's background.*

Editor Pollock believed he had performed a remarkable salvage job. Walter Wanger—who would later in his career have his own confrontations with Fritz

---

*Hel—Freder's mother—had been loved by both Rotwang and Joh Frederson; and Maria reminds them both of her. The fact that Hel died in childbirth lies at the heart of the rift between son and father. A monument to Hel's memory, an enormous, totemic statue of a woman's head, was one of the famous images deleted from the U.S. version. The oft-given explanation for excising Hel is that the German word for "hell" is "Hölle," so Germans were "innocent of the fact" that in America Hel would connote "hell" and therefore "create a guffaw in an English-speaking audience," as Randolph Bartlett reported in the *New York Times*. This was for a marketing strategy destined to fail in America: Wouldn't English-speaking moviegoers drawn to *Metropolis* in the first instance be sophisticated enough to swallow their guffaws?

Lang—wasn't so sure. "You did your best," Wanger told Pollock, "but the damned picture is [still] nothing but machinery."

Paramount's publicity tried to put a positive spin on the drastically revised *Metropolis*. Pollock, declaring he had given the film "my meaning," was sent around for interviews. "The trimming of this production is said, by those who saw it in its original form, to have improved it," reported Randolph Bartlett in the *New York Times*. "I am willing to wager that *Metropolis*, as it is seen at the Rialto now, is nearer Fritz Lang's idea than the version he himself released in Germany."

The influential Gilbert Seldes, writing in *The New Republic*, acclaimed the film as a visionary work of the first order, but, like others, criticized the scenario's odd "lack of balance." Reaction in general was measured. Ironically, the film that was supposed to conquer the market for Ufa was released in one of its most bastardized forms in the United States. The director himself never wavered in his opinion of the version that was distributed in America under his name. The *Metropolis* editing was handled "dictatorially and carelessly," Lang said on more than one occasion. "They had slashed my film so cruelly that I dared not see it."

Indeed, the film was dictatorially and carelessly slashed everywhere after its Berlin premiere. Foreign negatives were often different from domestic negatives—to save money, different "takes" rejected for domestic release were often inserted into foreign negatives, so that subtly and dramatically different prints made their way around the world. Local and government censorship in other countries added to the confusing variety of versions.*

Dr. Enno Patalas of the Munich Filmmuseum took on the Zeus-like assignment of restoring the original form of *Metropolis* in the 1980s. Using press synopses, a copy of the original screenplay, a piano score with written instructions, censorship records, East German archival copies, and three photo albums of the still photographer Horst von Harbou, Patalas and his staff restored a version that ran very nearly two and a half hours.

The definitive version—Fritz Lang's—can be said to have been presented only at the Berlin premiere and possibly at the Ufa-Pavilion an Nollendorfplatz—for no more than ten weeks—according to *The Ufa Story*. Yet *Metropolis* continues to be revived annually at film festivals, in college towns and major cities around the globe. Although it exists in all these disparate variations, Lang's film stands as one of the few silent-era classics whose spellbinding appeal has never waned.

---

*To add to the profusion of variations, Giorgio Moroder, the music producer, film composer, and arranger, released a widely seen re-edited version of *Metropolis* with a newly incorporated background score—featuring rock songs by Freddie Mercury, Pat Benatar, and Adam Ant, among others—in 1984.

Already, as the filming of *Metropolis* drew to a close, Fritz Lang and Thea von Harbou were planning their next film. "The Ufa crisis did not exist for them," recalled Erich Kettelhut. "They made their plans as if everything would continue in the future in its old way."

Far away in Hollywood, Erich Pommer wrote to tell the director that he could arrange a comfortable studio contract for him if Lang wanted to come to America. Lang had been linked so closely to Pommer that they were constantly mentioned in the same breath, but in 1927 he hardly gave Hollywood a moment's consideration. For one thing, as actor Willy Fritsch put it in his memoirs, Lang was "more patriotic than a German nationalist Junker." According to Fritsch, who would be the male lead of the director's next two productions, "When he found out I drove a Cadillac, he hit the roof. Fritz Lang believed it was the duty of every good German to drive a Mercedes."

February and March 1927 were taken up with publicity and personal appearances on behalf of *Metropolis* elsewhere in Europe. Lang and von Harbou traveled to Vienna for several days, shared tea with members of the press at the Hotel Bristol, signed autographs for two thousand fans for three hours on a Sunday morning. "Luckily," reported *Mein Film*, "the two artists are used to working hard and after signing the umpteenth autograph they were still in the same good mood [that] they were in at the beginning."

The Ufa crisis by now was out in the open, and people were whispering that Lang would never again work under the company's logo. Would he turn to one of the smaller, independent outfits that still managed to thrive in Germany? Or would he, like Pommer, try his luck somewhere else in the world?

The answer did not become clear until June, when Lang announced that he had formed his own company, Fritz-Lang-Film GmbH, with offices at Friedrichstrasse 224. He took on two partners: Hermann Fellner, who had worked behind the scenes at May-Film-GmbH, and Joseph Somlo, another executive with long experience in the German film industry. But on screen the title of "producer" would be Lang's alone.

"Fritz Lang is Staying in Germany!" headlined the *Film-Kurier* on June 19. "It was feared that Fritz Lang also, because of his American successes, would follow the numerous offers which were made to him," reported Germany's screen world publication.

Ufa was able to turn the development to its advantage. In exchange for modest investment guarantees, the company sewed up control of all domestic and foreign exhibition of all Fritz-Lang-Film GmbH productions. Even so, Ufa feared Lang's excesses would cut into potential profits. It ordered Major Grau to initiate "as soon as possible a discussion with Mr. Lang about his next film. All production details should be spelled out as precisely as possible and recorded in the files so that constant supervision of Mr. Lang's production is possible and cost overruns can be prevented."

Advertising and publicity would also be left to Ufa, under Rudi Feld, the energetic head of promotion. Ufa was an acknowledged leader in commercial and publishing tie-ins, souvenir programs, spectacular promotions, showy premieres, expensive parties. Lang's films had always received deluxe treatment from Ufa, and it was to his benefit to exploit the company's expertise in this area.

Ufa would pull out all stops on the Berlin premieres of the Fritz-Lang-Film GmbH films of the next several years, transforming the cinemas with fantastical special effects. The facade of the Ufa-Palast am Zoo would be lit up for the premiere of *Spione*, in 1928, by a stylized giant eye, with floodlights beaming from the pupils, piercing the throngs of illustrious guests. And the Palast would be similarly transformed for the 1929 premiere of *Die Frau im Mond*, the building converted into a model of the universe. Above the facade, model rockets were shot out of a massive sculpted globe, disappearing into an artificial sky. High above the main entrance, neon lights spelled out the glittering lure—words the director treasured above all else: EIN FILM VON FRITZ LANG.

Even while speculation about their future was mounting, Fritz Lang and Thea von Harbou were immersing themselves in their next film project; as was her wont, von Harbou crafted novel and screenplay simultaneously. The new film, a thriller overflowing with intrigue and treachery, would be called, simply, *Spione* (*Spies*).

The director already had his new lead actress. Vienna's legitimate theaters, by 1926, had fallen on hard times, and Gerda Maurus wound up touring Germany with a revue she emceed wearing a tuxedo. In September Maurus found herself in Berlin, and fished out Fritz Lang's telephone number and address. She phoned Lang, who of course remembered her. He was busy filming *Metropolis*, but not too busy for such an enticing personality, and Lang made an appointment for her the very next day.

Right away the director began charming her, telling her how exquisite she was, and how he would find a part that would perfectly highlight her beauty. His ambition on her behalf was greater than her own, and instilled confidence. "Fritz Lang was the first person who made me get over my shyness of standing in front of the camera," Gerda Maurus said later. "I did a screen test, and I soon had a contract in my pocket. I was filled with enthusiasm . . ."

Gerda Maurus would make her debut as the "virgin star" of *Spione*, playing a "super-spy" named Sonia, assigned to track and destroy opposing agent number 326. Agent 326 is working on the side of good government, while Sonia is manipulated by "the most dangerous man in Europe," the arch-sinister Great Haghi. When Sonia and Agent 326 fall in love at first sight, Haghi's master plan begins to unravel.

Once again Rudolf Klein-Rogge would head the line-up as Haghi, a financial wizard and omnipotent spy whose Langian ambition it is to dominate the world. A bank serves as his respectable smokescreen; underneath lies "a city within a city, an amazing network of secret passages, a veritable maze of courts and rooms equipped with countless sending and receiving apparatus," in the words of von Harbou's novel. Haghi is in fact a Russian whose mustache and goatee make him look "not unlike Lenin."* But Haghi is also a master of disguises, unrecognizable as himself—the politics of the film is all facial hair.

Willy Fritsch would take over from Gustav Fröhlich as Lang's leading man, who in the novel is known only as Agent 326, but in the film is also called Tremaine. Tremaine fulfills the requisites of a Lang Galahad: nothing is known about him except that he lives alone in one of the best hotels with a man-servant, owns a handsome car, and is a fan of boxing (a recent fascination of the director's). "Some years before, he had appeared, faultlessly dressed, show-ing every sign of culture and breeding, and if not wealth—certainly something near it—had presented credentials from the highest sources and had requested a position in the service."

Actor-director Lupu Pick would play Dr. Matsumoto, a Japanese emissary and spy-master, while Fritz Rasp would portray Colonel Jellusic, a character modeled after the Austrian Colonel Alfred Redl, who spied for the czar and delivered sensitive information to Russia at the outbreak of World War I. The small but significant role of Kitty was set aside for Lien Deyers, Lang's other Vienna discovery. She too would make her debut in *Spione*, playing the ma-licious waif in Haghi's employ who is befriended by Dr. Matsumoto.** When she steals state secrets entrusted to Dr. Matsumoto, he is disgraced and be-comes one more hara-kiri victim of a Fritz Lang film.

Cameraman Fritz Arno Wagner rejoined the Lang team. Karl Vollbrecht and Otto Hunte stayed on, the latter despite his predictable friction with Lang; the two would prove as resourceful on the abbreviated schedule for *Spione* as on *Metropolis*'s endless one.

Production began at Neubabelsberg in December of 1927 and lasted for fifteen weeks, until March of 1928. If the budget wasn't exactly shoestring, the circumstances were more modest than under Ufa auspices, and adjust-ments had to be made. The director was quite capable of revising plans and budgets as long as he accepted the conditions—and capable of creating pro-vocative, quality films under stringent circumstances. It was creative suprem-acy, not financial freedom, that was Lang's true obsession—and his Achilles' heel.

---

*The pretext for *Spione* was a series of newspaper articles about Scotland Yard's raid of a spy nest operating under cover of a Soviet trade delegation, which caused a scandal in Europe in 1926. Klein-Rogge's Lenin look is the only allusion to this "backstory."
**Technically, Deyers appeared first in Germany's movie theaters as a girl-next-door type in *Die Heilige und ihr Narr* (*The Saint and Her Fool*). That film, directed by Wilhelm Dieterle, was released a short time before *Spione*, although it was actually filmed afterward.

Robert Spa visited the set for *Cinemagazine* and reported for its February 17, 1928, issue that, although *Spione* was "only a small film compared to *Metropolis*," the director's methods appeared unchanged. "Lang sees everything, makes everything himself, supervises the makeup of actresses (actors do not use makeup). He controls all the details of the costumes, furniture and props; he is 'infallible.' "

The director was generous enough with salaries, reported the Vienesse cast member Paul Hörbiger, but almost "wasteful" with film footage. In one relatively simple scene, Hörbiger recalled in his memoirs, he was required to knock on a wall. "This was done no less than twenty-three times before he really liked the knocking. I swear, each time I knocked exactly the same as the time before. And it was a silent film, you couldn't hear the knocking anyway."

The actors could expect to take out-of-the-ordinary risks. Curt Riess described one incident during filming: a scene where Agent 326 yanks Sonia to one side just as a bullet slams into the glass plate behind her. Characteristically, Lang himself insisted on aiming the bullet. "It would have been easy to film this scene without putting Maurus in danger," wrote Riess. "But Lang needed danger, so the actors could act out the danger of the situation. He was convinced that they had to be afraid to make the audience afraid." The shot was repeated some twenty times. "It turned out a revolver bullet did not make a noticeable hole," wrote Riess. "Lang tried with a shotgun, a sling shot, a pistol, all kinds of firearms, until he was finally satisfied."

The "virgin star," as usual, bore the brunt of Lang's perfectionism. As bad luck would have it, Gerda Maurus had to have her appendix removed during the course of production. "The doctors advised her to take it easy," reported Curt Riess. "Lang had never heard of the expression." The director had his leading lady sprinting over gravel through a tunnel, standing under open lights for so long that she developed severe conjunctivitis, then rehearsing with her eyes closed to the point of weeping from the pain. ("Didn't Lang see that?" mused Riess in his account. "Of course, but he must not have wanted to see it.")

Under exclusive contract to Lang, Maurus was obliged to do whatever the director said. After *Spione*, Lang informed her that she would have to don boxing gloves and learn to box for his next picture, in which she would play some kind of prodigy. Maurus was nothing if not plucky. She trained for three weeks, every morning at eight sparring with the noted Turkish boxer Sabri Mahir. "She amazed her male partner with her incredible physical strength," wrote Riess. "Looking at the ravishing Viennese girl you would hardly expect it."

As part of the arrangement with Fritz-Lang-Film GmbH, Ufa was required to lend Maurus a beautiful evening dress for Saturday night publicity appearances around town, for which she would be escorted by her tuxedoed director. Lang made a point of being seen with his protégée (the two of them sometimes accompanied by Thea von Harbou) at the Horcher, the Adlon, the Bristol. "When the violinist Georges Boulanger saw Lang coming into [the Förster restaurant], he started to play the 'Volga Boat Song,' " one of Lang's favorites, in the words of Curt Riess. "Then Lang, after detailed discussion with the waiter, ordered."

Not only would Maurus learn how to box, but the director taught her "how to eat oysters, how to dissect a pheasant, how to peel a peach, which wine is drunk with which meal," in Riess's words. "She had to learn how to hold a cigarette nonchalantly. And afterward there was a small Viennese bar where [they would go that] a Heurigen band played and performed Viennese songs, and Lang would get a little sentimental and sing along."

Sundays, Riess reported, Lang's Mercedes rested in the garage while the actress and the director went off to explore the Grünewald woods. Carrying backpacks, Lang and Maurus picked berries and joined the picnickers on the outskirts of Berlin.

Critics were divided over *Spione* when it was released in March of 1928. The socialist *Film und Volk* labeled Lang's newest film "a load of garbage . . . despite the flashy and extravagant effects, deathly dull," while others found the spy thriller, after the pinnacle of *Metropolis*, enormously entertaining yet somehow anticlimatic. This reception ensured that one of the director's most assured and engrossing silent films would also become one of his most underrated.

The film is like a cross between *Die Spinnen* and *Dr. Mabuse, der Spieler*, joining the juvenile spy nonsense of the former (invisible ink, buttonhole cameras, periscopes, and peepholes), with the solemn treason and telling real-life details of the latter (including the spectacle of socialites hooked on opium). Though the film's intellectual quotient drops as its plot complications mount, the suspense and furioso strokes never flag.

The director's mastery of montage is evident in the train collision climax, which is conveyed with impressive concision. Lang, who knew trains, constructed the scene ingeniously. The audience realizes that the train bearing Agent 326, cradled in a sleeping berth, is hurtling toward a train car abandoned in a tunnel. Fritz-Lang-Film GmbH could not afford a big-budget wreck, but the director found ways to capture what he wanted. Nighttime shooting provided atmosphere. Spotlights were fixed in pairs on a movable framework in a tunnel. The director shot close-ups of glaring light, and a whirlwind of terrified faces. Pieces of glass and metal were hurled at the camera lens. The explosive crash was followed by horrible shouts and cries, hissing and steam.

Agent 326 escapes by a hairsbreadth. After the crash, a hand pushes through the wreckage, clutching a religious medallion—in Thea von Harbou's book, an emblem of carved ivory representing "some unknown feminine saint"; in the film a Madonna and child, which the audience recognizes as a token of love given, earlier in the story, by Sonia to Tremaine.

Tremaine is miraculously saved, but Sonia is kidnapped by an angry, jealous Haghi. The hero and other enforcers search the interior of Haghi's bank, but are interrupted by a communiqué giving them fifteen minutes to withdraw from the site, or Sonia will be executed. The last-minute rescue is especially well done, clocks ticking and the bank filling up with poisonous gas as the frantic hero manages to hack his way through a solid span of wall, saving the heroine as she collapses gasping in his arms.

However, in one final twist, Haghi also manages to escape. A coda gives Rudolf Klein-Rogge the chance to seize the audience's attention alone and unhurried at center stage, beneath a spotlight in a crowded music hall. His villainous part as Haghi has been a virtuoso turn, every bit on par with his Dr. Mabuse. Now the director gives his consummate star—his wife's ex-husband—a sublime curtain call.

Haghi wears his last disguise, performing as a clown in whiteface. When Haghi realizes he has been found out—police are milling in the wings—his face turns sickly. Roaring with laughter, the surrounded villain shouts "Curtain!" produces a gun out of thin air and abruptly shoots himself in the head. He crumples to the ground, the audience erupts in applause, and a scroll announces THE END. It is the most public—and startling—of the numerous suicides that pepper the films of Fritz Lang.

The critics may have been split, but audiences everywhere were bowled over. Once again Lang's belief in a "virgin star" was upheld; at the premiere of *Spione*, Gerda Maurus's performance electrified the crowd. Alone, the actress was brought out on stage to take her bows at the Ufa-Palast. "The audience wouldn't even let her go," reported Curt Riess. "They clapped like crazy. They screamed till they were hoarse."

A short time afterward, Lang told Gerda Maurus that the scenario for his next production was ready to go. "By the way," the director informed his protégée casually, "she doesn't box."

Lien Deyers, the lesser of Fritz Lang's two discoveries for *Spione*, did not work out to the director's satisfaction. He was forced to shoot one scene, between her and Lupu Pick, some seventy times. Though he had befriended Deyers in Vienna, he took an instant dislike to the young lady on the set. "How I hated doing those scenes with her!" the director would complain, years later.

When the Nazis came to power, Lien Deyers, like Lang, fled to the United States, where her career never regained momentum. One day the director, firmly established in Hollywood, received a phone call informing him that Lien Deyers had run into trouble with the Los Angeles Police. Lang didn't really care. He enjoyed making trips to the police station to examine confidential crime reports or photographs of murder victims, but for Lien Deyers Lang sent someone from his office to take care of the matter. He himself couldn't be bothered.*

Gerda Maurus, on the other hand, could do no wrong. She is often featured in close-up in *Spione*, in lingering, beautifully lit shots that dote on her beauty. The love story between her and Agent 326—which Eisner criticized as "the sentimentalism of a pair of lovers, the contribution of von Harbou"—warrants almost reverential staging. The two lovers obviously spend the night together in one scene, but the treatment is surprisingly chaste; flowers are exchanged (de rigueur for any Lang courtship, on or off camera), and the hours appear to fly by with the two of them murmuring and holding hands.

Everyone in Berlin film industry circles knew the gossip that during the filming of the production Lang had fallen in love with the actress—so much

---

*The fact that Lien Deyers's first husband was Alfred Zeisler, the production manager who sometimes found himself in the position of Lang's nemesis, may have hardened the director's attitude toward the actress.

in love that he had moved Gerda Maurus into an extra apartment in his building on Hohenzollerndamm, as once before he had done for Thea von Harbou. This would have broken a lesser personality than his scenarist-wife. But von Harbou chose to shrug off the public humiliation.

It was also rumored that the affair between Lang and Maurus was the opposite of the idyllic, chaste relationship portrayed in *Spione*. On camera, Maurus was worshiped by Lang. Off camera, their affair was considered sadomasochistic.

Alfred Zeisler, in his oral history, was not the only person to claim that Lang was reputed to beat Maurus up "so badly that sometimes she could hardly walk—she was black and blue when she came to the studio." Rudolph S. Joseph, an assistant to G. W. Pabst who had been a close friend of Maurus's before she became a film star, confirmed this account. Joseph in fact took the actress aside one day and asked her for the truth about the rumors. "I asked her how she could stand his beatings, and she replied if she didn't mind no one else should either," recalled Joseph.

Friends of Lang have insisted that, if true, this sadomasochism presents an isolated case in the director's love life. The Lang-Maurus relationship was a folie à deux, these friends theorize, involving two people, well-behaved under most circumstances, whose unique chemistry together was destructive. Others strongly disagree.

For many years, Lang flaunted his "addiction to the kind of perverse behavior that we usually associate with post-war Berlin," in the words of one screenwriter, a contemporary of the director's in Hollywood, who spoke on condition that he not be identified. "I was told, and I trust the sources, that Lang was the guru of depraved sexuality in Hollywood for a period of about ten years. Young men in leather jackets would be handcuffed to posts and beaten, smoking of marijuana was de rigueur, young women and animals were corralled as sex objects, and Lang himself would be present in regal robes."

There is no documentation of the above. Yet that sort of behavior would be commonly ascribed to Fritz Lang throughout his career; and, especially when coupled with the stories about the fate of his first wife and his cruel treatment of Gerda Maurus, the gossip added nothing positive to his luster.

The director, his wife, and the actress with whom he was in love made a trip together to Vienna in April for a *Spione* screening hosted by the Austrian Theater Owners' Association.

Returning to Germany via the Vienna-Berlin Express, Lang fell asleep in his berth, dreaming. The director loved the night sleepers, where he could enjoy "the soft movement back and forth of the body, the whistle of the locomotive, the swarms of falling stars of its sparks, the consciousness of being carried from one place to another without having anything else to do but lie still, dreaming the dreams of youth." This night the sleeping coach "became a spaceship cabin, and a chuffing vehicle tied to rails . . . became a rocket racing through space," as Lang explained on one occasion.

Lang, of course, was fond of emphasizing the sudden moments of inspiration—through vision and dream—behind his films. Although of course, his wife and scenarist then von Harbou, just happened to be riding that "chuffing vehicle" too. Travel usually gave the duo occasion to discuss their future projects; so trifling a matter as Lang's affair with Gerda Maurus was not permitted to disturb their close working relationship.

If past experience serves as example, it is quite possible that von Harbou had already begun work on the film script Lang claimed to be dreaming. In this case, not only did von Harbou write one of her novels to accompany the film's eventual release, but the scenario credit, for the first time since 1920, was granted to her alone—a subtle indication of the growing estrangement between the director and his wife. Publicity for the film, notably, revealed that rocket travel was not exclusively Fritz Lang's hobby, but another of those youthful enthusiasms which von Harbou shared with her husband.

One of the stimuli for making a movie about rocket travel was the couple's friendship with Willy Ley, whom Lang had met early in 1927. Ley, in his twenties, had authored pioneering books about rocket travel, including *Die Möglichkeit der Weltraumfahrt (The Possibility of Space Travel)*. In July 1927, Ley became a founding member of the Verein für Raumschiffahrt (Society for Space Travel), among whose members was a recognized authority named Hermann Oberth.

It was Ley who suggested contacting Oberth, who lived in Medias (now Romania). A native Austrian like Lang, Oberth had drawn the first plans for rocket artillery while a member of the Austrian Army during World War I. His groundbreaking book *Die Rakete zu den Planetenräumen (By Rocket to Interplanetary Space)*, published in 1923, had stimulated rocket research throughout Europe, and influenced the theories of Ley, his junior in status and age. Oberth arrived in Berlin in the fall of 1929 to lend his authority to the scenario Thea von Harbou had developed.

The film became known by several titles; most commonly, *Die Frau im Mond (The Woman in the Moon)*, but also *By Rocket to the Moon*, or *The Woman in the Moon* in English-language translation. Von Harbou's story focused on the crew of man's first, experimental rocket expedition to the moon. They include a dedicated scientist who acts as the pilot; his weakling chief engineer; a brainy female astronomer; a devious representative of a shadowy organization of financiers; and an avuncular elderly professor whose pet theory—that gold abounds on the moon—has made him the laughingstock of the scientific community. A young boy, infatuated with science fiction magazines, also joins the group when he somehow manages to stow away on the flight.

Wolf Helius, the dedicated scientist of the story, is secretly in love with the female astronomer, Frieda, who is engaged to marry the chief engineer, Hans Windegger. Frieda finds herself increasingly estranged from her fiancé during the moon adventure, however. And the sinister character, Walt Turner, proves willing to stop at nothing to claim the gold deposits scattered across the moon.

In her novel, von Harbou devoted elaborate attention to the Walt Turner character, creating in him another arch-criminal and master of disguises. In the film, Lang treats the villain more as a pro-forma necessity, while his female lead, Frieda, played by Gerda Maurus, garners far more attention and interest. As intrepid as any male hero, Frieda gives a von Harbouish speech defending a woman's right to be included in the maiden moon voyage. She herself will earn her way as a documentarist, filming the lunar landscape for posterity. That gives Lang a chance to slip in some film-within-a-film footage, which was one of the director's trademarks.

The male lead, symbolically named for the Greek god of the sun, would once again by played by Willy Fritsch. Gustav von Wangenheim, who had a small part in *Metropolis*, would graduate to a featured role as the chief engineer. Fritz Rasp was recruited once more for a Lang film, portraying Walt Turner. Gustl Stark-Gstettenbauer, a trained circus performer who also appeared in *Spione*, played the stowaway boy, Gustav.

The photography was by Curt Courant and Otto Kanturek. Oskar Fischinger, an avant-garde painter known for his pioneering works of abstract animation, assisted with the camera and special effects. The indispensable Otto Hunte and Karl Vollbrecht, from *Die Nibelungen*, *Metropolis*, and *Spione*, were back on the job of production design.

Emboldened by the popularity of *Spione*, Lang envisioned *Die Frau im Mond* as more of a "super-film," like *Die Nibelungen* and *Metropolis*, and he lavished time and money on the creation and design of a massive rocket ship. The eye-popping liftoff, which in the novel is rendered in but a few pages, would be the film's first master-stroke. In truth, the only other memorable spectacle would be the realization of the moonscape itself.

To create a lunar landscape inside studio confines, a convoy of trucks was commissioned to ferry bleached sand from the outskirts of Berlin and dump it over the floor of a stage. Then Hunte and Vollbrecht went to work, sculpting the sand into evocative swirls and dunes (creating "the wonderful luminosity of the lunar landscape," in the words of Paul Rotha). When Lang looked back on his years in Berlin, those trucks ferrying bleached sand would loom in his memory. It was a high point to savor, a time when the director had the power to conjure his personal trip to another world.

The moonscape was magnificiently realized, yet unfortunately the human drama was lost among the fancy effects and technical rigmarole. Lang suffered from a tendency—which sometimes spun out of control—to stress authenticity, or "expert facts," over the drama in his films. More than once would the director lose his grip this way in courtroom scenes, whose protocol never ceased to mesmerize him. And more than once in *Die Frau im Mond*, with its overemphasis on procedural detail and pedantic science, does pseudo-authenticity overwhelm the story ("the critical eight minutes," according to one intertitle, "is the period of acceleration, which can be deadly for the human organism if it is greater than forty meters per second").

Willy Ley and Hermann Oberth proved ascendant, as it were, over Hunte and Vollbrecht. Lang, whose friendship with Willy Ley continued over the years, always chose to emphasize the "great help" the younger expert gave in developing the plausible concepts of space flight for *Die Frau im Mond*. After all, Oberth stayed in Germany and later contributed to Nazi scientific research; Ley fled the Nazi regime and settled in the United States, becoming a regular dinner guest at Lang's Hollywood home.

But Oberth was the film's main scientific adviser, and it was he who took the lead in simulating the rocket design and travel. Indeed, for a time Ufa helped finance Oberth's invention of a real liquid-fueled rocket as a publicity gimmick. According to a biography of Oberth, the publicity-minded Lang paid an estimated five thousand marks, at least half the cost of the experiments, out of Oberth's own pocket. Half the profits for any "commercial use" of Oberth's discoveries would go to the investors, according to agreement, until the year 2020. Problems arose when the costs mounted; and the final experiment fizzled before the October 15, 1929, premiere. Ultimately Oberth had to leave Berlin, stranding investors, while he himself was left "financially and morally ruined."

Seen today, the opening sequences—which laboriously recreate the preparations and blastoff—are more numbing than deep-thrilling. The crowd shots, which seem intended to liven things up, are extraneous and ineffective. It seems to take an eternity—half the film, virtually—for the rocket to shoot out of the hangar and rise into outer space. Afterward, the interplanetary glimpses are all animation and effects.

Once the rocket ship is aloft, the story of the film takes on familiar shades: two men in love with the same woman, and the agonizing consequences; gold discovered in the lunar caverns; the professor mysteriously killed; Walt Turner slain during a violent struggle with the hero; and finally, the return-trip oxygen supply damaged. One adult must sacrifice himself by staying behind so that the others have enough fuel to make the return trip. Helius and Windegger choose matchsticks—the short one losing: it belongs to the weak-willed chief engineer. Helius, noting Windegger's panic and Frieda's apparent anguish, gallantly removes himself in favor of his romantic rival by doping the two of them, then exiting the ship. Gustav, the stowaway, operates the blastoff.

But Frieda has made her own choice. Leaving the rocketship surreptitiously, she manages to hide out on the moon until the spacecraft is gone. Helius and Frieda, who up to this point didn't dare express their love for each other, thus find themselves marooned together, with only meager supplies to sustain them. A close-up shows their faces as they recognize the inevitability of death—and then slowly edge into a long-delayed embrace. With a strange serenity, Frieda cradles Helius, stroking the nape of his neck. Amazed by her decision to stay, he appears to be sobbing.

It was one of the most personal, tender, and vulnerable moments Fritz Lang ever allowed himself on film. The director's paean to rocket travel was really a valentine to his beloved—Gerda Maurus. Her face dominates the picture. Her scenes smolder. But the love story remained chaste, as it had in the case of *Spione*; before the ending the most prolonged physical contact between Frieda and Helius comes when the scientist, suffering an injury, collapses in her arms, his wounds salved by her tears.

Most German critics of the time were suitably impressed by the film's mixture of technical foresight and slow-burning drama. *Film-Kurier* hailed *Die Frau im Mond* as brilliant, awesome, unforgettable. *Der Tag* described Lang's newest epic as "a sensation, a major event," its creator "the biggest European director of our times." Berlin's daily *Morgenpost* found *Die Frau im Mond* a "colossal directorial achievement."

Ironically, some critics complained that Gerda Maurus had been forced by her mentor into a caramelized characterization that prevented her from realizing her true potential as an actress. Max Brenner wrote in *Film und Volk* that by contrast, under the direction of others—as in Johannes Meyer's film *Hochverrat (High Treason)*—Lang's "virgin star" appeared "suddenly liberated and at ease."

Not until 1931 did *Die Frau im Mond* arrive in the United States, re-edited and retitled as *By Rocket to the Moon*. American reviewers were less impressed by its novelty and more critical of its clichés. *Variety* called Lang's latest film "painfully draggy." "The rocket trip to the moon is surrounded by a hackneyed melodramatic frame," wrote the reviewer, "and a bedraggled romance."

That is closer to how the film looks today. Yet *Die Frau im Mond* is another of the director's works whose mystique has continued to grow—in part because for years after its initial release the film was withheld from distribution by the Nazis. Its continuing reputation is also due to the host of technical innovations forecast in the film, which were later adopted and taken for granted by space science—and imitated in countless other science fiction films.

Never mind the incongruities: that the rocket ship is moored in a water basin, or that the lunar explorers freely breathe the moon's atmosphere, or a divining rod is used to search for water on the moon. Other ideas the film got right: the figure-8 around-the-moon flight pattern, the multi-staged upright rocket, the weightlessness of the spaceship's passengers—even the celebrated backward countdown that eventually became a staple of blastoff protocol. These the director could claim as genuinely prescient.

As Willy Ley wrote in *Rockets, Missiles and Men in Space*: "Thinking back, I realized to my own surprise that it [the countdown] had first been used in the film *Die Frau im Mond*. This was a silent movie, and at one point the words 'ten seconds to go' flashed on the screen, followed by the numbers, '6-5-4-3-2-1-0-FIRE.' Knowing that Fritz Lang had been in the Austrian Army in the First World War, I asked him whether he had adapted some military practice which used a countdown. He replied that he had thought it up for dramatic purposes when working on the film; on the proving ground nobody would possibly think of that side effect!"

Die Frau im Mond was the reason, in addition to *Metropolis*, that the director was courted years later by many of America's top science fantasy authors, including Robert Heinlein, Ray Bradbury, Robert Bloch, and others. He was sought out, too, by scientists and scholars passing through Hollywood. It was the reason that a 1968 Space-Science Seminar, held at a U.S. government research center in Huntsville, Alabama, invited Lang as an honored guest. "The scholars, engineers, et cetera, gathered in Huntsville," the director wrote proudly to Lotte Eisner, "explained to me that they considered me in a certain way as 'the father of rocket science.' "

Lang knew *Die Frau im Mond* wasn't one of his best films, but he always retained a disproportionate fondness for his last silent work. In his mind the experience of making it was inextricably linked to his years of power and glory in Berlin—and to his passionate relationship with Gerda Maurus. More than once, later in life, the director kidded himself into thinking he might recapture that time, maybe even improve on the film, if someone would give him the go-ahead to remake it.

*   *   *

The disappointing box-office returns for *Die Frau im Mond* contributed to the final breakdown of Lang's relations with Ufa.

All along Lang had irritated studio executives by insisting on implementing his own ideas in advertising and publicity campaigns. An inveterate self-promoter, Lang wrote bylined articles, gave unauthorized interviews, and demanded the promotion of Fritz-Lang-Film GmbH—in the person of Fritz Lang—in every authorized mention of his work.

The final straw was the company's insistence that the director acknowledge "talkies" by adding last-minute sound effects to *Die Frau im Mond* ("at the moment of the departure of the rocket, and so on," in Lang's words). All along the company had resisted allocating sufficient funds to the development of sound; now Uta needed to catch up rapidly. Adding sound effects was not such a bad idea, but Lang, on a collision course with the new people in charge, adamantly refused. Post-synchronized sound, he told the Ufa bosses flatly, would violate the internal rhythms of the film's narrative.

Compromise was impossible without someone like Erich Pommer around to arbitrate. The contempt with which Lang treated the Ufa executives hardened their attitude; by the time *Die Frau im Mond* was released, the company that had made possible the director's greatest works no longer wanted anything to do with him.

Ufa refused to extend its contract with Lang, rescinding its investment in future films, and withdrawing from all publicity, advertising, and distribution commitments. Fritz-Lang-GmbH could not continue to exist without Ufa. Lang's dream—to head his own company and function as his own producer—was destroyed. The idea was not lost forever, but when the chance for independence returned, later on in Hollywood, it would go sour for much the same reasons.

Lang could wax maudlin about his Ufa years, which lasted roughly from 1922 to 1929. "That was the happiest time of my life," the director said in 1966, "and I wouldn't want to have missed it for anything. It was like a large college: we would spend long hours, after work, at the canteen, discussing film, my colleagues and I."

In another interview Lang recalled that he was so disheartened by the demise of Fritz-Lang-Film GmbH that he had briefly pondered another line of work. "I was disgusted, and decided to make no more motion pictures. At that stage, and most perversely, I wanted to become a chemist. I don't know why. It was one of those stupid ideas."

But he couldn't have been serious. In fact, the director had already met with another producer, Seymour Nebenzahl, and agreed to work with Nebenzahl under the banner of Nero-Film, one of the smaller producing companies that managed to flourish under Germany's system.

Nebenzahl was a flashy operator. Generally thought to be a European, he was actually a U.S. citizen, born in Spanish Harlem. As a young man he had come to Germany with his father Heinrich, related by marriage to the Siodmak filmmaking family. At first, Heinrich Nebenzahl made his way selling American films with subtitles for German-language territories. Later, he produced several adventure films starring the popular actor Harry Piel.

The younger Nebenzahl, meanwhile, had become a successful stockbroker during the inflation period, making enough money to found his own bank. In the mid-1920s, Heinrich Nebenzahl formed Nero-Film. Although his partners included Richard Oswald (a Vienna-born director, who in his youth had performed at one of Lang's haunts, Café Fledermaus), the Nebenzahl family controlled the company's assets.

By the time Seymour Nebenzahl and Lang joined forces, the younger Nebenzahl had forged a reputation by producing two films—G. W. Pabst's *Die Büchse der Pandora (Pandora's Box)* and Robert Siodmak's first film, *Menschen am Sonntag (People on Sunday)*. Still, it was a coup for the fledgling Nero-Film to affiliate itself with the director of *Die Nibelungen* and *Metropolis*.

A killer businessman, Seymour Nebenzahl had a habit of talking poor toward the end of filming, and infuriated people with his financial sleight of hand. Nonetheless he would prove a first-rate producer who believed in creative filmmaking, a man of intuition and imagination as unique in the business as the more idolized Erich Pommer.

What would this new conniver and Lang, Ufa's ingrate, choose to do together? With sound exploding all over the screen, would the director attempt a "talkie" next?

Late in November of 1929, Fritz Lang and Thea von Harbou (sans Gerda Maurus) traveled once again to Vienna for the weekend premiere of *Die Frau im Mond* at the Ufa-Tonkino. They arrived by train, were greeted by "a large number of cheering fans, members of the press, and public figures," then were feted at a gala dinner hosted by Ufa director Wilhelm Karol.

At a press conference, the two were asked about the advent of talking pictures, and their future prospects. Neither Lang nor Thea von Harbou were willing to commit to doing a film totally equipped with sound. According to an article in *Mein Film*, von Harbou expressed their mutual reservations. "She is just as unenthusiastic about one hundred percent talking pictures as Fritz Lang is; he believes that a special style must be developed before talking pictures can be made . . . that are artistic and effective."

Lang, however, offered tantalizing remarks. He said his next motion picture would be vastly "influenced by sound." Even more intriguing, Lang assured *Mein Film* that the subject matter, which was already settled and promised to be "especially interesting," would satisfy those clamoring for him to direct a film with "roots in Vienna." This is a fascinating hint that *M*, Lang's masterpiece—which started out as a story about a writer of poison-pen letters— might have taken its first form with a Viennese backdrop.

1930

CHAPTER 8

1931

For the first time in years, Rudolf Klein-Rogge was out of the running—perhaps because Fritz Lang and Thea von Harbou found less and less to agree on. The director wanted another "virgin star" for his first talking picture, a different personality, someone who might fit snugly inside his own psyche, like one of those Russian nesting dolls that were sold, then as now, on the streets of Berlin.

The man Lang settled on was short, almost stunted, as pure and vaguely odious as a piglet. He had a moon-shaped face, sad eyes, and a low-pitched, silky purr of a voice. When the squeeze was put on, his eyes bugged out; his face transformed with fear and pleasure; the voice accelerated into a squeal. And then this deceptive Milquetoast of a man lashed out.

Born Laszlo Löwenstein in 1904 in the remote Carpathians, Peter Lorre possessed a background Lang could identify with. His mother had died when he was young; his father had moved to Vienna, where Lorre was raised. The father was straitlaced; Lorre fought with him, left home, clerked for a while in a bank, then clowned in restaurants for meals and slept on Prater benches while pursuing his dream of a life in the theater.

Little by little, Lorre found acting jobs in Vienna, Breslau, and Zurich. He improved, but it wasn't until the actor came to Berlin in 1928—proverbially, with ten marks in his pocket—that his sly, mercurial presence found its natural constituency.

Almost immediately Lorre became one of the rising lights of the Berlin avant-garde theater. He gave a brilliant performance in a controversial play, Marie Luise Fleisser's *Pionere in Ingolstadt*, performed in April 1929 at one of the two theaters of the Volksbühne, or the People's Theater. Jacob Geis was the nominal director; hovering in the wings was Bertolt Brecht, who dictated the casting (one of the leading roles was played by his wife, Helene Weigel), guided the staging, and urged rewrites. Although far from established, Brecht was already Berlin's most talked-about playwright; the Volksbühne, created by German socialists in 1890 and subsidized by the labor unions, was one of the city's most important theater groups. Lorre's association with Brecht and the Volksbühne would have commended him to the critics, even if the actor did not immediately evince the habit, later carried over into motion pictures, of stealing the show.

Pionere in Ingolstadt, in which Lorre portrayed a sex maniac in the Austrian Army, might to some extent have inspired Lang. Later the director, who liked to boast of his casting discoveries, claimed he "discovered" Lorre, as he phrased it when speaking to Gene D. Phillips, after having seen the actor first in an improvisational theater in Vienna. But it is more likely that Celia Lovsky, who was in love with Lorre, brought them together.

Celia Lovsky—Cäcilie Lovovsky, before her name was anglicized—was Lang's connection to the rising young actor. A pretty actress, Vienna-born and well-bred, she boasted a father who was a composer, a mother who was a cellist. She was well-known as an actress, at the Burgtheater in Vienna and for Max Reinhardt in Berlin, specializing in refined, ladylike roles.

After *Pioniere*, Lorre played an exotic gangster in Brecht and Kurt Weill's production of *Happy End* in the summer of 1929, while preparing another controversial role, the teenager Moritz Stiefel in Frank Wedekind's *Frühlings Erwachen* (*Spring's Awakening*). This play about father-son strife focused on the teenager's shame at his sexual awakening, his moral conflicts and eventual suicide. It was the film version of this play, in 1929, that was to provide Lorre with his screen debut.

Lang valued the work of Cesare Lombroso, who pioneered the theory of the "criminal type" and used phrenology to "prove" antisocial tendencies by measuring face shapes and the bumps on people's heads. Lombroso's *Atlas of the Criminal Classes* presented the classic murderer as a hulking beast with big shoulders and furry eyebrows. A maxim of Lombroso's—"There are no criminals, only crimes"—was cited by Lang more than once in interviews as the philosophical kernel of *M*.

Yet when Celia Lovsky brought Lang and producer Seymour Nebenzahl to a dress rehearsal of *Frühlings Erwachen*, they saw an actor of hunched size and tiny shoulders, the opposite of Lombroso's type. Lorre's size was, however, in contrast to his emotional intensity. The actor took people by surprise, on and off the stage. His every move was feverish. Like a caged snake, he coiled and uncoiled ceaselessly, throwing off nervous energy.

Many years later, in 1963, Lang would say in an interview that with *M*, "I started to become interested in human beings. I wanted to make a psycho-logical film." With this film, the acknowledged master of scope and spectacle needed something elemental—not thousands of extras, but one man who could hold a mirror up to humanity and reveal the torments of the inner soul.

Lang and Nebenzahl went backstage after the rehearsal and met with Lorre. They told him the script for Lang's next project was still being prepared, but the leading role loomed as available. As to the subject matter, the director felt obliged to act secretively. He could only tell Lorre this: the film would be about an unforgivable crime.

The actor had a nodding acquaintance with the famous director, having crossed paths with Lang at restaurants that were hangouts for Berlin's Viennese colony. But Lorre was noncommittal at first, even skeptical. "It never occurred to me that my puss could be photographed," Lorre told Lang.

His aloofness made Lang all the more certain of him. On the spot, Lang said later, he promised Lorre the part, on the condition that Lorre would vow not to accept any other screen offers in the meantime. Lorre agreed, according to the director. But this was likely another exaggeration by Lang: Lorre would appear in one other film besides *Frühlings Erwachen* in 1929—further deflating the director's claim to have "discovered" him.*

Lang concentrated on the scenario, while Lorre maintained his busy momentum on the stage—a role in a timely play by Karl Kraus, which failed; followed, in early December of 1930, by another Volksbühne production, a part in Valentin Kataev's five-character *Die Quadratur des Kreises (Squaring the Circle)*. Lotte Lenya was also in the cast of this love story, a satire amid a Russian housing shortage, in which Lorre played a Communist youth.

Lorre was performing nightly in *Die Quadratur* while rehearsing with Bertolt Brecht during the day for a forthcoming presentation of Brecht's *Mann ist Mann (Man is Man)*, when Lang kept a second appointment with the actor, now with script in hand. Principal photography was scheduled to begin in just a few weeks. History does not record Peter Lorre's reaction to the news that he would be playing a murderer of little girls, but one feels certain that the actor issued one of his hesitant smiles.

The director offered, on various occasions, different versions of the inspiration for *M*. He sometimes denied that a certain real-life case had shaped or influenced him; other times he admitted that, why, of course—that very case had not only influenced the scenario but dictated some of the storyline's defining moments.

Lang and Thea von Harbou had begun the script with the vague intention of focusing on an antisocial villain, a "writer of poison letters." It is conceivable that the setting of the story, initially, was Vienna, although the actual setting of the finished script would be obscured—so that the events could be taking place anywhere. A German would recognize it distinctly as Berlin, but like *Dr. Mabuse*, the film of *M* would have a universality that accrued to its advantage, addressing moviegoers of every origin.

One day ("I don't know what made me do it ... I said, 'Wait a moment ... ' ") Lang was hit by a lightning-bolt idea—as if he were once again glimpsing the Manhattan skyline for the first time, or dreaming of rocket ships in a sleeping car. The director must have been perusing the newspaper as usual when, not for the first time, his eyes fastened on recent reports of the exploits of mass killer Peter Kürten, whose dirty deeds in the Düsseldorf vicinity had led the press to dub him the Monster of Düsseldorf.

Kürten's name resounded throughout Germany in 1930. Lurid daily headlines catalogued Kürten's crimes, offered interviews with eyewitnesses, trumpeted new theories from police. The story developed dramatically, leading to his arrest that May. Though Kürten killed both adults and children, one of his final victims would figure into *M*; in newspaper articles, this victim was shown to be an eight-year-old girl, who was slain behind a church, her body covered with knife wounds, doused with petrol and burned.

---

*The film version of *Frühlings Erwachen* was produced and directed by Nero-Film partner Richard Oswald. Lorre also appeared in *Der weisse Teufel (The White Devil)*, filmed before *M*, in 1929.

One of the first times Lang formally reminisced about the genesis of *M* was in response to a questionnaire, sent to him by a Princeton University scholar, which he filled out in March of 1948. Lang admitted that although Germany was suffering a wave of "unconnected sex crimes and mass murders" around this time, the Monster of Düsseldorf was the criminal who most grabbed his attention while he was developing the script. (Thea von Harbou, interestingly, goes unmentioned in this account.)

Lang remembered noticing a remarkable item in the *Berliner Tageblatt*. This particular report described how the underworld organization of Düsseldorf, upset that their "legitimate" criminal activities had been disrupted because of the intensive police investigation, had taken it upon themselves to help stalk and arrest the killer. A beggars' organization had assisted the underworld group.

This twist was not all that unique, however; it had manifested itself on the stage in Brecht and Kurt Weill's 1928 *Dreigroschenoper (The Threepenny Opera)*, which went on to be filmed all but contemporaneously with *M* by G. W. Pabst, for producer Seymour Nebenzahl and Nero-Film. Members of the Düsseldorf underworld may not have attended Brecht and Weill's celebrated ballad-opera; Fritz Lang and Thea von Harbou most certainly did.

The *M* script was revised and completed with Peter Kürten in mind. The original poison-pen concept was salvaged and survives in the film in diminished form, with Hans Beckert, the killer, writing anonymous boasting letters to the press and police. Not only did Lang and von Harbou draw on the rash of daily newspaper articles about Kürten, but the director maintained regular contact with the police headquarters on Alexanderplatz and was permitted access "to the communications and secret publications" of Berlin's force—which enabled him "to document exactly the police procedure used to capture such a criminal." Von Harbou's secretary Hilde Guttmann confirmed that the director and his wife not only visited Alexanderplatz but traveled to London, where they consulted and compared notes with Scotland Yard. They also toured prisons and lunatic asylums to observe and interview sex offenders.

The news items, the underworld angle, the access to police files, the procedural authenticity—all this contributed to the script's transformation into "a synthesis of facts," in Lang's words. For it was growing increasingly important to Fritz Lang that his scripts were fundamentally factual and verified by eyewitness testimony, police documents, and newspaper clippings; in his eyes, it gave his work a claim to respectability. (How ironic, then, that in the case of some of his best films, such as *M*, the factual underpinnings do not matter—indeed, seem almost irrelevant—to an appreciation of the film.)

One source of Lang's who went unacknowledged in later interviews was a journalist named Egon Jacobson, who had compiled a detailed report about the underworld quest for the Düsseldorf murderer in Berlin's tabloid *B. Z. am Mittag*. Jacobson was mentioned prominently in the original publicity and advertising for *M*; his name was even etched on the screen, acknowledging articles of his which derailed the poison-pen scenario and sent the script flying off in a new direction.*

---

*Also, according to Friedemann Beyer's book *Peter Lorre*, a special edition of *Kriminal-Magazin*—

There were in fact three other names, including editor Paul Falkenburg, cited for assisting with script suggestions. But the actual scenario was officially credited to Thea von Harbou alone. Once again, significantly, Fritz Lang's name was missing.

The director rarely bad-mouthed von Harbou directly. But he proved clever at undercutting her on occasion, as when he left her out of the Princeton questionnaire—and, too, when _Films in Review_, in 1954—shortly after von Harbou's death—asked him about _M_. " 'I took no credit for it,' he [Lang] said in an odd tone," writer Henry Hart reported. "I was surprised to see him bow his head. 'The script credit went to my wife,' he said softly, and he added, with ever so slight a break in his voice, 'She went over to the Nazis.' "

No doubt the director worked "very closely" on the script, as he insisted on occasion—especially on "some of the speeches of the policemen and the underworld figures." Citing an example, Lang recalled one of his specific contributions. A Volksbühne actor, Hans Peppler, had been cast as Schränker, the ringleader of the Berlin underworld. Peppler, a character actor who could credibly evoke the criminal type, died in December of 1930 at age forty-one. Filming had not yet begun, and the role had to be recast. When Gustaf Gründgens, already famous as a stage director but an unknown quantity on the screen (he later became closely linked with the Nazi regime), was selected to succeed Peppler, Lang and von Harbou hastened to revise the dialogue to reflect Gründgens's dapper sophistication.* Schränker became more of an "international type," under Lang's prodding, as compared to the common criminal incarnated in an earlier script draft. "Only one sentence was necessary to distinguish him from the other criminal types," remembered the director in one interview. "The sentence that came to me and which I added to the original dialogue was 'The best man between Berlin and Frisco.' "

"Gründgens only had one big scene, where the other characters had the most lines, and he was only required to put in a word at the end," wrote Curt Riess. "But, as a cold-blooded, stony-faced gangster boss, in his stiff-brimmed hat, black gloves, and black leather coat, he was breathtaking, frightening—and unforgettable."

Lang could provide such expert lines and vignettes, but if he had ever functioned as a solo writer—from beginning to end of a scenario—he did so no longer. The director was by nature more editor than writer, and his contribution to _M_ and all subsequent films often had as much to do with what he chose to discard as what he decided to put in.

Although, for distribution purposes, Peter Lorre dubbed his lines in French and English as well as German, the lead character of _M_ actually has scant dialogue until the "kangaroo-court" scene. For long, tense stretches, the only audible sound is that of Hans Beckert's heavy breathing. In this director's first

---

the kind of magazine Lang followed attentively—devoted approximately thirty pages to what was known of the ongoing Peter Kürten investigation in early 1930. "It was as though one was reading the synopsis of the film with the scenes and details precise," observed Georges Sturm.

*Gründgens was well-known as a stage actor, as well as director, and later would lend his prestige to Nazi stage and screen productions. Hungarian director István Szabó's 1981 Oscar-winning Best Foreign Film _Mephisto_, based on a Klaus Mann novel, is all about Gründgens and his Faustian pact with the Third Reich.

talking picture, the dialogue would be minimized and the sound strategically muffled. It was a style Lang continued for many years after sound came in, in this way stubbornly remaining a director of silent pictures even after he proved capable of bridging the transition.

When actor Theo Lingen, who visited Lang at his home in Dahlem during the preproduction phase of *M*, espied the script, he was nonetheless struck by its "enormous bulk . . . he had never seen a script of such thickness." The script, for Lang, was more than the amount of dialogue he—or anyone else— set down on the page. The pages were always crowded with his infinitely changing notations: lighting and camera arrows, actor's diagrams, set decoration, reminders for editing.

Thea von Harbou's secretary was likewise amazed at the cumulative detail. "The thoroughness of Fritz Lang and his wife can hardly be described," Hilde Guttmann said. "I saw many other film manuscripts, but never one which could compare with the manuscript for *M*. Two typewriter ribbons were stuck together to give us three colors: one black and red, and the other blue. The camerawork and the action were typed in black, the dialogue blue, and the sound, where synchronized, was typed in red. No rubbing out was permitted; even if it was dealt with [with] the greatest skill, Fritz Lang and his wife spotted it immediately and the whole page had to be done again."

That is the script Fritz Lang "wrote." The camerawork and action, down to even the most trivial movements, were described to such an extent that Hilde Guttmann could not help wondering, was there anything left for the actors to do? Or for anyone besides the director?

With portly Otto Wernicke as Police Chief Inspector Lohmann, the major casting was completed. Peter Lorre, Theo Lingen, and Wernicke, who had a reputation as an "actor of the people," were all raided from the Volksbühne.

Lohmann was based on the famous Commissioner Genath, Berlin's "star detective," who scored his biggest coups through the relaxed questioning of murder suspects during extended, gemütliche coffee-and-cake sessions. (His brother was Ufa makeup artist Otto Genath.) The "star detective" had entered the Peter Kürten case toward the end, and some of the character detail was faithful to his legend. Wernicke had the same build: part muscle, part fat. In one scene, exhausted by the search, Lohmann sits at his desk; the camera shifts to reveal that he is soaking his feet in a bucket, as Genath was known to do.

The easygoing Fritz Arno Wagner, by now Lang's "right-hand man" (in Lotte Eisner's words), was enlisted once again as cameraman. Wagner would be asked to perform magical feats with exteriors, low lighting, and virtual darkness. Otto Hunte had finally washed his hands of Lang, and Emil Hasler took over with Karl Vollbrecht. (A journeyman assistant to Hunte and Walter Reimann, Hasler had proved himself with his moon craters on *Die Frau im Mond* and, independent of Lang, had helped craft memorable sets for *Der blaue Engel*, or *The Blue Angel*.) Since the film did not have the luxury of Ufa support, the director who had taken over a year to shoot *Metropolis* now faced a schedule of roughly six weeks, from January to March 1931. An unused zeppelin hangar at Staaken was leased for the scene where the beggar organization corners the murderer, and a Schnapps factory was used for the kangaroo-court climax. These limitations proved a strength for Hasler and Vollbrecht: the wanton grime, eerie emptiness, and run-down conditions became central to the film's ambience.

The original title was intended to be *Mörder unter uns* (*Murderers Among Us*). The director decided to change it during filming, influenced by a striking image: one of the beggars outlines an M in chalk on the palm of his hand and transfers it to the shoulder of Hans Beckert, making it easy for his pursuers to identify and stalk him.

There was another reason for the title change, according to the director. Lang said in interviews that when he went to make arrangements for the Staaken hangar, he was treated coldly and refused space. The place was not available for a film with a title such as *Mörder unter uns*, the caretaker insisted. "Without realizing it," recalled the director, "I had grabbed him by his shirt— 'Why shouldn't I make this film?' And all of a sudden I saw that there, on his lapel, was the Party insignia with the swastika."

The pin on the man's collar identified the caretaker as a member of Hitler's National Socialist German Workers' Party, and he was mistakenly convinced that the title referred to his beloved Nazis. Lang had to appease the man by reassuring him that the title referred simply to a sole, demented child murderer. It's an anecdote that has been swallowed whole by many Lang enthusiasts, as well as by no less a personage than Siegfried Kracauer. Although it requires a certain suspension of disbelief (could a mere title be so easily mistaken?), it made a good tale and provided an early point in chronology for Lang to polish his political credentials.

Lang told another publicity-wise story about the kangaroo-court scene, for which there also was his word only. Some of the members of the jury and some of the spectator extras, Lang claimed, were actually real-life members of the Berlin underworld, who were fugitives from police. The director maintained that he had made it his business to seek out these types and therefore was able to recruit at least twelve to fourteen criminal acquaintances. Their photos, Lang knew, were already on file with the police, so why shouldn't they agree to flaunt themselves in a motion picture?

As Lang told it, however, the police got wind of the gimmick and laid plans to raid the film set at the crucial moment. The director, who prided himself on his relations with authorities, argued with the police that he badly needed his true-life extras, so they agreed to postpone their raid until a certain precise hour, when the scene would be finished. Then, in the service of art, Lang deceived the police. "We worked faster than usual that day," said the director. "When the police came, everything was packed up and my 'actors' had two hours' head start."

Few outsiders were privileged to visit the set as M launched into production. Lotte Eisner was one, an observer for the first time on a Fritz Lang film. Having studied archaeology (she had written her doctorate on Greek vases), Eisner had become a stringer for *Die literarische Welt* and a freelance interviewer for *Berliner Tageblatt*. Initially disdainful of the motion picture medium, she had scorned Lang's version of *Die Nibelungen* when she first saw it.

"I didn't yet think of film as an art form. I felt it was something for the lower orders." When Eisner fell in love with movies, however, she became, like a religious convert, one of the most devout. Now, since 1927, she had been working for the prestigious *Film-Kurier*, whose approving coverage of any new production was considered essential to its chances of box-office success.

Although Eisner became more of a worshiper than a chronicler, she was also insightful about Lang from the beginning. She diagnosed him as a "complex character," egotistical, insensitive, and "a show-off," but beneath it all, "shy and unsure of himself."

There would be little other reportage in advance about this landmark film. Although Nero-Film did not command the publicity apparatus of Ufa, that limitation proved another strength. An aura of mystery suited this project, with its misleading working title. Lang's new "find," Peter Lorre, was permitted few interviews, and warned to divulge nothing of the provocative story line, even to his friend, the inquisitive newspaperman Curt Riess. "I swore not to! If I tell you anything, I'll be kicked out of the film," the actor told Riess.

Lorre proved reluctant to give up his niche in the theater and commuted to and from Staaken, trying to keep up with performances of *Die Quadratur des Kreises* as well as rehearsals for *Mann ist Mann* (which would shut down, as it happened, after a couple of performances). At night, therefore, the actor found himself performing in a farce, while during the day he was obliged to plumb the depths of his darkest impulses.

Lang grew to admire and genuinely like Lorre—an unusual empathy for him where his leading men were concerned. Later, in Hollywood, Lang would be mystified by Lorre's ambivalent attitude toward him; the director never seemed to register how badly he treated people on the set, and his selective memory sentimentalized relationships.

He and Lorre had a curious ritual on the set of *M*. Everyone steeped in the theater knew of the old custom in which well-wishers spit over the shoulder of an actor three times, often uttering the words "toi-toi-toi"—to which any reply was strictly forbidden by superstition. Max Reinhardt was one of the stage directors said to employ this ritual for good luck on opening nights. Now Fritz Lang, in deference to Lorre's love of theater, adopted this ritual—spitting on his star's back before major scenes.

The spitting was not the worst of it. Lang bore down on Lorre during the filming. Pushed to the limit, the actor grew weary of Lang's demands, and finally, one day, pleaded physical exhaustion to get out of coming to the set. Crowd cutaways for the kangaroo-court scene were scheduled that day, and Lorre's presence did not really seem necessary. But the director threatened Lorre with an injunction, and the film's star was forced to show up and stand around, simmering with rage.

Cameraman Fritz Arno Wagner told German film historian Gero Gandert that in the kangaroo-court scene Lorre was tossed down a flight of stairs ten or twelve times, at Lang's insistence, until the actor was reduced to pleading for mercy. This might have been the payoff for trying to escape Fritz Lang's dominion. Lorre's genuine misery was evidenced by the bruises on his body. Producer-director Gottfried Reinhardt, a longtime friend of Lorre's, said in an interview, "Fritz Lang was a sadist, a bona-fide sadist, and Lorre could have killed him. He made him suffer all through *M*."

It is hard to say what the actor's performance would have been like without the grueling treatment. Some of the well-known actors in Fritz Lang films (Henry Fonda, among them) insisted that their performances would have been precisely the same—or even better—without Lang's brutalism. But there can be no doubt that Peter Lorre was catapulted to international fame by this role, which forever after defined him as a murderous sociopath in many filmgoers' minds.

Writhing under Lang's direction, Lorre developed a performance as skin-crawling as a clammy sheen of sweat. The actor's intense empathy with the character brought out all the uneasy human insight of the script, making Hans Beckert more real and pitiable than his victims. The actor's performance reached an apotheosis in the unforgettable scene in which he defended himself before the court of lowlife:

"I can't help myself! I haven't any control over this evil thing that's inside me—the fire, the voices, the torment!

"Always . . . always, there's this evil force inside me . . . It's there all the time, driving me out to wander through the streets . . . following me . . . silently, but I can feel it there . . . It's me, pursuing myself . . ."

Beckert falls to his knees, sobbing. "Who knows what it's like to be me?"

This was the latent theme of many Fritz Lang films—the uncontrollable beast that forever lurks within the heart of man—in its clearest and most poignant articulation. Ironically, it was Thea von Harbou, the emerging Nazi, who wrote such a compassionate, pinpointed speech. The director took no credit. Lang confirmed this fact freely, publicly in interviews and privately in letters, declaring for the record to Lotte Eisner, "Every word is hers and not one syllable is from me. Amen!"

The job was never quite completed for the perfectionist director. "When Lang finished working," observed cameraman Erwin Hillier, whose first important job was as an assistant to Fritz Arno Wagner on *M*, "he was always going through his script, checking things over. I don't think he ever relaxed. There was too much at stake. Being the outstanding director of the time, he knew the public expected something special from him. There was no holiday on the picture, ever. Just constant hard work."

When the filming was over, the editing got the same treatment, but in this case Lang had to meet a hasty post-production schedule, for Seymour Nebenzahl had slated the Berlin premiere for May of 1931.

Lang, with his dislike of music, ruled out any conventional soundtrack. The only music would be the "Hall of the Mountain King" theme from Edvard Grieg's *Peer Gynt*, as whistled recurrently by the killer. Peter Lorre tried the whistling but Lang wasn't satisfied. Von Harbou gave it a try; so did editor Paul Falkenberg. Nothing pleased the director—until, surprise of surprises, he tried it himself. His whistling suited perfectly, giving the protagonist of *M* an additional personal flavor. "I am a musical moron who can't carry a tune but I decided to dub the whistling myself," Lang said in one interview. "It was off key and turned out to be just right since the murderer himself is off balance mentally."

It is a curious sidelight of film history that, while Lang's subsequent film, *Das Testament des Dr. Mabuse*, would run afoul of German censors, the far more condemnatory *M* passed the Filmprüfstelle, or censor board, unscathed. Although the Filmprüfstelle was politically conservative, the Nazis were not yet fully in charge in 1931. Lang recalled that he and von Harbou worried and waited for two hours while the board debated *M's* merits, feeling "like schoolboys who have done some homework and are waiting for a good grade or a lousy grade."

Lang turned the experience into another of his self-congratulatory anecdotes. When the censorship officials finally appeared, according to Lang, they announced, "Mr. and Mrs. Lang, this film shows everything which we are opposed to showing in a picture, but it is done with such honesty and integrity that we don't want to make one cut."

It was a motion picture that might, actually, have moved the stone hearts of censors. A film from 1931 whose power and originality seem startling and fresh today—a film that has not dated—*M* evidences not only the most advanced command of camera, lighting, and editing technique, but philosophically probes into the depths of sin and criminality, hate and redemption. It contains what must be ranked, still, as one of the ten greatest performances in the history of cinema. Imagine all this, and one begins to imagine *M*.

Lang's direction was never more fluid. The film is intricately constructed of inert close-ups (maps, official documents, the beloved array of clocks and stopwatches); clever cross-cutting; long, orchestrated setups as well as brisk vignettes. It is the chain-linking of images that gives such force to the masterful scene in which the director depicts the murder of a trusting little girl. A mother, in quick, silent, ominous cuts, calls out her child's name. The audience is shown an empty flight of stairs, a yard at twilight, an abandoned table setting. A child's ball rolls to a dead stop in the grass. Then comes the final, arresting shot—a small balloon (which the audience knows to have been purchased earlier by the molester) tangled on telephone wires.

Sound is ingeniously limited. The strategy of cutting away from dialogue to a literal symbol for what was happening in the story was a technique that seemed at once archaic and modern. Working with dialogue, especially in problematic group scenes, for the first time, the director acted decisively. The method of having the actors thrust their faces into extreme close-up and speak directly to the camera lens had been utilized in previous Fritz Lang films. In *M*, it was employed to a heightened, almost Brechtian effect.

The director's camera stalks unrelentingly. The suspense is breathless. Killer is juxtaposed with victim, police with criminals, until there are no distinctions, and the audience is roped into sympathy with "this monster who doesn't deserve to live."

Parts of the film are fablelike. There is a wishful reverence for smart technology and noble justice. The underworld network of beggars and criminals is almost Runyonesque. Other parts of the film are so grimly realistic as to be nearly unbearable.

It was by acclamation his greatest achievement yet. Fritz Lang had done it without the backing of almighty Ufa. And, in Germany in 1931, he was without peer in Germany.

One appreciative viewer was the soon-to-be master propagandist of the Third Reich, Joseph Goebbels. Having seen *M* with his wife Magda shortly after its gala premiere, Goebbels made a notation in his diary of Thursday, May 21, 1931: "Fantastic! Against humanitarian soppiness. For the death penalty. Well made. Lang will be our director one day."

Goebbels had arrived in Berlin—"the monster city of stone and asphalt," in his words—one cold winter evening in 1926, alone and afraid, carrying one shabby suitcase and limping from a club foot. His papers, signed by Adolf Hitler, appointed him the Gauleiter of Berlin's virtually nonexistent National sozialistische deutsche Arbeiter Partei (NSDAP), the National Socialist German Workers' Party. Goebbels, in the intervening five years, had built the local Nazi branch, with its program of rant, hatred, assault, and bloodshed, into a fearsome bulwark of the organization.

How cozy was Lang with Goebbels and the rising Nazi Party? This is a question that has haunted Langians, and which hangs over Fritz Lang's life story like the bloated shadow of a zeppelin. Evidence lingers on either side of the issue, and the many people who hated Lang needed little proof to believe the worst.

According to Gottfried Reinhardt and Harold Nebenzal*—the son of Seymour Nebenzahl—a Nazi banner was first raised over Lang's house in Berlin in the early 1930s. The gesture may have been Thea von Harbou's, yet both Reinhardt and Nebenzal later insisted that Lang was lax in tolerating the Nazis and flirted with Party approval.

Reinhardt swore that one day in the mid-1930s, by which time they were all living in Hollywood, Peter Lorre ("who loathed Fritz Lang") showed him a photograph. "I'll never forget it," said Reinhardt. The photograph showed Lang, Goebbels, and von Harbou together, smiling for the camera—"the big bluffer in the middle, flanked by his Brunhild and Dr. Fafnir." Just a publicity tableau for a gala premiere, or something more sinister?

This much is clear: By 1931, Goebbels had done his job well, and the Nazis were a bully force to be reckoned with in Berlin. Lang, who had been sleepwalking politically for most of the 1920s, couldn't help but notice the fresh converts springing up around him. Rudolf Klein-Rogge was an early NSDAP partisan, and presently Thea von Harbou began to tilt in that direction.

Lang's wife had always been a conservative nationalist, while at the same time she demonstrated progressive tendencies; she was an early, outspoken advocate of legalized abortion in Germany, an activist for reform in sex-discrimination legislation, a proponent of equal rights for women. Throughout the 1920s she worked tirelessly on behalf of these causes, behaving in some ways as the very opposite of an extreme right-winger.

Now Thea von Harbou, according to people who knew her, grew infected

---

*A U.S. citizen in the first instance, Seymour Nebenzahl renounced Germany and changed the spelling of his last name to the Americanized "Nebenzal" after the family emigrated to the United States. His son, a first-rate film producer (*Gabriela*) and novelist (*Café Berlin*), is Harold Nebenzal.

by the Nazi vision. The fatherland's defeat in World War I was a trump note in NSDAP propaganda. America's cultural invasion of Germany, especially in the motion picture field, was also a bothersome issue raised by the nationalists. Von Harbou admired the Nazi pageantry and symbolism. Gradually, so gradually that, for a while, it escaped Lang's notice, his wife was swept away.

Lang did not think very long or deeply about the Nazis, not early in the game. He regarded politics as not only beneath him, but remote from his own island-world of power and privilege. He was "unpolitical," a word that a friend of his, the Berlin journalist Paul Erich Marcus (aka PEM), used in one of his books to describe those among Germany's artists and intellectuals—most of them, really—who woke up late in the day to the horror of Adolf Hitler.

Lang, according to his own point of view, thought of himself as Catholic and a German patriot—"entirely Aryan," in Gottfried Reinhardt's accusing words, "which he [Lang] only half was." In his mind Lang had set aside his family—and, naturally, along with them the Jewish background of his mother and her parents. Although, from his very arrival in Berlin, Goebbels was well-known for his anti-Semitic ravings, the fundamental threat—and evil—of the Nazis would take time to dawn on the director.

"It was not like [Siegfried] Kracauer and the others say," said Cornelius Schnauber, a fellow German who landed in the United States and became the director's close friend rather late in Lang's life. "Lang was rather indifferent [to the Nazis] and a little bit stupid."

It was no longer as easy to sleepwalk by 1931. Events would soon jar Fritz Lang awake.

The love affair with Gerda Maurus ended, probably sometime during the production of *M*—a work unique in Lang's canon for the absence of a female character of any import. How the relationship ended the director never said, though his mention of Gerda Maurus was often accompanied by a heartfelt sigh, and for her, above all, he reserved nostalgia.

"It was one of the cases where there was the most emotion in his voice," said Pierre Rissient.

"He [Lang] would talk about other actresses," said David Overbey, "sometimes with massive disdain. But her he always talked about with a kind of tenderness."

His relationships had a habit of ending before they led to awkward impasses. Lang's girlfriends, even if they were actresses, usually became frustrated by the director's dedication to work; and by his womanizing, which did not cease on anyone's behalf.

Peter Heiman, a lowly *Dramaturg* and assistant director for one of Max Reinhardt's theaters, told this story: Heiman was in an elegant Berlin bar, circa 1929–1930, sitting with a young lady he was in love with—"blond, blue eyes, very German, very good-looking." The young lady was made extremely uncomfortable by Fritz Lang, who was sitting at another table, staring at her unrelentingly. When Heiman visited the men's room, Lang took advantage of his absence to send over his calling card, formally asking if he might come to the lady's table and pay his regards. Before she could think to reply, the director had scurried over, and Heiman returned just in time to hear him ask, "May I please be allowed by Madame to introduce myself?"—as if Fritz Lang weren't instantly recognizable. Angrily, Heiman told the famous film director that his visage was well-known to him and his companion, but they were entirely uninterested in making his acquaintance. Lang, somewhat embarrassed, beat a swift retreat.*

Probably it was Gerda Maurus herself who broke off the love affair with Lang. For his part, it must be remembered, Lang was still married, and there could be no question of a divorce. Understandably, the director was reluctant to sever close ties with Thea von Harbou—no matter how Nazi-leaning— because he was bound to her by the basic and continuing needs of his profession.

He confided to some friends that he received a cherished farewell memento from Gerda Maurus—a doll-like wooden monkey, about two and a half feet tall. Lang dubbed the monkey "Peter." Where did the name come from? The director made an odd joke of it, when people asked; he had had so many girlfriends in his busy life that after a while he just chose to refer to them *all* as "Peter."

Very quickly, after Gerda Maurus's disappearance, another woman materialized in Lang's life, whose ultimate significance overshadowed that of the star of *Spione* and *Frau im Mond*. Perhaps this new woman precipitated his breakup with Maurus, as Lang sometimes hinted. There was always a whiff of mystery about this newcomer, whose name was Lily Latté.

Like Peter the monkey, she had an obscure story behind her name. Lily Latté was indeed her name in 1931 (according to Eisner, her snobbishness made her remind people of the "accent aigu" over the *e*). But Latté was her *married* name, from her second marriage. Her first married name had been Bing; her maiden name was Schaul. As if these weren't names enough, Lang had a habit of calling her Mickey, a play on "Maus" or mouse, a German term of endearment, not unlike "honey."

Lily Schaul Bing Latté was ten years younger than Fritz Lang. Born in Berlin in 1901, Latté was tall, with well-shaped legs and high cheekbones. Everyone who knew her commented on her resemblance to Marlene Dietrich—which was amusing to the director and annoyed Latté, who had known Dietrich in grammar school. In later years, as Dietrich kept dropping years off her age for publicity's sake, Latté's irritation mounted. She knew for a fact that she and the star were born in the same year.

Like Dietrich, Latté was a blonde—perhaps. That is a minor aspect of the mystery. One of her closest surviving relatives insisted that Latté was a brunette at least up through her twenties. "I remember that my parents could not believe their eyes when they saw [Lily as] a blonde [in Hollywood] in the winter 1947–1948, after the many years of separation," said Latté's first cousin, Clemens Auerbach.

---

*Some weeks later, Heiman accidentally ran into Lang during the lunch hour at Ufa's, Neubabelsberg, walking toward him across one of the spaces between stages. One of Lang's producers, accompanying the director, came up to Heiman and offered to introduce him to the director. "Before I could say anything, Lang stretched out his hand toward me to say, 'Good day. Mr. Heiman and I met before.' And we shook hands. What could one do? In other words, he behaved as properly, at the moment, as one possibly could. It shows the power of Lang's character."

Latté's father was a businessman with contracts for Berlin's lucrative sanitation business. Albert Einstein is said to have been a distant relative. More closely related was Erich Auerbach, her mother's brother. After fleeing the Nazis and ending up in America, Auerbach became a noted educator, philologist, and literary critic, whose book *Mimesis: The Representation of Reality in Western Literature* is still widely regarded as one of the twentieth century's key works of literary history and criticism.

Lily Latté grew up in an affluent neighborhod in a culturally oriented family well-positioned in Berlin society. She was well-educated, having attended a Humanistisches Gymnasium, a liberal secondary school emphasizing a classical education, not customary for young girls at the time. "A rich, spoiled young woman," is how she described her position in the 1920s, according to lawyer Marlene Hucklenbroich, who many years later handled Latté's compensation claims against the post-Nazi government of Germany.

Latté drifted into the periphery of the film business in her early twenties. What she did professionally, if anything, is murky. Some think she briefly performed set-decorating chores; others, that she flirted with journalism. Apparently she did not work at much of anything for very long before marrying a prominent Berliner, Richard Bing, in the mid-1920s, by whom she had a daughter, Susanne, born in 1927. There was also a stepdaughter from Bing's previous marriage, who, thereafter, faded from the scene. Latté's 1984 obituary in *Variety* would describe Bing as "a scientist who died of cancer in the early 1920s."

Lily was still married to Bing when she spent some time as Conrad (a.k.a. Kurt) von Molo's mistress—his last girlfriend before he left Germany traveling to India in 1927. Latté had a luxurious flat on the Kurfürstendamm where she entertained boyfriends during the daytime. "She was unusually stately, a real lady," recollected von Molo, who would eventually become an assistant editor to Fritz Lang. "I adored her."

Conrad Von Molo was closely affiliated with Lang during the brief, intense period between 1931 and 1933, figuring directly in several pivotal episodes. He worked as Lang's assistant editor on *M* and also on the eventful production that followed—the second *Mabuse*. It may have been through von Molo, in fact, that the director met Lily Latté, sometime during the making of *M*.

Von Molo was the son of Walter von Molo, renowned throughout Germany as the president of the Prussian Writers' Academy, whose membership included Hermann Hesse, Thomas Mann, Alfred Döblin, and other distinguished authors. Von Molo, while a young man in his early twenties, had met the well-known newspaper editor Theodor Wolf at his father's house in Zehlendorf, and talked his way into a modest starting position at the *Berliner Tageblatt*, one of the city's largest and most reputable dailies.

It was during this time that von Molo carried on in an affair with Lily Bing. When he developed an interest in India and decided to live there, von Molo arranged to send articles back to the newspaper, reporting on India and Gandhi's campaign of noncompliance against the British. For a couple of years in the late 1920s, in fact, von Molo lived with Gandhi at his ashram, sharing his life of abstinence and poverty.

Residing in Calcutta in 1929, von Molo saw one of the first American "talkies," *The Singing Fool,* and decided to return home to Germany and to try to forge a career for himself in this exciting new medium. Arriving back in Berlin, he made phone calls to old acquaintances; one of the first people he phoned was his ex-mistress, Lily Bing, who after the death of her husband had remarried and taken the name Latté.

The man she had married was Hans Latté, an architect and inventor who helped to spearhead the all-important Tobis sound system. Once on the periphery of film, Lily Latté now found herself pitched into the middle of the Screen world at one of its most exciting crossroads. Hans Latté was in an unusually advantageous position because the technique of talking pictures was so novel. His expertise in sound engineering was vitally important to Tobis, which provided technology and qualified personnel to all the major German film companies in the early years of sound.

"Some of the fields were separate from studio operations in those early days of sound," explained von Molo. "Whoever made a picture in the studios wanted sound, so Tobis was obliged to offer them not only the technology, but people who understood how to use it: the sound engineer, the cutter, and the cutter's assistant."

Lily Latté told Conrad von Molo that he might be able to get a starter's job in this burgeoning field, and that he should come right away and meet her husband. The very next afternoon, he came to her place in Grunewald, was introduced to Hans Latté, and accepted a spot as an assistant cutter. His physical relationship with Lily Latté was perforce over, and a friendship with Hans Latté began to blossom. "I was hired by the studio [Tobis], starting off right away as a sound cutter—to be hired out to whoever wanted to produce films there."

One of the people coming to terms with the newfangled technology was Fritz Lang, fast at work on his first sound film—*M.* Hans Latté sent von Molo to meet Germany's most auspicious director and to be interviewed for a job as one of Lang's sound-editing assistants.

Lang knew the name von Molo, of course. Although he made a point of informing the director that he wanted to make a future independent of his father—a gesture Lang admired—the young novice came with a sort of pedigree.* "It was the reason I got a job with him at the time," von Molo said. "In a way it was a little snobbishness that had to do with the name of my father. I'm quite sure, without my ever saying it. Fritz Lang never mentioned it, and he knew he mustn't, or otherwise I wouldn't be pleased."

Right away, von Molo began to work alongside the director, helping to assemble *M,* "more or less all the time . . . day and night," even staying overnight at Lang's house as the schedule warranted. The director's energy never flagged; he worked as long and hard as the editors, and von Molo learned editing from the directors as much as from Fallenberg.

---

*Conrad von Molo's twin sister was also well-known in Berlin. Trude von Molo was an actress involved in a highly publicized romance with Lang's fellow film director Kurt Bernhardt.

"I learned a lot through Fritz Lang, for instance, the 'wipe.' We had the negative of two images, and Lang had the idea of taking a razor blade and a ruler, of splicing the two things together, and then sending the negative back to the lab to be reprinted."

Thea von Harbou often stopped by the editing room. If Lang and his team of editors were working overnight, von Harbou kept them company and brought them some food from Berlin's best restaurants—or soup she had cooked herself—to keep them going.

"Thea was a wonderful person," remembered von Molo. "She was quite a unique type, a personality, who in her way knew what she wanted. A severe person, very upright and Prussian—again and again, one must say 'Prussian'—but beyond criticism. She and Lang were just like one team. It was more than just 'belonging together,' more than love, they were a real combination, and the idea was impossible that there would be a row between them. They were absolutely one entity."

Meanwhile, the rapport grew between Lang and his new assistant. It was a "real friendship," remembered von Molo. "I liked him. I admired him. He was very arrogant and not easy to have as a friend, but somehow we became quite natural friends."

When M was completed, it seemed quite natural that von Molo would continue to spend time with the director, aiding with plans for his next motion picture and enjoying some time off together. Lang and von Molo attended athletic events, and visited clubs and restaurants, often accompanied by Thea von Harbou. Lang, who prided himself on his physical toughness, had a boxing ring installed in his second home on Podbielski Allee in Dahlem, and was earnestly taking boxing lessons. He and von Molo got in the ring sometimes and sparred with each other. "Lang wasn't too athletic or a great boxer," said von Molo. "He would have liked to be, yet he was quite strong."

It was between 1931 and 1932, especially, that the Nazis solidified their creeping foothold on power. Nineteen thirty-two was fated to be the last year of the Weimar Republic. Adolf Hitler was spreading his message in rallies one hundred thousand strong. Goebbels was shipping footage of Hitler to village meetings halls and mass-mailing recordings of his inflammatory speeches. In the July 1932 elections, the NSDAP captured the largest voting bloc in the Reichstag. Communists and Nazis escalated their bloody battles in the streets, and unemployment rooted in the slump of 1929 spiraled to six million.

It was alarming how the political scene in Germany had shifted without, at first, Lang's and his assistant's taking any real notice. But now they couldn't help but heed the virtual civil war taking shape around them. The director and von Molo shook their heads, more than once, over Thea von Harbou's steady rightward drift. Von Molo was a committed Socialist, and Lang gave many the same distinct impression.

Finally, the director and his assistant decided they didn't know as much as they should about the Nazis, and one evening spotted an opportunity to witness Hitler's deviltry with their own eyes. It was one night in 1932 that Lang and von Molo went off to one of Hitler's harangues at the cavernous assembly hall in the Potsdamerstrasse. They sat through one of the future Führer's screaming, gesticulating speeches. Both had the same reaction: it was as if they had glimpsed a monster, a Mabuse personified.

"Everyone rose, at the end of the speech, so we did too," von Molo recalled. "Then came the great moment when they all shouted, 'Heil Hitler!' I just couldn't do it. And Fritz Lang didn't either. Neither he nor I lifted our arms. We stood there as though thunderstruck but nobody hit us or took notice of the fact that we didn't raise our arms. We couldn't—it was as if our arms were nailed down."

All this time, during 1931 and 1932, Lily Latté seemed omnipresent, on and off the studio premises, dropping in on von Molo to say hello, or bumping into him and Fritz Lang on the nightclub, party, and film premiere circuit.

Latté, before her death, told actor Howard Vernon that as a young woman she had attended a private party at the apartment of family friends. There, through an open door, she spotted a man with a monocle who looked at her with frank sexual interest. The host told her it was Fritz Lang, the famous film director. "At that moment," Lily Latté told Howard Vernon, "I thought, I'll get that man!" It took some time, but she would accomplish her goal.

Von Molo, for his part, was convinced that it was he who had introduced Lang and Latté, and that he quite unwittingly facilitated their love affair, which bloomed under his very nose. "It hurt me to realize it because Hans Latté had also become a friend of mine," von Molo recalled.

Now the background becomes more complicated, like one of those flashbacks-within-a-flashback that Lang favored in his silent films.

Conrad von Molo lived modestly in a three-room Berlin flat with a roommate by the name of Ayi Tendulkar. Von Molo had gotten to know Tendulkar, who was a University of Paris graduate, early in the 1920s at evening get-togethers for journalists. Tendulkar, born in India, had been entrusted by the intellectual left-wing weekly *Die Weltbühne* to write about Gandhi, nonviolence, and political events in the Far East.

A dapper, impressive-looking young man (Hans Feld remembered his "magic eyes," like those of the psychic Rahmigani, or Dr. Mabuse), Tendulkar had a degree in mathematics from the Sorbonne and had studied engineering in Berlin before getting sidetracked into journalism. He did not make much money working for *Die Weltbühne*, so he ended up staying with von Molo, after von Molo returned to Berlin, between 1931 and 1932. Von Harbou had become solicitous of von Molo by this time, so it seemed quite natural that she would stop by his flat now and then, when she happened to be in the neighborhood, just to say hello or to bring him one of her care packages.

Through von Molo, Ayi Tendulkar was therefore introduced to Fritz Lang's wife, and Thea von Harbou—whose behavior in marriage had always been decorous—fell madly in love with this unlikely man, young enough to be her son. "She had had no relationship with anyone else but Lang until the Indian arrived on the scene," confirmed von Harbou's secretary, Hilde Guttmann.

Slowly, it dawned on von Molo that Lily Latté had become Fritz Lang's mistress, and that Thea von Harbou and Tendulkar were likewise developing an intimacy. Worse, his nonviolent, left-wing friend Tendulkar (who, like von

Molo, once had lived for a spell in Gandhi's ashram), began to spout the same National Socialist nonsense as Thea von Harbou. The NSDAP had made an unlikely alliance with the Indian community in Berlin and elsewhere in Germany. The two groups were united in their hatred of the British, and the Berliner Gandhians were willing to overlook anti-Semitism and other hard-line Nazi atrocities in return for unconditional support for their Nationalist revolution at home.

Others in Berlin also noticed the signs that pointed to von Harbou's torrid affair with the young Indian journalist. Lang, as smug in personal affairs as he was in political ones, meanwhile carried on blithely with his mistress of the moment, Lily Latté, without an inkling that in his life a bomb, just lit, was about to detonate.

The first talk of a sequel to *Doktor Mabuse, der Spieler* may have been spurred by a vacation in Istanbul that Lang and Thea von Harbou took, with author Norbert Jacques in 1930.

The director always claimed that he had long resisted the idea of making another *Mabuse* film. He emphasized that it was his producer, Seymour Nebenzahl, who sweet-talked him into creating a follow-up to the 1922 bipartite success, which ended with the madman Mabuse in police hands. Another Mabuse film, Nebenzahl argued, was guaranteed to strike box-office gold.

The burgeoning rift between Lang and Thea von Harbou may have made the writing of a new, entirely original scenario problematic, and the dusting-off of a familiar property attractive. Following on the credits of the 1922 film, this *Mabuse* would be credited to Lang and von Harbou together. Some people believe the director's contribution to the scenario was more comprehensive than it had been in the earlier work, especially in view of the fact that von Harbou was secretly preoccupied with her love life.

The sequel would start with Mabuse institutionalized. Locked in a padded cell, he busies himself filling up notepads with rambling hieroglyphics. That eerie image provided the film's title: *Das Testament des Dr. Mabuse (The Last Will of Dr. Mabuse)*.

Someone in the outside world appears to be doing Mabuse's insane bidding. Some omnipotent, unseen figure has taken over his malevolent crime organization and is masterminding wanton destruction—burning and bombing attacks on railways, chemical factories, banks, croplands. This "surrogate Mabuse" turns out to be none other than Dr. Baum, Mabuse's keeper in the mental ward; while researching abnormalities in the supercriminal's brain, Baum has experienced an apparition, perceived his own reflection in Mabuse's ghost, and become possessed of his patient's evil traits.

Chief Inspector Lohmann—the same character and actor returning from M, but with a likable spin—provides counterpoint and humor. The story endows him with humanizing traits—he is fat and a snorer—but Inspector Lohmann is also an ace detective whose very name terrorizes criminals. The sequel would also introduce a predictable hero, Kent, who is tortured by the fact that his self-respecting sweetheart, Lilli, doesn't know he is a member of Mabuse's gang. Anguished by his secret, he is looking for a chance to quit the crime business.

The script would exploit incidents and trends drawn from real life—astrology and clairvoyance (voguish among Berlin's aristocracy, no less so among Nazi leaders); newsreel-like scenes of unemployment lines and urban street life; up-to-date police procedural details (to the usual point of near excess); and reportage of "authentic events," as the director termed them in a letter to author Norbert Jacques.

"Thefts of explosives and mysterious thefts of poisons from a number of pharmacies in Berlin had been noticed, and no suspects had been found," the director wrote to the *Mabuse* author, explaining how the sequel was being developed. "The threats from a deranged mind that I integrate later in the film had already been done in the sense that threatening letters from an unknown person had been received in the town of Magdeburg. All of these things I collected from newspaper clippings."

The screenplay was thus given a relevance that was thoroughly up-to-date, reflecting a Germany that writhed—even more than in 1922—in the grip of sociopolitical crisis.

The project dictated that Rudolf Klein-Rogge would be brought back to reprise his role as Dr. Mabuse. Otto Wernicke returned as Inspector Lohmann. Oskar Beregi played the insidious Dr. Baum, and Gustav Diessl and Wera Liessem portrayed the romantic couple, Kent and Lilli.

Although nobody realized it at the time, the set for *Das Testament des Dr. Mabuse* was a kind of final reunion. This was Klein-Rogge's swan song for Fritz Lang. Willy Ley and other friends soon to leave Germany for political reasons dropped by during shooting. Von Molo was again the director's helpful assistant; and when *Das Testament* went before the cameras in October of 1932, Emil Hasler and Karl Vollbrecht, who had reached such creative heights on *M*, were again made responsible for the art direction.

For the last time Lang's "right-hand man" would be Fritz Arno Wagner. In a later interview, the cameraman recalled that the pride of working on a Fritz Lang film always had to be measured against the inherent danger. "This seems exaggerated, and yet it isn't at all," said Wagner. "Of all the chief German cameramen [of Lang's], I am certainly the one who most often came within a hairbreadth of death. I filmed the most complicated scenes in mountains or in general bumpy terrain. I was persuaded by I don't know how many of my colleagues that, if they were in my place, they would have made out their will—especially for the filming of *Das Testament des Dr. Mabuse*."

The only time he felt a genuine "instant of fear," Wagner explained, was during one scene which had been elaborately prepared for one of those explosions Lang savored—a scene where a chemical factory is blown up by Mabuse's henchmen. The cameraman sat next to the director on a perch some thirty feet up in the air, waiting for everything to be ready and for the director, true to form, to ignite the explosion himself.

"Next to me was a gadget with some red buttons, connected to the factory, which was lit up by several spotlights. It was only at the instant when Lang pushed on the buttons, which was followed by an incredible explosion sending everything two hundred forty feet into space, that I realized the danger we were all in. I still get the cold sweats when I think about it."

By now, Lotte Eisner was on such good terms with the publicity-conscious director that his chauffeur-driven Mercedes was dispatched to pick her up and bring her out to a nighttime location on the outskirts of Berlin. She was present as an attentive observer during the filming of one short scene, set at night in a forest, between Inspector Lohmann and Kent. The *Film-Kurier* report she filed would be later recycled (six weeks after she fled Germany in May 1933) in a French periodical.

Hasler and Vollbrecht had created "a fantastical kind of reality, a forest of scaffolding built into the real forest," wrote Eisner. "Scaffolds bearing enormous klieg lights and gigantic rigging towers arrayed with an army of ladders and covered with scores of thousand-watt lights tower up into the sky. Lang looks lovingly up at this monster scaffolding—a pity, he says, that he can't put the structure in the film; a pity it is only a means to an end.

"Light streams through the forest; the lamps light up all around on command—700-watt and 500-watt lights. A loudspeaker is used to communicate with the lighting crew instead of a megaphone, since they are so far up above. Like giant roots in a primeval forest, or like snakes, the cables are everywhere. They wind through the grass on the moldy forest floor, as if they were a part of it—all thirty thousand meters of them.

" 'We're using 140 klieg lights—the other studios are really going to be mad,' laughs Rath, the location manager.

"The lights gleam, silvery leaves hang from the branches, the tree trunks shine, the grass glitters. Lang's painterly eye looks upon it all with delight. 'I have always wanted to film in a forest at night, lit up this way—nobody has ever done this before.'

"But the forest has not yet been filmed. It turns into Birnam Wood out of *Macbeth*. Felled trees are dragged around, masses of them walk through the forest . . . they are carried on wooden planks and then planted again at spots where Lang the creator decrees they should stand. Lang himself gathers a few branches, placing them where he needs them. Long bunches of grass are planted singly. Lang watches the work and lo, he deems it not yet good enough and things are rearranged again. Using nature's living material, his hand creates a landscape according to his will. And then he sits on Fritz Arno Wagner's camera and drives over the [camera] track, peering closely through the lens the whole time, making corrections; his eye seems to be inside the camera lens.

"Lang says sincerely, 'It's a pity that there is still a difference between the human eye and the camera; I need a few eyes on the side of my head too.'

"They rehearse and rehearse again. Time slips away hour by hour. Again and again Lang jumps up to show exactly how he wants every movement and every glance. His eye sees everything . . . he explains every change he makes. The shot is repeated over and over again. Countless times Diessl and Wernicke have to struggle through the forest, stop at a clearing and look around them, then race off with the sound of a faraway car in hot pursuit.

Diessl and Wernicke are almost out of breath and sweat is running down their faces, which are not made up. "I want you that way." Lang nods enthu-siastically . . .

Everyone is sweating, but everybody is happy. All the electricians toil away, and somewhere someone says, "We got Wernicke from the Volksbühne. Boy, do people envy him for being able to make a film with Lang." Lang and Wagner debate keenly; one after the other they climb onto the sighting seat of the camera . . .

Diessl and Wernicke struggle on through the tangled brush while two peo-ple stand next to the tracks holding heavy branches in front of the camera. Lang corrects them repeatedly: "Kids, look how you're holding the branches." But during the short breaks, between the rehearsals, while Diessl and Wernicke catch their breath with us, Lang comes over and chats and jokes, only to get stuck again in the job a few moments later.

The lights flash; the midnight shoot starts after hours of rehearsals. Still Lang doesn't get the shot over within a couple of takes. He drives down the track over and over again, stops the camera suddenly and tries again. After six attempts, Lang says that possibly a shot might have worked out.

Not all the high drama was on the set. Sometime during the production of *Das Testament*, according to sources interviewed for this book, the director came home earlier than usual and found Thea von Harbou with Ayi Tendul-kar—in his own bed. By now the director seemed just about the only person in Berlin who did not know what was going on behind his back. Discovering the truth in this manner—in the way Lisa Rosenthal had intruded on Thea von Harbou and him ten years earlier—was one amazing irony. That his wife should betray him with an Indian lover, a native from that ancient civilization that had so long engaged his imagination, was another.

"That was the end of the marriage," said editor Rudi Fehr. "There was a big scandal. Everybody heard about it."

The director threw von Harbou out—or, at least, she promptly left, taking up new quarters at Gelfertstrasse 52. Von Harbou in any event knew all about Lily Latté; plus she had known about and lived with the knowledge of all the others. At last, she had her own romance, an affair with a younger man to whom her attraction was both "sexual and maternal," according to Tendulkar's nephew Vinayak Tendulkar.

Word flashed around film industry circles in Berlin, and the news was re-peated at parties and dinner tables; many seemed to relish the director's hu-miliation. "It hurt Lang," said Vinayak Tendulkar, "because in his eyes my uncle was just a poor Indian student. The difference in age—my uncle was seventeen years younger than Thea von Harbou—was also embarassing to Lang."

Lotte Eisner wrote in her memoirs that this treachery hit the director dou-bly hard because it coincided with a low point during the production of *Das Testament*. Seymour Nebenzahl had run short of completion money. Accord-ing to Eisner, Lang then had to go hat in hand to Erich Pommer, who had returned to Ufa activity, and who quietly volunteered the necessary finishing funds "out of his own pocket."[*]

---

[*]"I never heard of that," said Harold Nebenzal, suggesting that Pommer's rescue of *Das Testa-*

For the first time, Thea von Harbou failed to turn up regularly on the set of a Fritz Lang production. Naturally, the director wouldn't discuss the devastating breakup. "He [Lang] was too proud to go into this as a topic of conversation," said Conrad von Molo.

One can only speculate whether this incident added to the texture of *Das Testament*, a story already laden with paranoia and nihilism. But it could not have been entirely coincidental that sometime during the middle of the photography the director began talking to his assistant about leaving Berlin and creating a new life for himself in Paris.

"It became natural to speak about going away and not having anything to do with the Nazis," recalled von Molo. "What I didn't know was that apparently he [Lang] had tried, without ever telling me, to get on the right side of the Nazis. I have a few reasons to believe that because of what I've heard and read afterward about things he did—or reportedly did—of which I didn't know anything personally. If I were to speak only from my own experience, I never would think and say that he ever doubted for a day what he would do. Between him and me it was made quite clear that we'd leave the country right after the film was finished."

Filming ended. Post-production began. Nineteen thirty-three dawned, a watershed year in the history of modern Germany.

Adolf Hitler became Chancellor of Germany on January 30. The dissolution of the Reichstag came on February 1. The Reichstag fire on February 27 gave Hitler the excuse to seize more widespread powers, and after the March 5 elections, when the Nazis received 44 percent of the popular vote, he assumed full dictatorial control.

Many artists and intellectuals left Berlin immediately following the Reichstag fire, which Hitler blamed on the Communists, and which the Nazis used to whip up public furor. Anxiety about the headlines could not help but filter into the editing room, where, two or three years earlier, Lang had seemed unmindful of the Nazi movement. But now he suddenly admitted finding himself "terribly interested" in the goings-on.

Seymour Nebenzahl was Jewish; so was Erich Pommer, as was widely known. ("Pure Jewish—everyone knew that," in the words of Conrad von Molo.) These two were scarcely alone. The Nazis ascribed Jewish lineage to a majority of motion picture figures, from the obscure to the most illustrious people. A Nazi Party tabulation in 1932, quoted by Helmut Heiber in his Goebbels biography, claimed Germany's motion picture distribution companies were 81 percent Jewish-run, with 41 percent of the scenarists, 45 percent of the composers, and 47 percent of the directors classified as Jewish, according to the Nazi racial arithmetic.

Lang himself rarely mentioned his mother's background; when he did, it was a circumstance he played down, or misstated, or—in the most generous interpretation—regarded as irrelevant for most of the first half of his life, until history decreed otherwise. He steadfastly referred to himself as Catholic,

---

ment, as recounted by Lotte Eisner, was perhaps another Lang anecdote concocted to reflect poorly on his father.

though, ironically, many people in Germany's film world took it for granted that the director of *Metropolis* and *M* was Jewish.

With the rise of the Nazis and their hate-filled propaganda, anti-Semites—often with more than one ax to grind—made it their duty to ferret out ancestral clues and pigeonhole people as Jewish. And Fritz Lang had already begun to be mentioned within that category. The French magazine *Ciné-monde*, for one, had referred to Lang as a Jew in its December 19, 1929, issue. "Although Jewish," reported the magazine, discussing the pros and cons of the director's latest motion picture, *Die Frau im Mond*, "Lang possesses all the qualities and faults of the Germanic race: patience, scientific application, reasonable temerity, but also grandiloquence, bombast, pride, chauvinism."

Lang would not have missed such an indiscreet item, and he would have to worry about its resonance in an increasingly Nazified Germany. There may have been similar squibs locally in Berlin. Several people interviewed for this book mentioned a rumor that they remembered circulating in Berlin early in 1933, a revelation, much bruited about in film circles, which alleged as fact what many of them already presumed—that Fritz Lang, the leading director in all of Hitler's Germany, was a Jew. "Some malicious tongue came out with the story that Mr. Lang's grandmother on one side or another was Jewish, and he fell out of favor," remembered Harold Nebenzal.

Some attributed this rumor to Thea von Harbou, Lang's estranged, Nazi-leaning wife—she who knew the family history. To whatever extent von Harbou was a Nazi, however, there is no hint of her acting spitefully toward Lang, nor any record of anti-Semitic words or deeds on her part. And the director, in any case, would not have to look far to find any number of enemies who might have enjoyed exploiting a bit of inconvenient knowledge.

Add to this situation the fact that Joseph Goebbels had begun to assume control of all Third Reich media and culture. Goebbels, whose reputation as an anti-Semite was second to none, was also "a great friend of film, who never had a home without a special room for the previewing of movies," according to Helmut Heiber's Goebbels biography. And the Nazi leader was an avowed fan of Fritz Lang's work.

Early in 1933 Goebbels had raised the stakes by calling for a wide-scale boycott of all Jewish businesses. Shortly after the Nazis took over, Goebbels commandeered control of all radio operations, introducing new guidelines and restrictions, while denouncing Jewish ownership and themes. Everyone anticipated that his next move would be aimed against the "Jewish" film industry.

But Goebbels proved more cautious about this medium for which he had such a twisted affinity. For some time after Hitler took office on January 30, "traditional German censorship [of motion pictures] continued without a break as if nothing had happened," wrote Swedish historian Gösta Werner, analyzing the fate of *Das Testament des Dr. Mabuse* in *Film Quarterly*. "It was not until six weeks later, on March 14, that the Ministerium für Volksaufklärung und Propaganda (National Ministry for Public Enlightenment and Propaganda) was set up, with Dr. Joseph Goebbels as its head."

Even then it was unclear what Goebbels would do, and how the not-yet-monolithic screen community would respond to any dictates. Lang had no real reason to suspect that he or his own films would be specifically targeted. Indeed, in mid-March of 1933, the editing of *Das Testament des Dr. Mabuse* was just entering its final stages. It was an unfortunate coincidence of history that it would become one of the first films submitted for consideration to the Third Reich's new Minister of Propaganda.

On March 21, the Ufa publication *Der Kinematograph* reported that the upcoming premiere of *Das Testament des Dr. Mabuse* had been confirmed for Friday, March 24, at the Ufa-Palast am Zoo. Two days later, March 23, *Der Kinematograph* reported that the premiere had to be delayed until government censors could pass on the film. The very next day, on March 24, *Der Kinematograph* reported that the premiere of Fritz Lang's new film had been indefinitely postponed for "technical reasons," and that a work of "national resurgence dedicated to the German people" had been substituted—*Blutendes Deutschland* (*Bleeding Germany*), a compilation film propagandizing the history of Germany since the end of World War I and the Versailles Treaty.

Lang's name was prominently displayed in a public announcement three days later, on March 27, listing film figures who had taken part in the founding of the "directors' unit" of Nationalsozialistische Betriebsorganisation (NSBO). This was part of the psuedo-union movement of National Socialist-minded workers, which was in the process of becoming the sole, Nazi-ordained union in Germany. Other listees included Carl Boese, a successful comedy director; Viktor Janson, a young director for whom Billy Wilder had written a number of scripts; and Luis Trenker, an actor and director known for his nationalistic "mountain pictures." At least twenty-six directors were listed as "zealous" members of the new National Socialist set-up.

This is the most damning scrap of evidence that Lang, hoping to stave off the moment of confrontation, cozied up to the Nazis. The director's partisans insist that his name could have been added to the list without his direct approval. It could have been published expressly as Nazi publicity. Lang rarely addressed the issue, except for an assertion in a 1962 interview that he held no "managerial position" in any type of pro-Nazi organization.

The very day after the NSBO item appeared, on March 28, Goebbels hosted a conference of luminaries of the German film industry at the Hotel Kaiserhof. People who attended the summit meeting have given differing accounts of what transpired there. Lang himself gave the impression, on more than one occasion, that Goebbels used the event to announce the censorship of *Das Testament des Dr. Mabuse*, which is patently untrue.

Fellow director Kurt Bernhardt, who detested Lang before *and* after the summit gathering, remembered bitterly that Lang was not only present, but sat alongside the new propaganda minister, lending him his prestige (Lang "never admitted being Jewish" then or any other time, Bernhardt made a point of adding). As one of the most recognizable personalities in Germany's film industry, the director may have had little option.

Goebbels, on this occasion, made some public remarks, introducing himself as an "impassioned devotee of cinematic art" and exhorting the German film industry to live up to "the power and ingenuity of the German spirit." Goebbels sought to reassure those present by declaring, "We do not want to bother cinema or put boundaries on its creators."

His speech singled out four favorite films as models to which good German filmmakers should aspire.* One was Greta Garbo's *Love*, a 1927 silent film based on *Anna Karenina*, Tolstoy as rendered by the MGM director Edmund Goulding; another was Sergei Eisenstein's *Potemkin*, the classic Russian film about a mutinous episode in the 1905 revolution; the third, *Der Rebell* (*The Rebel*), about the Tyrolean struggle for freedom against the Napoleonic occupation army, was a German film from 1932, co-directed by Luis Trenker and Kurt Bernhardt. The fourth was Fritz Lang's *Die Nibelungen*, which the Minister of Propaganda singled out for effusive praise: "Here is an epic film that is not of our time, and yet it is so modern, so contemporary, so topical, that even the stalwarts of the National Socialist movement were deeply moved."

"What a backstairs joke of film history, of world history almost!" Paul Erich Marcus wrote, years later. Eisentein, Bernhardt, even Lang—according to common knowledge—were Jewish. Edmund Goulding, an Englishman, and Luis Trenker were the only gentiles among those listed by the anti-Semitic Goebbels. It was a chilling irony, and the Jews among the crowd realized their days in Germany were numbered; many resolved then and there to flee at the first opportunity.

Following Goebbels, Adolf Engl of the Reichsverband der deutschen Lichtspieltheaterbesitzer (a national organization of theater owners) gave a speech, laying down "the hard line," according to David Stewart Hull in his book *Film in the Third Reich*. Engl called for an end to the influence wielded by the foreign-owned Tobis, non-German distributors, and the "Friedrichstrasse crowd" (a veiled reference to pioneering Jewish producers who had their offices on that street). Arnold Raether from the Ministry of Fine Arts concluded the program by telling the gloomy audience that in the future the government would issue permits only to companies and cinemas able to demonstrate conclusively their Nazi principles.

"No one at the meeting protested Goebbels's declaration because the walls of the room were lined with storm troopers," recalled Kurt Bernhardt. "If you said anything, you were dead."** With Bernhardt at the meeting was Conrad von Molo's sister Trude, who had starred in his 1931 film *Der Mann, der den Mord beging* (*The Man Who Murdered*).† "She was very beautiful," recalled Bernhardt, "and Goebbels wanted to greet her. He got up and started toward us. I asked her what to do. She said, 'Let's walk out.' Trude took my arm and we walked in the same direction as Mr. Goebbels—parallel to him—toward the exit."

According to some accounts, Goebbels took Lang aside after this conference for a few words, sotto voce. That is how Lang himself told the story sometimes, and it is conceivable that Goebbels did whisper to the monocled director that

---

*Some accounts report that he named a fifth: *Die letzte Kompagnie*, a 1930 feature directed by Kurt Bernhardt, which took place during the Napoleonic era and saluted rear-guard bravery by a Prussian troop.
**One ex-Berlin journalist liked to inform people in Hollywood, years later, that Fritz Lang attended the Goebbels conference dressed in a Nazi outfit—a widespread tidbit for which there is no confirmation.
†The screenplay for *Der Mann, der den Mord beging*, incidentally, was by Thea von Harbou.

he wanted him to come and speak to him in private about *Das Testament*—perhaps the very next day.

Lang sometimes told it the other way around. According to Curt Riess, producer Seymour Nebenzahl, anticipating the blow of censorship, had asked Lang, against his own better judgment, to have a word with Goebbels. "His producer, who happened to be Jewish, had asked him to," wrote Riess, "because one of the first things Goebbels did was ban *Das Testament des Dr. Mabuse*. The producer was sure that Lang would be able to get that ban lifted. Lang's conversation with Goebbels took a different turn."

Harold Nebenzal said in an interview that his father put a further twist on that anecdote—that it was Lang who volunteered to intercede with the new Nazi propaganda minister. According to Nebenzal, the director assured his father, "Don't worry about a thing [about *Das Testament*]. Dr. Goebbels is a personal friend of mine. He's the head of the so-called Reichsfilmkammer [Ministry of Film]. He will take care of the whole thing."

The public event was over, in any case. Thea von Harbou was also at the Kaiserhof on March 28, 1933. Fritz Lang always remembered that it was the last time he ever saw his wife.

On the following day, March 29, the German Board of Film Censors announced that *Das Testament des Dr. Mabuse* had been banned from exhibition. The only reason given was that the film posed "a threat to law and order and public safety—in accordance with a regulation to be found in the Law of Censorship," noted Gösta Werner in *Film Quarterly*.

Ironically, the film was okayed for distribution in foreign countries: in Budapest, it would be shown at the end of March; in Vienna and other German-language markets, it was presented in May.

The version that premiered in France in April was Lang's—unexpurgated—its final assembly overseen in Paris by editor Lothar Wolff, working with producer Seymour Nebenzahl. According to Harold Nebenzal, his father was an early and fervent anti-Nazi, who in the early 1930s was already warning his Jewish friends to heed the ominous threats of Goebbels and the demagogic Gauleiter Julius Streicher and liquidate their businesses. Seymour Nebenzahl was under no passport restrictions because he was not a German citizen; fearing what was about to happen under Goebbels, according to his son, the producer loaded the negative of *Das Testament* into the trunk of his Mercedes with Dutch license plates and drove it across the border.

Another event on March 29, the day after the Kaiserhof meeting: The Ufa board convened, and the largest film company in Germany signaled its capitulation to the Nazi regime by firing all Jewish employees.

Rounding out the month of March, the government made the first of a series of announcements opening its internment camps. The first would be at Dachau, near Munich: "Here, all the Communist, and where necessary, the Republican and Social Democratic Party officials who are a threat to state security will be brought together." Evidence exists that the director took early note of the alarming news: With his contacts among police and officials, Lang had no difficulty in obtaining copies of the long-range Nazi plans. One ten-page document, which is preserved among the director's papers on deposit at the University of Southern California, outlined the projected rules and regulations in the new concentration camps. Lang went through the document, dated January 8, 1934, marking up key points and underlining the sections describing the punishment that was to be duly meted out to "Jews and other people who are considered harmful to the State."

Indeed, it must have been a rude awakening, all of a sudden, for the high-powered German film director to be forced to think of himself as an ordinary human being—and a Jew.

It was either the "end of March," according to some accounts; or, more frequently, "early in April," that Goebbels and Lang sat down face-to-face at the Ministry of Propaganda on Wilhelmsplatz, across from the Chancellery and the Hotel Kaiserhof. Writing his story into the annals of posterity, it was crucial for the film director to fix the date as early as possible in 1933, to make it clear that he had faced up to the Nazis at the first opportunity.

In one version, which Lang gave to *Movie* magazine in 1962, he stated that Nazi henchmen had approached him, threatening the censorship of *Das Testament*. Cocky, perhaps with the knowledge that his trusty Browning was near to hand, he mustered a curt riposte: " 'If you think you can forbid a Fritz Lang picture in Germany, go ahead.'

"Then I was ordered to go to see Dr. Goebbels. I put on striped trousers and my cutaway jacket, stiff collar. I didn't feel very agreeable. It was in the new Ministry of Propaganda. You go down long, wide corridors, with stone flags [tiles] and so on, and your steps echo, and as you come round the corridor, there are two guys there carrying guns. It was not very agreeable. You come to another desk, a third desk, and finally to a little room and they say, 'You wait here.' So now you are perspiring a little. The door opens on a long, long office, and at the end of the office, there is Dr. Goebbels. He says, 'Come in, Mr. Lang,' and he is the most charming man that you can imagine."

Lotte Eisner's version of these momentous events related that Lang "followed a humiliating obstacle course through empty corridors and empty rooms with bodyguards screaming 'Heil Hitler' behind him, so he was almost done in when he was finally told to sit down eye to eye with the Reichspropagandaminister."

Lang, interviewed by American director William Friedkin for a film documentary that was never completed, recalled that the Ministry corridor "had great squares of cement, the walls were black—no pictures; no inscriptions. The windows were very high, [so high] that you couldn't look out of [them]. I walked and walked on these cement squares. Every step echoed constantly." Goebbels's office was big, with four or five big windows spaced along one wall, and the Minister of Propaganda, when the film director was ushered in, was sitting at his desk in his party uniform, "very, very far away."

Goebbels stood up and stretched his hands out to greet Lang.

Exchanging formalities, the propaganda minister and the famous film director settled down for a long talk. How long? Well, a very long talk, because Lang was watching the hands of a huge clock, outside one of the windows, and the clock hands moved very slowly as the afternoon went by.

Goebbels, however, was charming. Lang always made too keen a point of Goebbels's charm—the Nazi propaganda minister was "a man of unbelievable charm," the director told Joseph Addison for the July 1945 issue of *Screen Stars* magazine. He could turn on "friendliness like a faucet," he told Friedkin for his footage. Lang, on his part—as he said on more than one occasion—was perspiring with nervousness right from the outset.

According to the *Movie* version, Goebbels profusely apologized for having to ban *Das Testament.* "Look, I am terribly sorry," Lang quoted Goebbels as saying, "but we [have to] confiscate this picture. It was just the ending we didn't like." According to John Russell Taylor, who also interviewed Lang in 1962 for *Sight and Sound,* the propaganda minister "took a surprisingly sophisticated view of it [the film]. There was nothing wrong with the development, he said, only it needed a Führer to defeat Dr. Mabuse in the end and save the world order from those who would destroy it by perverting the true ideals."

This point was a relative mainstay of the Goebbels legend. According to Lang, the propaganda minister's primary—if not sole—objection to *Das Testament des Dr. Mabuse* was its inconclusive ending. The villain should not have gone insane; that was not punishment enough. He ought to have been "killed by the fury of the outraged mob."

The implication was that if Lang altered the ending, the film might yet be okayed for general release. Easy enough, theoretically—but this was a director who could not even be prevailed upon to add a layer of rocket noise to *Die Frau im Mond.* And was the ending really the only problem?

On to more important business. The propaganda minister told the director that the Führer was one of his most avid fans. The Führer had "loved" *Metropolis,* which he had seen at a low point in his career, and of course *Die Nibelungen,* too whose majesty had apparently caused the Nazi leader to break down and weep. Lang quoted Goebbels quoting Hitler: "Here is a man who will give us great Nazi films!"

Hitler, in short, wanted Lang to serve as the head of a new agency supervising motion picture production in the Third Reich. He would become the Nazi's Führer of film.

The way Lang usually told the story, it was here and now that he suddenly realized the depth of trouble he was in. From that moment on he knew that he had to flee Germany. Now the director was really sweating—he liked to stress the sweating; if it had been a scene Lang was directing, this would have been the moment for a close-up. The director perspired so heavily he felt "drenched." Goebbels did not appear to notice.

Lang's first thought was whether he might be able to escape Goebbels's presence in time to make it to the bank and withdraw some needed money. But the banks closed in the midafternoon. Lang watched as the clock neared two, then, two-thirty. Then it was "around toward three" (according to the version Lang later gave John T. McManus in *PM*), or "four" (according to Lotte Eisner). In some versions, it was even later—Goebbels talking on, clock hands moving, Lang sweating veritable rivers ("wet all over my body," as he told Friedkin).

" 'How am I going to get out of here?' I wanted to get some money from the bank. Outside, on the other side of the window, there was a huge clock, and the hands were moving slowly . . ."

Lang plunged into murky waters. Astonishingly, according to published accounts, he himself ventured to mention his Jewish ancestry. "Mr. Minister, I don't know if you know that my mother, who was born Catholic, had Jewish parents." (Even if that wasn't quite the story.)

This could be overlooked, Goebbels replied, in light of Lang's service during the Great War.

There were many hand-me-down versions of this critical portion of their afternoon-long exchange. Director Billy Wilder, quoting one, told what happened next: Goebbels "brushed aside Fritz Lang's own objection that he wasn't a 'pure Aryan'—[reassuring him that] something could be arranged." Lang included a self-complimentary remark in his telling. "We know about the 'flaw' you have," Goebbels replied, "but your qualities as a film director are so exceptional that we intend to make you the president of the Reichsfilmkammer."

The director could have become an *Ehrenarier* (honorary Aryan)—of which there were a considerable number in Germany in the arts, especially before the last alarm bells went off in 1939. Lang probably could have avoided directing any explicitly Nazi propaganda films. Goebbels was perfectly in favor of the occasional Ehrenarier—and of innocuous entertainment. The "vast majority" of the films cranked out during Nazi rule were "light and frothy entertainments set in urbane surroundings and cozy circles, places where one never sees a swastika or hears a 'Sieg Heil,'" in the words of Eric Rentschler, author of *The Ministry of Illusion: Nazi Cinema and Its Afterlife.*

But could Fritz Lang imagine himself an Ehrenarier directing light and frothy entertainments?

"Mr. Lang, we decide who is Jewish or not," Goebbels interrupted Lang's private thoughts, even more emphatically reassuring the director about his future in Hitler's Germany.

Then is when Lang truly made up his mind—to get out of there, out of that office, out of Berlin and Germany posthaste. The director tripped over his words as he tried to figure out how to deceive the Nazi propaganda minister. "I am tickled pink, Herr Minister," he replied, according to one of his interviews. ("What else could I say?") "I am somewhat dazed," he answered in others. All the while: "He [Goebbels] was very charming. I said 'yes' to everything."

The clock "moved *and* moved and *moved*," Lang told Friedkin. Those hands turned ever so slowly. The banks were all closed by now; with a sinking feeling Lang realized he would have to leave without his life savings. But still he had a major problem to confront: What to tell Goebbels?

"He stalled Goebbels, saying he would think it over and get in touch with him as soon as possible," wrote Lotte Eisner. Within "twenty-four hours," in one version.

"When I left," Lang picked up the story in one of his interviews, "it was too late. I couldn't get any money. I went home and said to my servant, 'I have to go to Paris. Prepare what will be necessary for a few days,' because from that moment on I didn't dare tell the truth to anyone. And when he wasn't watching me, I took everything a man could carry—a gold cigarette case, a gold chain, cuff links, the money I had in the house, and I said, 'Take this to the Bahnhof, and buy a ticket. I will be there soon.' "

The financial particulars had to be numerically exact—like the sum of money Detective von Wenk has in his pocket, which is guessed precisely by the mass hypnotist in *Dr. Mabuse, der Spieler*. No matter that the particulars often changed: Lang told Frederick Ott that his getaway treasure amounted to five hundred marks, a gold cigarette case, and "a few pieces of jewelry." He told Gene Fowler, Jr., he had the equivalent of $2500 stashed away in his house. He told William Friedkin it was five one-thousand-mark notes hidden away in his Japanese netsuke. John T. McManus, writing in New York's *PM*, reported the cash on hand as three thousand marks. "That would suffice," wrote McManus, "the rest could go—home, belongings, fortune—none of them seemed to matter. The only thing that mattered was getting out of that office."

Afraid of being followed, the director took care to arrive at the Bahnhof just moments before the train was to depart, at exactly 8 P.M., according to the Friedkin interview. "I looked over my shoulder," Lang said other times. "It was like being in a bad film."

This time there was no passport shuffling. Lang's travel documents were in order, he explained in interviews, because he had been making regular trips to England and France, as well as to German-language countries, for film business and premieres.

Still, trains were fraught with risk and jeopardy. Frederick Ott compared Lang's behavior on that trip to the actions of a character in a thriller by Maurice Dekobra or Graham Greene. "As the locomotive steamed out of the station," Ott narrated, "Lang slit the carpeting of his compartment with a razor blade and hid a portion of the currency; then he taped the jewelry to the pipes in the lavatory; in the dining car, now empty but for employees, he tucked a wad of bills behind a varnished box which contained the refund book." This done, Lang returned to his compartment, closed the sliding glass door, took his seat "and may have looked pensively at his reflection in the window."

Lang even remembered and noted the color of the tape he used to hide his belongings. The tape was white, he told William Friedkin.

According to actor Dan Seymour, the executor of Lang's estate after his death, his secret money was not tucked behind a refund book after all, but hidden behind a picture frame on the bathroom wall. The director told Seymour "many times" how he had had to loosen the screws with a "nail file."

According to the Friedkin interview, Lang tried first to cut a hiding place in the carpet with a razor blade, in order to conceal "a portion of the currency," only to be foiled because the carpet was glued to the floor. That is why, instead, he went to the dining room, where there was a "little glass box on the wall and in this glass box was the book of complaints." When nobody was watching, Lang took the book out, slipped in his (fluctuating) quantity of bills, and went back to the safety of his compartment.

Dan Seymour added this intriguing nugget: All the time Lang was on the train, the director was accompanied and helped by a "girlfriend." The girlfriend would never be cited in any of Lang's expansive public reminiscences;

even the servant got more conspicuous billing. But there *was* a girlfriend; and this girlfriend, of course, was Lily Latté, who "repeatedly" put herself into the story—never in front of Lang, of course, never contradicting him—when speaking to close friends and relatives. It was Lang and Lily Latté together who made a "joint precipitate departure," from Berlin to Amsterdam and from there to Paris, in the words of Latté's cousin, Clemens Auerbach.

Some people believe Lily Latté was especially alert to Hitler because she was more left-wing than Lang, even leaning toward Marxism; and that in America later on her thinking began to influence the progressive sociopolitical perspective of the director's motion picture output. Other people are astonished by this assessment, and assert that Lily Latté never uttered a political sentiment in her life.

No matter. Lily Latté was Jewish and, unlike Lang, highly conscious of her Jewishness—highly conscious, earlier than the director, of the insidious Nazi ideology. "I think Lily Latté had something to do with Lang leaving Germany [when he did]," said Cornelius Schnauber, "because she was Jewish and she was already his mistress. She told me she warned him, 'One day they will also be after you.' "

According to Dan Seymour, Lily Latté not only urged the director to leave Germany, but accompanied him partway on the train until they fell into an argument, at which point she got off and took a return train to Berlin. Then Lang, according to what he told Seymour, engaged in another one of those suspenseful border crossings—pretending to be drunk in order to walk across the line to France unchecked.

"Next morning," Lang continued in one of his interviews, "I was in Paris, and things were quiet for a bit. Then a letter came from the income tax people, saying, 'There is a slight difference in income tax for the year 1927. You need to come back as fast as possible.' I was intelligent enough by now to know what that was about, so I wrote a very polite letter, saying, 'It cannot be very important, but I will come back, but not at the time you want me to. I am just here trying to get a job which cannot be got in Germany; I will be back in eight to ten days.' Eight days later I got a letter saying that they had confiscated all my money. Then they confiscated *M* and took everything."

No mention of any special meeting with Fritz Lang is made in the published versions of Goebbels's diaries for March or April 1933, or any other time in that year—curious, given Goebbels's thoroughness and inclusiveness. Why would he leave out such a meeting?

Lang himself did not mention the Goebbels proposal publicly until 1942–1943, in the midst of World War II—nearly ten years after the fateful encounter, making the chances of rebuttal highly unlikely. Goebbels had other things on his mind by then; he would soon be dead, his ambition of a thousand-year Reich destroyed. Lang's listeners were then mostly American journalists united in their antifascist sentiment, and eager to gobble up this savory anti-Nazi morsel of history.

After Lang's death, the director's passport for the early 1930s was purchased by the Stiftung Deutsche Kinemathek in Berlin. The seller was Lily Latté, and no doubt the transaction supplied her with some vital income shortly before her own death. But might she have had an underlying motive, a subconscious desire to wreak deflating revenge on Lang's greatest legend?

Examination of Lang's passport shows no visas or exit stamps for the months of February and March 1933. Between April and July, however, the passport does contain a considerable number of visas for entry into England, Belgium, and Austria. During this same period, Lang is marked down as purchasing foreign currency repeatedly at the Weltreisebüreau on Unter den Linden in Berlin, the sum totaling 1366 Reichsmark. The travel visas and currency transactions, duly noted in his passport, indicate that the director was still in Berlin as late as the mid-summer of 1933.

The only exit visa for Lang during the June–July period which is applicable to France was made out by police headquarters in Berlin and dated June 23, 1933. It was valid for up to six months. "Up to that date [June 23, 1933]," wrote Gösta Werner in *Film Quarterly*, "Lang had therefore never left Germany [for France]."

Even after that date, according to the passport notations, Lang appears to have returned to Berlin, making additional currency transactions. In fact, the final German exit stamp does not appear until July 31, 1933, roughly three months after Lang's supposed face-off with Goebbels, the Führer-of-film proposition, and that "overnight" train to Paris.

The first public notice that Lang was relocating to Paris came in *Mein Film*, the Viennese publication to which the director maintained close ties, in its August 24, 1933, issue. *Mein Film* reported, in present-tense language, that the director had been summoned to Paris by Erich Pommer: "Fritz Lang is leaving Berlin . . ." Nero Films had gone "into liquidation," according to the article—which contains no mention of National Socialism, or the banning in Germany of *Das Testament des Dr. Mabuse*.

What really happened?

Lang didn't make stories up out of whole cloth; he exaggerated, edited, embellished. He could be struck by inspiration, or "dream something up"; but he was at his best when taking a good first-draft of a script, or the highlights of a real-life incident, and using them as a foundation for his storytelling improvements.

The storytelling in these anecdotes could betray itself, however—like "being in a bad film," as Lang put it—with the overripe scent of melodrama. Note the attention Lang paid, in every telling, to the size, number, and color of things, to the ticking clocks, to the ministry-of-fear and cloak-and-dagger trappings. Note how the Berlin episode, with its echoes of Lang's 1914 letter from Paris, came replete with servant, train schedule, and border-crossing suspense. Note how, as Georges Sturm has astutely pointed out, Goebbels's pronunciamento ("Mr. Lang, we decide who is Jewish . . .") compares with the widely quoted remark of Vienna Mayor Karl Lueger from the time when the director was a youth—it had virtual status as a proverb even then—"Wer Jude ist, bestimme ich" ("I determine who is Jewish").

Most likely the foredoomed encounter with Goebbels was actually an extended series of meetings, brief and casual and relatively congenial. Probably the one climactic meeting between the two never did take place, in exactly that way. Perhaps the meetings, whether they occurred three o'clock in the afternoon or late at night, carried on for some time after March or April 1933.*

Perhaps Lang dithered and dallied, trying to decide whether to accept Goebbels's offer, or how to get out of it gracefully. Perhaps he struggled with the question: How Jewish am I?

Lang's cameraman Fritz Arno Wagner told film historian Gero Gandert an anecdote about sitting in a limousine with the director, one day, on the way to some unnamed film location. Lang told his favorite cameraman plainly that Goebbels had offered him the dictatorship of the German film industry. And Lang asked Wagner, "Should I accept?"

Although for years the Goebbels legend was acepted wholesale by film fans and the press, one group that always regarded it skeptically were Lang's fellow refugees from Germany who wound up in America. Gottfried Reinhardt was one of several who stated in an interview, "Lang could have stayed in Germany, there's no question about it, if they hadn't found out that he was half-Jewish. He tried to stay. He was a dishonorable man, a totally cynical man. I don't think he gave a damn [about politics]."

As Lang refined his story in interviews, it annoyed the émigrés all the more. Twenty years after his death, it still inflames Germans in Germany, where Lang—for better or worse—remains central to the cultural heritage. A new generation of film historians and journalists there have investigated the Goebbels story, accusing Lang of slowness or indifference where the Third Reich was concerned, while noting the self-serving as well as political reasons he had for leaving Berlin in 1933.

In its November 26, 1990, issue, the German magazine *Der Spiegel* went to the lengths of publishing a sensationalistic article ("Ein Schlafwandler bei Goebbels") analyzing the director's 1933 passport. The article, written by editor Willi Winkler, summarized Lang's version of events, compared dates with the passport, and concluded that the director had falsified the facts.

"Lang knew exactly how, his whole life long, to style his own myth," wrote Winkler. "His biggest success was the Goebbels number. He was the only witness." The dawning came late for the "apolitical Lang." The director realized that he was "half-Jewish" and that "the Nazis might start to get serious about race politics." The German national weekly casually discounted Lang's Jewishness as the root motivation for his departure: "The real reason [he left Germany] was his hurt male pride."

In the end, even the director's closest friends and defenders grew doubtful and weary of the gussied-up story, which Lang trotted out at gatherings public and private.

"He [Lang] prepared for the [Berlin-to-Paris] trip much more than he said," admitted Pierre Rissient. "First he made sure he had a deal with Erich Pommer."

---

*One of the earliest published versions of the Führer-of-film anecdote—in 1942—states unequivocally that "it was at one of those midnight inquisitions which Mr. Goebbels delighted to conduct," in Lang's words, "that I made up my mind that the sooner I got out of Germany the better." That version, quickly discarded by the director, would not have served the train-catching climax of his story so conveniently.

Fritz Lang as a boy in turn-of-the-century Vienna. The custom of the era was to dress boys in girls' frocks. *(Courtesy of Friedrich Steinbach)*

Fritz Lang's paternal grandmother, Johanna Lang, gave the future film director his surname, a deeply rooted Catholicism, and a mystery at the heart of his lineage. *(Courtesy of Friedrich Steinbach)*

Lang's parents, Anton and Paula, led a "thoroughly bourgeois" existence. Their attire here suggests a vacation at a tourist site. *(Courtesy of Friedrich Steinbach)*

While Fritz led a cushioned life, his older brother, Adolf (right), was not as fortunate, and was treated almost as an outcast within the family. *(Courtesy of Friedrich Steinbach)*

Die Spinnen (1920), an adventure cliffhanger, was a schoolboy's recipe that nonetheless hinted at the brilliance of a budding master. *(Photofest)*

Rudolf Klein-Rogge, von Harbou's ex-husband, in his prototypical Lang role as Mabuse in *Doktor Mabuse, der Spieler* (1922). *(Photofest)*

Bernhardt Goetzke (as Death) and Lil Dagover, Lang's first major "virgin star," in *Der müde Tod* (1921), the director's first great collaboration with Thea von Harbou. *(Photofest)*

The memorable scene in
which Siegfried (Paul
Richter) slays the dragon in
the epic saga *Die
Nibelungen* (1924).
(Photofest)

The ill-destined
Kriemhild
(Margarethe Schön)
with Siegfried (Paul
Richter) in a scene
from *Die
Nibelungen.*

Lang with producer Erich Pommer aboard the S. S. *Deutschland*
heading to America for the first time: October 1924.
(Courtesy of John Pommer)

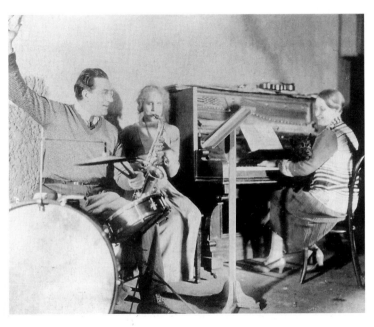

A musical break: Lang,
Helm, and Thea von
Harbou (at piano) on
the set of *Metropolis*
(1927). Von Harbou
actually played the
piano well, and occa-
sionally accompanied
the filming; Lang, by his
own admission musical-
ly ignorant, was more of
a publicity virtuoso.
(British Film Institute)

Prestigious visitors to the *Metropolis* set: (left to right) boxer Jack Dempsey and his wife, American actress Estelle Taylor; producer Erich Pommer; Thea von Harbou; and unidentified others flanking Fritz Lang. *(Courtesy of John Pommer)*

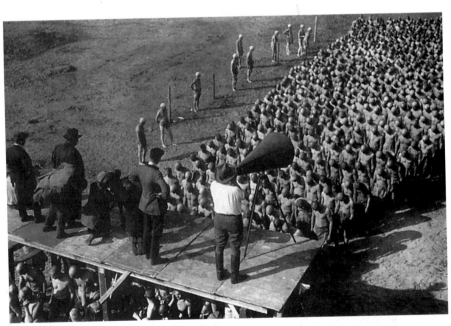

One way or another, the director got his way: Lang enslaving the bald-headed extras in the Tower of Babel scene. They were then optically multiplied to meet his arithmetic of thousands.

Lang and Karl Freund (garbed, characteristically, in white) held aloft by crew members during the floodtide of *Metropolis*.

Cameraman Gunther Rittau (in profile) and art director Erich Kettelhut at work on the *Metropolis* miniatures. *(Courtesy of the Stiftung Deutsche Kinemathek)*

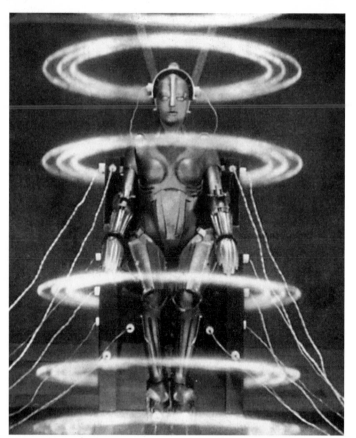

Brigitte Helm suffered through hours of painstaking photography for one of the most famous moments in Lang's cinema, when the robot-Maria is brought to life.

The futuristic *Metropolis* cityscape, inspired, according to Lang, by his first glimpse of the Manhattan skyline. The miniatures, which took months to prepare, yielded an image that lasted only a few seconds in the final film.

Lang bending Helm to his will on the set of *Metropolis* (with Gustav Frölich at left).

BELOW: The robot-Maria is burned at the stake in the film's unforgettable hellfire climax; many on the set feared for the actress's safety as the all-too-real flames licked at her body.

Gerda Maurus, the Lang "find" who starred in *Spione* (1928) and *Die Frau im Mond* (1929), with whom the director had his most passionate—and, reportedly, sado-masochistic—relationship.
(Courtesy of the Berlin Document Center)

Lang (gesturing at right) directing Gerda Maurus and others in *Frau im Mond*. In barren years, Lang would fondly remember the moment when he had the power to conjure his own moonscape. *(Photofest)*

Lang at his self-designed desk in his Berlin home—an office, Lotte Eisner noted, not unlike that of the Master of Metropolis. *(University of Southern California)*

An early 1930s snapshot of Fritz Lang and Thea von Harbou, as their marriage—and professional partnership—began to wear thin. *(Courtesy of Hilde Guttman/London Museum of Jewish Life)*

Lang at an early 1930s event—perhaps a press ball—with his *M* producer Seymour Nebenzal (in glasses) and other unidentified partygoers. *(Courtesy of Stiftung Deutsche Kinemathek)*

The film's emblematic scene: Lorre, discovering the "M" chalked on his shoulder by one of his stalkers.

Hans Beckert (Peter Lorre) with his potential child-victim in *M* (1931), Lang's first sound film and an acknowledged masterwork. Two of the director's best American crime dramas—*The Woman in the Window* (1944) and *Scarlet Street* (1945)—also began with scenes of innocent window-shopping.

A rare snapshot of Thea von Harbou with her Indian lover, Ayi Tendulkar. *(Courtesy of Hilde Guttman/London Museum of Jewish Life)*

Klein-Rogge, as Mabuse, rises from the past in the sequel *Das Testament des Dr. Mabuse* (1933). It was destined to be Lang's last film in Germany for twenty-five years. *(Photofest)*

Charles Boyer and Madeleine Ozeray in *Liliom* (1934), Lang's only French production—one of his rarest films today, and to the end one of his favorites. *(Photofest)*

Lang with Spencer Tracy, the star of *Fury* (1935). Publicity smiles, though, often belied behind-the-scenes tensions during Lang's American years.

Marlene Dietrich was one of Lang's most note-worthy amorous con-quests—or was it the other way around? It lasted briefly, and Dietrich moved on to Douglas Fairbanks, Jr.—who turned to Lang for advice on wooing her. *(Photofest)*

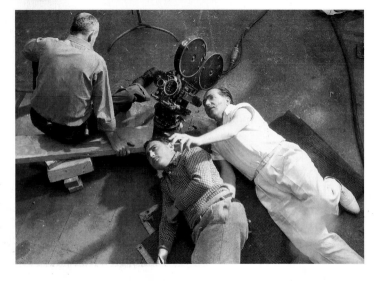

You Only Live Once (1937): Lang and cameraman Leon Shamroy work the Germanic angles. *(Photofest)*

One of Lang's first formal sittings, with monocle and scarf: MGM, Hollywood.

"There is no doubt that the meeting [between Lang and Goebbels] did take place," wrote Lotte Eisner in her memoirs, "but Lang probably slightly exaggerated the danger that he thought he was in, because he liked to style himself afterward as someone who had suffered political persecution and had been martyred by the Nazis."

"He [Lang] always told the story a little different," conceded Cornelius Schnauber. "It was a pretty much stable story, but it wasn't the whole truth. The next day [after speaking to Goebbels], he escaped, maybe, but he came back to pick up some stuff, which he never told people. The letters and the passport prove it."

"I never bought the Goebbels story," echoed David Overbey. "I have no evidence of any kind, but deep in my soul I never bought it. For one thing, I heard him tell it in greater and greater detail. There were no [major] inconsistencies ever in his telling, but by the time I heard it for the eighteen millionth time I thought it was a piece of stagecraft—the aria in the opera. The color of the carpet as he walked into Goebbels's office would change. It depended on who he was selling it to, and what audience."

March and April were certainly hectic months: the banning of *Das Testament*, Goebbels in public and private, tight train schedules, and the dissolution of the marriage between Fritz Lang and Thea von Harbou.

"It was a case of two characters growing apart," Lang said about his divorce in a published interview. "In the beginning we were interested in the same thing, German culture—books, music, movies . . . It is so often that way in the beginning. But life is fluctuant. Time passes and things change."

"Our separation was amicable," Lang said in another interview. "The only thing that divided us was National Socialism."

The divorce rocked Berlin's film scene. Even in America the news was reported in the press, giving as one of the causes of their separation the revelation that Fritz Lang was "not Aryan."

In fact, according to the court papers and corroborating interviews, it was Lang who sued for the divorce; this director, so preoccupied with the subject of guilt in his motion pictures, asked that his wife be declared the "guilty party" for not fulfilling her marital obligations. Von Harbou did not even submit a petition arguing the point.

Divorce papers were finalized on April 20, 1933. By then Lang and von Harbou were maintaining separate residences; there was not yet any indication that the director was away from Berlin or residing in Paris. Lang still listed his home at Schorlemer Allee 7a, while von Harbou was living nearby at Gelfertstrasse 52. The disputed value of their joint estate was estimated at 40,000 Reichsmarks, or close to $10,000, roughly.

The divorce papers provide some intriguing details: The date of the couple's separation is formally stated as October 1931—between the filming of *M* and *Das Testament des Dr. Mabuse*. Lang attested that his wife, "following the last marital relations, which took place over one and a half years ago, persistently refused, without reason, to fulfill her marital obligations and did, despite repeated warnings, continually decline to engage in marital relations."

The official investigation confirmed Lang's side of things. "She [von Har-

bou] admitted upon questioning that the petitioner did, after the last relations, repeatedly express the desire for relations with her, but that she
continually refused, without however giving reasons to justify this behavior."
The judgment was that her "stubborn refusal is a serious offense," and that
the Lang–von Harbou marriage ought to be dissolved.

The divorce papers itemized a number of the valuable works of art that, as
of April 29, 1933, would revert exclusively to Lang. There were eight Egon
Schiele paintings, including one landscape, one drawing, and four oils: *Auferstehung (Resurrection)*, *Die Eremiten (The Hermits)*, "*Marterln*" *(Memorials)*,
and *Tafelrunde (Company at Table)*. There were also several Oskar Laske paintings, including *Das Narrenschiff (The Ship of Fools)*, *Die Vögelpredigt (The
Sermon to the Birds)*, *Die Fischpredigt (The Sermon to the Fishes)*, and *Die
Arche Noah (Noah's Ark)*.

A separate contract providing for the artwork was drawn up on May 31,
1933, with the typewritten date later crossed out and a new date—November
27, 1933—written in by hand. It was signed by both Lang and von Harbou.
An official stamp at the top of the new first page, dated November 28, 1933,
suggests the possibility that the director may have visited Berlin as late as that
time in order to append his name.

This November 28, 1933, contract explicitly stated that objects belonging
to Lang, which were being kept by von Harbou in the apartment where she
had moved prior to divorce proceedings, were nevertheless to be regarded as
the director's exclusive property. The contract also stipulated that "conveyance
of these objects from Frau von Harbou, who has them in her possession, to
Herr Fritz Lang, has been agreed upon," but if the transfer did not take place
within the agreed-upon time, or, if she chose to place the objects into storage,
Lang was obliged to collect them within four weeks. Otherwise, von Harbou
was free to dispose of them.

There is a striking omission in the divorce papers of any mention of National Socialism; or, for that matter, of Ayi Tendulkar. Many people interviewed for this book agree with *Der Spiegel* that "hurt male pride" had as
much as anything—as much as Goebbels—to do with Fritz Lang's decision
to run away to Paris.

After Lang left, German film interests tried to salvage *Das Testament* by man-
dating the shooting schedule of some additional footage that would please
Goebbels, including flashbacks with the Inspector Lohmann character. "There
was a lot of money involved," explained Andrew Marton, the man brought in
to perform surgical editing, who was himself Jewish and who would later escape to England and join the exodus to America, where in time he became a
prominent second-unit director.

"I remember a Nazi emissary was sent—he came in uniform and stood over
my back," recalled Marton. "In the first scene I had to insert, the detective is
celebrating an anniversary of [his] retirement. He's asked to tell about his most
interesting case, and he says something like, 'There was one case, but it was
in the old days when lawlessness was rampant, and the Jews were running the
country . . .' Then Lang's picture starts.

"In order to insert the new scene, I had to tear the film open. The Nazi guy jumped on me—'I caught you! I caught you! Sabotaging the film! I caught you sabotaging—'

"I said, 'Man, just take it easy. In order to insert it, I have to open it up, don't I? There's no other way of doing it.'

"Those are the kind of guys the Nazis sent. They had no idea what film is. I inserted the flashbacks throughout the picture, but they didn't have much effect. The specific weight of the flashbacks was so flimsy, the minute one was over, you were back in Fritz Lang's vision. Like a mosquito bite, you forgot about it. You scratched it twice and you were back in the story, in the suspense. You forgot you were interrupted. Everybody who came out of the theater who was asked about those flashbacks said, 'What flashbacks?' They couldn't even remember them."

The film is studded with shoot-outs, burnings, bombings, explosions. On the purely cinematic level, *Das Testament des Dr. Mabuse* contains some of Lang's most spellbinding work, including an eerie high-speed automobile chase at the climax, with streaks of highway and ghostly tree branches whizzing starkly by.

But no matter how dazzling the film-craft, no matter how "exceptionally profitable" (in the words of Klaus Kreimeier) the film might prove in other German-language countries, the director's version could not be shown in Hitler's Third Reich. *Das Testament des Dr. Mabuse* was like a spinning tornado, with Germany at its dark vortex, and Mabuse an apocalyptic purveyor of doom. In fact, Fritz Lang's 1933 film would not receive its first public showings in Germany's theaters until after World War II, in 1951.

According to Heinrich Fraenkel and Roger Manvell in their book *Doctor Goebbels, His Life and Death*, Goebbels explained on one occasion, "I banned it [*Das Testament*] because it proves that an extremely determined group of men, whether they seriously want to or not, are perfectly capable of unhinging, no matter which State, by using violence." But that was short of calling the 1933 film, outright, an explicit anti-NSDAP parable.

Goebbels, in private, appears to have been the film's unlikely champion. When Lang went away to Paris, the propaganda minister saw no contradiction in celebrating his thirty-sixth birthday, in October of 1933, with a showing of *Das Testament* for privileged guests at his official residence. Since Goebbels styled himself a cineast, no doubt this was the "flashback-less version" denied to the German masses.

Indications are that Goebbels may have taken pains to watch *Das Testament* at least once again. Before the Reichsfilmkammer, on March 4, 1938, the Nazi propaganda minister made reference to a film he had re-viewed recently, which necessarily would continue to be banned "for political reasons." This film, historians have surmised, was probably the *Mabuse* sequel. To the conclusion of the war, wrote Helmut Heiber, "Fritz Lang and Marlene Dietrich were special favorites, and Goebbels would have put aside all racial and political objections had he been in any position to use them."

By 1938, the "political objections" would have included, uppermost, Fritz Lang's desertion of Germany in favor of the United States. By then, the director had made it clear that he would never return to the fatherland. He had been stripped of German nationality and had taken the U.S. pledge of citizenship, and he was conspicuously engaged in directing highly-touted movies in Hollywood, where he was widely reported by the press as a virulent anti-fascist opposed to Hitler's dictatorial regime.

Even so, over time Lang was spared the worst of the Nazi vilification suffered by Jewish and non-Jewish artists who chose to leave Germany. There seems to have been genuine regret in his case, as if the Nazi leaders also blamed themselves for fatally misreading the man who had directed their immortal *Die Nibelungen.* While most of Lang's films were banned outright, others—like *Siegfried,* reissued in 1933—merely had to be touched up by the Nazis.

Lang, however, was included indirectly in Fritz Hippler's 1940 pseudo-documentary *Der ewige Jude* (*The Eternal Jew*) which included scenes from *M* in its sweeping attack on "degenerate Jewish art." Hans Beckert's final monologue, inserted out of context, was presented as a Jewish confession, proving the race was incapable of controlling its base desires and unfit to live in a "moral society." One of the most memorable soliloquies in cinema, the final monologue was ironically the speech for which Fritz Lang always gave undiluted credit to his wife and collaborator Thea von Harbou, who was in fact in solid standing with the Nazis.

Thea Von Harbou and Ayi Tendulkar stayed together for several years. Ironically, when von Harbou and the native Indian she had converted to National Socialism chose to get married in Germany, sometime in the late 1930s, it had to be a secret marriage—because the state could not permit a lady of her renown to have marital relations with a dark-skinned Indian.

Very soon after her divorce from Lang, von Harbou tried directing—1934's *Hanneles Himmelfahrt* (*Hannele's Ascension*). It was not an altogether satisfactory experience, and she did not care to make a habit of it. The divorce with Lang coincided with the radical changes ushered in by sound film. "She was doubtless going through a stage which we today call a mid-life crisis," according to stage and screen director Arthur Maria Rabenalt, who worked with von Harbou on two German films in the mid-1930s.

Von Harbou remained one of Goebbels's favorites, and she turns up in his published diaries on a handful of occasions. In January of 1936, the propaganda minister made note of von Harbou's ideas for "a new anti-Bolshevist film program"—which apparently never came to pass. "A very clever woman," Goebbels noted in March of 1937, after giving the ex–Frau Lang a lift home after dinner at the French Embassy.

The last such mention of von Harbou in the published diaries falls in the summer of 1938, when Goebbels visited Emil Jannings's country house in the Salzkammergut, where a group of guests went sailing on the Wolfgangsee. Afterward, Goebbels, Werner Krauss (like Jannings, designated an "Actor of the State"), a certain "K.," and Harbou lingered, carrying on "long discussions about the cinema." Noted Goebbels: "A heated discussion. But finally everyone agrees with my point of view."

On several occasions, von Harbou acted as a liaison with Goebbels for people like Rabenalt when they aroused the government's ire. Rabenalt in a 1980 interview chronicled the fate of his third film, originally titled *Ein Kind, ein*

Hund, und ein Vagabund (A Child, a Dog, a Vagabond). After initially being approved by the *Reichsfilmkammer,* the film was seen by Hitler, who denounced it; and journalists who had made the mistake of lauding it were sorely reprimanded. When the foreign press began to celebrate the film as a cause, Goebbels summoned von Harbou to his office for advice. She told him she loved the picture and that with a little "fixing," Hitler too could accept it.

"Her attitude toward this film was very positive," said Rabenalt, "She loved the jokes in it, the satire, and the deeper meaning . . . its romantic, indeed surrealist, humor. In short, she loved what Hitler's arid National-Socialistic realism considered to be dangerous." Von Harbou suggested cuts and transpositions, helping "to conserve something of the spirit and nature of the film," remembered Rabenalt. "She decisively defended it." The once-verboten film was fixed up and released under the new title, *Vielleicht war es nur ein Traum? (Perhaps It Was Just a Dream?).*

Whether or not von Harbou was an "ardent Nazi," as Lang often insisted in interviews, cannot be said with certainty. She never stepped forward with programmatic statements in newspapers and magazines, like so many other screen personalities of the Hitler era. Her relatives insist—as von Harbou herself contended, in statements to Allied captors after World War II—that her ardor was purely patriotic.

But she did continue to be a prolific scenarist, and in the next ten years her career would not suffer. Under a regime where every film was a "state film," Thea von Harbou amassed writing credits on some twenty-six films, while giving uncredited assistance on countless others—including a handful with an indisputable Nazi stigma.

PARIS

1933
CHAPTER 10
1934

The express train from Berlin to Paris, with intermediate stops, took some sixteen hours in those days. It would be safe to presume that Lang spent some of that time thinking about what his next film would be. Already something like six months had passed since he had finished *Das Testament des Dr. Mabuse*. Ordinarily, he and Thea von Harbou would have had their next film project already plotted out. But Lang no longer had a wife, nor a scenarist devoted to his ambitions.

Perhaps the director worked a little on a scenario himself. If he had completed one, it would have been the first he accomplished on his own in over ten years. In Howard Rodman's fascinating if biographically inexact novel *Destiny Express*, which dramatizes Lang's final days in Berlin, the director is shown lingering in Germany, working on "Die Legende vom letzten Wiener Fiaker" ("The Legend of the Last Vienna Fiaker") while contemplating his flight from Hitler. (The novel's Fritz Lang also has Communist leanings, and is painfully in love with Thea von Harbou, who is having an affair with a mysterious left-wing American.)

This script, about the last fiaker driver of Vienna, was one that Fritz Lang mentioned wistfully in numerous interviews later in life. Charlotte Chandler, in the sympathetic thumbnail sketch of the director in her book *The Ultimate Seduction*, provided a concise summary of the story line: "That was the one film Fritz Lang always wanted to make. After World War I, life changed in Vienna. With the advent of the automobile, no one wanted to ride in a horse-drawn coach. On the great [Prater] avenue, the Hauptallee, the last coachman waited with his coach and horse, but no one came. He waited in vain until one day he died of a broken heart. Then his horse died of a broken heart, too.

"The coachman rose up to enter heaven, driving his coach. But when he got there, Saint Peter stopped him, saying, 'It is fine for you to come in, but you cannot bring your horse. There is a separate heaven for horses, you understand. He will be quite happy there.'

"The coachman said, 'You mean heaven is just like earth—a lot of rules. If my horse cannot stay, *I'm* not staying.'

"This caused quite a disturbance. God came to mediate. The rules were explained to the coachman, but he was adamant. Without his horse and coach, he would not stay. Then God got into the coach and said, 'You will be my coachman.'

"The coachman was very happy.

"In the last scene, the coachman drove off with God, and they vanished into the night sky filled with the Big Dipper and stars."

Lotte Eisner in her book about Lang noted that this script originated in 1933. But the only extant version of "The Legend of the Last Viennese Fiaker," which is typewritten in German, is a short treatment penned in Munich and dated October 1, 1962, when Lang, involuntarily retired from directing, was trying for one last comeback.

On publicity trips to Vienna in the 1920s, Lang had been urged by the press and city officials to feature their city in one of his films. But he never did make a film about Vienna, and his ideas for Vienna scripts—the "Last Fiaker" scenario, the turn-of-the-century musical comedy uniting Buffalo Bill and the emperor—were wishful contrivances that never got beyond their inarguably singular premises. They were like the New York City skyline as seen from a boat—only jumping-off points, not full-fledged yarns. A writer would have to fill in all the narrative components, and Lang, in 1933, was without this vital adjunct. Indeed, the director's quest for a compatible scriptwriter, someone who could identify wholeheartedly with his ideas and help him articulate the stories he wanted to film, would color the remainder of his career.

The date when Lang arrived at the Gare du Nord is impossible to know. The renowned director appears to have come and gone freely. Fifty years later, Lotte Eisner herself cast doubt on Lang's fabled spring of 1933 chronology in her memoirs: "When Fritz Lang arrived," she wrote, "I had already been in Paris for a year."

A multitude of other German film industry refugees had preceded Lang in their conviction that Nazism meant looming terror. So many had fled to Paris by May of 1933 that the Berlin correspondent for the *New York Times* filed a dispatch commenting on the subject. "So much turbulent political water has flowed by in recent weeks that a flood is about the only word to describe it," the *Times* reported. "And it has washed up the German film industry very efficiently."

A handful of Lang's former producers had already set up shop in Paris. Erich Pommer had arrived to produce films on behalf of Fox-Europa, and shortly had several projects in preparation. Joseph Somlo, behind-the-scenes on *Spione* and *Die Frau im Mond*, was ensconced there. So was Seymour Nebenzahl, who opened offices on the Champs Elysées. Hermann Millkowski had also retreated to Paris.

Hans G. Lustig, the Brno-born novelist and former cultural editor for the Berlin-based *Tempo*, was in Paris collaborating on a script for Marc Allégret. The budding screenwriter and director Billy Wilder had relocated to Paris by the spring of 1933. Eventually the list of German film industry figures hustling for a new life in France would directorial colleagues Joe May, Robert Wiene, E. A. Dupont, Richard Oswald, Berthold Viertel, Robert Siodmak, Douglas Sirk, Leontine Sagan, William Thiele, Kurt Bernhardt, and G. W. Pabst, among many others.

At the Hotel Ansonia, at 8 rue de Saigon, near the Arc de Triomphe, refugees pooled resources and bitter jokes. Peter Lorre, penniless once again, arrived in mid-1933, joining Wilder and fellow boardinghouse expatriates Oskar Homolka and Paul Lukas, screenwriter Walter Reisch, and composers Friedrich Holländer and Franz Waxman—all of them making a pit stop on the way to Hollywood.

Lorre did not speak to Lang for a long time after *M* was completed. The actor had managed to squeeze in eight additional German and Austrian films before fleeing Berlin immediately after the Reichstag fire. From Vienna, where he had gone to make *Unsichtbare Gegner (Invisible Enemies)*, Lorre had wended his way to Paris. When Ufa cabled him to urge his return, the actor reportedly cabled back: "There is not enough space in Germany for two murderers like Hitler and me."

Now Lorre was mulling various offers, while fretting about the typecasting that plagued him on the basis of *M*. The proposals were coming from all around the world, especially England and the United States, where Lang's 1931 film had made its star famous. Charles Chaplin, the gentleman tramp, had hailed Lorre publicly as one of the paramount actors in the world.

Among the flood of refugees were those who believed that Lang had lingered too long in Berlin and forever held the Goebbels fairy tale against him. It didn't help matters when Janet Flanner wrote in the April 29, 1933, *New Yorker* that his latest film, *Das Testament des Dr. Mabuse*, had been denied distribution in Germany because "though Lang is a Nazi, his backing was Jewish"—a reference to Seymour Nebenzahl.

It didn't help either that many refugees were forced to live like paupers, while Lang lived in unabashed luxury in a suite at the Hotel George V—which, in Janet Flanner's words, "blossomed like Aaron's Rod and is known as the Generalhauptquartier, or Parisian German G.H.Q." In short order the director would reassemble a small staff of servants (some believe he brought his own butler from Germany). The director of *Metropolis* and *M* was "not like the other emigrants in Paris," wrote Curt Riess. "He was, one could say, an emigrant deluxe." Resentment grew around him.

The enterprising Riess was waiting for Lang at the Hotel George V upon his arrival in Paris and he reminisced about the occasion in one of his books. "A tall, exceptionally good-looking man—the only thing that bothered me was his monocle, which made him look rather military—was sitting at the window and looking down at the street below," wrote Riess. "When I stupidly asked him what his plans were, he answered, 'I plan to buy a toothbrush! And some pajamas!'"

The toothbrush was like the slowly-moving clock hands—a detail the director remembered and retold, but with ever-shifting emphasis. One way or another, Lang mentioned the toothbrush on several occasions. In Curt Riess's telling, it was to stress the fact that he hadn't even *brought* a toothbrush. To others, like his American friend Gene Fowler, Jr., Lang made the point that he had left Berlin for Paris "with little more than his toothbrush." Either way, it was another of those fanciful details designed to suggest precipitate departure.

"As I looked at him puzzled," Riess's account went on, "he [Lang] continued, 'I am a refugee.' And he added, 'Now I am waiting for my luggage!'

"Which arrived promptly. Lilly Latté brought it, a beautiful, elegant woman, with whom he had been living for several years. In Berlin, of course. Despite her surname, she was from Berlin. She brought an enormous amount of luggage and also quite a lot of money, as I found out later."

Lang then recounted just a little of the Goebbels showdown, according to Riess, before continuing: "That was yesterday. And I knew I had to leave. I looked at my watch. If Goebbels lets me go within the next five minutes, I can make the Paris train. So I said something about having to think the whole thing over. But I didn't make it to the bank."

Not a clock, but a wristwatch. Not a girlfriend who had abandoned the train after an argument, but the indispensable Lily Latté, ever faithful, struggling with his luggage. Not a small amount of luggage, according to Curt Riess, but an "enormous amount." And Fritz Lang brought not a small cache of bills, but "quite a lot of money, as I found out later," according to Riess.

In his account Riess scoffed at the director's tendency "to dramatize things," Lang's overblown fear of immediate arrest if he lingered too long in Berlin. "He would have been arrested immediately. He arrested! He who had made *Die Nibelungen!*"

Unfortunately for later screen historians, Riess did not date this anecdote. In any event, Lang stayed at the Hotel George V only until he was able to find something more permanent. Erich Pommer was helpful in arranging a flat at 11 bis, rue Labie, near a wide boulevard in the seventeenth arrondissement.

When the daily work on *Das Testament des Dr. Mabuse* came to an end, Conrad von Molo had taken a job on another film for Ufa, *Walzerkrieg* (*Waltz Time in Vienna*); this was directed by Ludwig Berger, another well-known director of the era, born in Germany, who also happened to be Jewish. (Berger's contract would be nullified for that reason by the Ufa board at the close of production.)

But von Molo had kept in touch with Lang, stopping at his house some nights and most weekends. When Lang went to Paris, von Molo continued working at Ufa on the understanding that he would be engaged as Lang's assistant once again as soon as feasible. Von Molo could not recall the precise time frame either, in a 1993 interview, but "between us it was agreed that he [Lang] would summon me the very day that he had set up something with [Erich] Pommer."

One day Lang rang from Paris to say that he wanted von Molo to come and join him on a certain date. Von Molo could work as an assistant and editor on a film that Lang was ready to direct. Lang had already made all the travel arrangements and went over them with von Molo in his meticulous fashion, the director emphasizing that he wanted von Molo to depart on a fixed date from the Bahnhof Zoologischer Garten, where the train to France, originating from Lehrter Bahnhof, made a regular ten or fifteen-minute stop. Lang insisted he wanted von Molo to take that precise train, reciting the very hour and minute he ought to show up at the Bahnhof.

Von Molo gave the keys to his flat to a friend, packed only enough luggage so that it would appear he was going on a brief journey, and left for Bahnhof Zoo at the appointed time. "I had already stowed away my little trunk, knowing I would not be coming back to Germany, and I was carrying my winter coat, although it was spring (or summertime), because it would take up too much room in the luggage—when I heard my name called, 'Herr von Molo, Herr von Molo!'

"The housekeeper Fritz Lang had left behind, whom I knew, of course, came and said, 'Mr. Lang rang from Paris that you would be on the train and [asked] would you take the mail to him?' I said yes. As I told you, I had my winter coat with deep pockets and I stowed the letter and stuff that she gave me into the deep pockets and forgot about it."

Arriving for the first time of his life in Paris, he spotted Fritz Lang himself at the station, waiting for him. Lang stood with someone von Molo recognized but didn't know personally: Robert Liebmann. This writer, who, like Lang, had only one good eye (the other was glass), ranked as one of Germany's leading scenarists since his adaptation of *Der blaue Engel* in 1930. A former journalist and critic, Liebmann was expert at blending fantasy and realism, and in his career wrote, often in collaboration, over one hundred outstanding thrillers, musical comedies, parodies, adventure, horror, and crime films.

Liebmann, who was Jewish, also had fled Nazi Germany. He and his colleague Hans Müller had been victims of the March 29 Ufa-board purge of Jewish employees, and in fact were denied credit on the screen for their last script—the film von Molo had been working on, in fact, *Walzerkrieg*. Now Liebmann was adapting *Liliom* for Pommer and Lang.*

The first thing Lang said to von Molo, startling him, was, "Where is the money?"

"Not realizing, not being very clever myself," von Molo recalled, "I thought of the one hundred and not quite fifty marks that one was allowed to take out of Germany. That was all the money I had on me at the time. At the same time, the thought went through my head, blitz-like, have they already come down to that state of poverty?"

"Do you mean the hundred and fifty marks?" asked von Molo.

"Don't talk rot," Lang replied testily. "I mean the mail. Give me the mail."

Then it dawned on von Molo: He had risked his life to bring his director-friend money without even being apprised of the dangers. The precise amount contained in "the mail" von Molo never knew for sure, but he guessed by the size of the package that he had smuggled at least a hundred thousand Reichsmark to Lang.

"If I had been found out, or caught, it would have been my end," recalled von Molo. "That he had done that to me was just awful."

The director took von Molo to his flat, then advised him that all bets were off. Pommer, explained Lang, had refused to hire von Molo because he could still find work in Germany—because, unlike Lang, von Molo was a gentile.

---

*Liebmann was one German film refugee who never left Paris and whose fate became "unknown" after Nazi Germany occupied France in 1940. Only recently, French film historian Bernard Eisenschitz confirmed that Liebmann perished in a Nazi death camp during the war.

Von Molo regarded the news suspiciously. Not to worry, the director continued, von Molo could stay with him for the time being, "as a sort of holiday in Paris," until such time as he returned to Berlin. Von Molo, stung, never quite believed Lang's explanation. But he was alert enough to declare his refusal to holiday in Paris, or to return to Germany under any conditions.

"I don't know how many days I stayed on, but very few," recalled von Molo. "He [Lang] found a pretext that I had used too much soap in the bathroom. I was so furious I packed up and left the place and said, 'Never will I see you again!'"

Von Molo slept for two or three days on a park bench without any money in his pockets, until he chanced to meet another acquaintance from Berlin—Paul Dessau, a composer later to be closely affiliated with Brecht. Dessau took von Molo in and offered him a place to stay on and off for the next several months, until von Molo could find his professional footing and pick up steady work in Paris, which eventually led to jobs in England with Kurt Bernhardt and Alexander Korda.

Ufa's dismal financial straits, in 1927, had led the company to invite Erich Pommer back to Germany, where he was awarded his own autonomous production unit within the larger operations. Magic still surrounded Pommer's name. In 1929, he had produced one of the first all-talking pictures in Germany, *Melodie des Herzens* (*Melody of the Heart*). Then, in 1930, together with scenarists Robert Liebmann and Carl Zuckmayer, composer Friedrich Holländer, actor Emil Jannings, a young, rising star named Marlene Dietrich, and the director Josef von Sternberg, Pommer fashioned the early sound masterpiece *Der blaue Engel*, based on the Heinrich Mann novel about an elderly, upright professor who falls in love with an amoral nightclub singer.

Between 1927 and 1933, Pommer had one of the most productive phases of his career, supervising light entertainment films, love stories, musicals, and a classic of science fiction—*F.P.1 antwortet nicht* (*F.P.1. Doesn't Answer*). But the producer foresaw the end of his relationship with Ufa and for some time had been negotiating a deal with Fox to set up a European production and distribution arm. Pommer was on his way to New York in January of 1933 to finalize the deal when Hitler became Chancellor; he was on the high seas, returning to Berlin, at the time of the Reichstag fire. Arriving back in Berlin, he immediately offered Ludwig Klitzsch his resignation, which was refused. However, the day after the March 28, 1933, Kaiserhof meeting—which Pommer had skipped, although he had an invitation—Germany's best-known producer became one of the first terminated by the Ufa board.

Pommer sent his family ahead to Paris, and followed in late April. He started Fox-Europa, moving into modest offices in the *New York Herald Tribune* building. Then he leased stage space from the Studio des Reservoirs at Joinville, which was initially owned by French-Gaumont but had been purchased by Paramount in 1930.

Right away Pommer had set two properties in motion: a detective story called *On a volé un Homme* (*A Man Has Been Stolen*), and an adaptation of Ferenc Molnár's *Liliom*. Based as it was on a play that had been staged throughout Europe, *Liliom* was the better-known material. The bittersweet romantic fantasy, about a carnival barker who is given a second chance in heaven to atone for his transgressions on earth, was familiar even in America; Fox had produced an earlier screen version in 1930.*

Pommer had two directors on the string: Max Ophüls, a Viennese stage director who had turned to the screen with distinction, and the recently arrived Fritz Lang. Pommer gave the detective story to Ophüls, and chose Lang for the film that combined romance and fantasy. "In my mind, it was a double error," Ophüls is quoted as saying in the book *Spiel im Dasein*. "The reverse decision should have been made. Lang would have certainly made a remarkable detective film, and as for me, I probably would have succeeded in making a good romantic comedy."

But there is every reason to believe that Pommer gave Lang his preference, and that a working draft of the script had been completed by Liebmann by the time the director materialized in Paris. The case of *Liliom* testifies, if further testimony is needed, to the producer's superb instincts. Here, Pommer handed over material that on the surface might have seemed wildly inappropriate for the director of *Metropolis* and *M*; yet *Liliom* would prove one of the more bewitching—and Langian—films of the director's career.

Lang apparently did not know the playwright, Ferenc Molnár, personally, but he certainly knew of him: Molnár's bylined dispatches from the Eastern front had filled Vienna newspapers when Lang was hospitalized during World War I. Moreover, Lang had seen *Liliom* on the stage in the noteworthy Berlin production starring Hans Albers during the 1920s. Which came first: Lang's never-fulfilled idea for a film about the last fiaker, or the godsend of *Liliom*? Both were set in heaven; one might have compensated for the loss of the other. One might, in fact, have inspired the other.

As production geared up in the winter of 1933–1934, Pommer resorted to his old strategy where Fritz Lang was concerned: he assigned a go-between to act as the director's personal assistant, to help with local customs and cultural differences, and in general to act as buffer with the cast and crew. It was a necessary practicality for an over-extended producer but also a method of controlling Lang's anticipated excesses.

Gilbert Mandelik was another German film refugee with Jewish background, a dual citizen who happened to be fluent in French. When the Nazis assumed control of the *Film-Kurier*, operated by his stepfather, the Mandeliks retreated to Paris. (In time, Mandelik would marry the daughter of one of the executives of the short-lived Fritz-Lang-Film-GmbH, producer Joseph Somlo, and thereby forge a double connection with Lang.)

Although Lang had an affection for Paris, and spoke the language "with a fair degree of fluency," in Mandelik's words, in other respects the director was out of his element. Mandelik was assigned to help Lang with his limited "technical vocabulary," typing up a French-German dictionary of cinema words and expressions that the director might find useful. The assistant would pick Lang up daily at his apartment after filming began in December, and drive with the director to the studio at Joinville. He recalled a man for the first time tentative

---

*Much later, of course, *Liliom* would become the basis for Rodgers and Hammerstein's Broadway musical *Carousel*.

and defensive, attempting to learn a politesse more foreign to him than vernacular.

"In Germany, he behaved a little Prussian," recalled Mandelik. "He had
this reputation of being very hard on his people, but people did put up with
it because he also had a reputation as a great artist. The first time I took him
to the studio, he asked, 'What will they call me? In Germany they called me
Meister.' I said, 'They will call you M. Lang, or they might call you Patron.' "
The director nodded; this was acceptable. "I said, 'Later on, when you get to
know some of them better, they might call you something different. It's very
important that they like you, because that's the French spirit.' "

Liliom was probably the first Fritz Lang production for which the director
did not ordain the major casting—an augury of things to come. The title role
was bestowed on the well-known Frenchman Charles Boyer, a Sorbonne-
educated matinee idol of the stage; Boyer had worked with Erich Pommer in
a number of French-language versions of German films, appearing last in
1932's *F.P.1. antwortet nicht*. Madeleine Ozeray, from Louis Jouvet's stage
company, was cast as the female lead, Julie, a lovestruck girl whose troubled
relationship with Liliom leads to marriage, pregnancy, and tragedy. Among the
other faces in the cast was the surrealist poet, actor, playwright, and dramatic
theorist Antonin Artaud, in a small part. Years later Lang claimed in an interview that he noticed Artaud's "attractive face" when the avant-garde dramatist applied as an extra, and hired him on the spot.*

The cameraman was the creative, Cracow-born Rudolph Maté, who had
apprenticed with Karl Freund and worked for Pommer as a second-unit photographer in Berlin. For a production for which atmosphere music seemed
requisite, Pommer gave Franz Waxman his first soundtrack assignment. Waxman had worked behind the scenes as an arranger on *Der blaue Engel*, then
left Berlin after being beaten up by anti-Semitic thugs. In America, later on,
he became one of Hollywood's most renowned composers, winning Oscars for
his music for *Sunset Boulevard* and *A Place in the Sun*.

The producer spared no expense on this, his first announced vehicle for
Fox-Europa. In a French-language book about Lang, Waxman described the
lengths to which Pommer was willing to go, empowering the first-time composer to engage the best symphony orchestra then available in Paris; renting
the Théatre des Champs Élysées for the occasion; recording with several mi-
crophones experimentally placed in the dome of the empty theater to pick up
the effects of space and echo; and employing an electronic instrument called
'Ondes Martenot,' after the inventor whose "weird sound helped establish a
strange atmosphere for Liliom's heavenly and hellish adventure."**

Gilbert Mandelik recalled how Lang zealously prepared the rest of the production, turning out reams of his copiously annotated script pages and
sketches. The director was always refining his planning techniques, such as
moving miniature figures across a type of chessboard, or building scale models

---

*No matter that Artaud had played unforgettably in French silents like Abel Gance's *Napoléon*,
  as Marat.
**Invented by Maurice Martenot around 1918, the Ondes Martenot was a precursor of modern
  electronic music and used a keyboard and a ribbon to produce separate notes or a continuous
  tone.

with little periscopes and protractors to measure the angle of the lenses. In the case of this production he created special blueprints to suggest the sets, and, in order to visualize the shots, he would maneuver "V-shaped pieces of celluloid, each representing a different lens size" across the blueprints, in Mandelik's words.

The only deviations in the planning that Lang would accept were those of his own inspiration. "He ignored comments which anyone happened to venture, and even more, any advice that someone would have the audacity to give," recalled Bernard Zimmer, a French writer who contributed dialogue to the Robert Liebmann script.

For one sequence, set in a small suburb in the springtime, the director insisted on an over-the-shoulder angle from the point of view of a maybug perched on the branch of a high tree. "I pointed out to him that to see something through the eye of a maybug was fanciful," recalled Bernard Zimmer, "that no one knows how a maybug views the world, and in the end it was the eye of the spectator who would see what the maybug saw. But Lang held on to his '*Maikäfer* . . .'" Mandelik's runners went looking for the out-of-season maybug, but the only bugs they could find were dead. Mandelik informed Lang that he would have to wait until June to shoot the scene if he wanted a live one—unless he wanted to go with a fake maybug. Lang had a good laugh over that, then agreed to use a dead specimen, which nevertheless meant a lot of further searching on everybody's part. "We filmed the scene," recalled Zimmer drily. "I think it was cut."

Lang made repeated attempts to work through mealtimes, but skipping the dinner hour, Frederick Ott reported, "elicited a mild protest from his French co-workers. To remind him in a subtle way it was time to stop, one of the prop men followed the practice each day of boiling a saucepan of soup behind some flats stored in the studio, fanning the odorous fumes in Lang's direction. After a few minutes, the director would stop his work and dismiss the crew for lunch."*

More to the point, Lang drank coffee nonstop and continued to take his little pills to keep going. He had the luxury of having his own favorite meals delivered to him on the set, so that he could eat at his convenience while lights and cameras were being set up. Invariably, it was Lily Latté, stepping into the role Thea von Harbou had fulfilled in Berlin, who brought his nourishment to the *Liliom* set.

Mandelik was one who believed that "Mickey [Latté] helped him in all his work, in his planning and so on. I think she was very intelligent and had good taste." Latté also spoke fluent French—better than Lang's. Her English was better, too. In fact, she was generally better educated than Lang was, which irritated the director no end.

Latté had other uses. One day Lang needed an insert of a woman's legs. Lang considered himself an expert on the female anatomy, and no part of that anatomy excited him more than legs. However, no one's legs, among the many beau-

---

*This story was later reported, with variations, to have also occurred on Hollywood sets. Lang's behavior has been rationalized by his defenders: "The director was naturally unaware of local customs," or, "He did not realize that the labor unions had a contractual requirement of intervals for food or rest." Yet this was also a director who liked to reminisce about his appreciation for assassinated French Socialist Jean Jaurès, a staunch pre–World War I unionist, and who, in his Hollywood years, advocated many liberal causes, including pro-labor issues.

tiful and well-paid actresses on the studio premises, passed his muster. Finally, Lily Latté had to be located and brought to the set, and her legs became the chosen pair. Years later Latté would boast proudly of this moment. "Lily and I were talking about *Liliom* one day, having seen it just that afternoon," said David Overbey. " 'You know, I'm in *Liliom*,' she said. 'You are?' I asked. 'Those are my legs on the carousel!' I said, 'Ah, those are very beautiful legs.' She said, 'Yes, that is what Fritz was first interested in, before he lost interest . . . ' "

For his part, Lang liked to boast that his hands were used as an insert in every one of his films; those were his Hitchcockian cameo appearances. The director had large, graceful hands, always manicured, and a way of gesturing with them that was almost balletic. Paradoxically, he liked to use them in close-ups of strangling and hand-to-hand fighting. There was no way to confirm his boasting, but the director's catalog of various shots of his hands was convincing to friends.

Mandelik, as Lang's personal assistant, was drawn into the web of the Lang-Latté relationship, even though he, like many, couldn't quite figure it out. Lang and Latté regularly went out together after a long day of filming; often Mandelik helped form an uncomfortable triad. One time he was invited along with them afterward for a pipe of opium and some after-hours nightclub-hopping—an offer he civilly declined. "They had a warm relationship which they tried to hide," said Mandelik. "It was odd."

Lang and Latté lived separately. Hans Latté had joined his wife in Paris, bringing their young daughter Susanne; Lily's husband, too, had fled Germany for good. "He was a nice fellow who liked to fidget with things, to the point where we used to have dinner together at the studio, and I always arranged to have something with me or nearby that didn't work for Hans to fix, to keep his interest," recalled Mandelik.

At first the relationship between Lily and Hans seemed up in the air. For a while Lily lived with her husband on a side street not far from the Avenue Mozart; then she moved out and arranged her own apartment. The daughter stayed with her father. Lily's mother journeyed to Paris to help take care of the young girl. Finally, Lily's decision was made plain: she had picked Fritz Lang over her husband and daughter.

Hans Latté accepted the situation stoically. Conrad von Molo ran into him and began to see him periodically. "Hans tried to explain to me that he had given up Lily, he wasn't fighting for her. He never complained. He was such a nice person," said von Molo. To avoid awkwardness, things were arranged so that Lang and Hans Latté never crossed paths; meanwhile, according to von Molo, Lang was drawing on the income and savings of *both* Lattés in order to furnish his elegant lifestyle.

For the rest of her life, Lily Latté would remain devoted to Fritz Lang. But the director was already looking beyond her. "Fritz Lang was quite interested in women even though he had Mickey," said Mandelik. "He did play around. Not with girls in the film—although there is one that I'm not sure about. He met some girls at the studio who were doing a fashion short and he took their addresses. I knew about it because he asked me to take one of them some nice roses. He was going out with her in the evenings and so on, and I always tried not to show that I knew anything about it to Mickey. There was no point in getting her upset."

When Lily tried to extract information from Mandelik, he played dumb. Lang was busy tonight, he would tell her vaguely. Well, if Lang was busy tonight, why didn't Mandelik take her out? she asked more than once. Finally one evening Mandelik did agree to take her out, picking Lily up and saying an awkward hello to Hans Latté, who was there to see them to the door.

They went off to a show together. Mandelik had the distinct impression Latté wanted to go further with him that night; he had the impression, too, that it would have been just fine with Lang, who appreciated being relieved of some of the pressure of a waning affair.

All the while, Lily Latté was in and out of Paris, making mysterious trips. She knew bankers and lawyers in Berlin. She could make all the clandestine arrangements. She was not a public figure. Fritz Lang could not travel freely, but his mistress could.

The filming of *Liliom* was completed by late spring. Lang was at the editing table "for forty-eight hours without sleep on the day before the film was to be shown to his Fox-Europa producers," according to Gilbert Mandelik.

Conrad von Molo, whose life had achieved some equilibirium, made a point of confronting the director at the premiere in May of 1934. "That was quite an experience," said von Molo. "He saw me, he felt guilty, he realized at the same time that I was still there and had really made up my mind to emigrate. I went right up to him but didn't say anything. I just stood in front of him and looked him up and down as if to say, 'You swine.' I stood there for a long time. He didn't say a word. It was uncanny. Finally I turned my back and went out."

Right from the first showings, *Liliom* was maligned. The Catholic clergy and militant Catholic youth of France raised a protest. The scenes on earth were too sexually provocative, but even they were preferable to the jocular ones set in a cotton-candy heaven. The French Catholic Church decided that "the film was anti-Catholic and showed Fritz Lang's conception of heaven as being too much against that of the Church," according to Mandelik.

Mandelik recommended an insert or scroll at the beginning of the film explaining that the director was not presenting his own rigid interpretation of heaven, merely honoring the play as conceived by Molnár and as experienced by Liliom, in whose simple mind heaven is reflected. Lang, characteristically, refused to alter what he had signed and completed. Mandelik took up the issue with the producer, but Erich Pommer's involvement may have been weakened by the fact that he had to undergo surgery for colon cancer during the course of the production. In the event, Pommer admirably sided with Lang, declaring, "It is Lang's film and up to him."*

---

*Molnár himself, living in Paris at the time, renounced the picture, which was widely advertised as "A Fritz Lang Film." The playwright disliked the film intensely, not because of Lang's particular association with it, according to Egon Erwin Kisch in his book *Sensation Fair*, but "because the poster gave not Molnár's name as the author, but some German [Robert Liebmann] he had never heard of."

All this contributed to an unfortunate commercial fate for one of Fritz Lang's most personal works. At a time in his career when the director might have been thought to be vulnerable, anxiety-ridden, even floundering, he made the film in which he invested the most optimism and ebullience. What is *Liliom* if not Lang's most playful meditation on crime and punishment, and an ode to the second chance in life that every person wishes for?

The carnival barker was a figure out of his Prater childhood, a misbegotten anti-hero forced to atone for a crime that wasn't even a success. Charles Boyer, cast against type as a salt-of-the-earth figure, was never as charmingly despicable. *Liliom*'s relationship with Julie (who in both the play and film has a job as a portrait photographer's assistant) is unusually lustful. One scene on a park bench unabashedly shows Liliom fondling Julie's breasts.

Later on, in Hollywood, Boyer and Henry Fonda exchanged war stories about working with Fritz Lang. During his death scene in *Liliom*, Boyer told Fonda, the director positioned him on a bed with his bare feet stretched out of the camera frame. Lang stood nearby, behind the camera, whispering to him, "Charles, when I pinch your toe, close your eyes. Then, when I pinch your toe again, open your eyes . . ." Boyer was greatly perturbed. "I don't want to be told when to close my eyes and when to open them," the French actor told Fonda, adding, "But I must admit it is effective on the screen."

The carnival and outdoor scenes, filmed on soundstages, are a feast for the senses, fluidly staged and photographed. The knife fight, for which the sound track goes abruptly silent, is one of those rituals of death that the director staged, in film after film, with the intricacy of a dance routine. The scenes in heaven are spiked with humor, even if the Catholic Church failed to recognize their underlying reverence.

One could be forgiven for forgetting, after the solemn masterpieces of *Die Nibelungen*, *Metropolis* and *M*, that Lang possessed a sense of humor: It almost never quite carried over to his films. Privately, the director could hold forth with a stream of acid remarks, blistering observations, even rehearsed jokes— usually at someone's expense. With light comedy, though, Lang had difficulty expressing himself. In his American films especially, the humor came off "always a little heavy-handed," in the words of Gene Fowler, Jr., "very Germanic, more Katzenjammer Kids than Charlie Brown."

Yet there was sublime humor in *Liliom*. Lang kids himself throughout the film, which features allusions to passports, the stamping of identity papers, and droll undertakers of death with pale, knife-faces. The rules and regulations in heaven are even worse than those on earth. The director probably didn't feel comfortable with comedy unless it served a serious theme. In one highlight, Liliom is taken aback by a heavenly screening of film footage that documents the nefarious deeds of his life; after being forced to watch a stop-action of himself hitting Julie, he is chastised, then sent back to earth for one day to make amends. This moment of gallows humor is followed by a remarkable observation. "Film is like a memory . . . film is stronger than memory," the heavenly archivist expounds, a statement that might be taken as a motto for this director, to whom film was indeed a substitute—stronger and more reliable, more permanent—for memory.

Liliom was one memory Lang liked to dwell on. The film quickly vanished from sight in France and elsewhere; it was never released theatrically in the United States because of the prior version. For decades *Liliom* remained unavailable to cineasts. Thirty years after it was made, when he was living in Hollywood, Lang liked to surprise people by arranging a showing of the rarity at 20th Century–Fox. The director liked to escort privileged buffs—and old colleagues like Gilbert Mandelik, who also settled in Hollywood and remained friends with Lang and Lily Latté—to the studio's private screening room to see his sole Parisian film. He enjoyed their enjoyment. It was one of his old films—and there were not many—for which his tolerance was endless.

"*Liliom* I always liked very much," the director told an audience of American Film Institute students in early 1974. "Today I almost like *Liliom* best of all."

When work on *Liliom* was finished, Lang asked Gilbert Mandelik if he would stay on as "a kind of secretary" until the director departed for America. "He paid my expenses and then he left me some money. I was an expensive secretary but I did it really with a lot of goodwill because I liked him. I had phone calls to make, letters to write, conferences to set up with various people, et cetera."

According to Mandelik, Lang had several offers from Hollywood to sort through. And it was not immediately clear when or if he would go to the United States. He had contacts in London and meetings in Paris with a society figure, Mrs. Nimet Eloui-Bey, a wealthy Egyptian in Man Ray's circle, who was thinking of setting up her own film company.

Metro-Goldwyn-Mayer, the dream factory of glamour and elegance, may have seemed an unlikely home for Fritz Lang, but MGM had been partner to the Parufamet deal and knew the director's films firsthand. It was the first American studio to come through with a definite contract offer, complete with travel expenses and the promise of latitude for Lang to select his initial English-language project.

Producer David O. Selznick, the son-in-law of studio head Louis B. Mayer, took a trip to England and Europe in the spring of 1934, with his wife Irene, director George Cukor, and screenwriter Howard Estabrook. Selznick scouted locations in England for MGM's imminent production of Charles Dickens's *David Copperfield*, and made a side trip to Paris, disporting in a high-class brothel. Selznick made an appointment with Lang and, according to David Thomson in his Selznick biography, the producer signed the director to a contract, thereby launching the second, American, half of Lang's career.

According to writer-producer Joseph L. Mankiewicz, Selznick was actually the "closer" on a deal that already had been set in motion. "David, unofficially, but serving 'without portfolio,'" said Mankiewicz, "sold himself, MGM, and America—in that order."

Mankiewicz was an unabashed Germanophile (his father was a professor of German). Earlier in his career Mankiewicz had spent time in Berlin, briefly employed as a subtitlist of German films for exportation to America; he always claimed that Lang's films were among them. Now he was at MGM as a producer-in-training. And many others on the lot knew Lang's considerable reputation. Head of production Irving Thalberg—referred to by German film refugees as "America's Erich Pommer," just as they referred to Pommer as "Berlin's Irving Thalberg"—was said to be one of the staunch admirers of M.

Lang liked to tell one of his little stories about Thalberg. Hollywood's one-time "boy wonder" was so enamored of M, according to the director, that one day he had it screened for a group of studio scribes as a paragon of artistic filmmaking. The MGM writers were a little taken aback, since the film dealt with a highly unconventional subject by Hollywood standards. After the showing, the writers listened as Thalberg sang the film's merits. Then one of the writers raised his hand and asked the studio chieftain what his reaction would have been if one of his staff had written such a sordid story about a child murderer. Thalberg replied bluntly: "Probably I would have said, 'Go to hell.' "

Selznick was a born promoter and exceptional organizational type, and in 1934 he operated his own autonomous production unit at the studio. His publicity men beat the drums about his deal with Fritz Lang, one of the "scalps dangling from a metaphorical war belt," in the New York Times's phrase.

Things were arranged swiftly. On June 6, 1934, Lang, with the Selznicks and company, sailed from Le Havre, France, for New York aboard the Ile de France. The crossing was smooth and pleasurable. The director was at his most relaxed and charming, his most Viennese. His private, sociable self took over. "Fritz Lang could have been a diplomat," said fellow director George Cukor, who also took the 1934 crossing. "He was very formal and distinguished, a raconteur. He had his own kind of humor with an amusing slant on life. Lang commanded enormous prestige and authority. I liked and respected him very much."

The New York Times reported on the director's arrival on June 12, 1934. Besides Lang, Mr. and Mrs. Selznick, Cukor and Selznick's brother—agent Myron Selznick—the party included scenarist Howard Estabrook and British author Hugh Walpole (who would assist Estabrook on the David Copperfield script). Among the other "scalps" collected on Selznick's trip abroad were Leontine Sagan, the German director of Mädchen in Uniform (another reluctant exile, she was discovered running a little theater near Oxford); a nineteen-year-old English boy named Peter Trent, who would be tested to play David Copperfield; and British statesman Lloyd George, who had initialed an agreement with MGM permitting his war memoirs "to be brought to the screen."

Lloyd George's memoirs were never brought to the screen, Leontine Sagan never made a film in America, and Peter Trent did not pass the audition for David Copperfield. Selznick was a publicity-grabber; Fritz Lang was the only one of his "scalps" who would amount to anything in Hollywood. But subsequent events would prove that the producer understood Lang little better than he did his other discoveries.

Lang was described reflexively in the press as "the brilliant German director." According to the New York Times, Selznick persuaded Lang, "without much difficulty, to make his first [sic] trip to Hollywood." "Germany's loss is America's gain," Selznick magisterially declared.

Curt Riess, now transplanted to New York City, caught up once again with the director in transit. Interviewing him in his temporary hotel digs, he found a Fritz Lang proud and grateful to be out of Germany and finally on his way to Hollywood. On board ship, the director had acquired a convenient agent in Myron Selznick. But Riess stole a look at Lang's new MGM contract and didn't tell him that it was unimpressive compared to those of others in the German émigré community who had arrived in America before him. The contented Lang didn't seem to know, or care about, the difference, Riess noted.

Within days Selznick and company were all aboard the *Santa Fe Chief;* a week after the arrival and ballyhoo in New York, they were safely in Los Angeles. Many Germans familiar to Lang by acquaintance or name were already ensconced in Hollywood, including Erich Pommer, who had once again preceded Lang and was producing a Joe May film at 20th Century–Fox. One of Max Reinhardt's sons, Gottfried, although younger than Lang by two decades, was another relative veteran of American life, having arrived in Hollywood some months earlier. The scion of the great theatrical impresario was appointed by MGM to drive Lang around looking for a house.

Shortly, Reinhardt found an available place to which Lang gave his approval, and the director took up residence at 2141 La Mesa Drive in Santa Monica, west of the University of California at Los Angeles, near the Riviera Country Club, a mile or two from the ocean, and only a short hop by car from the Culver City lot.

Helping him get settled, Reinhardt was struck by how lonely and preoccupied Lang seemed to be. Europe's most celebrated film director was just like the other displaced people Reinhardt had been driving around—an ordinary human being, no better or worse for his mantle of fame, and profoundly subdued and disoriented now that he had reached his final destination.

HOLLYWOOD

Lily Latté came to America in lowlier fashion, without fanfare, entourage, or publicity. She had lingered in Paris for six months. The refugee flow did not abate, and one of the newly arrived was Peter Heiman, the Max Reinhardt assistant director who had become acquainted with Fritz Lang in Berlin in the early 1930s under curious circumstances. In Paris in mid-1935, Heiman met Latté for the first time and they became lovers. At first he even hoped that they might emigrate to America together. It took Heiman some time to realize that Latté had a prior attachment to Lang, who was already in Hollywood. The relationship with Lang had been temporarily broken off, but Latté was hoping their romance would resume in America. Meanwhile, Lang phoned Latté often, and "practically every second day a telegram appeared," according to Heiman. She was busy making arrangements for most of Lang's belongings to be packed up and shipped from Germany to France to the United States, and selling some items for cash. Heiman had difficulty getting his travel papers in order, and Latté sailed for America ahead of him.

Immigration and Naturalization records show that Latté crossed into the United States on December 20, 1935, from Calexico, California, near El Centro, along the Mexican–U.S. border. Her papers state that she was a "reporter" who would be taking up residence with Fritz Lang at 2141 La Mesa Drive. Her race: Hebrew. Her nationality: German. Her hair color (curiously, for those who remember her as Lang's blond archetype): auburn.

Her records—and the timing of her application, a year and a half after Lang had relocated to America—suggest that according to immigration law Latté had in fact *left* the country in order to re-enter with a permanent visa. It was common for German refugees with temporary "visitor's visas" to choose to re-enter the United States at Calexico, with sworn affidavits from people who guaranteed they would not become public charges. Thus it seems possible that Latté had continued to travel freely between Berlin and Hollywood throughout most of 1935, tying up loose ends for herself and Lang.

The loose ends Latté tied up in Europe included her marriage—she had gotten a divorce; her daughter Susanne, according to the 1935 immigration papers, lived with Hans Latté in Barcelona, Spain.

That Latté arranged for the transportation or sale of prized possessions Fritz

Lang claimed to have left behind in Hitler's Germany appears certain. In the very first, pre-*Fury* press release about the director, with the byline of MGM publicity head Howard Strickling, Lang is described as owning a "collection of objects of primitive art, principally South Seas and Negro, Chinese and Japanese," said to be "extensive and valuable." Other publicity items trumpeted the fact that the newly arrived director owned "one of the nation's finest collections of Polynesian art objects."* Another release announced: "Recently, he imported five thousand volumes of his personal library." There was no indication, as there would be in countless future interviews, that the director had had to sacrifice any of his art treasures, first editions, or signed works. Of course there was no mention of the Goebbels story, nor of Lang's distaste for the Nazi government.

The fate of Lang's art collection, conveniently itemized after his divorce and left behind in Berlin with Thea von Harbou for safekeeping, is especially mysterious. Otto Kallir compiled the definitive catalog on the works of Egon Schiele; according to his granddaughter Jane Kallir, the present-day operator of the Galerie St. Etienne in New York, "Lang confirmed in correspondence that four Schieles, as well as four Laskes, were left in trust ('zu treuen Händen') with Thea von Harbou when he emigrated from Germany. She apparently sold or gave them away, without his permission, sometime thereafter, and he never bothered to pursue the matter."

The best-known works in Fritz Lang's collection, the Schieles, vanished for a time after he left Germany. Von Harbou's secretary, Hilde Guttmann, who was employed by the scenarist until 1938, did not recall that they were ever displayed in von Harbou's home after Lang and his wife split up. Von Harbou's relatives adamantly maintain that she never kept or sold them for Lang. They were Lang's to do with as he pleased.

In Otto Kallir's catalog, four Schiele paintings—*Auferstehung, Begegnung, Mann und Frau* and *Tafelrunde*—are listed in Lang's ownership as of 1930. Interestingly, only two of the above (*Auferstehung* and *Tafelrunde*) appear on the list provided by Lang to the Berlin divorce court in 1933. Already by then, it appears, the director had sold the missing two—unless Lang was deliberately cheating the court inventory.

Both *Mann und Frau* and *Tafelrunde* (the latter, definitely owned by Lang at one time, was a Last Supper motif depicting members of Schiele's circle, including Klimt and Schiele himself) surfaced at auction after the war, their provenance a guarded secret. *Auferstehung* and *Begegnung* remain unaccounted for to this day. *Die Eremiten*—not in Otto Kallir's catalog as belonging to Lang, yet on the director's court inventory—is listed today among the holdings of Austrian art collector Rudolf Leopold. Yet Leopold, answering a query for this book, insisted that it had never belonged to Lang.

No doubt Lang did leave precious objects behind, and was forced to sell others. But the director, who exaggerated his flight from Nazi Germany "without portfolio," brought with him to Hollywood much more than he cared to admit. Not only did he bring art objects and a voluminous personal library,

---

*When a fire swept Lang's Santa Monica home in 1938, newspaper accounts emphasized the destruction of art objects worth an estimated $7,500.

Lang even found time to pack cherished production stills and memorabilia. He wrote a revealing memorandum on Nassour Studios stationery in the early 1960s, proposing an updated remake of his 1929 film *Die Frau im Mond*, and disclosing that when he fled Germany in 1933, he had "salvaged about four hundred stills" showing "the continuity of the picture, and how certain technical problems were worked out."

Even Peter the pet monkey, a sentimental gift from Gerda Maurus and a lucky charm from European days, made the trip to America safely. Writer and Lang friend David Overbey recalled his astonishment when, poring over photographs for Lotte Eisner's book in the early 1970s, he noticed Peter—by then a familiar figure to the director's associates—sitting on Lang's desk in Dahlem in the background of an old photograph. Though the director had not forsaken him, Peter would keep a decidedly low profile for over twenty years in Hollywood, hidden away for unexplained reasons, before surfacing again.

Right away, in Hollywood, Lang had to make adjustments.

For every European refugee who cannily adapted to the Hollywood system, there were many others, hapless as well as tragic, who did not. Leopold Jessner, formerly director of the State Theater in Berlin, couldn't get a decent job at the major studios; Max Reinhardt, the greatest name in German theater, directed only one film in America, and ended up running acting classes. Among Lang's illustrious colleagues who had been well-established abroad, Jacques Feyder was fired; E. A. Dupont was never able to find the right assignment; and Joe May, Lang's old nemesis, had only half a career in America, relegated to low-budget and horror pictures before he gave up and opened a Viennese restaurant.

Along with language and cultural barriers, the reasons for failure were as varied as the individual personalities. Granted, the Hollywood setup was magnificent in many respects. "The technical end was indescribably better [than in Germany]," Lang told Peter Bogdanovich. "Lighting and everything was ten thousand times better here." But for every Hollywood advantage, there was a corresponding disadvantage. If the technology was superior, this was offset by guidelines of lighting and camerawork that imposed each studio's preferred "style." Visual experimentation by directors was expensive and frowned upon. Realistic, stark, or gloomy photography was regarded as inappropriate. Actresses, especially, were expected to have their beauty accented, regardless of apparent light sources within a scene.

The contract staff of Hollywood studios were every bit as proficient as those Lang had worked with in Germany; by 1935, many included his former Berlin compatriots. But in Hollywood, studio executives chose personnel for each production based on who was under contract, available, and, in their estimation, appropriate. Costume and design staff answered to department heads, each sector a fiefdom. Cameramen were loyal to the studio, not the director, and most directors, in any event, left the visual elements of a production to cinematographers and their assistants, rarely even asking to peer through the camera lens. The editing rooms were almost strictly the province of editors and executives. Screenwriters usually worked independently of directors, crafting their scripts for producer, or studio, approval. The director was not ex-

pected to get involved until a script was already completed and needed mere
fine-tuning.

Hollywood actors and actresses may have been world-famous for their star
power, but here, too, things in America were different from Germany. In Germany the film itself was the star, as Lang had once deigned to inform Douglas
Fairbanks. Actors and actresses were subordinate to directors. Rightfully, Lang
could boast of having launched a number of German screen stars; their discoveries were part of his mythos.

In Hollywood, only the studio bosses (or, in rare cases, the audience) could
elevate an actor to stardom. Stars outranked directors in salaries and stature.
Directors had some standing; a very few, like Ernst Lubitsch, were virtually
one-man shows. But Lang never possessed Lubitsch's stature (not to mention
his likability) in the United States. The average American director had little
or nothing to do with the star-making machinery, and Central Casting juggled
player assignments for nearly all the supporting roles.

Unlike in Berlin, studio executives, boardroom officials, and behind-the-
scenes bankers were virtually invisible in Hollywood. A handful of key moguls
at the top of the studio hierarchy acted as benign father figures. But even the
moguls were stingy with their presences. They were busy, important people,
removed from the daily muck and mire, revealing themselves to studio employees only on cleverly stage-managed occasions. That left the daily power
plays to the producer, a species Lang had grown to revile. Most Hollywood
directors entered a production only *after* the screenplay was finished—and
under a producer's all-encompassing supervision.

In Berlin, according to Lang, filmmaking had been "a collective enterprise"—but it was a collective enterprise ruled, decisively, by the director. In
Hollywood, producers were the moguls' surrogates, the omnipresent bosses at
story conferences, production meetings, and throughout the shooting schedule. And, ironically, no studio in Hollywood was more of a "producer's studio"
than MGM, where Lang landed in 1934.

Now the director had to embrace a new religion of teamwork, diplomacy,
and compromise that was antithetical to his personality. At the same time
Fritz Lang, at age forty-five, faced the struggle of mastering English and adjusting to a foreign culture. He had always shown an adeptness at turning
misfortune into opportunity. How would he fare now, under the weight of so
many extreme and never-ending adjustments?

Hollywood was bigger, more industrialized, more citified than when Lang had
visited in 1925.

MGM's size and scale must have made it seem like America's Ufa. While
other studios were suffering during the Depression, MGM managed to flourish. It enjoyed a reputation, in 1934, as the Tiffany's of Hollywood, with its
vast lot and numerous soundstages, universally recognized stars, big budgets,
and generous shooting schedules. The studio relied heavily on a formula of
glittering love stories and glossy comedies, respectable stage and literary ad-
aptations, lush musicals and heart-warming family pictures, with little room
left for subjects outside that program.

Like most studios of that era, MGM maintained meticulous records of all productions, with copies for all concerned; and Lang kept memoranda and script drafts for the studio projects he was involved in, however tentatively, during his first year at MGM. The archivist and historian in Lang was always wrestling with the self-publicist.

Oddly, nobody rushed to exploit his talent. At first, Lang was able to work mostly at home, making appearances at the studio for scheduled appointments and story conferences. A bilingual secretary, Teddy Le Beau, was engaged to assist him, and various writers under contract were delegated to meet with him. Everything Lang proposed met with enthusiasm—or, seen in another light, with a kind of blanket indifference. Everything had equal priority, so nothing had real priority. He could work on one, two, three film projects at once; if none of them got finished, to whom did it matter? For Lang, such uncertainty marked a key difference between Ufa and MGM, Berlin and Hollywood.

It appears that Lang had busied himself on the ship to America working on a scenario that he was able to submit almost instantly upon taking up offices at MGM in early July 1934. When studio executives made ocean crossings, they invariably convened daily "bull sessions," where Selznick must have encouraged Lang's first story for American audiences, "Tomorrow," about "the universal evil of international traffic in arms."

The lead character of "Tomorrow" was a victimized hero of the type that would become Lang's stock-in-trade in Hollywood. A German World War I veteran is out of work, his spirit crushed by his wife's death. He is hired to work on a steamer bound for Shanghai, supposedly freighting pianos and other musical instruments. Once on board, he learns the steamer is part of the operations of a global munitions cartel and is actually smuggling a forbidden cargo of machine guns and rifles.

"Tomorrow" was a full-tilt spy-adventure story like *Spione*, which featured a Russian secret agent and one of the director's clandestine, all-powerful organizations (the "Asiatic Committee"). One can seize on the victim-hero, an icon of defeated Germany, brooding over his wife's death, and see in him a disillusioned Lang, betrayed by the fatherland and trying to recover from the emotional loss of Thea von Harbou.

Lang's sixteen-page treatment, written in German, had to be translated for Selznick's benefit. It lavished detail and shot-by-shot descriptions on the opening sequences, then skipped ahead and leaped over the middle to the ending; the middle stayed sketchy. It was the vast, ambiguous middle for which the director always needed help.

It appears from studio memoranda that writer Joseph Mankiewicz, under MGM contract, first met Lang at this juncture, and helped him polish an English-language version of the "Tomorrow" treatment. "Probably because of my fluent German and knowledge of pre-Hitler German culture and mores," recalled Mankiewicz in an interview, "I was among the first writers assigned to help Fritz find or develop a viable project."

When Lang submitted the treatment to Selznick, he typically assured the producer that everything in the scenario was based on documented fact. Yet Lang offered to append a "happy ending" if the facts were deemed too harsh. But that was not necessary; Selznick's interest in "Tomorrow" was only half-hearted anyway. It was just something to occupy the time of the newly arrived director. The producer took a pass.

In Germany Lang had had the unusual experience of seeing nearly every one of his envisioned films brought to fruition. In America, with its volume of production and complicated decision-making bureaucracy, script ideas were a dime a dozen. The director would spend much of the next twenty years trying to guess which of his ideas were best suited to satisfy the constantly revolving smorgasbord of Hollywood tastes.

"Tomorrow" was filed away, and Lang went to work on another scenario that likewise contained elements of his previous German successes. This one, entitled "The Man Behind You," was a Jekyll-Hyde story marbled with many of Lang's pet notions. The director worked alone on the story in July and August, then signed it over to Selznick and MGM, officially, late in the summer of 1934.

The story featured a doctor, head of a private hospital, engaged to a young actress. While giving testimony at a criminal trial, the doctor becomes obsessed with the existence of a "second ego," an impulse that compels someone to commit murder. He enters an insane asylum to study the lunatics. When his fiancé finds herself drawn to another, less fixated man, his life unravels. Fascinated by vice, the doctor himself becomes an insane murderer, unwilling or unable to leave his "second ego" behind.

No likelihood of a happy ending with this grim pastiche of *Dr. Mabuse* and *M.* And Selznick also rejected this Lang idea. But the director felt strongly enough about "The Man Behind You" to wangle the rights to it back from MGM when he later left the studio, and to revive the project in discussions with producers periodically into the early 1940s. Like many of Lang's would-be films, though, "The Man Behind You" never got beyond the lengthy-treatment stage.

Lang was at an obvious disadvantage in trying to jump-start his first Hollywood production with a script he had devised himself. He had not written a film—without Thea von Harbou—for ten years; now he was faced with the assignment of creating, on his own, a project "American enough" to suit a strange new marketplace. It was a job that called for expertise in a culture and language he understandably didn't possess. Perhaps, with more time, he would have succeeded, but his immediate failure at MGM would make the Americanization of his films a permanent source of insecurity. Selznick had little choice, in the late summer of 1934, but to assign a homegrown writer to assist Lang.

Oliver H. P. Garrett would walk Lang through the manufacture of an Americanized script. Garrett was one of Selznick's stable, a bon vivant and cynic often employed by the producer; later, notably, he was one of numerous script doctors for *Gone With the Wind*. A former New York newspaperman, felicitously enough, Garrett was one of those "beat reporters" who came to be valued by Lang for their observational skills and streetwise experience. Relying on newspapermen would become even more crucial for the director in the United States, where Lang constantly had to reinforce his knowledge and comprehension of the society.

"Hell Afloat" would be the director's first official MGM production. Lang himself may have picked the story out of the newspapers; the script would be modeled after the notorious S.S. *Morro Castle* disaster of September 1934, in which 124 persons perished off the coast of New Jersey in a suspicious fire. The director spoke eagerly about the inferno he could mount for the story's climax. Selznick, who had crossed the Atlantic with Lang, had no trouble making the connection between this particular director and a shipboard fire.

For the first time the producer seemed to be taking a Fritz Lang project seriously, and Selznick himself showed up in story conferences. A brief first draft entitled "The Journey" (it also shows up in various accounts as "Tell No Tales" or "T.N.T.") was executed by Garrett in early November of 1934. A series of meetings between the director and the scenarist, with Selznick sometimes sitting in, followed throughout the end of the year.

After the initial draft, Lang and Garrett cooked up a more intricate plot, interweaving three groups of ship's passengers, all of whom bear the director's stamp: Several pirates conspiring to commit arson and steal a cache of gold; a star-crossed divorced couple; and a group of ruthless arms dealers, left over from the aborted "Tomorrow," smuggling ammunition in pianos. Only when a hellish fire engulfs the ship are the three groups forced to join up, and the stories begin to interlock.

It was probably Lang who suggested a title change to the more lurid "Hell Afloat." So much is indicated by a memo from Selznick, rejecting "Hell Afloat" on behalf of MGM's advertising and publicity departments. "They think it will keep women away from the cinema," the producer wrote his trophy-director on November 13, 1934.

Lang didn't have much experience kowtowing to studio marketing departments, and he had probably never had one of his handpicked titles rejected before. But he and Garrett proceeded dutifully, and a revised draft, co-signed by both and still stubbornly bearing the title "Hell Afloat," emerged from their labors a few days before Christmas of 1934. "Selznick liked it very much on Christmas Eve," the director told Peter Bogdanovich. "Three days later, it was the lousiest thing he had ever read."

The production records show a slightly different sequence of events. Indeed, Selznick did reject the draft shortly after Christmas. His reader, Lenore Coffee, an able scenarist who had started out as a title-writer in the silent era, told the producer the various story threads had to be more believably intertwined. The principal characters were "too unpleasant and too bad," she reported, and there were "too many minor characters."

Garrett, who had a script pending for producer Sam Goldwyn, was relieved of the project in February. Selznick contacted Philip Barry, the playwright of *Holiday*, and dangled an unusually high fee to coax the noted stage writer into doing a revision. Lang was warned by Selznick that Barry worked best alone, and didn't need any input from the director. This had to gnaw at a man accustomed to close collaboration, though in the end it is unclear whether Barry did much work at all. Hollywood producers batted a low average when trying to coax a film script out of Barry, who preferred to concentrate on his thriving Broadway career.

Lang, for his part, determined to try and fix the script himself. Selznick thought it would be fine for the director to continue tinkering with "Hell

Afloat"—just so long as he didn't get the impression that he would be getting paid extra for any ad hoc script work. The producer reminded Lang, in a memo of February 14, 1935, that "any time spent making any changes that I may want on the script is part of your contract."

Lang poured all his time and energy into "Hell Afloat." Teddy Le Beau, the first of the director's Hollywood secretaries, was crucial in helping him put things into proper form. Lang established a pattern, dictating or "spitballing" ideas while his secretary took dictation—tidying up the language and arranging the scenes structurally. After his secretary had typed up a neat, ordered draft, Lang really went to work. Crossing things out, making pencil notations and changes in the margins, he became an editor extraordinaire. After endless alterations, an inevitable parade of further dictation and drafts would follow.

From his first days in Hollywood, Lang liked to say, he had rejected the German language. "From that moment I never spoke German again," the director told Charles Higham and Joel Greenberg. That is not entirely true; Lang did speak German to other Germans, and often wrote or dictated his script drafts in German, right through to the end of his life. But he did make a strenuous effort to master English, especially to pick up the colloquialisms that fascinated many émigrés forced to speak and write in a new language. Silent pictures may have been universal, but the language of Hollywood's early sound films was sprinkled with up-to-date jargon, grassroots vernacular, and subtle innuendo.

"I read only English [after coming to America]," Lang told Peter Bogdanovich. "I read a lot of newspapers, and I read comic strips—from which I learned a lot. I said to myself, if an audience—year in, year out—reads so many comic strips, there must be something interesting in them. And I found them very interesting."

Other European émigrés also studied American newspapers, comics, songs, and jokes. Some, like Billy Wilder, became walking volcanoes of slang. Lang had always read newspapers and comic strips; now old habits found their excuse in fresh surroundings. But he also had more trouble than some émigrés. The German language was deeply ingrained in his psychology, and Lang often made simple mistakes, in person and in script drafts, that came off comically as well as poignantly. "Cadillac" became "caddyac." "John Doe" became "Joe Doe." "Elephants never forget" became "the memory of a hippopotamus."

"You can't imagine what emigration means for someone who, like me, lives in the midst of the language," said Lang once. "You are lost, you start again with the babbling of newborns, you don't feel enthusiasm, you don't have an inkling, you don't have a style. Before getting to the point of being able to think and dream in English, you don't amount to anything."

Idiomatic English was one key route to Americanizing his scripts. Lang's early scripts were covered with penciled queries about slang that sounded inscrutable to him. "What does this line mean?" was a recurrent plaint. When Lang would volunteer an alternative phrase out of his own knowledge, it was not necessarily an improvement. "When he tried to use [American] vernacular, it would either be from the 1920s, things that he picked up in the movies— or something that was just not applicable," said Gene Fowler, Jr.

"Hell Afloat" was tentatively placed on the schedule for filming in March or April 1935, though Selznick continued to hedge his bets. The director traveled east in April to assess the *Morro Castle*, where she was beached at Gravesend Bay in Baltimore, on the theory that the abandoned hulk might be used for cutaway shots. By the time the director returned, however, the final draft, dated June 21, 1935, had been submitted, and Selznick's verdict was in. Lang's third project was also unceremoniously shelved.

By the time the decision came down, the director's future with Selznick was also moot. June was the month Louis B. Mayer's son-in-law resigned from the studio. He would soon form Selznick International Pictures, and leave the MGM lot.

All that time wasted. Now Lang lost patience. He complained vehemently to Eddie Mannix, the studio vice president, who was one step below Louis B. Mayer—the "second almighty," in screenwriter Salka Viertel's words. Mannix was a former Pacific Palisades bouncer, a tough character with a soft streak, the key man for contracts and assignments. Out of one side of his mouth Mannix expressed sympathy with Lang. Up to now, the director had been under Selznick's sole charge. With Selznick vacating, Lang would be transferred to the general roster of studio directors, and reassigned.

Lang had to start again at the bottom of the ladder, toiling on one of those iffy properties that were being nosed along by the story department. By midsummer of 1935, the director was immersed in "Passport to Hell," whose story had been originated by James Warner Bellah before being turned over to studio writers Leon Gordon and Humphrey Cobb.* The project was being supervised by contract producer Lawrence Weingarten.

"Passport to Hell" concerned a small-town American falsely accused of corruption, who must go to the ends of the earth to clear himself. A love triangle, an oil strike, a get-rich-quick scheme in a Persian Gulf kingdom—all these ingredients were tossed into the stew without much regard to narrative coherence. Lang's job, in July and August of 1935, was to work with the writers in sorting out snags and finding that most elusive element—an exciting "through-line," a plot that threaded the storyline together.

Bad luck hampered their progress. One of the writers had to bow out for a spell when he came down with malaria; others were brought in, pitching in ideas with Lang for a day or two, but the faces kept changing. Although Lang tried to show interest in the material, he was dismayed by how contrived and scattershot the process was, and he and writer Humphrey Cobb had long, soul-searching conversations about their mutual predicament.

Lang, who realized time was slipping by, complained about the melodramatic elements of the script, the too-convenient coincidences, the obligatory romance. Cobb advised the director to look on the positive side. He tried to convince Lang to view "Passport to Hell" as an "entering wedge" in the all-important realm of American box-office viability. Its completion and success would give the director "greater freedom in the future than if you give them

---

*Humphrey Cobb had just written, in 1935, the novel *Paths of Glory*, later to be filmed by Stanley Kubrick. Leon Gordon had borrowed the working title of the Lang project ("Passport to Hell") and some of the plotline from a Fox picture of the same name that he co-wrote in 1932.

[producers] a work of art which is above their heads and which they don't understand," Cobb told Lang, according to memoranda of their discussions.

Lang listened earnestly, but he had to cope daily with a producer who rubbed him the wrong way. Lawrence Weingarten didn't like the Leon Gordon–Humphrey Cobb treatment; he wanted a brand-new "through-line" and he wanted it fast, even if he insisted on approving all major story revisions personally. After Weingarten rejected Lang's initial script solutions, he complained that the director was torturously slow in coming up with alternatives. Insisting that he was working very hard every day, Lang once again appealed to the "second almighty," Eddie Mannix. Mannix stepped in as peacemaker between the director and producer, though he advised Lang to start keeping a secret log of his daily progress.

Although Lang himself had helped to foment the situation, now he worried that he would be trapped between Mannix and Weingarten, perennial rivals in MGM's court intrigues. Always the conspiracy theorist, the director decided he needed to bring his agent in as witness to his innocent motives. It fell to Myron Selznick to inform Weingarten that Lang was recording his daily progress, *not* because the director was trying to undermine the producer, but under Mannix's explicit orders.

Records show that throughout the summer of 1935 Lang worked several hours a day with Gordon and Cobb, and sometimes alone, dictating continuity suggestions to his secretary. "Trying to find a new [story] line," was the constant refrain of his summary reports for Eddie Mannix.

Scant progress was made. The project was a low priority in the first instance; and now Weingarten, irritated at being superseded by Mannix, began to treat Lang shabbily. The producer made himself unreachable on a daily basis. In mid-August Lang complained to Mannix again, asking to be excused from the uninspiring assignment. "I told him [Mannix] I wanted to be frank with him," said Lang in one of his memos, "and told him there was certain studio routine I had to fight against and I'd appreciate him backing me up. He said he surely would." Mannix advised Lang to keep attending to "Passport to Hell," while feeling free to rummage through other available properties in MGM's story files.

In the last week of August, 1935, a still sympathetic Mannix forwarded several other properties to Lang. The director occupied himself reading treatments for "Whipsaw," "His Brother's Wife," and "The Charlatan of Paris." Although the first two would become MGM productions in the next twelve months, they were hardly the pick of the litter. The director idly jotted down his own ideas for a film about Genghis Khan. Meanwhile Humphrey Cobb's option was dropped, and Weingarten let "Passport to Hell" wither on the vine.

As Lang was having problems fitting into the studio system, so too was he having problems mingling with the burgeoning European refugee community in Hollywood.

Lang was hardly the only foreigner manhandled by Hollywood. The newcomers from Germany and elsewhere, famous as well as obscure, huddled together in living rooms throughout the town, surrounded by secondhand furniture and precious souvenirs of the past, swapping anecdotes and sharing their common straits. Even those like Lang, who had nice jobs where every day brought sunshine and optimism and a bountiful paycheck, were struggling with the unfamiliar lifestyle. The money seemed little compensation for their psychic suffering.

Europeans in Hollywood had to learn to eat their way through "the sweet cake of forced laziness which Hollywood presents so freely," in the words of composer Friedrich Holländer. Brecht would describe America's motion picture capital as a "mausoleum of easygoing." Vladimir Pozner, a French screenwriter of Russian descent, called it a "luxury mining town." Said Gottfried Reinhardt, "The ghetto was so imponderable, its contours so amorphous, that many occupants did not perceive it at all."

There were a few places where everybody was made to feel welcome. The home of Salka Viertel, a red-haired former actress from Galicia who had been prominent in Berlin, was thrown open to newcomers on Sundays. The wife of poet-playwright Berthold Viertel (he had also collaborated auspiciously on an F. W. Murnau film), Salka was Greta Garbo's closest friend and the scenarist of several of her Hollywood pictures since 1928. She lived at 165 Mabery Road in Santa Monica, on a winding road overlooking the ocean. At once elegant and down-to-earth, Salka acted as "a kind of universal mother" to her endless number of guests, in the words of John Huston.

The armchairs were frayed but comfortable. The food was excellent, the wine flowed freely. The talk usually concerned society and politics. The people included such displaced titans of German culture as Franz Werfel, Thomas Mann, Lion Feuchtwanger and Otto Klemperer. Film industry sophisticates and celebrities came regularly for these occasions, which were unique in Hollywood. It wasn't surprising to find Charles Chaplin in the same room with Albert Einstein, absorbed in small talk.

It was "neutral ground" for European refugees, and Hollywood intellectuals, according to Reinhardt, "one of the few clearinghouses between the inmates and the guardians." Fritz Lang came to Salka Viertel's salon frequently. Writer Peter Viertel, Salka's son (then a teenager), observed Lang there, dressed characteristically in his elegant blue suit, shirt, and tie. Never, on such occasions, was he without his monocle. Sometimes he was accompanied by Lily Latté, whom everybody knew; she was as personable and well-liked as Thea von Harbou had been. When Lang came alone, in contrast, he seemed remote, unapproachable, sitting off by himself and nursing his martini. Distinctly uncomfortable in the group setting, he always behaved with meticulous formality.

The people at Salka Viertel's came from all walks of life—science, education, art, music, and literature. The director may have met some of the world-famous figures, but he knew few of them intimately in Germany. To move among them, made equal in their shared plight, was a humbling experience. One couldn't always talk about motion pictures with such people, even if one was lucky enough to have a "current project." Many of these refugees were first-class intellects and didn't really know or care about movies. Lang liked to think of himself as an intellectual, and he genuinely admired intellectuals. But these people were beyond his customary experience.

Worse yet, there were other German refugees, those who had failed to find any work in Hollywood's thriving film factories, who resented the luminaries such as Fritz Lang who had immediately secured comfortable niches. They were not likely to be captivated by tales of well-paid mistreatment.

The German émigrés were a fractious group from top to bottom, arguing incessantly about everything, especially politics. People violently disagreed about whether Germany was inherently a totalitarian society, or whether a sizable percentage of "good" Germans would be able to effect the overthrow of Hitler. Black marks were registered against people who left Germany later than early 1933, and blacker marks still against those who arrived with fortunes and their career momentum intact.

Lang's reputation as the visionary of Germany's silent screen—of dubious value in the studio corridors of Hollywood—was almost a liability in the gathering places of such refugees. For every person who admired the director, there was another who knew nothing; or, worse, one who had written a screed against his work back in Germany and thought only worse of Fritz Lang upon hindsight and reflection. The director was also suspect politically; many of the refugees were Jews who wore their Jewishness on their sleeves; in Fritz Lang they saw someone who was Germany personified—and who continued to make a point of declaring himself a Catholic. Here was someone to whom, it was rumored, Goebbels had offered the high command of the German film industry. Nobody was certain how or why Lang had turned down Goebbels's proposition; the director was still working out the details of the legend, including that pivotal turn of conversation about his mother's matrilineage.

Rumors flew that Hitler had planted people inside the American motion picture capital as spies and informants. Some German stars and directors, on sabbatical from the fatherland, did return home after sojourns in America. Some were even Bund supporters. Would Lang turn out to be one of these Nazi sympathizers, an informant, a fake émigré?

Some in the refugee community also knew the personal scuttlebutt. And Lang had vocal enemies who leaped to provide a case history against him. Ernst Jaeger, a former Berlin correspondent for *Variety* and one of those journalists the director never won over, was convinced that Lang had murdered his first wife, and reminded anyone within earshot of the murky incident. Jaeger's attack was two-pronged; as Lang's American career progressed, he kept up a critical onslaught against the director, writing newspaper pieces published in post-war German newspapers excoriating the director's "trashy" Hollywood films.

Having known Lang in Berlin, in many cases, eliminated any possibility of having a close relationship with the director in Hollywood. If the relationship wasn't poisoned already, Lang often found cause to wreck it in America. He was wary of past ties. He was never known for his largesse. The deference he demanded in Germany was no longer obligatory, and it was hard to patch up old relationships under a dramatically changed balance of power.

Harold Nebenzal recalled how the director's attitude changed toward his former producer, Seymour Nebenzahl—with whom Lang had vacationed, as well as made two of his most famous films. "Lang avoided him, spoke badly of him, and I discussed it with my father and my father's friends, and decided it was because my father knew who he was in Berlin; knew that he flew a big swastika flag from his house." Past familiarity was a debit in the case of Seymour Nebenzahl.

The nature of Lang's job had always meant that he had few intimate friends anyway. Inevitably new acquaintances were people beneath him in status, willing to serve his goals faithfully, or else people who were completely removed from his customary sphere of influence. He had walled himself off from people; few among the émigrés, few colleagues, few friends could claim they really knew him.

"I don't think he was particularly liked, even by his fellow émigrés," said Gottfried Reinhardt, who helped many of the refugees with "trivial matters" in order to help them reestablish themselves in America. Reinhardt made no bones about disliking Lang. "He had of course this name—the greatest name in German silent films. But not for me."

"Anyone who tells you that they knew Fritz Lang is a liar," said director André De Toth, a Hungarian refugee who came to Hollywood sometime later, in the early 1940s. "Fritz Lang didn't know himself. So how the hell should anybody else know him?"

Fritz Lang had plenty of time to sightsee in 1934 and 1935; starting then, and for many years after, he took long, pleasurable automobile trips during which he spoke with "every cabdriver, every gas station attendant" in a diligent effort to soak up American daily life. His very first MGM press release makes the point that "his [Lang's] principal diversion is driving to small towns and large cities, absorbing the details of the lives of the American people."

The director drew arrows on maps to classic Western locations, and began a habit of visiting the sites he had read about in dime novels and Karl May books. As with his claims about East Asian travels, the director may have exaggerated things when he told interviewer after interviewer that he lived among the Navajos in Arizona for "six or eight weeks," and also photographed their sand paintings (which was "almost forbidden"). But he did visit Indian reservations, he did take photographs and compile 8-mm footage of Western Americana, and he did journey to more than a few historic places.

Lily Latté may have been his dutiful companion on some of these trips. But she did not have the same unflagging appetite for Americana, and it didn't take Lang long to meet and coax other women along on his road adventures. A succession of young women and secretaries to whom he was a kind of father figure—as well as a regular parade of girlfriends—accompanied him on his travels. These excursions always had their professional component, as Lang carried on his informal study of Indians and Western folklore.

By late summer of 1935 Fritz Lang had traveled widely, seen quite a bit of the American Southwest, and improved his awkward English. Yet the director had been in Hollywood for over a year, and he had yet to direct his first feature film.

The cornerstone of Fritz Lang's Hollywood career is *Fury*, his first realized production for MGM—his first American picture. The fact that some critics consider *Fury* his finest U.S. film overall made it all the more important that over time Lang recreate the behind-the-scenes story of its creation as part of his mythomania. As with other parts of his life story, the director crafted an account that erased certain painful memories and turned the events into a triumphant fable starring himself.

"I wonder sometimes if it serves any purpose to rake up these old arguments," the director would say, sighing, to an interviewer. "Still, one likes to have the facts straight."

In such self-celebratory interviews the film director usually referred to *Fury* as a little-or-nothing "B" project contrived by MGM executives to occupy its lower orders—the studio minions slaving away to sustain the upper echelon, as in *Metropolis*. For Peter Bogdanovich, whose *Fritz Lang in America* is regarded as the definitive book on Lang's American career, he lowered the level: *Fury* was a "C" picture, which the studio was almost absentmindedly producing, affording Lang the opportunity to flex his creativity and override Hollywood conventions with an artistic surprise.

Lang told Charles Higham and Joel Greenberg that *Fury* came about when the director, meeting with Eddie Mannix, finally raised his voice to demand a worthwhile project. Lang knew of a writer on the lot, Norman Krasna, who had come up with a germ of a story about a man wrongly accused of a heinous crime; the man is cornered by a faceless mob, and appears to be lynched; yet he escapes and, eventually, orchestrates the courtroom conviction of his own would-be murderers. "It was I who chose the subject," the director informed Gene D. Phillips definitively. According to Lang, Mannix, heeding his demand, allowed him to work with Krasna on developing the through-line of the scenario "as long as we wanted to."

Bartlett Cormack came aboard to help with the dialogue writing, according to Lang's version of events, at the director's own behest. Admittedly, Cormack did most of the actual dialogue. "I must point out that I gave advice and we talked it over," Lang told Bogdanovich, "but that the written words were mostly by Cormack—naturally, I could write some lines—or were taken from newspaper clippings."

The two of them were supervised by the studio-appointed producer, Joseph L. Mankiewicz; but Mankiewicz, also one of Hollywood's consummate screenwriters, came "late to the project," and was actually something of an encumbrance, according to Lang. (No Hollywood producer could ever be an asset to Lang. "You must have worked with producers who facilitated your work sometime in your career?" American Film Institute students asked the director in 1974. "Look, a producer can be a great fellow . . ." responded Lang. "If he leaves you alone?" prompted the questioner. "No, if he helps," answered Lang. "Offhand, I didn't find anyone [in Hollywood]" . . .)

The rivalry between Cormack and Mankiewicz made some of the story sessions "tense," Lang told Peter Bogdanovich. The director would have preferred the story to be about a "white woman raped by a colored man," as Lang phrased it, but the studio (by implication, Mankiewicz) was too backward for that kind of social commentary. Nonetheless Lang tried to insert into the scenario various vignettes featuring black characters, only some of which were actually filmed. Louis B. Mayer personally had the racially-charged material cut out as "not necessary"—the studio head was convinced that black people should only be shown in menial occupations.

Lang implied in interviews that it was *he* who shaped the major events and characters of the screenplay. He told Peter Bogdanovich that he distinctly remembered arguing for the lead character to be a lawyer—because, this son of the middle class explained, "I felt that a lawyer could better express his feelings and thoughts than a working man, a laborer." It was Mankiewicz, in the act for which even Lang had to give him credit, who suggested the hero be an ordinary man: "John Doe—a man of the people," in Lang's words. "I thought, here is a kind of sign of a democracy. . . . This was something [I] learned here for the first time, and I think it's absolutely correct."

This made for a kind of synchronicity with *M*—the first film in which Lang had shown any curiosity about the psychology of ordinary human beings. In Germany, under the influence of Nietzschean philosophy and military power— even before Hitler, with the emperor—the hero of a film always had to be a superman, according to Lang. American democracy, the director told Bogdanovich, mandated a different kind of Fritz Lang hero.

"In a totalitarian state, or in a state governed by a dictator, an emperor or a king, this leader himself is, in a way, a superman; he can't do wrong—at least he couldn't in those days. So over there the hero in a motion picture should be a superman, whereas in a democracy, he had to be Joe [sic] Doe."

Lang claimed in some interviews that he had "complete freedom" to make this "B" or "C" film. In others he dwelled laboriously on the studio hindrances strewn in his path.

The MGM waters turned out to be shark-infested. "To begin with, I was a co-founder of the Screen Directors Guild and therefore a black sheep in the eyes of executives like L. B. Mayer," Lang told Gene D. Phillips.* The director therefore encountered "a great lack of cooperation from various quarters," right from the start of filming. If Lang happened to check on the construction and design of a certain set before he went home for the night, he might return in the morning and discover that this set had been mysteriously dismantled, "allegedly because some of the parts were needed elsewhere in the studio. If I needed a car with four doors, I got one with two doors—or vice versa."

Lang's altercations were sometimes strangely reminiscent of his experiences in France, with MGM cast and crew forced to skip meals because the director still overlooked the presence of unions. "I had some trouble," Lang would admit. "For example, in Europe I was accustomed to finishing a scene no

---

*This politically correct canard of Lang's cannot be substantiated. According to a definitive article in *Variety* on the origins of the Directors Guild Association, King Vidor summoned eleven prominent film directors to a secret meeting at his Beverly Hills home on December 23, 1935. The identities of the twelve DGA founders have been established: Vidor, Rouben Mamoulian, Frank Borzage, Howard Hawks, Henry King, Rowland V. Lee, Lewis Milestone, A. Edward Sutherland, Frank Tuttle, Richard Wallace, Herbert Biberman, and William A. Wellman. (Conflicting accounts, without mentioning Lang's name, list thirteen or fourteen.) Neither is Lang listed in various news reports of the temporary officers or leaders at the nascent organization's second secret meeting. When the first general meeting of the Guild convened in mid-January of 1936, the *Hollywood Reporter* listed all eighty-four attendees by name. Lang's does not appear on that list either.

matter how much time was needed. Still, I was very considerate of my crew, and the crew always loved me . . ."

Lang tried sincerely to find ways to get around the necessities of working with such a large union force. "I didn't have to halt filming after five hours so that extras or the crew could eat," Lang told Charles Higham and Joel Greenberg. "I'd dismiss, say, half the crew, and the cameraman, and I would continue working in the studio with a sandwich or something; then, when the half-crew came back from their meal, we'd send out the other half." American customs were so peculiar. "Nobody told me that here in America there's a law that you have to send your crew to eat after a certain time," the Bogdanovich version continued. "As a matter of fact, there's a law in California that every five or five and a half hours, all the extras have to be fed. I didn't know that."

Imagine a law that extras have to be fed! Lang couldn't. "One of my greatest enemies in this matter was Mr. Spencer Tracy," Lang told Peter Bogdanovich. "If somebody would have said, 'Fritz, look, in America it's important—so and so,' I would have done it. But no one told me anything and so in this case it was very disagreeable work."

L. B. Mayer, Joseph L. Mankiewicz, Spencer Tracy—all enemies. Enemies and saboteurs lurking everywhere. One of the most bitter pills was the film's "happy ending," one of those symbolic clinches that worked for *Metropolis*, but that Lang had decided he loathed—at least in this instance. It was Mankiewicz, the director's bête noire, who insisted that the leading man and lady hug and embrace in the final moments—after all the terrifying incidents that had gone before in the film. And Mankiewicz got his way, according to Lang.

It was a miracle that the film even got made—but it did, largely through Lang's subversive tactics. One of the director's favorite stories, competing with the Goebbels whopper, brought him to an appointment with Eddie Mannix after one of the first studio screenings of the film. Mannix couldn't believe what his own eyes had witnessed. He called the director on the carpet, accusing Lang of filming something other than the approved script. Lang begged to differ. Mannix, in a fit of pique, sent for a copy of the shooting script to make the comparison.

"I was in the doghouse," Lang told Peter Bogdanovich. "I sat there near the secretaries five quarters of an hour and everybody knew I was in the doghouse. Nobody even spat at me. I saw secretaries going in with highballs—nobody offered me one. So I sat at the bench—the accused." Finally, after the "five quarters of an hour," the elusive script was procured. Mannix waved it in front of Lang. "You are right, it's here," the studio vice president told the director, "but it sounds different on the screen!"

No matter how exceptional the film did turn out to be, the MGM front office stood arrayed against Lang. An executive in the front office—maybe Mannix; Lang shied from naming names—even told W. R. Wilkerson, publisher of the *Hollywood Reporter*, to skip the scheduled preview. It was just an embarrassing "B" or "C" film by a son-of-a-bitch director. But Wilkerson knew of Lang's German mystique; he attended the showing anyway, and became one of the first to spread the word about Lang's triumphant U.S. debut.

But it made no difference. MGM did everything possible to thwart *Fury*, despite good reviews everywhere. The film flopped. Fritz Lang's American debut, a virtuoso performance, was spoiled.

The director became convinced that there had existed a conspiracy against him. Everything Lang did in Hollywood thereafter was tainted by that conviction.

Joseph L. Mankiewicz was right in telling French author Michel Ciment that Lang's skewed version of events added up to a "fairy tale," tinged with paranoid delusion. Lang himself kept the precise day-by-day *Fury* story files and memoranda, and they subtly contradict much of his oft-repeated account.

The concept behind *Fury* definitely originated with Krasna. A former errand boy for the *New York World* and legman for a motion picture journal, Krasna started out as a press agent for Warner Brothers, where he had cultivated a reputation for pulling outrageous stunts. At night he wrote plays and scripts, winning a contract with Columbia as a junior writer. For the rest of his career, Krasna would divide his career between stage and screen; he was headed to New York to try out *Small Miracle*, in the summer of 1934, when he stopped in at MGM to have lunch with Mankiewicz.

Over lunch he and Mankiewicz discussed a recent headline-grabbing incident—one of those crime stories Lang would have filed away himself if he had even been in America when it happened. On November 27, 1933, a mob of vigilantes had broken into a jail in San Jose and lynched two suspects in the kidnapping and murder of a widely known department-store heir. News bulletins and photos of the hangings—the dangling victims stripped nude—stunned the nation. There were several unique angles: The kidnapping was never satisfactorily solved, with the alleged ringleader, one of the two lynching victims, maintaining his innocence up to the bitter end. The governor of California shamed himself by endorsing the lynching. And when the lynching case was brought to court, the locals stuck together, refusing to identify the mob members. Only one person among hundreds was indicted, the charges dismissed in February of 1934.

Over a cup of coffee, Krasna rehashed the headline incident with Mankiewicz. Both were outraged by the lynching. Krasna, normally a comedic writer, pointed out that a mistaken lynching would make a powerful screen drama; on the spot he improvised the semblance of a storyline. Mankiewicz, who had been trying to get Louis B. Mayer to let him direct, grew excited by Krasna's concept. When they parted, Krasna agreed to let Mankiewicz explore the subject's potential.

Time elapsed. Mankiewicz spoke to studio officials, who encouraged an initial story treatment. By the time Krasna returned to Hollywood, however, he had already forgotten the plot as he had pitched it.* Mankiewicz took it upon himself to write an initial ten-page treatment, which bore the title "Mob Rule." Krasna would eventually receive a fee of $15–25,000 for that treatment,

---

*Krasna's fabulous career included Alfred Hitchcock's only screwball comedy, *Mr. and Mrs. Smith*, a play and screenplay in collaboration with Groucho Marx, and a number of hit romantic comedies for the stage and screen. But he was not the only one in Hollywood notorious for brainstorming a story premise, selling the film rights, and then letting other people, coming along later, fill in the holes.

as well as an Academy Award nomination for Best Original Story (the only Oscar honor accorded *Fury*), without ever having penned a single word. That was okay with Mankiewicz. His goal was to direct.

Mankiewicz made his case in person to Louis B. Mayer, but the mogul of moguls turned him down. Mayer had bigger plans for Mankiewicz. He reminded the screenwriter that MGM was a producer's studio, and insisted Mankiewicz become a producer instead. One of his first jobs would be the decidedly "A" production of "Mob Rule."

All this took place late in the summer of 1935. As Lang was cooling his heels, waiting for an audience with Mannix, Mankiewicz was gearing up. Knowing Lang was available, he asked for the former Ufa director, in his eyes the best man for the job. Though Lang believed him a friend and booster, Mannix was already fed up with this perpetually aggrieved director who had yet to make a single picture in Hollywood. Behind his back Mannix was wont to refer to Lang as "that Teutonic son of a whore" ("which wasn't quite accurate," Mankiewicz liked to add). There was nothing else on the horizon for Lang, so the director was assigned to "Mob Rule."

With Mankiewicz came the casting of his friend Spencer Tracy, at this point an admired leading man but not quite a star. The producer had always envisioned Tracy in the principal role of Joe, the man falsely accused of a crime and attacked by a mob; indeed, all of the earliest drafts of the scenario refer to the actor by name.

Mankiewicz's initial treatment was understandably sketchy. The character of Joe had several brothers, who are prospering because of illegal activities; Joe, an honest lawyer, is ironically the only one suffering through the Depression. He has a dog ("like Spencer Tracy—beaten but with an innate courage" in the language of the script) that becomes the only fatality of a mob-incited jail fire. In later interviews Lang complained about the dog as one of the imbecilic details—in any case, meant ironically—that peppered early drafts. But Lang dwelled on such minor issues in his mind, then exaggerated their importance for posterity.

After Joe is nearly killed by the mob, according to Mankiewicz's treatment, his passion for vengeance nearly drives him crazy. Meanwhile, Mary, Joe's wife, resigning herself to the fact that Joe is dead, falls in love with the prosecuting attorney—her husband's professional rival. A climactic showdown between Joe, Mary, and the district attorney takes place at the penitentiary. The mob participants are about to be hanged. Joe, showing up to savor their execution, refuses to step forward and reveal the truth: that he has survived the mob's fury—that the murder for which they're about to pay never happened. When the prosecutor discovers him and pleads with him to come forward, Joe pulls a gun.

Mary interposes her body between him and Joe, so that Joe won't shoot. She and the district attourney manage to flee the room in time to stop the hanging. As Joe hears their footsteps hurrying away he sinks to a chair, his head in his hands. He says, "But they killed my dog—didn't they?"

Lang did not know—or, in later interviews, conveniently forgot—that this first treatment had been written up by Mankiewicz, and that it was the producer who vigorously championed him as director of the promising material.

Krasna was never involved in a single script conference with the director, and the skeleton of the storyline was firmly established before Bartlett Cormack ever joined the project.

But "Mob Rule" did need help. Studio records show that the first script session—on August 20, 1935, as prospects for "Passport to Hell" were dwindling—was a meeting between Lang and Leonard Praskins. Praskins was a brash New Yorker who had penned short stories and vaudeville sketches before coming to Hollywood in 1929; he had a prestigious credit on *The Champ* and had just done duty on *Call of the Wild*. An MGM veteran, he was expected to carry the ball as the senior writer. Lang may have considered Praskins the initial "story editor" on the project—a phrase he later used in describing Mankiewicz's predecessor. The director was conveniently oblivious to Mankiewicz himself.

Lang and Praskins met for nearly two weeks, but the Lang-Praskins sessions, as detailed story conference notes make clear, proved virtually worthless. Joe, they temporarily decided, would become an idealistic lawyer with a shady partner. His brothers were given connections with gangsters. Characteristically, Lang spent a lot of time on the visual construction of an intricate opening sequence. His camera would focus on a stray dog, ignored by the heartless brothers but befriended by Joe as he stands in a breadline. The opening sequence (later jettisoned) promised to be impressive, but the arc of the story— the through-line—remained vague and unfulfilled.

The director's faulty grasp of English, the imperfect chemistry between the two men, and the time pressures conspired to deprive the team of viable story solutions. Lang's notes indicate that he was asking all the right questions about the leading character and the elusive through-line: "What changes this man?" Lang wrote; "Fear—danger—injustice—personal experience." The director wanted Joe to be an easily understood character, recognizable to audiences, but how to bring this about? Lang knew his strengths as a visual filmmaker, and argued to minimize Joe's lines. "Short scenes can give us this man's character. Need no long dialogue scenes."

But Lang had no answers to the bigger questions. For two weeks, all the main story points of "Mob Rule" were juggled, crossed out, reassembled—to no avail. Frustrated with their stagnation, Mankiewicz showed up for his first story conference on September 3, 1935. Right away Mankiewicz focused on the main problem: "Who is the most important character?—the man, the wife, the district attorney, or the mob?" he asked Lang and Leonard Praskins. "Maybe the man should not be a lawyer," the producer mused. "He should be very bewildered and puzzled while in jail . . ."

Mankiewicz drifted in and out of story conferences during the first week of September, a crucial week during which the film's focus sharpened considerably. Most days, Mankiewicz proffered his ideas early, then left the room for errands and duties while Lang and Praskins carried on, trying to implement his suggestions.

On September 5, Mankiewicz and Lang launched into a discussion about Joe and his crime-connected brothers. Lang, with his predilection for underworld characters, insisted that the gangster ties added excitement to the script. Mankiewicz remained firm. "I see these kids not in touch with gangsters," the producer said. "To me, they are ordinary kids out of work." After that story conference, for the first time, the lawyer and gangster angles were dropped, and Joe became a "typical American," a John Doe. In the finished film this became a central premise.

The title was changed to *Fury*. Mary's name was changed to Katherine; she became Joe's fianceé, not his wife, and in the film her character would no longer fall in love with the prosecutor, though a hint remains that he has a crush on her. The brothers, as well as the prosecuting attorney, would be played down in the final form.

Fury's third act would switch from the penitentiary to the courtroom, where a town of John Does goes on trial, à la the San Jose indictment. Lang relished courtroom procedure, and citations and clippings from the studio's legal department kept him apprised of the most up-to-date court motions and maneuvers. With Joe "dead"—though in the film he sends coded messages from hiding, like the child killer of *M*—the weight of the drama would also shift—to Katherine.

Indeed, at the September 7 story conference, Lang made a case that the Spencer Tracy character was not sympathetic enough, and that *Fury* ought to be equally a woman's picture—told from Katherine's perspective as much as Joe's. This key suggestion was accepted; Joe became more likable, and Katherine's belief in the system of law became an important thematic counterbalance to Joe's vow of retribution.

Even with these strides, the draft Leonard Praskins produced on September 11, 1935, was woefully inadequate, carrying over many of the gaps of the treatment and early story conferences. The project needed a better-attuned writer, and the script continued to hobble along until, in mid-September, Bartlett Cormack entered the equation.

Cormack had just been signed by MGM. Mankiewicz knew him from New York, and considered him a friend. Cormack was one of the Ben Hecht crowd of unrepentant newspaper reporters from Chicago, the author of a hard-edged play about gangsters called *The Racket*, which had created a sensation on Broadway during 1927 and 1928, giving lead actor Edward G. Robinson, who would go on to star in two Fritz Lang films, his big break. A Phi Beta Kappa member who also wrote college musicals and short stories, Cormack had been brought out to Hollywood by Paramount; during his brief lifetime (he would die in 1942 at age forty-four), he wrote screenplays for a number of entertaining films that included *Gentlemen of the Press*, *The Front Page*, *Half-Naked Truth*, and *The Beachcomber*. "The melodramatic subject matter and his dramatic skills matched perfectly," said Mankiewicz, who lobbied strongly for Cormack, just as he had advocated Lang.

Now it was Cormack, Mankiewicz, and Lang. Cormack's first draft was turned over within two months, by November 12, 1935. There was indeed a tremendous amount of social awareness in the early versions, which featured breadlines, black characters, even a settlement house where Katherine worked. Cormack's first rewrite cleared away some of the social commentary; more would disappear as he honed the script.

Cormack's initial draft included one consciousness-raising scene, set in a movie theater, where a newsreel showed politicians from Western states debating over foreign entanglements (the kind of scene Lang, fond of film-within-a-film gimmickry, may have proposed). A mule-headed Joe gets into a political argument with someone in the audience, shouting his opinion, "It was the people who made this country what it is today!" An "elderly, bespectacled Negro" provides a capper, leaning over a row of seats to comment caustically, "Brothah, you ought t'get around more!"

This vignette would be eventually dropped, as part of the narrowing, parabolic focus on Joe. So was the scene which featured a shoeshine attendant listening to an argument about the Constitution; shining and slapping shoes, he nods his head in agreement at the liberal remarks of customers bemoaning the state of the nation.* Fritz Lang always maintained that these and other Negro scenes were deleted against his better judgment. But it appears unlikely that he raised any objection at the time. On the contrary: Lang's own publicity betrays a marked racial insensitivity during his first years in America. When Lang was "between pictures" in the 1930s, he kept press agents busy promoting his name in newspapers and magazines with innocuous items and not-so-innocuous jokes—often at the expense of "colored people" he supposedly knew.

Sample from Hedda Hopper's column in the *Los Angeles Times* of October 17, 1940: "Director Fritz Lang overheard his Negro cook asking her visiting boy friend, 'Wheah you all been?'

" 'Lookin' foah work,' said he.

" 'Man! Man!' exclaimed the cook, 'Youah curiosity's gonna git you in trouble yit.' "

There are other examples of such dubious racial humor in Lang's carefully preserved professional papers. In 1935, the film director had roughly the same slant on African-Americans as on American Indians, a perspective that was condescending and, at best, politically naive. Of the two, Mankiewicz—whose outrage over the San Jose lynching had inaugurated the project—was by far the more conscientious urban liberal.

The director's most substantial claim to political sensitivity—that at some nascent stage he had tried to turn *Fury* into a film about a black man accused of raping a white woman—is especially absurd, given both the historical record and the social environment. It was always Spencer Tracy, never a black actor; nor could it have been a black leading man at MGM or any other major Hollywood studio in 1935, when the film studios were still deeply beholden to the theater-owners and segregationist exhibitors in the Deep South.

Making *Fury*, though, did have the side effect of furthering Lang's political Americanization. It was through research for the production that Lang received his education about the long and shameful history of lynching black Americans being lynched. MGM's research department would provide for the director materials chronicling several notorious lynchings of blacks—including the murder of Henry Argo in Grady Country, Oklahoma, on May 31, 1930, which prompted the indictment of some twenty-three people.

---

*It is interesting that this character was a shoeshine attendant, considering that Lang often claimed in interviews that the scenes involving black characters were excised, because Louis B. Mayer thought black people should be shown only "as shoeshine people or as porters in a railroad car." In actual fact, that is how they were portrayed in all the earliest drafts of *Fury*.

The racial issue would bother Lang more in retrospect than it did in 1935, when he embarked on *Fury*. After the film was finished and had been released, he would become only too aware of its social failings. Critics like Kenneth Fearing—writing in *New Masses*, one of the left-wing journals to which Lang was just beginning to subscribe—opined that *Fury* was "one top-notch picture," albeit "with two or three mediocre ones tossed in on top of it." The first half was "fine anti-lynch stuff," Fearing wrote, "though not as pointed as it could have been—remember—we have to sell these pictures in the South."

As time passed, the director was often asked by people who admired *Fury* whether he had ever considered making the film with a black star as the falsely accused victim. He came to believe in his own mind that he had considered that brave option. Such a move would have been unpalatable to the reactionaries who ran MGM, Lang told fans of the film's message. This made sense to people, though all available evidence suggests that Lang operated strictly from wishful hindsight.

It was an issue that bothered Lang, because in spite of everything *Fury* always remained one of the director's favorite works. He used to screen it— along with *M*—for the heavily left-leaning office staff of his independent production company in the mid-1940s. They didn't have to qualify their heartfelt praise. Lang would then surprise them by acting so defensively about the film. "I was a coward," the director would confess in conversation. "I should have had it be about a black man."

Bartlett Cormack wrote several drafts before the screenplay was finally approved for filming in April and May of 1936. Coming almost two years after Lang's arrival in America, *Fury* then became such a battle royal—between Fritz Lang and nearly everyone else on the MGM lot—that it has achieved the status of Hollywood folklore. No matter how the director tried to make others out to be the villains, however, he himself was clearly at fault—if nothing else, for indulging in the kind of high-handed behavior that had always, in Berlin, been his accepted personal style.

He had only one full-fledged ally, and that was Sylvia Sidney. The actress, whose intelligent, dignified presence allowed her to portray everything from Oriental royalty (*Madame Butterfly*) to overworked working girls (*Dead End*), had recently left Paramount, the studio that had made her a star. After sifting through numerous offers, Sidney, more interested in proving herself an actress than in resting on her laurels, agreed to appear in *Fury*. From Norman Krasna, whom the actress had dated, she knew in advance about the film. Spencer Tracy was an up-and-comer she wanted to work with, and she was one of the Hollywood minority already aware of Fritz Lang's name. "I knew about his work in Germany," Sidney said. "I turned down many, many pictures for twice the money because I preferred to do *Fury* with Spencer Tracy and Fritz Lang."

In later interviews, the director could be gently deprecating about Sidney. He enjoyed telling this anecdote: For the scene in *Fury* where Katherine arrives at the jailhouse as it is being burned down (apparently with Joe trapped inside), Lang couldn't get a strong enough expression of fright out of the actress. So the director arranged for a prop man to stand behind Sidney with two revolvers and to shoot them off during the take. Lang pleaded with the actress,

"Please ... I know you don't like to do it ... overact in this scene ... for once!" Lang called action, the guns went off, and Sidney went through her motions—without the slightest unrehearsed twinge. When Lang called "Cut!" she turned to face him. "What was all that racket?" she asked mildly.

But Sidney's loyalty fortified Lang in the 1930s. After *Fury*, her say-so was instrumental in getting the director jobs on his next two features: *You Only Live Once* and *You and Me*. The actress completely accepted the director's methods, however crudely inflicted. "There was always someone who was his patsy," Sidney realized. "He [Lang] became a very dear and close friend," she said in a 1994 interview. "I loved him as a friend, and worked with him three times. He was bright, he was witty, he was giving. I still have a picture of him stuck up in my kitchen—with a monocle."

Not too many other people on the *Fury* set found the director bright, or witty, or giving.

"Spencer Tracy, together with the entire cast and crew, loathed Fritz Lang," said producer Joseph L. Mankiewicz.

"During *Fury*," echoed Gottfried Reinhardt, "Lang was the most loathed man on the lot."

"He's [Lang] a German through and through, a real sadist," said camera-man Joseph Ruttenberg. "He puts on a worse front than the dragon he had in *Siegfried*. He was hell on everybody—actors, technicians, everybody."

Choosing the right cameraman was still a priority for Fritz Lang. He was more fortunate in this category than others in America, and the director usu-ally got the cinematographer he wanted; cameramen were one of the bones tossed to Hollywood directors. Whether Lang always got along with his man was another issue.

On this initial outing, the director was permitted to supervise a series of screen tests for photographers under studio contract. Joseph Ruttenberg, a Russian-born veteran whose career dated back to silent features in New York during the post–World War I era, was familiar with the Expressionism of German films, and he wanted the job. Skilled at evoking depth, dimension, and atmosphere, Ruttenberg deliberately established a "cockeyed setup," with the camera perched at a severe low angle. The director went for the bait. "I vont that cameraman vor me," Ruttenberg remembered Lang commanding.

The director's way was the only way; there could be no other, as cameramen working under Lang were always obliged to learn. But to arrive at his final decision Lang loved to instigate a long process of debate and argument. This was as true in America as in Germany: agreement was acceptable, but argu-ment was thrilling.

Ruttenberg preferred not to argue. On one occasion, "after a long, hard day's work," Ruttenberg remembered, Lang called him in and put on an amaz-ing performance, "actually crying" for Ruttenberg's benefit. "Joe," Lang com-plained, wiping away tears, "What's the matter? You don't argue with me!" "Fritz," replied Ruttenberg, "there would be no use arguing with you. It would be only one-sided."

In the courtroom scene which takes place at the end of *Fury*, a newsreel photographer sets up a projector to show 16-mm footage of the mob riot.

Shades are drawn, the courtroom darkened. Citizens are picked out on the screen, lighting cigarettes that flicker on their faces, waving burning torches that highlight contorted features.

It promised to be one of the film's cinematic flourishes, and augured a technical challenge that whetted the director's appetite: How could Lang dim the lights gradually, without losing focus, in order to simulate the effect of those descending shades? Today it sounds like a minor challenge, but in the mid-1930s no such illusion could be taken lightly.

The director wanted to film the scene by somehow dimming the huge arc lights that would already be in place, but Ruttenberg believed there was no way to dim arc lights incrementally. They had to be turned on or off, all at once. Ruttenberg told Lang he had an idea to get the same effect using "different means," but stalled when the director pressed him for details. "I wouldn't tell him," the cameraman explained in an interview, "because I knew if I had he wouldn't like it."

This precipitated a crisis. A meeting with Mankiewicz and other higher-ups was called, where Ruttenberg spoke up. He would achieve the desired result by shutting down the lenses for a brief moment, as the shades were drawn; then, changing the exposure, he would reopen the lenses in the newly darkened room. Not only would his method approximate gradual darkening, it would be cheaper than Lang's experimentation. Cheaper: everyone (except Lang) liked that. Everyone backed Ruttenberg. There was no further argument. Lang was simply overruled—by a cameraman. He was furious. "The scene was photographed, and it was a beautiful scene," recollected Ruttenberg. "And Fritz said, 'Very good, but it wasn't what I had in mind.'"

There were worse crises than differences of opinion with Ruttenberg. The lynch riot would be like a mini-excerpt from *Metropolis*; Lang, typically, insisted on joining the frenzy himself. Although it meant intruding on the province of the property men, Lang would not only direct the scene, but act the provocateur, tossing small "smoke bombs" at the front doors of the building where Spencer Tracy was supposedly jailed. In the heat of the fray, however, one of the director's smoke bombs accidentally struck Bruce Cabot, who was playing one of the mob ringleaders. The scene was being filmed after midnight, and Cabot "had been imbibing against the cold of the night," according to Mankiewicz; the furious actor had to be physically restrained from throttling Lang.

That wasn't the director's only confrontation with an actor. Spencer Tracy was, contrarily, on the wagon, and in fact on probation with MGM, after having engaged in a nasty public altercation with director William Wellman late in 1935. Now Tracy—usually known for minding his business, learning and saying his lines with perfect emotional pitch, often on the first take, and then hiding out in his dressing room between setups—had to contend with Fritz Lang.

Lang liked to lord it over his stars—it was his instinct as a pack leader— and even Tracy, rarely flustered by a director, lost control of himself. The director's penchant for repeated takes and endless minor adjustments at first baffled the actor, then began to unnerve him. Finally Tracy was driven to the edge. Nothing would satisfy Lang, and the director ran roughshod over his star in full view of everyone, yelling directions like a kaiser.

In one scene, where Joe is fleeing in the middle of the night from the burning jailhouse, Lang had the actor, his loose overcoat flapping behind him, running along in front of a camera cart the director himself elected to steer. As Tracy huffed and puffed, Lang shot take after take, calling out, "A little faster . . . a little faster . . . faster!" as he sped dangerously close behind his star. Lang "almost drove him [Tracy] to drink," said Mankiewicz. The director had his leading man "terrified and quite rightly so."

The director's habit of working straight through lunch, regardless of the stomach growls of cast and crew, eventually caught up with him. Lang typically had "a pill and a glass of cognac brought to him on a silver platter by his secretary, who was nicknamed the Iron Butterfly," according to Mankiewicz. Ruttenberg confirmed that Lang's lunch consisted of "some kind of pill that was equivalent to a full meal." Interviewed later, Lang remembered more benignly that he usually had a sandwich to tide him over. Probably it was all three—a pill, cognac, and one of the director's preferred sandwiches faithfully assembled by Lily Latté, who was on the books as an "extra."

Every day, the assistant director argued with Lang that they really ought to make time for a lunch break. Every day Lang resisted. "I just did eat," he would say, "I'm not hungry." Spencer Tracy observed all this with mounting displeasure. One day, with the cast and crew griping ever louder, Tracy took the bull by the horns. "We have just come up with a plan," he told Lang. "We are all hungry. Can we go eat?" To which Lang, his authority challenged by a mere actor, replied, "It is I and no one else who will decide that." "Tracy looked him in the face very nicely," recollected Mankiewicz, "passed his hand over his face, smearing his makeup, and yelled, 'Lunch!' and left the set." The cast and crew followed suit, the lights were turned off, and Lang and Lily Latté, who was present for the showdown, were left alone on an empty stage.

From then on there would be lunch every day, but otherwise the daily schedule became a grueling race in which Lang struggled to meet both the studio's deadline and his own perfectionist demands. Most days filming began at 7:30 A.M., and carried over until 2 or 3 A.M. the following morning. Saturdays were even longer. The crew worked on the soundstages throughout Saturday morning and afternoon; then Lang would mount his exterior shots at night, filming until daylight interceded early Sunday morning. Sunday was a guaranteed break, but early each Monday morning everyone had to report back on call.

The crews were accustomed to long, brutal hours; other Hollywood directors were every bit as tyrannical. Trampling over people was part of a director's job description, all the more so for tunnel-visionaries like Lang. But Fritz Lang in America did not command the same authority that he had in Germany, and he would collect few allies over the years. He never thought to insulate himself with courtesies or endearments, and his offenses were many.

One night—again it was after midnight—tension on the set reached a flashpoint. Mankiewicz was awakened by a phone call at his home. Everybody was fed up. The electricians, irate over their terrible treatment, had rigged "a big arc [light] to fall on Fritz Lang," in Mankiewicz's words. Or maybe it was a sandbag rigged to plummet on the director's head—or both; Lang's enemies also have their conflicting lore.

Pulling on clothes, the producer hurried to the set. The assistant director was tearing his hair out. Tracy was threatening to walk off. The crew was standing around idle, murmuring ominously. Lang hadn't liked the look of a certain stack of oranges piled up in the background of a scene; hurling into a tantrum, he had knocked them to the floor, no matter that it would take two hours to rehabilitate the set. Now Lang was strutting around snapping at people, oblivious to the danger he had put himself in. Mankiewicz drew a deep breath and went about the work of calming everyone. He saved the director that night, he claimed—as he would save Fritz Lang, his own worst enemy, several times during the production.

From the onset of filming, the front office had exerted pressure on the producer to replace the unpopular director. Mankiewicz bent over backward to accomodate Lang, even indulging the director's unusual solution to one of the demands of the script—how to convey the guilt that haunted Joe. Lang chose to make the image literal, filming "ghosts shooting up from behind trees and chasing Tracy, twenty years after they appeared in *Caligari*," in Mankiewicz's words. The producer never thought that scene would work; Tracy hated it. Nonetheless it stayed on the schedule and in the film. "All of this made me crazy, but the rushes were brilliant," remembered Mankiewicz.

To Lang, Mankiewicz was the eternal viper slithering behind his back. To those in the know, however, the producer was regarded as the director's only legitimate defender. "It was purely Joseph Mankiewicz's doing that he wasn't taken off the picture," said Gottfried Reinhardt.

In the end Mankiewicz even permitted Lang free reign in the editing room. The sneak preview at nearby Palmdale, happy ending notwithstanding, represented the director's best cut of *Fury*—complete with all of Lang's embellishments, including the symbolic ghosts of guilt, a cherished conceit that appeared in several of the director's German films and would stubbornly recur in *Scarlet Street*. All the top MGM executives were in Palmdale, along with the director and producer, for the first public showing.

After the ghosts came on, "the public didn't stop laughing during the last two reels," according to Mankiewicz. In the lobby afterward, Eddie Mannix foamed at the mouth and ordered Mankiewicz to re-edit *Fury* and expunge all the "Walt Disney nonsense." According to the producer, the exasperated Mannix would have liked to fire the director on the spot.

Poor previews and studio re-editing were par for the course—but not for Fritz Lang. "Boiling with rage," in Curt Riess's words, the director insisted on bringing his case to the court of highest appeal—Louis B. Mayer. It's a measure of Lang's marginal status that he had never exchanged more than a half dozen pleasantries—the obligatory handshake and hallway hellos—with the top man. Throughout his Hollywood tenure, Lang would find himself largely isolated from the top moguls. Now, according to Riess, he made the rare mistake of trying to bully the boss.

"Mayer smiled at him, said he wanted to sign a new contract with Fritz, a much better one, he loved the new film, it would be a huge success," reported

Riess, "And Fritz shouted so much at Mayer that the most important man in Hollywood fell backward into his chair. Mayer is supposed to have said later, 'Even if it costs me a million, or two million, this man is not going to make another movie for MGM.' "

The Mayer incident took place in private. But another violation took place in public, at the Hollywood premiere, after the audience was bowled over by the revised version of *Fury*, which had been unassumingly reedited by Joseph Mankiewicz.

Lang always remembered "the bad things better." One of the bad things that stuck deepest in his craw was the film's re-editing—and especially the "happy ending," which to him became symbolic of everything the director had put up with. Lang had no quarrel with Joe giving himself up to prove that he was alive, as he told Peter Bogdanovich, but he believed that Joe's action couldn't be motivated by social consciousness alone. "I think this man gives himself up because he can't go on living with an eternal lie," explained the director. "He couldn't go through life with it. It's too easy an explanation to say social consciousness makes one do something. One acts because of emotions, personal emotions."

All along Mankiewicz had insisted that Joe and Katherine be reconciled at the end of the story, so the film could conclude with the standard fade-out—a romantic clinch, an approach that was almost axiomatic in Hollywood. Lang fought this ending, even the muted version Mankiewicz dictated, in which Katherine absolves Joe with a brief hug and a smooch. The only trouble with the ending, really, was that it was Mankiewicz's, not Lang's. The director wasn't averse to dreaming up his own happy endings, but he couldn't bring himself to forgive this trespass on his artistry.

Mankiewicz, who had done his best to forge an alliance with Lang, met the director on the sidewalk outside the Brown Derby after the premiere. Lang walked arm in arm with Marlene Dietrich. The producer stuck out his hand, saying, "Fritz, we had some problems, but now we have a very good film on our hands." "You have ruined my film," Lang replied, brushing by, refusing the olive branch.

Hollywood people might have been of mixed minds about Eddie Mannix and Louis B. Mayer, but the generous, witty, and self-effacing Mankiewicz was widely liked in the film industry. Word traveled quickly about this disgraceful treatment of the man who had all along given Lang his ardent support. Lang was stuck with this incident for the rest of his life. Mankiewicz, like one of Joe's ghosts, could not be banished from his mind.

"MGM was truly a test for Fritz," said Mankiewicz sympathetically in 1994. "It must have been difficult to have been the superman, the Übermensch, who directed *Metropolis*, and then to find yourself having to abide by union laws with regards to the hours of meals."

Years after, asked in an interview about *Fury*, Lang made an uncharacteristic confession that by not reconciling with the well-meaning producer he had done "a stupid thing."

The U.S. reviews were uniformly favorable. MGM could feel proud that it had produced "if not the year's most important film, at least as forthright a drama as the screen has concocted," in the words of the *New York Times*. Reaction around the world echoed the American assessment. In England, Graham Greene wrote that Lang's first Hollywood feature was "the only film I know to which I have wanted to attach the epithet of 'great'."

Lang came as close with *Fury* as he would ever come to winning a major U.S. film critics' citation. When New York critics met to cast their ballot for best achievements of 1936, the selection for the year's Best Director was "the most protracted contest" of the three-hour session, according to the *New York Times*. Lang received six votes for *Fury*—the most of any candidate on the first ballot—but several other directors earned enough support to warrant further voting. Nine ballots were necessary, the tallies swinging back and forth, before Rouben Mamoulian (for *The Gay Desperado*) gained momentum and defeated Lang with a final tally of twelve votes to six. But the director was quite right in boasting to columnists that *Fury* came "within an inch" of winning the New York Film Critics' prize for Best Direction of the Year.

The film starts quietly enough in a succession of Midwestern snapshots. Katherine (Sylvia Sidney) has a job prospect and must leave her boyfriend to improve her station in life. Joe (Spencer Tracy), honest, hardworking, is saving up to buy a gas station, planning marriage, looking optimistically toward the future. They bid each other an emotional farewell in a railroad station. Lang knew from train-station good-byes.

The character of Joe is tagged with a running joke in the film, a riff out of the director's daily life of ceaseless adjustments to his new home in America: He has a mental block about the word "memento," which he mispronounces "momentum."

The little dog of the earliest treatment made it into the film. "You look the way I feel," Joe tells the dog, "lonely and small." But the dog appears only briefly in the story, and the bruited-about Negro characters are barely represented. A black woman singing as she pins up laundry in the backyard is closer to caricature than social commentary. After a year's separation, Joe sets out on the road to meet up with Katherine and get married. Driving his new automobile, he is stopped in a small town on suspicion of kidnapping a young woman. Peanuts in his pocket circumstantially incriminate him, and he is jailed. Emotions run high. The arrest—and the Constitution—are debated by barbers with foreign accents. (One of the barbers confesses having an impulse, every now and then, to slash the Adam's apple of a customer that he is shaving.) Lang finds humor among a group of gossiping women, their scene intercut with footage of clucking hens, and makes a joke at the expense of newsreel photographers savoring the news potential of the upcoming riot.

These early scenes, in the first act of the script, are almost circumspect in their force and rhythm. It is as if Lang is settling in, digesting unfamiliar surroundings, lulling the audience into calm and expectation. Then the townspeople begin to whisper, pass word, collect in small groups. One of the key inciters—the script makes a big point of it—is a strikebreaker from another town. An outsider. An alien. Just passing through. Given Lang's personal history, the burning of the jailhouse cannot help but evoke the Reichstag fire. The jailhouse inferno was expertly mounted. The death-dealing faces are jubilant, demented, transfixed. Newsreel photographers race around gleefully, compiling footage. A fellow munches an apple. A woman holds up her baby for an unobstructed view. Another lady kneels, murmuring a prayer.

That richness of visual detail was not in the script. And its impact is intensified by the total absence of musical accompaniment during this and most of *Fury*. There is only the crackling of the fire as the wondrous, upturned faces watch the flames rise higher.

Joe, meanwhile, has crawled out alive. Only his little dog dies. His "fury" toward the perpetrators ("I could smell myself burning") is what takes the film to its next emotional summit.

Spencer Tracy was incapable of a mediocre performance. But here, prodded and goaded by a director he despised, his transformation—drenched in fear and rage—becomes startling. Sylvia Sydney is also directed well: She is idealized, sympathetic, quietly affecting, her Katherine one of Lang's rare decorous heroines.

The police, the prosecutors, the judge are not very colorful. Lang's belief in lawful authorities was sincere, but the drama in his films usually emanated from the lawless.

The final twist in the story is triggered by the word "momentum" in a letter of unknown authorship. Katherine figures out that Joe is still alive, hiding, conspiring with his increasingly reluctant brothers to rig the verdict. A door opens dramatically onto Joe and his brothers, with Katherine framed in the doorway. (Lang also knew from scenes where women walked in the door unexpectedly.) Joe, torn by Katherine's accusations, storms away and takes a long walk, peering in department-store windows. Stricken with conscience, he hears voices, is plagued by ghosts of the mob who tried to destroy him. Though Mankiewicz trimmed and shortened these scenes, they are still represented in the film, heightening the mood and suspense.

Joe makes a well-timed, eleventh-hour appearance in the courtroom. He delivers a strong speech, excoriating the mob without absolving himself. The final kiss between him and Katherine may be unnecessary. But it does not spoil the haunting power of what has gone before.

People not to be trusted; guilt not to be assumed; a man, ordinary, even good, who is transformed into a beast. With *Fury*, as with M, Lang had a subject to which he was perfectly suited. And yet, ironically, the film would cement Tracy's name—ensure that the actor would vault to stardom—while the director would sit idle, a Hollywood leper, for the next several months.

Not that Lang was entirely idle during the rest of 1936. It didn't necessarily help his cause, but he busied himself giving interviews protesting MGM's treatment of *Fury*. He met with freelance screenwriters and took appointments for possible directing jobs that, as it happened, didn't pan out. He also kept himself in the gossip columns with items tracking his appearances at nightclubs and premieres, arm in arm with girlfriends who sometimes, conveniently for the gossip columnists, happened to be as well-known as he. Every month dozens of these items were clipped and sent to the director's home by publicists on retainer.

For a time after her arrival in Hollywood in late 1935, Lily Latté had resided in a beach home near the director's. Yet, as Lang needed her less meaningfully, he tried to exclude her from his life. He made it clear their relationship was suspended. It was a shock to Latté; but she was not so easily brushed off.

Peter Heiman visited Latté when he arrived in Hollywood in 1937, and Latté made it clear to him that she was still in love with the director, even though her role in Fritz Lang's life had been greatly circumscribed.

She remained the director's financial adviser. She read scripts and filled in whenever his regular secretary was off hours or off salary. Because she had sacrificed so much for him, and worked so tirelessly to effect his transition to America, he felt beholden to her. He felt guilty, even while trying to remove her at a distance.

Lang's love life was always at its busiest between films. During the 1930s, he embarked upon a series of publicity-rich romances with some of Hollywood's most glamorous stars. A number of these were duly memorialized in the gossip columns. Other were more private affairs. But Lang was not modest about his sexual exploits, and what eluded the gossip columns usually came to light in conversations with acquaintances.

Actresses Miriam Hopkins and Marlene Dietrich, later on, Kay Francis; these and other famous fair ladies went in and out of Lang's life. (This list did not impress writer-producer Gottfried Reinhardt. "He [Lang] was a megalomaniac. It was an occupational disease. All his girlfriends were nymphomaniacs. To have an affair with one of these actresses was . . . well, how could you avoid it? I slept with one or two of them myself. They were all no-conquests.")

One of the stories the director relished telling over the years concerned his fling with Miriam Hopkins. It seems that Lang encountered Hopkins on one of his cross-country train trips to New York City, which he took once or twice annually to catch up with Broadway highlights. This one was at Christmastime, perhaps 1936. They met by chance in the dining room and sat down together for a long candlelight dinner. Lang did his best to charm the actress, and at such times the director could be quite endearing. Hopkins was not shy, and following after-dinner drinks, surprised Lang by making the first move. "How would you like me for a Christmas present?" the actress asked. And he and Miriam Hopkins spent one memorable evening together, Lang liked to boast, in one of those locomotive sleepers he liked so much, nestling close as they crossed the American West on the Twentieth Century.

Marlene Dietrich, his date the night Lang refused to shake Joseph L. Mankiewicz's hand—a gesture designed to raise a Dietrich eyebrow?—was an even more noteworthy conquest. Lang had made Dietrich's acquaintance in Paris, back in 1934. In Hollywood she sought him out, wanting to make the director feel at home. Dietrich was well-known for her hospitality, mothering refugees by serving up crawfish dinners and goulash for a houseful of guests; afterward, sentimental over Germany, they would break into old cabaret songs.

Sometimes, for Lang, sex was preceded by a long courtship that might have doubled as—or be mistaken for—friendship. The director was seen around town with Dietrich often in 1937—a critical juncture in her career as well as his (she was leaving behind director Josef von Sternberg and their Svengali-Trilby period). Lang and the actress spoke vaguely about doing a film together one day. They were confidential with each other, sweet and supportive, although in Lang sweetness was genuine softness, whereas with Dietrich, any emotion—or none at all—might be lurking beneath her brittle mask.

Judging from memorabilia in the Marlene Dietrich collection at the Kinemathek in Berlin, their romance peaked in the spring of 1937. Lang sent bouquets of roses to the actress, a gesture he knew the actress would recognize as the properly romantic way to introduce an affair. He sent a telegram at Easter:

UBER MEINEN EIGENEN SCHATTEN LAUF HINTER MIR SELBER HER UND VERSUCH MICH SELBST ZU FANGEN STOP HAB EINEN WUNDERLIEBEN OSTERHASENTAG*

The Hollywood community—especially the refugee colony—buzzed with the image of these two Teutonic icons entwined in each other's arms. Was Lang chalking movements on the bed? Was Dietrich, as was her habit, correcting the lighting?

At Salka Viertel's salon, Oliver Garrett, briefly Lang's collaborator on "Hell Afloat"—Viertel's onetime boyfriend and a regular there—titillated people with the widely repeated remark that Lang was reputed to be able to reach orgasm only with the taste of blood in his mouth. People from Germany who knew about Gerda Maurus were able to believe it. Yet the reality, in the case of Fritz Lang's affair with Marlene Dietrich, appears to have been relatively tame.

In his third incarnation, after Vienna and Berlin, Fritz Lang was a subtly changed man—politically, professionally, perhaps sexually. None of Lang's girl-friends and lovers in America have recorded any claims of unseemly behavior. If anything, there is testimony to the opposite effect: that the director was uncommonly courtly and gentle, even docile, in bed. To close friends he made clear his passive preferences, including fellatio. "It is less hard work," the director liked to say.

In her daughter's biography, *Marlene Dietrich*, Maria Riva writes that the sex-symbol actress also preferred fellatio to intercourse. "It put into her hand the power to direct the scene," wrote Dietrich's daughter. (The bedroom was one of the few places where Fritz Lang might abrogate that right.) "Besides," Maria Riva added, "European women were expected to have great skill in that department." For Dietrich as well, fellatio offered "less hard work"—and more territorial control.

The actual physical relationship between the two apparently lasted about as long as it took them to wake up in the morning and have sunshiny second thoughts. "The fling ended," wrote Steven Bach in *Marlene Dietrich: Life and Legend*, "when Marlene reached across the pillow and picked up Lang's phone to make a date with another man." Lang was one jump behind. "It was a race to see who would dump the other one first," explained screenwriter Silvia Richards, one of the director's lovers in later years.

Still, no unpleasantness transpired between Dietrich and Lang. The affair

---

*Translation: "Running after myself over my own shadow and trying to catch myself STOP Have a wonderful lovely Easter rabbit day."

was a badge of honor for both. Dietrich added Lang to her long list; the director took pride in having stolen Dietrich away from rival director Josef von Sternberg. "He [Lang] liked to say that his cock was bigger than Josef von Sternberg's," said his Parisian friend, Pierre Rissient. (Sometimes Lang put it differently: "Von Sternberg had a very tiny penis.")

The director continued to hold Dietrich's hand and give her romantic counsel where men were concerned—when, for example, she was suffering through her crush on Ronald Colman. And Lang might offer similar expertise to Dietrich's men—among them Douglas Fairbanks, Jr., the son of the man who had first squired the director around Hollywood in 1925, and a friend of the director's who, in the early 1940s, became one of Dietrich's more determined and longer-lasting beaux.

After confessing to Lang his inability to handle the mercurial actress, Fairbanks was offered "terribly frank romantic advice, how to handle certain clever situations. 'Don't do this . . . do it that way . . . don't call her up so often.' " But the director was discreet, too; to Fairbanks, he never once mentioned his own bygone affair with Dietrich.

Not everybody could see beyond the monocle to appreciate the director's sexual magnetism. "That's something about Fritz Lang that was a mystery to me," said his longtime agent Sam Jaffe, "why women would be attracted to him. I only knew the nasty side of him. Apparently, however, some women did find him attractive."

Actor Dan Seymour said there was a beguiling side of Fritz Lang that, like Goebbels, the director could turn on or off like a faucet. Sitting moodily in a bar, the director would spot a woman across the room, then excuse himself and go over, adopting his most charming manner. Under these circumstances, said Seymour, the charm invariably won out, and Lang would end up taking the lady home with him.

Douglas Fairbanks, Jr., remembered that when he was wooing Marlene Dietrich it made good sense to consult with the director, because Lang seemed so much the "beau gallant" in matters romantic. "He was all man and a yard wide, not a dainty character," said Fairbanks, "very masculine in manner and attitude. He could be rather forbidding and frightening, because of his monocle and authoritarian way of speaking. But when you got to know him, you understood he was really very soft and kind and humorous underneath."

Once he had slept with a woman, Lang retained a fondness for her. It was true of Thea von Harbou. It was also true of Marlene Dietrich. Lily Latté, for one, grew weary of hearing the Marlene Dietrich stories—what incomparable legs she had, as Lang liked to reminisce tirelessly. (A subtle rebuke to Latté, so proud of her own legs.) They were like the Goebbels stories; the more you heard them, the more suspicious the details seemed.

Dietrich would betray Lang some years later, in much the way she seemed to turn on everybody. It was one of the betrayals that hurt Lang the most— a deep, emotional wound. After that betrayal, which occurred when the two committed the mistake of making a film together, the director's stories about his lover Dietrich took a poisonous turn.

"She wears three layers of makeup," Lang told Gene Fowler, Jr., "one for the stage, one for the street, and one to go to bed with."

"She had terrible breasts," Lang would tell others. (Never mind the incomparable legs.) "If you want to go to bed and worship someone, she's all right."

How many in the director's circle must have wondered if the same couldn't have been said of Lang as well? ("Fritz was never good in bed," Lily Latté would tell more than one listener after the director's death.)

But Fritz Lang's eyes could grow momentarily moist at the mention of Marlene Dietrich. The director knew most of her signature songs by heart; they were Berliner songs—his songs too. And if the mood was right, he wasn't beyond singing a few words of one himself. For this compatriot and paramour, who befriended him at a vulnerable point in his life and career, he never lost his sentimental attachment.

Sylvia Sidney, one of the few who survived *Fury* in good humor, came to the director's rescue. The actress had signed an exclusive contract with producer Walter Wanger, who was preparing to star her in a story about a Bonnie-and-Clyde-like couple fleeing from justice. Sidney was the prime mover in recommending Lang as the film's director.

Wanger was something of an anomaly in Hollywood. While many of the ruling elite of the motion picture studios hailed from shtetls and had dropped out of high school, he was Jewish but socially advantaged and Dartmouth-educated. After producing Broadway plays early in his career, Wanger had served as an intelligence officer during World War I and was a member of President Woodrow Wilson's staff at the Paris Peace Conference. Returning to civilian life, he filled successive executive positions at Paramount (where he had supervised the U.S. release of *Metropolis*), Columbia, and MGM.

When talkies came in, Wanger had turned producer, guiding a number of noteworthy films, including the Marx Brothers' debut in *The Cocoanuts*, the politically explosive *Gabriel Over the White House* and *The President Vanishes*, and Rouben Mamoulian's luminous *Queen Christina* with Greta Garbo. Dapper and charming—"the most elegant and learned of the movie satraps," in Ben Hecht's words—Wanger was widely known for taking chances on films that explored social ills and topical themes. He was a stalwart New Dealer, who wore his bleeding heart on his sleeve.

Like Selznick or Goldwyn, the producer functioned best autonomously, outside studio channels. Wanger's strength lay in selecting worthwhile material, handpicking a cast and crew, then molding all the ingredients into an attractive box-office package. Unlike Selznick, Wanger did not hover over his writers and directors. He didn't fire off endless script memos; he was notorious, in fact, for his lack of interest in story conferences (and was "almost completely devoid of story sense," according to Ben Hecht). He concentrated on managing the the financing, budget, post-production, exhibition, and distribution.

Wanger had just made an audacious career move, quitting his studio job at Paramount to set up an independent production unit under the distributorship of United Artists. The producer had signed several up-and-coming personalities, including Joan Bennett—younger sister of the more established actress Constance Bennett—and Henry Fonda, a gangly newcomer attracting attention. And Wanger had also managed to lure away one of Paramount's stars, signing Sylvia Sidney to a contract that gave her desirable loan-out approvals.

According to Sidney, the genesis of what became Fritz Lang's next film, *You Only Live Once*, might have been a chance encounter between her, Wanger, and novelist Theodore Dreiser. The actress and producer were dining out together one night, when the author of *Sister Carrie* and *An American Tragedy* stopped by their table. Dreiser mentioned he had been researching the mid-1934 Southwest robbery spree of Bonnie and Clyde for a magazine piece he intended to write, and commented that if anyone ever made a film about the two bank robbers, Sidney would be perfect to play the role of Bonnie Parker.

As it happened, a Paramount screenwriting team, Gene Towne and Graham Baker, had written a 1935 Sylvia Sidney vehicle, *Mary Burns, Fugitive*, which had Bonnie and Clyde overtones. Wanger had produced the film. Now, starting out as an independent, the producer made a point of stealing Towne and Baker away from Paramount to rework their earlier hit shamelessly.

Towne and Baker had a reputation as "two of the most colorful screenwriters in Hollywood," in the words of Matthew Bernstein, author of the biography *Walter Wanger, Hollywood Independent*. They were madcaps known for using toilet paper to post notes on the walls, and working in bizarre costumes, bathing suits, sometimes even brassieres. Their scripts were churned out with astonishing alacrity; one journalist remarked that they made the notoriously speedy Ben Hecht and Charles MacArthur "look like snails."

Towne had been a title writer and gag man for Mack Sennett; Baker was an ex-reporter and cartoonist for New York newspapers. They met at Warner Brothers sometime in the late 1920s and had been a team ever since. Towne was the "hyperactive idea man," according to Bernstein, while Baker functioned as the "quiet, more dignified sounding board." Their credited pictures ranged wildly, from *Ali Baba Goes to Town*, a musical satirizing the New Deal, to the atmospheric love story *History Is Made at Night*.

Although Wanger later claimed that "the entire film was my idea," it appears that Towne and Baker freely developed the fugitive-couple script harking back to newspaper accounts of the Bonnie and Clyde saga. Their scenario featured a paroled three-time loser named Eddie Taylor, facing his last chance to go straight. He marries Joan Graham, a secretary in the public defender's office, but can't find a steady job. Accused of driving a getaway car for a gang of bank robbers, Eddie is arrested. He protests his innocence. Joan believes in Eddie; so does a priest and a public defender (the latter nursing a crush for Joan). But a jury finds Eddie guilty. Joan helps him break out of jail. The police keep up a relentless pursuit of the two, and their desperate flight ends in a bloody shoot-out.

Lang was not hired until the mid-summer of 1936, by which time a working draft of the script already existed. Wanger heard the director out about what had happened on *Fury*, and the two came to terms: This would be a tough-edged film without any sugarcoating at the conclusion. The producer gave Lang all the creative assurances he wanted to hear: Nobody but the director, Wanger vowed, would tamper with the footage, right through the final editing.

Lang went to work in August and September, honing the script with Towne and Baker. It was another ideal subject for Lang, giving him opportunity to indulge his preoccupation with criminals, courtrooms, and prison life. The director arranged an invitation to San Quentin, and attended a prison band recital there on Sunday evening, August 23, 1936. Others concentrated on the musical recital; Lang made a side tour of the execution room, noting individual touches ("here hung a pair of shoes . . . of a Negro, hanged some times [sic] ago") and making sketches of the iron walkways and cells that would inform the verisimilitude of *You Only Live Once*.

According to Matthew Bernstein, revisions of the script under Lang produced "some of the most powerful moments in the finished film," including changes in the dialogue that takes place on Eddie and Joan's honey-moon night. This thematic scene gave Lang the chance to articulate a philosophy of fatalism that he had espoused as early as *Der müde Tod*. In the scene, Eddie explains to Joan that he first started out on the path to crime when he was sentenced to reform school for beating up a kid who tortured a frog. He tells her this parable: When one frog in a mated pair dies, the other one always dies too. Then Eddie picks Joan up, kisses her tenderly, and carries his sweetheart in his arms up the stairs to their bedroom.

Eddie's allegory is echoed at the film's climax. According to Matthew Bernstein, Baker and Towne's script originally concluded with Eddie and Joan, shot down by police, entwined in a "kiss of death." It was the director who reconfigured the action to remind the audience of the parable of the mated frogs. "In the film's final moments," wrote Bernstein, "Fonda again carries Sidney in his arms and stands holding her after kissing her and being shot," evoking the earlier image.

Filming took place in November and December of 1936. Lang, though keenly interested in choosing the players in his films, was left out of the major casting, as he would be throughout much of his Hollywood career. All along Henry Fonda had been touted by Wanger as the man to play Eddie Taylor. And the director's published boast that he was the one who "brought over Sylvia Sidney" to play Joan was the opposite of reality; in effect, Sidney had brought over Fritz Lang.

There was more truth to Lang's remark that "the other parts were filled by General Casting." The supporting players in *You Only Live Once* would include Barton MacLane as Stephen Whitney, the sympathetic public attorney; Jean Dixon as Joan's steadfast sister Bonnie; and William Gargan as Father Dolan, the Catholic priest who befriends Eddie.

Cinematographer Leon Shamroy, whose creative photography gave him industry-wide standing, would handle the camerawork. Shamroy was another Walter Wanger alumnus, with previous credits that included *Mary Burns, Fugitive*. Alexander Toluboff, a capable Russian-born art director who worked for MGM before signing a contract with Wanger, would handle the scenic design.

Once again, the director went into production as if into battle, armed with research, notes, sketches. Everything was blocked out on paper, and in the director's mind. Fritz Lang at work was a human bulldozer—ferociously energetic, everywhere at once, determined to stake his claim on the material and roll over any opposition.

Shamroy found the director intelligent, but perhaps "too camera-wise." Lang, the cameraman recalled, was "fantastically meticulous," like a single-minded artist painting the same canvas over and over again, "covering one painting with another."

The interiors were filmed at United Artists facilities on Formosa Avenue, but other scenes took place in Los Angeles exteriors, and many were locations at night. Often the filming would go past midnight, giving the director the atmosphere and shadows that established his tone.

"We'd work every shot out in detail," recalled Shamroy. "I'd tape it from mark to mark, and at seven in the morning Lang would be back again after only four hours away, a long drive and maybe two hours sleep, and he'd say to me that the shot I'd prepared at that fantastic early-morning hour wouldn't work. 'It hasn't . . . the possibility.' I was furious. I always believed that the audience didn't care about all those finicky details he insisted upon; that all you needed was to be an impressionist, to create an illusion, a mood, that matched the way the characters were thinking. He didn't agree."

The orchestration of all minutia was important to Lang—more so sometimes than to his audience. The breakdown of scenes into tiny, seemingly extraneous details was part of his regimen, the way he conditioned his fantasy. So scrupulous was his idea of what he *intended* to film that he became prone to confuse the *actual* setup, in interviews years later, with the *imaginary* one he recalled from memory. He believed his memory to be infallible, but was capable of remembering nuances that never quite made it to celluloid.

Sylvia Sidney was hardly given an easy ride on her second Fritz Lang film. But she was friendly with the director by now, and she was a self-effacing actress willing to take whatever Lang could dish out. In the event Lang focused most of his venom on Fonda, to whom the director took an instant dislike and found weak in his role.

Fonda was another actor's actor noted for doing his job quietly and diligently, and he—like Spencer Tracy before him—was ill-prepared for Lang's assault. The director seemed oblivious to the fact that his star had just been wed—in September—and took a particular delight in summoning Fonda, who naturally preferred to spend nights with his new bride, to remote places after nightfall. As with Tracy, the director demanded repeated takes and insisted on picayune interpolations, forcing Fonda to vary himself endlessly.

"Lang took a whole day to shoot a simple scene between Sylvia Sidney and me," Fonda complained later. "It's the wedding supper, and the camera starts on an insert of the marriage certificate, then dollies back, sees the plates where we have finished our dinner, and finally sees us. The scene is what we say to each other, and Fritz was all day shooting it.

"He would dolly back and shoot, then he would stop and take the spoon from my dessert, move the ice cream round a little bit and dirty the dish, and then he would do it again, dirtying her dish a little bit, and then do it again. Then he would move the cup this way and do it, then he would tilt the marriage certificate and do it. He would do it fifty-five times, he would stand and blow smoke into the scene or something."

Fonda resented the repetition, the second-guessing, the niggling. "It just doesn't occur to him [Lang]," the actor mused, "that actors are human beings with hearts and instincts and other things. He is the master puppeteer, and he is happiest only when he can manipulate the blank puppets. He would actually manipulate you with his hands. If you were cutting that close, he would manipulate your hand while you were sitting there looking at the camera. That in itself isn't too bad, but if you are trying to work from here, from 'inside,' it's disconcerting to have somebody else doing something that has become automatic for you."

Sidney remained patient under the director's exacting methods. In one interview the actress shed light on how Lang used his friendship with her to manipulate Fonda's anxieties. "What he [Lang] would do," remembered Sidney, "was take me across the set from where Fonda was sitting, and would whisper in my ear. He had a thermos with homemade soup in it and he would pour some for me, all the time speaking softly. Well, Fonda knew that Fritz and I had worked together before, and he assumed that Fritz was giving me preferential treatment; giving me extra coaching, you know, that sort of thing. Well, Fonda would fume and mutter, 'That son of a bitch' (I *assume* at Fritz), while all Fritz was doing was telling me how he had made the soup. And Fonda sort of said, 'The hell with him. I'll show him,' and he gave one hell of a performance.

"And," the actress added, "you know how clever and manipulative Fritz was, he would sometimes do the same thing to me with Fonda, and he was so good that I believed they were talking about me and *I* got furious. Fritz was one of a kind."

Walter Wanger's rule of thumb was never to interfere, as long as the dailies showed quality and progress. Lang intimidated him besides, so the producer's forays to the set were spaced out with care. "He [Wanger] was a man of great tact and resource, and much taken up with the problems of our community," Lang said in one interview. "Just how tactful he was I can illustrate, for once when I had spent three days more than the schedule allowed over a fog scene, he contented himself by sending me a blues record entitled 'Lost in the Fog.' "

The scene where Eddie and Joan discuss the mating of frogs is photographed in a mirrored pond, and concludes with a frog leaping into the water to shatter their reflections. Lang insisted on having a real frog jump into the water on the precise dialogue cue. The prop men were stumped. They tried shooting off guns. They dangled bluebottle flies on horsehairs. Finally someone wired electricity under the frog, and the firing button was handed to the director. That coincided with a rare Wanger appearance on the soundstage. Fritz Lang ceremoniously handed the button to the producer, and for once someone other than the director triggered an explosive charge, however minor.

The frog jumped. The shot had taken all day. But what could the snookered Wanger do but grin? Lang knew a few such tricks; some Hollywood traditions—the production interrupted for birthday cake on the set, duly photographed for publicity purposes—were made to order for his occasional public displays of charm-to-spare.

Fifteen days of retakes were needed, adding up to forty-six days of shooting (the average film took closer to twenty-five or thirty). But Fonda's complaint to an interviewer that Lang took "forever, sixteen weeks or longer" to film *You Only Live Once* is an exaggeration. Other, more diplomatic directors could—did, all the time—get away with delays and overruns, but Lang's hard-hearted behavior left no fond afterglow. The production in fact came in under its $589,403 budget, was edited by Lang in businesslike fashion, and *You Only Live Once* was readied in time for planned release in late January of 1937.

You Only Live Once begins with scenes that are like outtakes from a soft-hearted Warner Brothers prison programmer. Hardened convicts in a penitentiary are playing a game of baseball, booing the umpire. The ump, likable Father Dolan, is a priest, one of Eddie Taylor's few friends.

Eddie, a beaten-down, habitual criminal, is paroled. At first, the character seems to demand more steel and vitriol than Henry Fonda brings to the part. Fonda emphasizes the angst, as Eddie attempts to carve out an honest life, taking a job as a truck driver, with all the petty bias and logic of the script stacked against him.

Joan is the angelic character, admirably carried off by Sylvia Sidney. She marries Eddie and prays for his luck to change, even when their honeymoon is ruined by people who read pulp crime magazines and jump to unfortunate conclusions.

In Germany, until *M*, Lang had made films about people who were rich or powerful—playboy-adventurers, industrial bigwigs, scientists, inventors, master criminals, spies. Fleeing Germany, Lang turned to characters who were helpless John Does, conflicted American everymen. Society became the villain in his films, not evil geniuses.

Lang's feeling grows for the increasingly embittered character as Eddie goes through his doomed motions. Henry Fonda's performance, too, grows more haunting. Violating parole, Eddie pals around with ex-cons. The film implies his involvement in a tautly staged bank robbery, a tour de force of montage: torrential rain, watchful eyes seen only through a window slot, tear-gas bombs, a wild shoot-out with police.

When Eddie is arrested, a jury hears his case. He claims innocence, but is found guilty. The director's faith rested in higher law, not juries—certainly not in "the people," who might shed their own innocence at any time and become a hydra-headed mob.

Meanwhile, Joan becomes pregnant. A desperate Eddie, in jail awaiting execution, pleads for her to slip him a gun. Joan, distraught, considers killing herself, but decides to go along with the plan. Their prison scenes together are well-staged, strongly acted, intricately woven together by close-ups, a shadowed setting, and utilitarian dialogue.

Eddie fakes a suicide attempt, escapes with a doctor as hostage. The priest blocks his getaway in the prison courtyard, then is inadvertently shot by Eddie. With his dying breath the priest lies to ensure Eddie's escape. It is a neat twist, the priest's falsehood, and a measure of the noble Catholicism Lang could bring to a story.

Joan is just about to mix herself a poison potion when she learns of Eddie's escape. Throwing aside moral qualms, she joins with him in his flight from justice. They do anything to keep on the run, even pull a gun on a gas station attendant. Headlines confer notoriety on them, and every conceivable crime is traced to their random movements.

The baby, finally, is due. The script has its imbecilities—among them a scene in which Eddie walks through a forest picking flowers while Joan gives birth, apparently unaided, in a country shack. Lang was no master of domestic verities, and censorship precluded realistic birth scenes. But *You Only Live Once* fights this and other inanities as Lang grows hypnotized by Eddie and Joan's fated folie à deux. The baby is left with the kindhearted sister and the district attorney, and finally the two lovers are chased down and cornered by police.

One of the climactic images is famous: Eddie, cradling Joan in his arms, struggling to get away, framed in the cross-hairs of a gunsight. Eddie is shot; he weaves and stumbles on ahead with his last dying breath. The backlighting suggests the opening of pearly gates. Over the soundtrack comes the gentle voice of the priest, Father Dolan, beckoning him onward—à la *Liliom*— "You're free, Eddie, the gates are open!"

Peter Bogdanovich asked the director if the ending was meant as irony or the truth. "As the truth," replied Lang. "You may laugh, but don't forget I was born a Catholic—perhaps I'm not a good Catholic according to the Church—but Catholic education (and probably any education which has to do with ethics) never leaves you. And I think it was the truth for those people—the doors are open now."

Lang was rarely an ironist. In many interviews he himself contributed to the impression that people like Eddie and Joan were intended as symbols of the struggle against fate's inevitability. Yet his message of a stoic and compassionate fatalism—in films such as *Der müde Tod*, *Liliom*, and *You Only Live Once*—often conveyed the opposite. People in Lang's films fight against police and courts, against misunderstanding, accusation, and guilt. But again and again this director ended his screen stories with his characters welcoming the liberation of a weary death.

When *You Only Live Once* was released, in January of 1937, the reaction was positive—although not nearly as extravagant as for *Fury*, to which Lang's newest film was inevitably compared. Frank Nugent of *The New York Times* stated the consensus among critics when he said that within the "somewhat theatrical limits" of the script, *You Only Live Once* proved "an intense, absorbing, and relentlessly pursued tragedy which owes most of its dignity to the eloquence of its direction."

Unfortunately, according to Matthew Bernstein's book, the relentless tragedy failed to connect with theater audiences and return a profit on its production costs. Furthermore, box-office failure brought differences between the producer and director into light.

Although Wanger had not been infatuated with the laborious "German direction," he had been true to his word, permitting Lang his final cut. The director, on his part, used interviews publicizing the film to shore up his political credentials. Even before the premiere, Lang was telling reporters that *You Only Live Once* would have been improved if he had been permitted to incorporate a prologue showing the unfair social conditions that forced Eddie Taylor into his ill-fated life of crime. The person who had prohibited the prologue, Lang warned potential moviegoers, was the film's producer, Wanger, who, though he was well-known as a crusading liberal, was in reality an admirer of the Italian dictator Benito Mussolini.*

The director was alert to the fact that *Fury* had launched him as an American social critic. It was a mystique he would do his best to cultivate; even his innocuous Westerns, he would later declare for publicity's sake, were meant "to interpret the cowboy in the light of the social and economic forces of his time." One of the truisms upheld by Langians is, as David Thomson writes in *A Biographical Dictionary of Film*, that in his films the director profoundly depicted "how far society was estranging its nobler heroes, forcing them into crime, vengeful violence, and conspiracies like those of corrupt governments. Look past the melodrama and simplicity of Lang's films and he is the most stringent of political filmmakers."

However, the director's claim about the vetoed prologue seems to be just another rewrite of history. Considering that other Fritz Lang films have theme-setting prologues, it's not beyond the bounds of possibility that he at least contemplated such a device.** Matthew Bernstein's book investigated the production memoranda, however, and ascertained that "in fact, no such scene appeared in the script drafts." One would be hard-pressed, in fact, to name a single Fritz Lang film, including any of the handful over which he exerted complete control, where such a prologue mitigated a criminal's actions by illuminating his social background. (Not to mention the fact that the "misunderstood criminal" of *You Only Live Once* has a number of well-placed societal benefactors in the story, including a frock-wearing representative of the Catholic Church and a duly-appointed district attorney.)

Lang was often too quick for his own good, compulsively assigning credit and blame, publicly disavowing his film's deficiencies. Ironically, Henry Fonda's performance—like Tracy's in *Fury*—was universally applauded by critics; it became one more notch in Fonda's climb to stardom. For Wanger, too, *You Only Live Once* could be counted a feather in his cap—one of the productions that established him "squarely in the front ranks of progressive and innovative Hollywood filmmaking," according to Matthew Bernstein.

Once again the director shot only himself in the foot; the stories about his unacceptable behavior on the set and his negative stance toward Wanger, afterward, followed him around the motion picture industry. Although he had only been in Hollywood for two years, he had already notched a formidable enemies list. This time, almost half a year would elapse before Fritz Lang would be offered another contract.

* * *

---

*That was true enough. Wanger was as foolish about Mussolini in 1936 as Lang had been about Hitler in 1933.

**In later years, Lang told associates that one draft of the film was written by ex-convict-turned-screenwriter Robert Tasker, one of the founding members of the Hollywood section of the U.S. Communist Party, who is credited with another prison picture, *San Quentin* (1937), around the same time as *You Only Live Once*. This may be the "prologue" Lang was referring to— perhaps suggested by Tasker. But there is no evidence that Tasker's ideas were ever incorporated into any draft of Towne and Baker's script.

To his credit, Lang showed no irresolution and plunged into work on his own diverse ideas.

It was the director's dream that in Hollywood he might head up his own independent company—as he had briefly with Fritz-Lang Film-GmbH in Germany. First he had to have a script that somebody would care to underwrite for financing. Through the winter of 1936 and spring of 1937, Lang worked from scratch on several new projects. How humbling; whereas in Berlin he had grown accustomed to having his films made at the snap of his fingers, now this onetime lord of creation was forced to scrounge around in his old trick bag, looking for an attractive bauble with which to curry some producer's interest.

With Teddy Le Beau helping him, Lang collected clippings about the daily routine of an American police squad; the life of a drum majorette; a hobo's existence; the career of gangster Al Capone—who never ceased to intrigue the director as a possible screen subject, and the exploits of notorious Depression-era bank robber John Dillinger.

For a brief period of time, Lang worked with German refugee Vicki Baum, author of *Grand Hotel*, on a couple of story ideas: one about women in an old-age home, another about a Works Progress Administration (WPA) work gang bringing the technological miracle of water to the desert of Arizona. Neither came to fruition.

Baum was an exception. Lang generally worked with American scriptwriters—because his English was inadequate (he continued to dictate in German), because he thought it wise to propose American subjects, and because the émigré community still gave him a cautious berth. His collaborators were often ex-playwrights or newspaper reporters, and always writers outside the studio loop, without competing contractual obligations. They had to be inexpensive, too, for Lang was paying them out of pocket.

The four projects that occupied most of the director's time in 1936–1937 indicate the extent to which history and politics had invaded his thinking. One was a fictitious portrait of the wife of Napoleon III, on which Hy Kraft, a Broadway playwright who passed in and out of Hollywood toiling on film scripts, worked with the director.

The second was a panorama of recent American history with a pioneering feminist at its center, a character roughly modeled after Josephine Roche, the female president of one of Colorado's largest coal companies. "American Cavalcade" was one of the director's most ambitious scripts, and he poured a lot of effort into the project. The contours of the story attested to the side of Lang that condemned men as the destroyers of the world, while extolling women as the heart and conscience of humanity.

"American Cavalcade" focused on the daughter of a Midwestern senator, a young woman whose feminist consciousness and desire "to make the world better" after World War I leads her into social work. Her boyfriend, a newspaper reporter, flirts with revolutionary ideology and becomes a spokesman for a militant union. She herself becomes politically disillusioned and marries a mining industrialist—whose maltreated workers are led out on strike by her onetime boyfriend.

Riots and sabotage ensue. Her husband is killed, and she inherits his mining empire. She proves a capable capitalist, and tries to use some of her fortune to perform good works for society. History whizzes by—Prohibition, the Crash, the Depression. Her former boyfriend becomes a labor boss, her avowed class enemy. He is indicted, falsely, for syndicalist violence. She sticks by him, and the story concludes with another one of those "happy endings" that Lang professed to hate.

George O'Neil, an ex-playwright whose Hollywood screenplays in collaboration included *Magnificent Obsession* and *High, Wide and Handsome*, worked with Lang on the story for several months between studio assignments. But too much history was shoehorned into the script, and once again the director couldn't come up with a satisfactory through-line. So "American Cavalcade" was moved to the back burner, while Lang took up a third possibility, an equally ambitious epic about the American cigarette industry.

That was "Virginia," based on events that led up to the dissolution of the American Tobacco Company early in the twentieth century. That Lang took "Virginia" seriously is evidenced by the casebook in his personal archives: cigarette workers' pamphlets, tobacco-industry health documentation, guides to Virginia localities, tobacco-auction reports, photographs, newspaper and magazine articles. The storyline was inspired by an actual incident the director uncovered in his research, in which a group of armed farmers rioted and took over an entire town in Kentucky, burning stockpiles of American Tobacco–owned tobacco.

Three characters dominated "Virginia," two men and a woman. One of the men was a simulacrum of James Duke, the guiding force and controlling stockholder of the American Tobacco Company; the other a former backwoods lawyer who successfully sues to dissolve the tobacco monopoly. The third character would be "a Joan of Arc of the Kentucky hills," in the words of the script—a heroine of the people. But "Virginia" was also fraught with difficulties, and had to be set aside unfinished. Lang's American sagas had large-scale problems which all the clippings in the world couldn't resolve: apart from the whopping budget considerations they would warrant, they never seemed to boil down into a simple, compelling story. And only rarely—not in the case of "Virginia" either—did Lang complete a fully-fleshed script.

The director frequently claimed, later in life, that after *M* "I became tired of the big pictures," as he put it to Peter Bogdanovich. "I've always turned down the so-called big pictures" in Hollywood, he said, "the spectacles with the huge mass scenes." Even putting aside the example of *Fury*, with its full-throttle crowd scenes, Lang's rejection of the epic in America also represented his failure to get something large-scale under way.

In the spring of 1937 Lang beat a creative retreat. The last, more typically Langian, project that occupied him was a contemporary story of patriotism and treachery, of American heroes fighting foreign spies and villains. "Man Without a Country," his own original story, was hardly low-budget; but it mined Lang's familiar strengths—espionage, secret weapons, police, government cabals, and, yet again, a brave young heroine.

The writer Lang hired for this script was Martin Mooney, a veteran Hearst newspaper reporter who in Hollywood specialized in G-man stories and "B" crime films. Lang and Mooney constructed a rudimentary draft about an international espionage organization stealing secrets from American factories and military centers. The characters included a U.S. government clerk determined to stop the villainy, and a female secret agent—an American Gerda Maurus—who assists the case while falling in love with the clerk. On the villainy side, there was one of Lang's mysterious spymasters (complete with Russian accent) and a German count peddling inhumane weapons.

"Man Without A Country" has been reported in published articles and books as one of the director's first, unrealized anti-Nazi stories. But in fact it was an informal American update of *Spione*—the kind of comic-book potboiler that Lang liked to elevate with his direction. Although the scenario predicted a coming world war fought with lethal weapons of mass destruction, Germany itself was mentioned only in passing. The super-secret annihilation weapon, dubbed F-222 in the script, was, like the rocket ship of *Die Frau im Mond*, drawn more from futuristic fiction than political reality.

But Lang had great expectations for "Man Without a Country," and on one of his train trips to New York he made a point of going backstage to speak with actress Katharine Cornell, one of the leading lights of the American theater, about playing the lady counterspy. Casting Cornell, who had never appeared in motion pictures, would have been quite the coup. Anointing a star from outside Hollywood, as he used to do with impunity in Berlin, would give the director an added measure of distance from the governing studios.

Lang had been adrift for almost half a year—from January through May 1937—when he used "Man Without a Country" as an entering wedge for contract talks with Paramount. With every dry spell, the director lost an agent and acquired another with fresh zeal. Now Charles Feldman, a pal of Wanger's and one of Hollywood's fastest-talking deal-makers, agreed to represent Lang, brandishing Katharine Cornell's name in the negotiations, and offering "Man Without a Country" to the studio as part of a multi-picture contract.

Paramount seemed, in prospect, a more comfortable fit than MGM. The studio had a plethora of Hungarians and Viennese on its roster, and the camera and design departments especially—under Ufa veterans such as Ernest Fegté and Hans Dreier—were known for setting standards of opulence in Hollywood films.

The director had to meet with production head William LeBaron and studio chief Adolph Zukor in order to pass muster, but Lang was always the soul of civility at such meetings, and easily established a rapport with both executives. Could this be the fierce, uncooperative megalomaniac everyone in town was gossiping against?

Feldman was an extremely persuasive agent. Out of favor elsewhere in Hollywood, Lang received a two-year contract at Paramount. The terms called for him to direct three films, at a salary of $2,012.78 a week, or a total of $210,000 for two years. In addition, the director was given the travel perks and vacation allowances (four weeks after completion of each film) expected by a first-rank director. Lang was personally assured by Zukor that he would be functioning at Paramount as the de facto producer of his own projects. However, the studio would control all advertising and publicity. "A Fritz Lang Production" was guaranteed top billing on all his Paramount films.

The studio contract came just in time. Lang had been sinking his own money into script development; he had cash and valuables squirreled away, but, like most directors of the era, he was reluctant to spend too much of his own money on illusory projects.

Once again Sylvia Sidney played a role as Lang's benefactor. Paramount, the actress's former studio, was eager to lure her back for a picture. And screenwriter Norman Krasna, who had conceived the original story for *Fury* and stayed friendly with Lang, also figured in the package. Krasna had come up with a thirteen-page treatment for a romantic comedy that would take place in "a typical department store of any large American city." The head of the store makes a point of employing ex-prisoners and parolees; a man and a woman, concealing crooked pasts from each other, fall in love. A second, lengthier synopsis added some song ideas, and *You and Me* began to shape up as an unlikely Fritz Lang film: a quasi-musical.

It was miles from the director's usual stuff. These characters were decidedly Runyonesque. But the out-of-work Lang wholeheartedly embraced Krasna's idea, pronounced the film a prospective *Lehrstück* ("teaching play") in the manner of Bertolt Brecht, and immediately began campaigning for Brecht's onetime collaborator, composer Kurt Weill, to contribute the songs and music.

All this was tacitly understood when Lang was hired. *You and Me* would be his first Paramount picture, and, if things worked out, "Man Without a Country" his second. Of all of Lang's major studio projects in America, *You and Me* is the one he had the most time and freedom to shape—and the one that proved the worst disappointment.

Krasna stuck around longer than usual, doing outlines and treatments for eleven weeks; where he left off, Virginia Van Upp took over, collaborating with Lang on revisions for thirteen more weeks. A contract writer, Van Upp was a former silent screen actress who had worked her way up as script girl, editor, casting director, and agent, before making the switch to screenwriter (among her previous Paramount credits were the W. C. Fields vehicle *Poppy* and Mitchell Leisen's film of *Swing High, Swing Low*, a drama with music about a trumpet player that related quite well to the Lang project).*

Lang liked Van Upp; he met and lunched with her daily, usually at his home, throughout the summer of 1937. The work progressed—very slowly. When the studio complained, Lang blamed the pace on Van Upp, so Paramount authorized the hiring of another writer, Jack Moffitt. Some days Lang worked with both writers on different scenes, alternating one in the morning with the other in the afternoon.

Lang met simultaneously with Kurt Weill, who instantly understood what the director was aiming for: "a Lang picture with a light touch." Weill understood much more. Hired in mid-May for $10,000, Weill was treated as a "sacred totem" by the director. Nonetheless, Weill wrote to his wife, actress-singer Lotte Lenya, on May 29, 1937, "Lang makes you want to puke. Nobody in the whole world is as important as he imagines himself to be. I completely understand why he is so hated everywhere. He's still trying to be very nice to

---

*Eventually Van Upp advanced to producer, becoming one of Hollywood's few women fulfilling that role, notably on *Gilda* (1946) and other Rita Hayworth vehicles for Columbia.

me, because he knows that I don't need him, and I always let him know it, too."

The songs were going to have Brechtian/Weillian titles like "Song of the Cash Register" and "The Door-Knocking Ballad." But Weill couldn't work too far ahead of the script, and Lang's story conferences, which the composer hated, were endless. The script puttered along with little seeming urgency. At the end of June, Weill left for New York City, where he had other obligations, and where, presumably, he would await delivery of the final form.

Nobody at Paramount supervised Lang's time, at least initially. While he was supposed to be working on the *You and Me* screenplay, the director was also squeezing in remedial sessions with George O'Neil on "American Cavalcade," trying to whip that reluctant scenario into shape. But *You and Me* ought to have been the priority, and as the summer flew by, production chief William LeBaron grew impatient. He called Lang into his office and insisted the director quicken his pace. As Lang had done at MGM, he went over LeBaron's head, personally appealing to Adolph Zukor to delay the start date until the script was "perfect." Zukor gave the director the benefit of the doubt, and a calendar extension.

Sylvia Sidney took a look at the situation and elected to fill some time in a Ben Hecht play (*To Quito and Back*) opening in New York. Although she remained penciled in as the star of *You and Me*, anxiety mounted in Paramount's executive suite. Lang saw the actress's moonlighting as a further excuse to postpone the schedule, while he made additional script improvements and engaged in the type of prolonged preproduction he preferred. The director even took time to travel to New York, making the rounds of plays, and meeting there with Sylvia Sidney and Kurt Weill.

When the Ben Hecht play closed abruptly on November 13, Paramount acted decisively. The start date of principal photography was summarily announced for January 12, 1938. That would make almost half a year since Lang had signed his contract.

With all of Lang's emendations, the script had ballooned to 170 pages. And now the music had to be rushed to keep up with the revisions. Lang continued to slavishly court Kurt Weill, who with Lotte Lenya paid an extended visit to Hollywood in December (the director's ingratiating "Merry Christmas" telegrams were delivered at successive westward train stops). But at the same time Lang had begun to hedge his bets, making an alliance with Borris Morros, the studio's musical director, to navigate Paramount's concerns.

Weill stayed for the first weeks of shooting, his dislike and distrust of Lang mounting.

Lang picked as his cameraman Charles Lang, Jr., the leading craftsman on the lot. At Paramount for much of his fifty-year span of activity, Lang (who was no relation to the director) was admired in Hollywood as much for his subtlety as his dazzling variety of work. He would notch a record eighteen Oscar nominations for best cinematography in his distinguished career, working with such top directors as Frank Borzage, George Cukor, Henry Hathaway, and Billy Wilder. He would also become one of the few American cinematographers to work more than once with Fritz Lang.

George Raft had been cast to star opposite Sylvia Sidney, boosting the film's marquee power. Harry Carey would play the department store owner, with newcomer Robert Cummings and Barton MacLane from *You Only Live Once* in supporting roles.

Lang's sparring with the studio only accelerated. Paramount had released publicity items referring to him as the director of its upcoming production of *You and Me.* Lang, employing a personal publicist, released competing items referring to himself as the "producer-director." The studio objected that Lang was only the director, *not* the producer. Lang protested that when he signed his Paramount contract, Zukor had assured him he would be serving as de facto producer. William LeBaron advised the director to reread his contract, the cold print of which stipulated no such guarantee.

Emphasizing its authority, Paramount assigned a production manager to supervise Lang. But the production manager was not the tactical genius required by the situation. He made the mistake, for example, of suggesting Lang utilize a "dialogue director for rehearsal." The director could match memos with the best, and now he shot one back—characteristically addressing himself in the third person—proclaiming that Fritz Lang had personally never used a dialogue director, and "doesn't need one."

With the extra writers, long preproduction, and elaborately designed musical numbers, the estimated budget had crept over $700,000 by the time photography began. To compound the problems, Lang ordered last-minute modifications in the sets. Cast and crew were exhorted to work all the harder to make up for lost time. Most days everyone had to report to the set from nine to midnight, and people also had to work Saturday nights—and at least one Sunday—as filming fell behind.

The director did not endear himself to the cast or crew with his customary autocratic attitude. Sylvia Sydney proved agreeable once again, but George Raft bristled under Lang's strict regimen, giving a performance even more stilted than usual. To the studio's dismay, the filming kept falling behind, and when photography finally wrapped in late March the director had dropped seven days behind Paramount's projections.

In April, when Kurt Weill launched into recording and dubbing music, he found a director for whom the "sacred totem" had lost its status. Now Lang refused to see Weill in private and in meetings with Boris Morros sided with whichever way the studio winds were blowing. In his letters to Lotte Lenya, Weill complained of the "lack of culture I have to struggle against" in Hollywood, saying his worst enemy was Lang, "who opposes me at every opportunity and is so incredibly unmusical it makes you want to tear your hair out."

Weill saw an early compilation of scenes and privately declared it "zu Lang" (i.e. over-long and "too Lang"). Over his objections, filler music was parceled out to Boris Morros, and lyrics assigned to Sam Coslow, a studio tunesmith (who in his autobiography admitted he found the project "uninteresting"). Although he was determined to do his best, Weill's hatred of Lang was now undisguised, and he took pleasure in every opportunity to face the director down.

Not for the last time had Lang badly miscalculated the prestige of his Berliner ties. After the first preview in May, Kurt Weill left town, then his songs underwent such "ruthless surgery," according to Les Symonette and Kim H. Kowalke in their book *Speak Low (When You Speak Love): The Letters of Kurt Weill and Lotte Lenya*, that the music in the final cut would evince "nothing of his Weill's formal conception."

Still, the studio tried to put the best face on the production as the release date of *You and Me* approached. Paramount posed Lang in a series of photographs highlighting his monocle. Publicity statements issued to accompany the photos tried to "humanize" the monocle with amusing explanations of how and why the director wore it. Later on, in a more humble phase in the 1940s, Lang would try publicity photographs without the monocle; even, still later, with eyeglasses. He liked to supervise his own publicity shots, and there were endless variations: with cigarette, with cigar, with pipe . . . few other Hollywood directors enjoyed the posing as much.

In another Paramount handout, Lang's perfectionism was painted as a laudable strength. Sure, the director had spent an hour and a half giving Sylvia Sidney a lesson in penmanship: "He kept her rehearsing and rehearsing, and between rehearsals he would rub out what she had written [on a chalkboard], trace barely visible lines for her to follow, and get her to try it again. The lady was so tired she misspelled the word 'trucks' three times, and when it was all over she could hardly lift her arm."

Sure, he was tough on the crew. "Lang is all over the place, criticizing the props, changing the set dressing, supervising camera setups and lighting. At one moment he is lying face down on the floor, poring over the script; at the next he is up on the catwalk with a finder-lens, looking for an odd angle to photograph the scene."

Sure, he was a demon of energy. "He waves his arms, sputters, whispers, acts, cajoles, argues, but through it all he never drops his monocle. He drinks from twenty to thirty cups of coffee during a working day, takes no food but a little soup alone in the vast soundstage while the rest of the company is at lunch, and if he had his way he would make each production a nonstop affair."

The studio tried to stay optimistic, and nobody seems to have realized what an out-and-out stinker *You and Me* was until it was shown in theaters in June of 1938.

It was a strange, tortured pastiche of Lang and Brecht, Frank Capra and Damon Runyon.

The songs were intriguing, but oddball. From the opening montage, it was clear that Lang's reach exceeded his grasp. An array of wine, food, cash registers, statues and pistols, set to a toe-tapping tune about the power of money, was visually arresting; inanimate objects were, after all, one of the director's specialties. But the first song was long and nebulous, and one of several whose contrived effect was ultimately tedious.

There is some quirky visual humor in *You and Me*: the department store owner, Mr. Morris (Harry Carey), scratching his head in his inner office, while outside the window, the upper torso of a massive Langian statue makes the same gesture.

There is also one of the more tender shots in the Lang canon: When Joe (George Raft) and Helen (Sylvia Sidney) head in opposite directions on an escalator, their fingers entwine momentarily in close-up. The director knew all about illicit affairs.

The musical numbers are enthusiastically filmed, each number designed to impart one of Lang's little morals. The camera swings overhead, takes extreme angles, zooms into close-ups. In a nightclub sequence, women wriggle as they dance out of martinis. The best of the musical interludes is "The Big Shot," in a prison setting, in which the inmates communicate through knock-knock codes and a whispering chorus.

Sylvia Sidney endeavors gamely to appear a sweet young thing. But Raft, who could sometimes play wry comedy, fails to pull it off for Lang. All the Hays-Code scenes about courtship and sleeping arrangements—who beds down where—fall flat. Fritz Lang, as worldly as anyone where sexuality was concerned, must have been holding his nose while he filmed this nonsense. And the motivation for the second half of the film (Helen's elaborate charade to keep her illicit past secret) doesn't jell. The mistakes were embedded in the script, and the film was doomed by Lang's failure—before filming—to weed them out.

The denouement has its moments: When the other department store parolees gang up with Joe to rob the store on Christmas Eve, Helen finds out and betrays Joe by alerting the police. The good-hearted Mr. Morris lets them all go with a blackboard lecture about virtue and common sense, from Helen. Robbery's a racket run by the guys at the top, she explains. No one really makes a profit except the highest boss. "The big shots aren't little crooks like you—they're politicians!" It's a passing moment of social commentary, couched in the most lighthearted context.

At the end of the film Helen has a baby, and the reformed gang members coax Joe into a reconciliation. The director wasn't opposed to a happy ending for such a vehicle, but nothing else about the experience of *You and Me* was particularly happy. The work stands in Lang's career as a signal case of misjudgment—"a failure between intent and achievement," in the words of Lewis Jacobs.

The director admitted to Peter Bogdanovich that *You and Me* was "an unfortunate affair from the beginning." And he told Charles Higham and Joel Greenberg, "It was—I think deservedly—my first real flop."

"A combination of second-hand movie stuff and a Y.M.C.A. spirit of 'Let's all get together, boys,'" commented the *New York Post*.

"Totally unconvincing," declared the *New York Daily Mirror*.

"It is hard to believe that the same man who staged the memorable *M* guided this motion picture through its fantastic convolutions," wrote Howard Barnes in the *New York Herald Tribune*.

Paramount took its time coming to the inevitable conclusion that it was all Fritz Lang's fault. The studio gave the director his contractual four-week vacation with pay in June, then another four-week leave of absence in July. It was generally agreed that *You and Me* had not been "right" for Lang. But what was right for the director of *Metropolis, M,* and *Fury?* The studio dithered while perusing the available properties.

In the meantime Lang revived "Man Without a Country," and Jonathan Latimer was assigned to work with the director on a revision of the Lang–Martin Mooney spy script. Latimer was an adept writer of mystery fiction who would have a sterling career in Hollywood, first writing suspense films (including *The Big Clock*), then as a prolific scripter of episodes of "Perry Mason" and other television series. He and Lang worked together from late summer into the early winter of 1938, retooling the scenario.

Notes and memoranda from their sessions indicate that Lang felt frustrated by the superficial melodrama of the story he himself had conceived. No matter how many scenes they "fixed," "Man Without a Country" still lacked any inner drive.

Typically, Latimer did the actual writing, while Lang "polished" scenes with his editing suggestions. The director was up to his usual habits, fussing with slang ("Darn!" crossed out and changed to "Rats!") and adding some tainted humor (cutaways of Negro servants). Under Lang's tutelage Latimer made the story's villain more Rotwang and Mabuse-like with each draft, until the final version had the character blinded by his own death-ray machine and left alone in jail, "going mad, tortured by the knowledge that the terrible doom which he sought to let loose on the world is his own."

When the revision of "Man Without a Country" was completed, the director got back in touch with Katharine Cornell, but she continued to play the shy bride and ultimately proved less interested in Hollywood and Fritz Lang than Kurt Weill had been. And Paramount was noncommittal about the upgraded film script, signaling its waning interest by closing out Jonathan Latimer's contract just before the end of 1937.

Relations between Lang and the studio now reached a nadir. He was feuding with the front office about seemingly everything. Paramount had decided it wanted Lang to check in daily on the lot. The director reminded the studio of his contract which stipulated that it was not necessary for him to set foot on the lot "unless sent for." The studio responded by asking Lang to check in daily by telephone, at least. The director countered with his own procedures: his agent, Charles Feldman, would take any calls the studio wanted to have forwarded; the director's secretary would call Feldman's secretary twice daily, at noon and 5 P.M., checking on any urgent queries. (Lang liked making such arrangements as complicated as possible, like the spy business in his films.)

By 1939, six months had elapsed since *You and Me*, and still there was nothing on the docket for the director. Sometime early in the spring, Paramount tired of the aggravation and negotiated the close-out of Lang's contract. Almost two years had gone by since he joined the studio, and only one film had materialized, a debacle with none of the luster of *Fury* or *You Only Live Once*. Now Paramount could be added to the list alienated by Lang. If the director was a leper before, now he was king leper.

Historically, 1938 proved a crossroads. Mussolini made overtures to Hitler. "Kristallnacht," Germany's nationwide rampage of anti-Semitic arson, pillage, and homicide, shocked the world. Austria was annexed. In Spain, with Hitler's help, Franco's fascists had destroyed Guernica and launched their final offensive.

No question that Fritz Lang had turned antifascist. The director made no secret of the fact that he had repudiated the Third Reich and intended to become an American at the earliest opportunity. Ironically, even this fervent opinion could be held against Lang, at heart still the native Austrian. Few German refugees were so quickly prepared to abandon their deeply ingrained love of the fatherland, all Nazi evils aside.

But Lang took his exile personally. The Nazis were not only ruining Germany; they had tried to ruin his life.

Soon after arriving in Hollywood, Lang had begun to take political action unprecedented for him, diving into antifascist and allied causes. While still at MGM, he had become friends with actress Ruth Chatterton, a big star of the late 1920s and early 1930s, now a militant anti-Nazi. A capable amateur pilot, Chatterton took the director up in her plane and they flew over Bund rallies in southern California to drop anti-Hitler leaflets on mass meetings of people trying to drum up U.S. support for Germany.

The anti-Nazi movement in Hollywood was closely affiliated with other crusades: campaigns against joblessness and racism, defense committees for the Scottsboro Boys and other courtroom causes, support for the Soviet Union, and aid to the Loyalist side in the Spanish Civil War. It was a time of curious bedfellows and widespread solidarity. Lang's involvement in antifascist activities brought him into contact with many of the prominent progressives in the screen community and contributed to his growing sophistication in politics.

The broadly structured "umbrella" organizations of the era were spearheaded in Hollywood by "a small nucleus of activist-celebrities [that] launched the main effort," in the words of Larry Ceplair and Steven Englund in *The Inquisition in Hollywood*, "which was then run on a day-to-day basis by a salaried executive director, a small staff, and a host of anonymous volunteers." Lang became one such prominent "activist-celebrity." Like most, he was too busy for the spadework, but gave his prestige and letterhead willingly; he could also be counted on for modest donations. Preoccupied with his career, uncomfortable in large group discussions, the director mainly plugged into what was going on at small meetings and private dinner parties, where everybody was on a first-name basis.

Fritz Lang lent his name to the legal effort on behalf of San Francisco labor leader Harry Bridges, whom the U.S. government was trying to deport back to his native Australia on the grounds that Bridges was a Communist. With Walter Wanger and other Hollywood figures, Lang sat on the advisory board of Films for Democracy, a short-lived organization instituted to promote educational as well as theatrical films with democratic themes. Lang gave donations to FDR's 1936 reelection campaign, to the association which published *The Nation*, to the United Negro Veterans of America—to most of the popular left-wing associations and issue drives.

Hy Kraft was one of Lang's "closet writers"; he was also a behind-the-scenes workhorse helping to organize the first important all-industry group devoted to antifascist goals: the Hollywood Anti-Nazi League. A private meeting was arranged between Prince Hubertus zu Löwenstein (exiled leader of the Catholic German Center Party) and Hollywood luminaries—including Lang—in 1936. Then the Popular Front organization was launched in style, with a hundred-dollar-a-plate banquet at the Victor Hugo restaurant. Lang was one of those announced as a founding father.* Studio chiefs signed on; so did bankers, American Legion officials, even the Archbishop of Los Angeles.

The Anti-Nazi League was prolific in sponsoring its own newspaper, radio shows, panels and educationals, demonstrations, and letter-writing campaigns. When Vittorio Mussolini, the Duce's nephew, made a well-publicized trip to Hollywood, the League waged a campaign against the man, who was heading the fascist film industry in Italy. Then, late in 1938, German actress-director Leni Riefenstahl came to Hollywood to show *Olympische Spiele*, her documentary about the 1936 Berlin Olympic Games. Riefenstahl was the Third Reich's most prestigious filmmaker, holding the status, if not the actual position, supposedly proffered to Lang by Goebbels—a Führer of film. Her acclaimed documentary had been personally ordered by Hitler, and many considered it, in Leslie Halliwell's words, "a hymn to Nazi strength." Lang was one of those spearheading the fight to make Riefenstahl persona non grata— limiting her Hollywood appearances and criticizing her contacts with film folk who were Nazi sympathizers.

Even before the European Film Fund was formally established, Lang had made a point of writing letters and sending money on behalf of notables stranded overseas. When, after 1939, the film fund got going, Lang kept Lily Latté and his secretary busy on behalf of people whose plight was usually brought to his attention by others more resolutely in the forefront of activity: Salka Viertel, agent Paul Kohner, or the William Dieterles. They were the real activists; Lang's leadership role in the film fund has been exaggerated. Yet the director's concern was genuine, even if his involvement was low-profile—even if he sometimes played one cause off against another. (Dunned by the United Jewish Welfare Fund in April 1939, Lang apologized for his small contribution. "I cannot make it a larger amount as I personally am taking care of so many refugees," he explained, "that I have tripled my budget for contributions.")

If Fritz Lang was once thought too snug with the Nazis, now the director was careful about his German associations. Paul Kohner kept in touch with German director Luis Trenker, while continuing to admonish him about his National Socialist leanings.** Trenker was one of those Germans who protested to the end of his life that he never embraced Nazism, even though his career prospered under the Third Reich. From Berlin, Trenker corresponded with Kohner, making occasional noises about a career move to Hollywood.

A forthright Kohner reminded Trenker that his name didn't mean much in Hollywood, considering that his recent films were such "fascist propaganda" (i.e., *Condottiere*) that they'd have drawn only rotten eggs in the United States. In his letters Trenker, a member of the same National Socialist–front group for directors that in 1933 had boasted Lang among its members, kept reminding Kohner to pass regards on to his colleague. In October of 1937, Kohner wrote back, "In all of your letters you ask me to give regards to Fritz Lang.

---

*Other celebrity founders of the Hollywood Anti-Nazi League included writers Dorothy Parker and Donald Ogden Stewart, actor Fredric March, and lyricist-librettist Oscar Hammerstein II.
**Kohner, who was Jewish, had produced Trenker's *The Prodigal Son*, which is now shown as a Nazi film, ironically.

I just want you to know that Lang is not a friend of yours. He thinks you are now a Nazi. So, from now on, don't send any more regards to him."

Many of the German émigrés treated Lang's new political awareness with skepticism, while others, in the spirit of the times, accepted it wholeheartedly. Political friendships brokered professional ones in Hollywood, and the director was able to take advantage of the atmosphere of goodwill on the political front to mend certain fences temporarily.

When the Anti-Nazi League sponsored a Sibelius concert on behalf of Finnish relief in December of 1939, one of the organizers was Joseph L. Mankiewicz. It was Ernst Lubitsch who brought the estranged producer and director of *Fury* together at a Finnish fund-raising party held at his home. This time the two shook hands, signaling a truce between them. Afterward, Lang wrote Mankiewicz saying he regretted what had transpired at MGM, and apologized for the "senseless situation between us," adding, "the sooner forgotten, the better."

It had been almost a year and a half, however, since Lang had directed a film. Anti-Nazi and other political causes kept him busier during the late 1930s than ever again, but all indications are that these merely filled the time—and that by December of 1939 the out-of-work director was profoundly and uncustomarily demoralized.

1939

CHAPTER 13

1941

At this peak of anti-Nazi fervor, this professional low point, Fritz Lang became an American citizen. His citizenship papers were finalized on August 14, 1939. The two official witnesses were his secretary Teddy Le Beau and the director's writer-friend Hy Kraft. Filling out a naturalization petition with details about his background, Lang declared his race and nationality as "German." He noted his height as five feet eleven, his weight as 180 pounds. The director stated that he was divorced from Thea von Harbou, though he made no mention of any other previous marriage.

Lang had been in Hollywood only five years. Most European refugees were slowly adjusting, still uncertain about their host country. Lang was quicker than most to abandon his once-prized German citizenship and pledge his allegiance to the United States.

Lily Latté, for example, waited a little longer—until the spring of 1941. Her witnesses were Le Beau and Pasadena Symphony Orchestra conductor Richard Lert, the husband of Vicki Baum. On her citizenship papers, Latté stated her occupation as a "collaborator and secretary" of film director Fritz Lang.

After coming to America, Latté had had rocky years. Her daughter Susanne died suddenly, of diphtheria, while vacationing in Italy with her grandmother Schaul in 1936. In the meantime Latté had been trying to persuade her mother to leave Germany and come to the United States, but her mother—convinced that the idiocy of Hitler would not last—returned to Germany and passed away there in the summer of 1937.

Lily's ex-husband Hans Latté died in Barcelona, Spain, in April of 1938. Either he was "killed while covering the Spanish Civil War" as a photographer, as Latté told some people; or he died of typhoid, as she informed others. Lily never forgave herself for the fate of her daughter, whom she had sacrificed to her husband in favor of her ambiguous relationship with Fritz Lang.

By 1939, Latté was alone in life, and heavily reliant on Lang. In letters and conversations with ex-Berliners, the director stressed the emotional difficulties Lily had been experiencing since her arrival in America. He never mentioned whether he was affected by his own father's death, which also occurred during this time.

In September of 1939, a deaf and very nearly blind Anton Lang was brought by his doctor to the doorstep of the Convent of the Sisters of Charity, whose nuns cared for the sick and dying in Gars am Kamp, the Lang family's rural retreat in Austria. There he would live out the few remaining months of his life, emaciated and infirm, suffering from glaucoma. On February 14, Lang's father suffered an attack of pneumonia. He died, after receiving Extreme Unction from a Catholic priest, on February 28, 1940, at the age of eighty.

Although Fritz Lang had very little contact with his father, he, the favored son, was named heir to three-eighths of the estate, with five-eighths going to Anton's widow, his second wife, Malwine Löwenthal Lang. The eldest son, Adolf, received nothing.

Anton Lang had married again in 1922, eighteen months after the death of Lang's mother Paula—which may have increased Lang's alienation from his father. Malwine Löwenthal was a divorcée, also with Jewish ancestry; and now that Austria was controlled by the Nazis, this affected the final dispersal of the Lang estate.

The family assets had been whittled down to the villa at Gars am Kamp and four small fields east of Vienna, in Prinzendorf and Ort an der Donau. According to the Nazi racial laws, Anton Lang had been listed as "married to a Jewess," and his widow had trouble even obtaining a lawyer to claim her rightful share. Her "non-Aryan" classification made holding on to the property all but impossible. A lawyer represented Fritz Lang's interests at the reading of the will, and it was very swiftly arranged that the family possessions be auctioned off to pay debts. The house sold locally. The share set aside for the director now residing in America was 5285 Reichsmarks, but it is unlikely that this small sum was ever transferred overseas to his bank account.

As for Malwine Löwenthal Lang, neither she nor her destiny was ever publicly acknowledged in any interview by the director. For a time Fritz Lang's stepmother was sheltered in a convent; she was then transported by the Nazi-controlled state to Poland, where it is believed that she perished in a death camp.

In late 1939, Sam Jaffe brought stability to Lang's career. Jaffe was a cultured man, one of Hollywood's premier art collectors. His sister Ad had married B. P. Schulberg, the onetime head of Paramount. After holding executive positions at Paramount, RKO, and Columbia, Jaffe had gone into the talent agency business as a partner of Charles Feldman in 1934. Their client list included Humphrey Bogart and Joan Bennett.

When Feldman and Jaffe split up, Jaffe established an independent agency under his own name and took some of the agency's clients with him (including Bogart and Bennett). Jaffe was on the lookout for new clients; his roster would eventually expand to include such future Lang collaborators as writer Albert Maltz and émigré-come-lately Bertolt Brecht. When Jaffe heard that Lang, now sans an agent, had secluded himself in his home in Santa Monica, he resolved to visit personally the man everyone said was washed up. "It's hopeless," Lang told Jaffe as they sat down to talk. "I don't think they want me in Hollywood."

Jaffe found to his surprise that he liked the newly-Americanized director.

In his own living room the monocled Lang, about whom the agent had only heard horror stories, won him over. Obviously, Lang was knowledgeable about art; more intriguing, the director spoke keenly about the culture and history of Indians, which appeared to be something of a passion for him. Jaffe had a brainstorm. Wouldn't it be an interesting idea, he thought, to get this refugee from Hitler a contract to direct an American Western?

20th Century–Fox, Jaffe knew, was planning a sequel to *Jesse James*. Henry King had directed the previous film about the poor, misguided outlaw, a slice of Americana that had stirred audiences and critics alike in 1938. But King would not be directing the follow-up. Jaffe knew all this from the man who was going to produce the 20th Century–Fox film—Kenneth Macgowan. Jaffe and Macgowan were friends, and together they had arranged art shows and exhibits in the Los Angeles area.

Macgowan was one of the Hollywood folk who knew and admired Lang's German career. A Harvard-educated former drama critic from the East, Macgowan had been one of the triumvirate, along with playwright Eugene O'Neill and designer Robert Edmund Jones, that was responsible for the glory years of the Provincetown Players in the 1920s. A producer with a writer's sensitivity, he would eventually leave the film industry behind, become a college professor, and author a number of works of nonfiction, from scholarly surveys of theater to psychological explorations of marriage.

Proposing Fritz Lang as the director of a Western might sound ridiculous on the surface, Jaffe knew. But if Jaffe could bring the director together with Macgowan for lunch, he was certain the two would find common ground . . . which is the way it happened. The producer was impressed by Lang, and, with Jaffe's connivance, promoted the idea to 20th Century–Fox production head Darryl Zanuck. Zanuck thought the gimmick of Lang directing his first Western was publicity-rich and asked to meet the out-of-work filmmaker, face-to-face.

One thing: Jaffe did not like Lang's monocle. He thought, especially in the anti-Nazi atmosphere of the times, that the monocle was dangerously misleading. "I said to Fritz, 'Fritz, the monocle represents Nazi Germany,'" recalled Jaffe. "'It's not an attractive character trait. You talk with a German accent too. Together these things don't go well. I would please urge you not to wear the monocle [when meeting with Zanuck].'"

That wasn't the first time the monocle had been pointed out as a handicap. Why Lang persisted in wearing it was baffling. It was much more conspicuous than eyeglasses could ever have been. "Of course it was for effect," said Hilda Rolfe, the director's secretary during the 1940s. "He always said he didn't understand why he had a terrible reputation. He'd talk about that once in a while, especially if he had a drink. 'I don't understand why everybody is afraid of me.' I'd say, 'It's the monocle.' He'd say, 'If I thought that, I wouldn't wear it.' But he'd wear it—*especially* on the set."

But for this crucial appointment, his pride momentarily suppressed, Lang took Jaffe's advice and donned eyeglasses. Zanuck was predictably enchanted by the director, and soon the trade papers were alerted to the news that the legendary refugee director Fritz Lang had been signed by 20th Century–Fox to direct his first Western, *The Return of Frank James*. The contract guaranteed $2,500 a week for ten weeks—for one picture only, just to see how things worked out.

In his published interview with Charles Higham and Joel Greenberg, almost three decades later, Lang made a point of declaring his contribution to *The Return of Frank James* "extended also to the script, although in a minor capacity; for *Western Union* I wrote much more." In fact, typical of his Hollywood experience, Lang's employment came only after a first draft, including all the major story points, was already completed.

The film had been set in motion in September of 1939, before Lang's hiring. Nunnally Johnson, who wrote the script for *Jesse James*, also whipped together an outline for a sequel that would focus on Frank James, the James brother who outlasted his real-life outlaw sibling—and outlasted the storyline of the first film as well. Johnson then bowed out, and Sam Hellman was brought on as screenwriter.

Another former newspaper reporter and editor, Hellman had worked for the press in Saint Louis, the James brothers' stomping ground in the mid-1800s. A 20th Century–Fox contract writer since the early sound days, Hellman had collaborated on a number of films including *Little Miss Marker*, which helped elevate Shirley Temple to stardom.

Twenieth Century–Fox was a producer's studio like MGM, but only one producer really mattered there—Darryl Zanuck. As was customary at Fox, Zanuck, himself a former writer, had been involved in *The Return of Frank James* script from the earliest stages. A pint-sized whirlwind with a Napoleon complex, Zanuck steeped himself in every phase of production. "No one who ever ran a studio was as completely involved as Darryl Zanuck," wrote Garson Kanin.

Zanuck was anxious not to fashion a too-pat sequel. Indeed, he disliked the very word "sequel," and instructed the publicity department to stress that *The Return of Frank James* was not a strict sequel, since it followed a character who had clearly played a subordinate role in the original film. Hellman delivered his initial treatment in December, and his first draft in February of 1940. Macgowan and Zanuck heavily supervised the revisions. Lang did not materialize on the lot until February, so the first draft that could have reflected anything of his input was the last one—dated the first week of April.

Under the circumstances, Lang was restricted to a modest contribution. The director proposed some dialogue suggestions—again, fiddling with the slang. He had been in America long enough now that his ideas were occasionally an improvement, if rarely earth-shaking. (When Lang questioned the wording of shots calling for cutaways to "pickaninnies," his substitution was the slightly more up-to-date pejorative "colored boys.")

There was no way around the casting of Henry Fonda. The rising star whom Lang had tortured during *You Only Live Once* played Frank James in the first film, and he was going to play Frank James in the "non-sequel." Both Macgowan and Zanuck had pressed this worrisome issue with Lang. He assured them that he could make amends with the actor. "He [Lang] knew how I felt and came up to me with tears in his eyes, great big crocodile tears," recalled Fonda, "and said he had learned his lesson and so forth. I finally went along and said, 'Okay.'"

The other cast members would include Gene Tierney, a sleek Eastern aristocrat making her screen debut, and former child star Jackie Cooper. Tierney would play a newspaper reporter writing up the Frank James legend while falling in love with him (although, as the project progressed, Zanuck insisted on playing down the romantic angle). The teenaged Cooper would portray the orphaned son of a deceased gang member. The cast was rounded out by the villainous stalwart John Carradine, playing Jesse James's assassin, Bob Ford.

Cameraman George Barnes (who had entered motion pictures with Thomas Ince and evolved into one of Hollywood's most celebrated cinematographers), assisted by William V. Skall, would accompany the director on his first Wild West excursion—which also would mark his Technicolor debut. A Fritz Lang more inclined to cooperative gestures made friends among the studio departments, including Wiard "Bill" Ihnen, who teamed up with Richard Day to create the design and scenery of this as well as many other 20th Century–Fox features.

Day was a Canadian who had experience with another monocled director: He had begun as an apprentice to Erich von Stroheim, working with von Stroheim on *Foolish Wives*, *Greed*, and *The Merry Widow*. Ihnen, the husband of costumer Edith Head, became one of the director's "useful" friends, and would work closely with Lang in the future on several productions. Ihnen could also, in a pinch, deliver an intelligent opinion on the merits of a screenplay.

It was one of those Lang friendships that included a hint of malice. Ihnen, who became a frequent visitor to the director's house, sometimes took the brunt of Lang's "hurtful sense of humor," in screenwriter Charles Bennett's words. "He [Lang] enjoyed making fun of people to their faces, providing he considered them mentally beneath him." Bennett, the director's neighbor later on in the 1940s, occasionally accompanied Ihnen on his Lang visits, and remembered that one night "everything was fine until Fritz started to practice his sardonic sense of humor on Bill, chuckling openly at his own 'wit' and reducing poor, entirely intelligent Bill into a state which made him look like a buffoon."

Lang was thrilled to have the job. That *The Return of Frank James* was a Western was cause for extra happiness.

With little time left for preproduction, the director dived into research and location planning. Studio edict would make this one of Fritz Lang's rare "exterior" films, with most of the outdoor scenes to be shot northeast of Los Angeles, near the Sierra Nevadas. Adapting to the new Technicolor process was another of the challenges.

"As an example," Lang explained on one occasion, "let's say it is night, and a woman lies in bed with her head against a white pillow, and a man stands against a dark wall. You have a close-up of this woman, who is well-lit by a lamp on the night table and, with the white pillow, you have a bright background. Now you cut to the man against a dark wall. White—black. Shocks you. Therefore, with a little thought and experimentation, I learned that if you had consecutive close-ups with the backgrounds lit in a similar way, your eyes weren't shocked.

"Another thing (which became especially important later when you were shooting in Cinemascope) was that if you have a shot in subdued color of, say, a woman with an apple in her hand—every painter can tell you that your eye will immediately be attracted to the red apple. So I learned to avoid points of bright light, of reflecting glass or bright color."

Photography started on May 8, 1940. On location, Lang resolved to wear the studio straitjacket as snugly as possible. He didn't dare change the script beyond what Zanuck had approved, nor tamper with the carefully prepared schedule and setups.

Sadly, Lang's love for the American West never really came through in his own Westerns, *especially* the two he made for 20th Century–Fox. He often told interviewers about a letter from an old-timer's club in Arizona praising the truthfulness of his Westerns, but his pride in authenticity was almost comical in the fantasy world of that genre. Around town, people told funny anecdotes about Lang trying to adapt to the Western format. The joke went through 20th Century–Fox that the director showed up on the set of *The Return of Frank James* one day, peered into a viewfinder, and asked, "The third cow, move her a little bit to the left, please." Editor Gene Fowler, Jr., conceded there were many such gaffes, as when Lang cried, "Bring in the mools," then screamed his head off when people didn't understand it was the "mules" he wanted.

No matter that he was on his best behavior; Lang encountered some friction with the actors, who proved less malleable than cows and mules. Inevitably, Lang and Henry Fonda clashed again. "Not only was it [*The Return of Frank James*] a wrong picture for him to have done, a Western, but he hadn't learned any lessons at all," said Fonda. "He killed three or four horses on location. He was riding them too hard, making the wranglers ride them too hard up hills and at an altitude. Anyway, that was Fritz Lang."

Fonda had a reputation for never raising his voice in anger. "I saw Henry Fonda with veins about to bust out of the side of his head, screaming at Fritz Lang," recalled the film's co-star, Jackie Cooper. "I mean, yelling and pounding and slamming and kicking and screaming, because the man had no respect for actors at all. He wanted everybody to be a puppet. He would tell you when to put your elbow on the table and when to take it off. He would tell you how to read a line. Everything was picture to Fritz, and actors were not important at all."

Cooper admitted that he didn't get along very well with Lang either. "It's the first time I ever walked off a set," Cooper added, "and had to make a director apologize, and so on and so forth. It did me no good, because most of the picture he was on my back."

If he had not been powerless to do so, the director might have opposed the casting of Gene Tierney, Darryl Zanuck's own "virgin star." Lang made it clear he didn't think the onetime debutante could act worth beans. When the director deigned to speak to her, his words were freighted with hostility. "I tended to keep my lower lip open when I wasn't talking, the kind of habit that can look so unattractive on the big screen (unless you were Marilyn Mon-

roe),” Tierney wrote in her memoirs. “The director, Fritz Lang, stopped one
scene and barked at me, ‘You little bitch! When you have no lines, keep your
mouth shut.’ ” Henry Fonda rushed to Tierney’s rescue, upbraiding Lang. But
Tierney was one member of the cast who thought the director was not entirely
off-base. “Actually the tip was a useful one,” Tierney recalled. “As the work
went along, everyone, including Fritz Lang, tried to be helpful, and I began
to feel that I belonged.”

Back at 20th Century–Fox, what mattered was the budget, the schedule,
and the dailies. Zanuck liked what he saw. He had no illusions about the
picture, which was always regarded as a “shaky A” production, but after supervising the final cut, Zanuck couldn’t help but be pleased. It had all gone
as he had hoped. At the end of May, the personnel department was ordered
to draw up new, extended terms for the director.

“I remember Zanuck was very sweet to me on that picture,” recalled Lang,
“contrary to later on. Everybody had great respect for him, not a respect that
I would like or accept—but fear.”

This docile Fritz Lang was not simply putting on an act. The time he had
spent without work had chastened him. The director was earnest now in wanting to succeed in Hollywood—and on Hollywood’s terms. The setbacks and
reversals he had suffered during the 1930s had engendered the seeds of self-
doubt, and even consideration, in his psychology. Though his instincts would
continue to war, practicality would increasingly be the winner.

For people who met Fritz Lang during these years—even more markedly,
for old acquaintances who had known him in Berlin—the director must have
seemed astonishingly different from the dictatorial Teuton of legend. He
spouted leftist ideas with the zeal of a true believer. He had traded his monocle
in for eyeglasses and cowboy boots. He spoke hopefully about upcoming contract assignments and endorsed such studio bromides as the “wienie”—one
or two snappy sentences that could succinctly summarize a screen story—and
the once odious happy ending.

Curt Siodmak had emigrated to the United States from Germany and become a science fiction author and screenwriter who in Hollywood occasionally
crossed paths with Lang. One day Siodmak met his fellow expatriate in one
of the studio commissaries and reminded him of his visit to the *Metropolis*
set over ten years previously, when Brigitte Helm had nearly been burned
during the stake scene, and Siodmak, then a cub reporter, had been tossed off
the set. “He didn’t remember,” said Siodmak, “and denied that the robot
even caught fire.”

Carl Zuckmayer, the German poet, playwright, and scenarist, spent an evening with the director, and informed Lang that he was on the verge of rejecting
a lucrative offer from Warner Brothers producer Hal Wallis to write a Don
Juan picture starring Errol Flynn. It was going to be “some typical movie
nonsense,” Zuckmayer recalled, “and I had neither the talent nor the urge for
that sort of thing. Fritz Lang, who wished me well, was horrified.

“ ‘In Hollywood, you never said no to anything, no matter what was asked
of you,’ he advised me. To refuse an assignment was to be fired. And how
could I ask for anything better than this offer? It would keep me occupied for

years; that kind of expensive costume spectacular went slowly, so that I could count on staying on for the length of my contract, which provided for an increase in the weekly check from year to year. I ought to rent a nice house and hire a Filipino couple as domestics, buy a car on installments, bring my family here, and be 'happy.' Besides, I would have a three-month holiday every year during which I could do my own writing. 'For God's sake, be reasonable and say yes,' Lang urged me."

When *The Return of Frank James* was released, in early August of 1940, the box office and reviews were good. Many reviews commented on the exceptional outdoor photography and the novelty of Lang as director. If one behaved agreeably to the Hollywood critics and columnists, they behaved agreeably back, and Lang knew how to woo the press. One of the people he cultivated was Louella Parsons, who wrote in her influential, nationally syndicated column that *The Return of Frank James* was superlative entertainment, in many ways better than the original.

Looking at the film today, though, one is struck by its total absence of personality. It is as bland and pedestrian as anything Fritz Lang was capable of turning out.

Henry Fonda had the upper hand over the director, and his performance is distinguished only by copious spitting of tobacco. So much for authentic Americana in Lang's debut Western. To be fair, Fonda's character was also unremarkable in the script, and the actor held his own alongside John Carradine's showboating and the simpering from Gene Tierney (cited by the *Harvard Lampoon* as "Worst Female Discovery of 1940").

Working in a milieu he had adored since boyhood, Lang's direction was bereft of his trademark style and invention. No extreme close-ups, few overhead shots, darkness banished in favor of sunshine; even the crowd scenes were perfunctory. There were racist caricatures, plot implausibilities, and a dull, drawn-out courtroom sequence at the film's climax. The whole point of the script was that Frank James was an innocent; in the course of the entire story, he never kills or even mistreats a single person.

This was Lang without teeth—Lang effacing himself.

Nonetheless, *The Return of Frank James* proved a solid hit.

The director had a clause in his contract barring him from any publicity not originated or approved by 20th Century–Fox. But there was a loophole allowing personal publicity, publicity between films, and activities unrelated to the studio.

Sam Jaffe's nephew was Henry C. Rogers, just starting his lengthy career as a Hollywood publicist. (Rogers would go on to head one of the film industry's high-powered firms, Rogers and Cowan.) Recommended to Lang by his uncle, Henry Rogers was hired to publicize the director's name; with Rogers and Jaffe on retainer for the next decade, Lang would have a stable continuity of personal management.

Rogers had the unusual publicity challenge of having constantly to remind people in Hollywood who Fritz Lang *used* to be, without in the least appearing passé. Accordingly, items were manufactured toasting the fact that Lang had more motion pictures in the permanent collection of New York City's Museum of Modern Art—seven—than any active director; others cited European polls attesting to the director's global reputation.

It was eternally frustrating to Lang that he had to reintroduce himself to Hollywood and America over and over again. "He was not regarded in those days as the great German genius in the way he became recognized years later," said Henry Rogers. "He was just another director, somebody else who had come over from Germany. He was not Fritz Lang the Great at that moment in time. This bothered him. That Hollywood didn't recognize his genius. He wanted people to know about his accomplishments in Germany, but nobody really cared. Nobody made a big fuss."

Romantic squibs in the press added luster to the professional tintype. After the release of *The Return of Frank James*, these "love-life bulletins" accelerated in variety and quantity. Lang, his career revitalized, was out and about more than ever, conspicuously wining and dining the screen colony's eligible beauties.

Kay Francis and Lang were one such item during the summer of 1940. The chic leading lady, whose finest films, dating back to the late 1920s, were gay comedies or throbbing romances, had been acquainted with the director for at least a year. They probably met through Miriam Hopkins, one of their circle of mutual friends.

Lang had escorted Kay Francis to the premiere of the original *Jesse James* in January of 1939; the actress was also his date, a year and a half later, for the "non-sequel" he directed. Together they attended the December 1939 gala premiere of *Gone With the Wind*, and the invitation-only party afterward at the Jock Whitney's. In March of 1940, they attended the first showing of Walt Disney's *Pinocchio*. Dozens of gossip-column items in Lang's archival deposits evidence the rising parabola of their public outings—dinner and dancing, trips to Hollywood Park, stage and screen shows.

By late July of 1940, the director and actress were "seen together practically everywhere," according to the parlance. They could be glimpsed in "the darker corners of restaurants," columnists reported. When Lang made his annual theater-going trip to New York, Kay Francis was there on the train station platform waving good-bye. Their romance had definitely entered the "Torrid Zone," wrote Jimmy Starr in his regular column. By late September the news was sensational: Danton Walker confirmed in his regular "Broadway" feature that "Kay Francis will become Mrs. Fritz Lang very shortly."

Such gossip, typical of the Hollywood publicity mill, cannot always be verified. But it so happens that Kay Francis kept a journal of her daily life in Hollywood in the 1930s and 1940s, complete with an oft-explicit record of her sexual activity. These journals, on repository at Wesleyan University in Connecticut, confirm that the actress and director had an affair in the summer of 1940; indeed, the journals confirm the precise date of the couple's first sexual encounter: July 13, 1940. "Fritz and I home and at last we got together," reported the actress. "And very nice too!"

As her diary attests, Kay Francis was a sexually liberated woman, who pursued several lovers and relationships during the time she knew Fritz Lang. (At the time the director was romancing her, the actress had another lover, a

German named "Erik," which Lang seemed not to mind.) She and Lang had been close friends for some time before their friendship evolved into physical intimacy. The actress knew a side of the director that not very many people would recognize: the sensitive, sweet-souled Fritz Lang. Again and again in her journal, Francis commented on what a fascinating talker and thoughtful listener her dear friend, the director, was. "What an angel!"

Her journal pinpoints the director at various private occasions in 1939 and 1940, giving an idea of their social circle. The two of them went to restaurants and dinner parties with Lang's colleague, director Lewis Milestone (another Selznick veteran); with Berlin-born Warner Brothers producer Henry Blanke, who had trailed Lubitsch to America as his assistant; with Hungarian director Michael Curtiz; with *Fury* scenarist Bartlett Cormack.

It is possible that Lang did float the proposition of marriage to Kay Francis. The director was more than capable of acting the dewy-eyed romantic. "The Viennese are supposed to be very sentimental, which they are, and that was his attitude about women," said actor Howard Vernon. "Lang was over-courtly and sincere about women. For him, the word 'woman' was written in capital letters. To him, women were something on a pedestal. They never returned that to him. There were actually very few women who paid him back."

But the director also had a short attention span. Although he and Kay Francis stayed friends for a long time after they went to bed together, by December their torrid romance was already over. By then it was another actress, Virginia Gilmore, who was being glimpsed "everywhere together" with Lang, without any published explanation of what had transpired to hinder the impending Fritz Lang–Kay Francis nuptials.

A beautiful, leggy blonde, Virginia Gilmore was born in El Monte, California, in 1919 with the unlikely name of Sherman Poole. She had German ancestors. After graduating from high school in 1937, she performed in little theater groups in San Francisco. No older than twenty when she met the film director—Lang never said how or where they met—she became "his protegée," in the words of her son Rock Brynner.

Lang might have seen her in a play in San Francisco and stopped backstage to introduce himself. That is the way it would have happened in Europe. Rock Brynner said that "at Lang's suggestion" Gilmore auditioned as a Goldwyn Girl. Producer Sam Goldwyn paid for her dance lessons and orthodontics. Goldwyn's publicity department announced that the newcomer's legs had been insured for a million dollars, and Gilmore won the annual trophy sponsored by the Physical Culture Foundation of Hollywood for having "the best legs in the industry." Hence her nickname: "Gams Gilmore."

But legs were only part of the package. "She was known to enjoy highfalutin' literature," wrote Rock Brynner in the biography of his father Yul Brynner, "at a time when ingenues were not generally recognized for their cognitive faculties. Her poetry, coached by Lang, was remarkable, at least for a teenage Goldwyn Girl. Samuel Goldwyn himself described her as 'an honest-to-God American beauty with brains who even writes poems.'"

Leaving aside, for the moment, the curiosity of Lang coaching Gilmore's poetry, people were taken aback to see the two of them together—the young, leggy Goldwyn Girl in constant company with the fearsome director who was old enough to be her father. At Salka Viertel's they created a stir, all the more because everyone was under the impression that Lily Latté, also a salon regular, was herself still in love with the director.

"Virginia was a very attractive girl, but somehow I could never understand the relationship between the two," said Henry Rogers who, as Lang's personal publicist, was responsible for churning out the press items about their love affair. "He was so much older than she was. They didn't seem to fit at all. She looked like a typical all-American high school girl, while he was a Prussian with a monocle in his eye."

The director was just "out and out in love" with the aspiring actress, remembered Gene Fowler, Jr. Indeed, Lang pressed Darryl Zanuck to accept Virginia Gilmore as the leading lady of his second film under the 20th Century–Fox contract. The director could be clumsy about pushing the actress's career, however, making casual references to her as "my mistress," according to his agent Sam Jaffe. "You don't use that term in America," Jaffe cautioned Lang.

After leaving the Goldwyn Girls behind, Gilmore paid her dues with appearances in "B" films. Then Jean Renoir zeroed in on her for his first American production, *Swamp Water*, also filmed at Fox. Although Zanuck had initially leaned toward Brenda Joyce, he began to listen more attentively to Lang's lobbying, and finally approved Virginia Gilmore to co-star in Lang's next picture, *Western Union*. It was a rare return to what had been Lang's accustomed practice back in Germany—discovering and molding a "virgin star."

In his interview with Peter Bogdanovich years later Lang quoted producer Erich Pommer: "Never have an affair with an actress." "He [Pommer] didn't obey it," said Lang matter-of-factly, "I didn't obey it. But I never did it—and never do it—during a picture. What happens afterward is my private business. But that during the shooting somebody should say to me, 'Last night you said, 'Sweetheart,' and 'Beautiful,' and today you order me around!'—nothing doing."

Lang had forgotten his own publicity!

During this period—the late 1930s and early 1940s—Lang continued to travel widely throughout the American West. His cache of "home movies," on deposit at the American Heritage Center of the University of Wyoming, show trips to the Rockies, Jasper Park, Bryce Canyon, Santa Fe, and the Petrified Forest, as well as other tourist meccas.

It cannot be said with certainty that the University of Wyoming holds the full catalog of Lang's home movies, nor that their content is characteristic of what the director, in his spare time, chose to photograph with his 8-mm Kodak. More personal footage in these home movies, sold to the archives by Lily Latté, may have been purged from the collection; that was par for Lang's memorabilia after the director's death. However, the ten-to-fifteen-minute home movies were still in their original packaging when seen by the author, and did not appear to have been disturbed by any handling since their stamped laboratory dates.

The home movies, oddly, are impersonal, almost entirely scenic. The footage shows oil fields and train tracks, sunrises and sunsets, mountains, forests, hot springs, bridges, tunnels, and caves, sometimes filmed out of the front window of an automobile whose hood ornament is glimpsed in the foreground of the frame. Repeatedly, Lang set his little camera up on a tripod and took long, static shots of sculpted rock, desert flowers, and peculiar cacti. (One of the American magazines the director faithfully subscribed to over the years featured color layouts of Western flora and fauna.)

The filmic content is notable for its absence of people. A close-up of the face of an Indian boy, during a panoramic shot of a clay dwelling of Native Americans, is almost startling. A glimpse of a woman—probably Virginia Gilmore—dozing on the front seat of Lang's car is another rare exception. The director himself is seen fleetingly, once or twice, in one home movie, posed adoringly with his pet dogs, like any ordinary person.

The director was all over the newspapers in 1940: making his first motion picture in two years, squiring around a series of mistresses—and enduring public accusations of being a Communist sympathizer.

The director had come a long way since 1933. The September, 1939 start of the war in Europe had reinforced his leftward drift. His political credentials were by now solidly established in Hollywood. A grand jury convening in Los Angeles in the summer of 1940 heard a witness, described as a former "chief functionary" of the local Communist Party, identify a list of forty-three secret Communists or sympathizers who were attempting to advance the "Red" cause in the American film industry. The personalities named included well-known actors Fredric March, Franchot Tone, J. Edward Bromberg, James Cagney, Humphrey Bogart, Lionel Stander, and Francis Lederer. Fritz Lang was one of only a handful of directors on the list, his name prominently mentioned in the August 15, 1940, front-page articles.

Curiously, the functionary, one John L. Leech, testified that he had gone with Franchot Tone to visit Lang years before to let the director know "he was betraying the working classes by lending his name to the type of propaganda" articulated in *Fury*, which "was opposed by the Communists." That was how Lang, whose politics were all gut-instinct, confused people: *Fury* was a singularly hard-hitting anti-lynching film, but it wasn't Marxist-Leninist enough for the Communists; it couldn't even be considered populist, since "the people" were depicted as a cowardly mob, and with just a nudge, Spencer Tracy, the John Doe character, metamorphosed into a Mabusian vengeance-seeker.

In New York City, when the headlines broke, Lang conferred with his publicist Henry Rogers, and they quickly drafted a press statement. In the prepared release, interestingly, the director made one of his few public references to any previous impeachment of his politics. "A few years ago I was accused of being a Nazi," Lang declared. "As a fugitive from Nazi Germany, the charge was ridiculous. This charge is even more ridiculous. I hate Hitler—I hate Stalin—I hate all dictators and dictatorships!" The previous December, when he became a U.S. citizen, Lang's statement continued, had proved the proudest day of his life. "I swore to uphold the Constitution and the American flag," the director stated. "I know no other allegiance. I respect no other flag."

Arriving from Texas, Martin Dies, the chairman of the congressional panel investigating subversive activities, convoked a secret hearing into Communist organizing in Hollywood and the swirling allegations of sabotage, espionage, and treason. The motion picture industry, however, reacted strongly to the unwelcome federal investigation, and united in support of the big names. A smiling Humphrey Bogart was pictured on page one of the August 17, 1940, *Los Angeles Times*, wagging his finger at Congressman Dies; shortly thereafter the chairman left town, having overestimated his issue. The "Hollywood Reds" furor appeared to blow over, and Lang's publicist assured the director that his statement, duly printed in all the local newspapers, rated as among "the best" and most convincing of the denials by the accused.

Some denials had cleverly sidestepped the issue. Some of those named by John L. Leech *were* Communist Party members or sympathizers, in spite of public protestations to the contrary. (It was Party policy to keep one's membership clandestine.) Not Lang, apparently; all the former Hollywood-section members of the Party who were interviewed for this book said the director aligned with them on many issues of the era, but was too aloof, too career-oriented, to actually join up.

In spite of his statement opposing Stalin, Lang stayed friendly with the American Communists, among whom he had friends and associates whose politics were no secret to him.

The Dies Committee (predecessor to the House of Representatives' Committee on Un-American Activities) controversy caused only a ripple. Zanuck seemed to think the coverage added up to more swell publicity. Nobody could have predicted at the time that the 1940 grand jury naming Fritz Lang and others was the opening sally of what would turn out to be a prolonged, intensive, and destructive anti-Communist crusade in Hollywood.

In December of 1939, Curtis Kenyon and Kenneth Earl had handed in the first outline for *Western Union*. A treatment executed by Robert Carson followed in February of 1940; then, in June, came a temporary script. All along director Irving Pichel, assigned to the project, worked closely with Carson, shaping the script. Lang was busy wrapping up *The Return of Frank James*, and uncertain—until that film was finished and his contract re-negotiated—that he would be involved in any other 20th Century–Fox production.

Carson was one of Hollywood's dependable screenwriters. A novelist and short-story author whose books included *The Magic Lantern*, an account of the pioneering days of the motion picture industry, Carson shared an Oscar with William Wellman for his original story for *A Star Is Born*. Thereafter he worked frequently with director Wellman while continuing to market his story-telling knack elsewhere at the studios.

Once again, Zanuck participated heavily in the script's evolution. The film was envisioned as a virile saga about the construction of the Western Union telegraph line across the inhospitable miles of the American frontier in the 1860s. In fact, Zanuck was tempted to excise all the women from the story ("This should be a man's story about men," the producer opined), which is one of the reasons why Virginia Gilmore's role in the final product seems almost tacked on. An initial impulse to give the project a documentary aura was also considered, then rejected, after some of Zanuck's ideas—camels instead of horses as an appetizer for audiences—proved historically baseless.

Commercial instincts prevailed, and the eventual script was bolstered by Indians, outlaws, and a lovely lady made lovelier by scenes that focused on her presence. What little drama there was would center on the telegraph-laying operations and two of the empire-builders, a tenderfoot and a manlier cowboy with a secret agenda, who compete for the affections of the boss's sister. A raffish outlaw gang would trail along after the operations, rustling cattle, stirring up Indians, and fueling the various levels of conflict.

Because Zanuck was worried about the script being too talky, Horace Mc-Coy, whose hard-boiled novels included the minor classic *They Shoot Horses, Don't They?* was brought in to trim and consolidate the final version of the script, dated September 7, 1940. All of this essential scenario development took place without Lang even on the premises. The director did not return to the studio under his newly-extended contract until mid-August, with principal photography slated to begin on October 17.

Right away Lang seems to have recognized that the studio "preferred to give an audience the same old thing—with some new trimming," in his words. The architectural blueprint was prepared; now all he had to do was serve as builder. Except for Virginia Gilmore, the director made no inroads with Zanuck's casting. And above all, Lang had to resolve to follow the studio head's dictum that an effective picture be made "just as economically as we made *Frank James.*"

The director was still in an obliging mood, however. When cast and crew decamped to locations near Kanab, Utah, Lang could breathe a sigh and do his best to enjoy himself. He visited nearby Indian reservations during shooting breaks. The box-office popularity of *The Return of Frank James* and the constant presence of Virginia Gilmore made the production pleasant, and the chore relatively simple.

The cameraman was a bonus. Edward Cronjager, who had been on and off the set helping out with *The Return of Frank James*, got along remarkably well with Lang, and would work with the director again on *House by the River.* Cronjager was from a family of cameramen, and among his disparate specialties were Sonja Henie's ice-skating pictures and many of Fox's Technicolor Westerns produced on location.

In later years, the director would remember one shot in *Western Union*, engineered by Cronjager, with considerable pride: A camera pans up a telegraph pole to reveal a loose wire cut by an Indian war spear, then a ninety-degree pan reveals a nearby troop of Indians arrayed in war paint. But in general the production minimized the director's pictorial strengths. Lang in the wilds was surprisingly restrained, almost subdued in the face of God's surroundings; and he didn't warm to color, ironically—not in his previous Western or this one—until he moved indoors to shoot *Moonfleet* many years later.

After filming was finished, Lang was distressed to learn that Zanuck had ordered retakes—approximately fifty shots' worth. In a nine-page memo, Zanuck explained that some refilming was imperative to give him "coverage" in postproduction; Zanuck was notorious for reassembling pictures in the editing room, and additional close-ups and angles would multiply his options. Lang had already experienced his share of humbling Hollywood experiences, but nobody had yet second-guessed him so totally.

The director had little choice, however. The tension in the screening room was palpable when Zanuck stopped by to look at assembled scenes and growl his instructions. Lang's smile was increasingly forced. The editing warranted more Zanuck participation than usual, and for the first time the director was overruled on the ultimate selection of takes—another new humiliation for him to swallow.

That is one of the reasons Lang's relationship with Gene Fowler, Jr., started out awkwardly. The director mistakenly diagnosed Fowler, an assistant editor on *Western Union*, as one of Zanuck's toadies. The son of Gene Fowler, a colorful ex-newspaperman and Hollywood gadabout, Fowler was on the studio payroll but also knowledgeable about Fritz Lang. As a boy his father had taken him to see *Metropolis* at the Garden Theater in Jamaica, Long Island, and he had admired Lang's work ever since.

Fowler's introduction to Lang occasioned a yelling match. The director accused the assistant editor of hiding a particular piece of film footage that Lang wanted to watch on the Movieola, a clip Fowler insisted did not exist. If such footage existed, Fowler told Lang, it was only in the director's imagination. Lang was amazed that an assistant editor would dare to stand up to him. Later, Lang sidled up to Fowler and apologized for losing his temper. "I blow up every once in a while because I'm trying to get this picture perfect," the director said. So the two became fast friends.

Fowler would prove an important ally for Lang. He tried to mediate in the editing room and help the director accommodate the studio without losing control of the film. But Fowler ranked low as a cutter, and couldn't do much on *Western Union*. The director had to go along with Zanuck, and finish the job with his most good-natured shrug.

Nonetheless, *Western Union* isn't such a bad picture. It's quite agreeable, really, the opposite of the intended rugged saga, and instead as much of a lark as Lang could muster.

The actors gave relaxed performances. Randolph Scott, who played the reformed desperado Vance Shaw, was the kind of leading man Lang seemed to prefer—wooden and taciturn. But Scott was comfortable in Western costume, and delivers an appealing performance.

Robert Young plays the tenderfoot, Richard Blake, who is trying to live up to the expectations of his rich father (Dean Jagger). The film makes fun of Blake, a bumbling outsider, but the character proves his mettle with heroics in the end. Lang in the right mood could endorse such a type and see in him a bit of himself—the tenderfoot in Hollywood.

Sue Creighton, the Virginia Gilmore character, is treated graciously, although she has little to do but bat her eyes at Shaw and Blake every now and then. A good-hearted type, she believes in the reformation of bad character. "Mistakes can be corrected," she philosophizes. (Vance Shaw delivers the Langian response: "Not always.") Her rival suitors behave toward each other in unusually civilized fashion, which rings true from a director accustomed to wishing his girlfriends well in other men's arms.

The director's personality was gently sublimated in favor of the Old West atmosphere. There is shopping for Paris fashions on a frontier Main Street, coded messages sent by telegraph, a forest fire less spectacular than Lang's usual conflagrations. (It was filmed by the second unit.) A brief scene in which Vance Shaw forces his wrists into a campfire in order to burn off the ropes that tie them together, leaps out as a flash of the director's old sadistic streak.

The film's Oglala Indians, whom Lang professed to revere, come off here as embarrassing stereotypes. Their stumbling-drunk behavior, the clichéd drumbeat whenever they appear, a routine where they are tricked into grabbing telegraph wires to shock themselves electrically—these were unforgivable lapses of reason as well as taste. No doubt all of this was in Zanuck's master plan, but Lang showed no hint of subversion.

On the other hand, *Western Union* has three times the humor of any other Fritz Lang film. Much of it is picaresque, some is corny. The surfeit of cutaways to the grizzled cook (Slim Summerville), whose exaggerated facial expressions are intended as comic relief, were in fact dictated by Zanuck. The studio chief's list of retakes called for additional close-ups, "quick take-ems" of "that sickly smile whenever he [Slim] hears of a death."

At the end of the film there comes a rather surprising twist of plot. The cattle-rustling villain Jack Slade (Barton MacLane) turns out to be Vance Shaw's brother. A well-choreographed shoot-out ensues, leaving both brothers dead. The camera offers a final Fordian tribute to Vance Shaw, with a shot that peers over the grave toward a line of telegraph wires stretching into the sunset. It was a little reminder that Fritz Lang the craftsman had shown up for work, even if the artist stayed home.

Once again the director had managed to rein himself in. Zanuck was satisfied, and the box office for *Western Union* was even better than for *The Return of Frank James*.

Almost immediately, Lang's terms were stepped up and he was given a multipicture deal—making him, effectively, a 20th Century–Fox contract director.

It so happened that director John Ford, increasingly tied up with his own Argosy Productions, had just backed out of filming an adaptation of Geoffrey Household's 1939 novel *Rogue Male*. Especially well-received in England, the timely book was speculative fiction about a British aristocrat in Germany who, for the sporting thrill of it, stalks the biggest game of all—Hitler. He is discovered and tortured by Nazis guarding the Führer; though he escapes to England, the tables are turned and he becomes the hunted quarry, as the Nazis scramble to capture him and exploit his "assassination attempt" in order to justify their upcoming invasion of England.

Although Jules Furthman wrote the first treatment, Dudley Nichols took over the assignment, and throughout the fall of 1940 prepared the script with John Ford in mind. A Hollywood figure since 1930, Nichols would prove Lang's most outstanding scenarist in the United States. Raised in Michigan, Nichols had a background as a radio operator on the Great Lakes and a minesweeper in World War I; after the war he spent the decade of the 1920s in New York at the *Evening News* and *World* newspapers, covering the news and drama scene while studying Latin and Greek in his spare time.

Nichols and Ford had developed into one of Hollywood's greatest writer-director teams—responsible for *The Informer, Stagecoach, Mary of Scotland, The Plough and the Stars,* and *The Long Voyage Home.* Among Nichols's other stellar credits were screwball comedies *(Bringing Up Baby),* and even a Fred Astaire–Ginger Rogers vehicle called *Carefree.* His best scripts were not only beautifully constructed as stories, they were social treatises. He was a crusader who hated injustice, and brought a humanist approach to each project.

In his autobiography French director Jean Renoir, who worked with Nichols on *Swamp Water* and *This Land Is Mine,* told an anecdote about a script conference at which a producer deigned to bestow the wisdom of his story craft on Nichols. "What your script lacks," the producer said, "is a good, old-fashioned love scene—the riverbank, trees in blossom, and the girl in her lover's arms—naturally, all bathed in romantic moonlight." Nichols hated such fluff scenes. "Dudley Nichols, during this exordium, had turned from pink to scarlet," wrote Renoir. "He rose slowly to his feet, and, turning his back on the speaker, said simply, 'The moon is rising.' Then he led me out of the room."

When, in early December, Ford bowed out of the *Rogue Male* project, Zanuck turned to the producer—Kenneth Macgowan, who had also supervised Ford's film *Young Mr. Lincoln*—and asked him who might be the best candidate to get along with Nichols and replace Ford. Macgowan recommended Fritz Lang. Serendipity all around.

With Nichols involved, Zanuck would be more likely to grant more of the creative freedom Lang desired. The subject—the European locales and anti-Nazi slant—was up the director's alley, a more natural vehicle for his personal vision than Westerns. Lang had proved himself, and now the director would be rewarded with a prestigious project.

Studio records show that the basic draft of the script was completed before Lang was even assigned to the production, but that he immersed himself in subsequent story conferences, eagerly applying his visual ideas to Dudley Nichols's pages. With the director participating, a revised draft was prepared on January 20, a final draft a month later, and one more draft, a shooting script, ultimately produced on March 7.

One story conference, which included Zanuck, took place on February 4, 1941, and touched on a scene in which Thorndike, the British aristocrat pursued by the Nazis, topples from a ridge. The director's expertise with inserts, virtually irrelevant in the earlier Westerns, proved useful. Lang made the suggestion that, in shooting the scene, the camera should aim upward from below the ridge: "We should see the knapsack with broken strap hanging on the limb of the tree" that breaks Thorndike's fall. "Excellent," Zanuck judged.

In another scene, later in the film, Thorndike hides in a cave. Lang, perhaps stimulated by his own zest for caves, proposed "that the cave stuff should be played for the most part from Thorndike's angle," with the voice of the Quive-Smith character, his Nazi nemesis, coming from the outside, "to give the effect of a trapped animal." Zanuck also found that Langian suggestion excellent, but, typically, asked for editing room "insurance coverage" from Quive-Smith's point of view.

Lang was also more involved with the general casting than he had been on the prior Fox productions. After watching William Wyler's screen test of a twelve-year-old British child actor evacuated during the London Blitz, the director made a strong case for lowering the age of the character Vaner, a ship's mate who aids the fugitive during his escape to England. Everyone agreed, Vaner became a cabin boy—a key change that Dudley Nichols made on Lang's behalf—and Roddy McDowall earned his first American role.*

For the part of Thorndike, Walter Pidgeon was borrowed from MGM. According to studio publicity, Lang "felt that this departure from Pidgeon's usual light vehicles would be a splendid opportunity for him," but the director didn't have much say in the matter. Walter Pidgeon was one of the elements set in stone before Lang was assigned.

In pre-Lang drafts of the script, Nichols had supplied a major female part not in the book—a Cockney streetwalker named Jerry who risks her life to befriend the fugitive Thorndike. Lang, that connoisseur of prostitutes, heartily approved—but the Production Code office didn't, and officials insisted that all reference to prostitution be excised from the script. According to the director, this set in motion a series of decisions that compromised the character, while postponing the choice of actress.

The prostitute implications had to be toned down. A sewing machine had to be planted in the character's apartment as an obvious sign of her respectability. "Thus she was not a whore, she was a 'seamstress,'" wryly explained the director in one interview.

In one of her scenes, however, the character was supposed to adopt the mannerisms of a streetwalker in order to give Thorndike an alibi to keep him from getting nabbed by the Nazis. This surreal situation (a character the studio couldn't allow to be a prostitute, *pretending* to be a prostitute) nonetheless teetered on the Production Code tightrope, and Zanuck targeted the scene for further revision. Lang fought to preserve the scene, defying the studio head to defend his objections. "He [Zanuck] gave me a very characteristic answer," recalled Lang. " 'When a whore plays a whore in front of the man she loves— that is not tragic. When a decent girl plays a whore, then it is tragic.' Now I couldn't even discuss this kind of thing—for me, it is too silly—and I couldn't have convinced Zanuck anyway."

The character's occupation had to be left maddeningly oblique, but the role was still a substantial one. The right actress would supply the missing inferences. Zanuck wanted Lang to test Anne Baxter for the role, and the director obliged; he liked Baxter, and would return to her in his thinking over the years. Before long, though, Lang and the studio gravitated to Joan Bennett, another Sam Jaffe client, conveniently, who was trying to break out of the mold of her typecasting.

Joan Bennett, born into a veteran show business family in 1910, had attended a finishing school in Paris before launching her career as a screen

---

*Technically, *Man Hunt* became Roddy McDowall's U.S. screen debut. John Ford's *How Green Was My Valley* was filmed afterward, then released first.

actress in 1929. She spent most of the 1930s in the shadow of Constance Bennett, her sister, a bigger box-office star. Though early on Joan had played a fresh-faced blonde in films such as George Cukor's adaptation of *Little Women*, she had lately matured, gone brunette, and now leaned toward playing seductive femmes fatales. Off-screen, only a year earlier, in January of 1940, she had married one of Lang's producer bêtes noires—Walter Wanger, who was her third husband.

In Dudley Nichols, Lang had the only American screenwriter with whom he was able to forge a partnership that succeeded beyond one film—and also one of Hollywood's best. The director's relationship with Joan Bennett would prove equally fortuitous on several levels. The actress was able to provide a sex appeal that had been oddly lacking in his American films up till now. The care the director took in lighting, the scrutiny of the camerawork, the emotional undertow of *Man Hunt*—all suggested a man who was drawn to his leading lady as Fritz Lang had not been drawn since the time of Gerda Maurus.

Rogue Male was filmed as *Man Hunt* in the spring of 1941. There were few exteriors; German and English locations were shot using soundstage replicas. That was all right with Lang, who still preferred his own embellishments to the natural order of the universe.

Everything about the production rose a notch. Arthur Miller, the cameraman, was a long-term 20th Century–Fox employee who went straight from working on *Man Hunt* to photographing John Ford's *How Green Was My Valley*. Miller had started in silent films in 1915, then gone on to photograph films for Ford and for other leading directors. He was a cameraman who prided himself on hyperrealism, deep shadows, and glossy highlights, which suited a project the director aimed to be "deliberately Germanic in style."

Richard Day's art direction (with Wiard Ihnen) produced lush sets of the type that would earn the art director seven Academy Awards in his lifetime and comparisons to the style of Edward Hopper. Travis Banton, noted for his stunning gowns for Marlene Dietrich at Paramount, was now ensconced at Fox; he had supplied Western wardrobe for *The Return of Frank James* and *Western Union*, but was more in his element evoking the European costuming of *Man Hunt*. Lang would recruit Banton some years later to design the costumes for one of his few independent pictures in Hollywood, *Secret Beyond the Door*.

The director had been gradually reasserting his authority—and reintroducing his monocle. Not only did he have a proficient crew and a competent cast, but a producer, Kenneth Macgowan, who trusted his judgment enough to indulge his whims.

Unfortunately, Macgowan left the production midway through the filming. Zanuck diverted him to another Western, *Belle Starr*, which needed bailing out. But it may also have been a crafty maneuver on Zanuck's part: The studio chief would have been right to suspect Lang of being fundamentally insubordinate, and Macgowan of being a pushover for the man.* The staff producer

---

*Macgowan lasted a few more years as a Hollywood producer before retreating to academia, named

who took over was more of a nuisance than anything else, but he took every opportunity to second-guess Lang, and to report the director to Zanuck.

Lang was forced more than once to tiptoe around the studio to get the job done *his* way. When it came to the scene where the Joan Bennett character pretends to be a streetwalker, the director fell back on a clever ruse to win the day. Lang went into a huddle with the unit manager and cameraman. He told them he wanted to try the scene as originally envisioned, despite Zanuck's orders. The unit manager complained that he couldn't authorize spending a penny on anything Zanuck hadn't approved, but Lang had a strategy around that: With the empathetic Arthur Miller, he conspired to shoot the scene on a standing set, with the background fading away into fog and mist.

When Zanuck saw the dailies, according to Lang, he didn't even realize that the director had gone behind his back. He didn't care that the scene had not been dropped, nor substantially altered; he was too bewitched by the visual imagery. "Where the hell's that set?" Zanuck kept asking. The scene stayed in. It's another Lang anecdote that may be apocryphal, but its portrait of behind-the-scenes chicanery reflects a larger truth about the journey of *Man Hunt* to the screen.

Lang completed the rare semblance of a team by requesting Gene Fowler, Jr., as an assistant editor. The senior editor assigned by the studio was Allen McNeil, a veteran from the Mack Sennett era, who was close friends with Fowler; McNeil's silent-era expertise was instrumental on the purely visual sequences, while Fowler again came in handy, as he did throughout Lang's Fox stay, as a closet conspirator.

Fowler recalled what a painstaking editor the director could be, demanding that the cutters "take two frames off here, put another frame in there, and so on. I didn't mind doing that because I was learning." But the head of the 20th Century–Fox editing department complained to the staff producer that Lang's vacillation was holding everything up ("which wasn't true," according to Gene Fowler, Jr.), and got the director banned, for the first time, from the editing room of one of his own productions.

Fowler's chummy relationship with McNeil enabled him to intercede, though, on Lang's behalf. They arranged for the director to sneak back on the lot in the evenings, when nobody was around, and work alongside Fowler without the knowledge of higher-ups. "I'd work with him [Lang] on the thing and nobody knew any different," remembered Fowler. "He knew exactly what he wanted. If he wanted a couple of frames trimmed here and added there, it was for a reason, not playing around."

The net result of all this serendipity, compromise and calculation, hard work and sly manipulation is that the powerful *Man Hunt*, released in June of 1941, is the only one of the director's 20th Century–Fox productions that can be called decisively Langian.

The opening scene must have riveted 1941 audiences: Thorndike (Walter

the chairman of the newly created Department of Theater Arts at UCLA. He stayed friendly with Lang, invited him to lecture to UCLA, classes and showered him with compliments in his comprehensive history of film, *Behind the Screen: The History and Techniques of the Motion Picture* (New York; Dell, 1965).

Pidgeon) has crawled to a perch high in the mountains above Salzburg, over-looking Hitler's Berchtesgaden. He draws a bead, through the crosshairs of his rifle scope, on the puffed-out chest of Adolf Hitler, strutting around below.

The trigger clicks empty. It is a "sporting stalk," and Thorndike has not loaded any bullets. He is sorely tempted, though—before he is hauled off by Nazi guards.

He is dragged before the Nazi official Quive-Smith—George Sanders, a contract villain in the first of several appearances in Fritz Lang films. Thorn-dike is interrogated and tortured. The Germans, the better to propagandize their forthcoming invasion of England, want him to implicate his older brother, an English lord. But the evil of the villains is disappointingly bland, and some aspects of the story are downright naive, considering that *Man Hunt* was filmed in 1941 by an antifascist director who must have been aware of the dire reports from Europe. Indeed, the political statements are trite, and Hitler is referred to as a mere gangster, a Little Caesar. Once in London, moreover, the Nazi villains become stock Lang characters—spies and traitors with their carrier pigeons, familiar at least as far back as *Spione*, reappear conveniently here.

Lang's brusque methods did little to toughen Walter Pidgeon up, nor to bring complexity to his characterization. There are people who think his is a marvelous performance, but it was only a stiff, respectable one, with no interior dimension. *How Green Was My Valley*, filmed later that year at Fox, shows what the actor was capable of, under a more sensitive director, in more creative circumstances.

The scenes between Thorndike and Jerry (Joan Bennett's character) are, partly because of the Hays Code, oddly formal. Sexual implications are kept in check—although there is no mistaking Jerry's disappointed look when, after some dangerous adventures, Thorndike tells her to get some sleep, and curls up, at gentlemanly remove, alone on a couch. The socially superior man mixing with a woman of low repute was a time-honored Lang conceit, and the director had the ability to make it plausible.

Joan Bennett pulled out all stops. Her Cockney accent was coached by Queenie Leonard, an English music-hall performer, and the actress felt unu-sually well-rehearsed—"it was the only movie I ever made in which I knew the entire script, like a play, beforehand." Because of the Hays Office restric-tions, she had to hold back in some scenes, overdo it in others. It was a brassy job; she snorted her accent, and overflowed with tears. But the role was a marked departure for Bennett, and it was obvious Lang had alighted on a character—and an actress who aroused his instincts.

The film has a slow but beguiling rhythm. A series of long, ingenious se-quences, in the forest and out on the water, uses wind effects, dogs barking, waves lapping, and other natural sound effects to transform the interiors into outdoor landscapes. In scene after scene—a breathless chase in the woods, an escape on choppy seas, in murky London streets and claustrophobic caves—the dialogue is unimportant. It is the lighting, the angles, the cutting—Lang's fluent vocabulary of visual effects—that tell the story.

In the end Jenny is killed (a faked suicide staged off-camera by the Nazis). After some tedious speechifying the story climaxes deep in the forest, where a wounded Thorndike fashions a crude bow and arrow, aims it into a cave hole, and kills the cornered Quive-Smith with a shaft tipped with the dead woman's brooch.

But there is also a coda, and it is a memorable one, which packed a wallop in 1941. Lang's final image shows a coldly determined Thorndike bailing out of a plane over Germany, carrying a rifle with him, and vowing this time to go through with the extermination of Hitler.

When *Man Hunt* was released in late June, the reviews were almost unanimously positive. "Lang gets depth in every scene he makes," wrote Otis Ferguson in *The New Republic.* "He is a careful and thorough man with detail; and his first concern is with the rightness and immediacy of each fragment as it appears to you, makes its impression, leads you along with each incident of the story, and projects the imagination beyond into things to come."

"The adaptation gains in thrills what it loses in plausibility," wrote Anthony Bower in *The Nation.* "The director, Fritz Lang, seems able to give a few lessons in the technique of suspense even to Alfred Hitchcock, and has created out of a maze of improbabilities, inaccuracies, and poor performances a really exciting picture."

In England, where people might have been forgiven feeling proprietary about the novel, the reviews were also complimentary. Dilys Powell, writing in the *Sunday Times,* found *Man Hunt* praiseworthy. "Lang, almost alone among the European directors who have gone to work in Hollywood, still remembers the cinematographic language of Europe," Powell wrote, "despite the absurdities of a London background with pearlies at every corner and street-walkers living in mansions."

At the end of the year *Man Hunt* was named one of the ten best films of 1941 by many U.S. critics, cementing Lang's "comeback" as a Hollywood studio director.

Seen today, the film has tarnished slightly. The artistic compromises stick out; its antifascism seems shallow. Hitchcock would have given the proceedings more show business. Ford would have given the ending the emotional uplift that too often eluded Fritz Lang. Still, *Man Hunt* was the director's best picture in five years—the best since *Fury*—and perhaps the praise was understandable from critics around the world rooting for Lang and happy to wish for the demise of Hitler.

What next? As *Man Hunt* was being prepared for release, the director was already reviewing the possibilities. He put in some work on an original Western based on the true history of the lost Superstition Mountain mine. He told people he would like to direct a musical starring a promising singer-dancer named Rita Hayworth (he professed to have "many new ideas about the genre"). And records show that he was just a couple of months away from holding meetings with Bertolt Brecht about another anti-Nazi drama.

The rhapsodic reviews for *Man Hunt* revived Lang's hauteur. He had worked off his gratitude to Zanuck. The director felt that he should have been promoted, been offered better projects, and rewarded with power, but Zanuck continued to treat Lang the way he treated most people—as a mere employee.

"You listened to Zanuck," said Gene Fowler, Jr. "Zanuck was the man. His conversation was orders. He treated Fritz that way too. He was very cold to him. There was no love lost between Fritz and Zanuck."

The director was still under a multi-picture obligation to Fox, and there was fated to be no personal confrontation between the director and head of production. "Fritz was contentious with anybody and everybody," said his agent Sam Jaffe, "but the smaller man [in particular] he diminished and mistreated. The upper man he was afraid of—of course. He wouldn't tackle a Louis B. Mayer or Goldwyn [or Zanuck]. But someone who wasn't so certain or sure, he would sense it and be cruel."

Instead Lang played a different game: he waged for the rest of 1941 a passive-aggressive war of memos, deception, and guerrilla skirmishing.

Even as *Man Hunt* was being released, Zanuck handed Lang a new project: *Confirm or Deny*, based on a story contributed by future director Sam Fuller. Fuller's treatment, in collaboration with Henry Wales, told the story of a wire service in England trying to maintain its news-gathering operations during destructive aerial raids; a hard-nosed editor determined to report the scoop of a Nazi invasion of London; and the editor's romance with a patriotic Londoner, a teletype operator, equally determined to stop the newsman from breaching government censorship.

Wales, a former war reporter for *The Chicago Tribune*, helped Fuller, who had never been to England, with the London milieu. "I wrote ninety-two pages in fifteen hours," remembered Fuller in one interview. "Hank made me coffee and cognac cocktails. 20th Century–Fox bought the story, entitled 'Confirm or Deny,' for twenty thousand dollars. Hank and I were very happy to learn that Fritz Lang was going to make the film. An incomparable creator, Lang remains a symbol full of meaning for all filmmakers."

The project seemed a natural follow-up to *Man Hunt*, with its scenes showing the bombing of London, a story line that rumored a large-scale land invasion by the Germans, and a Lang alumni cast that included Joan Bennett (as the teletype operator) and Roddy McDowall (playing a newsboy watching the skies for bombers).

The temporary script by Jo Swerling was finished by mid-March. Rouben Mamoulian originally had been assigned to helm the film, but Lang was rotated into the job in mid-May. The timing was so abrupt that the director had to miss the final studio script conference of May 26 because he was in New York at the Waldorf-Astoria, giving interviews to promote *Man Hunt*. The revised script and set sketches had to be rushed to him there by mail.

Lang hadn't minded being inconvenienced before, when his career was in a woeful state, but this time he felt he deserved more respect. Under the circumstances he was able to make only remedial notations in the script margins (trying as usual to sharpen the slang). He opposed the casting of Don Ameche, usually a light comedian, in the role of the wire service editor. The part called for more of a hard-boiled Clark Gable type, the director thought. But Ameche was Zanuck's candidate, and as ever, there was no room for disagreement.

Reluctantly, in late July, Lang appeared on the set to preside over principal photography. "The whole thing, as the studio envisaged it," the director informed Charles Higham and Joel Greenberg, "was very phony." Fortunately, he told Higham and Greenberg, he suffered a gall-bladder attack after four or five days. "I was delighted that I was unable to shoot," he explained, "and told a very good friend, who acted as a go-between between all the shooting companies and Zanuck, that my doctors had put me out of action for three or four days, or a week. So when he came one day shortly after and told me that Zanuck had taken me off the picture, I couldn't have been more pleased."

Production records tell a slightly different story: Actually, Lang filmed scenes for at least two weeks of the ten-week schedule. Lang did suffer from periodic gallstone attacks, but it seems likely that the seriousness of this well-timed illness was exaggerated. Joan Bennett in her autobiography stated flatly that Lang "walked out."

Why? It's a nifty little film—less artistic, perhaps, but no more or less "phony" than *Man Hunt*. And contract director Archie Mayo, who finished up the directorial chores, gave *Confirm or Deny* a brisk pacing and unpretentious humor that would probably have been lacking under Fritz Lang.

Meanwhile Lang fed his resentment of Zanuck, while the head of production entertained doubts about the director and his alleged illness. When Lang's two-month layoff ran out, on October 20, he was immediately ordered back to work.

This time Zanuck thought he had a project that would tempt Lang into renewed good humor. Jean Gabin, the archetypal French leading man, had finally reached the United States, among the eminent flotsam and jetsam washed up by Hitler. Gabin had signed with 20th Century–Fox, which had swiftly arranged for him to make his Hollywood debut in *Moontide*, from a novel about a seaman who befriends a suicidal waif. Ida Lupino would co-star in a script that was penned by novelist John O'Hara. Mark Hellinger, the well-known journalist and columnist, would function as the studio's producer.

According to her daughter Maria Riva's book, it was Marlene Dietrich, behind the scenes, who encouraged Gabin to request Fritz Lang as his director. Gabin was the actress's current lover—perhaps the love of her life, if one prefers the storybook version. Who better to direct her current lover than a former beau? And after all, Lang had always been a discreet and supportive friend to Dietrich.

But the director was in a rapidly disintegrating mood. Contributing to his sour disposition was the fact that *Moontide* was slated to be photographed on soundstages with "an artificial indoor quay on the Fox lot," as Lang recalled. The director had happily made do with indoor wharfs for *Man Hunt*; he *liked* artificiality. Yet now he fought this point, and losing to Zanuck—as usual—only made his temper worse.

O'Hara's final script was already completed by the time Lang returned to the weekly payroll. Predictably, said script displeased the director. Nor did the script gratify Gabin, who barraged Zanuck with memos criticizing its verbosity. Producer Mark Hellinger threw up his hands, and Zanuck had to get involved personally to force results.

Looking for a way out, Lang turned a card calculated to spur a crisis. He took Gabin aside on the set one day and had a "man-to-man talk" with him, in Maria Riva's words—boasting of his own previous affair with Dietrich. Gabin stormed away, incensed.

This is what happened next, according to Riva: "He [Gabin] came home one day and accused her [Dietrich] of having had an affair with Lang, to which she replied, utterly amazed, 'That ugly Jew? You must be joking, mon amour,' and enclosed him in her embrace. Throughout her life, Dietrich did that constantly—erased lovers from her memory as though they had never existed."

Lang liked to disclaim *Moontide* as a production he worked on for only the briefest period of time. (According to Lotte Eisner: "Only four days.") Again, the studio log tells a different tale: Shooting went from November 24 of 1941 through to February 7, 1942. But Lang directed *Moontide* for almost three weeks, until December 12.

Records indicate that the production then shut down for three days while 20th Century–Fox scrambled to assign a new director. Lang's footage was preserved. Archie Mayo picked up once again where the disgruntled Lang left off, and turned out an uneven picture that pleased no one and permitted his predecessor to congratulate himself on a well-timed exit.

As 1942 dawned, these events were still fresh. After being dropped from *Moontide,* Lang left the studio under a cloud. Zanuck was happy to mediate an escape clause with Sam Jaffe that permitted the director to explore his options elsewhere, on the proviso that he owed 20th Century–Fox a future film at some mutually convenient time.

The director was free romantically as well. His affair with Virginia Gilmore had waned. Gilmore had moved to New York at the beginning of 1942, intending to study acting and try her luck as a Broadway actress. Lang was still fond of his former protegée, and talked vaguely about starring Gilmore in his next production, whatever it happened to be. Meanwhile, he helped put her up in an apartment in Manhattan.

It was in New York that the actress met Yul Brynner and fell in love with the magnetic aspiring actor. Typically, Lang felt saddened, though also relieved. The director gilded the lily whenever he spoke about Virginia Gilmore in later years. "Fritz always claimed that when she married Yul Brynner," said Pierre Rissient, "that was because he would not marry her, and that at the beginning of her marriage [to Yul Brynner] she was still coming to sleep with him from time to time."

The director told people that Lily Latté had busted up his relationship with the pretty actress. That was one of his constant refrains; he—Fritz Lang— would have married any number of beautiful women with whom he was deeply in love if only "the Latté," as he sometimes referred to her, had not conspired to interfere with his love life.

While he was employed by Fox, Latté's usefulness had been eclipsed by services provided by the studio. In 1939, she had moved away from Lang, taking an apartment in the avant-garde complex designed by the Vienna-born architect Richard Neutra, on Strathmore Drive in Westwood. But when Lang found himself alone in 1942, Latté was drawn back into his life.

It was Lily Latté after all, who hired his household help, took care of the director's clothing needs, supervised his personal correspondence, watched over his finances and investments. It was she who arranged Lang's daily menu and ran his dinner parties, which were mostly payback events for occasions the director had been invited to. At Christmastime, she was responsible for buying Fritz Lang's gifts, and for having the distinctive crystal and porcelain treasures elegantly wrapped for distribution.

Latté became his "domestic manager," in the words of screenwriter Silvia Richards. His "glorified *Hausfrau*," according to the director's secretary, Hilda Rolfe. His "general factotum," in the words of writer-director Peter Bogdanovich.

He owned her, treating her with contempt: "Dumme Gans!" She worshiped him: "Yes, mein Herr." Most people noticed the glaring inequality. Especially in the émigré community, where Latté was well-known and generally better-liked than Lang, it was a black mark against the director. "He was so abusive to her," said Lang's own agent Sam Jaffe. "She was so frightened. She hovered over him. She trembled."

At the same time it was indisputable that Lang needed Lily Latté, couldn't exist without her. "He was somehow always dependent on women," said Cornelius Schnauber. "He needed Lily. He needed her probably more than she needed him. I know that sounds strange. I know that she must have agreed that he could still have his affairs, but he needed her; he needed a woman who took care of him not just physically, but mentally. Apart from everything else, Lily informed his thinking. In return he could be very nasty. I don't know if it was in his subconscious, but there was always a kind of 'having revenge.' A revenge, I had a feeling, for his dependence."

"She looked after him—like a mother, as far as I'm concerned," said Andries Dienum, one of Lang's production assistants in the 1940s. "And she took a helluva lot from Fritz. But there was a sort of dislike [for him on her part] there too."

"To women," said his actor-friend Howard Vernon, "he was absolutely passive, passive in the way of letting them treat him the way they did and wanted. Lily manipulated him, so that he stayed her creature. To me she was a negative person. They were together by necessity, but she didn't do all that out of kindness and a good heart. To her, it was more a means to keep him under her wing. And I am sure a lot of these love affairs never took a more solid form because of Lily Latté."

When Peter Heiman, the assistant theater director from Berlin, came to Hollywood in 1937, he tried to pick up where he had left off with Lily Latté. They always seemed to click when they met, as they first had in Paris in 1935. Nor did the director seem to take offense when Heiman moved in temporarily with Latté. Lang even went out of his way to help Heiman with job referrals, introducing him to composer Kurt Weill—who helped Heiman land a job as a stage director with the West Coast branch of the Federal Theatre Project.

Lang, in fact, acted almost *indebted* to Heiman. Heiman had the impression that the physical relationship between Latté and Lang was over. "That the sexual relationship between these two was ever of great importance, I have good reasons to doubt. I deduced this from my own relationship with her. Mine came in where his ended."

If Lang was indulgent of Latté's private life, she was still jealous about his. The director conspired to keep her infuriatingly in the dark. He enjoyed complicating the subplots in his life. Whenever he and Latté had to make a social appearance, Lang's latest girlfriend was banished for the occasion, whereas Latté was perfectly welcome to bring Peter Heiman along for a night on the town—making an awkward triad with the director.

Lang even went one step further, propositioning men on Latté's behalf. The director would take male friends aside and let them know reassuringly that they shouldn't feel shy about approaching her. There was nothing physical between Lang and "la Latté," nor had there ever been, the director would assure them. The latter was definitely a lie; about the former, no one ever felt absolutely certain.

1941

CHAPTER 14

1945

When the Japanese bombed Pearl Harbor on December 7, 1941, America had no choice but to abandon its isolationism and enter the rapidly escalating war. The very next day the United States government declared war on Japan, and within a few days America's list of enemy states had expanded to include the other Axis powers, Italy and Germany.

Directors were in the forefront of those in Hollywood who contributed to the war effort. Yet Fritz Lang, curiously, never volunteered any military-related duty in the fight against the nation he had once embraced and which he now reviled. True, Lang had served before, on the side of Germany in World War I; true, he'd turned fifty-one by the time hostilities commenced. But Lewis Milestone and John Ford, both only five years younger than Lang, were among the veteran film directors who hastened to enlist in the armed services.

Lang claimed once in an interview that he tried to join the U.S. Office of Strategic Services (OSS), precursor of the Central Intelligence Agency (CIA), when it was formulated in 1941, but was rejected because of his age. But there is no record of his claim, never repeated, and made as part of the publicity campaign for *Cloak and Dagger*, the director's first post-war film, which was about the OSS network.

Indeed, Lang would exploit the war for publicity and career advantage. It was during these years that his Goebbels story first surfaced in the press, in interviews and articles promoting his quartet of war-inspired productions: *Man Hunt, Hangmen Also Die, Ministry of Fear*, and *Cloak and Dagger*. That is one of the reasons why some people, especially émigrés, associated the director's story with self-serving opportunism.

Articles and interviews timed to coincide with the release of *Hangmen Also Die* revealed to the public for the first time the Lang-Goebbels saga. It made good copy: the story of how the director had been ordered by the Third Reich's Propaganda Minister to prepare propaganda films presenting the National Socialist Party in a favorable light, because the Führer "had decided that Lang was the man for the job of making the epic film of National Socialism. The hero was to be the Nazi brownshirt. The villain was Communism. The theme: the Nazi new order."

The director told the U.S. Communist newspaper *The Daily Worker* that his frightening encounter with Goebbels marked "the first moment in which he became fully aware of the stark reality of Nazism." Like most other German progressives, Lang explained, he had recognized the Nazi movement as a mobilization of corrupt forces, organized by big industrialists and popularized with free beer and demagoguery. "He [Lang] was a keen student of social affairs with a liberal, international outlook on life and of course anti-Prussian and anti-Hitler long before Hitler smashed the Weimar Republic," noted *The Daily Worker*, "which explains the sociological character of some of his early German films."

The U.S. premiere of Lang's last German film—the banned-in-Nazi-Germany *The Testament of Dr. Mabuse*—was conveniently timed for March 1943, to coincide with release of *Hangmen Also Die*. In interviews the director could bracket both films: his latent anti-Nazism of 1933 blended with his vociferous anti-Nazism a decade later. Lang in fact helped with a new prologue to *Testament*, declaring publicly for the first time that the film "was made as an allegory to show Hitler's processes of terrorism."

The director assured the press that he had "made the picture as an anti-Hitler picture, putting all the Nazi slogans into the mouth of criminals. That is what angered them so much." According to the publicity line he adopted, Lang's goal was "to expose the masked Nazi theory of the necessity to destroy everything which is precious to a people so that they would lose all faith in the institutions and ideals of the State. Then, when everything collapsed, they would try to find help in the 'new order.'"

In none of these accounts, tellingly, did Lang make any mention of his own Jewish heritage. In fact, publicity went out of its way to describe him as an "Austrian director" who was in fact the opposite of Jewish. "While many famous Jewish directors had to flee Germany because of the 'Aryan' work decrees, Lang, a Christian, fled only because he is a believer in democratic government," reads Fritz Lang's entry in *Current Biography*, which also came on the heels of *Hangmen Also Die*, in 1943.*

To those émigrés who knew something of Lang's personal story, and who remembered the chain of events that prompted him to leave Germany in 1933, this was soft soap. To those who were Jewish, it showed insensitivity to anti-Semitism, and indifference to one of the most heinous Nazi policies. Lang's politics hadn't shed their blinders. It's ironic that the director's most famous Hollywood films tend to be his World War II features, because that is how Fritz Lang spent the war years—consolidating his career.

Of the World War II films, *Hangmen Also Die* was the only one based on Lang's original story, and the only one to come into existence of the director's own volition. It is among his most celebrated, most scrutinized films, not least because it involved the participation of Bertolt Brecht.

Brecht was every bit as famous as Lang, and if anything, more of a mythomaniac. But there was something poignant as well as comical about the man: the deliberately unsanitary habits; the forelock combed forward suggesting

---

*It was standard for *Current Biography* to consult the subject, and Lang cooperated with his profile. An advance copy of the text, in his USC files, shows no emendations—rare for Lang.

Napoleon; the tunic, very much like a latter-day Nehru jacket, evoking the look of a commissar. At Brecht's side there usually stood a secretary who doubled as his mistress, along with his wife, actress Helene Weigel; with Brecht, they made an awkward triad. The secretary was usually an unsung collaborator, of whom Brecht had many in his career. He tended to crush collaborators.

The production of *Hangmen Also Die* is often presented as an instance of Lang's largesse. Brecht, down on his luck and only recently arrived in America, was scrounging for recognition in Hollywood. Lang had made it a priority to help raise money to bring Brecht over from Finland, where the playwright was hiding out from the Nazis. He and Lily Latté joined early on in organizing the support of the European Film Fund, writing letters and soliciting contributions on Brecht's behalf.

Lang had attended Brecht's plays in Berlin, though he knew him primarily through Peter Lorre, whose adoration of Brecht counted with Lang. Perhaps Lang really did believe that Brecht was "the only genius among us," as he sometimes said. Or maybe he was simply quoting the exiled novelist Lion Feuchtwanger, a friend of Brecht's who said it first, and whose opinion carried more weight with Lang than even Lorre's.*

When Brecht arrived in Los Angeles in July of 1941, the director was preoccupied with his deteriorating situation at Fox. But because of their Berliner ties, Lang began seeing Brecht almost immediately at parties and occasions at Alfred Döblin's house, the Feuchtwangers', or Salka and Berthold Viertels's, throughout the fall and winter of 1941–1942. Lily Latté gave Brecht's daughter a white dog, and Lang and Brecht took walks, communing together on the beach.

The playwright kept a journal of acid-etched recollections of every place he went and everyone he encountered in America, and Lang was no different— no luckier—than the rest. On October 21, Brecht wrote for the first time of visiting the director at his home. The playwright was appalled, as he was, generally, everywhere he went in Hollywood.

There "grown adults, refugees, sit and listen to the British court astrologer (a former novelette writer for the Berlin illustrated weeklies), a fat booby who identifies the constellation of stars in May 1940 as the cause of Hitler's victory over France." Astrology struck Brecht as a bourgeois pastime left over from decadent Berlin. The astrologer "gets very angry," continued Brecht's journal, "if anybody suggests that with Hitler's superiority in tanks and planes, April or June would probably have done just as well."

In conversations with Brecht, Lang propounded his vision of America as the new Atlantis. As he had with Carl Zuckmayer, the director glorified the Hollywood lifestyle. The more Lang repeated his mantras, the more it appeared that he actually believed them. But not everyone was dining at the trough. "He [Lang] sees a special lifestyle where I only see high capitalism," wrote Brecht in his journal. "Possible that I can't see the 'real Atlantis' for the high capitalism; but he just obscures it."

---

*Reflecting on Lang's connection with Brecht, Martha Feuchtwanger added this interesting tidbit in an "oral history" on deposit at UCLA: actress Helene Weigel was the film director's old friend from Vienna theater circles, to whom he used to lend money during hard times in Berlin.

Brecht's journal collected émigré gossip, and early on in their newfound friendship—in November of 1941—Brecht reported that actor Fritz Kortner had shown up Lang as the source of an anti-Semitic remark. Kortner, with roots on the Vienna stage, was a household name in Germany before (and after) his exile in America; but he was nobody's favorite in Hollywood, and "is generally feared here as the great Thersites who rails with biblical (or maybe Lutheran) power and vividness," wrote Brecht. A longtime Lang nemesis, Kortner had been known to refer openly to the director as a "murderer," according to Brecht's journal—a rare published allusion to the fate of the first Frau Lang. It was an incident that Kortner, whose activity in German films dated to the pre-1920s, would have known about.

Despite such hearsay, Brecht felt grateful to Lang for his largesse, and seemed glad whenever he was thrown into the director's company. The playwright noted in his journal that his first Christmas in America was celebrated at the Feuchtwangers' home, gathered around the tree with actress Elisabeth Bergner, director Paul Czinner (Bergner's husband), and actor Alexander Granach. Stopping by later in the day was Fritz Lang.

Many years later the director told Axel Madsen, revealingly, that "it was only because of an impassioned plea from Lion Feuchtwanger that the refugee playwright [Brecht] got the bread-and-butter writing job" on *Hangmen Also Die.*

Brecht's journal leaves no doubt that Lang's career was almost as desperate for a shot of adrenaline. On April 27, 1942, Brecht wrote up his version of what had recently transpired at 20th Century–Fox during the back-to-back fiascoes of *Confirm or Deny* and *Moontide.* Lang had the two films "taken away from him, one after the other because he got involved in disagreements," according to Brecht's journal, "or because a French actor demanded an American director." The recent contretemps had put Lang in a momentary professional bind, and apparently in dire need of a cash injection.

Everybody knew, Brecht wrote, that Lang had oodles of money stashed away, and that he had asked former Berlin theater critic Rolf Nurnberg "to give him back $80,000 he had been looking after for him, for savings." Eighty thousand dollars was a lot of money in 1942, but Nurnberg, after an "unamusing attempt at suicide," confessed to Lang he had spent it over the years on necessary expenses, according to Brecht.

Added to Lang's professional and money woes, according to Brecht, was his rocky love life, and a new development: Lily Latté (referred to by Brecht as Lang's "girlfriend and secretary for some years") had taken up romantically with a German journalist-critic, Hans (John) Winge, a mutual acquaintance more devoted to Brecht than to Lang.*

Worst of all, according to Brecht's journal, during the last month of his Fox contract Lang had gone to visit an eye specialist, and confirmed the fact

---

*Winge later wrote an influential article about Brecht's experiences working with Lang on *Hangmen Also Die.* The article appeared in *Sight and Sound* after Brecht's death in 1956 ("Brecht and the Cinema," Winter, 1956–57). Although it was Winge's opinion that the director had emasculated the film with his compromises, to him Brecht's contribution gave it stature and *Hangmen Also Die* "remained superior to most Hollywood pictures of the European resistance."

that his right eye—the one sans monocle—was going bad. "He [the eye specialist] covered one eye and wanted him [Lang] to read off the letters," Brecht recorded in his journal. "L. said, 'you'll have to switch on the lamp.' The lamp had been on all the time. Now he knows, or suspects, that his other eye is threatened by blindness too, like his father."

His checkered career, his rocky relationships with women, his faltering eyesight: Lang had his share of troubles in the spring of 1942. Linked by common anxieties, he and Brecht had drawn closer, and were talking tentatively about collaborating on a film. The Kurt Weill experience was forgotten by Lang; in any case Weill's grumbling wouldn't have mattered to Brecht, who was himself well and truly estranged from the composer.

Almost six months had gone by since the director left 20th Century–Fox, and a year since he had completed *Man Hunt*. Though Fritz Lang had proclaimed his independence, he had no office, no offers, no script nor pending project. But he did have one thing: a new producer enthusiastically scurrying around to scare up the necessary financing. Wouldn't investment be twice as attractive with a Fritz Lang–Bertolt Brecht billing?

The producer—later blamed for everything, and credited for nothing—was a prime mover behind the scenes. Arnold Pressburger was a native of Bratislava (now in Slovakia) who had been a cameraman in Austria before World War I and, later, a producer in Vienna, London, and Paris. In fact, Pressburger had served as a production executive of Sascha Film in Vienna after World War I. The director may first have met Pressburger there in that capacity; that could have been the source of Lang's inevitable animosity.

A recent refugee from Europe, Pressburger had arrived in Hollywood in 1941 and produced Josef von Sternberg's *The Shanghai Gesture*: all the more reason for Lang to badmouth Pressburger behind his back. Lang had a set of derogatory expressions for producers; in Pressburger's case, he was a mere "line producer," according to Lang, only a fund-raiser and controller. Nonetheless, the director sorely needed a bankroll, and he and Pressburger had been in a courtship dance since early spring.

A native of Czechoslovakia, Pressburger had lived in Prague as a young man. Dispatches reporting the May 26, 1942, assassination in Prague of Reinhard Heydrich, the Reichsprotector chief of Bohemia and Moravia, in charge of Czechoslovakia, caught his eye—as well as Lang's. Heydrich, a ruthless Nazi official known as "The Hangman" who had played a leading role in Kristallnacht, had been responsible for the widely reported repression of the Czech resistance. Shortly after Heydrich's assassination, in June of 1942, the Nazis would retaliate by liquidating inhabitants of Lidice, a town outside Prague thought to harbor the assassin.

Pressburger's eagerness for an anti-Nazi film set in Prague was an important factor. And in interviews of the time, the producer pointed out that when the *Hangmen* script was being prepared it was he who suggested the character of a quisling—based on a Czech general, Jan Sirovy, who had turned traitor. The quisling was adopted by Lang and turned into one of the characters pivotal to the film's story line.

Bertolt Brecht, who wouldn't have known otherwise because he was kept at arm's length from Pressburger, believed the project was the director's sole inspiration. It was May 28, 1942, according to Brecht's journal. He set the scene: Lang and he were lying on the Santa Monica beach. Near them, under a big bath towel, were two young people lying close together, "the man on top of the woman at one point, with a child playing alongside," in Brecht's account. "Not far away stands a huge iron listening contraption with colossal wings which turns in an arc; a soldier sits behind it on a tractor seat, in shirtsleeves, but in front of one or two little buildings there is a sentry with a gun in full kit. Huge petrol tankers glide silently down the asphalt coast road . . ." It was then and there that Lang raised the subject of the Hangman's assassination as a possibility for a film.

A week passed after their beach-blanket brainstorm, during which time Lang no doubt conferred with Pressburger, and received a go-ahead. Lang later claimed in one interview: "In a matter of days—four or five at most—we produced a short outline between us. I was sure I could sell Arnold Pressburger the idea of making such a film . . ."

The "selling" of Arnold Pressburger included a demand for suitable compensation for Brecht. Lang lobbied for $7,500—"twice what Brecht asked for," in the director's words. Then, throughout June and July, the director and playwright worked on a scenario, developing characters and a plotline based on the newspaper accounts.

War films were new for Brecht; the prickly ideologue wrote in his journal that they could be treated as Westerns—"Wild East" counterparts to Wild West fables, with guerrillas substituting for cowboys. He couldn't decide whether to take Lang seriously, though, when the director began to suggest dialogue and stage business that Brecht associated with the hoary melodrama of the silent film era. But Brecht was determined to hold his tongue as long and tightly as possible. He wanted the Hollywood credit and he needed the money.

Brecht's journal takes up the chronology:

June 5, 1942: "try to sketch a story 'silent City' with lang. about prague, the gestapo and the hostages, the whole thing is of course pure monte carlo."

June 29, 1942: "i usually work with lang on the hostage story from nine in the morning till seven in the evening. there is a remarkable term that always crops up whenever the logic of events or of the continuity cries out to be discussed: 'the public will accept that.' the public accepts the mastermind of the resistance hiding behind a curtain when the gestapo searches a house. and commissars' corpses falling out of wardrobes. And 'secret' mass meetings during a period of nazi terror. lang 'buys' that kind of thing. interesting too that he is far more interested in surprises than in building up suspense."

July 20, 1942: "with lang all the time, working on the hostage story to earn my bread. Supposed to get $5000, plus $3000 for further collaboration."

July 27, 1942: "what an infinitely dismal fabrication this hostage film is that i have to occupy myself with these days. what a load of hackneyed situations, intrigues, false notes! the only respectable part of it is that i have confined myself strictly to the framework of a bourgeois-national rising, and now there is the cast on top of it all. i looked at a book with photos of all the actors we can have, or rather who are on the books here—faces from the program at the municipal theater in ulm."

Already by the end of June, Lang and Brecht had registered a 32-page treatment with the Screen-Writers Guild called "437!"—the title referring to the number of Czech civilian hostages shot by the Gestapo in order to force someone to betray the Hangman's killer. The treatment had all the embryonic elements of the film: the assassination, the love story, the quisling, and the hostage camps. A longer, more detailed, treatment would follow, with a more assertive title: "Never Surrender!"

Lang signed his 23-page contract in late July. Brecht might have envied the director's terms. Lang would receive $10,000 for his contribution to the original screen story, for which he would retain full ownership. His $40,000 salary as a director might be less than he had received at 20th Century–Fox, but Lang would earn $5,000 in bonus money after all costs, loans, and obligations were repaid, then 25 percent of net profits in perpetuity. According to the contract language, Lang would be credited as "producer-director" on the screen, and (no trivial clause) in all advertising and publicity.

But by the time these contracts were signed, in effect, Lang and Brecht had already halted their collaboration. Lang said later that one of the reasons was that Brecht spoke "very little English." That caused no problem in communicating with Lang, but Brecht was unable to supply the very touches that the director desired most from a writer—the commercial script flourishes and American jargon with which the director hoped to strike a chord with audiences.

More importantly, the playwright aimed as always for a didactic approach. Brecht wrote in his journal that the things about the script that interested him most were "an intelligent presentation of a modern tyrant," the workers' sabotage, scenes with the hostages evincing "class differences," and "displays of anti-Semitism in their midst." Brecht was optimistic that the film would be "constructed in the epic manner." And, as recorded in his journal, he intended that one of its lessons be that the mistakes of the underground movement "are corrected by the broad mass of the people, et cetera."

Brecht was in the camp of ideologues who persisted in believing that a people's rebellion would rise up to defeat Hitler in Germany. This political plank, as well as others of Brecht's, seemed like nonsense to Lang. Brecht's storyline had evolved as a hymn to popular resistance, but the director could hardly put his wholehearted trust in such a creed; as he had demonstrated in previous films, to him the collective will of "the people" held as much potential risk as promise.

Worst of all, no personal affinity developed between the director and Brecht. Lang prided himself on getting along with writers, but after Thea von Harbou (and excepting Dudley Nichols), his writers were all subordinate to him. Brecht was the director's equal, cunning and bitter-minded about pushing his own ideas and resisting Lang's.

"They didn't get along together very well," said Lion Feuchtwanger's wife Martha, who observed them on occasion, "because they had such different ideas." Whatever the director said, according to Feuchtwanger, Brecht would reflexively come up with the opposite. "It was a kind of hypnosis, almost, that when he heard something, it inspired him [Brecht]" to contradict Lang.

"I remember when both were here [in our house] once and they told us about their plans. It was Brecht who always went up and down the room and had his ideas, one good and one bad or so, and Fritz Lang said, 'They wouldn't buy that,' or 'That I buy.' "

"I admire Brecht very, very much," is what the director told Peter Bogdanovich, "but in films I had more experience and I knew more about what the American audience would swallow; also, I had certain ideas, so really we worked hand-in-glove."

If only for the briefest time . . .

After hand and glove parted ways, it was Lang's decision to bring in a third person to further commune with the mercurial Brecht, and fill out the screenplay along more traditional Hollywood lines.

In late July, Lang contacted an industry veteran, John Wexley, at his home in Bucks County, Pennsylvania, summoning him to California. Wexley knew German, so he and Brecht could hold daily sessions, work out the nitty-gritty of scenes, and save Lang some aggravation. A former playwright, Wexley had written *The Last Mile*, an exemplary prison drama of 1930. In Hollywood off and on since the early 1930s, he had written the antifascist *Confessions of a Nazi Spy* and noteworthy Cagney vehicles for Warner Brothers, including *Angels With Dirty Faces* and *City for Conquest*.

Wexley was also a staunch left-winger, which was as important as his professional credentials to Lang. However, the director would later deny knowing the writer might in fact have been a member in good standing of the Communist Party. According to Wexley, however, Lang did hire him because "I was kind of an expert politically."

At first, Brecht and Wexley hit it off. According to Wexley, Brecht listened agreeably while Wexley propounded scenes. (According to Brecht, it was he who did the propounding, Wexley the listening.) Hanns Eisler would come by and play the music he was composing for the film, and they would all recite Brecht's lyrics. As each scene was finished, Wexley would make a show of reading the pages aloud. "Brecht would love to hear the screenplay scenes read," said Wexley. During breaks the two writers passed a good deal of time playing chess.

As August progressed, the work escalated. Now Brecht kept daytime hours at the United Artists studio, where Pressburger had leased space; he drove into Hollywood in the morning and usually worked until late afternoon, when he had to return to Santa Monica in time for the twilight curfew required of "enemy aliens." Then it was Wexley's turn to make the trip by car to Brecht's house, where they resumed sessions in the evening.

Hiring Wexley, a buffer between Brecht and himself, had been a canny move on the director's part. At the same time it engendered simmering rivalry and bad feelings. Brecht's journal took note of Wexley's superior salary ($1500 a month) and status.

Brecht's journal, August 5, 1942: "he [wexley] is supposed to be very left and decent. i first go through a sequence with him, and he dictates it to the secretary. she makes four copies, and when i ask for one he makes childish excuses. at the top of the page stands 'john wexley' and the date, and there is no name against the individual suggestions. in one scene he needs a german translation; so he puts handwritten additions on one copy and hands it to me. i take the sheet with me. then there is some phoning around, he says i took a sheet he needs, he can't get on with his work. it would seem that these tricks are highly paid."

Brecht, already suspicious of the director, tried to recruit Wexley as *his* ally. "When he'd hear that Lang would cut something out, he became furious," remembered Wexley. "And he began to call him names, like he had 'gone Hollywood,' he was commercial, and so on . . . which was true. Lang had cottoned up to the producers." Brecht suggested that the evening sessions be spent on an "ideal" version of the Heydrich script, as an antidote to what loomed as Lang's more commercial version.

Brecht's journal continues: "September 14, 1942: work on our film (which i would like to call *trust the people*) is going better now that it is wexley and not lang with whom i am discussing how to convert the outline into a script (in the process i also correct his work). above all i have got wexley to come home with me in the evenings and write a completely new, ideal script, which will later be shown to lang. i have naturally laid the main emphasis on the scenes with the people."

October 5, 1942: "very typical procedure; i hear that wexley demanded a bonus for working in the evenings and on sundays. he got it and lang told me i should do the same. i did and after some to-ing and fro-ing it was granted, the to-ing and fro-ing having to do with my demand that mine must be the same bonus. but the next day lang came along and demanded that we write the main script in the evenings and leave the "polishing" to the end. the result is that i cannot get wexley to work on the ideal script anymore. there are only seventy pages of it."

October 16, 1942: "just now, right before shooting, lang hauled poor wexley into his office and screamed at him behind closed doors that he wants to make a *hollywoodpicture*, and shits on scenes that show the people, et cetera. the change in the man once $700,000 [brecht's notion of the production budget] is in the offing is remarkable. he sits with all the airs of a dictator and old movie hand behind his boss-desk, full of drugs, and resentment at any good suggestions, collecting 'surprises,' little bits of suspense, tawdry sentimental touches and falsehoods, and takes 'licenses' for the box office. for an hour or so—i am naturally condensing all this—as i sit in my treacherously pretty garden and force myself to read a detective story, i feel the disappointment and terror of the intellectual worker who sees the product of his labors snatched away and mutilated."

October 22, 1942: "i now notice that this work on the film has almost made me ill. these 'surprises' which consist in impossible things happening, these 'moments of suspense' which consist in withholding information from the audience, these underground leaders who stand bleeding behind the curtains while the gestapo searches a house, these indignant shouts of 'why should i give the line to a worker whom i am paying $150 when there is a professor standing beside him whom i am paying $5000!' these effects from the rose theater anno 1880, these eruptions of a tainted imagination, of sentimentality which reeks of money, of deep-seated reaction triumphant, the persistent wild resentment at having supposedly to make a great film when in actual fact you are just part of a composite production . . . ''

Neither Brecht nor Wexley wrote concisely, and between them the screenplay swelled to 220–250 pages. The two writers were too preoccupied with adding new scenes to subtract any old ones. Lang, for his part, was so busy with other aspects of the production that he couldn't apply the major editing the script warranted. As the start of principal photography approached, the director therefore hired another writer—ex-newspaperman Milton Gunzburg—to trim scenes behind the backs of Brecht and Wexley.

Wexley was philosophical, accepting it as part of the Hollywood game. But Brecht deplored the cuts made at Lang's insistence. He knew he had written a hard-hitting story, filled with "scenes of prisoner camps" and a realistic depiction of Nazi anti-Semitism and anti-Communism. In the very first treatment, the character of Heydrich had complained, "Everything is contaminated with Jews and Communists!" But that line would be cut, along with a scene that brought Brecht tremendous pride—a scene set at a mass grave, which would have constituted the first on-screen depiction of Jewish victims of the Nazi terror.

According to Wexley, the director himself made a point of cutting out the mass-grave scene* and all explicit references to Jews. There would be no mention of the Jewish victims of Nazis in Fritz Lang's *Hangmen Also Die* . . . although among the prisoners in the death camp the film would flaunt a Catholic priest bravely administering last rites.

Arnold Pressburger had collected an ad hoc group of European investors, but with costs adding up since late spring, he extracted a gentleman's agreement from Lang to leave certain scenes out of the screenplay when it was reviewed by them; later on—at least that was how Lang chose to remember it—the director could film those scenes anyway.

The tight budget forced Lang to start "a month sooner than we expected," according to the director. That was Pressburger's fault, in Lang's view, and gave him the excuse he wanted to treat the producer contemptuously. "He slaved him [Pressburger]," said Sam Jaffe. "He was so terrible to this man. This man was afraid, intimidated, and felt very inadequate around Fritz Lang. That of course was the wrong signal. If you showed that kind of attitude toward Fritz Lang, he took advantage of it."

On this production Lang had to function as virtually a "one-man show," as he complained to a journalist. He had no studio apparatus. He had to organize and oversee all the casting and hiring of crew, and do all preproduction planning himself.

The production designer was the erudite Hungarian-born William S. Darling, who had won an Academy Award for 1932's *Cavalcade* and spent most of his career as a supervising art director with 20th Century–Fox. And Lang went out of his way to hire James Wong Howe, reputed to be among the highest-paid cinematographers in the industry. A Chinese immigrant raised in

---

*The mass-grave scene was actually filmed *and* photographed for publicity purposes, before Lang thought better of it and excised it from *Hangmen Also Die.*

the state of Washington, Howe had been a professional pugilist before he got a job as a Beverly Hills bellhop and later found a job as an assistant cameraman. An innovator and perfectionist in the industry since 1919, Howe was considered an expert at atmospheric black-and-white photography.

The casting depended on both budget and availability. Brecht thought he had a vote, Pressburger chipped in with his suggestions, and each decision became a three-way tug-of-war, with Lang—more so than on any of his previous Hollywood films—ultimately prevailing.

The director announced a policy of casting only actors *without* mittel-European accents in the Czech roles; he wanted to "Americanize" the heroes of the film, and didn't care to tip the audience off to the villains. In what might have been a reflection of his own sensitivity as an accented émigré, Lang was inclined toward Midwestern types (he called them "middle Americans"), or British actors with flawless diction. In practice, ironically, this partiality would homogenize the casting in the two anti-Nazi films over which the director exerted the most influence—*Hangmen Also Die* and *Cloak and Dagger*.

A minor star who often played villains, barrel-chested Brian Donlevy, won the hero's role of Svoboda, the medical doctor turned resistance hit man sought by the Nazis. The production needed a marquee name, and Donlevy happened to be obtainable; but the character he played had nothing of Lang's usual victimized air, and the hero was the least interesting role in the film.

Walter Brennan was another marquee name—not a star, but a quintessentially American actor; he was hired to play Professor Novotny, a resistance sympathizer who is caught up in the Nazi dragnet. The director tried to hire another well-known character actor, Thomas Mitchell, for the role of Emil Czaka, the quisling who betrays the resistance movement, but Mitchell turned him down flat. A veteran vaudeville and stage performer, Gene Lockhart, stepped into the part, which grew so dramatically in the course of the production that it would ultimately dominate the film.

The lead female character was Mascha, Professor Novotny's daughter, whose political ambivalence is tested when she is caught up in the Nazi dragnet. For a time, the director held out hope for his all-American girlfriend, Virginia Gilmore, but by 1942 it was clear her sights were set elsewhere. He considered taking a chance on John Barrymore's daughter Diana, a "virgin star" to whom he had taken a liking, but couldn't make up his mind. At Pressburger's urging, Lang took a look at footage of British actress Anna Lee, a rising star in the United States on the basis of her performance in John Ford's *How Green Was My Valley*. Lang agreed to hire Lee, but never warmed to his own decision, and Anna Lee became one more cause to inveigh against Pressburger.

Lang's "Americanized" casting drove Brecht crazy. All the actors he knew and preferred—including his own wife, Helene Weigel—had European accents. But the director wouldn't consider any of them them for a part, no matter how inconsequential.

From Brecht's journal: October 17, 1942: "[fritz] kortner is hurt because i did not get him a part in the lang film, though i tried all I could to get the role of czaka for [oscar] homolka; in other words, I tried to get him for the part. lang has all sorts of personal grudges against kortner, who once said unpleasant things to him in company when he was defending freedom of opinion in democracies, e.g., that he was talking with his weekly paycheck in his mouth. lang seemingly has less against homolka, mainly the fact that he is a good actor."

Kortner was a Brecht insider, Homolka another veteran of Brecht's plays. The director was not about to stock the production with Brecht's allies. Nor would he deign to give the small role of the vegetable woman, Miss Dvorak— whose chance encounter with Mascha casts her in a suspicious light with the Nazis—to Helene Weigel, a onetime star of the Berlin stage who had been reduced to giving acting lessons in Hollywood. Brecht always maintained that Lang promised to set aside the part for his wife, then reneged. Lang said he did no such thing, but at the least he handled the delicate situation ham-handedly.

Brecht wrote that the director "made a hasty voice test [of Weigel], promised a full screen test, made her wait and work for it, then simply filmed the first scene with somebody else without even letting us know." It stung Brecht all the more when he learned to whom the part had gone: Sarah Padden, a British character actress whom Lang used more than once in his productions. Perversely, Padden went ahead and adopted a vague European accent for her character anyway.

There was only one conspicuous former Berliner, and he played the film's villain. For the part of Alois Gruber, the Gestapo detective spearheading the investigation into the Hangman's assassination, the director settled on Alexander Granach, a leading actor in Berlin during the pre-Nazi era, who had emigrated to Russia, then eluded the political purges by fleeing to America. Alexander Granach and Gene Lockhart, the rotten characters, both were permitted to operate with thick foreign accents.

By the time filming started in late October, Brecht was virtually as unwelcome a presence as Arnold Pressburger.

Not that Brecht had any illusions in the matter. Composing the words to the Hanns Eisler theme song, "Trust the People," the playwright had set down the lyrics in his journal because he thought they were otherwise unlikely to survive Lang's meddling. Later, Brecht chronicled just how it happened: The director employed "a highly paid *hitparademan*"—Sam Coslow, left over from *You and Me*—to translate the song into Tin Pan Alley "Americanese," combining a few of Coslow's lines with Wexley's to produce "a piece of incredible crap," from Brecht's point of view. The bowdlerized lyrics then were handed over to an actor who was the opposite of the type envisioned by Brecht for the song.

But Brecht couldn't be denied; he was a world-reknowned figure, not a mere producer. Lang sought to avoid a confrontation with him, and Brecht, mindful of his fee, registered his own politesse. Once the production got underway, the playwright was obliged to pay a ceremonial visit to the *Hangmen Also Die* set. Afterward he returned sickened by how his ideas had been cannibalized to create a Hollywood product designed to please.

From Brecht's journal: November 2, 1942: "lang's secretary called to say that shooting has started and i was "invited, more than invited." the first scene lang shot was one wexley and i had cut; the heroine is arguing with her aunt about her wedding dress—she wants a deeper decolleté. the heroine is cast with a fifth-rate english actress, a smooth doll with no character. the lord of the lens is sitting beside his camera, unapproachable, while beside me a german refugee doctor waits to give him his vitamin injections. lang, of course, gives me an unconvincing wave and says half-audibly. 'hi, brecht! you'll be getting a script tomorrow.'

November 4, 1942: "for two weekly paychecks ($3000), wexley has torn down what it took ten months to build. i had almost managed to eliminate the main idiocies from the story and now they are all back.

i see the scene in which the assassin, after wandering around for hours, comes to the historian's house looking for somewhere to hide. before his entrance the hairdressers and tailors pounce on him, oil his locks, block specks of dust off his jacket. and the girl, the mother, the aunt, the father are only left alone by the hairdressers when the bell goes, and the take starts. the rooms are vast halls, the furniture is imitation museum pieces (whose originals were themselves fakes. in short, an 'ideal' world.

The city of Prague had to be recreated inside the boundaries of General Services Studio. Because of wartime restrictions, there was a five-thousand-dollar ceiling on the construction of individual sets; the director petitioned and received permission to exceed that amount, arguing that the sets could be preserved for future productions with European settings. But inevitably other shortcuts were taken because of the inadequate budget.

The director's growing displeasure was transferred to the actors once photography started. Lang couldn't bully Brian Donlevy, who was built like a boxer and would have sparred back. (Sadly, Donlevy also acted like a boxer in the film.) But Alexander Granach took verbal blows, as did the extras. Yet extras were ducks in a pond. and ultimately it was leading lady Anna Lee who caught the brunt of Lang's foul mood.

From the moment she stepped onto the set, Anna Lee was treated as an unwelcome substitute for Virginia Gilmore. To Lang she was hopelessly unsuitable for the part. The actress had made the mistake of assuming she would play her character with the hint of a Czechoslovakian accent, but the director was offended by any affectation that went against his "middle-American" policy. To her surprise, Lang informed her sharply that she would have to undergo extra hours of coaching in a Midwestern voice.

"From the word go, he was determined to make this as unpleasant for me as possible," remembered the actress. Lang himself heavily acted the mittel-European; he wore not only his monocle on the set but Prussian boots with heavy heels. Yet he ordered the actress to take off her own shoes, claiming that they made her walk like a duck. So Anna Lee had to play her scenes barefoot, while he hovered around her, "deliberately," she believed, crunching her feet with his boots. "I've still got a scar," she said in an interview four decades later.

It seemed to Anna Lee that the director watched for opportunities to bully her unmercifully. "We had a scene where I had to put my hand through a carriage to shout for help on the way to the Gestapo," she remembered. "So the time came to do the scene and the prop man came up and put gelatin stuff in the window, and Fritz said, 'No, no, no. We must have real glass.' So they put real glass in.

The crew was already "ready to kill him by that time," according to Lee. "Well, we started the scene and I put my hand through the window and it went right through, clean, without even a scratch. It was a perfect shot; and everything in the scene was fine. Everybody sort of sighed with relief, and Fritz looked at it, and said, 'We do one more.' And they couldn't believe it, because there was nothing wrong with the scene at all. So back came the glass, and this time I wasn't so lucky. I didn't hit a big vein, fortunately, but I did hit a smaller vein and there was a lot of blood. And all of a sudden this strange man, Fritz Lang, comes running, 'Oh, my darling, my darling!' and he starts sucking the blood from my hand like an old vampire.

"The next day the crew sent me this huge bouquet of flowers with something very nice written on it, and he [Lang] was so angry. Well, he was really working up for a storm, because by this time they [the crew] hated the way he was bullying me."

Lang had promoted his friend Gene Fowler, Jr., from assistant editor to editor, and Fowler was on hand to watch as the director ran people ragged. Lang thought Anna Lee was "one of the worst actresses in the world," remembered Fowler, and in one scene made her repeat a line of dialogue over and over again until she was nearly dizzy, screaming at her when she got it wrong. Nobody, including Fowler, had the faintest idea what Lang was reaching for. "What the hell he wanted I don't know," said Fowler. "We didn't have a clue how he wanted her to say it. It was like a loop running over and over again. He gave her emphatic line readings, until she began to say it with a German inflection." Finally, the director was satisfied. Standing on the sidelines, Fowler realized that the actress had only managed to please the director when she began to sound like Fritz Lang himself—this director who had refused to cast anyone with an accent like his own.

People took umbrage on Anna Lee's behalf. "One day he was directing a scene with some extras," recalled the actress, "and there was a big, tall Texan. I always remember because in those days I was very fond of Texans. And he said something to him about his accent, something like, 'Why do you not speak good English!' I mean, this from Fritz Lang! He got into a fight, and this Texan slammed him, glasses on and all, and he fell over. Not one of the crew came forward to pick him up. They all just sat there. Nobody picked him up."

The producer could do little. Once filming began, Arnold Pressburger was ignored. Lang tried to banish him from the set altogether, but Pressburger insisted on his rights, and just for good measure brought his tag team of investors, perched on special bleachers, to watch the oft-horrific proceedings.

Not only horrific, but prolonged and expensive. Pressburger took to writing Lang memos complaining about the extra shots and finicky details slowing the film's progress. Nothing infuriated the director more than memos from a producer. Lang wrote memos back blaming everything on a slow cameraman, malfunctioning equipment, and the long hours he had to put in trying to upgrade Anna Lee's performance. "The continued harassing every day while I am shooting is very disturbing," the director scribbled at the bottom of one such memo, "and tends to slow me up and accomplish nothing."

When the main photography was completed, Lang would take advantage of Pressburger's oral agreement to spend an inordinate amount of time shooting "wild lines" and "inserts," entailing further overtime expenses. Lang did relish filming inserts, but he may also have enjoyed the thought of the producer's tearing his hair out over further delays and costs.

Afterward, Lang retreated to the isolation of the editing booth, where he could work alone with Gene Fowler, Jr., and Fowler's assistants—including Marjorie Johnson, screenwriter Nunnally Johnson's daughter, whom Fowler was destined to marry.

The three of them were a pocket coalition, pitched to battle a world conspiring against Lang. At one point, when the producers wanted to see the picture before Lang was ready to reveal it to them, the director convinced Marjorie Johnson to grab up the reels and make herself unavailable by disappearing into the ladies' room.

They worked all night, and the work was fun. There was a little coffee shop called Lillian's around the back of the studio, and Lillian gave them a key for after-hours; they'd take a break around midnight, send Marjorie over to get some coffee and sandwiches ready. "Fritz and I would climb the fence, go in, and we'd eat and then climb the fence and come back," recalled Fowler. "It was funny, Herr Director Lang climbing a fence!"

One of the reasons editing always took longer than anticipated was that, with Lang, there were always "a lot of takes of the same [shot]," in the words of Fowler. "Fritz Lang sure as hell had a big ratio," recalled the editor. "Wellman, I think, was probably the most economical [of Hollywood directors]. I think Fritz probably shot the most."

Fowler remembered the director's resourcefulness in a scene where a resistance member leaps to his death through a window. Such scenes usually utilized breakaway glass to avoid injury, but as before, the director preferred real glass. This time the actor was Lionel Stander, however, a bonafide tough guy who wasn't about to let himself be pushed through real glass simply to please Fritz Lang. So the director chose to film Stander's scene without *any* glass. It was bound to look fake in the dailies, but that was okay with Lang; he would fix the scene somehow during editing. "In order to make the jump realistic," remembered Fowler, "we ordered a fine-grain print, and the two of us handanimated slivers of flying glass into the scene. The effect was startlingly good, and I believe more dramatic than if we had used the real thing."

Although the pressure was on and the release date was closing in, Lang was in his element toying with footage, trying out endless variations of the same sequence. One night Lang and Fowler halted work to experiment on an issue whose significance would have eluded, if not baffled, most directors. Lang had been wondering how many frames "one should hold on a piece of film after a sharp look by an actor, and before cutting to his point of view," recalled Fowler. "After many trials, and at three in the morning, we came to the conclusion that seven frames was the correct length."

* * *

Before the release of *Hangmen Also Die,* the script credits had to be formalized by the Screen Writers Guild. Brecht put in for equal credit on the story and screenplay, fighting for his name on material that had been mangled practically beyond his recognition. Wexley contested with a claim for solo script credit, so the Guild was obliged to convene a hearing of its arbitration committee.

According to Lang, Arnold Pressburger refused to come to the hearing and speak up for Brecht, which hurt Brecht's case. Lang always claimed that the producer was still furious with Brecht over his exorbitant money demands. Therefore it was left to Hanns Eisler and Lang to defend Brecht. But the director's anecdotes were always holding producers to blame, and this one was hardly definitive.

Brecht's version: January 20, 1943: "the sight of spiritual mutilation makes me ill. it is scarcely possible to stand being in the same room with these spiritual cripples and moral invalids. a session of the Screenwriters Guild, whom i had to call because Pressburger and lang gave me no credit for my work on the screenplay—wexley was against it. he [wexley] sat there with half a hundredweight of manuscripts and maintained that he had hardly spoken to me. the credit would possibly enable me to get a film job, if things get really bad."

Screenwriter Maurice Rapf was chairman of the Guild's arbitration panel. He recalled that Brecht's version was accurate where Wexley was concerned: "The wily Wexley had put his name on all the pages written in English and the committee had to conclude that those pages—representing the bulk of the final screenplay—were written by Wexley. He won the arbitration. I think that Wexley got away with a credit he didn't deserve."

Wexley was awarded the sole screenplay credit. Brecht would share with Lang two separate credits—original story and adaptation—with Brecht's name appearing first.

In its letter of January 23, 1943, awarding the official wording, the arbitration board stipulated that "the placing of Mr. Brecht's name before Mr. Lang was suggested by Mr. Lang in the hearing before the Committee." Lang, always deferential before tribunals, had completed his beau geste.

Under such circumstances it was hard to keep track of who actually wrote which scenes. In his authoritative book *Bertolt Brecht in America,* James K. Lyon analyzed script drafts and decided that Brecht's influence was most evident in Walter Brennan's speeches, a series of scenes in the hostage camp, and the poem that is read at the end of the film. But Brecht thought that he had written much more, and felt betrayed.

"Brecht got a raw deal here," was all Lang would say to Axel Madsen for *Sight and Sound* in 1967. "There were endless fights with producers and so on." "If pressed," Madsen added, "he [Lang] will add that their acquaintance was casual, that Brecht's Santa Monica house was a weird place full of émigrés forever playing chess . . . and that he himself is no Brecht fan. 'I mean, François Villon did all that five hundred years ago, n'est-ce pas?' "

Sometimes Lang was his own worst public-relations enemy. Before the release of *Hangmen Also Die* he complained to a journalist for *Look* magazine that

"Anna Lee is very bad in our picture—too wooden," and that he had a tremendous challenge trying to mold her to the part.

An astonished Arnold Pressburger admonished the director, who also received a letter of protest from Paul Kohner, Anna Lee's agent. Lang tried to save face: He denied ever having uttered such foolishness to *Look* or anyone else, and went on the record, officially, as being "pleased and happy" about *Hangmen Also Die* and Anna Lee's performance, insisting it was "her best American picture" to date.

In the film, Dr. Franz Svoboda (Brian Donlevy) sends red roses to Mascha (Anna Lee) as a way of identifying himself as the assassin. In order to patch things up with Anna Lee, Lang sent the actress a dozen white orchids. A few years later the leading lady of *Hangmen Also Die* met the director socially at Joan Bennett's house, where, off the set, he behaved toward her with surprising civility. "You know, you were an awful bully in those days," Anna Lee told Lang. "Well, no more, no more," Lang answered.

Joan Bennett took Anna Lee aside and told her that the director had been ill during the filming. Perhaps that was true, the actress mused. "He had a doctor [on call] and he kept taking pills," she remembered, "and I think he was hyped up or something."

One can detect Anna Lee's discomfort in the film. All of the delicacy is squeezed out of her performance. The actress strains for effect; she is pitched too high. At times, her character resembles Maria in *Metropolis*, flinging out spasmodic movements.

The script of *Hangmen Also Die*, which did not help her, was in the end a disappointment. As Brecht put it in his journal, all the character logic is thin, the melodrama overripe, the fingerpoints obvious. People race around, dash off, crouch behind doors, burst into rooms. The machinery of the plot—its elaborate pretense of coded messages and eavesdropping coincidences—creaks like a revolving stage.

The Nazi ideology, so important to Brecht, was snipped out by Lang. Even the torture and violence is quick and unconvincing. In the prison camp the hostages seem complacent, even well-fed; like Brecht and Wexley, they pass the time playing chess.

The villains were not only permitted European accents, they showed all the personality—guzzling beer on the job as they sign and stamp their endless forms, à la *Liliom*—that other characters lacked. Brecht's nasty sense of humor and Lang's paranoia come together in jovial Nazis surrounded by ceiling-high files, making their lists of victims to be exterminated.

The Inspector and Czaka dominate the last, most compelling act of *Hangmen Also Die*. That is when the turncoat who has supplied the citizen lists is elaborately fingered by the underground, and the Gestapo is tricked into believing Czaka a double agent—a railroad timetable conveniently providing the incriminating evidence.

The Inspector is killed in one of Lang's drawn-out slugfests. Czaka goes mad with fear, crawling toward the safety of a Catholic Church narthex as Gestapo gunfire nips his heels and finally cuts him down. Lang's last-ditch attempt to imbue the quisling with humanity isn't quite enough, although in the end that character obviously fascinated the director more than all the other wise people and noble deeds in the script.

Lang was proud of the final words on the screen: "NOT the end."

Nonetheless, the Nazis were everybody's favorite enemy, and *Hangmen Also Die* swept to success on a wave of American wartime fervor.

United Artists rounded up publicity blurbs from war correspondent William Shirer ("superb and unforgettable") and novelists Fannie Hurst ("a picture so eloquent that it makes everything we are fighting for clearer and dearer") and Rex Stout ("If words are weapons, so are pictures. This one shoots as straight and true as a P-40 blasting a Messerschmitt.").

The critics competed with superlatives. Howard Barnes of the *New York Herald Tribune* proclaimed *Hangmen Also Die* "a director's picture, indelibly marked by Lang's craftsmanship." Alton Cook in the *New York World-Telegram* wrote, "From the fierce passion of a man driven from his homeland, Fritz Lang has drawn a monument of venom and hatred for the Nazi conquerors of Czechoslovakia. Audiences will emerge from [the] theater at once more shaken and more stirred than by any other picture the war has produced." "One of his finest jobs of direction," rhapsodized Archer Winsten in the *New York Post*. Joy Davidman of the *New Masses* wrote it "may well be America's finest artistic comment on the war."

Indeed, *Hangmen* was among the early contenders for Best Film of 1943 in the balloting of the New York Film Critics organization. "Eight directors were nominated," according to one published report, "but it was evident from the start that there were only three serious contenders—William Wellman for *The Ox-Bow Incident*, Fritz Lang for *Hangmen Also Die,* and George Stevens for *The More the Merrier*. Mr. Wellman and Mr. Lang ran a nip-and-tuck race up to the fifth ballot, when Mr. Lang lost all but two of his votes and Mr. Stevens came behind to tie Mr. Wellman at seven." Stevens finally inched up to defeat Wellman, and the winner was *The More the Merrier*.

But *Hangmen Also Die* was wiped out in 1943's Academy Award nominations, and there were a few fault-finding heretics. Manny Farber in *The New Republic* was one who found *Hangmen* a "grim, awkward film." Wrote Farber: "The plot's windings are endless and sometimes fantastic. Much of the playing is beginner's stuff. The lighting is awful. The dialogue contains such clumsy 'German' as 'Stay right where you are or you get a slug in the guts,' and such weird 'Czech' as 'Don't let yourself get snowed under at Valley Forge.' Nowhere are human beings examined deeply enough to find the ideologies this movie is presumably about."

Brecht entertained no illusions about the experience. It was, after all, merely a job of work. In his journal entry of June 24, 1943, just after *Hangmen Also Die* was released to theaters nationwide, Brecht expressed contentment in the knowledge that his well-paid effort on Lang's film "has given me enough breathing space [to work on] three plays."

Nor did Lang entertain any illusions. The director always set a film aside in his mind once it was completed, and in New York in the spring of 1943, while doing interviews to promote *Hangmen*, he meekly accepted a studio offer to film a project whose screenplay was already completed and approved by higher-ups. Though *Hangmen Also Die* had given him a refreshing glimpse of auteurism, now he was once again a hired hand.

The director had always admired the novels of Graham Greene, and at the start of his career, reviewing movies for London's literary weekly *The Spectator*, Greene had shown an appreciation for Fritz Lang. About *Fury*, Greene had written: "No other director has got so completely the measure of his medium, is so consistently awake to the counterpoint of sound and image." (Greene also wrote that a Lang melodrama was "infinitely more expert" than a Hitchcock one.)

In New York City, Lang read an adaptation of Greene's novel *Ministry of Fear*, replete with ticking clocks and roaring trains, séances and spy rings, mysterious Nazis with Viennese backgrounds, and a lead character who has just been released from an insane asylum after serving time for his wife's mercy killing (which turns out, actually, to be a covered-up suicide).

Paramount owned the screen rights to Greene's novel. It is also true, and not unimportant, that Lang owed the studio a film dating back to his 1938 deal. The job paid $50,000. Lang signed an agreement in his hotel, then returned to the West Coast.

In later interviews, Lang said he was "terribly shocked" by how the script had worsened in the meantime. "I did everything I could to get out of making that picture, but Paramount wouldn't cancel the contract," he told Gene D. Phillips. "That was one of the times that my agent had failed to get me a clause in my contract that allowed me to work on the script."

Actually, Lang rarely had such a clause. This script had been closely nurtured by the Paramount producer, and it couldn't have changed all that drastically after Lang took the job, since the producer, Seton I. Miller, was also the screenwriter.

Miller, a Yale graduate who had entered the film business initially as an actor, was one of Hollywood's top scenarists. A friend and frequent collaborator of director Howard Hawks, Miller contributed to *Scarface*, *The Criminal Code*, and other Hawks productions dating back to the early days of sound. A contract writer throughout much of the 1930s, Miller wrote *The Adventures of Robin Hood*, several James Cagney vehicles, and a slew of prison, gangster, and boxing pictures for Warner Brothers. He had a reputation for taut plotting, snappy dialogue, and creating masculine characters.

With *Ministry of Fear*, Miller was branching out as a producer. Paramount records indicate that Lang signed a contract on the basis of the May 18, 1943, version of Miller's script. There would be only one more version, dated the week filming started—July 8, 1943. But Lang's input was even slighter than usual, given Miller's dual powers over the script. It is interesting that the only time the director ever clashed with Hollywood writers was when they dared to assume the added mantle of producer, giving them an unwonted edge.

Other issues besides the script upset Lang. The cast and crew were entirely under the studio umbrella. Paramount stalwart Ray Milland already had been secured as the film's star. The studio was giving Marjorie Reynolds a big push, and the director had no choice but to accept the actress—once a brunette, now a blonde for her Viennese impersonation—as his female lead. The cameraman, Henry Sharp, was capable—he had been a great pictorialist of the silent era—but answerable to the studio; and the creation of the phony-England sets was already fait accompli. Paramount was not about to repeat any past mistakes with Lang; the package bestowed on the director was already tightly bound and wrapped.

In Seton Miller, too, the director found a producer he could not intimidate. Although Miller had to fight Lang on almost a daily basis, and was obliged to give the set a wide berth, dropping by only to watch certain key scenes, the novice producer was determined to hold Lang to script, budget, and schedule. He bombarded the director with memos whenever Lang strayed. Miller refused to back down, and Lang knew the producer had the full weight of the studio behind him. The producer would win all substantive arguments.

The writer-producer had finessed a breezy adaptation of the Graham Greene novel, treating the story as Hitchcock might have—glossing over the puzzling clues that didn't quite add up, the alarming leaps in continuity, the superficial characterizations. Everything was sacrificed to the style and momentum of a slick Hollywood thriller.

The principal photography was finished by September 1. Even with Miller prodding him every step of the way, Lang took the production nine days over schedule and some $44,000 over its projected $700,000 budget. Afterward, he had no Gene Fowler, Jr., no secret ally in the editing room. The "supposed producer," as Lang liked to refer to Miller, presided over assembling a final cut that would meet studio approval.

Graham Greene detested the resulting film. So did Fritz Lang. It was his compulsory imitation of Hitchcock. Yet Lang's feelings for his old films were intertwined with his subjective memories and distant emotions; his dislike could be out of proportion to the work itself.

Actually, *Ministry of Fear* is an eminently watchable film. It has the studio patina that *Hangmen Also Die*—and Lang's weak-budgeted "independent" films—lack. The production is handsome, the scenes atmospheric and beautifully mapped out; and the director accomodated the suspense with a bitter, surreal, and truly dark point of view.

The story jump-starts with Stephen Neale (Ray Milland) leaving an insane asylum, haunted by voices in his mind whispering about a mysterious killing, poison, and frozen clocks. He stops at a bizarre country fair, buys a cake on the advice of a fortune-teller, and is thrown helter-skelter into a riddlesome plot. He gets hooked up with a network of dowagers that is a front for Nazi sympathizers, and meets a Viennese beauty (Marjorie Reynolds) and her brother (Austrian-born actor Carl Esmond).

The plot hurtles along. The Viennese lady is revealed to be a sunny innocent, her gentlemanly brother a covert Nazi agent. At suspenseful intervals, out jumps Dan Duryea, an actor making the first of three memorable appearances in Fritz Lang films, playing a Hitlerite rat who, when finally cornered, impales himself on a pair of scissors.

There is only a thimbleful of political thesis. Most of the film is breathlessly cut to action. But the camerawork is dazzling, with marvelous Langian setups of winding and crisscrossing steps, apartments with statuary and masks, and deceptive mirrors; one scene offers a glimpse of one of the director's old haunts, Scotland Yard, as viewed murkily from the back seat of an automobile, with rain pouring down everywhere.

The ending was one Lang particularly disdained: A dark, stormy rooftop shootout, with Scotland Yard to the rescue. It afforded the director one of his mini-fireworks shows, full of exploding light and noise, but whatever impact it might have had was undercut for Lang by the coda scripted by Miller, which showed the two leads motoring along the coast. They are cooing romantically over each other as they debate what kind of cake—cake, which had started the whole business—to serve at their wedding. It made for a weak fade-out.

Ministry of Fear was one experience Lang refused to dwell on. The director regarded his work as utterly impersonal, the film a botch. "I saw it recently on television," Lang told Peter Bogdanovich in 1967, "where it was cut to pieces, and I fell asleep."

On his very next production, ironically, the director would encounter again the same situation: a screenwriter who had become his own producer.

Nunnally Johnson had been at 20th Century–Fox when Lang was on the lot; he had penned the first treatment for *The Return of Frank James*. A Southerner, a former newspaper reporter in Georgia and later in New York City, Johnson had achieved national recognition for his *Saturday Evening Post* short stories. Arriving in Hollywood in 1932, Johnson joined Fox as a contract writer and swiftly established himself as one of the most prodigious scenarists in the business. Gifted with a folksy touch, Johnson collaborated memorably with director John Ford on several films, including Ford's acclaimed adaptation of John Steinbeck's *The Grapes of Wrath* in 1939.

Unlike Seton Miller, Johnson was no tyro as a producer. He had been producing many of his own scripts since 1934, but now Johnson had rejected the highest wage ever offered a studio scribe—a reported guarantee of $4500 a week, fifty-two weeks a year, for five years—in favor of declaring his independence from Fox. He had formed his own company, International Pictures, which would release films under the aegis of Universal, and for his first outing had chosen to adapt *Once Off Guard* by J. H. Wallis, a novel about a mild-mannered professor who gets mixed up with a femme fatale.

The popular thriller had undergone several printings since its publication in 1942. Johnson in his adaptation stayed close to the novel, but changed the professor's field from English Literature to Criminal Psychology. The novel had hinted that the female lead was a prostitute; Johnson made the character more ambiguous, but still obviously a rich man's mistress. The project's new title: *The Woman in the Window*.

After finishing the screenplay in the fall of 1943, Johnson went to work wooing Fritz Lang. He convinced his partner Bill Goetz (a former Fox executive who was, like David O. Selznick, another Louis B. Mayer son-in-law) that Lang was the right director for the project. Before even approaching Lang, Johnson had contacted Edward G. Robinson and set in motion the other major casting; Robinson had read the novel and very much wanted to play the part of Professor Wanley, which was made to order for his personality.

Joan Bennett was also Nunnally Johnson's idea, though, surprisingly, she was not anyone's first choice to play Alice, the rich man's mistress. The writer-producer had flirted with the possibility of Tallulah Bankhead, the raspy-voiced Broadway star who never quite made a fluid crossover to motion pictures. Lang, who had seen the legendary performer on stage and considered her "a great actress," gave Bankhead his vote. But she proved elusive, so Johnson swung over to Bennett, partly because of her past connection with his chosen director.

Because it was an independent production, and because Nunnally Johnson was not one to hover over the director, Lang was able to throw himself into preproduction planning, which buoyed his spirits. The director took one of his jaunts to New York and prowled the streets, sketching houses like the one where the woman in the story might live, and visiting the Hudson Parkway, where in the film Professor Wanley has an encounter with a toll-booth attendant. The exteriors would be replicated on soundstages, and the interiors were places that Lang himself knew well—automobiles, men's clubs, the apartment of a "kept" mistress.

Lang had an amenable art director, Duncan Cramer, and he found another felicitous match in his cameraman. Milton Krasner was a Philadelphian whose long career paralleled the development of the craft. He had worked his way up since starting out as a lighting assistant at Vitagraph in 1919, and was known for a multiplicity of styles: adept at black and white as well as color, the standard format, and, later on, the wide screen. In his career Krasner photographed a broad range of genres at nearly every Hollywood studio. Krasner ended up getting along so uncommonly well with Fritz Lang that he signed up for his next project—working consecutively with Lang on the following film—which only happened with a cameraman and this director twice in America.

Again Gene Fowler, Jr., was hired to edit the film. His assistant again would be the producer's daughter, Marjorie. Early into production, Fowler had to resign to enter the Army, and Lang championed Marjorie to replace him. *The Woman in the Window* would become her first full credit as editor. "Fritz was a manipulator," she recalled, "and I know perfectly well that he assumed if I could keep [scenes] in sync, the picture would be cut because he'd tell me how to do it. Which would make him very happy."

The story of *The Woman in the Window* opens with Professor Wanley pausing one evening to gaze at the portrait of a beautiful woman in a shop window, only to find, Alice, the model herself, standing at his side. Uncharacteristically, he invites Alice for a drink and winds up in her apartment, where their platonic idyll is interrupted by a man raving with jealousy. He tries to attack the professor. In the ensuing struggle, Alice hands Wanley a pair of scissors, and he impulsively stabs the man to death.

The professor must hide the body and, even harder, conceal his guilty conscience. The dead man turns out to be a well-known financier. The professor's friends become intrigued by the unsolved crime, and one of them, a district attorney, begins to add up the clues. The financier's bodyguard turns up, begins to blackmail Alice, and must be dealt with. Professor Wanley, feeling himself trapped in a nightmare, decides to commit suicide.

"We started out, of course, with the advantage of having one of the most perfect scripts I have ever been associated with, by Nunnally Johnson," exclaimed Edward G. Robinson, when he was interviewed by David Overbey a few months before his death in 1973. "It was so good that there were absolutely no changes made in it." When Overbey drove over to Lang's house and repeated this comment to the director, Lang snapped, "How the hell would he know about the script? I fought like hell with Nunnally Johnson over that script. Robinson saw only the final shooting script. Even then there were at least minor changes. There always are."

Writers and directors naturally have competing memories. Shortly after the film's release, Lang was already telling interviewers that Professor Wanley should have remained a professor of English, as in the book; and that he would have preferred Alice to be presented as "a lower character." In fact, the director had little to do with the script. Except for the much-debated ending, his changes mainly affected the "tone" of scenes.

In later interviews, Johnson always insisted *The Woman in the Window* was a funnier story on the page. "I hardly know what to say about Fritz as a director," Johnson told Tom Stempel in an "oral history" for the American Film Institute. "His record is too formidable, you know, to dismiss him, which I wouldn't be trying to do, but he offered various suggestions that I thought were so corny that I thought he must be laughing. He wasn't. He's a humorless man . . ."

There was one scene with newsreel footage that showed a Boy Scout talking about how he intended to use the reward money for tracking down the killer to pay his tuition to Harvard. That ought to have been a solid laugh, according to Johnson. Lang filmed it as "a piece of exposition," according to Tom Stempel in his book *Screenwriter: The Life and Times of Nunnally Johnson*. Other "comic touches that were supposed to add to the tension do so," Stempel added, "but without being in any way comic. What Lang did was simply emphasize the elements of the script he sympathized with and ignore those he did not."

Another scene had Professor Wanley driving along the highway with the dead body in the back of his car, when a motorcycle cop pulls up alongside him at a red light. "Fritz, somewhere in his past, had heard that story of the man who went to call on J. P. Morgan, Sr., and was advised not to look at Morgan's nose," Johnson recalled. "Morgan had a fat, ugly, pitted nose, and he was very sensitive about it. An old, old story in which the man is so bent on not calling attention [to the nose] that he lost track of things and he said, 'Well, I'll tell you this, Mr. Nose . . .' Well, it was an old story and Fritz said, 'Wouldn't it be funny if the cop came in and looked in there and said something or other, and Eddie answered in the same way, like, 'Yes, I'm a murderer.' "

Johnson, a humorist of some repute, didn't think so. Although Lang's strength was decor and design, the director committed curious stylistic anachronisms too. The writer-producer nearly exploded one day watching dailies, when Joan Bennett strolled into a scene carrying a cigarette holder that had gone out of fashion in 1920s Europe. "Oh my God," Johnson complained, "I forgot to write, 'She did *not* carry a two-foot cigarette holder.' "

Their big fight—the one significant script change over which Lang prevailed—was about the ending. More than anything, Lang took beginnings and endings to heart; the director slaved over them in each of his films. But everybody else in Hollywood fretted about beginnings and endings, too, and invariably they came in for tampering.

In this case, according to Marjorie Fowler, studio executives didn't like her father's original ending, faithful to the book, in which the guilt-ravaged professor despondently commits suicide. "The problem that immediately came up was how to get around the problem of the suicide, a story 'solution' discouraged by the Production Code," wrote Tom Stempel in his Nunnally Johnson biography. "[William] Goetz insisted that the story be revealed at the end to be a dream. Johnson felt that kind of ending was a cheat, but Goetz was insistent, and Fritz Lang, the director, agreed with Goetz."

"It had to be a happy ending," said Marjorie Fowler. "This was strictly studio practicality."

Acting on Goetz's suggestion, Nunnally Johnson devised an alternative that the writer-producer never wholeheartedly embraced: After drinking the poison, Professor Wanley wakes up, having dreamed the whole escapade. There follows a little scene in which the audience meets the people who were in his dream: the murdered husband is actually the men's club hat-check man; the club doorman is the blackmailing bodyguard, et cetera. Lang championed this ending, siding with Goetz against Nunnally Johnson, the "so-called producer."

One suspects the director regarded the scene as an excuse for a virtuoso camera turn—a brilliantly executed sequence that Lang was able to recite, shot by shot, for French cineasts twenty years later. Professor Wanley is in his bedroom in a dressing gown, slumped in a chair; the camera pushes slowly in as he prepares to drink the poison. The actor was wearing a breakaway robe, prepared for what would happen next.

At the moment Wanley's head slumped forward, stagehands standing out of camera range jerked the dressing robe off, and the camera edged slowly out of focus and began to pull back. As it did so, the entire room split in half and was pulled away to reveal a second set inside of the first one. Professor Wanley awakes from his "dream." It was all done in one take, without any cuts. Extraordinary.

Lang told Peter Bogdanovich that the *Rahmenhandlung* "framing" of *The Woman in the Window* reminded him of *Caligari*—where, similarly, the whole story is revealed to have been a nightmare at the end. ("This was unconscious—I didn't even *think* I was copying myself at the time.") But the "dream" ending wasn't sufficient; the story also needed a postscript, another device Lang loved. He told Gene D. Phillips that he devised a special epilogue so the story could fade out on a "healthy laugh."*

This brief scene shows Professor Wanley returning to gaze at the window, and encountering another luscious type à la Joan Bennett, who asks him, "Have you got a match?" Professor Wanley gives a start, fleeing in horror. "I personally felt that an audience wouldn't think a movie worthwhile in which

---

*Lang told Gene D. Phillips that he had thought of this particular "happy ending" himself. No matter that it is also in the J. H. Wallis novel, where one of the professor's friends—not Wanley, who is dead—has a similar run-in with a young beauty, eerily reminiscent of how the story has begun.

a man kills two people and himself just because he had made a mistake by going home with the girl," Lang explained.

A few months earlier, Lang had fumed about the comical epilogue forced on him for *Ministry of Fear*. Now, a light chuckle at the end of a grim film didn't seem so bad after all.

Although the script disagreements were private, it was hardly a happy set. The director preferred tension—created and stoked it, the better to foster a Langian tone.

Lang labored over Joan Bennett, blocking her every gesture, every tilt of her chin. The director was "very careful with externals," in the words of Edward G. Robinson. "He snapped his fingers when they [actors] were to turn their heads, snapped his fingers for looks, cued 'em like puppets," echoed Majorie Fowler, "[Gene was] always cutting finger snaps out. He [Lang] knew the timing he wanted, and he wasn't going to rely on *them*."

Joan Bennett was aware of the perception that she was a second-rank actress. That was part of Fritz Lang's power over her; her insecurity made her vulnerable to him. To Edward G. Robinson the director behaved more respectfully, although when David Overbey interviewed the star on the subject of Lang in 1973, he left with the distinct impression that the feeling wasn't mutual. Robinson's attitude toward Lang was grudging.

"He [Lang] was part of everything, not just in the direction of actors, but to the point of doing the makeup," remembered Robinson. "He would even sweep the floor of the set. During *Scarlet Street*, the light wasn't hitting the floor exactly the way he wanted it to, so he had it washed. It still wasn't right, so he put dust all over it and then swept it himself.

"Fritz was a very civilized, erudite man, and he could be jovial," Robinson continued, "But he could be seemingly cruel, especially with the crew. When he was particularly hard, I called him aside, and said, 'Now Fritz, I love you, but you know Hollywood boasts some of the finest craftsmen in the world. You don't have to treat them this way. They'll give you more if you loosen up on them a bit. It upsets me.' He wasn't really cruel. He was just concerned with the film and only with the film. For a while he would mend his ways. Then he would revert to type again."

Lang would defer to Edward G. Robinson—a star of his magnitude—but everyone remembered that the director refused to soften his callous treatment of an English actor named Edmund Breon, who portrays Dr. Barkstone, one of Professor Wanley's friends.

The director seemed to relish turning the screws on this mild-mannered, elderly character actor. On one occasion, in a long dialogue scene where Dr. Barkstone had to share ice cream with Professor Wanley and the district attorney (Raymond Massey), Lang insisted on using real sundaes. Then he insisted that Breon eat away at his sundae each time the camera rolled. Breon was in delicate health at the time, according to Gene Fowler, Jr., yet the director demanded an unseemly number of retakes.

The director's reprehensible behavior toward Breon inflamed people, and Nunnally Johnson said he feared that some crew member might take it upon himself to exact a violent revenge—shades of *Fury*. "I'd heard him bawl out

a fine old actor, embarrassing to have him shout at this old Englishman,"
remembered Johnson in his AFI "oral history." "And everybody around there
hated his guts. He called me at the end of the day [when filming was finished].
He said, 'Look, we're going to have a little party on the set—closing out. You
know, five o'clock, something like that.' I said. 'If I were you, I wouldn't go
to it.' He said, 'What do you mean?' I said, 'Somebody is going to drop something on your head, Fritz. You know, the picture's over. You won't be the
boss.' "

In her job as editor, Marjorie Fowler could be counted on to be on the set
most days and at the editing table most nights, working nearly round the clock.
She remembered using the dressing rooms on the lot to change clothing some
mornings, and catching up on her sleep over the lunch hours in a couch in
the ladies' room.*

Lang took his time with the editing, though, hovering over Marjorie and
trying to do as much as possible himself. When Nunnally Johnson complained
that the postproduction was falling behind, the director blamed the slow pace
on—who else?—the producer's daughter. Johnson did not hesitate to call the
director's bluff: If the novice editor was causing any undue delay, then Lang
ought to fire her straightaway. The director backed off, and with Lang at her
side Marjorie Fowler swiftly finished the editing.

All such discord was set aside, and professional smiles painted on, after the
picture was finished. The previews, in October of 1944, augured well. The
initial box office was the best Lang ever had. "Nearly every review of the
picture commented negatively on the ending," wrote Tom Stempel, but that
didn't affect the film's overall success. *Ministry of Fear* also had been released
that fall, and suddenly the onetime leper of Hollywood, who had never had a
big hit, was enjoying an annus mirabilis.

The Woman in the Window was a film in which Lang invested a great deal
of himself. The character of Professor Wanley represents another of his civilized alter egos—the private, Viennese side of Lang. An Old World gentleman,
the professor loves art and literature, after-dinner drinks and cigars. (In the
book he also enjoys popular songs and comic strips. "It would be more agreeable," the character muses, "to read about Superman and his associates than
about Hitler and Chamberlain and Roosevelt.") During the story his wife happens to be conveniently away on summer vacation in Maine, and it may not
be entirely coincidental that Wanley is feeling lonely, undergoing a mid-life
crisis; so was the director. "I hate this solidity, this stodginess I'm beginning
to feel," Wanley says. "To me, it's the end of the brightness of life, the end
of spirit and adventure."

Edward G. Robinson was the closest Lang would come to finding an Amer-

---

*Marjorie Fowler's assistant was Sam Fields, and *his* assistant was Verna Hellman, daughter of
Sam Hellman, who had written Lang's film *The Return of Frank James*. When Verna Hellman
married Sam Fields, she became Verna Fields, and worked one more time for Fritz Lang as the
sound editor for *While the City Sleeps*. After that, she became a full-fledged editor on numerous
Hollywood features, coming into her own in the 1970s with *American Graffiti*, *Paper Moon*, and
Jaws, which brought her an Oscar.

ican Peter Lorre. A subtle actor capable of comedy, tenderness, and sudden bestiality—sometimes all knotted up in the same character—Robinson specialized in the placid Milquetoast pricked by rage, or surprised by romance. He could be a quite humorous performer, but it is true that some of Nunnally Johnson's comedy is squandered in the scenes where three old friends sit around discussing the art of murder. The director preferred to emphasize the long introspective sequences, without dialogue or music—and certainly without any humor—in which the professor is besieged by his conscience.

The film really wasn't Joan Bennett's showcase, but her performance was a striving one, and Lang's camera doted on her even more obviously than before. Two glowing performances, uncommon for the director in Hollywood, gave *The Woman in the Window* a solid core around which the director hung the clever story of manslaughter, blackmail, and guilt.

The reviews for *The Woman in the Window* were wonderful, although many contemporary critics disliked the dream ending and said so. Lang hotly defended it, telling Philip K. Scheuer of the *Los Angeles Times* that the Production Code could not be crossed—and anyway, Bill Goetz had been proved right. The happier ending "made a difference of a million dollars more in receipts," the director declared proudly.

Fritz Lang, with his newly consolidated position, now entered into negotiations to direct one of Hollywood's hottest actresses for the producer who originally had brought him to America.

In November of 1944, David O. Selznick—on a hot streak himself after *Gone With the Wind*—signed Lang to a tentative term deal, calling for the director's services for forty weeks out of the next year, starting with a project called "Dawning" being written by Dore Schary for Ingrid Bergman. Lang worked with Schary for three weeks, when, as with another Selznick project ten years earlier, "Dawning" was summarily called off shortly before Christmas—ostensibly because Bergman had decided in favor of a more immediate loan-out offer.

"Dawning" was placed in abeyance, and Lang's contract with Selznick also went into a gray zone. It was an unusual agreement to begin with, filled with all sorts of clauses designed to exploit the director's talents while heading off his faults. Lang was obliged to make himself available to Selznick for cutting expertise on any of the producer's films, but Selznick himself would oversee the editing of any Fritz Lang picture; if, after an inconclusive preview, Lang wanted to reedit, he could do so to his heart's content, but Selznick would not be obliged to compensate him for his time.

When Bergman dropped out, Lang explained to Charles Higham and Joel Greenberg, "Selznick wanted to pay me out for less than the amount specified in my contract. I protested, but my lawyer—a wonderful guy—urged me to make a generous gesture in the hope of winning Selznick around. 'What kind of a gesture?' I asked. 'Tell Selznick,' he advised, 'that you don't want anything at all.' I told Selznick that, whereupon he just said, 'Thank you very much,' and I didn't get a penny compensation for the entire four weeks I'd worked for him."

What actually happened, according to records in the David O. Selznick

Collection in Austin, Texas, is that the Lang-Selznick arrangement had some stubborn wrinkles that could not be ironed out. For one thing, the director had made "demands for extraordinary credit" (Selznick's words) on the screen as well as in advertising and publicity. Lang balked at pledging his services on any lesser Selznick vehicle, and tried to lobby for a second project on par with the first ("with Ingrid Bergman or someone equivalent," in Lang's words). Assurances from Selznick meant nothing in the absence of mutual trust.

Indeed, Selznick offered Lang a fifteen-thousand-dollar severance, and indeed Lang rejected it, on the grounds that it was "an insult to a person of my standing in the industry." The lawyers moved in to dissolve the contract in the spring of 1945, by which time—months wasted—the director was already deeply involved in formation of an independent production company with Joan Bennett and her husband, producer Walter Wanger.

One must be careful in writing about the relationship between Fritz Lang and Joan Bennett. The actress was married to Walter Wanger from 1940–1965, and maintained, for the public record, that she was never unfaithful to him during their marriage. In fact, during the period when she worked most closely with Lang, Bennett and Wanger had two children—a daughter, born on June 26, 1943, shortly before the filming of *The Woman in the Window*; and another daughter, born on July 4, 1948, shortly before the filming of *Secret Beyond the Door*.

Yet several close friends and associates of Lang's asserted in interviews that the director and his leading lady carried on an intermittent affair right under her husband's nose. "Fritz was in love with Joan Bennett," said Lang's friend, editor Gene Fowler, Jr. "She was married, but that never stopped him. I don't know if Wanger didn't notice or overlooked it. Wanger wasn't one of the brightest people in the world."

Both *Man Hunt* and *The Woman in the Window* took Joan Bennett's persona and eroticized it to a degree rare for the director; and *Scarlet Street*— the first of Fritz Lang's films in formal partnership with the actress and her producer-husband—was the only one of his films to run afoul of the Production Code and other censorship boards.

Actor Edward G. Robinson recalled a time during the filming of *Scarlet Street* when the director spent an hour "rearranging the folds in Joan Bennett's negligée so she would cast a certain shadow he wanted." Editor Marjorie Fowler recalled another day "toward the end [of the production] where Bennett was lying across a bed, and Fritz was fascinated. He had to have a particular take that showed the rise of her breasts. And he was very articulate about it! That was the take we were going to use, and we were going to play the hell out of it. I figured he was in love with Bennett."

Speaking to friends in private later on, during his retirement, Lang was known to aver that it was half-expected of a director in his era to try to go to bed with his films' female stars; but didn't Lang really mean that he half-expected it of himself?

If Lang was cuckolding Walter Wanger, it might seem odd that he steered his way into a business partnership with him. But this director thrived on intrigue and complications. He would have realized the pragmatic benefits of a love affair with Joan Bennett. The actress was able to motivate her husband, and it was definitely she who brokered the creation of Diana Productions, the joint company the three announced together in the spring of 1945.

Lang believed he could dominate Wanger. As he envisioned it, the new arrangement would allow him to capitalize on Wanger's prestige—his entrée to studio hierarchy and departments—without actually having a meddling producer in his hair. Lang thought Wanger merely a businessman; behind his back, he was distrustful, even dismissive of him.

"He thought Walter Wanger was not very smart and a phony liberal," remembered Lang's secretary, Hilda Rolfe. "They didn't love each other. As soon as Walter would walk out of the bungalow [where we worked], he would make some negative remark, and I wouldn't be surprised if it didn't work the other way, too."

Lang had no illusions about Joan Bennett's acting prowess, but she did have audience value. The director had grown genuinely fond of her, and perhaps under his wizardry she would achieve a modicum of greatness. "If it's true [they had a love affair]," said Hilda Rolfe, "then I understand why he used her, because he didn't think she was a good actress. He would make negative cracks about her all the time around the [Diana Productions] office."

The World War II years—a time when Hollywood was depleted, other directors were engaged in military service, and Lang was achieving his rare string of successes—gave the director his only opportunity to become once again the head of his own company.

Universal Pictures would be Diana Productions' sponsor. Wanger had been a staff producer there since 1941; now he was given the chance to head his own semi-independent unit inside the studio. With the combination of Fritz Lang and Joan Bennett—especially on the heels of *Man Hunt* and *The Woman in the Window*—Diana Productions would have greater box-office prospects than any project Wanger could count on coming from Universal itself. "Twelve-and-one-half percent of a Lang picture may well be worth more than fifty percent of a Joe Doakes picture," Wanger's attorneys advised him.

Although the Wangers succeeded in naming the company Diana Productions, in honor of Joan Bennett's eldest daughter (from her first marriage), Lang would do his best, contractually and otherwise, to turn the company into a reborn Fritz Lang-Film-GmbH.*

Protracted negotiations resulted in the following formula of ownership: Joan Bennett retained 316 of a total 1000 shares; Lang took seniority with 506. Sam Jaffe and attorney Martin Gang, who represented Lang's legal interests, were allotted thirty-three shares each. Lily Latté was among a handful of other parties granted fifteen shares each. According to Matthew Bernstein's biography of Walter Wanger, Gang joined with Lang in insisting that Wanger not be allowed to hold any stock, though, "unbeknownst to Lang, it was actually Wanger's money that Bennett invested in the company."

Wanger was less concerned with any strict ownership than with ensuring a

---

*The director's proposed name: New World Pictures.

trusting atmosphere among the partners. Privately the producer conceded that he had decided to give Lang stock seniority because "this was the only way to build the man up so that he wouldn't have this inferiority complex and be so difficult. The idea was that if people once showed confidence in him, he would be very easy to handle."

For the first production under the Diana logo, Lang would be paid a salary of $75,000, with a boost to $100,000 when the company made its second film. Although the producer would receive only $40,000 (and Bennett, $50,000), Wanger would earn twelve and one-half percent of all net profits as a deferred salary bonus and dividend.

The official duties of company officers and each person's formal screen credit required long, continuing debate. Finally, it was agreed that every Diana Production would be introduced by the title card, "Walter Wanger Presents a Fritz Lang Production," offset by the separate card, "Produced and Directed by Fritz Lang."

As president of the company, Lang was empowered to preside over the board meetings, with Wanger designated as "executive vice president." The board meetings consisted only of Lang, Wanger, and Joan Bennett (usually one or the other), Sam Jaffe, Martin Gang, and a secretary. Lang took the procedural rituals very seriously, others less so; again, Wanger didn't mind humoring the director.

By contract, Lang had to agree to consult with Wanger "in connection with problems arising in the course of production," while the director extracted a clause giving him final judgment "with respect to matters of a purely artistic nature." Wanger meanwhile was given supreme decision-making power concerning "all financial aspects of the production, including all matters involving any substantial increase in costs."

At the outset, the wordings seemed judicious, the relationships rosy; everyone was inclined to be optimistic about the future of Diana Productions.

At first, Wanger was happy enough to leave the director alone. *Scarlet Street*—close to a masterpiece—became Lang's single most autonomous production. Even so, it appears that it was the producer, not the director, who had the foresight and wherewithal to pluck from studio files the property on which *Scarlet Street* was based.

The French novel *La Chienne* (literally, *The Bitch*) was the work of Georges de la Fouchardière, a French playwright and novelist who had a second career as a pseudonymous columnist for *Paris-Sport*, *La Liberté*, and *L'Oeuvre*. De la Fouchardière's novel was published as *Poor Sap* by Alfred A. Knopf in the United States in 1930, and Jean Renoir had directed the first film version in France in 1931. Another ex-Berliner, Ernst Lubitsch, had bought the American screen rights some years afterward, but the property had languished in the face of Production Code and other obstacles.

The novel concerns a henpecked bank cashier who dabbles as a painter. On the way home one night, he impulsively rescues a lady of low character getting knocked around by a man in the street. The lady—conspiring with her shady boyfriend—pretends to fall in love with the cashier. The cashier begins to embezzle funds to keep his "mistress" in style in an apartment, where he paints her portrait. The shady boyfriend pilfers some of the cashier's paintings and sells them on the sly; unexpectedly, the Sunday painter's works are discovered and acclaimed by art-world experts. When the cashier finally realizes what is going on—and that his "mistress" is making a fool of him—he murders her. In the end, he escapes punishment by shifting blame onto the boyfriend. But he is condemned to live out his days tortured by guilt.

Dudley Nichols, who had impressed Lang with his diligent script for *Man Hunt*, was the first scriptwriter to be approached by Diana Productions, but Nichols was busy with a writing-directing contract at RKO. He exchanged letters with Lang the first week of March 1945, saying he was sorry to beg off; he hoped they could collaborate on something else in the future. Nichols added a compliment for Lang's latest film, *The Woman in the Window*— though "like any realist I got a jar from the dream business, but of course it was Hays Office, and cleverly done once you had to swallow it . . ."

Lang actually dictated the initial outline of the screenplay to Gordon Kahn, one of those writers who occasionally served as his "ghost," in mid-March of 1945.* In this thirty-three-page outline, Lang sketched the Greenwich Village setting, the background of the characters, and the first couple of scenes which took the cashier through his initial meeting with the streetwalker. The title Lang floated at this stage was "Pomander-Walk."

That Lang identified with the main character is apparent by the background he sketched—far different from the illuminating societal prelude of the type he claimed to have championed for *You Only Live Once*. The director's outline described the character as a man whose youthful ambition to become a painter had been thwarted by his father. "Probably his father had no understanding for such kind of a useless profession, and has curbed his ambitions and has put him into some practical and respectable business," the outline stated. "Probably there the tragedy of the cashier's impeded life started."

In an early scene, the timid bank cashier stops and observes two decorators in a department store looking at "scantily clad mannequins and semi-nude dummies" as he strolls home. Prudish window decorators note his gaze and draw the curtain, insulting him. "The overabundantly imbibed alcohol and the just-mentioned insult get this little bourgeois into the mode where even he wants to start a fight."

At home, the cashier has a snoring wife who humiliates him with household chores; he is forced to indulge his artistic hobby in secret. "I am fooling around," noted Lang in his outline, "with the idea that he has to sit in the toilet on the johnny, having his canvas tacked to the door in front of him." It was important to show the cashier's alienation, Lang added, presaging the violence to come and establishing "a definite mean streak in his character."

In Lang's outline, the shady boyfriend, who acts as a kind of pimp for his

---

*With Lang and Kahn, it was a rare case of mano-a-monocle. A journalist and prolific writer of mostly "B" pictures, the Hungarian-born Kahn was also known as one of the few people in Hollywood who, like Lang, wore a monocle. "Gordon was small in stature," said fellow screenwriter Ring Lardner, Jr., Kahn's friend, who later worked with Lang on *Cloak and Dagger*, "and he liked to say that without the monocle he was just 'that little Jew writer,' but with it he was 'that little Jew writer with a monocle.' "

girlfriend, lives with his father. This character was also a curious creation for a director who aspired to social consciousness. The son of "honest, hard-working people," the boyfriend is nonetheless contemptuous of hard work. He despises his father, and has a fixation for his deceased mother. Crime attracts him, and his big ambition is "to live plush and in velvet."

Lang wanted to suggest that the girlfriend was a prostitute, implying just enough to get the point across while satisfying the Production Code. Having faced the problem before with *Man Hunt*, he knew he had to be elliptical. "We must find some nice business, characterizing the way such a girl lives and what she is doing, indicating laziness, poverty, but always emphasizing the great attractiveness of this young lady."

It was Wanger who had the unorthodox idea of hiring Ludwig Bemelmans to shape the adaptation. Bemelmans, an Austrian-born American who had come to the United States in 1914, was flitting in and out of Hollywood during this time. He was already widely known for his watercolors and drawings for *The New Yorker*, and for his droll writing—especially his classic 'Madeline' series of children's books, which debuted in 1939. Wanger thought the Lang-Bemelmans collaboration would be a publicity windfall, and expected these two famous former Austrians to get along famously. But Lang's checkered experience with Kurt Weill and Bertolt Brecht had reinforced his preference for a more native American résumé.

Bemelmans was hired in late March. After Lang held initial story conferences with the ex-Austrian, he left the Gordon Kahn-penned outline with Bemelmans while he took the Super Chief train to New York to scout Greenwich Village and make drawings of locations and settings. When Lang returned from New York, however, he couldn't locate Bemelmans, and had to spend several days hunting the writer down. The director was in high dudgeon, yet when Lang finally located Bemelmans he "made no reproach to Bemie—was very nice to him—asked him how things were going," in Lang's words.

Bemelmans explained that he had been distracted by recent upheavals in his life. Instead of working on the script, he had written thirty-six pages of personal notes, including "his private adventure with a shell-shocked crazy man he has hired as a butler," according to Lang. Contrite, Bemelmans vowed to work fast and make up for lost time.

For about a month they met every day at Lang's house, but Bemelmans did not enjoy the traditionally servile role of screenwriter; he did not like Lang's ideas, and Lang did not like Bemelmans's, but they seemed to work under the polite understanding that the director was always right.

Abruptly, Bemelmans disappeared again. On April 11, 1945, he sent Lang a telegram: "Dear Fritz, I love you dearly and I hope I will know you all my life. I hope that some day we will have time in plenty to work on a story. In the meantime, I yesterday completely lost my taste for this one. I don't like your method of working. I don't like your advice on the sad fellow [the cashier]. Am not overly fond of sitting in a rat trap and listening to the pronouncements of the pedantic professor that you are."

The wire arrived midmorning on Thursday, April 12. Secretly relieved, Lang immediately contacted Dudley Nichols again, pressing for a Saturday lunch.

Nichols was reluctant to break into his weekend, but now felt he might be able to free himself up for the project and pledged to read the book as soon as possible. The director sent *Poor Sap* over to Nichols, who agreed to get together with Lang for lunch early the next week.

Early next week, however, Bemelmans's agent finally located his client, who admitted to being drunk when he quit. Once again Bemelmans was apologetic, and anxious to resume work.

Lang balked. He told the agent that he had worked with Bemie primarily because of Wanger's faith in him ("Walter has tremendous daring to take on a man like Bemelmans"). But Bemelmans "talked in curlicues and detours," according to the director. The writer ceaselessly complained that he didn't believe in the characters; why, Lang had to escort him down to the Los Angeles police station one night, securing "some police records which I showed Bemie of pimps and prostitutes," in order to convince him that such lowlife actually existed.

According to a transcript of their conversation, Lang told the agent: "The evening before I left [for New York] he called me up, drunk as a fish, saying 'I am sorry you are going away. Walter Wanger is a jerk . . .' I said, 'Walter loves you. He has respect for you. I have not read anything you have written, but I know your reputation as a very interesting man and out of respect to Walter I talked to you to see if you wanted to do the job or not.' Bemie replied, 'I have no need to work. I am a rich man.' "

Agent: "When he says, 'I am a very rich man,' you must remember he is essentially a Bohemian man. (If Bemie has ten thousand dollars he thinks he is a rich man.)"

Lang: "Let me tell you something: He submitted certain titles which he had just taken out of other plays and which could never be used. We were sitting here before I left discussing titles and wrote out certain streets of Greenwich Village and one of the names was Carmine Street—a real street in Greenwich. Someone said 'Scarlet Street.' Bemie did not like it and told Walter he thought it was rotten. Everyone likes the name—Walter tried it out on several people—they all like it. That night Walter met Bemie at Romanoff's when Bemie said he still didn't like it and thought the title 'Playboy' better. But 'Playboy' doesn't mean anything. When Walter told me this it worried me. Walter said, 'I think Bemie is fine when you are here.' But . . . if I have to direct and produce I cannot be a maid for a writer. I shall be worn out—without attempting to write also."

Nevertheless, the agent insisted that Bemelmans wanted to stay on the job. Indeed, Bemelmans declared himself ready to move into the spare bedroom in Lang's own house to finish the script. And when the director arrived home on Tuesday evening after lunching with Dudley Nichols, he found an apologetic offering—an original *New Yorker* cover signed by Bemelmans.

Lang felt stuck in an awkward position: Over lunch and a handshake, he had already effectively hired Dudley Nichols. It was left to Wanger to wade in and settle things all around. Nichols would eventually be paid $50,000 to write the film, along with nominal shares and standing as a board member of Diana Productions. As for Bemelmans, he was given a severance fee. From his one-month stint on the script, only one thing was salvaged: a title Bemelmans neither suggested nor liked. The adaptation of *La Chienne, or Poor Sap*, would be called *Scarlet Street*.

Dudley Nichols was a fast worker—so fast that the final script would be ready for shooting within two months, leaving the director free to concentrate his focus on all the other aspects of production: casting, camera and lighting, sets and costumes.

Bemelmans's pages were worthless, and Lang's thirty-three-page outline merely provided a background for the opening sequences. As Nichols went to work, he kept some of Lang's ideas while jettisoning others. He returned to the well-constructed de la Fouchardière novel, which zeroed in on the three main characters, represented with different points of view in alternating chapters ("He," "She," and "The Other"). The through-line for Nichols's scenario would follow the novel almost scene by scene. The close adaptation was "really one hundred percent Dudley Nichols's creation," Lang told Charles Higham and Joel Greenberg.

The cashier's unsympathetic-father background was dropped; so was his "mean streak," which clashed with Nichols's humanism—making the cashier more of a Milquetoast and less of a Liliom. The mistress's profession would remain intriguingly obscure; she tells the cashier she's an actress. (Her roommate is a girdle model.) The pimp would have no credible working-class background and would become a shiftless type the audience could easily hiss.

The script's nickname for Joan Bennett's character capitalized on the director's attraction to well-turned heels. Probably it was Lang who suggested it. "Lazy Legs" stuck with fans of the film, also becoming shorthand for the actress who played the part.

Lang had seen Renoir's version of the de la Fouchardière novel at the time of its release, but claimed in later interviews that he purposely never rewatched the earlier film. Production records show that the director and his dutiful screenwriter tried hard to locate a print of *La Chienne*, without clarifying, however, whether they were successful.

Nichols didn't mind Lang's penchant for endless discussion, but he was independent-minded and knew his craft. When he disagreed with the director, the arguments became heated. Lang thought it was all fun, part of the process. For Nichols, who had missed out on that friction on *Man Hunt*, it wasn't as enjoyable.

One thing the director could add unstintingly to Nichols's finished script was the unmistakable Fritz Lang "tone." Renoir's version also had followed the original de la Fouchardière novel rather closely, but *La Chienne* had a savagely ironic and Gallic sensibility that would be replaced in *Scarlet Street* by Lang's somber fatalism.

Milton Krasner would serve again as Lang's cameraman. The art director, Alexander Golitzen, came from Universal (where, many years later, he would become art director of *Play Misty for Me* and *Breezy*, two of the first films directed by Clint Eastwood). The editor was Arthur Hilton, who would become friendly with Lang and a regular drop-in visitor at his house over the years. With Edward G. Robinson, Joan Bennett, and Dan Duryea returning from their stint on *The Woman in the Window*, it was almost another Ufa-style team.

The bank cashier's paintings were a crucial part of the story. They were produced by John Decker, a versatile artist who made a sideline of Hollywood sittings—including a famous rendering of W. C. Fields as Queen Victoria and a widely reproduced portrait of John Barrymore. Decker was a rogue who seemed to be everyone's friend, including Lang's; his studio on Bundy Drive was a bohemian hangout for actors and artists—"an artist's Alamo," in the words of Gene Fowler, Sr. Decker's work for *Scarlet Street*, personally overseen by the director, amounted to a curious Chinese-puzzle situation: a would-be painter instructing a paid, real-life professional in the creation of amateurish paintings—all for a fiction about another would-be painter.

All along the lead role of the bank cashier had been earmarked for Edward G. Robinson, forging a link with *The Woman in the Window*. The director's original outline mentioned Robinson by name; the script gave the character the punning name of Chris Cross. Robinson had proved unflappable on his first Fritz Lang production, and his hundred-thousand-dollar salary, exceeding Lang's, ensured he would once again be treated decently.

Joan Bennett would play the sex kitten, appropriately named Kitty. The actress was by now thoroughly under the director's spell. The director and his third lead, Dan Duryea—playing Johnny, the pimp-boyfriend—had a companiable relationship; on the set they held long discussions on what it meant for an actor to base his career on playing "the incarnation of evil." "The audience always remembers the villain," Lang assured Duryea.

All the technical contributions were outstanding. The sets owed a large debt to the director's imagination. The office complex, the cashier's flat, the Greenwich Village apartment—these were outfitted with all the clutter and trimmings of Fritz Lang's aesthetic. All the exteriors were of course soundstage recreations; it was not only easier and less expensive but, as usual, Lang, the celebrated realist, preferred an indoor shoot. The Greenwich Village of *Scarlet Street* would prove all the more effective for seeming eerily artificial and claustrophobic.

Walter Wanger rarely appeared on the set. Under nobody's supervision except his own, Lang worked for fifty-six days, from July 23 through to October 8, 1945, as the budget crept up to $1,228,770. Although he went five days over schedule and $200,000 over projected costs, according to Matthew Bernstein, "neither Universal nor Wanger tried to restrain him." When Wanger was informed of the overruns and schedule delays, the producer behaved with decided graciousness, forwarding to Lang a copy of the complaining studio memo, with this attached note: "Here is [the] key as to how to make quarter of a million dollars. Put this under your pillow."

According to Universal's contract with Diana Productions, however, the director was obligated to complete postproduction within sixty days after principal photography had shuttered; the studio then had the right to "recut and reedit said photoplay" to meet any legal, censorship, or commercial requirements. Wanger's responsibilities kicked in during postproduction, and when editing proceeded more slowly than expected, inevitably the producer came into conflict with Lang.

The length of the film was a concern, but the director hated to lose bits and pieces of scenes. One key vignette he ended up deleting wholesale: Chris, atop a telegraph pole, watching the voltage drop at the time of execution and crying out exultantly at the moment of Johnny's death. The director agonized over this scene, which was filmed but eventually eliminated, according to Lotte Eisner's book, because Lang himself "rightly felt that this might have an un-intentional comic effect on the audience."

Even the musical score piqued the director's interest more than usual. Universal suggested Hans Salter from the studio's roster, on the presumption that another native Viennese would click with Lang. Salter had worked for Ufa in Berlin in former years; in fact, he had conducted the original score for *Frau im Mond* at afternoon and evening performances at the Ufa-Palast am Zoo. Perhaps for such sentimental reasons the director did work closely and smoothly with his fellow Ufa alumnus.

Literal-minded about music, Lang envisioned a score composed chiefly of sounds emanating from real-life sources: radios humming in the background, songs blaring from phonographs. Salter liked the idea, which recurs in several of the director's films, and tried to accommodate Lang. Only upon hearing the end theme did Lang raise any objections. "He said, 'The idea of my film is that crime does not pay, and your end title is too hopeful. I want it more downbeat,'" recalled Salter. "So we discussed this for a while and then I gave in and said, 'Okay, I'll write a new end title,' which was really downbeat. That stayed in the film. It was one of my best scores all around."

At every stage, the director invested himself emotionally in *Scarlet Street*. That is one reason why he ended up taking too much time with editing and postproduction. But in Hollywood, too, Lang often hedged his bets, running out of finishing time (and money) on one film, while hurrying off to launch into preproduction work on another.

It was vital, for financial reasons, to finish and release *Scarlet Street*. But after six months Lang's salary had run out, and such was his own professional insecurity that almost immediately he turned his gaze to another opportunity. In November, he quietly entered discussions with producer Milton Sperling, and signed for a directing job at Warner Brothers. The fact that Lang left Universal to go to another studio—before the final editing was completed on his first Diana Production—infuriated Wanger, and may have encouraged the producer to tamper with the final form of *Scarlet Street*.

Aided by Arthur Hilton, Wanger himself delivered the "final cut." According to Matthew Bernstein, who made a comparison of the shooting script with the released version, there were significant elisions that eliminated "redundancies and character motivation cues from the story," wrote Bernstein. "They also diminish the extremity of Chris's idealism, his humiliating infatuation with Kitty, and his degradation at the conclusion of the film." One expunged scene had Chris finding a copy of *Romeo and Juliet* that Johnny has bought Kitty as a prop for her charade as a struggling actress, and reading from the balcony scene as Kitty rolls her eyes in exasperation.

Universal executives were pleased at the first studio screening. But Lang's disappointment at what he saw quickly escalated into accusations that Wanger had stabbed him in the back with changes that diverged from the director's punctilious guidelines. Wanger consented to reinstate some footage, but not all. It seemed to Wanger that the director blew the tiniest cuts out of proportion. The fight "just took up the goddamnedest amount of time and became the most annoying thing," the producer said later.

Surprisingly, the Production Code office approved *Scarlet Street*—with its unsavory characters—with only a minimum of recommendations. Partly through the combined prestige of Walter Wanger and Dudley Nichols, the film eluded standard Hollywood censorship. But censorship could happen at any time or in any place before a motion picture's release, and *Scarlet Street* encountered its most extreme reaction when the film was finally completed and ready to ship to theaters nationwide.

The Legion of Decency announced its classification: The film would slip by with a "B" rating, "objectionable in part"—an acceptable box-office category but nonetheless a black mark. The Legion listed numerous complaints: close-ups showing Kitty in a slip and negligee; the number of bedroom scenes, including one where Kitty undresses and has her toenails painted by Chris; dialogue that implied that Kitty liked men to beat her up; and the scene where Chris stabs Kitty.

Taking their cue from the Legion of Decency ruling, New York censors manufactured similar complaints. The New York State Board of Censors, which operated the State Education Department, rejected the film "in toto." This unusually drastic action was especially threatening because it gave a clear signal to numerous state and local censor boards. Indeed, Atlanta and Milwaukee, two metropolises with considerable box-office muscle, quickly followed suit, banning *Scarlet Street* from theaters.

Lang was by now deeply involved with his next production, and willing to leave the fight to Walter Wanger, urging the producer to contest the censorship all the way up to the Supreme Court if need be. Since they both were already known as "stinking liberals," Lang informed Wanger, it was time they earned their liberalism "without the stinking."

In a letter to Wanger, Dudley Nichols sheepishly noted that some of the requested eliminations were lines he himself had intended to omit; in their haste, secretaries piecing the final script together must have folded in earlier, unedited drafts. Funny that nobody noticed the transgressions. Or could it have been that the director himself had reinserted left-out scenes? "This is in no sense an alibi," wrote Nichols, "for I believe the censors are all wrong and should be vigorously opposed, but I only point out that in my own judgment they should not have been included in the shooting script. The script itself was always walking a tightwire and needed careful scrutiny."

In his letter the writer succinctly stated the moralistic theme of *Scarlet Street*: "It asserts that there are higher moral laws which cannot be violated by any man. It says even if you fool the police you are caught by the judgment of your own conscience, that no one can escape it, and that it is far less terrifying to be punished by police courts and the executioner. It says the real judge, jury, and executioner lie hidden within ourselves.'*

---

*Lang told Charles Higham and Joel Greenberg that he personally debated the morality of *Scarlet*

"Films have remained adolescent for so long because Hollywood has not fought for freedom of the screen as publishers have fought," Nichols argued eloquently. "You don't have to have freedom of the screen to make profits—that is why suppression is so dangerous. But you have to have freedom and moral responsibility if you are to have self-respect and respect for the screen among all intelligent men everywhere."

While cooperating with censorship guidelines *inside* the industry, Hollywood usually united against after-the-fact tampering by outside condemners. It was one thing to tidy up the offensive portions of a scenario before production launched into photography quite another to limit audience numbers in the marketplace. Wanger swung into action, while Universal mobilized support from politicians and the other motion-picture studios.

With editor Arthur Hilton, Wanger flew to New York on January 22, 1946, armed with *Scarlet Street*'s favorable reviews and clippings. He met on January 23 with Dr. Irwin Conroe, acting head of the state censor board. "The negotiations that ensued between Wanger and Conroe were remarkable," wrote Matthew Bernstein. "As Conroe suggested nominal cuts which would make the film acceptable, Wanger conferred with Hilton, who advised Wanger of the cuts' potential effects on story and visual continuity, and whether alternate shot angles of a scene were available.

"Hilton and Wanger finally agreed to cut one line of dialogue—'Where's the bedroom?', Johnny's first question when he and Kitty inspect a new apartment—and the repeated stabbings of Kitty by Chris Cross (instead of seven, there remained only one)." (As Lang would muse in a later interview with a Pittsburgh journalist, "Is it immoral to stab a woman four times—moral to stab her only once?")

Conroe was induced to make a public statement saying that the artistry of the film had been misunderstood, *Scarlet Street* was given New York's stamp of approval, and Lang's film had its Manhattan premiere on February 20, 1946, in Loew's Criterion theater near Times Square.

Wanger also flew to Atlanta. After much brouhaha, the local morality board reconvened, saw the film en masse and deadlocked on a decision. Universal appealed, and a local judge reversed the initial ban on a technicality. *Scarlet Street* could be shown. The city of Atlanta continued to appeal, all the way up to the State Supreme Court, finally winning its case on a procedural flaw—by which time the film had only one unfulfilled booking in the vicinity. Other American cities fell in line.

Real censure would have had negative box-office implications, but the newsworthy controversy and subsequent victory over public guardians made for a press agent's dream. Critics devoted more than usual space to *Scarlet Street*, their disapproval of prior censorship augmenting their enthusiasm for

Street with Production Code official Joseph Breen, using his Catholicism as a wedge in the argument. "Look," the director told Breen (according to Lang), "we're both Catholics. By being permitted to live, the Robinson character in *Scarlet Street* goes through hell. That's a much greater punishment than being imprisoned for homicide. After all, it was not a premeditated murder, it was a crime of passion. What if he does spend the rest of his life in jail—so what? The greater punishment is surely to have him go legally free, his soul burdened by the knowledge of his deed, his mind constantly echoing with the words of the woman he loved proclaiming her love for the man he'd wrongly send to death in his place . . ."

the picture; across the nation audiences flocked to the much-discussed film, making the first undertaking of Diana Productions profitable.

"I cannot really say why," Lang told Gene D. Phillips shortly before his death. "Somehow a certain film just seems to click, have all the right touches, and turn out the way I hoped that it would. This is difficult when there are obstacles to one's creative freedom."

Lang never wavered in his regard for *Scarlet Street,* one of his favorite films, and one of the few that had turned out almost exactly the way he had hoped.

The film touched any number of chords that marked it as a product of the Fritz Lang psyche. Typical was its mix of contempt and pity, for the hopelessly married bourgeois overshadowed by a smug monster of a wife (played to the hilt by Rosalind Ivan). The smug wife likes to listen to "The Happy Household Hour" on the radio; but the household is anything but happy, and her first husband, a cop whose portrait hangs above the fireplace, despised her so much that he faked his own death.

The Chris Cross character happens to have the same occupation as a brother the director barely acknowledged. All of Chris's joys are furtive: not only does he paint behind closed doors, but like Lang he derives furtive pleasure from gory items in the newspaper. Under such oppressive conditions, who could blame a fellow for taking on a mistress? Chris's sympathetic boss has one, the audience learns. Why not one for him; or you, or me?

But extracurricular sex can lead to entanglements. Kitty, the woman Chris meets by accident, is a hellcat, no less the bitch of the title they couldn't use. She knows her power over men like Chris, and comes on like a strong perfume or a slug of booze. All the same it is strange that she is such a purring fool for Johnny.

"You're never appreciated in your own country," she tells Chris, praising his painting. Behind his back, she scorns him; it would be better, Kitty complains to Johnny, if he was "mean or vicious or if he'd bawl me out or something, I'd like him better." Part of her attraction to Johnny is that he is willing to slap her around. Few other directors of the era would have conceived of, much less gotten away with, this Langian equation of violence with desire. It is taken one step further in the scene where Johnny makes it clear that Kitty should sleep with Chris—or even an art critic, if necessary—to keep the two of them in clover.

It had taken Fritz Lang a while to find his stride with personal subjects; whereas in Germany he had been the epic ringmaster, working in a language of exaggerated flourishes, in Hollywood he was obliged to adjust his vision gradually. *Fury* is practically German in its scope and ambition. *The Woman in the Window* was his first chamberwork. But the first to show a mastery of the delicate scale, of the human canvas, was *Scarlet Street.*

The director's mesmeric dark atmosphere and camerawork are still dazzling half a century later. Almost every shot ends tightly. In one scene, the camera glides through a room and out a window, hovering overhead, before swooping down from high branches into a picturesque courtyard, showing Chris and Kitty as they share a cup of coffee. There is never any hint of life outside the frame. There are only He, She, and the Other, and their lives in microcosm.

The end of the story was, as usual, all-important to Lang. Chris is found out—ironically, for embezzlement. The benevolent boss forgives him, but meanwhile Johnny goes on trial for Kitty's murder. The court scenes are handled quickly for a change, with Chris a voyeuristic spectator on the sidelines. Though Johnny protests his innocence, he is condemned to the electric chair. And the bank cashier exults.

In private, Lang took the Catholic point of view that the electric chair was a barbarism of the state. In the film it is the tool of a brutal justice: The no-good Johnny is executed for a crime he didn't commit. In a train scene, a reporter coming back from the event leans over and strikes up a conversation with Chris. He tells him that, no matter the truth of the case, everybody possesses their own internal judge, jury, and courtroom. "The problem just moves in here," the reporter says, referring to his conscience, "where it never gets out."

This is how Dudley Nichols—Lang himself—perceived *Scarlet Street*. It was a story about the punishment of guilt, not ill-fated love. "I read somewhere that the Hays Office had been created by a Jesuit," he told Peter Bogdanovich. "And Hays himself was a Catholic.* I had not the slightest difficulty with this picture—because Robinson *was* punished—a great punishment."

For Lang's unlucky cashier, time never forgets. Chris goes steadily downhill after Johnny's execution; he tries to commit suicide by hanging himself, botches the job, loses his home, wanders the Bowery. At the end of the film a cop prods him off a park bench, and as the onetime bank cashier drifts down a street, he spies one of his paintings—a transcendent reminder of Kitty—as it is carted off after purchase.

The camera rises for one of the director's eagle-eye views of humanity. The whispering voices in Chris's ears build to a cacophony, the people around him evanesce, and the scot-free killer shuffles on down the street, head bowed, in pathetic, unrelieved misery.

The only thing that stopped the film from being truly great was the director's coldness. Renoir's compassion had turned *La Chienne* into a social tragedy. Ultimately Lang's attitude was a superior one, and his introspective jewel of a film pitiless and unforgiving.

Victory over Germany had come on May 8, 1945, as *Scarlet Street* was in preparation, and V-J day arrived during its filming on August 14. The Axis was defeated. World War II was over, but the director was one of millions who harbored no forgiveness for the Nazis.

"I thought that on V-E Day I would feel very happy," Lang told Maxine Garrison for her *Pittsburgh Press* column in early June 1945. "But when it came, I could not rejoice. For Roosevelt, who should have lived, was dead, and V-E was an incident, not an ending. And now we are knowing what must come. I tried—I tried so hard to convince people. 'You must kill five million Germans,' I told them. But they said, 'You have been too close to it, Fritz, you are bitter.' Now they see Buchenwald in the newsreels, and they know."

The remark about killing five million Germans was not idle rhetoric. Al-

---

*Actually, Lang is in error—Hays was an elder of the Presbyterian Church.

though he may have balked against electrocuting criminals, he was of a mind to obliterate the fatherland. Colleagues remembered that Lang, although personally against the atom bomb, more than once remarked that it should have been dropped on Germany instead of Japan. "He used to say to me the only way you ever change the German character is to drop a bomb on the whole country and decimate it," his secretary Hilda Rolfe remembered. "That was always a terrible thing to hear, but [at the time] I believed he was right."

On the home front Lang was one of the most vehement of the ex-Germans. "As a matter of fact, he was not at all homesick for Germany," said Gene Fowler, Jr. "He hated the Germans. He was very much against Germany. He was sorry he even had to speak German."

When in late 1944 director Fred Zinnemann made *The Seventh Cross*, about concentration camp escapees aided by German resistance fighters, Lang spoke out against the film to the press, saying that it was too soon to celebrate any good in the German character. While others made plans to return to Germany to help the U.S. military rebuild the film industry—Erich Pommer, among them, working on behalf of the U.S. government in the occupied zone—Lang swore that he would never go back, whatever the circumstances.

When people asked him, as they often did, if he pined for Germany, Lang's reply was simple. "I miss walking down the street and being called Meister."

One day after the war a man came to his offices on the Universal lot and spoke with Lang about the new Germany and inviting him over to help to make new films there. Lang had been led to believe that the man was a progressive, but when the man suggested that the future of Germany would rest with the indoctrinated Hitler Youth, Lang exploded. People nearby remember hearing the conversation, which had begun politely in English, switch abruptly to German. Voices rose, ending with Lang shouting, "Raus! Raus [Get out]!"

Indicative of the ambivalence with which he viewed Germany—and the extent to which he had embraced Hollywood—was the reception he accorded Paul Kuttner. Kuttner was the son of Dr. Paul Kuttner, Sr., Ufa's medical doctor-in-residence, who had treated the director for minor ailments in old times, and whom Lang recalled warmly. Kuttner, Jr., who had spent his teenage years in Great Britain, came to America and visited Hollywood for the first time after the war.

Kuttner was hoping Lang might help him find some employment in Hollywood. Lang invited him to lunch in the Universal cafeteria, and they shared a table next to actor Fredric March, who was eating with two friends. While Lang and Kuttner were reminiscing about the German film industry of old, Kuttner couldn't help but observe March, noticing at one point that the actor had extinguished his cigarette in his mashed potatoes.

"Having recently arrived from a poverty-stricken post-war Great Britain," recalled Kuttner, "I was incensed by this wasteful disregard of food and I got up and berated (rather childishly) Mr. March about 'the crime of destroying good food while millions of people were starving to death.'

"Mr. March stared at me as though seeing a ghost and his two companions gaped at me openmouthed, then at him [Lang]. Probably no mortal of my low stature had ever addressed a world-famous star in public in such a scathing fashion and no response for this outburst had ever been contemplated or written.

"It was Fritz Lang who came to everybody's rescue. He first apologized to Fredric March for this uncalled-for behavior on my part, then explained that I had just arrived from Europe, which was impoverished at the time, and that he hoped Mr. March would understand the short-tempered outburst of a young man. He had broken the ice. Mr. March got up and shook my hand, saying he'd try to remember not to extinguish cigarettes in his food in the future, and Mr. Lang and I left the studio restaurant."

As with a Fritz Lang film, the anecdote ends with a tone-changing coda. "Back in his office, Mr. Lang's magnanimous behavior changed drastically," recalled Kuttner. "He dressed me down, with good reason, for embarrassing him in front of one of Hollywood's greatest stars and added that my father would have given me a good thrashing if he had still been around. (He was killed in the Theresienstadt concentration camp in 1943.) Then Fritz Lang settled back, opened a box of Whitman chocolates, took out a piece for himself, chewed it pensively, closed the box and gave it to me."

The director swiftly ushered Kuttner to the door and advised him to move to New York City, since there really was no Hollywood opening for him in the foreseeable future.

At the same time, the end of the war did mean the opening up of long-sealed channels. Lang was interested in the issue of restitution—hoping to recoup some of his lost income and wealth from Germany's new government. So was Lily Latté, who might, however wishfully, have been anticipating a chance to get out from under Lang's hammerlock.

Although the director himself did not care to go to Germany, he also had an interest in the issue of foreign copyrights. To others heading overseas he gave letters to be delivered to Thea von Harbou, inquiring about the legal rights to their works. One film that especially interested him was *Die Frau im Mond.* For the first time, in a spate of arranged interviews, the director spoke to U.S. journalists about remaking his silent classic, updating it for Hollywood.

In interviews Lang waxed exuberant about the farsightedness of the film's rocket ship and other technical inventions, which "were so accurate that in 1937 the Gestapo confiscated not only all the models of the spaceship but also all foreign prints of the picture." Lang contended that Hermann Oberth, one of those who became an "ardent Nazi"—like his wife—set these confiscations in motion when he went to work for the Third Reich on rocket research and development.

"First thing he [Oberth] did was to confiscate all our movie plans and models and then he called in from world release every print of our film, apparently in the belief that it might contain some workable information. I don't think it did, and I hope it didn't, but the fact remains that nowhere in the world today can be located a copy of *The Girl in the Moon,*" Lang told a Hollywood columnist in widely published remarks in 1944.*

---

*There was no indication how Lang knew this. Lotte Eisner repeated this tidbit in her authorized book about Lang's career. What interested the Nazis, principally, about *Die Frau im Mond* was

In lieu of a remake of *Die Frau im Mond*, there were other projects from the past that might be revisited. In private with his associates, Lang mused about seeing Austria again. He revived talk of the "Last Fiaker" film, or one that would be set in Vienna's Prater fairgrounds.

It was a side benefit of the war's conclusion that old acquaintances from the pre-war era felt comfortable getting back in touch. Lotte Eisner—Jewish, anti-Nazi, a political refugee—had had a rough time of it in France during the war. She was briefly interned, lived under a false name, dodged Nazis from town to town while working for the Cinémathèque Française. Now Eisner wrote Lang from Paris, renewing their acquaintance and opening up a correspondence. Berlin journalist Paul Erich Marcus and Julius Singer, both living in London now, were two other past friends who reestablished contact.

After several years without communication, Lang's brother Dolf wrote from Vienna, somewhat pathetically asking for financial assistance. Because he had been categorized as part-Jewish by the Nazis, according to Friedrich Steinbach, Dolf had lost what little resources he had before the war. His brother the Hollywood director wrote back, lamely, that he hadn't much to offer. To Lily Latté was delegated the task of sending Dolf and his wife occasional, rudimentary, care packages of food and household goods.

The various emissaries to Thea von Harbou never fulfilled their mission. Lang would never see nor speak to his ex-wife again. No letters were delivered, none exchanged.

All famous people who had joined the NSDAP were suspect in Germany after the war, and Thea von Harbou was detained in Staumühle, a prison camp run by the British, from July 10 through October 10, 1945.* Von Harbou's relatives insist that she was held so long in part because she had written a novel championing pro-India independence and thereby had offended British authorities.

A nationalist she was, however, and the Allied interrogation papers itemize her admitted memberships and activities during the Nazi era. In her own defense von Harbou insisted that she had only joined the Nazi Party in 1941 in order to assist Indians in Germany and Indian prisoners of war, that she never worked "explicitly" for the Party and "despite repeated warnings, never attended Party meetings." Her direct work on behalf of the government consisted, she claimed, entirely of volunteer welding, making hearing aids, and emergency medical care. In fact, she received a medal of merit for saving people in two air raids.**

---

the experimental rocket that Ufa had contracted for publicity purposes (in which Lang had invested and would have been owed money, on profits). It was "the first combustion chamber for a liquid-fueled rocket," according to Rainer Eisfeld in "Technische Vision and psychologisches Zeitbild," his essay accompanying the most recent German edition of Thea von Harbou's *Frau im Mond* novel (Munich: Heyne, 1989). Yet Oberth's 1929 model was one—hardly the only, or most advanced—prototype for further rocket developments.

*By comparison, Leni Riefenstahl was held for only a few weeks, though she later underwent extensive post-war scrutiny by the Allies.

**The NSDAP enjoined its members to perform "Boy-Scout type good deeds to endear the Party to the people," according to Richard Grunberger, in his A *Social History of the Third Reich*.

Whether von Harbou or her interrogators jotted down the comment in her detention papers that she was divorced from "the Jewish director Fritz Lang" is uncertain, but otherwise her former husband did not come up in the questioning. Von Harbou denied any anti-Semitism, denied involvement in any Aryanization of Jewish property, noting instead several instances where she had acted as a good Samaritan—helping people out of Germany or out of trouble with Goebbels (including her Jewish secretary Hilde Guttmann* and actor Alfred Abel, who had played the master of *Metropolis*). "Although I am unwilling to mention things that I once found a matter of course," von Harbou told the interrogators, "I don't think there is anyone who can claim that I hurt or insulted them because of their race."

It is sadly true, however, that she prospered during the Nazi reign. Von Harbou worked with dedicated Nazi filmmakers such as Gustav Ucicky and Veidt Harlan, the latter the director of the infamous *Jud Süss* (1940)—a film described by historian Richard Grunberger as "the cinematic curtain-raiser for the Final Solution." She seemed at the beck and call of that Staatsrat, or "Artist of the State," actor Emil Jannings, one of the most prominent Nazi enthusiasts, and a friend from the time of her salad days in the theater. Von Harbou acted as a "script doctor" or consultant on several Jannings vehicles. And she wrote the script for at least one film (1943's *Die Gattin*) starring one of Goebbels's actress-girlfriends, Jenny Jugo.

Her annual income, which she listed for the American questionnaire, ranged near 120,000 Reichsmarks a year, or close to the tremendous sum of $50,000. The spring of 1940, when she admitted to joining the party, was actually a propitious time to become a Nazi: Things were going well in the war, and it might not have seemed like any kind of risk.

Significantly, even in the formal statement she made in her own defense, von Harbou didn't distance herself from the Nazi ideology, nor express any repentance for Third Reich wrongdoing. This was something that always bothered even some of her close relatives. Her nephew, Vinayak Tendulkar, lived with her as a boy for almost two years after the war. "She never criticized in any way," said Tendulkar, "never mentioned any dislike of the Nazis. She must have known, because she was moving in Germany's high society, of the inhuman rule of the Nazis—the treatment of Jews and others."

Von Harbou's indomitable, upbeat personality did not change. In prison she directed a version of *Faust*. Once released, the scenarist of *Der müde Tod, Die Nibelungen, Metropolis,* and *M* toiled as one of the *Trümmerfrauen*, or "rubble women," for a solid year, from October 1945 to October 1946. To earn her food rations and coupons, she stooped among the rubble, separating the good bricks from bad, helping to rebuild Germany.

People in Hollywood remembered Lang cackling when he learned von Harbou had been reduced to collecting bricks from Berlin rubble. Yet her interrogation papers point out that, at age fifty-seven, she would have been exempt from this back-breaking work: Von Harbou had volunteered. Moreover, she

*Hilde Guttmann, in fact, became a prime mover in the "Kindertransport" movement in England, helping to ferry Europe's condemned Jewish children to a new life there. Later in life, in speeches and interviews, Guttmann stayed loyal to von Harbou, whom she considered a Nazi—but not an anti-Semite.

would have worked at this task even longer if inflamed tendons hadn't forced her to stop. Upon quitting she received a commendation from a construction company in Charlottenburg as "a very hard worker, even at the hardest jobs," an exemplary German who had never missed a day.

She began to write again, living frugally and, at first, anonymously. "I can still see how she came to my more-or-less ruined apartment one day," said her cousin Dr. Anne-Marie Durand-Wever, "dressed in a faded summer dress and a scarf wrapped around her head. She was carrying a backpack with wood in it she had been collecting. She said this work was some adventure for her and really satisfied her and since she didn't have a contract with a publisher, she finally could write her own way."

Soon she was able to find a job dubbing U.S. films for audiences in Germany. There is nothing to say that she didn't dub one of Fritz Lang's—or repatriate one of her own, for German films once banned by the Nazis were gradually becoming available once again. Nor can it be guessed what went through her mind as she performed this lowly job, light-years removed from the luster of yesteryear.

While Walter Wanger was fighting the good fight over censorship of *Scarlet Street*, Fritz Lang was at work on his next project: a film for Warner Brothers about the Office of Strategic Services (OSS). One might generously read into the director's involvement with *Cloak and Dagger* a desire to see at least one more war-related picture through to a satisfying result—a final nail in the fascist coffin, as it were. But in truth the jobs were drying up as Hollywood personnel flooded back from wartime service, and a nervous Lang saw no immediate prospects on the horizon. "Fritz took *Cloak and Dagger* because nothing else was available," said Andries Dienum, an assistant to Lang on the production who also became the director's confidant.

After the end of hostilities, there was a stampede in Hollywood to make the first feature about the exploits of the U.S. department of foreign espionage and propaganda that had performed undercover during World War II. Eventually more than one project would exploit the OSS mystique—including Paramount's *O.S.S.*, starring Alan Ladd.

Cloak and Dagger was based on a book by Corey Ford and Alastair MacBain, "the inside story of General Bill Donovan's famous O.S.S.," whose screen rights had been snapped up by Milton Sperling, a journeyman screenwriter returning from Marine Corps duty as a documentarist in the Pacific. Sperling—like Seton I. Miller and Nunnally Johnson before him in Lang's career—was branching out as an independent producer. His United States Pictures was naturally going to be affiliated with Warner Brothers, for Sperling had the advantage of being married to Harry Warner's daughter Betty.

Sperling was a New York go-getter who had started out as a messenger boy and shipping clerk at Paramount's Astoria Studios in Long Island before coming to Hollywood in the early sound era. Initially a secretary for Darryl Zanuck, he had turned to screenwriting and amassed a number of solid credits. After the war, Sperling would produce films as often as he wrote them, eventually garnering an Academy Award nomination for his script of *The Court-Martial of Billy Mitchell* in 1955.

But Sperling would eschew script chores on his first independent foray. Two sets of writers—first Ben Maddow and John Gates, followed by Boris Ingster and John Larkin—had labored on the OSS scenario for several months before Lang was hired in November. From the beginning, it was clear the project desperately needed more of a plot. "Sperling had bought a title," explained the film's technical adviser, Michael Burke. "The book had no beginning, middle, and end. Rather, it consisted of a series of vignettes."

Lang's reputation for substantial war movies preceded him; he was also known to get along pleasantly with writers. Although the director was an unknown quantity at Warner Brothers, that amounted to a plus, considering how he had burned bridges at other studios.

By the time screenwriter Ring Lardner, Jr., the son of humorist Ring Lardner and an Oscar winner for *Woman of the Year*, joined the enterprise sometime in early December, Sperling had already set a date for start of principal photography. Still there was no approved script, but Warner Brothers was determined to be first out of the gate with an OSS picture. And the producer had little choice but to honor a tight scheduling commitment from one of Hollywood's top box-office names—Gary Cooper, who had agreed to play the film's scientist-hero, Professor Alvah Jasper.

Lang had just been put in charge when Lardner came aboard. Lardner's mission was to accomplish, at improbable speed, a marriage of earlier, unsatisfactory drafts. The screenwriter recalled a series of agreeable meetings with Lang, mostly at the director's house, in which the two hashed over the revisions. "I liked him," said Lardner. "He said funny things, mostly of a dry wit and mostly detrimental about other people. He was a helluva good talker."

The screenwriter also met with Gary Cooper, who informed him of one of the script prerequisites. "Look," the star told Lardner, "I want you to understand one thing. I'm supposed to be playing an atomic physicist in this picture, and the only way I can get away with playing an atomic physicist is if you keep the lines very simple, because I can't be convincing as an atomic physicist if I try to say anything complicated."

Gary Cooper as a brainy nuclear science professor was enough of a stretch; Lang also made him a Middle American teaching at a Midwestern college, improbably recruited for his dangerous adventure overseas. The character is virtually a collage of Langian in-jokes: Professor Jasper confesses, for example, to youthful dreams of becoming a secret agent (a cliché that would come in handy later, as the plot filled with secret door-knocking and coded whistling); and when the professor goes undercover in one scene and orders a dry martini, a Gestapo agent is prompted to sidle over and say he must be an American, judging by his favorite drink.

The script couldn't be written fast enough for Warner Brothers; indeed, another writer had to be inveigled to help out. Albert Maltz had refused an earlier offer from Sperling, but the producer kept badgering the writer, best-known for his adaptation of Graham Greene's *This Gun for Hire*, until Maltz caved in. Maltz also met with Lang on a regular basis throughout January, but wrote his scenes separately from Lardner, concentrating on punching up the last third of the film. It was a helter-skelter process that sometimes worked in Hollywood, though rarely with Lang.

*   *   *

None of these writers was a reporter, so an expert had to be brought on to authenticate the spy-trappings. Michael Burke was the real thing.* A former University of Pennsylvania all-American football player who had been with the OSS, Burke, in one famous exploit, had helped smuggle an anti-Nazi admiral out of Italy. Hired as technical adviser, Burke ventured a few sensible suggestions, and found himself gratefully "adopted" by Lang.

Andries Dienum also added a bit of expertise to the project. A native Dutchman and a friend of Milton Sperling's, Dienum also had OSS experience. At first employed as Sperling's assistant, an intermediary for the producer with Lang, Dienum also found a kinship with the director and was "adopted" by him. In part that was because Dienum was a young man just starting out in the business, in part because he was versed in German language and culture. His love of Karl May's books resonated with Lang.

Burke and Dienum became frequent dinner guests at Lang's house, where the only other person Burke recalled regularly encountering was Lily Latté, "a tall, poised, Slavic-looking woman" he knew to be Lang's "female secretary-companion." "Fritz was not a gregarious man and appeared to have few friends," Burke recalled in his memoirs, *Outrageous Fortune*.

One night when the three of them were dining together, the evening turned into a long forum about the best way to kill someone with one's bare hands. There was a particular scene in the movie that Lang fretted about, where Professor Jasper (Cooper) has a hand-to-hand set-to with a fascist, played by Marc Lawrence (with Gina, the film's female lead, tossing in kicks and punches from the sidelines). Lang had done that kind of scene many times before. He *loved* that kind of scene—the close-ups of clutching, clawing hands, with his own sometimes incorporated. But was there a novel, exciting way to stage the fight?

After dinner, Burke and Dienum, these two graduates of the OSS, rolled around on the floor for what seemed like hours, Dienum remembered, acting out variations of weaponless struggle. The director hovered over them, "making a square with his fingers," in Dienum's words, "to get the shots." It may be that this one scene interested Lang more than all the rest. According to Marc Lawrence, the fight was described by a single line in the screenplay. On the set, Lang spent *six days* filming the scene, "using extreme close-ups of my fingers poking and tearing at Gary's mouth and distorting parts of his face."

Once a month Lang and Michael Burke made a public excursion in the director's yellow Buick, driving, top down, to the Brown Derby—quite an experience, especially if the director himself insisted on doing the driving, as he sometimes did, because by this time he was already badly nearsighted. When driving, Lang would peer at the road through thick glasses, ignore other drivers, even stop right in the middle of traffic to consult a map, or point something out.

---

*Lang was tempted to see in Burke another of his "virgin stars": the technical adviser became one of the rare nonprofessionals for whom the director arranged a screen test, in Hollywood. But Burke didn't pass muster with Lang on camera.

"At the restaurant, as an attendant held the door, Fritz put his steel-rimmed glasses in the glove compartment, fingered a monocle from the breast pocket of his jacket, clenched it in his right [sic] eye, and, stepping onto the pavement, stiffened into a Prussian military posture," recalled Burke. "It would have been futile for him to have tried to pull in his stomach. The front door was held open for him, the velvet cord that restrained tourists waiting for tables was unfastened, and the maître d'hôtel deferentially bowed Fritz through."

They were always taken to a "conspicuous table, preceded by unnecessarily loud pronouncements that Fritz Lang was arriving." The director ordered imperiously—for himself and Burke. Autograph seekers who approached were whisked away. "There was no mundane nonsense about paying or signing a check. We were escorted out in the same ostentatious way, Fritz affecting a nonseeing disdain for the peasants. Once back in the car, the monocle dropped from his eye, normal glasses went back into place, and his heavy body fell gratefully into its normal slouch. It was a first-rate performance of its kind that everyone seemed to enjoy, including me."

The *Cloak and Dagger* script had to be hastily finalized as the first week of photography approached in March 1946. Ring Lardner, Jr., thought it had turned out a modest but competent job. Andries Dienum and Michael Burke thought it was earnest hooey. Albert Maltz was disgusted. More than once he tried to quit, and had to be cajoled into continuing by Milton Sperling.

"I had been led to believe that both Sperling and Lang wanted to make an important film out of this material," recalled Maltz in an interview. "But after a few weeks I realized that what they wanted to make was a melodrama with a patina of importance. When finally a script came together, putting together the work of Ring and myself, I felt that it was a very mediocre script, and indeed the film turned out that way."

Milton Sperling, who knew a thing or two about writing, was just about the only person left out of the story conferences. After Lang had passed muster with the producer and got himself hired, the director proceeded to treat Sperling like dirt beneath his fingernails. Lang thought Sperling's story suggestions were "awfully stupid," and said so. "Milton he [Lang] couldn't stand," remembered Andries Dienum. "He thought Milton was an incompetent little producer, although actually Milton had a long experience. It's a mystery to me why he was so nasty to certain people and nice to others"—unless, Dienum added, Lang "felt threatened" by Sperling. ("Myself, I have no complaints," said Dienum. "Fritz was always very nice to me, treating me like a son.")

Typically, Lang feuded with Sperling on several fronts at once. Sperling was unwilling to surrender all craftsmanship of the production to the director, nor was there time enough, with the script in disarray, for Lang's all-encompassing approach. It was another film where many of the design and budget decisions were made for him, doubtless to his frustration.

Sol Polito, an excellent Warner Brothers contract cameraman, was assigned as cinematographer. Max Parker was a studio art director whom Lang liked, but who had neither the time nor freedom to fully oblige the director. Christian Nyby was a quite capable editor, but his first loyalty was to Milton Sperling and Warner Brothers.

As the Italian guerrilla fighter Gina, the producer wanted to cast Lilli Palmer, a cosmopolitan actress from Germany, who had stage background in Berlin and Vienna, as well as experience in British films. Palmer was married to Rex Harrison, and had accompanied the actor to the United States on his first Hollywood trip. Because she had not yet made an American film, Palmer fit the Lang conception of a "virgin star"; and yet, resisting Sperling, the director initially opposed her casting.

The truth was that he'd made his own discovery. For a long time, the director held out for his own newcomer, an aspiring actress without any previous credits. But Sperling persuaded Lang to go ahead and make a camera test of Lilli Palmer on February 22.

In her autobiography *Change Lobsters—And Dance*, Palmer takes up the story. The director was waiting for her impatiently when she arrived at Warners. "He made a point of speaking only English and was reasonably friendly, in a curt sort of way. Authoritarian, though. Even moving my head from left to right turned into a third degree.

"Suddenly he said, 'Take her blouse off and get her a vest.'

" 'A What?'

" 'An old-fashioned undervest. What poor people wear to keep warm,' he growled impatiently.

"They got me a vest. The Warner Brothers wardrobe department, like that of all the other Hollywood studios, was a fully equipped department store where you could find anything, no matter how unusual. Modestly hidden by a screen, I exchanged my blouse for the undervest. Back in front of the camera, I felt naked and self-conscious. Lower down, I was still wearing my skirt, but above it, nothing but the awful woolen undervest. The lights blinded me . . . "

So Lang went along with casting Palmer, but afterward the familiar pattern prevailed: his resentment toward her was added to his list of grievances against the producer.

The Friday before the cameras were set to roll, Sperling tried to bury the hatchet. He called a top-level meeting, praised the script and tried to head off any further aggravated hostilities with the director. "Now," announced Sperling, "we're going to start shooting on Monday. We've had a lot of disagreements. There's been a lot of harsh words going back and forth. But that's all behind us now, and let's forget it. And Fritz," Sperling added jovially, "I look forward to seeing you Monday morning." "*That*," replied Lang sharply, "will not be necessary." And Sperling—like other Fritz Lang producers before him—was henceforth banned from his own set.

For Palmer, things worsened after her lighting test. For starters, the director took an instant dislike to her husband, and banned Rex Harrison from the set as well. Everyone else on her first Hollywood set seemed friendly and communal. "Not so Fritz Lang," the actress wrote. "He never ate with us and became more unapproachable every day. Any attempt to talk to him and 'break down the barriers' was greeted with an icy look and a curt reply."

Palmer made a mistake she could not have calculated, reminiscing for the director's benefit about her first acting role, as a teenager in school in

Germany, where she had recreated the Siegfried-dragon scenes from Lang's film *Die Nibelungen*. "One day during a break, my chair happened to be next to his, so I tried German on him. I told him of the unforgettable impression his film *The Nibelungs* had made on me and my classmates and of my first role as Siegfried and the dragon. He looked at me without a word. Perhaps he didn't believe me. To prove it, I sang the still unforgotten Siegfried motif from the silent film, and, when he still didn't react, the Hagen motif. Delighted at this sudden discovery of an unsuspected musical archive in my memory, I began the Volker motif.

"That was too much for him. He got up and brusquely interrupted me, in English. 'None of that interests me anymore.'"

At the end of the first week of photography the intimidated and bewildered leading lady went to a party at Walter Wanger's. Joan Bennett drew her aside and asked how she was doing on Lang's "drill ground." Palmer confessed that she lived in mortal dread of the monocled director. "Do you know how I used to greet him, loud and clear, every morning while we were shooting?" confided Joan Bennett. "'Good morning, Fritz, you old son of a bitch,' right in front of everybody. That took the wind out of his sails, and everything went swimmingly afterward. You've got to get it in first—you know what I mean?"

Joan Bennett didn't mention whether or not she was also sleeping with the director. Or whether, as Michael Burke recorded in his book, Lang's generally severe attitude toward the cast ("except for Cooper, with whom he was gentle-spoken and considerate") might have been made even worse in Lilli Palmer's case because, as gossip in Hollywood held, *Cloak and Dagger*'s female star had "rejected his invitation to bed."

Palmer was not the type to call the director a son of a bitch. In fact, she was at a loss for how to cope. Sperling was powerless to intercede, since Lang glared at his every approach; nevertheless the producer continued to hoist the white flag.

After holding a screening of some early footage, Sperling informed Lang, in an April 11 memo, that Warners production executive Steve Trilling wanted to use *Cloak and Dagger* "as an object lesson to Warner Bros. directors on how to set up shots with intelligence and imagination"—not that this would have endeared Lang to the other contract directors. Sperling raved on and on about Lang's extraordinary camerawork, but no soap; the producer was still barred from the set.

Gary Cooper did nothing about Lang's treatment of Lilli Palmer either.* Cooper, "the highest paid motion picture actor per production in the world," according to publicity for the film, had been guaranteed $500,000 for his participation—or ten percent of the world gross receipts, whichever was higher. This far exceeded Lang's salary, and accordingly the director gave his leading

---

*After the filming ended, Cooper apologized to Palmer for not sticking up for her against Fritz Lang. "Gary was waiting outside my dressing room, absorbed in a game of imaginary golf, practicing his swing," the actress wrote in her memoirs. "'Hey, kid,' he said, hitting a splendid drive, 'say, that business with Lang, you know—I probably should have ... uh, but you see, I'm ... not much good at that sort of thing, I never seem to find the right words. I need a script. Know what I mean?'"

man a wide berth. There was little communication between them, just a polite neutrality that dampened any hope of a performance.

The ordeal continued. "Sometimes he screamed," Lilli Palmer wrote. "But only at me. With the others he was curt, though he remained polite with Cooper, probably because he'd once spoken to him impatiently and Gary had just turned his head and looked at him as if he was hard of hearing. Which he actually was, in one ear. When he missed something, you never knew whether it was because he hadn't heard or hadn't wanted to."

Michael Burke agreed in his account of things that Lang's treatment of Lilli Palmer "became increasingly abusive. Maybe this was his formula to prod her best performance, or a sadistic impulse toward women under his professional control. Maybe some of each. Whatever, his verbal lashings made me cringe and one day sent Lilli bolting from the set in tears."

A month of filming had elapsed when one day, as Palmer put it, the boil burst. "I looked at the schedule one morning and saw with alarm that Cooper was off and I was working alone with two supporting actors [the actress recollected]. We were shooting a scene in a tavern which I, the doughty girl guerrilla, was defending, with the help of the two supporting actors, against a whole mob of fascist villains. The prop man handed me a live machine gun and showed me how to work it. The course lasted ten minutes, after which Mr. Lang decided that I ought to handle it like a veteran. It fired blanks, not live cartridges, but they burned very effectively if they hit you on bare skin. The script required me to race across the room—'I said *left* foot first,' yelled Fritz Lang—smash the window with my machine gun and start shooting.

"Once again I took off on the wrong foot, ruining the scene for Lang before we'd even begun. I then slammed the gun against the window too timidly— I was afraid of the glass splinters—so it didn't break at the first blow. And then, though I managed to pull the trigger, the blanks hit me on the legs, burning through my nylons, and I must have let out an anguished yelp. In any case Lang bellowed, 'Cut!' There then descended on my head such a torrent of abuse that from one minute to the next I became completely calm. Tense silence, while Lang awaited my apology. I put down my machine gun without haste and examined my burned stockings. Then I straightened my skirt, shook the glass splinters out of my beret, and walked past Lang and the camera to the exit."

Palmer retreated to her trailer, drew the curtains, locked the door, and fell on the sofa, sobbing into a pillow. Shortly, a knock announced three "representatives of the electricians', property men's, and cameramen's unions." They informed the actress that all their workers were walking off the set in solidarity with her. Rex Harrison rushed over. A studio nurse appeared, then a flurry of anxious agents and executives.

"The walkout lasted three days," reported Palmer. "The upshot was a compromise: Fritz Lang was to continue as director, but during every scene in which I took part, a special representative of the management would sit by the camera to ensure a 'suitable' working atmosphere. Was this acceptable to me? Yes."

For the rest of the film, "a gray-haired man in a slouch hat" sat unobtrusively behind the camera, sometimes snoring, always awakened by the sound man before each of her takes. "Mr. Lang never addressed another word to me except the briefest instructions. It didn't matter anymore whether I took off on my left or my right foot."

After the very last scene involving the actress had been photographed, Lilli Palmer found herself standing awkwardly next to the director, who filled the silence by speaking to her brusquely, one final time, in German. "Yes . . . well, good-bye. I'll do my best for you in the cutting room." To be fair, the actress added in her autobiography, "He did do his best, too. Even in my scenes with Cooper, he used as many takes of mine as he possibly could."

The final scene in the released version of *Cloak and Dagger* is not the ending Lang preferred—and not the one he filmed. This, too, became a sore point in his memory.

In the last scene as the film stands, Professor Jasper manages to elude death on the ground in Italy. He escapes by boarding a plane with an elderly scientist defector. But this was yet another "happy ending" foisted on Lang. It had been augmented in the original script by an epilogue in which the scientist dies on the plane from a heart attack brought on by the stress of events. A snapshot in his pocket then provides the only clue to the whereabouts of a fascist atom-bomb factory in the Bavarian Alps.

The last scene was intended to be one of Fritz Lang's superclimaxes: the American going back on one final secret errand, determined to destroy the German atomic-bomb factory. It was a wishful finale—reminiscent of the *Man Hunt* fade-out—but also a cry from the heart from a director who could not bring himself to forgive Germany, or look to its future. Lang had savored that scene when planning and preparing *Cloak and Dagger*.

Milton Sperling, Michael Burke, Andries Dienum, Willy Ley, and another adviser on the picture—a scientist from Los Alamos—all tried to talk Lang out of the scene on the principle that nothing of that sort had transpired during the war. Everyone knew the Nazis had fallen short of atomic capacity. Lang, only interested in authenticity when it served his purposes, was adamant. He wanted to make a statement against war and weapons of mass destruction. The producer, still bargaining for long-term goodwill, decided the wise thing to do would be to let the director have his way.

Lang took Gary Cooper and everybody out to Bronson Canyon, where Warner Brothers had built an imitation bomb factory and where for several days they filmed the superclimax—adding thousands upon thousands of dollars in budget costs. Planes flew overhead, paratroopers dropped from the skies, the bomb factory blew up for the cameras.

According to a plot synopsis prepared by the studio publicity department, this is how Lang's version would have ended: "They have come too late. The factory has been thoroughly stripped by the Germans, its equipment probably moved to Spain or Argentina, where the Nazis had a foothold. The picture ends with the lines of the American scientist [Professor Jasper]: 'God have mercy on us if we think we can keep science a secret! God have mercy on us if we think we can wage other wars without destroying ourselves.'"

After showing a rough cut to Warner Brothers executives in late August, however, Sperling decided to drop the expensive and historically dubious sequence. Lang, naturally, was already preoccupied with his next film, but the *Hollywood Reporter* leaked the news that the director was "sizzling" over the truncated ending. Sperling finally threw up his hands and wrote Lang a memo that sizzled back, insisting that the superclimax had always been optional, that it added to an already long (106 minutes) viewing experience, and that, according to the contract, the final cut was the producer's perogative. Furthermore, Sperling admonished the director, Lang's preemptive press remarks were beginning to hurt *Cloak and Dagger*'s box-office prospects, not to mention the director's long-suffering image in Hollywood.

Lang recently had suffered another gall-bladder attack, and it gave him the excuse to plead that he had been misquoted. He didn't really have enough energy to sizzle, Lang told Sperling. The director admitted preferring the original ending, "a plea for peace" that would have given the picture added prestige, but acknowledged their dispute over the ending as an honest difference of opinion. He closed by wishing the producer success.

"Do you know why the sequence was cut?" Peter Bogdanovich asked Lang in his book, some twenty years later.

"You must ask Warners, I don't know," Lang replied disingenuously. "Maybe because it was after Hiroshima and Nagasaki."

The picture was a bland realization of the script, competently filmed with no surprises. The Nazis and fascists were as interchangeable as the European locales. The camerawork was uninspired.

Ironically, the best performances came from Helene Thimig (Mrs. Max Reinhardt)—playing a lady scientist assassinated by her German "nurse"—and Vladimir Sokoloff, as the elderly Italian defector. Here, with these two veterans of the Golden Age of Berlin film and theater, the director conspicuously reversed the policy of casting "only Americans" that had driven Brecht to distraction on *Hangmen Also Die*.

Gina, the Italian guerrilla fighter, was both sinner and saint, ennobled more by Fritz Lang's Catholicism than by his politics. The film tries to celebrate her love affair with the professor, though both know the relationship is destined to be short-lived. She is a "whore," she weepily confesses, who must sleep with many men in the interest of her cause. "I want you to think I'm a girl in a white dress who has never been kissed before," she tells the professor. No matter how hard she tried, Lilli Palmer couldn't transcend such scenes.

The director's talismans are sprinkled throughout the film: the busts and sculptures of the Kaiser Wilhelm Institute; a cowboy folk song, which is sung by the lady guerrilla fighter—who has learned it from a downed U.S. pilot; a vignette with the professor hiding out in a carousel's hulk; and finally a group of nuns, collecting for charity, who betray the hiding place of the underground. (The nuns, of course, are impostors; the robed Catholics in Fritz Lang films were generally on the side of the angels.)

The hand-to-hand combat between the professor and the fascist (Marc Lawrence) is one scene, free of dialogue, italicized in the best Lang tradition. Festive music drifts in from outside while they slug it out in a stairwell. The fascist digs his fingernails into the professor's face. The American hero responds by bending the fascist's fingers back until there is an audible snap;

that sets off a scramble—a flip-over, a chin-kick, vicious arm-twisting, a knife knocked aside. The struggle ends with the professor seizing the fascist by the throat and slowly squeezing the breath out of him. The last shot in the sequence recalls *M*: Lang's camera frames a child's ball as it bounces down the steps and rolls to a stop on the landing, under which the professor and Gina are crouched in hiding.

The same critics who had gone overboard for *Man Hunt* saw emptiness and contrivance in this belated antifascism. Archer Winsten in the *New York Post* called *Cloak and Dagger* "a disappointment." Bosley Crowther in the *New York Times* thought it was loaded with "the baldest and most familiar of spy-thriller clichés." Howard Barnes in the *New York Tribune* dubbed it "melodramatic mumbo-jumbo."

If one or two scenes interested Lang more than the rest, one critical caveat also bothered the director more than others. In October, a letter arrived on his desk from a man in New York City, one of those average moviegoers whom Lang prized, commenting on a specific inaccuracy. In a café scene, where the diners are shown in an overhead shot, an actor in the foreground is seen cutting his food with his knife, then picking up a fork in his right hand, as is the custom in the United States. However, the setting was Europe, where the table etiquette, as Lang well knew, was quite different.

This letter caused a furor in the director's office. Lang walked around for days, vexed by the mistake. "Fritz thought about it and he became so upset, so angry with himself that he couldn't even answer the letter," said his secretary Hilda Rolfe. "He couldn't believe he had made such an error." The Americanization of Fritz Lang's films had proceeded to the point where even Europeans dined as if they were from the Midwest. Two weeks went by before Fritz Lang wrote back, alleging that *Cloak and Dagger*'s technical adviser had assured him that this American style was used in "certain sections" of Italy, and the director's own travels confirmed this. It was, of course, a little white lie.

Years later, reminiscing with Peter Bogdanovich about *Cloak and Dagger*, the director made the admission that he was wrong to have fought so much with Milton Sperling. "I should have had the intelligence to laugh about it," Lang said, the producer's stupidity, that is.

As for Gary Cooper, Lang said dryly, "Personally, I think it is more interesting to work with young actors . . . He [Cooper] has his limitations, right?" Lilli Palmer, surprisingly, Lang claimed he had fought *for*, against the wishes of the producer. Seeing the film later, he came to the opinion that she was "extremely good" in her part. "She has no heart," the director added matter-of-factly, "but that is something else."

Fritz Lang would salvage two important relationships from *Cloak and Dagger*.

One was with Dan Seymour, a burly character actor best known as Abdul the Arab, the doorman at Rick's in *Casablanca*. A native of Chicago, born in 1915, Seymour was a song-and-dance burlesque and nightclub comic before moving to Hollywood, where he usually played good-natured Middle Easterners or effete villains. Seymour, cast by Warner Brothers (not the director), was in the film playing the small role of Marsoli, a member of the resistance. One day, listening to Lang berate Lilli Palmer in German, he burst out laughing at one of Lang's crude insults. The director swooped down on him. "Why are you laughing?" he demanded. "Because I can speak German fluently," Seymour, uncowed, replied.

Later in the day, Lang walked up to the actor and asked him to dinner with him that very evening. Thus began another close, thirty-year friendship.

The other important relationship was off-camera, with a woman by the name of Silvia Richards. Born in 1916, Richards had grown up in Colorado and spent a lot of time in Santa Fe. Her father was an English professor who made a sideline of collecting cowboy songs. After the breakup of a bad marriage in the East, Richards had come to Hollywood and become first a radio writer, then, after a try-out at Warner Brothers, a screenwriter. Her first two credits were *Tomahawk*, which established her as a Western expert, and *Possessed*, which typed her for films about suffering women.

Richards was thirty, young enough to be Lang's daughter, and a vision of loveliness—tall, freckle-faced, copper-haired. She must have seemed a composite all-American.

Richards was active in all the left-liberal Hollywood causes. In a later interview she could not recall where she met Lang, but thought it might have been through Lion Feuchtwanger. She and Lang started dating during preproduction of *Cloak and Dagger*. Together they went to Actors Lab plays, and the director ended up hiring some of the *Cloak and Dagger* performers (including Marc Lawrence and J. Edward Bromberg) from those productions. When these same actors started complaining about the marbled dialogue of the *Cloak and Dagger* script (which "they couldn't get into their mouths," in Richards's words), Lang summoned Richards for some uncredited remedial writing. Add her name to the long recitation of the film's writers.

In fact, they had known each other for a few months before Lang suggested they work on a project together from beginning to end, and the director offered to hire Richards to write his next film for Diana Productions.

Sometime late in 1945, Lang moved from the house in Santa Monica, where he had lived since his arrival in the United States, to a new hilltop residence in Beverly Hills.

It was expected of the top Hollywood directors that they advertise their importance with the purchase of a big, beautiful house. Finally, Lang could afford that luxury, and the one he chose was a lovely Spanish-style, tiled-roof home at the end of a long road on a narrow section of Summit Ridge Drive, perched atop a promontory overlooking Pickfair, the fabled residence of retired silent screen star Mary Pickford. Pine trees dotted the grounds, and the director had a spectacular view of the city of Los Angeles.

Hungarian expatriate Paul László, one of the foremost architect-designers for the screen colony (among his other clients were Barbara Hutton, Sonja Henie, and director William Wyler), was chosen by Lang to coordinate the design and decor. László, like Lang, was fanatical about detail—noted for arranging everything "down to the last ashtray or built-in Kleenex holder," according to *Time* magazine. László's motto was simplicity with elegance, and accordingly the appointments in Lang's home would be tasteful but spare. It was like the decor of his American films, as opposed to the German ones, and different from the showplace Lang had shared with Thea von Harbou in Berlin; the director's American citizenship mandated a house that departed radically from the aesthetic of his time in Germany.

A stark whiteness, startling visitors, predominated. The living room was carpeted in white; a large, abstract coffee table (always stacked with books and periodicals) stood in front of a long, curved couch. An easy chair where Lang often read or dozed occupied a prominent spot. Unlike in the director's Berlin home, with its morbid masks and skulls and primitive art, few artworks decorated Lang's Hollywood walls; visitors remember one or two of Käthe Kollwitz's sketches, maybe a Matisse line drawing. A László-designed fireplace formed the centerpiece of the main room.

The dining room doubled as Lang's study, where the director would sit and work at a medium-sized table that comfortably sat four people. There was a large bedroom (with an animal-skin throw), as well as a sun room, and, perhaps the most individual feature of the house: a small bar with a linoleum floor.

On a shelf behind the bar Lang kept his collection of miniature carvings, statues, and crystal animals. On the wall was a mural, painted by the director, of bare-breasted women dancing out of martini glasses.

Lily Latté supervised the acquisition and furnishing of the new home. She engaged a full staff: a German cook who could make Lang's favorite dishes; a short, bald Scottish driver; a succession of gardeners. Usually roaming the house were Lang's two Sealyham terriers—short-legged, heavy-boned little beasties that looked like Scotties, named Mutt and Jeff for the comic strip characters. The director liked Mutt and Jeff so much, sometimes he couldn't bear to part with them for the whole day, and would bring them to the office, letting the two dogs romp around as he worked.

In those days, Lang's new house was a scenic outpost, its isolation a status symbol. Lang never renewed his aquaintance with his neighbor, Mary Pickford. Other nearby neighbors included film producer I. G. Goldsmith, who was born in Vienna and launched his career there before producing features in London and the United States; the screenwriter Charles Bennett, who wrote half a dozen pictures for Hitchcock in England as well as, later on in America, 1940's *Foreign Correspondent*; and the Honorable Cecil Howard, son of the Earl of Suffolk.

Howard lived in a house beyond Lang's, down a narrow dirt track. "The approach for either of them was a one-way one," remembered Charles Bennett. "I adored Cecil, but I knew him to be a stiff-necked aristocratic Englishman. One day he and Fritz met head-on in the alleyway, Fritz's car on the way out, facing Cecil's on the way in. It was a clash of wills. One had to retire, back away, to allow the other to pass. An arrogant German versus an equally arrogant Englishman. The tie-up lasted an hour. Finally it was Fritz who yielded, but he and Cecil, close neighbors, never spoke to each other again. Well, Germany lost the war too."

Lang's records show that while finishing up the filming of *Cloak and Dagger*, his attention was once again diverted—back to Diana Productions.

The success of *Scarlet Street* had emboldened the director. In the spring and summer of 1946, Lang expended vast amounts of time dictating company policy, hiring office staff, planning publicity campaigns, and attending board meetings (where he relished presiding). But the already strained relationship between him and Walter Wanger began to worsen—even before offices could be formally set up, the next project announced, a company logo chosen.

Lang hadn't found story material that felt "right." He blamed that on Wanger—complaining that submissions went to the producer first, leaving Lang with leftovers after Wanger had sifted through them for his own purposes.

Before there were additional credits, there was an additional credit crisis. Wanger had been cited as producer for *Scarlet Street*. Lang wanted equal billing as producer next time around. That was okay with Wanger. Their names also had to be the same size—also okay. But what about advertising and publicity? Lang wanted Wanger's name downsized, and he stipulated that he himself would oversee all future dummies and layouts.

In April Lang complained about items planted in Hollywood columns that referred to Diana's films as "Walter Wanger productions," calling a special board meeting to discuss the "hapless" or "bungled" announcements that tormented the director. (The calling of board meetings was entirely the company president's province.) Such erroneous publicity items, Lang complained, did "great personal harm" and injured "everything I stand for." Yes, Lang's name was usually mentioned as director; but what about his equally important titles as president of the company and producer?

Letters and memos flew to Wanger, insisting that the producer himself respond to each and every error in print. Lang told Wanger in forceful terms that Diana Productions must be represented as "an absolutely independent organization of which Fritz Lang is president." It was Wanger's obligation to clear these issues; certainly, as the director put it when one such mishap occurred, Wanger couldn't expect Fritz Lang to write "personal letters [to each columnist] (since my writing would give the industry the sad spectacle of my disavowing you)."

Wanger replied that he couldn't help it if journalists made slipups based on their own assumptions. He couldn't prognosticate every mistake. He didn't care about publicity for himself. Could he help it if gossip columnists referred to him as a producer? That's what he was. Nonetheless, Wanger vowed to do his best.

It fell to Lang to organize some new publicity that he could wholeheartedly endorse. This was easier said than done. Press relations were a mess of conflicting interests. The director didn't entirely trust the company publicist (Margaret Ettinger—a close friend of Joan Bennett's). Not only was Henry Rogers on retainer, but Lang had his own personal legman (Dave Kaufman). Added to this was the studio's staff, led by J. L. Kaufman, the associate director of advertising and publicity for Universal, whose instructions were to liaison with Lang, and let people know it was "Fritz Lang's Diana Productions" and not "Walter Wanger's Diana Productions."

Above all, publicity had to counter the negative image of the director that some people in Hollywood stubbornly seemed to harbor. The plethora of press agents were exhorted to compile memos of their attention-getting suggestions. During the period of time between *Scarlet Street* and the follow-up Diana Production, newspapers, magazines, and radio networks were bombarded with pitches for Fritz Lang interviews, articles featuring his byline, or "canned" stories that would prominently blaze his name. It was not lost on the writers assigned to these pieces that, as one Associated Press reporter noted, this particular Hollywood director was "as publicity-conscious as an actress."

Lang worked closely with the Ettinger agency in drawing up a list of all the proposed activity that would spotlight his name. There were literally dozens of such ideas in the spring of 1946, with *Cloak and Dagger* still in the process of being edited.

Ettinger reported that it had been arranged for Ideal Publications to shoot a layout of Lang at his home, "in which he would supervise preparation of several favorite dishes, and which would include 'party' shots of any group Mr. Lang might wish to entertain." In the same vein, material had been submitted to Erskine Johnson for his Mutual Network radio program that would feature Lang as an outstanding gourmet chef. (No matter that in real life the director rarely did the slightest amount of cooking.)

It was duly noted that Ettinger had made contact with Harold Ross of the *New Yorker* and "preliminary reaction to the suggestion and outline was excellent." A friendly stringer had been approached to freelance an article for *The New York Times*. The New York advertising agency Geyer, Cornell & Newell had been asked to include Mr. Lang in the Lord Calvert–Kodachrome series "Men of Distinction," and the managing editor of *American Home* had tentatively agreed to pen a piece for *Los Angeles Shopping News, House Beautiful,* or *The Woman. Movieland* planned a two-page spread of Joan Bennett paintings in connection with *Scarlet Street* and *Woman in the Window*, with a conspicuous display of Fritz Lang's name.

There were interviews pending with *Western Family*, the wire services ("based on Mr. Lang's theories concerning the future of rockets and the possibility of flight through space"), *Photoplay*, Louella Parsons's column, *Maclean's* ("on censorship"), *The Vancouver Sun, Look, The Minneapolis Tribune and Star Journal*, and *Australian Women's Weekly*. There were also regular bulletin items churned out by the agency and sent to a hundred newspapers and columnists nationally, plus periodic house-organ mailings to six hundred addressees, with announcements to be used in the "chatter columns" of publications.

Someone had the bright idea of commissioning a name designer to create a "Diana" hat, taking a photo of Joan Bennett wearing it, then circulating the photo to syndicates and fan magazines. Lang liked the goal of appealing to the female sector of the audience. It was hoped that the actress and second-ranking stockholder of Diana Productions could be presented as a guest of honor at a national retail fashion show, while posters of her wearing the "Diana" hat were displayed in major U.S. department stores.

The ideas got wilder and more gimmicky: The Ettinger agency proposed a photographic layout of Lang "touring the Los Angeles East Side area looking for characters" to incorporate in the next Diana Production. Perhaps there could be a National Archery Contest to select "The Modern Diana" as a "living trademark." Commercial tie-ins were explored with Serta Mattress, Nescafé, the Troll Mint company, and Bradley Jay Perfume. A nationally publicized search for the Lost Dutchman gold mine in Arizona, headed "by planes equipped with radar," would recall the Ufa grand-style promotions—e.g., the experimental rocket trials for *Die Frau im Mond*. The radar planes would help focus attention on "Superstition Mountain," the historical Western script dating from 1940, which the director hoped to relaunch as a Diana project.

The publicity themes were fantastically varied: Lang and Western folklore, Lang and homemaking, Lang and women. In part this was just floundering. Lang sought a catchy nickname for himself—like Hitchcock's "Master of Suspense," but distinctive enough that he couldn't be accused of aping Hitchcock. The Diana publicists toyed with "Perfectionist Deluxe." They considered "the father of the psychological film, as the proponent of the adult film, based on honesty and realism." No consensus.

According to a June 1946 publicity summary submitted to the board of directors: "Although some excellent suggestions [for his catchy nickname] were included in the prospectus, Mr. Lang felt that the overall tone did not seem to strike exactly the right tone for Diana publicity. 'Master of the Unusual,' for example, seems to connote a mastery of film trickery which bears no relation to the realism which is an outstanding characteristic of Mr. Lang's direction. It is his feeling that no phrase should be used which can be compared with 'Master of Suspense,' the Hitchcock tag, or 'The Lubitsch Touch.' It was generally agreed that a new slogan should be created which will be more representative of the kind of pictures Mr. Lang will produce and direct for Diana."

It was hard to come up with a slogan without being able to pinpoint Diana's next production. "Although Diana pictures are aimed at adult audiences, it was the consensus at this conference that the slogan 'adult pictures for adults' is a trifle presumptuous, as well as dull and condescending. A picture which bears the Diana trademark must certainly be adult, but the publicity approach should be made not only on the basis of an appeal to the adult, intelligent, discriminating moviegoer, but even more—an appeal to the average moviegoer who can be persuaded that the person who likes Diana pictures is among the intellectual upper-crust."

Nobody seemed to notice that the publicity language, quoting Lang, sometimes amounted to gobbledy-gook. "Mr. Lang believes that motion pictures are an art of—and by—and for the people. Diana productions, therefore, are 'of the people' in the sense that they are about real persons and real situations with which the audience can identify themselves, and thus be understood and believed—which adds up to solid box-office."

It was a constant dilemma for his publicists that Americans were generally not as knowledgeable—or appreciative—of Fritz Lang as they ought to be. "It was pointed out," the minutes continued, "that Fritz Lang pictures have far greater prestige, and Mr. Lang enjoys far greater personal acclaim in Europe—especially England—than in the United States. This is evident from reviews of his pictures, magazine articles, and box-office returns."

The board members were doomed to spend a lot of time discussing ways to develop adequate name recognition for the company president—who, more than anyone in Hollywood, "unites the culture of Europe with the highly specialized technical achievements of Hollywood," according to the minutes. Dudley Nichols, the forgotten man in the organization, came to board meetings once or twice in the early stages, got a dose of the proceedings, and thereafter disappeared from Diana Productions.

The implication had been in the air that Nichols might write the follow-up to *Scarlet Street*, but he was ambivalent. When Lang championed Silvia Richards instead, Wanger was disappointed, and Nichols probably secretly relieved. The screenwriter could smell the coming disaster. Nichols cooled his heels for several months—until Lang's next film, *Secret Beyond the Door*, was almost completed, in fact—then wisely bailed out of the company, selling off his stock to the other principal partners.

For the first and only time in America, Lang was able to assemble a genuine team of his own—a small office team, but a team nonetheless. From all accounts the group loved and admired him. With them he was warm and charming; in the office, his monocle was always tucked away in his pocket.

Lang employed a couple of energetic young assistants. One was Jan Read,

a student from England who was a nephew of social commentator and journalist Malcolm Muggeridge; another was Andries Dienum, who had been spirited away from Milton Sperling's side and now worked for Lang while studying
for a master's degree.

Dienum was a member of the U.S. Communist Party, although it was a
covert membership, and he was never sure whether Lang was aware of it. In
fact, Dienum kept a straight face when one day the director took him aside
and quietly advised a man of his political convictions to join up. "He himself
wasn't a member of the Party," said Dienum. "I would have known that. There
are ways of knowing. I think he liked his way of living too much and always
thought there was something risky about joining the Party."

It was de rigueur that members of Lang's office be, if not Communist, then
leftist, or at least staunchly progressive. "I don't think it's incidental that most
of the people who worked in his [Lang's] office were Left," noted Dienum.
"He didn't have to hire us. He hired people because he wanted to have people
like that around."

Leading up to 1948, they were all supporting Henry Wallace and his independent left-of-center campaign for the presidency. The Wallace cause was
popular in Hollywood. Many celebrities involved themselves, including director
William Wyler, Charles Chaplin, Edward G. Robinson, Katharine Hepburn,
and Burt Lancaster. Lang himself made a show of publicly pledging a hundred
dollars a month to the campaign.

Lang liked to discuss political issues with his office team, and with Dienum
in particular. When the director realized Dienum knew who Jean Jaurès was,
Lang brought up the French socialist's name often, proclaiming that he felt
under the influence of Jaurès, whose assassination precipitated Lang's enlistment in World War I. Dienum became the conduit for people approaching
the director for contributions to left-liberal causes. Representatives of workers'
groups, black veterans' organizations, and other ad hoc committees were slotted for appointments, and given small donations.

Dienum helped Lang with another extracurricular activity. Sensitive to a
problem he himself had experienced, Lang was eager to encourage anyone
trying to arrange the distribution of foreign-language films in America.
Dienum said the director was instrumental in helping arrange showings of
Roberto Rossellini's *Open City*—a grittier *Cloak and Dagger*, about an Italian
resistance leader in Rome hunted down and killed by Nazis. At Universal,
Lang hosted a VIP screening of "an uncut version with a lot of torture
scenes," recalled Dienum, and Gary Cooper was coaxed into attending. "I remember at that screening Gary Cooper cried so hard he could barely contain
himself," said Dienum. "I think the success of *Open City* [in the U.S.] had a
lot to do with Fritz's support. He was very enthusiastic about that film."

Lang's secretary during the early 1940s, Luanna Kekkonnen—who had replaced Teddy Le Beau—had moved on, and care had to be taken in replacing
her. Lang's secretaries were required to be highly efficient, preferably good-
looking, able to balance personal and professional needs. They had to work
from dictation on the script as well as on Lang's correspondence, answer the
phone and handle appointments, arrange restaurant reservations and social
engagements.

Hilda Newman Rolfe had been a secretary for writers Irving Stone and Albert Maltz at Universal.* Her mother was Austrian, a fact Lang duly noted. She too was left-wing; a member of the office workers' union, Rolfe had been on the Warner Brothers picket line during the industry-wide Conference of Studio Unions strike of 1945–1946, where she was hit by a tear-gas canister during one of the violent confrontations. She also was continuing her higher education, a pursuit Lang respected in young people.

And she was beautiful, though Lang never made any romantic noises about Rolfe. The opposite: He behaved in fatherly fashion, cautioned his secretary on her love life, and invited her to his home to dinner to make sure she was eating properly. Her name filled out the guest list whenever one of his unattached male friends was coming over to dine.

Dorothy Hechtlinger, persuaded by Lang to leave her longtime position as Darryl Zanuck's assistant, was briefly the director's office manager, but Hechtlinger didn't stick it out for very long. So Lang needed to find someone else to run the day-to-day business—taking care of all contracts and financial affairs, hiring people, communicating with his agent, his lawyer, and his accountant. A Lily Latté for the office.

Rosemary Foley, Walter Wanger's executive assistant, recommended Min Selvin, who had been one of the leaders of the Screen Office Employees Guild in the studio strike—in fact, had been arrested a couple of times on the picket lines. When the office workers were beaten, one of Selvin's jobs was to amalgamate the strikers and scabs, in effect putting herself out of a job. Selvin was one of the people who had organized the shop-steward system at Universal, which meant that she knew everybody on the lot, and Foley thought she was a sharp lady who could hold her own with Fritz Lang.

The director came over from the set of *Cloak and Dagger* in April of 1946 to interview Min Selvin. He wore his monocle, playing the scene for what intimidation he could muster, but Min Selvin was one up on him. Married to a well-known lawyer, she knew Martin Gang, Lang's longtime attorney, socially. When she gave Gang as a reference, the director made a point of calling her bluff and phoning Gang on the spot, mentioning casually that Min Selvin was there in his office. When Gang told him to say a warm hello to her, Lang's eyebrows raised. "He [Lang] was not a very good bluffer," Selvin said, "so he never again questioned me."

Hiring a woman to run a production office just wasn't done in those days, according to Selvin. The director wasn't sure what her title should be; it didn't matter to Selvin, but titles were important to Lang. The first meeting they had was a long, drawn-out discussion over her title, Lang finally warming to "Executive Assistant to Mr. Lang."

Joining Hilda Rolfe and Silvia Richards, Selvin found to her surprise that women were in the majority in the Diana Productions operation. "The thing that struck me about him [Lang] in our relationship was that he was such an ardent feminist," she recalled. "He really stuck up for women. In having me

---

*Hilda Newman became Hilda Rolfe when she married writer-producer Sam Rolfe, creator of the "Have Gun, Will Travel" and "The Man From U.N.C.L.E." television series.

carry out various and sundry duties, any time any man acted as if I was just a secretary, he'd put them in their place, just like that."

Rolfe took a slightly different perspective. "Mostly he did gravitate to women," remembered Lang's secretary. "I have a feeling, looking back, he could push women around a little easier than he could men. He did not get along well with men."

Men did not lend themselves as easily to publicity hooks, either. *Liberty* magazine, for one, was interested in interviewing Lang "on why the majority of his business associates are women." It was not only political consciousness; it was a journalistic angle. As the minutes of one Diana Productions meeting reported, "Mr. Lang's respect for women—their intuitive understanding, their efficiency and intelligence—might well be used in seeking publicity outlets among the women's magazines."

Besides being young, female, and left-wing, a number of the Diana Productions staff were Jewish; naturally, many of the writers, directors, and producers stopping by were also Jewish. Lang liked to joke that he was the only Catholic in the office. In that post-war time, when there was much talk about the Jews, the Holocaust, and the struggle to inaugurate the state of Israel, the director never mentioned his Jewish heritage.

"If I think about it, nearly everybody in the organization was Jewish," said Rolfe. "Yet he never told me that he was Jewish, knowing that I was. He had many opportunities—at his home, at dinner, in a car with him alone. Instead he often talked about having been raised as a Catholic and having a good, regimented, ethical education."

The director's offices were at the far end of the back lot, on top of a hill—the last bungalow on studio grounds, on the edge of wild country. Next door to the bungalow was a gym, where studio employees could work out or visit a steam room in the morning before work. Far down the hill, in the main section of the lot, was Walter Wanger's bungalow. The location seemed to emphasize Lang's aloofness.

The bungalow opened onto two smaller offices for Hilda Rolfe and Min Selvin. Lang and Silvia Richards worked in a large executive space furnished with a living room and desk. There was a kitchenette at the back, with a refrigerator and liquor. The atmosphere was informal; Lang was known some mornings to shave in the bathroom.

For a very short time, the office was indeed like a household, and the staff not so much a production team as a tightly knit family, devoted to their august father figure.

For a year, Lang searched for story material that would equal the depth and quality of *Scarlet Street*.

As usual, newspaper clippings were among his prime sources. One of Hilda Rolfe's jobs was to cut articles out and file them away. For a time, Lang thought about doing a film on serial killer William Heirens, who terrorized Chicago in 1945–1946; he also avidly followed the case of the "Black Dahlia" murder, which rocked Los Angeles in 1947. Rolfe collected a stack of clippings on that still-unsolved crime. Lang had tried to develop close ties with the Los Angeles police, but they were not always as accommodating as those on Alexanderplatz.* Still, local police officials indulged the director on a number of trips downtown to the central police station, where he pored over photos of the mutilated Black Dahlia victim. "He had an attraction for bizarre deaths," Hilda Rolfe recalled.

The director had a yen to do another Western, and in February of 1946, his next project was announced: a Fritz Lang film about "Billy the Kid and the famous Lincoln County cattle wars," according to *The New York Times*, which "will be filmed in late spring or early summer, probably in New Mexico or Arizona." But that was just a burst of optimistic publicity. There was no screenplay for such a subject.

For a while the director fixated on reviving his 1940 treatment called "Superstition Mountain." Lang's treatment brought the Spanish legend into the present day, focusing on the trial of a prospector who has murdered his partner in a fit of gold fever. The story featured a young gold hunter named Dan Webster; a cigarette girl; Jim, the young man's stepfather ("oily, churchgoing . . . and ever since Jim's marriage to Mrs. Webster, Dan and his mother have become estranged"), and Dan's rival, an engineer.

Lang tried to talk it up as a Diana Production in late 1945, and went shopping for a Western author to write a full-fledged script. He met with Stuart N. Lake, Paul Kohner's client, who proved unenthusiastic about "Superstition Mountain." But in their meetings it emerged that Lake had written another story, a treatment for a Western called "Winchester '73" about a vengeance-seeking cowboy obsessed with tracking down a man—and his stolen gun. The treatment, envisioning the film as a series of separate but cleverly interconnected episodes, languished in story files at Universal.

Subsequently, in January 1946, Diana Productions purchased the rights to "Winchester '73" for $30,000 from Universal, then paid out another $35,000 to Lake—half of the money for transfer of legal rights, the other half for ten weeks of work on the screenplay. Lake was optimistic he could deliver some sort of first draft by mid-1946.

So confident of the property was Lang that "Winchester '73" was stated in legal memoranda as Diana's first obligation under its new two-picture deal with Universal. The Western would be budgeted at an estimated $1–1.3 million, and was guaranteed for delivery to the studio by December 31, 1946.

While Lake worked on the script, Lang kept busy with *Cloak and Dagger*, Diana board meetings, and publicity schemes. In April, he asked to see pages. Lake showed him twenty-nine. Lang protested that he had expected two hundred; most of the twenty-nine, besides, consisted of a long introduction explaining the history of the "Winchester '73" rifle. The director moved to discharge Lake. But the author didn't go easily; he was angry (he thought he had been making reasonable progress), and his contract had an unusual clause granting him separate rights for a novel based on any storyline he devised. So after he stepped aside, Lake proceeded to craft the story of "Winchester '73" into a novel.

It appears that all along the director had been manipulating circumstances

---

*When Lang was working on "Man Without a Country" with Jonathan Latimer, he had also tried—and failed—to arrange a face-to-face meeting with Federal Bureau of Investigation head J. Edgar Hoover.

so that Silvia Richards could take over the assignment. By this time Lang had cemented a romantic relationship with the screenwriter, and decided she was going to write not only his next picture but his next *two*, fulfilling the Diana agreement with Universal. One would be "Winchester '73," the other to be decided later.

This upset Wanger. Given the pressures—and the fact that Lang and Silvia Richards were emotionally involved—the producer thought that two writers working simultaneously on different projects made better sense. The director insisted Richards could handle both. As Silvia Richards said in an interview, Lang showed "more ambition for me than I did for myself."

After fulfilling her Warner Brothers terms as of April 8, 1946, Richards took two weeks' vacation and then went to work for Diana Productions at $750 weekly. Her contract dictated specific obligations "broader than merely requiring her to render services as a writer." She would also be required to read material, search for stories, act as a story editor, and "to write articles in addition to the general obligations of a writer." The contract stipulated that "if for any reason Fritz Lang leaves Diana, Miss Richards is to be released" from her agreement.

For several months, "Winchester '73" remained the primary focus of Diana Productions. But Silvia Richards and Lang couldn't progress beyond a lengthy outline; and that is the main reason why the director turned his attention from this project—which became a landmark Western, later, in the hands of director Anthony Mann—in favor of the relatively obscure and unappealing *Secret Beyond the Door*.

Lang told Peter Bogdanovich that making *Secret Beyond the Door* "wasn't my idea"—that the blame rested solely with Wanger, who plucked the idea from some "old scripts" lying around. But there was no old script lying around; the story itself was not very old. The Rufus L. King serial had appeared in *Redbook* in December of 1945. Its screen rights were purchased shortly thereafter by Diana Productions for ten thousand dollars. By late spring, Lang had no choice but to postpone the script-troubled "Winchester '73," and come up with some quick alternative—*Secret Beyond the Door*.

Both Wanger and Lang would have been familiar with the works of Rufus L. King, though he was more the director's cup of tea. A popular author, playwright, and screenwriter, King specialized in murder, secret agents, and backstage mysteries. The generally "B" pictures made in Hollywood from King's crime stories included *Murder by the Clock*, *Love Letters of a Star*, and *The Victoria Docks at 8*.

The *Redbook* serial was about a millionaire newspaper magnate who recreates, in his mansion, rooms where notorious murders have occurred—his own Madame Tussaud's chamber of horrors. He strikes up a relationship with an attractive widow. It may have been purely incidental to Lang's interest that the widow's name is Lily, a "slender, well-groomed figure, the absolute prototype of so many women whose lives have been spent in the luxury resorts, both here and abroad"; or that another character in the story is an obsessive, disfigured, heroic secretary, held in thrall by the millionaire.

The millionaire is murdered by his brother, who covets his wealth and estate. The wife is framed, but grows to believe she has committed the murder while sleepwalking. She comes to the brink of suicide, before all the wrongs are righted in the nick of time.

Lang said in later published interviews that the story reminded him a little of *Rebecca,* the 1940 Hitchcock film that, to his surprise, had bowled him over. It annoyed Lang that Hitchcock was always getting so much attention and praise, especially considering that Lang felt Hitchcock copied him in some of his work. "Fritz hated Hitchcock because he felt that Hitchcock had usurped his title as king of suspense," said Gene Fowler, Jr. "He felt he knew suspense better than Hitchcock."

Never mind *Ministry of Fear; Secret Beyond the Door* would be his true Hitchcock film. "You remember that wonderful scene in *Rebecca* where Judith Anderson talks about Rebecca and shows Joan Fontaine the clothes and fur coats and everything?" Lang mused to Peter Bogdanovich. "When I saw this picture (I am a very good audience), Rebecca was *there,* I *saw* her. It was a combination of brilliant direction, brilliant writing and wonderful acting. And—talk about stealing—I had the feeling that maybe I could do something similar in this picture."

It was no secret, Silvia Richards said later, that she and Lang were in love. The director was pestering her to marry him.

All of her memories of that time, roughly from 1946 to 1949, are happy ones. "Fritz was a tremendous human being," the screenwriter said. "I was very fond of him." They are memories in which food, politics, and exploring the West together figure more prominently than *Secret Beyond the Door,* the scenario she and Lang happened to be working on.

Richards recalled how Lang liked to celebrate the early-spring season with a drink called Waldmeister, which was made from young, fragrant asperula shoots that grow in the forests of Germany. He was proud of growing the plant, also known as woodruff, in the shadow of the pine trees on his lot. He would place the asperula shoots in a large crystal tureen and moisten them with a bottle of Rhine wine and some brandy. Add tiny pink strawberries, let the contents steep for a week or two, then pour over a big chunk of ice.

The two of them made regular excursions into the desert for picnics—with Lang bringing along an insulated leather case containing bottles of iced wine and martini mix, spicy sausage, and rye bread. They'd eat a leisurely lunch, then head out to scout ghost towns and Western historical sites.

Lang had become enamored of American square dancing. "He wanted to try it out," said Richards. "We watched what the people did. Pretty soon we were do-si-doing." For a spell the director and his screenwriter-girlfriend were regulars at Los Angeles square dance events. "Fritz wore a wonderful Western shirt with a silver bull's head holding the kerchief, and cowboy boots," Richards said. "I wore ruffled petticoats and skirts. We went square dancing all over this town for about a year and a half. Let me tell you, there's nothing like a man square-dancing in a cowboy suit with a monocle."

Together with Willy Ley they attended meetings and conferences organizing protests against the building of atomic weapons. Lang was extremely

concerned about the issue of former Nazis sneaking into America, and especially those, Richards remembered, who might be brought over to work on
future weapons technology.

The summer and fall of 1946 drifted by as Lang and Richards picnicked,
square-danced, and held hands at political gatherings. The office pace was
leisurely. No one seemed overly busy. People stopped by, drank coffee, discussed current events. Dignitaries and personages were always popping in.
Anthropologist Margaret Mead paid a memorable visit. Dave Kaufman liked
to drop by to joke around with Lang; the director liked Kaufman, who would
plant articles about him in the *Hollywood Citizen-News*.

Lang convened office roundtables on subjects that interested him; murder
was one recurring topic. Jan Read, Andries Dienum, Hilda Rolfe, Min Selvin,
Silvia Richards, and anyone who happened to be visiting were corralled in the
director's presence for a couple of hours to muse about the whys and
wherefores of murder.

These discussions were sometimes channeled into publicity pieces. Jan Read
ghosted one such article for Lang called, "Why Am I Interested in Murder?"
Another manufactured during this period, with Lang's byline, repudiated the
extreme pessimism found in the director's early German films, and announced
his new philosophy of embracing audience-friendly "happy endings" where
appropriate.

Silvia Richards ghosted a few pieces. Certain of the articles about Lang and
women may in fact have been written secretly by Lang's lover; years later, she
didn't remember which she might have done. It would be another Chinese
riddle: the woman Lang loved ghosting articles about the kind of women the
director tended to fall in love with.

Any ghosted publicity was always discussed, revised, polished by the director
himself. Lang's myopia had reached the point where all such articles as well
as script drafts had to be brought up close to his face. "He made grammatical
errors and sometimes he didn't pronounce things correctly," said Hilda Rolfe.
"He pronounced things in the German way, especially if he was tired. If Silvia,
jokingly, would correct him, sometimes he'd get annoyed."

"He had mood swings," added Rolfe, "and if you got him angry he did
blow, which was kind of frightening because he was this big man. It's very
German—my mother did it too. It's a bully trait. If you yelled back at him,
he'd kind of back off and look surprised. He never did it to me, but I heard
him with others. He'd get out of hand and be horrible to people on the set."

"The office was low-key, very pleasant, no yelling," echoed Min Selvin.
Selvin stayed Lang's executive assistant for approximately four years, from
1946 to 1950, and he raised his voice to her only once. Lang was watchful of
his cash flow, and she remembered him screaming and yelling at her all day
on one occasion when she had made an accounting error. The director followed her to her car at nightfall, still screaming and yelling, until finally she
stuck her head out the window and asked, "What do you want me to do? *Kill*
myself over this?" That took Lang aback, and got him laughing.

One of the duties of Hilda Rolfe was to maintain his personal appointments
diary. One of her duties, therefore, was to keep Silvia Richards and Lily Latté

apart on the calendar. Latté's domain was the house; Richards's, the office. Where one saw Lang and Latté, one rarely saw Silvia Richards.

"I was a sort of go-between," said Hilda Rolfe. "Fritz used to say to me, 'I'm going out to dinner tonight with Silvia. If Mickey asks me where I am, you don't know.' So she would get angry with me. She'd grill me. 'What do you mean, you don't know where he is?' "

Latté was hardly a total martyr—except where Fritz Lang was concerned. According to *Los Angeles Times* film critic Kevin Thomas, a close friend of both Lang and Latté, her affairs with conductor Leopold Stokowski and actor Walter Slezak were open knowledge in the German-American community.

Peter Heiman had been in the U.S. Army for five years. When he came back to Los Angeles late in 1945, he again moved into Latté's apartment with her. (When Lang moved into his new home in Beverly Hills, Latté had moved from Strathmore Drive to a location slightly closer to the director's, taking a place on Kelton Avenue in West Los Angeles.)

Now Heiman, on the GI Bill, studied and worked at the Actors Lab. Once again, Lang treated him as a friend, at one point visiting rehearsals of a stage play he was directing to give Heiman the benefit of the Meister's advice. It was perfectly fine for Heiman to accompany Lang and Latté to public occasions or private parties, but it didn't work the other way around for the director's girlfriends. Lang's paramours spent those evenings at home.

Hilda Rolfe said she remembered being struck by the fact that most of Lang's close friends hailed from outside the industry. John Decker and Willy Ley were among those who dropped by frequently, or phoned. After work, Lang often saw animator Oskar Fischinger, who in the United States had contributed his skills to Disney's *Fantasia*; and—one of his more unlikely acquaintances—the Frankfurt-born philosopher, social theorist, and popular-culture critic Theodor Adorno. Few actors phoned or visited: Dan Seymour was one; Mady Christians, a Viennese actress, was another who kept in touch.

Even though he was busy and in mid-affair with Silvia Richards, Lang didn't always have an engagement in the evening. The director struck some of his office staff as a fundamentally lonely man. He liked to visit the Los Angeles planetarium and sometimes talked one of the staff into going along with him after hours; from there they'd go to dinner at the Brown Derby, where Lang would order his ritual meal of steak, asparagus with hollandaise sauce, and chocolate mousse for dessert.

When he decided he didn't approve of a Universal employee Hilda Rolfe was dating he arranged to give her a ride to work at the studio every morning so she would have independent transportation. Lang was happy to go out of his way for her. Apart from his charitable impulses, she had the impression that he took any opportunity to have company. And Lang himself was good company, Rolfe said. While driving along in his car, the director would keep up a running monologue, making acerbic comments out of the side of his mouth. One time, Rolfe remembered, he pointed to a blind man outside the car, fumbling along with his white-tipped cane, and said, "Lang—in twenty years." Recounting this, Rolfe added sadly, "It turned out to be true!"

* * *

Everything was going swimmingly—except the script for *Secret Beyond the Door*.

Lang had changed the millionaire newspaper magnate, Mark Lamphere, into an architect. The female character's name had been changed from Lily to Celia. A significant addition Lang made was to conceive of a prologue in Mexico, where Mark and Celia get married—a "framing" scene that did not appear in the Rufus L. King serial.

The prologue would begin with a flashback of Celia's Mexican sojourn. In Lang's version, no longer is she a widow; it's the death of her guardian brother that has left her wealthy, and alone in life. Watching two men locked in a knife fight over a woman in a town plaza, Celia experiences a voyeuristic frisson. "Death was in that street," her voice-over narrates, "and I thought how proud she must be." Then her eyes meet the architect's. Sitting at another table, he has been eyeing her.

A subplot about nasty boardroom infighting was excised. In the *Redbook* serial there was a secondary character, a musician just freed from a prisoner-of-war camp, who gave the story a topical angle; he was dropped. The millionaire is murdered in the *Redbook* version; this, too, was abandoned. Instead the architect becomes a suspected murderer whose homicidal impulses are triggered by the scent of lilacs, which remind him of his mother.

Lang had other strange ideas, such as suggesting that the voice-over narration be done by an actress other than Joan Bennett, to make a distinction between the heroine's "thought voice" and her "oral voice." The narration would at times be assumed by the architect, fantasizing about murder and misleading the audience into thinking he has murdered Celia. Through these techniques, according to the director, the film would probe the death-dealing impulses that lurked in everyone's subconscious. *Secret Beyond the Door* would become a kind of psychodrama, psychology being a topic that endlessly fascinated the director.*

In the end, though the idea of a spooky mansion with a murder gallery remained, so much of the story had been altered that it became almost unrecognizable as the Rufus L. King source material. Silvia Richards worked totally under the director's spell. She was learning some craft pointers ("Forget the shots: Long shot, close-up," Lang told her, "and just describe what we see"), but felt uncertain of the material, a fact she admitted only to herself.

Most of the time the director dictated the dialogue and scenes, with Richards trying to organize his flow of words. "I was working in a little office next to him," she remembered, "but I could never voice what I felt. I was working against the grain. My stomach was in a knot of disapproval the whole time. I had no feeling for the story. I wrote good English sentences, so the language looked fine on paper—at least to Fritz, and the people in the front office—but that didn't mean it would look fine on film. It was labor every inch of the way. I couldn't talk to Fritz about it. I swear I was too much in awe of him."

Lang appeared completely confident. If there were any deficiencies in the

---

*Lang had several friends who were psychiatrists and whom he liked to draw out on the subject of murder. He also devoured popular books by psychologists. Never, though, did he see a psychoanalyst for his own benefit.

scenario, he would make up for them through his artful direction. That is what Richards also hoped. "I think the reason he was fond of me," the screenwriter mused, "is that he could be the great director in my eyes. The failures he didn't want to dwell on."

Hilda Rolfe, typing up the pages as they progressed, also thought the script was mediocre, but, like Richards, put her faith in Lang's talent. "I thought that he had a vision and could make it work," recalled Rolfe. "I couldn't believe that they couldn't see what they were doing was just awful."

It was not only a mediocre script; it took forever to write—almost *all* of 1946. When given enough rope, Lang liked to stretch out every phase of a production. The drawn-out schedule meant extra costs for the extension of rights, interest on loans, and of course office overhead and salaries. And Lang had insisted that his own fee be raised to the contractual maximum of $100,000, so he was well-paid in the meantime.

Universal, Walter Wanger, and Joan Bennett were all getting jumpy. With the studio weighing in on his side, Wanger was able to pry "Winchester '73" away from Lang. The producer insisted that another writer, Howard Dimsdale, be employed on a weekly basis to work on the Western, so that, theoretically, "Winchester '73" would be ready to go before the cameras by the time Lang polished off *Secret Beyond the Door*. For its part, the studio agreed to extend additional seed money for the Fritz Lang Western, but—a cautionary noise—only until October 31, 1947.

By September 1946, when Joan Bennett made her preliminary wardrobe selections, Lang and Silvia Richards still had only the first fifty pages of *Secret Beyond the Door* ready. Those pages concerned mainly the extensive Mexican prologue—one of those intricately prepared and extensively revised openings the director hated to let go. A completed first draft of the script was not approved until November. This was one of the fatal delays that "drove up Diana's overhead and weakened its bargaining position with Universal," wrote Matthew Bernstein.

Since late spring, Lang had been making attempts to cast the part of Mark Lamphere, Celia's husband, with an actor whose star power would equal Joan Bennett's. The director had a penchant for British actors; one certainly couldn't fault *their* English. Originally, Lang tried very hard to interest James Mason in the leading man's part, but that wasn't easy without a script to wave around. Instead, the *Redbook* serial had to be bundled up and sent to Mason in London.

It was accompanied by a Walter Wanger letter, actually dictated by Lang and transcribed, then polished, by Silvia Richards. While conceding that the *Redbook* serial offered evidence of "the very barest skeleton for a psychological study," Wanger's letter promised thought-provoking drama from a world-renowned director not shy about evoking comparisons between *Secret Beyond the Door* and one of his earlier world-renowned films. "We are convinced," the letter read, "Fritz Lang will create, even more powerfully than in his classic *M*, a story which throws light on some of mankind's most sinister emotions, arousing in the audience that irresistible combination of terror and pity."

James Mason was not sufficiently tempted. But Michael Redgrave, another cultivated Englishman, had spent time as a student in Heidelberg, and Fritz

Lang had been "a hero" ever since Redgrave watched *Die Nibelungen* in a dingy, smoke-filled cinema there. Min Selvin had seen Redgrave—as a ventriloquist possessed by his dummy—in 1946's *Dead of Night*, which the Rank Organization, in a reciprocal relationship with Universal, screened for people on the lot. Selvin urged the director to see the decidedly Langian film noir. He did, and the fifty pages of script were dispatched to Redgrave—enough to convince him to come to Hollywood.

It would be Redgrave's American debut, making him the "virgin star" of *Secret Beyond the Door.** Silvia Richards sat alongside the director during interviews with other actors for the supporting roles. Everybody in the office chipped in with suggestions. Lang was in a buoyant mood. His cast would be an extension of the happy office family.

Employed for $66,675, Redgrave arrived in Los Angeles in January of 1947, wearing a new wardrobe purchased for him by the Universal publicity department. Dave Kaufman had alerted all the newspapers, then brought his own camera along to be sure that Lang got the kind of stills he wanted: the famous film director greeting the soon-to-be-major star of his forthcoming production. When the director, formally attired in a camel-hair coat and fedora (and, naturally, sporting his monocle), met Redgrave at Union Station, the actor was impressed and flattered, preferring to see "an act of Old World courtesy" in what was actually an exercise in New World publicity.

Stepping off the train, Redgrave shook hands with Lang, then was introduced to the pretty, freckle-faced woman at his side—screenwriter Silvia Richards. Instinctively, Redgrave swept her into his arms with a hug. "Thank you for your wonderful script!" the actor said. Silvia Richards murmured a thank-you, thinking to herself, oh dear!

As a principal stockholder of Diana Productions, Joan Bennett had been booked in advance as the leading lady, her salary raised to $75,000 for the duration.

The script was tailored for her, no doubt. Every scene revolved around her character, even if Celia Lamphere was a victimized woman and a saint, unlike the aggressive sinner Bennett had played in *Scarlet Street*. There were unusually explicit scenes showing the actress engaged in openmouthed kissing, taking a bath, and flaunting her cleavage, which alarmed the Production Code, and required all of Wanger's pacifying skills.

But a curtain of frostiness had descended between the actress and the director even before principal photography began. Lang's staff remember that Joan Bennett visited the office bungalow only once or twice throughout all of 1946, and rarely phoned. Silvia Richards was now the love of Lang's life, and although Bennett accepted the fact, still tensions mounted.

The first alarm came when the actress sided with her producer-husband in the choice of Stanley Cortez as the film's cameraman. The director had sought Milton Krasner again, but Krasner had taken another job when the scriptwriting dragged on, and Cortez, under contract to Wanger, proved eminently

---

*It was conveniently arranged that Redgrave would also star, almost simultaneously with *Secret Beyond the Door*, in Dudley Nichols's adaptation of *Mourning Becomes Electra*, filming at RKO.

available. Cortez, the brother of actor Ricardo Cortez, had photographed another film featuring a many-roomed mansion—Orson Welles's *The Magnificent Ambersons*. He was considered a master of experimental long takes, and of the exploration of space and depth. As a former portrait photographer, Cortez was also widely regarded for his glamorous lighting of actresses, a logical reason why Joan Bennett might favor him.

Cortez was first-rate, but he wasn't Lang's pick. The director did secure his other choices: Arthur Hilton as his editor, Max Parker from *Cloak and Dagger* as his art director, the highly regarded Miklos Rozsa as the film's composer. But Lang remained peevish about Cortez, and their relationship would start out on the wrong foot.

By February 10, 1947, when shooting finally began, the bad feeling was pervasive. Wanger felt the pressure of Universal, increasingly anxious about its investment. The estimated budget for the film had somehow risen above $1.3 million. The remaining cast and crew had to be tossed together as quickly as possible—ironically, considering all the time that had elapsed since Lang completed *Cloak and Dagger*.

The director bore down vengefully on Joan Bennett. Darryl Zanuck had once warned the actress that when Lang was riding high he was "impossible." It was failure that made him a prince; success transformed Fritz Lang right back into the beast.

On their previous outings, the actress recollected in one interview, Lang and Bennett had engaged in "thrilling arguments," always with constructive results. Now at production conferences Lang behaved in a "rebellious" manner while on the set he was "outrageous and demanding." "Fritz was a real Jekyll-and-Hyde character, calm and purposeful one moment and off on a tirade the next," Bennett remembered.

In his autobiography, Michael Redgrave described filming of the first scene, the marriage in a Mexican church—which was Lang's special contribution to the scenario. From behind the camera the director kept up a monologue lambasting the actress's tiniest movements. "Don't close your mouth, Joan. No, *don't* close your mouth. I said DON'T. Cut! Do you think you could leave your mouth a little open, Joan honey?" According to Redgrave, the female star stalked off the set after the shot finally proved adequate, muttering, "He treats me like a puppet."

Filming another scene, the director raged that Bennett didn't seem able to drink out of straws without ruining her dainty expression; after countless takes and sarcastic reproaches, Lang simply stepped in and Scotch-taped the straws together to keep them out of the way. The actress, sitting there sucking on Scotch-taped straws, could do little but fume.

Michael Redgrave began to have misgivings. The actor thought to himself, "But Lang *must* know what he's doing . . . " After all, Redgrave reflected, in the director's previous films with the underrated actress, Bennett gave "very polished performances."

Redgrave himself came in for punishment when the actor proved inadequate to the subtleties of the character the director himself had created on the page. It didn't help to give the actor line readings, or chalk his footsteps. Redgrave still disappointed Lang, and the director resorted to the usual carrying on. Min Selvin visited the set one day and was astonished by Lang's tirades, which she had never witnessed in the office. She took her employer aside and advised him to stop shouting at the distinguished actor. "He always took my advice very seriously," said Selvin, "but paid no attention to it."

Joan Bennett loved the way Stanley Cortez was photographing her. He made her shimmer with loveliness, she thought, and that only fueled Lang's fire. Cortez was painstaking, and, following instinct, took his fair time photographing each scene. Lang fought him. Cortez fought back. Lang tried to have the headstrong cameraman deposed. Crisis meetings ensued. Bennett stood up for Cortez—the final betrayal. "In the end, Joan Bennett irritated the hell out of Fritz," said Silvia Richards.

Lang ended up opposing everybody. The minute the prop men left the soundstage, he'd go in behind their backs and rearrange the props. One day, he screamed and screamed at one of the set decorators, halting production and ringing up postponement costs until Lily Latté could be chauffeured from his house on Summit Ridge to take a look at the carefully appointed set and correct whatever the perceived stupidity was.

Wanger, as was his wont, tried to keep out of the director's hair. He had left the board meetings and publicity to Lang, the company president. He had left the script to Lang, vaunted shaper of scripts. Except for Stanley Cortez (who was more Joan Bennett's call), he had left the determination of cast and crew to Lang, the director and co-producer of *Secret Beyond the Door*. Wanger had stayed calm and collected for almost a year.

Now, on March 5, 1947, the producer sat down and dictated a memo because "it is easier for me to crystallize my thoughts in the form of a letter than by oral statements." By March 5, Wanger stated, the production was already five days behind schedule, and the producer had been prompted by the comptroller to urge "less rehearsals and fewer takes" in order to save money. Every day the production was falling farther behind, in spite of the fact that the morning call was at 7:30 A.M. and the crew usually was not dismissed until about 7 P.M., "which makes it a very long day," in Wanger's careful words.

The producer was particularly concerned because—the diplomatic Wanger phrased it delicately—"the remedies are so difficult of application." By now the producer realized he was essentially powerless: "Whether you can defer any doubtful sequences until you have assembled the picture; whether you can make any further eliminations from the script; or whether the number of takes can be minimized is a matter almost completely under your control."

As of the first week of March, Wanger noted, only 74 of a projected 125 scenes had been finished, or 32 of a projected 43 script pages. "I notice that in most every setup, an early take is printed, then another later take is printed, then finally a twelfth or fourteenth take is printed," Wanger wrote, implying the randomness that fellow Fritz Lang producer Erich Pommer had detected as far back as the director's Ufa days. "This procedure consumes very much time and footage. Also, rehearsal time and lighting time seems excessive." At the end of the letter, Wanger tried to make a hairpin turn with a gracious reversal in tone and some conciliatory phrases. "I cannot let this memorandum go without saying I personally think what you have shot is of exceptional quality and dramatic interest and I like it better than anything you have done in a long time."

It was too late for tact. Coming on March 10, Lang's reply, a three-page, single-spaced, point-by-point rebuttal, was blistering, yielding not an inch of argument. The director blamed the slow progress on Stanley Cortez, who had insisted on using a mobile camera but had much to learn about focus and lighting ("I have never had so much trouble with a cameraman")*; an "inefficient crew;" the "incredibly bad work" of costumer Travis Banton (whom we are "overpaying"); airplanes flying overhead; actors blowing their lines. Some delay could even be ascribed to the producer's wife: Joan Bennett had recently undergone an operation, the director reminded Wanger, forcing Lang to forego close-ups of his distaff star after 5 P.M. Some of this was true enough; some of it was Lang making Langian excuses.

The director defended his script, wielding Wanger's own laissez-faire attitude against him. "On numerous occasions before we started shooting," Lang wrote, "I asked you for specific suggestions for cutting the length of the script. You never had anything to offer except generalities. You also said that you didn't see any possible cuts after the Mexican sequence, that the rest of the script was tight and impossible to cut. Nevertheless I eliminated more than one thousand words of the dialogue from the final script."

The director insisted that Wanger's cost estimates of cumulative delay were "meaningless," since a producer couldn't possibly gauge the degree of creativity represented by the footage. To Wanger's reminder that Diana Productions was obligated to pay back all cost overruns, Lang responded caustically, "I am surprised to learn that you have just now discovered what was in the contract. I talked to Norman Tyre [Martin Gang's partner], who tells me that this originated in a discussion with Peery Price, your lawyer, and that it was brought to the attention of everybody before the contracts were signed."

In response to Wanger's assessment of the footage thus far as "exceptional," the director added a final retort to his itemized memo. One word: "Thanks."

Enemies and spies everywhere. The director had built into the script another scene that wasn't in the *Redbook* version of *Secret Beyond the Door*: one of his house-afire catharses. When it came to filming that scene now, he refused to utilize doubles for either Michael Redgrave or Joan Bennett. These two stars would bleed white for Fritz Lang. He made Redgrave crawl out through the smoke "185 times, it seemed," according to onlooker Min Selvin, "telling him to do it over and over again, and not very politely." Joan Bennett remembered: "We fled, terrified, through scorching flames, time and again . . ."

The filming concluded on April 19, eighteen days over schedule.

Things did not settle down when the photography was finished. The editing went fine under the reliable Arthur Hilton, but Lang found himself locked in a war of memos with Universal over publicity and postproduction decisions.

In August of 1947, as *Secret Beyond the Door* was being assembled, the

---

*To be fair, Orson Welles, director of *The Magnificent Ambersons*, also commented more than once in interviews about Stanley Cortez's slowness.

merger of Universal and International Pictures had resulted in a new company, Universal-International, with executives William Goetz and Leo Spitz newly in charge of production. Lang knew Goetz from *The Woman in the Window*; he was a hands-on operator like Zanuck. Spitz, a lawyer who handled contracts and legal issues, immediately renegotiated all semi-independent contracts to make the principals subject to cross-collateralization costs. "This meant combining the profits and losses of *Secret Beyond the Door* and 'Winchester '73,' " wrote Matthew Bernstein.

This put Diana Productions further into a hole with the studio, pairing costs for two projects that had not yet shown any income, much less profit. Lang insisted that Universal was adding on unfair operating expenses, and that the studio had failed in certain obligations, including an unsatisfactory buildup for Michael Redgrave. (Publicity had extolled the cerebral Redgrave as "the clean-limbed, all-weather type of Englishman." One handout began: "He's tall—he's rangy . . .")

It may not have occurred to Lang that at the same time that he was attacking the publicity department, he desperately needed their cooperation. The director did not in the least endear himself to the people responsible for the advertising, marketing, and distribution of his forthcoming latest film, Lang believed he had the right idea to oppose all their wrong ones. Behind his back, the Universal publicity and marketing people referred to him sarcastically, as "The Genius."

The thankless search went on for a publicity tagline for the director—or, at least, this film. The psychological trend had passed in Hollywood, and was "no longer box office," in Lang's words. What had begun as a Hitchcock-style story—or, as the director liked to phrase it, a work of "psychological realism"—had developed into neither fish nor fowl.

More than once in his career, Lang would fall back on the canard that his films were "social problem" exposés. Nearly every film could be read thus. Sometimes, genuinely, the films *were* socially conscious; just as often, though, it was an absurd description, as when Lang defined *The Woman in the Window*, in interviews promoting its release, as a "problem film" that warned: "Be on guard for women."

After a series of meetings, Min Selvin summarized Lang's position in a memo to the Universal publicity department: *Secret Beyond the Door* was, after careful consideration, also a "problem picture." She wrote: "Mr. Lang felt an exploitable angle for *Secret* is the fact that it is a picture which shows the resolution of a problem. Other films have depicted a specific problem—*Fury* and the recently released *The Locket*, for example—but *Secret* shows how a compulsion to murder is frustrated. This is done, not through violent actions, or props, but out of the people themselves. Thus suspense is built on the characterizations in the film, so that murder and violence are sidestepped . . . Because of this, *Secret* marks a new kind of film for Fritz Lang."

If that didn't make much sense (and it didn't), then the director proposed an alternative in line with previous Fritz Lang publicity: *Secret Beyond the Door* as received wisdom about women. "A second exploitation angle was offered for consideration—the woman's angle," noted Min Selvin. "*Secret* shows a woman putting up a desperate fight to maintain her marriage vow—'for better or worse.' Instead of running away from danger—away from the possibility of being murdered—Celia Lamphere is determined to solve her problem by finding the reason for it. It was suggested that Celia Lamphere's determination to make her marriage a success might be tied in with the overall problem of easy divorces in Hollywood and in the United States."

While the publicity department puzzled over this strategy, studio executives urged Lang to hurry up so they could view a rough cut of the film. Lang had his Berliner friend Oskar Fischinger working on an animated "dream pool" for the film's opening-credit sequence. When Fischinger failed to deliver, however, the Walt Disney studio was approached to fill in. Min Selvin was sent over to talk to Disney animators, but she couldn't articulate what Lang wanted. Lang went over himself, but he couldn't articulate it very well either. Regardless, the Disney animators did their best, on short notice, whipping up some appropriately evocative footage to preface the film.

The special credit sequence delayed progress further. It was late summer before a public final cut was approved by Lang, and then fall arrived before a public preview could be slotted on the calendar. Still, Lang acted supremely confident, and everybody else crossed their fingers . . .

Until Universal had one of the all-time disasters of a preview. The audience rating cards were unanimous: "Poor." "Beyond human endurance." "It stinks."

"It got wrong laughs, the most dreaded thing in moviedom," recalled Silvia Richards. "Let's face it, even to me, it was just a sticky idea—a guy smells lilacs and goes crazy, with all those rooms under the house. It had no believability. None."

"We were absolutely sick about the fact that it was such a bad picture," recalled Min Selvin, "We were in terrible, terrible shock."

Lang and Richards walked down the street together after the preview, and found a bar where they could hide out and order drinks. Mulling things over while nursing a martini, Lang voiced a heretical opinion: the audience must be wrong—they were just unsophisticated young people. "Fritz analyzed that they were just bobby-soxers," said Richards. "He hadn't yet come to his opinion that the audience was always right."

A second preview proved "more favorable," according to Matthew Bernstein, but Lang did not have the muscle or goodwill to forestall Universal's drastic action. "Goetz simply took Lang's print and began recutting it," reported Bernstein. "He added bits of voice-over narration supplied by a different screenwriter, and had Bennett dub the entire voice-over track, originally recorded by another actress. To make matters worse, Goetz requested that Lang await the completion of his cut before viewing the film."

Out the window went a lot of the early material, including Celia's trip to Mexico and her honeymoon with the architect. Wanger knew these sequences were dearest to Lang: shadowy, packed with detail and intricate camerawork. But the producer was "conspicuously passive" during the reediting disputes, in Bernstein's words. Lang had jeopardized Wanger's own position at the studio, and the producer would depart from the Universal lot by the fall of 1947.

Lang was so infuriated that he threatened to remove his name from the reedited version of the film. Compromises were instituted. "But the ill will, between Diana and Universal, and between Lang and Wanger, was now irreparable," reported Matthew Bernstein.

From start to finish, *Secret Beyond the Door* had fared an utter failure. When it was finally released, in January of 1948, the film would receive the worst reviews of Lang's career. The *New York Daily News* called it "puerile." *PM* remarked on its "stupefying silliness." The *New York Herald Tribune* called it "warmed-over goulash," and *The New York Times* found it "pretty silly."

It was Universal's "lowest-grossing film in a terrible business year," reported Bernstein. The studio had already backed off from any future commitment to "Winchester '73," and canceled all guarantees to Lang, Wanger, and Diana Productions.

"When Lang found he could not control the course of his film's postproduction," wrote Bernstein, "he shifted his strategy to obtain control of the corporation. He took the high moral ground and accused Bennett of violating 'her duties and obligations as a stockholder' in dubbing the new narration for Goetz. His desire to see Wanger resign was by this time open."

The Wangers' desire to part company with the director was also out in the open. The director managed to hold on to "Winchester '73" for a few months longer before he was forced to sell the story rights. In the meantime Diana Productions was formally dissolved.

Wanger had gone into the partnership half-believing that Lang had been "an abused soul" over at 20th–Century Fox, "and if he only had a company of his own where he could get a chance to express himself, it would make a new man of him and remove all his inhibitions." Afterward, he privately wrote his attorney that Lang's mischief-making had been "beyond human belief. The man is a Prussian to the fingertips when it comes to detail, and worries about something that's been said in a column about him . . . Although he wouldn't even write a letter without my dictating it for him, he wanted all the credit."

For Wanger, it was the end of "two and a half years of misery." Joan Bennett "parted friends" with Lang, because after the failure of the film the director instantly reverted to his "adorable" self. But he and the actress would never work together again. In one of the few times Bennett ever commented in an interview on *Secret Beyond the Door* she labeled it an unqualified "disaster"—and an emotional mistake on the director's part. "Fritz had fallen in love with the woman who was writing the script."

"Joan Bennett wanted to divorce her husband" was the different reason Lang gave when Charles Higham and Joel Greenberg asked him why the film was so lousy. "Lots of things like that went wrong," he added.*

---

*Indeed, Joan Bennett did divorce her husband, but not until 1965. In 1952, in one of Hollywood's more notorious scandals, Wanger was jailed for several months after being convicted of shooting and wounding the actress's agent, Jennings Lang, in a fit of jealousy. Jennings Lang, incidentally, was one of the agents working out of the office of Sam Jaffe—Fritz Lang's as well as Joan Bennett's agent.

1948

CHAPTER 17

1952

It would have been understandable if Fritz Lang, approaching sixty, had entertained thoughts of slowing down, or even retiring. Diana Productions and his association with Joan Bennett had ended ignominiously in late 1947. His love affair with Silvia Richards was ebbing. His sight continued to fail, and he was coming to rely on thick eyeglasses to replace the monocle.

Adding to these anxieties were revived attacks by the House Un-American Activities Committee (HUAC) on Hollywood's left-wing community. Lang, erstwhile sleepwalker though history, stirred as political lightning flashed on the horizon.

The congressional committee, which had first targeted Lang in 1940, again rolled into Los Angeles in May of 1947. The investigative hearings coincided with a widely publicized Wallace-for-President fund-raising gala attended by screen figures. While the left-liberal half of Hollywood turned out publicly for Wallace, reactionaries were massing behind closed doors to testify about the creeping Red takeover of American movies. Among the fourteen "friendly" witnesses who regaled the HUAC staff with questionable tales of Communist cell-groups and propaganda in the movies were Warner Brothers studio chief Jack Warner, actor Robert Taylor, director Sam Wood, actor Adolphe Menjou, and Lela Rogers, the mother of actress Ginger Rogers.

Committee chairman J. Parnell Thomas (R–New Jersey) vowed to follow up the spring testimony with public hearings in the fall in Washington, D.C., openly confronting screen figures suspected of Communist leanings. Under Thomas and his successors, HUAC would pursue hearings over the next ten years. Hollywood offered a glamourous quarry. Prominent people could be publicly browbeaten into confession and capitulation. Some were able to make payoffs to escape the witch-hunt. Others resisted, and saw their careers destroyed.

One of the first subpoenaed, in September of 1947, was the German exile Hanns Eisler, the former collaborator of Brecht's who had orchestrated the music for a number of Hollywood films, including Fritz Lang's *Hangmen Also Die*. Eisler, an internationally recognized composer, was confronted by HUAC interrogator Robert Stripling, who accused him of being "the Karl Marx of Communism in the music field." To which Eisler replied, "I would be flattered"—while denying he ever held any Communist Party membership, either in Germany or America.

But Eisler's brother Gerhardt was an avowed Communist ideologue, and their sister, Ruth Fischer, rebelling against family and Stalin, functioned as a HUAC authority on the evils of Marxist-Leninism. So the committee treated Hanns Eisler shabbily, haranguing him and ordering his deportation; eventually, Eisler was allowed to purchase his own airplane ticket and leave for Czechoslovakia. (On the other hand, his brother, who freely admitted his politics and *wanted* to leave the United States, was briefly imprisoned before he jumped bail and stowed away on a ship heading for another country.)

A month before the "Hollywood Nineteen" were subpoenaed Hanns Eisler served as a cautionary cause célèbre. Lang closely followed the Eisler prelude. Among his personal papers he kept a copy of Martha Gellhorn's article "Cry Shame!" from *The New Republic* of October 6, 1947—widely distributed as a pamphlet by the Arts, Sciences and Professions Council—which excoriated Eisler's predicament as a disgrace of justice.

Eisler's treatment stirred the German exile community, while Hollywood at large turned its attention to the next act in the HUAC drama. When writs were issued to nineteen "unfriendly" writers and directors, requiring them to appear under lights and cameras in the nation's capital in October, the industry made a stab at rallying defenses. A small group led the fight behind the scenes, spearheading a campaign to unite against HUAC's threatened political housecleaning.

The founding meeting of the Committee for the First Amendment took place at the home of songwriter Ira Gershwin. Fritz Lang was probably there; certainly his name was added to the list of supporters, who sponsored a subsequent series of advertisements and programs counterattacking HUAC. The Committee for the First Amendment covered a wide array of screen talent, including notable producers (including Walter Wanger, William Goetz, and Jerry Wald) and recognizable stars (including Humphrey Bogart, Danny Kaye, Katharine Hepburn, Henry Fonda, and Myrna Loy).

A handpicked contingent of members flew from Los Angeles to Washington on Sunday, October 26, to host a national radio broadcast ("Hollywood Fights Back") on behalf of the First Amendment Committee. The Hollywood celebrities gave interviews and provided a splash in the press to coincide with the launch of HUAC testimony on the following Monday morning.

What happened, starting with the shouting defiance of the first "unfriendly" witness, screenwriter John Howard Lawson, was a disaster that couldn't have been predicted. Only eleven of the nineteen "unfriendlies" actually made it to the stand, much less gave testimony, over the insults and recriminations of congressmen determined to impugn them. The first ten to have their names called out were cited for contempt of Congress and packed off to threatened jail terms (though they managed to stall that threat, for the time being, while appealing their sentences). They became known as the Hollywood Ten.

The eleventh was Lang's collaborator on *Hangmen Also Die!*: Bertolt Brecht. The slippery Brecht managed to evade the worst by slyly changing the subject and pretending his English was inadequate, then delivering an obscure lecture on the arts, with a final disquisition on ancient Japanese theater that left committee members slack-jawed and scratching their heads. It was, someone later quipped, as though apes were examining the zoologist. After his tour de force, Brecht hopped on a plane for the German Democratic Republic.

It was painfully clear to the Committee for the First Amendment that most, if not all, of the Hollywood Ten were in fact present or former members of the Communist Party. It was a situation the cheerleaders for the First Amendment, in their speeches about freedom and the Constitution, had not counted on; and the handful of truly passionate liberals in Hollywood dedicated to defending the accused—even if they *were* Red believers—were left high and dry by a mass panic.

On November 24–25 studio producers and executives were summoned to a secret conclave at the Waldorf-Astoria Hotel in New York City. There, Eric Johnston, president of the Motion Picture Association of America, and Dore Schary, head of RKO—both previous outspoken advocates of civil liberties—hammered out a consensus statement of capitulation. Within a month, the industry had reversed itself totally, ushering in over ten years of vicious widespread blacklisting.

Humphrey Bogart was one member of the Committee for the First Amendment who was forced to backslide publicly, confessing in the March 1948 *Photoplay* that he had been a "dope" for supporting the "unfriendlies." The court appeals of the Hollywood Ten eventually ran aground; one by one, in 1950, the abandoned martyrs trooped off to jail.

Of course Lang knew Brecht all too well. The director had also worked with two of the Hollywood Ten, Ring Lardner, Jr. and Albert Maltz—both on *Cloak and Dagger*. And others who had figured in Lang's life, personally and professionally, were cropping up on the sudden rash of Reds lists drawn up by various ad hoc organizations and freelance fanatics.

The director was not the only one among the German émigrés who experienced a disturbing sense of déjà vu when comparing Germany in 1933 with the political climate of post-war America. "American conservatives," in the words of Anthony Heilbut's *Exiled in Paradise*, "were about to inflict the punishment that the Nazis had been cheated of." Twenty years earlier, Lang had awakened to the realization that he was "half-Jewish," according to the Third Reich. Now, according to the reckoning of HUAC, the director might be considered "half-Communist."

It was a period of enormous instability in Hollywood. The Justice Department forced the major studios to divest themselves of theater chains that had guaranteed their profit margins. Television was stealing audiences away. Box office showed dramatic erosion. HUAC was gnawing at the industry's heart and soul.

It was a mark of the director's character that he forged on, in fact remarkably multiplied his efforts. In the eight years that followed the failure of Diana Productions, Fritz Lang would direct ten motion pictures. These would become the years of his greatest productivity in America.

After the failure of *Secret Beyond the Door*, Lang had to snare a new producer willing to go to bat for him. His producer relationships were doomed to be about as short-lived as his romances, however. The latest suitor to come along was Howard Welsch, one of the eager new beavers who were fitting into the fast-changing Hollywood landscape.

Welsch's Fidelity Pictures had financing from the Bank of America and production-distribution deals with several major studios. Aided by New York financial partner A. Pam Blumenthal, Welsch had emerged in the late 1940s with several credits, including *Woman on the Run* for Universal and *The Groom Wore Spurs* at RKO. Fidelity Pictures was headquartered at Motion Picture Center Studio on Cahuenga Boulevard, and now Lang moved over there to set up headquarters.

The director had his formidable reputation to offer Welsch—along with the promise of a film that would star an aging but still potent sex symbol whom Lang could claim as his friend. In the dying days of Diana Productions, Lang and Silvia Richards had concocted a treatment for a Western called "The Legend of Chuck-a-Luck" that would help assuage the loss of "Winchester '73." From its inception the project had been intended as a vehicle for Marlene Dietrich, who had given the director her verbal commitment.

Sam Jaffe made a deal with Fidelity Pictures covering two new Fritz Lang films. Welsch himself owned the first property, a suspense story called *House by the River*, based on A. P. Herbert's 1921 novel *Floodtide*. Mel Dinelli, who had just received a Writers Guild nomination for his work on 1949's *The Window*, did the script. Lang would work to finalize the screenplay for "Chuck-a-Luck" while *House by the River* was being produced.

House by the River was a bizarre project, but pure Lang. The drama involved two brothers. One is a failed mystery writer who strangles the household maid; the other a gimpy-legged accountant, decent but weak, unable to appreciate the artist in his brother. Together the brothers conceal the murder, filling a sack with the maid's body and dumping it into the river that edges by the house. The body won't sink or wash away, and bobs up to betray them.

Louis Hayward would play the evil brother, Stephen. Lee Bowman would portray the weak-livered John. Jane Wyatt was Marjorie, the wholesome lady unaccountably married to the villainous brother, who, as the story progresses, finds herself ineluctably drawn to the stodgy-but-sweet John.

Welsch had already sold the package of cast and script to Republic Pictures. Nicknamed "Repulsive," Republic, one of the "minor studios" that churned out cheap quickies, was shunned by Hollywood's top echelon. On the credit side, however, its executives seldom interfered with the filmmaking: to those prepared to accept its meager budgets, Republic offered a challenge to their genius. John Ford, Orson Welles, and Frank Borzage all made memorable films there.

The director once again turned to Edward Cronjager as his cameraman, and Arthur Hilton as his editor. The production designer would be Boris Leven, with the settings confined to soundstages—the "house" a Victorian mock-up, the "river" likewise artificial.

Filming, which took place in mid-1949, was a dismal experience. Jane Wyatt remembered the director roaming the set with a seemingly permanent scowl on his face. The crew suffered Lang's belittling. The actors were well-advised to follow his atomized instructions. Both of the leading men wilted under his reign of terror.

The ladylike Wyatt, who had acted memorably in Frank Capra and Elia Kazan films, was astonished when one day, without provocation, the director's jaundiced gaze alighted on her. He found fault with one of her readings, and began to berate her uncontrollably. Her acting was amateurish! Everything she was doing was wrong. Was she trying to ruin his film? For the first and only time in her career Wyatt stalked off a set, and in a pattern that could not have been unfamiliar to him, Lang had to follow and apologize.

With everybody cowed or offended, the director concentrated on the look and tone of the production. The angles and lighting grew more reckless, adding Langian flavor to scenes while camouflaging catchpenny decor. Along with *Man Hunt, House by the River* would turn out probably the most Teutonic film Lang directed in Hollywood.

The film starts off with the mystery writer out on the lawn, reading. A beetle crawls ominously across a page. Stephen looks up, notices a light winking on in a second-floor bathroom. Upstairs, the audience is treated to an erotic reflection in a mirror as the maid steps out of a bath. His libido aroused, Stephen heads inside, waiting for the unsuspecting maid to patter downstairs wearing only a robe. She has anointed herself with his wife's perfume. And again, as in *Secret Beyond the Door,* a familiar scent triggers a deathly impulse.

The maid tries to dodge him. Stephen grabs her, squeezing a little too hard, and she succumbs. But maybe he deliberately meant to kill her; later, he cannot hide a peculiar, gratified look whenever the maid, mysteriously "missing," is mentioned. And the murder does serve to inspire his first breakthrough novel.

Stephen's literary success infuriates his brother, the accomplice plagued by guilt. An inconclusive inquest, suicidal musings, and apparitions of the deceased ensue. Though Lang's camera lingers attentively on Stephen, who acts as a square-dance caller at a party (recalling the director's own hobby), the direction betrays little compassion for any of the characters. The people are bland puppets in a plot whipped to a stylistic froth.

Light splashes off surfaces, moonlight spills through frosted windows, water glistens, the wind riffles the trees and curtains. Everything in the film is dark and shiny and foreboding. Scene after scene shows the director at the height of his ingenuity—working out of the depths of his own despair. Lang's direction was never so lush or smothering.

In the end no outlandish claims should be made for *House by the River,* Fritz Lang's real descent into the "B" world. But the director did make something peculiarly riveting out of the material he was handed. Howard Welsch was satisfied: the *Hollywood Reporter* called *House by the River* "an unusual and powerful" drama, and the film performed reasonably well in U.S. theaters. Outside America, where it was poorly distributed, *House by the River* has come to be regarded as the rarest of the director's Hollywood titles.

Years later, whenever *House by the River* was mentioned, Lang surprised people by speaking warmly of it. "He talked about *House by the River,* a film no one in France had been able to see, with enormous emotion in his voice," said Pierre Rissient. "He could describe shot by shot the first ten, twelve minutes of the film. It was almost as if we were seeing the film. When people speak of the coldness of Fritz Lang, it's true, but in this case there was also enormous emotion."

Work proceeded slowly on the Marlene Dietrich Western, in part because the director was still entertaining other offers. One of the distinct benefits of Lang's pact with Fidelity was that it was nonexclusive. Years later, Lang said in interviews that one of the offers, late in 1949, came from his former German producer Seymour Nebenzahl: Would Lang consider directing an American remake of *M*? The director claimed he was instantly appalled by the notion, and gave Nebenzahl a flat no.

According to Lang, he then entered into a dispute with Nebenzahl over who controlled the copyright. As the director explained later to Peter Bogdanovich, the rights to *M* were cloudy because his lawyer in pre-Hitler Germany had ended up becoming an "ardent Nazi" and "years later when I asked for the contracts [he said], 'We were bombed out—I can't remember anything.' "

On his part, Seymour Nebenzahl had kept in contact with Thea von Harbou, whom he never regarded as a full-fledged Nazi, but as a misguided German patriot. Her name alone had adorned the original screenplay—and she gave permission for the Hollywood remake.

According to Nebenzahl's son, Harold Nebenzal, no overtures were made to Lang in any event. The director Seymour Nebenzahl approached had strong left-wing as well as show-business references: Joseph Losey. Losey had made a name for himself working in the theater with Brecht and Charles Laughton on *Galileo*, and he was an up-and-coming entity in Hollywood on the basis of such early films as *The Boy With Green Hair*, *The Lawless*, and *The Prowler*.

A half-skeptical Losey took the job. He selected David Wayne, from *Finian's Rainbow* on the stage and *Adam's Rib* in movies, to play the role Peter Lorre had blazed around the world. Nebenzahl had already commissioned an updated script from Norman Reilly Raine and Leo Katcher, setting the story in modern-day Los Angeles.

When Losey's hiring was announced, Lang complained to one of the German journalists with whom he continued to maintain friendly relations. The rift between Lang and Nebenzahl was first mentioned in an article published in Germany. Lang insisted in the article that a Hollywood remake would have no credibility, since there were no beggars' organizations in 1950s America as there had been in 1930s Germany. The original director of *M* made no mention of having been offered the remake. Nor was there any citing of contracts destroyed in wartime bombing.

The ugly "hassle" between Lang and his former producer was then aired in the United States in Ezra Goodman's nationally syndicated newspaper column. Picking up on the published account in Germany, Goodman consulted both parties. "Lang maintains that he was producer-director of the original picture and that Nebenzahl was only involved in a financial capacity," reported Goodman. "Lang further states that he owns the rights to *M*."

Nebenzahl's reply to this assertion was a letter published in its entirety in Goodman's column. The producer stated he had "controlled entirely" the Nero-Film A. G. Corporation. He had originally acquired the *M* screenplay solely from Thea von Harbou.

"Mr. Lang functioned as director and director only," said Nebenzahl. "Mr. Lang makes the statement that the old picture was built around the sex criminal being caught and tried by a group of organized beggars in a kangaroo court. He also says that because there is no organized group of beggars in the United States, therefore the premise of the original film is not valid here.

"I am surprised to hear that the matter of organized beggars should be the premise of the old picture. I always thought, and still think, that the problems connected with a sex criminal of this type, his menace to the community and the treatment of such criminals, was the basic premise of the story—a problem which is much more acute today in the United States than the few isolated cases were in Germany in the early thirties.

"Mr. Lang states that he owns the rights to the picture and he casts doubt on my legal rights to the film. I can calm Mr. Lang's doubts. I have all legal rights to *M*.

"He says further that the original contracts for the film were in Berlin, but they have probably been destroyed in the bombing of the city. Mr. Lang had the time to take his papers with him *when he finally decided to leave*. [Author's emphasis.] Fortunately, my contracts were not destroyed in the bombing of Berlin and are right here."

Planning for the remake went ahead, while Lang—unaccountably, if indeed Nebenzahl had proffered *M*—elected to direct another, impersonal project to which he admitted indifference from the start.

American Guerrilla in the Philippines would be Lang's fourth World War II film, and his first since the concluding peace treaties.

The project was based on a novelized account of the exploits of a Navy ensign who joined with guerrillas on the island of Leyte to help fight a rearguard action against the Japanese. Ira Wolfert, who had won a Pulitzer Prize in 1943 for his dispatches from the Solomons in the Pacific, wrote the book, which was snapped up by 20th Century–Fox and molded into a screenplay by Lamar Trotti.

The initial film deal took place in the spring of 1945. Henry King had been set to direct, yet with peace closing in fast, Darryl Zanuck worried that the studio might be "too late with that kind of picture." Script revisions continued right up to the brink of principal photography in August of 1945—but with the arrival of V-J Day, Zanuck felt obliged to cancel the production.

Early in 1950, *American Guerrilla* was revived. 20th Century–Fox needed a Tyrone Power vehicle in its upcoming line-up. And the studio gambled that by shooting on location in the Philippines, they stood not only to save money on union salaries, but to add to the film's travelogue appeal. One of the ways Hollywood countered the ogre of television was by playing up the kind of exotic, faraway locales that might prove an irresistible magnet to audiences.

Lamar Trotti was reassigned to the project as producer. A mild-mannered Southerner, he had worked as a reporter and city editor in his native Atlanta. Employed exclusively by 20th Century–Fox during his career, he was admired throughout Hollywood for his screenplays of lofty Americana such as John Ford's *Young Mr. Lincoln*, William Wellman's *The Ox-Bow Incident*, and

Henry King's *Wilson*. But this was one Lamar Trotti script that didn't quite jell—one reason why Zanuck had mothballed *American Guerrilla* for five years.

The original idea had been to give the history-based story a semi-documentary flavor, but the scenario kept drifting toward fiction. The real-life Navy hero became "a composite of various American guerrilla leaders." And the hero got a sidekick, taking advantage of the availability of Tom Ewell, the studio's all-purpose character comic.

Studio records show that Zanuck himself, working with his secretary Molly Mandeville, revised Trotti's script. Trotti never got very involved, and appears to have skipped the Philippines location altogether. All the casting was also Zanuck's.

Micheline Presle, who had electrified European audiences as the lover of Gérard Philipe in *Devil in the Flesh*, would play the requisite heroine in the story (her name respelled "Prelle" for the benefit of English-speaking audiences). When she arrived in Hollywood to take up her role, Presle met with producer Trotti, and gave him her candid opinion of the script. "I told him I didn't think the script was very good," recalled Presle, "and that it wouldn't make a very good film. He didn't say anything. I remember he just sat there and looked at me. I suppose he was amused. Perhaps he was afraid of the studio."

Although he had shrugged off the prospect of a reunion with Nebenzahl, Lang apparently leaped to reconcile with Zanuck. The director still owed 20th Century–Fox one film, according to his 1941 contract. His fee would amount to $50,000, though he had managed to pay himself *twice* as much to direct *Secret Beyond the Door*. Only by his own company, Diana Productions, would Lang ever be paid more than $50,000 to direct a film in Hollywood.*

Not long after the initial previews for *House by the River*, Lang appeared on the Fox lot for a January 31, 1950, story conference. At first he was all cooperation and civility; the production was already in high gear. The studio had shipped cameras, cranes, booms, and generators aboard the *President Harrison*. Cast and crew would follow later in the spring. Filming would take place around Subic Bay and at isolated locations deep in the tropical interior.

Once the company landed on Luzon Island, however, Lang underwent one of his personality turnabouts. Hiring Filipino workers, native actors, and extras was cheaper than shipping people all the way from Hollywood, and it did serve the aims of authenticity, but working with local amateurs also meant nothing went smoothly. Apart from everything else, Zanuck had sent along an editor, posing as a location manager, whose job included sending back confidential reports on Lang's "coverage." (All the unprocessed film had to be flown to and from Hollywood for development.) When the director found out he became furious. It wasn't long before he started acting like his old self, waging war on his inferiors: especially the cameraman and crew.

---

*By comparison, around this time George Cukor was earning $4000 weekly—whether he was actually directing or not—under contract to MGM. Directors Frank Capra, George Stevens, and William Wyler were guaranteed $3,000 a week, and up to $156,000 per picture, after Paramount took over their independent Liberty Films Inc. And Alfred Hitchcock, Lang's bête noir, had just signed a four-picture deal with Warners promising him close to $250,000 a film.

You and Me (1938), Lang's first real flop, with co-stars George Raft and Sylvia Sidney. Paramount was upset, but Sidney stayed a loyal friend.

With composer Kurt Weill (at Lang's right) and Paramount musical supervisor Boris Morros (looking over his left shoulder) in the recording studio for *You and Me*. The director was a failure at studio politics, and Weill's disgust with Lang presaged that of another eminent German émigré—Bertolt Brecht. *(Courtesy of the Kurt Weill Foundation for Music)*

When 20th Century-Fox gave Lang another chance, he was forced to play humble when reunited with actor Henry Fonda—who detested him—on *The Return of Frank James* (1940).

Lang out on the town, proud to be photographed with one of his glamorous inamoratas—actress Miriam Hopkins.

A beauty young enough to be his daughter, Virginia Gilmore got pushed to star in Lang's *Western Union* (1941)—and later broke his heart (he liked to say) by marrying Yul Brynner.

Another time, another inamorata: With actresses Kay Francis (at right) and Constance Bennett, the older sister of Joan Bennett, another Fritz Lang on- and off-camera leading lady.

Lang was obsessive about preproduction. Here he plans his camera movements using a miniature set for *Hangmen Also Die* (1943), his ill-fated collaboration with Bertolt Brecht.

Joan Bennett and Walter Pidgeon in *Man Hunt* (1941). Serendipity, compromise, and skillful cunning made it the only one of the director's 20th Century–Fox films that could truly be called Langian.

Lang's editing allies: Gene Fowler, Jr., and Marjorie Fowler. Marjorie got her break editing *The Woman in the Window* (1944), produced by her father, Nunnally Johnson; Gene, her editing supervisor, later became her husband. (*Photos by Hal McAlpin*)

A mass-grave scene in *Hangmen Also Die*, which Lang may have filmed as a gesture toward the politically minded scenarists (Brecht and John Wexley), was cut from the final film.

Playwright and screen-writer Clifford Odets visits Lang during the making of *The Woman in the Window*. Lang would later film Odets's play *Clash by Night* (1952).

Lang in a publicity pose with producer William Goetz (Nunnally Johnson's partner in International Pictures) and his most empathetic star, Edward G. Robinson, during the filming of *The Woman In the Window*.

Lang loved murder and hand-to-hand struggle scenes, and spent hours working up the choreography for them. Here he instructs *Scarlet Street* co-star Dan Duryea on how to assault Joan Bennett. (*Archive Photos*)

The happy partners of Diana Productions before *Scarlet Street* (1945) led to success and discord. From left: Producer Walter Wanger, screenwriter Dudley Nichols, Joan Bennett, and Lang. (*Archive Photos*)

Lang could drive actors crazy with his fussy habits. Here he endlessly adjusts the teacups on a table before filming a simple scene
with Robinson and Bennett.

Lang at work on *Cloak and Dagger*, guiding Lili Palmer and Gary Cooper
through their paces. Neither warmed to him, and the film fell flat. *(Photofest)*

All-American, left-wing, and a capable screenwriter to boot, Silvia Richards clicked romantically with Lang; between square-dancing excursions, they collaborated on the disastrous *Secret Beyond the Door* (1948). *(Courtesy of Silvia Richards)*

Meanwhile, Lily Latte was always there, hovering in the background--the love of his life, his occasional muse, or his oppressed Hausfrau, according to varied opinions. Here "la Latte" joins Lang and his dogs in a 1940s pose. *(Courtesy of Kevin Thomas)*

An old-world gesture that
made for new-world pub-
licity: Lang made a show
of greeting his *Secret
Beyond the Door* star,
Michael Redgrave, when
he arrived by train from
New York. *(Courtesy of
Hilda Rolfe)*

Lang's big house
afire in *Secret
Beyond the Door*:
The flames were
too close for com-
fort, and Redgrave
and Bennett fled
for their lives —
repeatedly, at the
director's insis-
tence.

The three stars of
Rancho Notorious.
Lang finally got his
chance to work with
Marlene Dietrich;
with co-star Mel Ferrer
and producer Howard
Welsch, she intrigued
endlessly against the
director. Only Arthur
Kennedy ended up on
his good side.

Lang specialized in
detecting the chinks
in people's armor,
and the usually
steely Barbara
Stanwyck proved no
exception. He is
photographed with
the actress on the
set of *Clash by
Night* (1952).

Perfume triggers a killing, when Lee Bowman accidentally strangles Dorothy Patrick in the director's first descent into "B" territory, *House by the River* (1950).

An elegy of suppressed feeling: Stewart Granger (right) and Jon Whiteley in *Moonfleet* (1955). The French received it as one of Lang's masterpieces, while American critics were all but dismissive.

Lang got a new lease on life with Harry Cohn at Columbia, and directed Gloria Grahame and Glenn Ford in *The Big Heat* (1953), a crime story that proved a high point of his late career.

The director with Bert Friedlob, his last (and, in Lang's eyes, worst) producer, sharing a publicity-minded slice of birthday cake on the set of *While the City Sleeps* (1956).

Lang with Joan Fontaine and Dana Andrews during filming of *Beyond a Reasonable Doubt* (1956). His last American film was, in part, a graceful and intelligent reprise of favorite themes—but he'd lost the will to fight his daily battles.

A *nouvelle vague* homage to an old master: Brigitte Bardot reads a relevant book in the bathtub in Jean-Luc Godard's *Le Mépris* (*Contempt*, 1963). *(Courtesy of USC Cinema-Television Library and Archives of Performing Arts)*

His final work: Lang directing Peter von Eyck and Dawn Addams in *Die tausend Augen des Dr. Mabuse* (1960). The disappointments of the experience finally broke his spirit. *(Photofest)*

Lang went to India, briefly reviving his career and rediscovering the passions of his youth in *Der Tiger von Eschnapur* (1959), a two-part, big-budget epic that some critics rate with his best work. Here he coaches actress Debra Paget for her ritual dance scene. *(Photofest)*

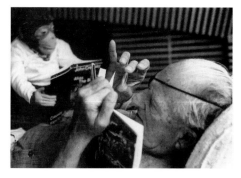

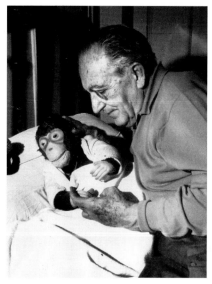

A day with Fritz Lang and Peter. The director enjoyed his little joke, and the poses with Peter were infinite. (*Courtesy of Howard Vernon*)

Meeting of the titans: Lang finally met fellow director Luis Buñuel, who regarded him as a cinema hero, at a reception in the spring of 1973. (*Courtesy of USC Cinema-Television Library and Archives of Performing Arts*)

BELOW: Lang and the ever-devoted Latte in one of their last pictures together, in the 1970s. (*Courtesy of Kevin Thomas*)

Beset by the illnesses and enfeeblements of
age, Lang at the end remained a figure of
courtly dignity to those who met him.
(Archive Photos)

"When he got to the Philippines, he put on the monocle," said Sam Jaffe. "I knew that was the beginning of the end. He got difficult again."

The director knew better than to take out his anger on Tyrone Power, who was one of the studio's box-office heavyweights. Micheline Presle, for a different reason, received his courtly respect—she could share his fond reminiscences about Paris. And among the cast members she alone would emerge on the screen with her dignity intact. The director warmed to her character with indulgent close-ups, including one vignette, characteristic of Lang's occasional sentimentality, in which she sings a French Christmas song.

"He [Lang] didn't like the film," recalled Presle. "Neither did I. I don't remember very much about it. The crew did not like him altogether. I couldn't understand why. He and I became very friendly. I remember sitting on a boat with him, we two Continental souls, talking about European filmmaking and how much we hated Hollywood."

Whenever in later years *American Guerrilla* came up in the chronology of questions in an interview, Lang waved on another title. "It was an awkward time to be making a film [in the Philippines]," was all the director told Charles Higham and Joel Greenberg, "because there were big clashes going on involving the Communist Hukbalahap forces."*

Not that it wasn't filmed competently—if nothing else, as an excuse for some picturesque scenery. But the hero (Tyrone Power) was dull and virtuous, one of the dullest of a type Lang still did not believe in. The film had no credible wartime atmosphere, and its history was vulgarized. Lang made a point of heroically positioning the Catholic Church; as in *Metropolis*, the film's climax would take place in a cathedral—a religious sanctuary invaded, and turned into a battleground. Even an altar boy pitches in during the final shoot-out against the Japanese.

By the time the director returned to America, Lang was already persona non grata at 20th Century–Fox. Zanuck took over the editing, but there was little anyone could do to hurt, or improve, the film. Released in mid-November 1950, *American Guerrilla in the Philippines* received some of the director's worst reviews of his Hollywood career.

"You would gather that MacArthur's well-known determination to return was motivated principally by a desire to attend the Tyrone Power–Micheline Presle nuptials," wrote Robert Hatch of *The New Republic*. *Time* said the film was "hackneyed as a comic book adventure yarn and not nearly so well played." "Perfunctory and artificial," observed Bosley Crowther in *The New York Times*.

It probably *is* Fritz Lang's worst film. But the pragmatic director developed a sense of humor about *American Guerrilla* over time. To Peter Bogdanovich, he offered the most direct explanation of why he had taken the job. "I did it because I have to eat."

In his twilight years, the director came to enjoy berating his acolytes, saying their high opinions of him were worthless since they inevitably revered every

---

*The Communist participation in the Filipino national resistance is one detail of history that is conveniently glossed over in the film. It was not an appropriate time to be singing Communist praises. The film's script prefers to stress the danger of "fifth-columnists," which in blacklist-conscious Hollywood was shorthand for Red sympathizers, spies, and traitors whose first loyalty was to the Soviet Union.

film he directed. "No, I *don't* like every one," one of them, David Overbey, ventured to say one day. "Which one don't you like?" the director asked, arching a menacing eyebrow. "*American Guerrilla in the Philippines*," replied Overbey. "It's shit—there's not a decent shot in the entire film." "*American Guerrilla?*" thundered the director, "*American Guerrilla*?! I never made such a film! It would never fit into the Fritz Lang world vision."

The only member of the Diana Productions staff to continue on with Lang at Fidelity Pictures was Min Selvin. The others could not be kept on salary and had to be let go. Lily Latté became more important to the director than ever.

No matter that Peter Heiman was still residing with Latté and that she, Heiman, and Lang still gathered together on social occasions. (They spent the night of Truman's election, with the Adornos, at Lily Latté's apartment, listening to the returns on the radio.) When, sometime in 1949, Peter Heiman asked Latté to marry him, she said she had to talk it over with Lang. The director told her, "Over my dead body!" Latté was afraid to go against Lang, and a disheartened Heiman opted, shortly thereafter, to move to New York.

Soon after that, Latté vacated her apartment and moved into Lang's house, so she could be there to help him as his career stumbled along and his eyesight degenerated.

After *Secret Beyond the Door*, Lang's love affair with Silvia Richards ran its course. The fact that she had two young children was always thrown up by the director as a smoke screen for his unwillingness to make her a permanent commitment. Richards worried about the director's getting along with her children on a daily basis. One day Lang half-seriously suggested installing Richards and her brood in a nearby house so that he could visit them daily. It would *almost* be like living together . . .

"Fritz didn't like children," noted Lang's secretary, Hilda Rolfe. "I remember Silvia bringing her kids to the studio once, and he was very annoyed and didn't talk to them much. I don't think he could communicate with children."

When Hilda Rolfe left Lang, she went to work at 20th Century–Fox as a secretary for the hard-boiled novelist and screenwriter A. I. Bezzerides. Then, before she took an extended trip to Europe, she played matchmaker between Silvia Richards and Bezzerides. Richards hit it off with Bezzerides, surprisingly, and they became a couple—which brought Lang both disappointment and relief.

One final time, Lang had asked Silvia Richards to marry him. His unexpected proposal came during a phone call from the Philippines during the shooting of *American Guerrilla*. Richards never forgot the wavering sound of his voice coming over the oceanic cables. "It was his last try," Richards said. "I don't think he expected me to say yes."

He certainly didn't. Michael Burke recalled Lang's astonishment and dismay when Burke informed the director that Burke was going to marry a woman he had been squiring around during the filming of *Cloak and Dagger*. Lang tried to dissuade Burke. "Why do you Americans always have to *marry* them?" the director demanded to know. There were some lengths to which Lang would *not* go to become an American.

☆   ☆   ☆

The remake of *M* opened in the nation's movie theaters around the same time as *American Guerrilla*, in the fall of 1950. Lang always claimed that when he returned from the Philippines he discovered that his normally "wonderful lawyer" had left him in the lurch on the issue.

Curiously, Lang's lawyer was also Joseph Losey's lawyer—Martin Gang. And Gang was emerging as the principal go-between for Hollywood ex-Communists who were caving in to behind-the-scenes pressure and making confessional statements to HUAC about themselves and their friends. Gang's advice was to cooperate with the Red-hunters. Losey would eventually ditch Gang, and—would be one of the Losey's last credits before getting blacklisted himself.*

Lang showed up outside a screening of the new *M*, and launched into a public shouting match with Seymour Nebenzahl. Lang hated the very idea of the unauthorized remake. He repeated over and over again to friends that the only reason he wasn't suing Nebenzahl was that his papers had been lost in Berlin. "It's theft!" the director would insist. What it really constituted was *emotional* theft. Lang could barely contain himself when his friend, UCLA instructor David Bradley, mentioned having gone to see the Losey version. After Lang had gotten all the angry words out of his system, a long silence prevailed. "Then a tear came into his eye which he blotted away with his fingers under his monocle," recalled Bradley.

Losey meant well; he recalled seeing Lang's masterpiece while a student in Munich in 1931, and made an effort to imitate certain shots and scenes, lodging them within Los Angeles environs. The picture as it turned out was compelling in its own right, but for the rest of his life Losey remained defensive about the *M* remake. "The picture was censored and totally banned in eight states and the people who did see it were mostly critics who knew the Lang film and compared it adversely with that," Losey told Michel Ciment. "The same thing happened in England. So it's kind of a dead picture, but none the less it contains some of my best work up to that time—cinematically, visually, and in terms of characterization—because of David Wayne's performance."

An important incident involving Lang, Losey, and other leading Hollywood directors took place in the fall of 1950.

Director Cecil B. De Mille, a superpatriot who was also one of the legends of the industry, led a faction of the Directors Guild in stirring up a debate about "fifth-columnists" in the membership. De Mille, in fact, tried to have Guild President Joseph L. Mankiewicz, Lang's old nemesis, recalled, after Mankiewicz protested De Mille's campaign to force every director to sign a loyalty oath to the U.S. government. While Mankiewicz was out of town on vacation, De Mille convened a board meeting to pass a loyalty-oath bylaw, a maneuver that sparked a members' backlash.

Joseph Losey was among the handful of directors who then spearheaded a

---

*The credits for the remake of *M* included several ill-fated blacklistees, who were hired by Losey and Nebenzahl at a time when such an act was pure bravery on their part. The writer credited with the script's final dialogue revisions was in fact one of the original "Hollywood Nineteen"—Waldo Salt.

petition drive asking for the membership at large to come together to censure De Mille, abrogate the loyalty oath, and demonstrate support for Mankiewicz. Lang was not among the twenty-five signatories of that petition, which included the names of such onetime Berliners as Billy Wilder, Walter Reisch, and Andrew Marton. But both he and Losey—the two directors of *M*—showed up at the emotion-charged gathering in the ballroom of the Beverly Hills Hotel on October 22, 1950. "The entire membership showed up," wrote fellow director Robert Parrish in *Growing Up in Hollywood*. "A record turnout."

Mankiewicz opened with a long, eloquent, rehearsed speech. De Mille replied—assailing the Guild president and his liberal supporters, defending "his faction's position as best he could, but he was not a good speaker and soon began to bore his audience, a thing he seldom did with his movies," in the words of Parrish.

"As his loss of ground became more apparent, he [De Mille] turned his fire on what he charged to be the questionable politics of his opponents," continued Parrish. "He singled out the twenty-five directors who had signed our petition. De Mille said that most of the twenty-five directors were affiliated with un-American or subversive organizations and theories and that many of them were foreign-born. When he said this, there was a gasp of disbelief, then some of the members started to hiss and boo."

Rouben Mamoulian, William Wellman, John Cromwell, and Delmer Daves took the floor to denounce De Mille. Fritz Lang was another who stood up, "quietly" confessing "that, for the first time, the fact that he spoke with an accent made him a little afraid," reported Parrish.

The meeting went on for several hours, with more attacks and counterattacks. At long last, John Ford stood up in his baseball cap, sucking on his pipe and casting humble glances at his tennis shoes. "He was an important man in the Guild, and everyone wondered what he thought," said Parrish. "He was also a master of timing."

Ford identified himself for the stenographer taking it all down. "My name's John Ford," the dean of American directors said. "I make Westerns." Ford's brief speech demolishing De Mille was drawn out by his practiced shtick of fiddling with his glasses and pipe as he spoke. "I don't like you, C. B.," Ford declared. "I don't like what you stand for and I don't like what you've been saying here tonight."

Ford demanded a formal apology, his motion was seconded, and the membership voted overwhelmingly that De Mille and the entire board resign, with Mankiewicz awarded a vote of confidence. There is no record of how Lang himself voted, but years later, Mankiewicz remembered Lang "courageously" sticking up for him on this occasion.

The fix was definitely in, however, and HUAC's marked victims were running scared. The next wave of congressional hearings was scheduled for the spring of 1951.

The Philippines film signaled the end of the relationship between agent Sam Jaffe and the constantly-fretting Fritz Lang. The director's paranoia was soaring. He was convinced that his phones were tapped no matter where he worked, that he was surrounded by studio backstabbers, secret agents writing up confidential reports to undermine him with producers. All no doubt partly true; the studios were notoriously authoritarian. Everyone else in Hollywood lived under the same rules, but Fritz Lang saw it as a personal persecution.

Ring Lardner, Jr., recalled a script conference in which Lang kept inveighing against screenwriter John Wexley for his duplicity. "He's a dishonest man," Lang complained repeatedly. Lardner, who wasn't overly fond of Wexley, still felt this was going too far. "What do you mean, he's a dishonest man?" Lardner finally asked.

"On the script for *Hangmen Also Die,* I told him the script had to be shortened by about twenty pages and he came back with a script that was twenty pages shorter," Lang explained, "but I found that only ten pages in actual length had been cut out, and the rest was by his instructing his secretary to put more lines on a page!"

"Now this is something I think writers had done since the beginning of time, and it was not exactly a crime," Lardner added to the anecdote, "But Fritz was very moral about it."

Lang and Sam Jaffe had been having circular conversations for far too long. Why wasn't Jaffe getting Lang better jobs? Why wasn't his agent getting him better publicity? Why wasn't Jaffe defending the director against the industry scuttlebutt that deeply wounded him?

"He was always complaining, 'You don't protect me,'" remembered Jaffe. "I'd say, 'What am I, a defense lawyer?' I had never heard anybody say anything like that. I couldn't translate it. If he had a bad reputation, he had a bad reputation. I couldn't dismiss it."

One day, Lang showed up at his agent's home. Jaffe wasn't there, but when his wife answered the door, the director took it out on her, screaming at her for several minutes. For Sam Jaffe, who had been loyal to Fritz Lang for over ten years, that was the last straw. "I finally gave up on him. He had a persecution complex. There was nobody against him. He was against himself. He would take a situation and instead of looking in a mirror and saying, 'What is wrong with me?' he would blame the source."

The political atmosphere in Hollywood in 1950–1951 certainly contributed to Fritz Lang's embattled psychology. To the list of producers and studios that considered Lang an "untouchable," he could now add the U.S. government, whose agents he knew to be scurrying around behind the scenes trying to pinpoint his political coloration.

In the fall of 1950, in fact, Peter Heiman had been visited by an FBI investigator asking about Lang. Heiman scoffed at the idea that the self-absorbed Lang would put the Communist Party or any political manifesto above his personal interests. Silvia Richards, being pressed hard by HUAC investigators, was another asked about Lang's ties to the Communist Party. Richards almost laughed at the idea of Lang as a Red, and told the investigators they were way off track.

A review of government files pertaining to the director, obtained under auspices of the Freedom of Information Act (FOIA), indicates that Federal agencies first began compiling information on Lang as early as 1939. The director's activities were sporadically monitored throughout the 1940s; then, in 1950–1951, when HUAC hearings picked up steam, a series of updates was filed on his associations and relationships.

Much of the material, in FBI, state, or military intelligence files, focused on Lang's friendly connections with émigrés known to advocate such sinister policies as Soviet-American friendship, or a post-war German government favorable to Russia. Heinrich and Thomas Mann, Lion Feuchtwanger, Hanns Eisler, Bertolt Brecht, and especially Otto Katz,* a casual acquaintance of Lang's, were also the focus of government surveillance; whenever Lang turned up at their homes for dinner—or on the same "Communist-front" masthead—another report on him was filed.

As researchers know, there is as much dross as gold in FOIA documents. In Lang's case there is also the customary degree of misinformation. An interview with a fortune-teller, prognosticating about the director, is included. Lang is sometimes confused with another man; the report refers to him as "alias Fred Lang," married and the father of one child. Typically, the FOIA papers offer more blacked-out sections, representing either covert sources or even wilder misinformation, than legible text.

Occasionally an on-target zinger is recorded. Although Lang is described in one report as having "a very bad disposition"—inclined to "yell, curse, and throw things around and display a violent temper"—he couldn't be labeled a Red. According to this undercover informant, "Fritz Lang always used politics in any way in which he thought it would benefit him." Another succinctly summarized Lang as "a talented director, but politically a child, a 'sucker' for organization, sponsor, and donor lists." Still, not a Communist.

When Lang went looking for a replacement for Sam Jaffe, he sought an agency that could help him out with this pressing problem of establishing his political naiveté. For a long time the Nat Goldstone Agency had included a disproportionate number of Hollywood's "fellow travellers" among its writer and director clients;** and Goldstone's partner, George Willner—considered the agency's driving force—was widely reputed to be a committed member of the Communist Party.

After the Waldorf statement of 1947, however, the Nat Goldstone Agency had undergone a curious schism characteristic of that "scoundrel time." The opposite politique was now ascendant, and the changing political winds made room for such vehement anti-Communists on the client list as Robert Taylor, Ginger Rogers, Robert Young, and screenwriter John Lee Mahin. Willner himself was on the verge of being blacklisted. He would be named first by another agent, Meta Reis Rosenberg, in the spring 1951 HUAC hearings; eventually his $750,000 interest in the agency would be relinquished for the bargain price of $25,000. Nat Goldstone bought him out.

Goldstone was the proverbial gray man—from all accounts a mensch but

---

*Katz, aka Rudolf Breda, was a supporter of Prince Löwenstein, who was deeply involved in antifascist causes. A longtime member of the German Communist Party, Katz lived for a time in Moscow and after 1933 made many trips to Hollywood, organizing campaigns and funds for the underground resistance. Later he was executed by Stalinists in Czechoslovakia, where he had ended up as minister of state.

**Among the longtime clients of the Nat Goldstone Agency were screenwriters John Howard Lawson and Lester Cole, two of the Hollywood Ten, and director John Berry, who directed the Hollywood Ten's fund-raising documentary before being blacklisted himself.

without any deeply held political beliefs. He would walk the tightrope—staying loyal to some blacklistees, leaving the hard cases behind. When necessary, Goldstone and others in his agency worked cheek by jowl with Martin Gang, patching up HUAC "misunderstandings."

Lang signed up with Goldstone's agency, but stayed loyal to the lawyer who had left him in the supposed lurch on the American M. Martin Gang never had so much business. Once known as a liberal, a Democrat, a member of the anti-establishment National Lawyers Guild, Gang had even signed the amicus curiae brief on behalf of the Hollywood Ten. Then Gang made his switchover. By mid-1951, Lang's lawyer had become "the symbol of collaboration" with HUAC's reign of intimidation, according to Victor S. Navasky in his authoritative book *Naming Names*. "In fact, he [Gang] represented more informers than any other single attorney in Los Angeles."

1952

CHAPTER 18

1953

It may be an exaggeration to describe *Rancho Notorious*, as the director himself did, as a "Western for adults"; as "an almost existential tale," in the words of one contemporary critic, its scenario probing "issues of personal identity and morality, the ephemeral nature of Man's quest for purpose"; or as a film that helps make Lang "the father of the psychological Western," in the words of Steven Bach.

But his third Western was the only one Fritz Lang developed from start to finish—in fact, the only original screen story apart from *Hangmen Also Die* that he conceived and executed in all his Hollywood years. Therefore it represents a personal breakthrough, as well as a film that on its own terms harbors rewarding pleasures.

The gradual breakdown of the director's relationship with Silvia Richards meant that "The Legend of Chuck-a-Luck" lay dormant for most of 1949–1950. The first treatment in Lang's files at USC is forty-one pages—without dialogue, without any mention of music, without the film's identifiable flashback structure. Lang's name alone is credited. Basically, Richards had acted as a stenographer for the director's ideas; she was certainly modest about her contribution, transferring all rights to the director for one dollar on September 13, 1949.

"Chuck-a-Luck" referred to a saloon game, a type of vertical roulette played with a turning wheel. ("I myself have seen it played in a Mexican border town," Lang told Peter Bogdanovich.) The Marlene Dietrich Western was supposed to start principal photography in November of 1950, according to initial publicity pronouncements, which misspelled the title "Chuck-o-Luck" (getting it spelled right was one of the title's drawbacks). Indeed, Lang did some location scouting in November and December in the Tucson area. "Bank of America financing guarantees didn't permit too much time" or "cause for brooding," in the words of *The New York Times*.

Yet the publicity was premature. There was no ready-to-go script, two years after the death of Diana Productions. The announced start date came and left; still no script. The director had tried crafting one himself, but, as ever, found he needed a compatible collaborator.

Enter Daniel Taradash. Taradash was a graduate of Harvard Law School who had won a national play-writing contest and come out to Hollywood on a Columbia contract in 1939. His first credit was a co-adaptation of Clifford Odets's *Golden Boy* for director Rouben Mamoulian. After spending time in the Signal Corps during World War II, Taradash returned to screenwriting. His post-war credits included *Knock on Any Door* for director Nicholas Ray.

Taradash received a call from his agent: Fritz Lang wanted him to work on a script. The "Chuck-a-Luck" treatment was sent over. Taradash liked it, but he was busy working on a "spec" project, a labor of love. So he made what he thought was an impossible salary demand of $1,500 weekly—and was taken aback when producer Howard Welsch, frustrated by the lack of script progress, agreed.

At his very first meeting with Lang, Taradash remembered, he informed the director of "a story notion that I had invented and that I almost had to insist on if I were to write the film. It must be noted that this was long before *High Noon* was filmed or shown. My idea was that instead of a narrator, we would have a cowboy ballad sung intermittently through the film, in which whatever story points we didn't make on the screen would be made in music."

Later on, in numerous interviews, Lang took pains to credit himself for that conceit: the repeated theme song of "Chuck-a-Luck" that cues scenes and motifs in the story line. ("I had the idea," he told Peter Bogdanovich, "and talked it over with the writer . . .") "No way he had the idea!" remembered Taradash. "I'd swear to that in court on a thousand Bibles. Not only was it my idea but I had to *sell* him on the idea."

The director, who *collected* folk songs, probably resented not having thought of the theme-song idea first. But Lang came around, and the "Chuck-a-Luck" song was approved. With Taradash, an intelligent younger man who admired the director's body of work, Lang would have his most productive relationship with a writer since Dudley Nichols.

"I had been told Lang was an ogre, a monster," recalled Taradash, "impossible to get along with. I can see how many people would say these things, but I found Lang none of them. Indeed, we became very good friends and remained so throughout the rest of his life.

"A considerable amount of my time on this project was spent at Lang's house, seated at a table across from him; he made dreadful coffee and he consumed about fifty cups a day; I found myself slowly swallowing this brew myself. He went over every centimeter of the script with me. I learned more about screenwriting from Lang than from anyone else.

"One of the reasons was that Lang wanted a rather special type of script, or at least the one to be prepared for the director. He insisted on working out every camera angle, from unusual angles to typical over-the-shoulder shots. I soon found out why. Lang disliked his producers and feared the production control they would have once the actual shooting started.

"He was very much afraid that after a few days or a week he would have some kind of terrible row with them and they would fire him and turn the script over to another director. And Lang was so fond of 'Chuck-a-Luck' that, as he told me, he was having the script prepared so that if he were fired, 'even an idiot could direct it.' "

✳   ✳   ✳

The script evolved to focus on a cowboy named Vern who is intent on re-
venging the rape and murder of his fiancée (a scene that takes place during a
store robbery in the opening credits). Driven by hate, Vern catches up with
Whitey, one of the two killers. But Whitey, Vern learns, is not the one who
actually perpetrated the crimes. Before he dies, Whitey can only manage to
gasp a mysterious clue—"Chuck-a-Luck."

From a chance encounter in a barbershop, Vern learns that "Chuck-a-Luck"
is connected with an aging salon singer named Altar Keane. Through other
encounters Vern learns more about Altar Keane: She is amorously involved
with a gunfighter named Frenchy, who happens to be cooling his heels in a
nearby town jail.

Vern gets himself arrested and tossed into Frenchy's cell. The two men
engineer a jailbreak, and Frenchy leads Vern to the sprawling ranch Altar operates with earnings from "Chuck-a-Luck" gambling. There the ex-saloon
singer presides over a haven for "wanted" outlaws. One of the rules of the
ranch is that nobody is allowed to inquire too deeply about the identity of any
of the other desperadoes.

Vern schemes to figure out which of the cowboy guests is the unknown
killer. He contrives to spend time with Altar, slyly interrogating her. Against
his better judgment, he finds himself attracted to the amoral saloon queen
and thrust into a romantic rivalry with Frenchy.

A bungled robbery brings Vern's mission out into the open. Vern realizes
that a man named Kinch is his fiancée's killer, and hands him over to the
local sheriff. Vern angrily confronts Altar, reveals his true identity, and con-
demns her indifference to her villainous friends. Meanwhile Kinch manages
to escape. A climactic shoot-out ensues at the ranch, with Vern and Frenchy
banded together against Kinch's gang.

Kinch is killed, but Altar steps in front of a bullet intended for Vern, who
realizes too late that he has fallen in love with her. She dies cradled in the
arms of both Frenchy and Vern.

The characters, plot, and structure were definitely Lang's, although in the
end Taradash would receive sole writing credit. The script reprised themes
that had intrigued the director for years: a secret buried deep in the past; an
innocent hero plunged into a nightmare and driven by revenge; a love triangle
revolving around a tarnished lady. The story is framed by an Ufa-style *Rahmenhandlung* and a series of flashbacks, including one scene, a human horse
race in a saloon, meant as a parody of Berlin decadence.

Frenchy was crafted to be as sweetly diffident a gunfighter as imaginable,
the kind of outlaw who pauses during a jailbreak to kick in a window on Main
Street and grab a bottle of perfume for Altar Keane. Nothing real about him;
he was Lang's fantasy.

Vern (played by Arthur Kennedy, the actor Lang ended up liking best
among the cast) would be the character awash in self-pity. The director's most
revealing characters had the same quality. Hans Beckert, Chris Cross, and
Dave Bannion—the police detective of *The Big Heat*—all believe, as Lang did
about himself, that they have been martyred by fate.

Altar Keane was intended to be Marlene Dietrich incarnate: half-Cleopatra,
half-Sphinx. Though, behind her back, the director referred to her as "a rotten

actress," Dietrich nevertheless stirred deep feelings within him. Lang always connected her with Berlin years and the shared times in Hollywood, thinking of her as a kindred soul.

The story the director told was that one day he ran into Dietrich in a stationery shop in Beverly Hills, where the actress was trying to finagle the sale of some stationery without paying the full amount. Casting her in his next project would amount to an "act of charity," thought the director. This may not be untrue: Dietrich's career was in a downswing. But the screen siren was someone who bartered prices in the best of circumstances, and the director was known to emphasize the desperation of others when it was he himself who needed the charity. The stationery-store anecdote is at odds with Daniel Taradash's recollection that Dietrich, fresh from recent appearances in films by Billy Wilder and Alfred Hitchcock, could still conjure a magical aura in Hollywood.

After the Jean Gabin incident on the set of *Moontide*, Dietrich had behaved coolly to Lang, but their friendship persisted. During the war, Dietrich entertained troops overseas, and in 1946 she had taken the time to let Lang know that a poison-pen writer had named him as a closet Hitlerite in a letter to a Paris newspaper. Lang sued the source, expressing his gratitude in a letter to Dietrich. The director saw less of the actress socially when she returned to America, but only out of circumstance.

His Western script was fashioned as an earnest tribute to her, as well as a sort of metaphor about himself. In the right mood, Lang could see himself in Dietrich's reflection. "She'd shut the door on a cattle baron if she had a fancy for a cowpuncher," the script says of Altar Keane; Lang was also a baron who fancied himself a cowpuncher. Altar Keane's narcissism, her code of honor, her incongruity in a distinctly American setting (everything must be "explained double" to Altar Keane, who is slow to fathom the lingo), her tough shell and sense of superiority—these were all quintessentially Dietrich, and quintessentially Lang.

Steven Bach, in *Marlene Dietrich: Life and Legend*, pointed out that the name "Altar" was a play on the German word "Alter," which translates as "an aging man," and was meant by Lang as almost a private joke, clueing some members of the audiences into the subtext of Dietrich's role as an aging star with fading sex appeal. It was a reference that reflected both Dietrich's career and Lang's own mid-life crisis. But Dietrich didn't find that in-joke funny, and it was one aspect of the script that spelled trouble from the outset.

The characters were not really as "unconventional" as some of the film's enthusiasts have maintained. After Lang's death, when the director's library was sold to the University of Wyoming's Special Collections, the inventory revealed a broad diversity of social history, atlases and reference books, crime stories, literature, political tracts, and sex-and-marriage manuals. But the director's library is also striking for its number of Max Brand, Eugene Cunningham, Zane Grey, Ernest Haycox, and other Western novels—many of them well-thumbed paperbacks. This was Lang's genre since boyhood. He *loved* the Western conventions.

But the trouble, for once, had little to do with the script—a solid, craftsmanlike job. The trouble was a budget that seemed to be constantly shrinking. An ample budget had never been much of an issue for Lang in Germany, but it was a luxury the director rarely enjoyed in America.

Lang hired a first-rate cameraman—Hal Mohr, a wizard with complex crane, dolly, and boom shots. Mohr had been one of the cameramen of von Stroheim's *The Wedding March*, then a longtime stalwart for Warner Brothers, an Oscar-winner for *A Midsummer Night's Dream* and *The Phantom of the Opera*. Lang got the art director he wanted, too: friend Wiard Ihnen, whose relationship with Lang dated back to late 1939 and his 20th Century–Fox contract films.

Mohr and Ihnen could be counted on to do their utmost, but inevitably money grew tight and the schedule abbreviated. After spending freely on his expensive director and even more expensive star, on the interminable script development and preproduction, and on a first-tier crew and supporting cast, producer Howard Welsch proved reluctant to dig any deeper into his pockets. Exteriors had to be skimped on, and interiors filmed at General Services Studio, with a few outdoor scenes at Republic's Western Ranch; the on-screen effect amounted to "an extremely cheap production," in Taradash's words.

The trouble was—as ever with Lang—a producer he could barely stomach. Welsch, sensing the propitiousness of a Marlene Dietrich western, chose to second-guess every directorial judgment. The producer had not supervised Lang's first Fidelity film, *House by the River*, delegating that chore to an associate; now Welsch plunged into daily decision making. Lang hated the fact that, of the two Fidelity partners, the producer liked to refer to himself as the "artistic head" of the production company. Characteristically, the director would show no diplomacy nor tactical shrewdness in battling Welsch, but grappled with him on each and every fine point.

Mel Ferrer proved every bit as troublesome. Casting Ferrer as Frenchy had been Lang's idea, ironically. Ferrer had been an editor, writer, dancer, producer of radio shows, and a feature film director before turning actor. He had made his screen debut in 1949's *Lost Boundaries*, then was noticed by Lang as the sensitive matador of 1951's *The Brave Bulls*. But Lang was always envying qualities in an actor's performances, glimpsed in another director's work, that he couldn't quite seem to coax forth in his own.

Once on the set, Ferrer, a man whose ego was equal to the director's, took umbrage at Lang's dictatorial methods—his customary barking commands, the way he stipulated an actor's every gesture and movement. Since Ferrer didn't really have the authority to buck the director alone, he teamed up with a disgruntled Marlene Dietrich to make things difficult for Lang. And in the film's female star he found a formidable ally.

Whenever the two went to Welsch with their complaints, the producer was only too happy to take their side. The "Unholy Three," as Lang dubbed them—after the larcenous trio of Tod Browning's silent film classic—intrigued against the director. Welsch overruled Lang on cost and scheduling issues, while Ferrer and Dietrich went through their numbers—sometimes stonily—on the set. Lang was accustomed to slugging things out on a film set; he always believed he could sort the footage out in the editing booth.

The trouble was—inevitably—Marlene Dietrich. She had been cast as an aging glamour queen, but, not surprisingly, she wanted none of the "aging." "I had the foolish idea, foolish because it led to a lot of unpleasant fights with her, of wanting to give Marlene a new screen image," the director told Charles Higham and Joel Greenberg. "In the script I'd described the character she played as 'an elderly dance-hall girl,' and she came on looking younger in each scene."

Dietrich would just as soon direct herself, since Josef von Sternberg was no longer acceptable. She recommended her own lighting and angles, pointedly informing Lang that her beloved von Sternberg would have directed scenes differently and better. Nothing needled Lang more than hearing von Sternberg's name over and over.

"Fritz Lang was the director I detested most," wrote Dietrich in her 1987 autobiography *Marlene*—in which she offhandedly refers to the director as "a Jew." "I became conscious of my feelings toward him in 1952, when we filmed *Rancho Notorious*. In order to be able to work with Lang, I had to repress all the hatred and aversion he aroused in me. If Mel Ferrer had not been there I probably would have walked off the set in the middle of shooting. But Mel was always near and helped to see me through those troublesome days.

"Fritz Lang belongs to the 'Brotherhood of Sadists.' He despised my reverence for Josef von Sternberg, and tried to replace this genius in my heart and in my mind. I know that because he confessed it to me.

"Before the order 'Everybody on the set' resounded, Fritz Lang would spend hours marking out positions on the ground. At the same time, we were not allowed to look down at the ground. In this way he was trying to prevent, at all costs, the actors from being quicker than himself, and he seemed to take a diabolical delight in making us endlessly repeat our movements.

"He was tall, and took long steps so that we could follow him only with the greatest effort. Mel Ferrer, an elegant man, but much shorter than Lang, took great pains to respect the markings and not step beyond them.* Despite my height, I was unable to do the same. But that didn't bother Lang one bit. 'Do it again,' he would scream, and have me repeat the same gesture a hundred times."

Perhaps actor Douglas Fairbanks, Jr., both a friend of Lang's and an ex-lover of Dietrich, would have made a better Frenchy, having played the part with both of them in real life. But Fairbanks said in an interview for this book, "Thank God I never worked for Fritz." Even the strong quaked before Herr Lang.

On the set of their first and only movie together, it was a stand-off: the director was the irresistible force, Dietrich the immovable object. Actresses usually buckled under, or rushed away in tears from Lang. Dietrich, more German than Lang, fought back tooth and nail. Dietrich protested endlessly. She snaked around behind Lang's back. And finally she opted to play her scenes differently or indifferently, his way or her way, her performance dictated only by her mood.

---

*Mel Ferrer's studio publicity puts his height at 6 feet, 2 inches, which, if precise, means that he was not "much shorter" than Lang, but actually *taller* than the director.

One day, responding to a repeated summons by the director, the actress appeared wild-eyed in the doorway of her dressing room. In front of the astonished cast and crew, Dietrich ripped off her dress, ruining the expensive costume while launching into a diatribe about the shortcomings of an outfit she had virtually designed herself. The temperamental star knew full well who would suffer the consequences of the costs and delay. By the end of production these two old compatriots, who once had engaged in pillow talk, spoke with each other only shrilly.

The anecdote is incredible, therefore, that one night, toward the end of the filming, Fritz Lang returned to the set to tinker with props and lights after everyone had gone home. All of a sudden he noticed a light in Dietrich's trailer. Drawn forward, the director glimpsed the actress through an open door, garbed in a glittering white tuxedo and top hat, preening in front of a full-length mirror. The way Lang's friends liked to tell the story—very cinematically—Dietrich turned and her eyes met Lang's; then they fell slowly into an embrace, and ended up making heated love. Without exchanging a single word.

As with Lang and Goebbels, there were no eyewitnesses.

The spring 1951 session of the House Un-American Activities Committee opened in Washington, D.C., as the Western Lang was still calling "Chuck-a-Luck" wended its way through postproduction. The hearings went more smoothly than the film. The HUAC script had been slavishly rehearsed. There were no limitations on time or budget, or "number of takes."

One of the people named in this second round was Lloyd Gough, the actor who plays Kinch, the killer of *Rancho Notorious*. But Gough refused to cooperate with HUAC, he was swiftly blacklisted, and the character—as well as the actor who played him went unmentioned in the official screen credits.

The star of the second round was Edward Dmytryk, one of the Hollywood Ten, freshly released from prison and scrambling to revive his career by purging himself of his tawdry political past. Among the two dozen of his former friends and comrades Dmytryk named as Hollywood Communists were Gordon Kahn, one of Lang's ghostwriters in the 1940s, and John Wexley, scriptwriter of *Hangmen Also Die*.

As other public penitents followed Dmytryk back on the career path, Wexley would become one of the most frequently named people in the HUAC sessions. This belied Lang's assertion, to American Film Institute students, that "we didn't know it that he was in the Communist Party." The "we" must refer to Lang and Arnold Pressburger—one of the few times the director of *Hangmen Also Die* gave the film's producer any credit. Everyone else seemed to know about the ideological Wexley, whose Hollywood career effectively ended with the HUAC purge.

In interviews where he discussed the blacklist, Lang never mentioned Silvia Richards; she was like von Harbou's Indian lover—the Ayi Tendulkar of this little episode. At HUAC's fall hearings, Hy Kraft (who had signed Lang's citizenship papers) was also named; like Wexley, Kraft refused to give "friendly" testimony and henceforth was blacklisted. Another, called before HUAC in the fall, was Robert L. Richards, Silvia Richards's ex-husband. He appeared on

September 20, 1951, refusing to affirm or deny Party allegiance. Also black-listed.

Now the pressure on Silvia Richards became unbearable. Everybody knew the committee was casting its net wide, swooping down on the families and spouses of "named" Reds. Lang was no longer in regular contact with his former girlfriend, but he was finishing a film with her name on the screen; through Martin Gang, the lawyer they retained in common, he was kept apprised of her dilemma. Gang advised Richards to offer sacrificial testimony expunging her past, incriminating herself and others.

Throughout the late spring and early summer of 1951, Lang and Welsch fought over the final cut of "Chuck-a-Luck." Welsch forced Lang to direct an alternative ending, with the two cowboys riding off into the sunset together, which the producer preferred against everyone else's judgment. When all the voting in the editing booth went against Welsch, the producer banned "Lang-men" from screenings—Wiard Ihnen and anyone else friendly with the director—because they voted in a bloc with Lang.

The director was convinced, as he said in a letter to Daniel Taradash, who was away on business in New York City, that Welsch "has accumulated such a hatred toward me that I am convinced he would gladly spoil the picture just to harm me and to hurt my feelings."

Although Lang later insisted to Peter Bogdanovich that Welsch had no right to edit the picture until after the first preview, Lang was prone to citing fantastical terms in ideal contracts that never existed. Welsch could and did have the right to edit, and Lang was crucially overruled by the producer he had gone out of his way to antagonize. Welsch wanted the film as short as possible, so exhibitors could squeeze in an extra performance on Sundays and holidays. Lang's optimal cut ran roughly one hour and forty-five minutes.

Of the two officers of Fidelity Pictures, Lang preferred the "financial head." In urgent telegrams to A. Pam Blumenthal, the New York partner, the director referred to himself despairingly as a humble "contract man," praying for the benevolent intercession of higher authority. Blumenthal, who had produced short subjects in Europe in the late 1920s, was the one who had helped forge the contract with the director. Now, unfortunately, Blumenthal was gravely ill (he would die in January of 1953, before the film's release), and in no position to intercede for Lang.

In the end the "artistic head" of Fidelity slashed Lang's Western to eighty-nine minutes. When Taradash, who had been absent from the worst hostilities, ran into the producer a few weeks after it was all over with, Welsch told him gleefully, "I cut the mood!"

The producer had always loathed the idea of a theme song, with its refrain repeated at intervals throughout the film. The director stonewalled the producer's arguments in favor of a more conventional score. When the "Chuck-a-Luck" song came in, Welsch couldn't stand it. It *was* a corny song: The guitar-strumming, the Langian lyrics of hate, murder, and revenge, the monotonous chorus. No degree of passion for the film can make the song "Brechtian–Weilian," as Lang wished to think of it. But "Chuck-a-Luck" *was* the film's title . . .

Until Welsch changed it. Lang and Taradash always blamed RKO and How-ard Hughes for changing "Chuck-a-Luck" to what Taradash called the "gaudy and less agreeable" *Rancho Notorious*. But this was Howard Welsch's ultimate revenge. The new title would torment the director more than anything else.

As he did so often during this last phase of his American career, when he always seemed to be working fast and furiously against time and paranoia, the director had already left "Chuck-a-Luck" behind to embark on another project.

In the fall of 1951, Lang hooked up again with Norman Krasna, with whom he had maintained friendly relations, and through Krasna with Jerry Wald. Wald, who became important to the director in the twilight of his career, was one of the industry's aging whiz kids, and one of Hollywood's unforgettable characters. His boundless personality and indefatigable energy made him one of the inspirations for Sammy Glick, the crude success-story hero of Budd Schulberg's 1941 novel *What Makes Sammy Run?*

Arriving in Hollywood as a refugee from journalism, radio, and fan maga-zines in 1933, Wald had swiftly established himself as a clever scriptwriter. But if the ideas gushed for him, actual writing came harder. Producing was his true forte; he was at his best cheering writers like a coach from the side-lines. A notorious fount of ideas, Wald had a mind like "a magpie's nest," in the words of fellow writer Philip Dunne, "crammed with situations, characters, and plot devices he had gleaned from his omnivorous reading of every writer from Euripides to Proust."

If one idea didn't work, Jerry Wald came up with another, and another, and another . . . That made the producer beloved by some, an impossible man to others. Director Jean Negulesco once described Wald as "a personality drawn by a caricature composed by a dreamer." Negulesco added, "He was sublime and horrible."

After nearly two decades at Warner Brothers, Wald, teamed with Krasna, was making his move into independent producing. In June of 1950, the two had formed Wald-Krasna Productions, and affiliated themselves with Howard Hughes at RKO in what *Time* called "the juiciest independent producing deal in movie history." Promised autonomy by Hughes, Wald and Krasna were contracted to produce twelve movies a year for the studio over the next five years. The first year of operations yielded precisely two: *Behave Yourself* and *The Blue Veil*. The second year would have to be better, and it would begin with *Clash by Night*, a Clifford Odets play that had been earmarked for Fritz Lang.

Odets was the Group Theater playwright whose proletarian *Waiting for Lefty* was a high point of New York theater in the 1930s. Odets had served time in Hollywood, and as his published diaries reveal, he was acquainted with Lang through Brecht and Salka Viertel; they saw each other socially during the period when Lang and Brecht were hashing out *Hangmen Also Die*. None-theless, *Clash by Night* was a lesser Odets play, Lang a peculiar choice as director, and the over-all timing odd, to say the least.

Odd, especially when one recalls that Odets had been conspicuously named as a Communist by Jack Warner in the October 1947 HUAC hearings. Odets would be named again in the spring and fall 1951 sessions, which were underway as Wald and Lang held their preliminary meetings. A rumor ran through show business circles that year that Odets was being leaned on by investigators and would eventually be forced to make an appearance before HUAC.

Odd, because the Odets play was ten years old and largely forgotten. The 1941 stage version had scored only a modest success on Broadway. It had starred Tallulah Bankhead, with Robert Ryan also in the cast, playing the small part of Joe Doyle. The title originated in the famous Matthew Arnold poem "Dover Beach": "And here we are as on a darkling plain/Swept with confused alarms of struggle and flight/Where ignorant armies clash by night."

Screen rights to *Clash by Night* had been purchased by an earlier RKO regime. Now the plan was to remove the "social background of unemployment" (Lang's words) and all the hard-edged political realism of the stage play. And sanitizing Odets would be the task of screenwriter Alfred Hayes.

A complex, erudite personality, Hayes cuts an intriguing figure in this equation. Born in London, raised in New York City, he had been a young Communist poet—didactic, not unlike Brecht—who was once extolled in *New Masses* as the "lyric poet of the New York working class." Hayes's stanzas eulogizing Joe Hill, the militant labor organizer for the Industrial Workers of the World executed in Utah in 1915, were adapted into a ballad by songwriter Earl Robinson; the song, "I Dreamed I Saw Joe Hill Again," would become a standard folk tune and rallying cry on picket lines.

After his years in poetry, Hayes became a crime reporter for William Randolph Hearst's *American* and *Daily Mirror* in New York. He served with Special Services for the U.S. Army during World War II, then stayed in Italy and "made a major contribution to Italian neo-realistic films," in the words of *The New York Times*. He helped to write such films as *The Bicycle Thief*, Vittorio De Sica's seminal neo-realist drama about an unemployed workman searching Rome for his stolen bicycle; and Roberto Rossellini's *Paisan*, an episodic reconstruction of the Battle of Italy, for which Hayes had received an Academy Award nomination. Recently Hayes had made his way to Hollywood, where, at the point Lang encountered him, he had just finished his work on Fred Zinnemann's *Teresa*, for which Hayes would again be Oscar-nominated.

Hayes was also a novelist, whose best-known work, *The Girl on the Via Flaminia*, a bittersweet romance between a lonely American soldier and a respectable Italian woman, also became a successful Broadway play. The versatile author was "a very interesting man," in Lang's words—"very intense—determined to do something good."

Hayes was also as determined as Clifford Odets to leave his Marxist credentials behind. With Jerry Wald breathing down his neck with story memos, Hayes tore apart and reconstructed the Odets play. Not much besides the main characters and the basic triangular situation—two men in love with the same woman—survived. Only a few lines of Odets's epigrammatic dialogue were salvaged; the rest of the text was pretty thoroughly tossed out the window.

The play had originally been set on Staten Island. Probably it was that man of gushing ideas, Jerry Wald, who had the passable notion of switching the setting to a Cannery Row–style small town. The female lead, Mae, arrives there, fleeing an unhappy, shadowy past. In a bar she bumps into a simple-minded fisherman, Jerry, and ends up marrying him not out of love but because she needs a new start in life.*

Jerry's friend Earl is a troublemaker, hot for Mae, and itching to slip off to the local Prater with her. The big revelation occurs to Jerry as he rifles through Mae's dresser drawers and spills some expensive perfume—of the type that seemed to proliferate in recent Fritz Lang films—on fancy new underwear that he never noticed before. Earl is a movie projectionist (a Langian detail actually drawn from Odets's play), and the story climaxes with a knock-down-drag-out between him and Jerry in the projection booth.

That's about it for plot. The actors would have to make it all come alive. One of Hollywood's most durable leading ladies, Barbara Stanwyck, was signed to play Mae. Burly former sportscaster Paul Douglas would portray the dumb cluck, Jerry. And stalwart Robert Ryan got a promotion from his stage part into the larger role of Earl.

The character of Peggy, one of Jerry and Mae's friends, was padded for a newcomer named Marilyn Monroe, on loan-out from 20th Century–Fox. Her boyfriend, the Joe Doyle character, would be played by another newcomer, Keith Andes. This was the prefabricated job repast presented to the director in the fall of 1951.

Lang had the best cameraman on the lot: Italian-born Nicholas Musuraca, who spent most of his career at RKO. Although absent from many reference books, Musuraca was a master of the *noir* aesthetic, with studio credits that included *Golden Boy, The Stranger on the Third Floor, Cat People, Out of the Past,* and *Blood on the Moon.* Carroll Clark and Albert S. D'Agostino, both under RKO contract, would handle the art direction. Clark would work with Lang more than once; for years he was RKO's supervising art director and later would go on to head the design department at Walt Disney (where he was nominated for an Oscar for his work on *Mary Poppins*).

The studio-assigned producer was Harriet Parsons, associated with RKO since 1943. Parsons was not only one of Hollywood's few female producers, but the daughter of screen colony columnist Louella Parsons. Harriet Parsons would supervise daily progress for Krasna and Wald.

Because *Clash by Night* was only the director's second filmed play, Wald encouraged Lang to hold rehearsals to capture an ensemble feeling among the cast. Then he put a bonus in the director's contract if Lang could wrap photography on time and under budget. As shooting started, Wald remained close to the production, monitoring the footage and issuing a stream of memos crammed with advice for Lang.

The producer urged the director to focus on the histrionic content and bring out the full emotional impact of the story. The last scene, for example—when Mae tearfully decides to stay with Jerry—should be "full of emotion," Wald advised. Lang should "not be embarrassed about allowing tears to well

---

*In the first scene of the play, by contrast, Mae is already married to Jerry and the mother of a newborn.

in Stanwyck's eyes as she plays her scene with Ryan, and also with Douglas . . . We must hit the audience in the pit of the stomach."

For once, Lang took a producer's memos in stride. He owed Wald a clear debt; this film had come at one of the shakiest periods of his career. Stanwyck, Ryan, and Douglas were seasoned professionals who worked well together, and all Lang had to do was to establish the right atmosphere. Only Marilyn Monroe, who was in the midst of a publicity buildup, was vulnerable—she was already the neurotic starlet of legend. "Poor Marilyn," said Lang, "was a scared girl, scared of everything."

One of the things that scared her most was Lang. The actress vomited before almost every scene and grew so apprehensive about her dialogue that she broke out in red blotches. It didn't help her standing with the director that Monroe was habitually late, or that she insisted on her personal dialogue coach Natasha Lytess being present on the set at all times. Or that newspaper columnists squired to the soundstage by RKO publicists ignored the veteran player, Barbara Stanwyck—not to mention the veteran director—demanding instead to interview, in Lang's words, "the girl with the big tits."

Indeed, Lang gave Monroe something to be terrified of. He banned her dialogue coach, then erupted whenever she bungled her lines, a regular event inevitably followed by the actress crumpling in tears. It may not have been coincidental that Monroe's erratic behavior provided a good excuse for the many retakes the director loved.

Lang could jangle anyone's nerves; he even detected a chink in the usually impenetrable armor of Barbara Stanwyck. One morning the star summoned Lang to her trailer to complain that a certain scene was so badly written she didn't think she could play it. It was the scene in which her character, Mae, anguishes over the falsity of her marriage to Jerry. Lang knew what everybody else in Hollywood knew: the veteran actress was involved in a painful ongoing divorce suit against her husband, actor Robert Taylor.

The director wielded that knowledge like a cudgel. " 'Barbara, may I speak very frankly and openly with you?' She said, 'Naturally,' and I continued: 'I think the scene reminds you of a rather recent event in your private life, and that is why you think it is badly written and you cannot play it.' Barbara looked at me for a second and then said slowly, 'You son of a bitch'—went out and played the two-and-one-half-pages-long scene so wonderfully that we had to shoot it only once."

In the end nothing much could be done about the film's running time, which crept up to approximately 105 minutes; but Lang came in on schedule, and earned his bonus.

With a straight face, Lang told Peter Bogdanovich that he had done "a lot of research" for *Clash by Night*, "about the faithfulness of wives. And I found in one of the leading women's magazines that seventy-five percent of married women betray their husbands with extra-marital relationships. This became the problem in the film."

If there was any "problem" Lang did not need to research, it was the unfaithfulness of wives. Around the émigré community, the director was known for befriending other men's wives—even if he was on merely polite terms with the husband; especially if the wife was pretty and youngish.

Sometimes his relationships with married women were platonic and paternal. Ruth Albu was a young actress in Berlin who had played a small part in one of Lang's German films, before her bit was squandered on the cutting-room floor. When she met up with the director again in Hollywood, he made a point of pursuing her; whenever her husband was out of town, Lang took her out for dinner, quietly, at some nice place out of the public eye.

They never had a physical relationship. Ruth Albu felt it was out of the question. For one thing, there was an age gap of some twenty years. For another, she was petite and brunette, and knew instinctively that Lang was interested in a different type. "I think he was somehow sentimental with me because I wasn't his type as a woman," Albu recalled. "People sometimes talk about him unsympathetically, but he was very sweet to me.

"I think he had what the Germans call 'Heimweh'—nostalgia for Berlin," Albu added. "He missed the coffeehouses. He missed the atmosphere of artistic intercourse. It's true he was a filmmaker and part of that circle in Hollywood, but he felt an outsider still. For him, I was 'nostalgia.' When he first met me, I had been very young, childlike, and in the swim in Berlin. I still personified Berlin, for him, and Berlin life, for all of us, was something very special."

In other instances, Lang's extramarital relationships were sexual. And sometimes they went tragically awry. At the same time that the director was preparing *Clash by Night*, and, according to his own account, researching "the faithfulness of wives," he broke off one of his long-standing affairs—with a onetime actress named Maria Ray, the wife of producer-director Gustav Machaty.

Machaty, from Prague, was best-known for celebrating the nude beauty of Hedy Lamarr in her 1933 film *Ekstase (Ecstasy)*; he was one of those émigrés whose career bottomed out in Hollywood. Maria Ray, a smoldering blonde who had been a society figure in Vienna, had starred in Machaty's 1934 film *Nocturno*. Unable to find work in Hollywood, Ray became a seamstress, helping to support her husband. It was widely known among the European community in Hollywood that she carried on a clandestine relationship with Fritz Lang.

The former actress ended up taking her own life, hanging herself in the cellar of her Hollywood home in October of 1951. Officially, it was reported that she was despondent over her health. Although she had other affairs, many émigrés believed the real reason for her suicide was that Maria Ray had been crushed by Lang's rejection.

"It was the talk of the town," said Gottfried Reinhardt, "because she was his mistress."

"That was quite well-known," echoed Peter Heiman. Heiman knew Maria Ray, and dared to ask Lang about the true story behind her suicide. "I heard it from him," Heiman said. "He was in a way very upset about it, but in a way not. He said, 'This is not my responsibility that this happened.'"

It was the just the wheel of fate: "Chuck-a-Luck."

* * *

On paper, 1952 looks like one of Lang's most productive years. *Rancho Notorious* was released first, in February.

Despite the last-minute title change, despite the film's being "cut to pieces," despite Dietrich's cold, metallic performance, this is the only one of the director's three Westerns that actually comes alive on the screen, and feels truly Langian.

Lang was obviously in a rare mood. The love scenes between Vern (Arthur Kennedy) and Altar Keane (Dietrich) were markedly romantic for this director, whose own vulnerability did not usually show through his reserve. Vern flirts with Altar in one scene, probing for information about the brooch she is wearing (it belonged to his slain fiancée). She warns, "The rules of Chuck-a-Luck are meant to be kept. And if you don't intend to keep them, you can clear out right now."

"It's hard for a man to look at you and keep any rules," Vern replies smoothly.

Alter eyes him appraisingly. "Did you just think of that?"

"No. I thought of that the first minute I saw you, grease and all."

"Like heat lightning, I suppose?"

"How'd you know?"

"And every time you see me you feel a little weak in the head, mmm?"

"No, I feel sorry for myself. Sorry I never met you before, sorry I never had a chance to give you a brooch like that."

"You're as smooth on the ground as you are on the back of a horse."

"Only when somebody irons me out—like you do."

"Vern, when you come to a fenced range, do you always try to climb over?"

"I always see if the gate's open first."

Vern draws nearer, kisses Altar. Taking a step back, she slaps him across the face. "That was for trying!" she exclaims. She slaps him again. "That was for trying too hard!"

Vern rubs his face ruefully. "It strikes me you're real unfair, ma'am."

"Why?"

"I got two slaps, only one kiss."

Altar likes his answer, flips him a little smile. A Langian woman, she doesn't mind a little brutality with her sex. The moment is italicized by the camera's dewy-eyed close-up of Marlene Dietrich—a miscalculation of the director, not the actress. Even so, the scene, from a screenwriter who went on to write one of Hollywood's all-time celebrated love scenes (Burt Lancaster and Deborah Kerr on the sand in *From Here to Eternity*) came closer to true passion than any other Fritz Lang film.

When Leo Laitin interviewed Lang for *Collier's* magazine shortly after the film's release, the director, fresh from the *Rancho Notorious* hostilities, made it clear that the female star was somebody "whose throat he would gladly slit." Marlene Dietrich had no real talent. She was lazy. Her singing left a lot to be desired. "For me she is just a tragic figure"—as empty inside as the robot-Maria of *Metropolis*. "Von Sternberg created a robot, and then, along the classic lines, the robot destroyed its creator."

It was a brutally candid interview. Lang discussed rumors that the actress had lesbian relationships as well as affairs with men. It was doubtful, according to Lang, whether Marlene Dietrich enjoyed sex with women *or* men. "He [Lang] did everything but tell me," wrote Laitin, "that he had had an affair with Miss Dietrich and had taunted her many times by telling her he did not love her. This is a man whose life obviously was very much involved with hers, personally and professionally. And a man who had come out on the short end of both relationships."

Lang told this devastating anecdote about Dietrich, whom he would never speak to again: "She still has the ability to catch the sex imagination of both men and women. She is still a dream fulfillment. But for how long? I saw her come out of the dressmaker's on the lot the other day. I am nearsighted but I noticed this woman, wearing slacks, jacket, and a saddle bag over her shoulder. I thought to myself, 'This is how Dietrich will look in ten years.' I was shocked when I came nearer and saw it was Dietrich."

When the article was published, the harshest and most indiscreet of these ungentlemanly comments were left out.

Clash by Night was scheduled for release in May of 1952. But first there was the matter of Clifford Odets. Surrounded by Red-hunters, the playwright hoisted a flag of truce. He became a "combative informer," in Victor S. Navasky's terminology. Odets appeared in executive session the last week of April, and then in open session on May 19–20, a week before *Clash by Night* opened in New York and Los Angeles.

It may be too much to allege, as David Caute wrote in *The Great Fear*, that "the release and success of his film *Clash by Night* was at stake," but certainly Odets's future viability was. The well-known writer tried to finesse his predicament, lecturing the HUAC members while naming only six names, the bare minimum, all dead or expendable people in his view. It was shameful, but it got Odets a passing grade; he was guaranteed work as a script doctor in Hollywood for the rest of his short, haunted life.

Likewise, film critics gave the overwrought *Clash by Night* its own passing grade.

Lang and Nicholas Musuraca had spent several days up around Monterey, in October of 1951, photographing swirling gulls, smelts being dumped and sorted, boats moored on the water—footage that was woven into a mesmeric montage to accompany the Roy Webb score in the opening credits. The long prelude, with its realistic sound, was a reminder of what a natural silent director Lang was.

Once the story starts, however, the film's evocation of daily life becomes theatrical and unconvincing. The plot remains stagebound. The only real villain is an abstraction—marriage. The only characters for whom love is grand are the non-marrieds—Peggy (Marilyn Monroe) and Joe (Keith Andes). Their relationship is also the most intensely physical. When Peggy admits that Earl turns her on, and Joe punches her in the face, she tastes the blood and grins—another female Lang character aroused by brute force. Marilyn Monroe's performance conveyed "a combination of brash carnality and skewed masochism," in the words of Donald Spoto.

Earl certainly has a poisonous marriage. He says he would like to stick his

...

wife, a burlesque dancer, full of pins, "just to see if blood runs out." (This Langian comment is also the way Earl talks in the Odets play, where he casually remarks that sometimes he gets the urge to "cut up" a woman.) Robert Ryan did his best to enrich such a character.

Paul Douglas, as Jerry, one of Lang's husbands emasculated by marriage, overdid the schmaltz. When he and Mae have a baby that is produced offstage and available at the contract minimum, what could the director do? What could any director do with a scene where Jerry hugs his baby and makes goo-goo talk in the moonlight? Or with that old chestnut, breakers crashing on the rocks, as metaphor for Mae's inner turbulence?

Barbara Stanwyck, playing one of many unfulfilled wives in the director's canon, was a gutsy actress, incapable of a bad performance. When Earl shows her some sympathy, she snarls back that he doesn't really know her. "What kind of animal am I? Do I have fangs, do I purr? What jungle am I from?" She was saddled with similar self-conscious dialogue, but like Robert Ryan did her utmost to wring emotion from it.

At the end of the Odets play Jerry strangles Earl to death. In the film, on the other hand, Jerry shakes his fists in Mae's face but can't bring himself to strike down his unfaithful wife. (He obviously hasn't seen too many other Fritz Lang films.) Later, in the projection booth, when Jerry, Earl, and Mae get all tangled up on the floor, Earl tries to conk Jerry over the head with a wrench. Then Jerry grabs Earl, and tries to strangle him. Mae, trying to separate them, is thrown violently backward against the projector. (No hint what movie is being shown.)

Unlike the play, the film version of *Clash by Night* had to abide by the cautious atmosphere of 1950s America. For the first time in any Fritz Lang film (disregarding the feebly comic *You and Me*), not a single person expires. Everyone turns apologetic. Earl is rejected by Mae, who reconciles with Jerry. The message was contrition and redemption.

After finishing *Clash by Night*, Lang liked to tell interviewers, he discovered that he had finally made the industry-wide blacklist that kept Communists and "pinkos" from working in Hollywood.

For "a year" (according to his interview with Peter Bogdanovich) Lang couldn't figure out what was going on. For "a year and a half" (per his interview with Bernard Rosenberg and Harry Silverstein in their book *The Real Tinsel*) he couldn't seem to land another job. Cornelius Schnauber and Lotte Eisner estimated thirteen months of "forced idleness," with the director unable to scrape up an assignment because of political persecution.

The irony of a fugitive from Hitler being blacklisted for Communist tendencies in America made good copy in later articles and books. The only difficulty is that the story was half Lang's paranoia, half a lie. For some time Lang had been well aware of the HUAC danger. His lawyer and agent had been working overtime to accomplish the same thing for Lang, in private, that Odets had carried off for himself in public: to put as much distance as possible between the director and former associates too closely identified with left-wing causes.

It was crucial, in the retelling, for Lang to have been "blacklisted" for as long as possible, just as it was crucial for him to have fled Nazi Germany as early as possible. His courageous self-image had to be preserved, once the danger and fear had passed. "I feel there was some self-pity in Fritz," commented screenwriter Daniel Taradash. "It's possible he *wanted* to feel he had blacklisting troubles. It would explain, to *him* as well as others, that his talent was unable to be used properly under the studio system (and even when working for independents). This is merely a hypothesis."

By mid-1952, Martin Gang and Nat Goldstone were busy writing letters on Lang's behalf to clearinghouse organizations and the American Legion, pleading the director's political innocence. Ten years earlier, his suspiciously close connections to Nazis were rewritten for publicity; now his Communist ties were swept behind closed doors. Martin Gang, Lang admitted on one occasion, was delegated to go see "the head man of the American Legion" in New York City. Nat Goldstone was empowered to draft a to-whom-it-may-concern letter stating that the director had "never belonged to an organization that was to my knowledge ever termed Communist." Like other Hollywood left-leaners who came in for unwanted HUAC harassment, Lang had to concoct sugary rationalizations for his seeming protean left-liberal activity.

The United Negro and Allied Veterans of America, Lang explained, included such all-American sponsors as Joe Louis, Sugar Ray Robinson, and Jackie Robinson, "who are all well-known as anti-Communists." Lang had made the mistake of milking newspaper coverage out of his pledged donations to Henry Wallace's presidential campaign. "But after I heard him [Wallace]," the director told Peter Bogdanovich, "the same night in Willy Wyler's house, I wrote him a letter saying that under the circumstances, because he had said some things about which I didn't agree, I couldn't give the money. But when we walked out of the house, we were all photographed."

Not only did the Red-baiters have a photograph of Lang at the Wallace meeting, they had his incriminating signature on Committee for the First Amendment petitions. In a letter of January 16, 1953, intended for studio-wide dissemination, Lang renounced his endorsement of the First Amendment Committee, which purely on constitutional grounds had supported the briefly defensible Hollywood Nineteen, before they became the repellent Hollywood Ten. Lang claimed that if he had known the group was "Communist-inspired, [he] would never had taken part in its activities or permitted them to use [his] name." This was effectively the same as Humphrey Bogart's "I-was-a-dope" line, if handled more privately.

Naturally, Lang had second thoughts about his name resurfacing on so many 1930s and 1940s petitions and mastheads. "I spoke English very badly," the director told Peter Bogdanovich, "but on the list [of these organizations] I saw Walter Wanger, Thomas Mann, God-knows-who, so I signed my name." This from a director so proud of assimilation, and particularly of the idiomatic English of his screenplays?

A handful of such exculpatory letters appeared among Lang's personal papers when they were donated to the University of Southern California after his death. Others vanished. Lang's friend, journalist Kevin Thomas, said that after the director's death some documents had to be summarily destroyed, following his wishes. Thomas described these letters as "the hat-in-hand type," which reflected poorly on the director. No doubt some were letters pleading for jobs, others confessing his left-wing sins.

After the McCarthy era, in fact, Lang tried to cement positive relations with the FBI. On at least one occasion, in the early 1970s, he went so far as to furnish information to an FBI investigator inquiring about the politics of one of the young people who flocked around him. Anything to prove his Americanism.

All accounts of Lang's life agree about what happened next: The tide turned in his favor when he won over Harry Cohn. Columbia's chief of production believed Lang when he said he was not a Communist. Cohn interceded on Lang's behalf, and got him a job directing *The Blue Gardenia*, an independent production for Warner Brothers.

Production files attest that Lang was at work on *Clash by Night* as late as the last week of March 1952, and on the rolls of *The Blue Gardenia* by mid-October of the same year—a total of no more than *six months* of "blacklisting" for a man who had been out of work in Hollywood for that long and even longer several times before in his career. Six months between films was standard for Fritz Lang.

But why Harry Cohn, and why did Cohn intercede for Lang on a film that would be shot at Warner Brothers, not Columbia?

Intriguing question, and there is no completely satisfactory answer. For one thing, Lang did not need Harry Cohn to make the connection to *The Blue Gardenia*; he was well-acquainted with author Vera Caspary, who wrote the story on which the film would be based. Caspary's longtime friend, whom she eventually married, was one of Lang's closest neighbors, producer I. G. Goldsmith. The director had always maintained cordial relations with Caspary, while feuding endlessly with Goldsmith.

When Lang was casting *Rancho Notorious*, according to Daniel Taradash, the director met Harry Cohn for the first time. Although Lang abhorred run-of-the-mill producers, he harbored a reverence for the larger-than-life moguls who eluded his acquaintance, the great puppet-masters behind the scenes. The only one Lang had worked with closely and long enough to develop any relationship was Darryl Zanuck, and even for him the director was known to express a grudging appreciation.

In early 1950, when Lang was searching for someone to play the character of Frenchy, he wanted to take an advance peek at Mel Ferrer's performance in Columbia's forthcoming *The Brave Bulls*. The picture had finished filming, but editing wasn't completed. Lang asked Daniel Taradash, who was on good terms with the studio—one of Harry Cohn's pet writers—if he could arrange something. Taradash phoned Cohn, who said, "Sure. Bring Lang over. I'd like to meet him."

"A few days later, Lang and I went to see Harry," remembered Taradash. "He was in his well-known office with all the Oscars behind him. When Lang and I entered we walked to his desk; Harry didn't get up to greet us; he said nothing but he seemed transfixed as he looked up at Lang. Fritz had the monocle in his eye. He wore a trench coat. He stood before Harry, ramrod-upright. He was at attention, staring over Harry's head. Harry looked up at

Lang and, in best–Harry Cohn form, spat out, 'You look like a fucking Nazi spy!' How Fritz kept the monocle from dropping out of his eye and how I kept from laughing aloud I'll never know."

As Taradash recalled, the relationship only improved from there. Cohn graciously ran the film in the private projection room just off his office, and indeed Lang ended up hiring Ferrer. It appears from studio records that Lang even consulted Cohn on the *Rancho Notorious* script, though Columbia had nothing to do with the production. Cohn saw a draft in late 1950 and dashed off a memo suggesting that Marlene Dietrich sing a song in one scene. "I rather like a community song—or one that everybody joins in," Cohn wrote. Dietrich probably would have gotten around to a song anyway, but the musical number was dutifully inserted—an enjoyable highlight of Lang's best Western.

At this uncertain moment in his career, in 1952, Lang launched into a peculiar near friendship with the man many considered the Dr. Mabuse of Hollywood. In the vulgar, abusive, and omnipotent Cohn, Lang saw qualities other people didn't, attributes he envied. The small-time operators Lang usually worked with were born losers, he thought, but a fellow like Harry Cohn had the instincts. Lang especially enjoyed relating Cohn's well-known method for gauging the running length of a Columbia release. After they finished screening a new film, Cohn would announce, "It is seventeen minutes too long." How did Cohn know, right to the minute? Lang loved the punch line: "That," according to Harry Cohn, "is when my ass started to ache."

Harry Cohn could get away with that and more, with Lang. Like Jerry Wald, he was among the few to whom the director owed gratitude. Now, with the director's career endangered by the blacklist, he went to have a long talk with the studio chief. Lang assured Cohn that he was no Red, and Cohn, who achieved "something of a reputation as the studio boss most willing to obey only minimally the anti-Communist crusade law," in the words of Larry Ceplair and Steven England's *The Inquisition in Hollywood*, promised the director that he would look into a film project for him. A few phone calls on Lang's behalf were all it took.

From the producer on down, *The Blue Gardenia* was hardly a top-flight production. Alex Gottlieb was a Russian-born producer whom Lang always referred to as "the man who married Billy Rose's sister"; in Lang's eyes, he was merely a husband trading on his wife's family connections. Gottlieb had worked for Walter Wanger in advertising and publicity early in his career, before going to work as a writer and producer of low-budget "B" comedies, musicals, and suspense films. *Hollywood Canteen*, a flag-waving pastiche with cameo appearances by Hollywood stars, was one of Gottlieb's better-known productions.

The trade papers announced on October 16 that Fritz Lang had been signed to direct Gottlieb's next project, a Vera Caspary short story that had been adapted by Charles Hoffman. Principal photography was due to begin the first week of December.

Charles Hoffman was a Stanford-and Columbia-educated writer who had sold his short fiction and novels to Hollywood before taking a contract at

Warner Brothers in the early 1940s. (Probably his best-known screenwriting credit was *Night and Day*, the Cole Porter film biography starring Cary Grant.) Hoffman had written a draft of *The Blue Gardenia* before the director was contracted, and there was little time for changes.

The scenario concerned a fashion designer named Harry Prebble who makes a sideline of painting calendar girls. Harry tries to seduce Norah, a telephone operator, with a technique that includes plying her with liquor and playing a silky Nat King Cole recording, "The Blue Gardenia." When Harry goes too far, she struggles with him, breaks a mirror and faints. When she comes to her senses, she finds herself surrounded by broken glass and, terrified, rushes off. Next morning's newspapers report that Harry has been found dead. And Norah wakes up in the apartment she shares with two other working girls, Sally and Crystal, her mind a blank. Is she the guilty party?

A police reporter named Casey Mayo made a convenient alter ego for the director. Casey carries a "little black book of women," and the centerpiece of his apartment is a bar of the type Lang had in his Summit Ridge home. Mayo's investigation, parallel with the official police inquiry, focuses on the "mystery woman" who was with Harry the night he was murdered. He makes a public appeal to learn her identity, and Norah agrees to a secret rendezvous with him. But the police find out and arrest her, before Casey, who instinctively believes in her innocence, can prove the facts.

Meanwhile, events reveal that Rose, one of Harry's spurned lovers, is the real killer. Rose attempts suicide by slashing her wrists in a music store, Norah is cleared, and Casey waits outside the jail to greet her when she is released. Still dazed from her experiences, however, Norah cannot commit to Casey, and their future together is uncertain.

The cast included Anne Baxter as Norah—Lang had wanted to cast her in a film as far back as *Man Hunt*. Ann Sothern and Jeff Donnell played her roommates, Raymond Burr was the lecherous painter, and Richard Conte the beat reporter.

The director had the same cameraman (Nicholas Musuraca) as for *Clash by Night*, but all the rest of the circumstances were sorely reduced. Photography took less than four weeks—Lang's fastest Hollywood production ever. The script wasn't awful; it had elements that ought to have intrigued the director—including the character of the spurned lover, who was an eerie reminder of Maria Ray Machaty, someone in his own life story driven to suicide.

But Lang's direction was humdrum. The murder mystery was neither convincing as reality, nor captivating as fiction. Richard Conte made another specious Lang hero-without-warts, and the working girls were the kind of phony maidens the director never really believed in. Where was Fritz Lang's celebrated psychological insight? Or his concern for fate and destiny?

The director himself knew *The Blue Gardenia* for what it was. "It wasn't much," he told Charles Higham, and Joel Greenberg, "but I was very happy with Anne Baxter's performance in it."

For the least accomplished of Fritz Lang's works there arise die-hard advocates. *The Blue Gardenia* is certainly among his lesser efforts, yet in France, future nouvelle vague director Eric Rohmer praised the film in print. Later, in Germany, aesthetes published a book that offered frame enlargements "as part of an eloquent illustration of Lang's methods of visual and symbolic condensation." Lang's 1953 film was eventually awarded a widely disseminated feminist interpretation by Anne Kaplan, and a noteworthy essay by Janet Bergstrom, published in France and the United States, that sang its merits as a film noir.

"Deception, betrayal, and psychological terrorism thoroughly permeate this McCarthy-era film," wrote Janet Bergstrom.

It was a film permeated by the McCarthy era, to be sure. It was Lang on probation.

Columbia had the welcome mat out for people who had been cleared by HUAC.

Hollywood Ten turncoat Edward Dmytryk, Elia Kazan (the most prestigious of the director-informers), and screenwriter Richard Collins (one of the original Hollywood Nineteen, who also snuggled up with the inquisitors) were among those who would turn up, after their "friendly" testimony, with Columbia contracts.

Jerry Wald and Norman Krasna helped facilitate Lang's rehabilitation. Meanwhile, they had grown disenchanted with Howard Hughes (and vice versa). Wald bought out Krasna's shares, and in late October 1952, with *The Blue Gardenia* in preproduction, Wald announced he had severed his RKO contract and been appointed a vice president of Columbia Pictures. He was moving over to Harry Cohn's studio.

After *The Blue Gardenia* finished filming on Christmas Eve 1952, Fritz Lang would also move into offices on the Columbia lot. The director's contract, starting date January 8, 1953, paid him $1,500 weekly and would run one year, with built-in extensions.

After Sam Jaffe resigned as Lang's agent, it was only a matter of time before Henry Rogers, the director's longtime publicist, quit too.

Lang would hire a succession of press agents in the 1950s, each in turn charged with the doomed search for a publicity moniker as strong as Hitchcock's "Master of Suspense." One strategy Lang liked, and kept returning to, was presenting himself as an expert on hard-to-handle actresses—not to mention women in general.

Some of the director's press statements were angled ill-advisedly. One, in 1947, called attention to his opinion that foreign actresses, especially British and European ones, were better qualified for challenging roles than Hollywood stars. "Take Lana Turner, Gene Tierney, and Ann Sheridan," Lang was quoted. "Any one of the three could do just as well as any of the other two in any role any of the girls has played. What I mean is, their acting is completely stylized. It isn't acting. They just go through picture after picture playing the same kind of glamour girl."

The director continued to act the fuss-budget about his "canned" publicity. The Bernie Williams–Kay Mulvey agency copied down Lang's words extolling Rhonda Fleming in *While the City Sleeps*: "Her figure arouses the male instinct and she displays it to great advantage in the picture." Afterward, reading the transcript, Lang brought out his pencil and scribbled little changes: "She arouses all the male instinct and she displays her physical assets to great advantage in the picture." This article, like others, was published under Fritz Lang's byline in a movie magazine.

In previous publicity incarnations, the director had been presented as a homemaker and gourmet chef. He had also expounded on the qualities of a perfect wife. From there, it wasn't too much of a stretch for the director to pose as an authority on women's fashions, cosmetics, and above all, perfume.

Perfume had figured into several of Lang's recent films, although it may not have been the world's greatest recommendation that a man was aroused to homicide by a fragrance in one (*House by the River*), or was prompted by an unfamiliar scent to discover his wife's infidelity in another (*Clash by Night*). Lang liked perfume, and women who wore expensive fragrances (Lily Latté always wore the same brand, Taboo). Who better to discourse on the subject?

Although it was more common for actors than directors to fill in for vacationing columnists, Lang was happy to parade his opinions in such a venue. In Lydia Lane's June 20, 1954 column in the _Los Angeles Times_ the director offered advice about how to enhance one's sex appeal with the right perfume. "With me, the obvious repels," Lang wrote. "I dislike a girl who deliberately raises her voice to be conspicuous, who wears her dress low to attract attention." The director claimed he could pinpoint the proper fragrance for any woman. Lydia Lane appended a note to her column, widely syndicated by the Mirror Enterprises Syndicate. "If you are interested in knowing what perfume Fritz Lang finds most appealing, get in touch with me," she advised.

After 1947, the focus of Lang's more philosophical articles also shifted, reflecting Hollywood verities Lang had culled from his rocky studio experiences. One of Lang's emerging beliefs was in the wisdom of audiences—that if a movie proved unpopular at the box office, the reaction revealed nothing but the director's own bad judgment. "I don't want to sound smug or stuffy," Lang told the _Hollywood Citizen-News_, "but the screen has passed through its experimental stage and today there is usually a relation between a picture's commercial success and its artistic worth."

Another was his surprising position that camera effects were no longer fundamental to filmmaking. Nowadays, Lang's publicity explained, the director tried to minimize camera virtuosity, whereas once he had been known as its greatest exponent. "The more the audience is absorbed in the story and the more they forget the camera angles, the little sly tricks of direction, and the director's 'touch,' the better the picture is," Lang was quoted as saying.

In Hollywood's new era of conservativism, the director's publicity also stressed how fast and economical he was as a director. Tight budgets? Limited preproduction time? No problem. "I have to work fast," Lang told Philip K. Scheuer of the _Los Angeles Times_. "Time has become an integral part of picture-making—and far be it from me to say the front office is wrong."

Gone was the "Perfectionist Deluxe." More up-to-date publicity stressed his efficiency and standard cost-saving gestures, such as photographing all scenes "in one direction, whether in or out of continuity—before turning the camera in another. This, he [Lang] estimates, lops a week off the schedule." Any technological innovation—such as a forerunner of the "crab dolly," a scuttling camera cart Lang devised for _Clash by Night_—was presented as a budget-trimmer that alleviated the producer's pocketbook.

Gone too, in publicity shots, were the monocle and the immaculate blue suits. Eyeglasses were now more common—and soon enough, the eyepatch over his right eye. Bulky sweaters made him look almost avuncular.

With publicity intended both to reassure Hollywood and keep his name in front of moviegoers, the new Fritz Lang entered an almost poignant phase of his lifelong self-campaign.

War—of any kind—was not a matter of winning or losing; it was about survival. A director, like a general, had to be a master both of attack and of rearguard action. Lang's Hollywood career was like the long, chaotic Lutsk retreat he had undergone on the Eastern front during World War I. Casualties didn't matter. A costly defeat or two didn't matter. Withdraw, regroup, watch for another opportunity.

Now at Columbia following this frantic period of quickies and misfires, Lang would stumble across a property that was made to order for him—one of those happy accidents of time and place that for the most part eluded the filmmaker after Germany.

The Big Heat was based on a novel by William P. McGivern, serialized in the *Saturday Evening Post* in seven parts from December 1952 to February 1953. A January 12, 1953, item in the *Hollywood Reporter* announced that the story rights had been purchased by Columbia for immediate development; that was the week after Lang arrived for work, cleared of any blacklist suspicions, at Harry Cohn's studio.

It is apparent from Lang's records that he was initially matched with a different Columbia project, before being reassigned by Jerry Wald to *The Big Heat* in mid-February. By then, the first draft script of January 20 was already completed, and *The Big Heat* had been scheduled to go before the cameras. Filming was temporarily delayed when Lang got the assignment, but even so photography would start on March 14.

McGivern's novels were both unusually brutal and profoundly moral. They provided the basis for several noteworthy motion pictures, including 1959's hard-hitting *Odds Against Tomorrow*, about a bank robbery; and later, the "Killer on the Turnpike" story which served as the basis for director Robert Altman's breakout telefilm *Chicago, Chicago* (a.k.a. *Nightmare in Chicago*). *The Big Heat* was a police thriller, and Sydney Boehm, who wrote the script, would hew closely to McGivern's novel—while making shrewd improvements.

Boehm, above all, was fortuitous for Lang. The scenarist had logged time as a police reporter on the *New York Evening Journal*, staying with the newspaper for some fourteen years. Studio publicity liked to stress Boehm's coverage of such headline events as the Lindbergh kidnapping and the activities of the German-American Bund, but his specialty was crime and corruption on a newspaper "whose front page was a virtual abbatoir of murder most foul," in the words of one source. As the end of World War II neared, Boehm walked away from the city desk and took a job in Hollywood, where he would specialize in film noir, eventually writing or producing more than fifty hard-boiled screenplays.

Sergeant David Bannion, the lead character in McGivern's novel, had originally been conceived as an educated policeman, able to quote Hume, Locke, and Kant. The erudition was one of the first of the novel's marginal elements dropped by Boehm. The scenarist made Bannion more of a representative citizen swept up in a nightmare, someone more in sync with Lang's middle-American complex; another character who became, like the mob victim of *Fury*, "close to John Doe," in the director's words.*

---

*Black characters sometimes figured centrally in McGivern's novels (Harry Belafonte played one in the film of *Odds Against Tomorrow*), and in his British Film Institute monograph on Lang's film, Colin McArthur pointed out that there was a conspicuous black character in the novel of *The Big Heat*, dropped from the film: a homicide suspect befriended by Sergeant Bannion. It is

The story follows Sergeant Bannion as he endeavors to investigate the suspicious suicide of a corrupt cop. Bannion is plunged into a series of horrific incidents. His own family car is rigged to explode, killing Bannion's wife and leading him to lose faith in the legal system. Though he bitterly resigns from the police force, he pursues his own quest for justice. He encounters nothing but obstacles and dead ends, until he is befriended by Debby, a gangster's moll. All the leads point to a crime lord who hides behind a facade of seeming respectability. But the hard evidence is insufficient, and a despairing Bannion must decide whether to take vengeance into his own hands.

Lang was able to work with Boehm on revisions for roughly four weeks in February and March. His script contribution was modest, a situation he had learned to accept. It would amount to "no more than the usual careful editing and modifications," in Lotte Eisner's words, " 'personalizing'—which were Lang's invariable contributions to any script." Producer Jerry Wald was also involved, issuing his customary flow of memos.

The scenario would emerge as a model. The structure was solid and suspenseful, the characters crisply etched, the themes clearly articulated. There was memorable dialogue—especially in Debby's scenes.* Boehm's work was the best of his career, and his screenplay would earn an Edgar Allan Poe Award from the Mystery Writers of America.

Columbia's casting of Glenn Ford was an indication of where *The Big Heat* stood in the pecking order. The actor, a poor man's Spencer Tracy, was the studio's meat-and-potatoes lead. *The Big Heat* wasn't quite the "A" list; it had been a long time since Lang had been on anyone's "A" list. But Ford was prized at Columbia, which had the actor under contract for only one picture per year.

The others in the cast—mostly from Columbia's payroll—included Gloria Grahame (as Debby), Jocelyn Brando (Bannion's wife), Lee Marvin (Vince, Debbie's gangster-boyfriend), Alexander Scourby (ganglord Mike Lagana) and Jeannette Nolan (Bertha Duncan, the dead cop's wife).

The black-and-white photography would be provided by Charles Lang, Jr., who had worked well with Lang fifteen years earlier on *You and Me*. The script called for a range of settings, including police headquarters, barrooms, terrace-top apartments, and an automobile graveyard. These would be expertly executed by set decorator William Kiernan and art director Robert Peterson, both longtime studio personnel.

As filming began on March 11, the director had to be acutely aware that *The Big Heat* offered a chance at a new lease on his career. "Lang said he had liked all the characters in the book," novelist William McGivern reported in

---

telling that Lang, who made unsubstantiated claims about wanting to cast a black man as the lynch-mob victim in *Fury*—and who once insisted he would have preferred the maid-victim of *House by the River* to be a "colored girl," in his words ("I fought like a Trojan but I couldn't get it")—failed in this instance to keep a black character already present in the source material. In fact, the roles for black characters would be negligible in Lang's Hollywood films.

*Samples: Debby's appraisal of Bannion's hotel room, where he is hiding out—"Early nothing." Her acid comment to Bertha, the suicide-cop's self-serving wife—"We're sisters under the mink."

a later article, "and although this wasn't essential to him in making a film, it gave him something special to work with." The truth, too, was that Lang had learned some hard lessons. In this last phase of his U.S. career, the reports of the director's riding actors and crew members dwindle. The only friction on the set was between Lang and Gloria Grahame.

Grahame was playing the sort of tainted lady Lang knew from experience. The director's special affection for tramps and hookers meant that she was in for some uncomfortable scrutiny. Lang's paradoxical attitude meant paying close attention to the character while abusing the actress who couldn't help but fall short of embodying the type.

Grahame had picked up an Oscar at the annual spring ceremonies for her role as the frivolous wife of William Powell in 1952's *The Bad and the Beautiful*—just as filming of *The Big Heat* got underway. Her career was on the rise. But she was also a notorious spitfire, and the studio was happy for a director tough enough to "tame" her.

The character of Vince, Debby's boyfriend, also interested Lang. The director "liked a certain evil in the quality of the character," and he warmed to Lee Marvin, who proved cooperative. While filming, Lang later told William McGivern, the director grew fascinated "by what he saw in the curve of Lee Marvin's upper lip, a suggestion of absolute evil and corruption." Filming the incident where Vince pitches hot coffee into Debby's face—after realizing that she has witnessed his humiliation by Bannion—Lang's camera gravitated not to the victim, but to the perpetrator. "It is not the spectacle of scalded, ruined beauty," McGivern later wrote, "but the evil of Marvin's face and lips, glistening and quivering in Lang's close-up of him, that gives realistic horror to the scene."

Lang knew to leave Glenn Ford and the others more or less alone. Though Ford was actually born in Quebec, the actor made a career out of archetypal American roles. Sometimes he could be a monotonous presence on the screen, but he was also capable of performing with surprising subtlety and distinction. In either case, Ford was a fiercely independent as well as introspective actor, and didn't require, or accept, much direction.

His part was written faultlessly. Bannion was in some ways the opposite of Hans Beckert—a symbol of decency, more able than any previous Lang character to make the grade as a shining hero, to move from despair and self-pity to "reintegration," in the terminology of Colin McArthur. With his own career regenerated, the director found himself embracing a character like Bannion, and able to endorse such an uplifting theme.

Speaking to McGivern some years later, Lang explained how "heated memories of his own experience" influenced *The Big Heat*. "He stressed," wrote McGivern, "that he felt the lead character in the book did *not* resign himself to evil, he did not believe all men had a price, he did not concede that all men must compromise. That one heroic man, the character played by Glenn Ford, stood up and fought back. He appealed powerfully to Lang's own sense of frustration and humiliation at being forced to leave Germany. In a sense, Lang said, he himself had stood up to Goebbels and Hitler, but did so by running away."

One of his greatest works, *The Big Heat* would also be one of the director's fastest, ironically, with its principal photography accomplished inside of four weeks.

A photograph of Silvia Richards decorated the March 26, 1953, front page of the *Los Angeles Times*, while *The Big Heat* was filming. Lang neatly clipped the articles and kept them among his records.

After agonizing over her decision, made partly because she worried about how to support herself and her children, the scenarist chose to cooperate with the FBI and testify publicly. Richards told HUAC representatives that she had first joined the Communist Party in New York City; that in 1943 she and Sam Moore, a former president of the Radio Writers Guild, had organized the first radio branch in Hollywood. But a series of unsettling incidents, including the Party's restriction on books she might read (Proust was taboo, according to Richards), nurtured her political disillusionment, which culminated around the time of the Korean War.

Among the people Richards fingered in her testimony were George Willner, the left-wing partner of Nat Goldstone's talent agency, and Howard Dimsdale, the writer who had followed her at Diana Productions in working on "Winchester '73."

All the Los Angeles papers played up photographs of the beautiful mother of two children, who in "friendly" testimony gave "an extremely articulate account" of her Red-speckled past, admitting to holding Communist Party cell meetings and fund-raising events in her seven-bedroom home in Santa Monica.

The Big Heat was previewed in August and released in October. The reviews were fair, the box office average. Yet almost overnight the 1953 film became one of Lang's most highly esteemed works around the world.

Cahiers du Cinéma in Paris gave the film three pages of complimentary coverage in January of 1954. The writer, François Truffaut—a fresh-faced pupil, like Buñuel in 1927, gazing with reverence upon an idol—titled his piece "Aimer Fritz Lang."* "It seems a long time since Fritz Lang gave us a good film," began the review of another future director, this one writing in England's *Sight and Sound*. Lindsay Anderson would go on to hail *The Big Heat* as "an extremely good thriller, distinguished by precisely those virtues which Lang's pictures in the past few years so painfully lacked."

From the first scenes it was apparent that this Fritz Lang film was going to be different. The film begins with an insert: a close-up of a .38 that is taken out of the frame to be used in a crooked cop's suicide. The suicide, which is shot with almost clinical detachment, sets the plot in motion, and is followed before long by the scene where the hero's innocent wife gets blown up in an automobile. Connoisseur of big bangs, Lang achieved one of his most gut-wrenching effects here, with a quick, off-camera blast. Lang marked a departure by focusing instead on Bannion's anguished reaction.

The hero's wife is probably the least convincing of the story's females anyway. Marriage was never a comfortable subject for Fritz Lang; here it was

---

*"To Love Fritz Lang."

cloying, destined to explode. Yet this is also the only time in the director's career when the erotic attraction between husband and wife is palpable, the marriage itself a solid bond.

The director's sympathy lay more with women on the periphery: the barfly whose inside knowledge leads to her death; the lame secretary who supplies Bannion with a vital clue; especially Debby (maker of perfect martinis). The director obviously *likes* Debby—and her likability became central to the film's stoic warmth and humanism.

The criminals are among Lang's oiliest. Crime lord Mike Lagana is a glib overlord, and there is no more psychotic villain in the American cinema than the well-groomed Vince, who matter-of-factly destroys Debby's looks in a scene whose violence is still shocking.

Debby aids Bannion in the final shoot-out against Vince, and is mortally wounded. Partly due to Debby, Bannion has slowly undergone a change of heart—and revenge feels bittersweet. Now, as she lies dying, Bannion cushions her head with her fur coat, the spoils of her misspent life, comforting her with words murmured as if he is coming out of a trance.* For the first time he begins to speak about his dead wife, about what she had meant to him. The words flow on as Debby ceases breathing. Bannion scarcely notices, lost in his reverie. The scene is beautifully poised on this ambiguity.

But there was also a second ending—one of those codas Lang couldn't resist. A postscript shows the rogue cop accepting back his badge and returning to work. Life goes on, the film appears to say. Not exactly a happy ending, nor a downbeat one, but a mixture of both. A deeply moving ending of the kind that had always eluded Lang.

The director's best works since 1934 (*Fury*, *Man Hunt*, and *Scarlet Street* among them) were mixtures of German style and Hollywood convention. Westerns had basically stymied him. But here, in the twilight of his career, he tapped into a genre every bit as American, yet as Langian as anything he had ever done, and he managed to make his most compassionate film: a gesture of grace and wisdom from an aging master.

The second film under Lang's Columbia contract ought to have been just as good as the first. The property was even more literary; the director had the same leads; he had time and freedom on the script and seemingly all the preproduction in the world. What happened?

Human Desire was based on the Emile Zola novel, *La Bête Humaine (The Human Beast)*, about the triangle of a psychopathic train driver, the married woman who lusts after him, and the husband she schemes to have murdered. It was first adapted in 1938 by Jean Renoir, and would mark the second time that Lang, who knew his French colleague only in passing, became involved with a remake of one of Renoir's films.

"The Human Beast" was the working title, and Maxwell Shane had penned its first draft at the end of 1952, before Lang joined the studio. Jerry Wald was the producer, and he assigned Lang to the film simultaneously with *The Big Heat*, bringing him into story conferences to discuss revisions. When, in

---

*This scene, McGivern emphasized in his article about Lang, was "taken directly from the book."

mid-February, Lang strongly critiqued the Maxwell Shane draft, arguing that the script needed more complexity and logical characterization, the long-term development was handed over to him.

The director, from this early stage, floated a pet idea: Peter Lorre might be right for the leading role of Jeff, the psychopathic train driver. Columbia was receptive, and Lorre was penciled in as the potential star. But Lorre, who was in Germany at the time fulfilling previous engagements, proved diffident. Lang refused to let go of his idea, however, hardly believing that the actor he had catapulted to fame in *M* couldn't be persuaded to reunite with his director.

The Lorre idea sidetracked "The Human Beast" for a while, and first Lang had to finish *The Big Heat*—on time and under budget. When he did so, and with the footage beginning to stir excitement on the lot, Lang had the leverage to bring in his own writer on "Beast," someone equally comfortable with Jerry Wald. That was Alfred Hayes, the adaptor of *Clash by Night*, who in April was asked to start from scratch and create an entirely new screenplay.

Meantime, Lang began planning, surprisingly, to photograph much of the film on location in Canada. When making *The Big Heat*, Jerry Wald had worried that the film had "too much indoor action and not enough outdoor activities," in Lang's words. Now the producer urged Lang to shoot scenes in an actual rail yard amid splendid scenery. The studio arranged for the director and Alfred Hayes to travel to Edmonton and Jasper in early May, scouting locales and inspecting the trains, bridges, and track lines of the surrounding districts.

Script problems continued to nag the project. Despite the fact that there was already a book as well as a previous film based on the book, disagreements arose about that thorny problem—a throughline. The story conferences were unpleasant affairs; it was apparent that Jerry Wald, who thought he was being groomed to take Harry Cohn's place, was in a subtle competition with the studio chief, who had no intention of relinquishing his ultimate authority. When Cohn sat in on meetings, he tended to one-up Wald's ideas and cut him off in mid-sentence. Lang had thrived on such group crossfire in Berlin, but in Hollywood, where he didn't preside, he was stymied. He pragmatically sided with the top man—in this case, Harry Cohn—but trying to play studio politics was always a no-win proposition for him.

Cohn hated the downbeat nature of the Zola story. According to Lang, Jerry Wald, trying to follow Cohn's mixed signals, balked at accepting a faithful version of the novel, which had featured three morally ambiguous and doomed characters. Instead Wald insisted on a regulation Hollywood femme fatale manipulating a love triangle.

According to the director, Wald called Lang and Alfred Hayes in at one point and said, "Everybody is bad in your picture." "Naturally," Lang responded, "because Zola wanted to show that in every human being is a beast." "You both don't understand it," insisted Wald. "The woman is the human beast." Lang's anecdote concluded: "What can you do against the producer? Hayes and I looked at each other and tried to convince him, and then we made a compromise and again it became a triangle story."

Revisions dragged on, affecting everybody's morale. Lang worked with Hayes on a draft throughout the summer of 1953. Sydney Boehm offered revisions in August, before Hayes returned in September for a final whack at the screenplay. As 1953 drew to a close, the usual anxiety was in the air over mounting investment in a year-old project whose shooting script had yet to be approved.

Lang's bluff had been the Peter Lorre idea; with Lorre, maybe the film could be darker than usual, more nihilistic. But it became apparent that casting Lorre was an illusion, and Lang and Alfred Hayes had to throw in their cards. The main character was revamped for Glenn Ford, and stripped of all pathology. The train driver would become a returned Korean War veteran, a John Doe good guy caught up in an evil morass—like Ford's Bannion, though not enough like him to make a difference.

Although Jerry Wald made overtures to Olivia de Havilland, the producer also settled, partly for convenience, on Gloria Grahame to play Vicki, the married seductress. Reuniting *The Big Heat* stars would stir some publicity interest.

But "The Human Beast" smelled like a loser even before the cameras were turned on. Wald had one foot out the door of Columbia. With the producer a lame duck, and Harry Cohn apathetic, the budget suffered cutbacks. After all the scout work, the Canadian sequences—including footage of crisscrossing tracks and trestles exquisitely photographed by Burnett Guffey—would be carefully rationed. After a moody *Clash by Night*–style opening, the production would be forced to retreat back into the soundstages.

Fritz Lang was at his worst when he knew he was wrestling with a production that was bound to fail. And foreboding reports from the set didn't help the director's rapidly crumbling status with Columbia.

Lang was back to his tyrant ways—behaving even more harshly toward Gloria Grahame than on the previous films, without finding any of the saving graces in the character she was portraying. Broderick Crawford, who was playing Grahame's husband, was an alcoholic; and at one point the burly actor, dangerously drunk and finally fed up, stepped in between the director and the actress, grabbing Lang by the shirt and lifting him threateningly off the ground. Photography had to be shut down while tempers cooled. When filming resumed, all Lang could muster was aloofness.

It was hardly a "fast" shoot, taking seven weeks in early 1954. Further watered down by its new title, *Human Desire* was in and out of theaters quickly in August of 1954. Lang was already gone from the lot, for Columbia had declined to renew his contract.

There is no faulting the visual quality of *Human Desire*. Burnett Guffey's work was at times poetical; and Robert Peterson and William Kiernan—also the unsung heroes of *The Big Heat*—dished up a bona fide American interiorscape, with rooms dominated by TV sets, parakeet cages, dime-store prints, and A-1 sauce on the kitchen table.

But the three main characters were ill-drawn by the script. The train driver, Jeff, ended up a muddled soul; Vicki was a bored-housewife caricature; and her sadomasochistic husband, Carl, the only Langian of the three, is sadly the least well-acted.

Vicki fears and despises Carl, who already has killed one person he suspects of carrying on an affair with her (prompting one of the director's familiar inquests, always frustrated in their search for truth). She seduces Carl's fellow trainman, Jeff, drawing Jeff into a conspiracy, and coaxing Jeff to help arrange an "accident" for Carl.

Stumbling home drunk one night along the railroad tracks, Carl is observed by the director from a lordly angle. Marriage has made a pathetic eunuch of him. Jeff lies in waiting, although, like the characters in another film that Jerry Wald had too much to do with—*Clash by Night*—he can't bring himself to carry out the murder he intends.

In the end Jeff spurns Vicki. A violent showdown occurs between Vicki and Carl in a train compartment. As the locomotive hurtles through the night, they perform one of Lang's strangling routines. At the controls of the train is Jeff, seemingly unaware, a hero reduced to emasculated bystander. It was the dismal anticlimax that capped a long, sluggish buildup.

"The French consider this [film] formally very beautiful," Lang liked to say about *Human Desire* with a deep sigh. "That's very nice, but it's not *La Bête Humaine*."

The director harbored no bitterness toward Harry Cohn. "He [Cohn] was always very nice to me," Lang told Peter Bogdanovich. "Mostly he is hated, very unreasonably." "With him, you could talk," Lang informed Bernard Rosenberg and Harry Silverstein. "He used very dirty language, but you could talk to him."

But it is also true that Columbia used Fritz Lang only as a contract director for studio-ordained properties. Harry Cohn proved cool to any of the director's original ideas. And the early 1950s was a particularly fertile period for Lang in this regard; he toyed with all kinds of ideas, many of them surprisingly "un-Langian." But despite these attempts to break free of his typecasting, none of his original stories got off the ground—not at Columbia nor any other Hollywood studio.

Harry Cohn mulled over "Scandal in Vienna," Lang's quasi-musical set in turn-of-the-century Vienna (intended to star Rita Hayworth), but turned it down. Also rejected was "The Law and the Fly," a comedy about a fourteen-year-old winner of a national good-citizenship essay contest, "a clean-cut American youth personified" who becomes a folk hero when he accidentally smashes a racketeering ring. Most unlikely of all to have sprung from the brow of Fritz Lang was "Here Speaks LB2," a whimsical spy story set in post-war Europe, in which a mysterious voice broadcasting on a shortwave transmitter claims to be Hitler. Lang appended a note to his treatment, insisting that "LB2" was envisioned by him as an uproarious comedy. Also rejected.

There were other ideas, ones that plowed more familiar Fritz Lang terrain. The director made one of his periodic stabs at talking up a remake of *Die Frau im Mond*. He floated a Revolutionary War scenario involving hanged spy Nathan Hale. And he developed, with science fiction author Ray Bradbury, a prospectus for a half-hour television series in which a strange traveler in time would visit well-known historical figures (Christopher Columbus, Abe Lincoln, Jack the Ripper) and get mixed up with their lives. The time traveler would be a brilliant Rotwang-style inventor, accompanied by two adoring women, his sweetheart and secretary; the episodes would blend the new world with the old—allowing a big-game hunter to stalk a dinosaur, or Washington to cross the Delaware with an outboard motor.

All rejected around town. All neatly transcribed, typewritten, and stamped by Lily Latté as "the property of Fritz Lang." By the mid-1950s, she had become the entire Fritz-Lang-Film GmbH.

A feeler came, in the spring of 1954, from a most improbable source—Metro-Goldwyn-Mayer.

MGM, like most of the once-omnipotent studios, was in shell-shocked condition. Hoping to reinvigorate the studio, the board had ousted Lang's old nemesis, Louis B. Mayer, and slashed production and payroll. Bad memories had faded since Lang's *Fury* dust-up in 1936, and the director was offered—of all things—a swashbuckler.

Moonfleet was based on a novel by John Meade Falkner about eighteenth-century smuggling between England and France. The book had been purchased by the story department, scripted back in 1952, then left to stagnate in studio files, where producer John Houseman, rummaging around one day, came across this "sparse, rather somber tale of a boy and a gentleman-smuggler operating on the southwest coast of England."

"I needed to have another film in preparation," offhandedly explained Houseman in his autobiography, "and I had never tried my hand at one of this sort."

Born in Bucharest, Houseman had made his name with a fruitful, sometimes stormy partnership with Orson Welles, producing landmark plays in the 1930s. Like Welles, Houseman had made his way to Hollywood, and after World War II he took up offices at MGM where, as producer, he racked up a number of films characterized by their inordinate good taste and intelligence. Lang could not really dismiss Houseman as a "go-between," as he typically did with producers; Houseman was known as a worthy character, and his name dignified any relationship.

Once again the director had little contact with the scenarists, who were long finished by the time Lang was officially hired on August 2, 1954.* Houseman, for one, realized the script amounted to "a whole slew of eighteenth-century clichés," but hoped Fritz Lang might bail him out. Houseman had already organized the cast and crew.

A thoroughly respectable troupe was assembled, including Stewart Granger, Viveca Lindfors, George Sanders, Joan Greenwood, and Jon Whiteley, a blond Scottish boy who had scored a huge success the previous year in the British film *The Kidnappers*. The crew included cameraman Robert Planck, who hand-

---

*One of the scriptwriters, ironically, was Jan Lustig, formerly Hanns G. Lustig, who had written a particularly dismissive notice of *Die Frau im Mond* back in Berlin days. According to one of Paul Erich Marcus's books, Lustig managed to review the film without referring to it directly. Instead he wrote a society gossip report that ended with the sentence, "By the way, there was also the new Fritz Lang film *Die Frau im Mond*."

Lustig had crossed paths with Lang in Berlin and Paris, where he had collaborated with Billy Wilder, Antoine de Saint-Exupéry, and director Marc Allégret. He arrived in America after the fall of France, one of the beneficiaries of the European Film Fund, then became a valuable scenarist and "story doctor" almost exclusively at MGM.

somely photographed a host of MGM films of the 1940s and 1950s. And veteran Budapest-born composer Miklos Rozsa—whose music for *Secret Beyond the Door* was one of that film's few highlights—was called on to create a rousing score.

Principal photography, in fact, would begin a mere two weeks after the director was signed. Yet *Moonfleet* would be an "A" production, with all the studio gloss and appointments—Lang's first in the new Cinemascope process, and his biggest budget ever in Hollywood, set at $1.9 million. The director himself would receive $48,000 for ten weeks' employment.

With the start date coming up fast, Lang threw himself into last-minute plans and preparation. Gone was the time when he could spend more than a year shaping a superfilm like *Metropolis*. Rare now was the once-leisurely schedule of sketches and research and script drafts. One thing Lang had adapted to well in Hollywood was the ceaseless driving pressures.

Oceanside, Corona Del Mar, and Point Dume would substitute for the Dorset coastline. The director turned to Hogarth prints for visual inspiration. MGM's design departments swung into action—never mind what might have happened on *Fury* years before—and pulled together expertly. There would not be a tossed-off shot in *Moonfleet*; there would not be a more beautifully crafted work in all of Fritz Lang's career.

But the acting was a different matter. Stewart Granger was in the midst of his box-office vogue as a dashing leading man. He would make an earnest effort as the pirate Jeremy Fox—who befriends a little boy searching for his long-lost father—but Lang could only feel lukewarm about the actor. The character called for more emotional complexity. In his autobiography Granger complained that he wasn't helped much by the "once brilliant" director, who was "a little out of his depth" with *Moonfleet*.

This criticism was echoed by Viveca Lindfors, who said in an interview that the director barely spoke to her and others in the cast, just informed them where to stand and little else. "He [Lang] had everything worked out exactly the way he wanted it," recalled Lindfors. "He might as well have had puppets to play with. He really didn't like actors. He only told us to look this way, or look that way. It was very stylized, and you could say, in a way, that I was too inexperienced to fill in and make it interesting for myself. I hated it."

The emotional heart of the film is the little vagabond boy John Mohune, who never suspects that his true father is the pirate. This is where Lang concentrated his absolutism: the director swooped down on Jon Whiteley, the most innocent and fragile. The only person Lang really *directed* was Whiteley, screaming at the child performer, at times reducing him to tears. Then, when the production fell behind, Lang went further, blaming the worst of the delays on Whiteley—and on Stewart Granger, for not knowing his lines.

Houseman's policy, like Walter Wanger's, was to remain unobtrusive during filming. "To begin with," according to Lang, Houseman was "approachable and friendly." The photography was finished in mid-October, and Lang himself helped shape the "final cut" before taking his leave. Then: "Behind my back and certainly without my consent," Lang claimed in later interviews, Houseman reedited the film. "Producer's cuts," the director informed Charles Higham and Joel Greenberg, "not only drastically reduced Viveca Lindfors's part, but rendered certain sequences almost unintelligible." Once again, double-crossed by a producer. Privately Lang declared the result "abominable."

But the director could be wrong about himself and his films, and differences with a producer were apt to curdle his feelings. "Fritz was a tortured man, a perfectionist who never did get the perfection he wanted," explained Lang's friend David Bradley. "He sort of had a good memory," Bradley added. "But he would forget which things were cut and recut. He'd rather have the film pristine—his cut—even if that was only in his memory."

Some people believe *Moonfleet* is one of his most heartfelt works. The dead trees, murmuring ruins, and statues that dwarf the characters were ghosts summoned from the director's Germanic soul, while the pretty painted clouds and postcard skies recalled Lang's artistic roots in the sentimental decorative art of nineteenth-century Vienna.

Jon Whiteley turned in a surprisingly affecting performance. On occasion Lang was capable of finding within himself as much plucky boy as demented child murderer; and when the boy sings a folk song that stirs the pirate's deep-buried feelings, it is as if the same emotions are sweeping over Fritz Lang. Once again, the actor Lang treated most cruelly represented the character he empathized with most vividly.

The end of the film involves a frenzied sword fight and a runaway coach. Then a sensitive coda: Jeremy Fox, returning to John Mohune—whom he now recognizes to be his son—to spin one last lie. He has to go away on a trip (he doesn't mention that he is mortally wounded). As the boy watches from a window, his face trembling, the dying pirate boards a small boat and turns his craft into the rising wind. For Lang, as for Jeremy Fox, this film was an elegy of suppressed feeling.

In the United States, *Moonfleet* was all but dismissed. "Mr. Lang has got everything into *Moonfleet* except a reason for your slightest concern," complained *The New York Times*.

Abroad, on the other hand, it gradually found acclaim. Fritz Lang's *Moonfleet* took a while to weave its way across the ocean, but when shown in Paris in 1960, the film was honored with a newly created Prize of the Nouvelle Critique against competition that included Ingmar Bergman's *The Magician* and Robert Bresson's *Pickpocket*.

"Why, in Paris, they adore this film is beyond me," Lang liked to say. And he meant it. Still, the director recognized that the Europeans rated him very highly, while in Hollywood he still had to scrounge for contracts. As 1954 drew to a close, the director might have been forgiven for looking over his shoulder toward Europe—and especially old Germany.

A death may also have loosened Lang's psychology where Germany was concerned.

It was Thea von Harbou. She had been in unstable health for several years, suffering from high blood pressure, migraines, and neuralgia. While ill, she continued to write or dictate from her bed, invariably with a dachshund at her feet and a tomcat on her shoulder. Her visitors included screen personalities, students, and the *other* wife of Ayi Tendulkar.

Ayi Tendulkar, whom von Harbou had secretly married, had also been arrested and briefly interned, in India, after the war. He had returned to India sometime in 1938–1939, working on behalf of the well-known engineering company Allgemeine Elektricitäts-Gesellschaft (A.E.G.), intending to forge contacts there for the industrialization of India. After India won its independence in 1947, Tendulkar would become one of the first to obtain foreign contracts from Krupp's, the steel and armaments company.

Tendulkar himself never returned to Germany. He did marry a second time, in a ceremony presided over by Mahatma Gandhi. Since his first marriage had been kept secret, there could be no divorce, and the von Harbou liaison was hushed up. But Tendulkar never lost his passion for von Harbou, and spoke so warmly of her that his Indian wife, Indumati Tendulkar, went to Berlin to spend a year with her in 1952.

"She treated me as her own daughter, though I was the wife of her lover," recalled Mrs. Indumati Tendulkar, "and I considered her [as] my mother." Mrs. Tendulkar recalled that von Harbou often spoke of the richness of the time when she was Mrs. Fritz Lang. But there was no memento of the director in her apartment, whereas in her bedroom hung a framed photo of Ayi Tendulkar. Another wall displayed portraits of von Harbou's two polar-opposite political idols: Gandhi and Hitler.

Invited to the Berlinale as a guest of honor in 1954, von Harbou appeared at a showing of *Der müde Tod*, answering questions from the audience. A relative said later that her mood had been so affected by the film that she wasn't watching her step as she left the screening. Von Harbou stumbled and fell to the ground; rushed home, she developed a hip injury and was taken to a hospital, where a few days later, on July 1, 1954, she died. She was sixty-five.

Her funeral was attended by government officials, Ufa representatives, and "a high number of people involved in film and theater as well as a lot of fans," according to Elfriede Nagel, her last secretary. Director Ludwig Berger, once a refugee from Hitler but one of those who had returned to Europe, eulogized her as a "Queen in giving." Von Harbou was buried at Charlottenburg, and in time the city of Berlin assumed responsibility for care of her grave.

In America, it took two weeks for the news of her death to be published in *Variety*, but Lang had heard it almost instantly from German contacts. He blamed von Harbou in part for the American remake of *M*—she had given her consent to Seymour Nebenzahl—but otherwise his attitude toward her had softened. Though he might vary his remarks about her for interviewers, von Harbou was one of the few people for whom he felt an almost unconditional regard.

There were practical reasons for Lang to reconsider Germany. He and Lily Latté were extremely interested in the restitution money vouchsafed by the German government to those who had been victimized by Hitler. Together they began to explore their options. On Lang's behalf Lily Latté retained Berlin attorney Marlene Hucklenbroich, whose husband Volker was also an attorney. Marlene Hucklenbroich's father had been well-known back in Berlin's Golden Decade, representing many of the Jews in the motion picture industry. It was logical now for those who had fled to Hollywood to renew that connection.

Now Lang had professional possibilities to mull in Germany. Not only Peter

Lorre, but Gottfried Reinhardt, Kurt Bernhardt, Robert Siodmak, Hermann Millkowsky, Erich Pommer, Conrad von Molo, and many, many others whom Lang knew had been lured back to Germany in support of massive efforts to resuscitate the national film industry.

Many were making movies for Artur Brauner, a canny new-generation producer whose CCC Co. was committed to the German-language marketplace. Around the time *Moonfleet* was presented in U.S. theaters, Brauner contacted Lang, asking the director for his comments on a script concerning the unsuccessful July 20, 1944, plot to assassinate Hitler. It is tempting to perceive in Lang's response the changes taking place in his own attitude toward Germany.

The man who had scoffed at "good Germans" in Fred Zinnemann's *The Seventh Cross* now replied that he thought the moral of a Hitler-assassination-attempt scenario should be that "there were still enough people around, at this stage of the total war in a police state, who were prepared to risk their lives to prove to their own people and to the world that there were still Germans who did not identify with Hitler."

Lang felt there was too much of an implication in the present draft that the plotters were motivated by their own personal ambitions. More important to the theme of the film, according to the director, ought to be those "who had a very long, very heartfelt struggle with themselves" about Hitler and Nazi Germany. No doubt Lang had reasons of his owns, harking back to 1933, to dwell on such a theme.

But Brauner was moving too quickly for Lang, and the Hitler-assassination film had already gone into production by the time the director's letter was received in Germany.

In Hollywood, Lang knew, his career was winding down. He was sixty-five, and feeling his age. The motion picture industry seemed in bitter disarray. Production output had been drastically reduced, and many of the big-name directors and producers were winding down their careers. Only the new, fly-by-night producers seemed to be flourishing.

Lang's last producer was probably, in the director's opinion, the worst. Bert E. Friedlob was a parvenu businessman from Chicago, whose first marriage had given him access to the Annenberg publishing fortune. Friedlob pioneered roller derbies and midget auto races in Europe and the South Pacific before landing in Hollywood prior to World War II. His third wife was actress Eleanor Parker, and after their divorce Friedlob turned film producer—though not an entirely incompetent one, as evidenced by such credits as *The Star* and *Steel Trap*.

Friedlob was well-connected at 20th Century-Fox, Universal, and RKO, and though the director disliked him at first glance, Lang put on his practiced smile. He needed those connections. And he needed a script that somebody would finance through to production. Although Friedlob was not interested in any of the ideas from Lang's story file, he had two properties of his own ready to go, and serendipitously, one of them was based on the story of William Heirens, the Chicago killer whose exploits Lang had followed back in the mid-1940s.

A former Chicago reporter, Charles Einstein, had written a Dell paperback, roughly based on the Heirens killings, called *The Bloody Spur*. This novel—somewhat in "ze pulp" vein that Lang professed to enjoy—would form the basis of *While the City Sleeps*, the first film under his contract with Friedlob. The setting would be switched to New York City; Casey Robinson, a Utah-born, Cornell-educated professor's son, who had been around Hollywood since the silent era, was already immersed in scriptwork.

For Lang, it seemed a particularly serendipitous choice of material. The guilt-stricken Heirens, who scrawled "For heaven's sake catch me before I kill more . . ." in lipstick on mirrors in his victims' homes, was almost too reminiscent of Peter Kürten, the serial killer who had inspired *M*. "I saw great possibilities in it [the subject] as well as some things which I didn't believe in," the director told Peter Bogdanovich.

Lang enjoyed working with Robinson, whose reputable credits included *Tovarich*, *Dark Victory*, *King's Row*, *Now, Voyager* and *The Corn Is Green*. "We really worked hand-in-glove," the director told Bogdanovich. "Sometimes I invented a scene, sometimes he invented a scene, sometimes I improved, sometimes he improved . . ."

In true Lang tradition, the first Bert E. Friedlob production would be a honeymoon. The producer gave Lang and Casey Robinson room to breathe—which also meant time to second-guess themselves. Robinson had no journalism experience; and the script would lack the real-life versimilitude the director usually boasted. Instead it would be riddled with scenes and characters plagiarized from other Fritz Lang films.

The columnist racing his rivals to crack the news, the sluttish ex-newspaper lady who doesn't mind how she earns her fur coat, the publisher who has failed to live up to his father's expectations—the characters were scavenged from the Langian grab bag. In *M*, Lang had managed to convey empathy for a child killer. Here, in Eisenhower's America, Lang diagnoses the Heirens-prototype, Robert Manners, as but a Mama's Boy.

That character is the film's worst indignity. Manners is a mockery of Hans Beckert, just as the actor who played him—John Barrymore, Jr.—is a poor stand-in for Peter Lorre. Lang and Robinson conceived of a delivery boy wearing Brandoish leather, an aficionado of comic books and *True Crime* magazines. This was not far from the facts of the Heirens case, but on screen it made for shallow psychologizing.

One scene the director boasted about—Lang claimed he actually wrote it—took place between the newspaper columnist and the conniving newspaper lady angling to seduce him for inside information. Sitting on barstools, she attracts his curiosity by peering through an eyeglass at a photographic slide, chuckling and cooing lasciviously. "Pretty?" the newspaper columnist asks in a lascivious tone, "Would I like?" When, after some cuteness, she finally shows the slide, the camera reveals it as the snapshot of a bare-naked baby. This was the level of comedy to which Lang had descended.

One subplot has the columnist's girlfriend Nancy (Sally Forrest) going to great lengths to protect her virginity. The columnist keeps trying to smooth-talk her into bed, but she has trained her mind on a respectable marriage. After the killer's arrest, a coda shows the two of them on their Florida honeymoon—another "happy ending," like the one in *Ministry of Fear*, but one for which the director had only himself to blame. The film's coy last image—Nancy bouncing up and down invitingly on a motel bed—couldn't have been more out of context, or less Langian.

In truth most of the film was concerned—not with the grisly killer—but with the other, more familiar characters. Friedlob did not pinch pennies on the cast, and the "big-name" ensemble would include Dana Andrews, Ida Lupino, Vincent Price, George Sanders, Sally Forrest, Thomas Mitchell, Rhonda Fleming and Howard Duff. *While the City Sleeps* was shot quickly in the summer of 1955, and when it was released, almost a year later, in May of 1956, it was considered a taut, well-made suspense film.

"A top-flight job," noted *Variety*.

"A very commercial attraction," said the *Hollywood Reporter*.

"Three-and-a-half stars," cheered the *New York Daily News*.

"An extremely lively melodrama," wrote the *New York Journal-American*.

From the perspective of time, however, the film looks woefully thin and calculated, the director's misguided attempt to curry some final favor with his American audience.

Beyond a Reasonable Doubt, Lang's second film for Bert E. Friedlob, also came with a competent scriptwriter attached. Douglas Morrow was a former boy opera singer who had studied law at Columbia University before turning to screenwriting. He won an Academy Award for Best Original Story for 1949's *The Stratton Story*.

Morrow had devised a clever scenario about a novelist, Tom Garrett, who is persuaded by a newspaper publisher, Austin Spencer, to become a guinea pig in his campaign against capital punishment. When a burlesque dancer is strangled, the two men conspire to create enough circumstantial evidence to get Garrett arrested. The idea is to spring Garrett from the electric chair, at the eleventh hour, to prove the unreliability of death-sentence verdicts.

However, Spencer, on his way to free Garrett with documentation of their charade, is slain in a car accident. Garrett, protesting his innocence, is nonetheless scheduled for execution. Susan, the publisher's daughter—and Garrett's fiancée—mounts a campaign to free him, culminating in the discovery of a vital exonerating clue. But when she visits Garrett to tell him the good news, he slips up and reveals the murder victim's secret identity, making it obvious that he was the real killer all along. Shocked by this revelation, Susan lets the execution go ahead as planned.

Beyond a Reasonable Doubt was prepared simultaneously with *While the City Sleeps*, so Lang could divide his time with Douglas Morrow. The story of crime and punishment, of a reporter steeped in the story he is covering, of a respectable man mixing too closely with the dregs of society, was one that had inspired the director before. The story twists were modest ones, but the script that emerged was superior.

It is tempting to see this final Hollywood film as one that ultimately coalesced into an encore of Fritz Lang's American works. Like *Fury*, *Beyond a Reasonable Doubt* featured a man wrongly condemned. As in *You Only Live Once*, there is an attorney in the prosecutor's office, in love with the honest lady who steadfastly believes in her man's plight. And as in *Scarlet Street*, a convicted murderer is decreed to die in the electric chair for a crime he apparently has not commited.

Considering Lang's personal history, it would be interesting to know who planted the final turn of plot: at the eleventh hour, when the reporter is revealed as the true killer, the victim is revealed as his wife from a secret marriage. She is a nightclub dancer, which may have been the calling of the first Frau Lang—who also died under mysterious circumstances.

It is all the more intriguing that one of the film's weaknesses is the director's seemingly ambiguous attitude toward Garrett, who is never quite the malefactor warranted by the plot. Perhaps Garrett acted understandably, Lang mused in one interview. After all, the murder was "a crime out of despair," the victim a mere ex-girlfriend "who made his life unhappy."

Some contemporary critics, who admire *Beyond a Reasonable Doubt* as one of Lang's finest, see in it a deliberately unassuming style—"a visually drab and unyielding film, *about nothing else but its own subject*," in the words of Gilbert Adair (who chose it as *the* representative film of 1956 for *Flickers*, his book celebrating the centennial of motion pictures); "less the mise-en-scène of a script than simply the reading of the script, presented to us just as it is, without embellishment," according to Stephen Jenkins, writing in his British Film Institute monograph *Fritz Lang*.

The truth is, Lang approached the start of photography burdened with his own growing despair, and a mounting hatred of the producer he was forced to rely upon to succeed. The fighting and arguments that in the past had always been thrilling no longer seemed like challenges worth meeting. Lang knew his career was all but over. He no longer had the appetite for the fray.

The once severe taskmaster showed only apathy toward the cast members. "He [Lang] was on his good behavior," recalled Joan Fontaine, who starred as Susan, the publisher's daughter. "It's interesting, in the German character, where they can be bullies, they can then turn right around and be very obsequious. Well, he was going through this 'I-must-be-a-good-boy . . . yes, anything-you-say-Miss-Fontaine' kind of thing. So I found him a false character."

Dana Andrews, who had been part of Friedlob's packaging for both films, was a somber, monochromatic actor who presented problems that the director couldn't solve—and no longer had the energy to confront. Andrews was an out-and-out alcoholic, and the characters he played in both *While the City Sleeps* and *Beyond a Reasonable Doubt* tended to carry drinks throughout the stories. Off-camera, the star was "really on the sauce," according to Gene Fowler, Jr., showing up most mornings "with the most god-awful hangover in the world, and we couldn't get a shot out of him until eleven o'clock, when he was fed gallons of coffee."

Lang couldn't cope with the actor. The producer finally laid down the law and made Andrews promise to quit drinking. Just to make sure, Friedlob ordered an underling to tail the actor one day after work. Andrews drove at speed onto the freeway, then performed a sudden, illegal U-turn across the dividing strip, disappearing down an off-ramp. Friedlob's man was afraid to follow. Next morning Andrews showed up with a hangover, same as usual.

The actor's alcoholic haze added a further layer of insincerity to the film, remembered Joan Fontaine. Andrews was "finding it very difficult," the actress recalled in one interview. "So again, I'm dealing with false characters. It's very hard when you're playing in fantasy, playing dream characters, and then you're playing them with false characters [the actors]. You come home just feeling that you've been in a dust storm all day."

Lang, too, must have felt in a dust storm. Bone-tired. Tired of stupid producers. Tired of troublesome actors he couldn't replace. The director took his small pleasures where he could find them, spending time on the inserts and minor technical challenges, communing with the small group of friends he had managed to collect around him—his last U.S. "team."

Dan Seymour would play a small role in his fourth and final appearance in a Fritz Lang film—his scene, as a sleazy nightclub owner, is a highlight of *Beyond a Reasonable Doubt*. Carroll Clark, who had become Lang's friend, did his best with art direction on a low budget; and Gene Fowler, Jr., who was showing ambitions of his own as a director,* returned one last time to serve as Lang's editor and buffer with Friedlob.

The director and his editor cooked up a special effect for the scene where the publisher retrieves the evidence from his wall safe and gets into his car to go and clear Garrett. Backing out of the driveway, his car is hit by a truck, and he is killed. Throughout the entire sequence—one of those Langian visual sequences without dialogue—a radio blares up-to-the-minute bulletins about the ongoing trial.

"Fritz had laid it out very meticulously," said Fowler, "and he had a very elaborate shot where they took an automobile and welded an axle to it, longitudinally, which he wanted to photograph as the car went over. Well, that was the biggest megillah in the world, and if I used *any* of that shot . . . it just plain didn't work. The car spun around like a second hand on a clock. I mean, there was no impact or anything like it. So we printed every eighth frame to speed it up."

That was the way things went. Even the special effects fizzled.

Bert Friedlob monitored Lang like a cop, and calculated the expense of every insert and retake. He and the director had their final showdown over the ending, although what exactly happened remains murky, no matter how many times an aggrieved Lang told the story.

As the film stands, Garrett, abandoned by Susan, returns to death row to await his punishment. Friedlob wanted Lang to show the electric chair scene with the actual execution. The director refused: The audience was smart enough to realize the character was going to die off-camera. The wrong culprit had been executed in *Scarlet Street*, so that was no endorsement of capital punishment. Despite the twist that Garrett was in reality *guilty*, the director didn't want to be misunderstood as reversing himself.

But the producer insisted on a "really gruesome" execution ending, according to Lang. They fought over the ending during the script stages, and continued to fight throughout filming. Friedlob was one of those single-minded characters who never gave up, so every time Lang thought the issue was dead, the producer revived it.

The director had made a pit-stop at every major studio except Walt Dis-

---

*Fowler would turn director with 1957's *I Was a Teenage Werewolf*.

ney's, completing twenty-two feature films since arriving in Hollywood in 1935. He had been forced to accept inferior properties. He had lost control of casting. He had worked on pitiful budgets and ever-speeded-up schedules. His editing had been overruled. He had been fired, ordered to make retakes, had his titles second-guessed and altered. Now, another idiotic ending was being foisted on him.

So Lang filmed it his way—not an execution but Garrett at the moment of reckoning, collapsing in terror, being dragged toward his fate. One of those production spies who had haunted the director throughout his career was on the alert, and reported back to Friedlob, who came down screaming to confront Lang. But this time Lang didn't buckle under. Friedlob couldn't direct the scene himself*, so it was Lang's victory.

But it was a hollow victory; there was no euphoria. After the last scene he directed, Fritz Lang did something he had never done before. He walked away from the film. "You son of a bitch," he told Friedlob, "I don't want to have anything to do with you anymore or the American motion picture industry."

Fritz Lang would never again direct in Hollywood.

Lang left his friend Gene Fowler, Jr., to finish the cutting. "He knew exactly how I could cut the film," said Fowler. The director was sick and tired of the job. It shows in every frame. *Beyond a Reasonable Doubt* was shot "under duress," Lang told Charles Higham and Joel Greenberg. The director struggled in later interviews to blame the film's shortcomings on something other than his own collapse of will. His agent, perhaps? According to Lang, Friedlob had promised he could implement "certain script changes," but "owing to my agent's negligence, I had nothing to that effect in writing." Once again: a mythical clause was to blame.

"I hate it," Lang said of *Beyond a Reasonable Doubt*, "but it was a great success. I don't know why."

It wasn't exactly a "great success," but *Beyond a Reasonable Doubt* did fairly well, and received adequate reviews. And Lang could have kept working in Hollywood. It would have meant starting all over . . . but he could have done it.

He still pined to make a Fritz Lang film, based entirely on a Fritz Lang inspiration. If his inadequate screenwriting skills frustrated that idée fixe, he would at least create the illusion. Ghostwriters were employed to put his ideas on paper. And when he couldn't—or felt he couldn't—afford them any longer, Lily Latté took down his dictated stories and put them into fluent English. To conceal his identity as the writer long enough to fool producers, Lang registered his scripts under a pen name—Michael Latté.

Realizing that his mystique, especially in America, was based on films about crime, murder, revenge, and lust, Lang set aside his more whimsical stories, and in the months after *Beyond a Reasonable Doubt* focused again on his strong suit. One of the stories Lang worked hardest on, fitfully, was "Dark

---

*In fact, the producer was gravely ill, dying of cancer. In the final months of postproduction Friedlob underwent two operations; and shortly after *Beyond a Reasonable Doubt* was released, Friedlob passed away, at age forty-nine, on October 7, 1956.

Spring." It was about a teenage girl whose mother, a widowed actress, is on the verge of marrying a stranger. The daughter, resentful, grows suspicious of the new husband, and as events unfold, it becomes clear he intends to kill his wife for her insurance. Through the determined efforts of the daughter's boyfriend, the killing is aborted. The whole story is told in a *Rahmenhandlung*-style frame-flashback as the husband's weak-willed accomplice is being grilled by the police.

Lang accumulated a file of jokes, crime-story anecdotes, statistical background, and a list of various scene ideas for this scenario: "cast of characters," "opening situation," "the intermediate situation," "kill attempts," et cetera. But it was a painfully schematic approach, and though he compulsively mentioned the project to columnists interviewing him, he never followed through with the script. Boasting about the subject to one newspaper writer, Lang claimed "Dark Spring" was a very up-to-date "boy-girl story." Then irrationality kicked in: Though, sadly, there was nothing unique about his story, the director abruptly declined "to outline the plot, other than to say it was a tragedy even though 'it doesn't quite come to murder.' He said he fears that, since the plot is a simple one, someone reading it in the newspaper might steal it."

It was still rare in those days for directors to take their own option on a book—to gamble a lump sum of their own money. But the through-line of an already published novel was reassuring for someone having trouble fleshing out an original story. Such was Lang's state of mind that in 1954 he did purchase the rights to a Nedra Tyre book that looked promising. *Journey to Nowhere* was described in publicity leaks as the story of a young woman who, on a trip to England, begins to experience post-traumatic effects from a mysterious childhood car crash that killed her entire family. "Actually," according to publicity, "she is unwittingly the courier for certain valuable information coveted by sinister agents." Anne Baxter was touted as the director's likely leading lady when the project came to realization.

Lang's envy of Alfred Hitchcock, whose career was still going strong in the 1950s, extended to raiding one of his prized writers. The director's neighbor, the British-born Charles Bennett, who had covered sinister-spy territory for Hitchcock in several films, agreed to work with Lang in adapting *Journey to Nowhere*. But Bennett didn't get very far in his work on the script between 1954 and 1955.

"I visited him [Lang] and drank with him quite often," reminisced Bennett, "but he was a hard man to really know.

"The project fizzled, somewhat to my satisfaction. I liked Fritz, but I knew we would never get along together on a final script. I'm a stickler for my own ideas. So was he. We would have clashed. As I said, I liked Fritz, but not his arrogance and eternal self-satisfaction. He always concluded he was right. Often he was, but his general attitude would never have worked when it came to a meeting of minds. I imagine that most writers who worked for him did as they were told. Fine! It speaks for Fritz's genius."

Bennett chose to accept a more definite job in England, and Lang couldn't bring himself to seek a replacement. Another low-cost option was taken on a twenty-five-cent paperback novel called *Wiretap,* about the murder of a small-town judge, and an investigation that reveals a widespread wiretap racket. Again there were file folders of notes and clippings, drafts starting out in German and finishing up in English. Again, no script was completed.

Occasional job offers trickled in, but were they genuine? In September 1954, a telegram came from one Joseph Steiner of Waring Pictures in New York City asking Lang to consider directing an adaptation of Natalie Anderson Scott's 1947 novel *The Story of Mrs. Murphy*. Steiner had already commissioned a script. The story was about a dipsomaniac—lovable when sober, unscrupulous when drunk—who is loved by four different women. The book ends in debauchery, dope-peddling, jail, and matricide. The opportunity tempted Lang, even though he had to admit he found the story gloomy.

Telegrams and phone calls wooed him—but when the director checked up on Steiner, he discovered that the producer didn't own any soundstages. That worried Lang. Steiner assured him that the film could be shot mostly in real-life New York City locations. That was an alluring prospect—something Lang had never done—but also worrying. The director couldn't believe the producer could raise the necessary financing; yes, Steiner assured him in a series of letters, the money was virtually guaranteed.

Even after he was invited to New York for an all-expenses-paid story conference, Lang couldn't decide. Fearing that it was all part of some conspiracy designed to make him look foolish, he asked his friend, critic Herman Weinberg, to spy around and report to him confidentially on the viability of Waring Pictures. Weinberg did so, and his opinion was that the whole setup looked "dubious." The flirtation with Steiner ended with Lang writing that the script was too negative and advising the producer, "I don't think you should make this depressing picture."

After twenty years in Hollywood, Lang had no channels open to the major studios; all he had left to consider were teasing, worthless offers from nobodies.

His publicity and interviews, coinciding with the release of the two Bert E. Friedlob productions, had the feeling of valedictories. During an interview by Don Ross in the *New York Herald Tribune* on May 20, 1956, the director was asked what he considered "his greatest achievement in this country." According to the article, "he [Lang] at first had nothing to say. This was not, it developed, because he feels he has made nothing good here; it was because he apparently feels that nothing he's done comes up to the lofty standard set by *M*."

Still saying he yearned to preside over his own independent company, the director admitted he didn't know what he would do next in his career, if anything. "Mr. Lang thinks that people in real life—not just in his movies—are caught in a net. 'If I make a picture I don't like because I need money, don't you think I'm caught in a net?' "

The would-be project that briefly lifted his spirits was "The Pearl of Love," whose producer was not one of those unreliable Americans but a Bengali from India, Bishu Sen, an associate of Sir Alexander Korda. Korda had once hoped to make a film about the love story behind the construction of the Taj Mahal. Prodded by Korda, David Lean had explored the subject before abandoning it some years earlier. After Korda's death in 1956, Bishu Sen had formed a partnership with Captain Peter Moore, a television and film producer, and hit on the idea of approaching Lang.

The enticement for Lang was clear: It was India, the jewel of his imagination. The director had never actually visited his beloved India, and here were two British producers, with the magical name Korda attached, offering to fly him there—first-class—to scout the terrain.

It is unclear how much involvement the director had in the 25-page, 104-scene treatment for "The Pearl of Love." (The script is routinely attributed to Lang in books and articles, though his records indicate it existed independent of him; and advance publicity credited it to writer Gerald Savory.) Certainly the director contributed some Langian details, investing key scenes with his unmistakable visual imagery.

"The Pearl of Love" was a three-way love story, with two men subordinated in the drama to a heroic woman pleading for peace and unity in seventeenth-century India. One of the men is a budding architect who goes on to design and construct the Taj Mahal. The production was envisioned as an epic adventure with bandit raids, village massacres, harem-girl parties, crowded city-street scenes, and desert vistas. A human chess game, a polo match to the death, a corps of fearless female soldiers, and a final battle, led by an emperor propped up dead in his howdah and encircled by vultures, were among its highlights.

Shortly after he was contacted in late July of 1956, Lang journeyed with Bishu Sen to India as an honored guest of the state. It was the first time he had traveled beyond the American continent—excluding his Philippines trip—since leaving France in 1934. "Director Fritz Lang Is Happy to Be In India" blared the headline of the August 31, 1956 *Bombay Screen*, and indeed India's film world was happy for his visit.

Press conferences, interviews, official receptions, and parties in his honor bloomed in the director's path. The full calendar of events flattered his sense of importance. One Indian critic, upon meeting Lang, wrote that it was one of the most stimulating experiences of his lifetime to gaze upon "one of those masters whose name is forever engraved in the annals of cinema history," who in addition to being "one of the cinematic giants of all time," was a human being whose "humility, sincerity, and kindliness" was "a sign of the great intellect." A photograph caption described him as "Mr. Fritz Lang—Statesman."

The express purpose of the trip was for the director to study and collect data about the Mogul period "in order to catch the spirit of the age." Lang toured the studios of Minerva Movietone, Mehboob Productions, Filmistan, and Bombay Talkies, inspecting "the equipment and methods of working at these places besides talking to those on the sets." Catching up with the latest Indian films was part of the experience. During his stopover in Bombay, according to one account, Lang was known to watch "even two in a day. He was anxious to know the treatment, techniques, and standard of Indian films besides knowing the tastes of the Indian audiences."

At his press conferences, the director elaborated on the film he hoped to create. "Making a picture in India, on India, is a matter dear to his heart,"

India's *Screen* reported, because "he has heard so much about India as a place of enchantment, mystery, and wonder." Since "no Hollywood star will be able to do full justice to the role of Mumtaz Mahal, he is in search of an Indian girl who can take up the role."

In all, Lang and Bishu Sen had a three-week Cook's Tour. After Bombay, New Delhi, and Udaipur, the director visited the Taj Mahal in Agra. He was photographed in the nation's newspapers laying a wreath on the samadhi of Mahatma Gandhi at Rajghat. No matter where he stopped, his mood was jubilant, according to press reports. "He found everything wonderful and enchanting and he seemed to be in a kind of fear that he was in a dream from which he might have to awake to reality."

En route to India, Lang had made a connecting stop at the Düsseldorf airport. It was the first time the film director had set foot in Germany in more than twenty years, but it broke the spell. His thoughts had been increasingly filled with the so-called new Germany, and now, returning from India, Lang decided that the time was ready for his homecoming.

Lily Latté had disembarked at Düsseldorf on the trip over with plans to visit the Theodor Adornos in Frankfurt, and to prepare Lang's itinerary for when he returned.

When in September Lang returned to Düsseldorf, his first days were shadowed by a viral illness he had picked up in India. But word began to spread that Fritz Lang was back in Germany, and his curiosity about people and places revived with his health; the director decided to prolong his stay, meeting with old acquaintances and sniffing out professional contacts.

Lang spent several weeks shuttling between Frankfurt, Munich, and Berlin. Latté or Paul Erich Marcus—the director's travel guide from London—accompanied him everywhere. Brigitte Helm, Willy Fritsch, and Fritz Kortner were among the names from the past who arranged to see him. The director had a warm reunion with Fritz Arno Wagner and an emotional one with Gerda Maurus. His onetime leading lady and girlfriend had been briefly detained by the Allies after the war, then cleared of any Nazi taint; thereafter Maurus would appear mainly on the stage. The star of *Spione* and *Die Frau im Mond* made only a handful of films after 1945.

Representatives from Germany's film companies came to greet Lang wherever he went, vaguely outlining future prospects. Among the officials who met with Lang were Herbert Tischendorf, Germany's most powerful distributor, and Fritz Thiery (a former Ufa sound supervisor) from Bavaria-Filmkunst. CCC's Artur Brauner was another—and the most persistent. Brauner invited Lang to Berlin and energetically courted him there, but the director remained "skeptical and suspicious," in the words of Claudia Dillmann-Kühn in her book *Artur Brauner und die CCC*.

Germany's press trooped to interview the director, describing the man whose name was synonymous with the Golden Twenties as "tired, silent, defensive, beset by memories, a trifle stooped, shadowed by quiet melancholy." Writing in *Der Tagesspiegel*, Karena Niehoff thought the monocle had begun to look democratic on Lang—"a little professorial and middle-class." Her report added: "He sits in his hotel room with the Berlin press people, none of whom he knows, and gets lost in conversation so absent-mindedly that he could be back in the Romanische Café."

"Although one can chat with him charmingly about any topic," another scribe wrote, "there are some areas where he stops talking. He is not one of those who repeatedly praises the rebuilding of the cities and industry with astonishment . . . Now and then he expresses his feelings: 'What do you know about back then?' "

When the reporter from the *Frankfurter Neue Presse* wondered about his future intentions, Lang declared that, confronted with the country he "loved very much and hated very much," thoughts about film subjects that he might tackle crowded his mind: the story of Anne Frank, the problems of contemporary young people, tales of German working women. Maybe, one day, he would take one of these producers up on their ambitious offers, return to Germany, and make one final "Fritz Lang film." "And why shouldn't I make a film, if I found a subject that I thought I would get a kick out of? Most people just want me to suggest something to them."

The real reason for the trip to Berlin was an appointment with lawyers Marlene and Volker Hucklenbroich for the director and Lily Latté to make their official compensation claims. State-sanctioned restitution had been divided into several categories of eligibility. The highest bracket of claimants, which included both Lang and Latté, were people who could prove the most substantive loss. These could choose between receiving a pension of approximately 600 DMs every month, or a onetime lump sum of approximately 40,000 DMs. Pensioners had foreign income subtracted against the monthly sum, so it made sense for Lang to choose the onetime sum, while Latté, who entered claims not only for herself but for her late husband and other deceased family members, opted for the long-term plan.

The Hucklenbroichs remembered being struck by the fact that Latté had suffered more in the war years than Lang, and they saw how returning to Berlin had stirred up her pain and regrets. "I thought coming back to Berlin was harder for her," said Marlene Hucklenbroich. "She lost more. She lost everything. Under the circumstances, she lost her child, her family, and her social situation—much more than he did."

The brief optimism for "The Pearl of Love" evaporated all too quickly. Inevitably, Lang had spent too much time in the company of the producer, and they ended up quarreling about every facet of the ill-fated project. The director ultimately decided he hadn't the necessary script authority nor budget assurances to proceed.

Astonishing Lily Latté and others closest to him, Lang announced his irrevocable retirement, and proceeded to lapse into an unprecedented funk. Back in Hollywood, the days stretched into weeks, the weeks into months, as Lang hid out in his house, secluded and aimless. No script engaged his mind; no meetings with producers were scheduled; no projects loomed on the horizon. He didn't seem to care.

State and academic honors were beginning to drift his way. In March 1955, the first installment of Lang's professional papers was earmarked for deposit at the Cinémathèque Française in Paris, which was on its way to becoming a world-class film museum and study center. Lotte Eisner, who had been associated with the Cinémathèque and its colorful director, Henri Langlois, since arriving in France in 1933, brokered the acquisition. Thus began Lang's rapprochement with France—and the seeds of Eisner's book about him, the "official" summation of his life and career.

After the Indian trip, Lang had been scheduled to receive from Princess Margaret a British Film Institute award for "his unique contribution to the cinema," but was obliged to postpone going to England because of illness. Germany made a similar gesture, and Lang went to Washington, D.C., to receive the *Bundesverdienstkreuz*, along with fellow directors Richard Oswald and William Dieterle, with whom his life and career were intertwined in Vienna, Berlin, Paris, and Hollywood.

In Washington, D.C., of all places, Lang happened to find some peace at this lowest point in his life. A friendship with a woman he met at an official function there developed into a serious affair—so serious that when the lady in question came to visit the director in Beverly Hills, Lily Latté was asked to move out of the house and into a hotel, so that Lang and the woman could have privacy.

Despite his professional stagnation, Lang's appetite for women showed no sign of flagging. Sex, like martinis, afforded him a dependable pleasure. Screenwriter Daniel Taradash remembered his surprise when the director showed up at a story conference during *Rancho Notorious*, and announced, beaming, "I got laid last night." Lang's life after Silvia Richards had included a number of trysts, but for a long time no one he could claim to be in love with.

"Everyone looks for love," Lang confided to a female columnist in 1946, at a time when he was privately professing his love for Silvia Richards. "You think you have found it with someone and of course you lie to yourself. You try to persuade yourself. That's vanity. The greatest confusion rests with sex. It's a game, an illusion of love created to fight off idleness and boredom."

The director continued: "If I am sincerely in love with a girl, I want to share everything with her—swimming, skiing. Good God, there is a German word that means exactly that, but I don't know how to translate it: *Mitteilungsbedürfnis*.

"It's a word that means that a man needs to love in order to have someone else take advantage of his experiences. He needs to be able to say what touches him and what he believes is real, and that isn't easy. Driven by such a feeling, if you are in love, you want to share everything with the girl, from the highest to the most sordid."

One of the striking qualities of Lang's final Hollywood feature was its risqué sexuality. The newspaper reporter and his girlfriend have a refreshingly adult relationship in *Beyond a Reasonable Doubt*; though they are unmarried, it is plain that they are carrying on afternoon assignations. And the backstage scenes full of undressed burlesque dancers—unusually explicit for the 1950s— put Lang in his element.

Now the director was in love again. The Washington, D.C., lady was middle-aged, German, with some connection to diplomatic organizations. When her vacation ran out and she had to return to Washington, the director made an unprecedented gesture. He flew to the capital to be at her side.

The stay lengthened into weeks. Lang's onetime agent, Sam Jaffe, visiting Washington, was surprised to learn that his former client was living there. Jaffe, who always liked the charming side of Lang, looked up the director— and found that the monocle, and all its attendant pretensions, were gone. Lang was in such low spirits professionally—despite his thriving affair—that to Jaffe he seemed worse off than when they had first met in 1937. As in the old days, Jaffe tried to give the film director a pep talk. But Lang was remote and distracted. It was no good to think otherwise, he kept repeating: Hollywood didn't appreciate him. He was retired for good.

No doubt he would have stayed retired if Artur Brauner had not been so persevering. But the producer tracked Lang down in Washington at the end of 1957, and made him an offer too good to be true: Would the director consider returning to India and guiding a remake of *Das indische Grabmal*, the film stolen away from him by Joe May in 1921?

Why would Lang agree to remake this film on a subject which, as he himself put it, was no longer on his level? The answer, as he explained later, was that he felt something "mystical" at play. A circle was closing. That which he had been denied, almost forty years earlier, he was now being permitted. Remaking *Das indische Grabmal* was a way of remaking his fate.

Producer Artur Brauner was a man of character and accomplishment. A Polish Jew, he had survived the worst of World War II—maybe in Afghanistan, maybe somewhere else—and started over afterward with nothing. He had rented an old poison-gas factory and built the first post-war film studio in Berlin. Thriftily, he had produced his first-low-budget feature in 1947. He made a practice of collecting rights to vintage German films and rehabilitating screen artists who had toiled under the Nazi regime; he made it his business to lure back to the homeland many of the best-known refugee writers and directors and give them, in their twilight years, one last chance.

"The German film industry has a lot to thank him [Brauner] for," director Robert Siodmak wrote in his memoirs. "He was one of the few people who had faith in Berlin."

In Lodz, as a youth, Brauner had first become acquainted with the legendary name of Fritz Lang. He saw and admired all the famous films: *Der müde Tod*, *Metropolis*, *Die Nibelungen*, *M*, and especially the original *Mabuse*, which as a boy he had watched some twenty-three times. Brauner got hold of a movie magazine with the director's photograph, cut it out and hung it over his bed, next to Tarzan and Buffalo Bill—"the ultimate place of honor," in his words.

Brauner associated Lang with cinema history, technological innovation, and unparalleled dramatic sensation. Lang's story of rebuffing Goebbels struck an especially resonant chord with the Jewish producer, giving this director a status above all others.

After unsuccessfully trying to lure Lang with earlier offers, Brauner had contrived to acquire the rights to *Das indische Grabmal*—which, in fact, had been remade once before, by director Richard Eichberg under the Nazi regime between 1937 and 1938. Since Thea von Harbou had written the original novel, her estate was involved in the negotiations. Another curve was traced in the closing mystical circle.

After reaching a tentative agreement, Lang flew to Germany. The producer met him at the Tempelhof airport in Berlin, where Brauner was headquartered and the bulk of the production would be shot. "My heart was in my mouth," Brauner later wrote in his autobiography. "I was as excited as a seventh grader before his first school dance. That was a rather unusual reaction for a film producer waiting to meet his director, but on this day I was to fulfill a dream of my youth."

It had been announced that Lang's plane would arrive two hours later, but as it happened it landed on time. Brauner had postponed his trip to the airport, so the director piled into a taxi by himself, guiding the driver into a few detours on the way to the hotel so he could tour his old neighborhood and other once-familiar areas of the city, some still partially in ruin from the war.

The contract Lang signed on February 7, 1958, took his "star-director" status into account. According to Claudia Dillmann-Kühn's book *Artur Brauner und die CCC*, the contract was superior to any the director had enjoyed in America. It gave Lang control over casting and crew, script supervision, and of course the tag line "A Fritz Lang Film" on the screen before any other credits, and without any larger succeeding credits. This was the slogan, publicity or otherwise, that mattered the most to him.

Only in the area of salary was Lang still lagging behind. The contract awarded him 70,000 marks for directing, and a fee of 38,000 marks for his involvement on the screenplay—or, roughly, a total of $24,500—to which would be added a 7.5 percent share of any profits accrued by CCC. It was a bargain rate for a living legend. In America, Lang had never focused on his fee, preferring clauses that guaranteed his power and prestige. Even now, he did not think to pad his salary for retirement.

As before, *Das indische Grabmal* would be split into two films—*Der Tiger von Eschnapur* (*The Tiger of Eschnapur*) and *Das indische Grabmal*. Especially considering that Brauner, a self-described man "of modest circumstances," was the producer, the Indian films called for an extraordinary budget: some three million marks, when CCC's average was 750,000 marks per picture. There would be hundreds of extras, a top-notch crew, location costs in India, and expensive color processing. Lang's name would help attract French and Italian investors to offset CCC's higher-than-usual gamble.

In the early spring, the director divided his time between Frankfurt, Düsseldorf, and Berlin. He met with Werner Jörg Lüddecke, a former journalist who after World War II had become a much-praised screenwriter. Lüddecke's films included *Der 20. Juli*, (*The 20th of July*), the Hitler-assassination project that had originally been offered to Lang; *Nachts, wenn der Teufel kam* (*The Devil Strikes at Night*), a noteworthy 1957 thriller about a mass murderer directed by Robert Siodmak; and *Kinder, Mütter, und ein General* (*Children, Mothers, and a General*), an uncompromising 1955 anti-war film which happened to be Erich Pommer's last as a producer.

Lüddecke had already written a version of the *Das indische Grabmal* scenario, and now plunged into daily talks with Lang, bent on shaping the final draft. "It was not easy work," remembered Lüddecke. "Every day, Fritz Lang arrived very early at my house, the house of a late sleeper, dressed elegantly, noble in his demeanor, civil from the first greeting to the last 'drink' at the end of a battle over subject, over form, over the general overview, and the smallest details. He was a perfect worker, a perfect architect, a perfect tyrant, a perfect listener, critic, and furthermore, a man who could withstand criticism.

"More than once I got angry about his way of provoking an argument even over punctuation. Later, I learned that, even in the studio, he didn't change any of the punctuation except in a way that would integrate it into the direction."

Lüddecke added: "I had hoped to be able to write a parody on this well-worn subject. That wasn't possible. Fritz Lang considered himself wholly responsible vis-à-vis the interests put into play by an industry which didn't exactly have a lot of stability. The films made a fortune. It was because of him. I had to make concessions and I complained. He had to make a lot more and never said a word.

"He was obstinate, disciplined, and, in a certain way, young."

At the luxury hotels where Lang was holed up, young turks with film ambitions came to visit him, and journalists flocked to report on the famous director's German "comeback." Berlin's reporters commented skeptically on the forthcoming remake, while sketching a director who seemed troubled by any mention of the Golden Twenties. Some nights Lang attended screenings or went out to the theater (he picked supporting players Richard Lauffen and Sabine Bethmann from the casts of Berlin plays); other nights he accepted invitations to dinner engagements at people's houses.

His 1957 Berlin stopover had been whirlwind. Now he had time to linger, absorb, and digest. The city was being revitalized at astonishing speed; it cleaved his heart and assaulted his senses. It was Lang's nature to be stoic, but he couldn't deny the sadness, or the grudges he bore. His heart pounded whenever he saw the Reichstag, and he found the bombed-out Gedächtnis-kirche "deeply distressing."

"He didn't recognize this Berlin," remembered Brauner. "This was not his Berlin. It was a completely different Berlin. It was bombed, first of all, and secondly, all of the people were strangers to him. I can understand that one hundred percent."

"The Berlin of 1958 was a new city, which some, returning, would not recognize," recalled future filmmaker Volker Schlöndorff, who came to meet Lang and later dedicated his first short film to the director. "The Viennese accent of Lang, his monocle, his gentleman-farmer raincoat, his courtesy belonged to a Germany which no longer existed. Lang wasn't recognized. Not being able to go out without feeling like a foreigner, he closed himself in the international anonymity of a hotel room. He recreated the films of a different world."

Gottfried Reinhardt, also working for Brauner's CCC at this time, crossed paths with the director on airplanes and in hotel lobbies. "I had a strange feeling of depression on his part," recalled Reinhardt. "He didn't fit into Hollywood, but he certainly didn't fit into the new Germany. Mellow? Yes. But I never trusted any mood of his. I always felt he was a chameleon."

According to Lotte Eisner, Lang hoped to secure Fritz Arno Wagner as his cameraman, recapturing their chemistry on *Der müde Tod, Spione, M,* and *Das*

Testament des Dr. Mabuse. Brauner had an ongoing relationship with Richard Angst, however, and Lang let himself be talked into hiring Angst, one of the most talented of the Alpine cameraman.* Angst's career dated back to the silent era and included many nature films for Arnold Fanck, a pioneer of the Heimat film, who had made "mountain movies" with Luis Trenker and Leni Riefenstahl. The art directors would be Willy Schatz and Helmut Nentwig, and the latter's wife Ilse acted as one of the costume designers. The music would be composed by Michel Michelet (*Tiger*) and Gerhard Becker (*Grabmal*).

In Rome, where the Italian co-production firm, Gloria Films, was located, last additions were made to an international cast and crew. But the casting did not go entirely smoothly. Some actors echoed screenwriter Lüddecke's attitude that the material seemed old-fashioned. India had retained little of its former mystery in the present-day world of television and jet travel. The remake begged for perspective, ironic or otherwise.

The popular Vienna-born actor O. W. Fischer asked to be excused, saying he felt too old for the sort of project they were planning. Paul Hubschmid, who after World War II had worked in Hollywood as Paul Christian before returning to Germany, signed to play the architect Harald Berger, but he "wasn't especially enthusiastic," in Dillmann-Kühn's words. René Deltgen, whose Mediterranean looks enhanced his often hot-blooded roles, agreed to play Prince Ramigani, but he reportedly grumbled about it to Brauner: "Why in the name of heaven is he [Lang] making these films?"

For the female lead of the palace dancer Seetha, who unites a sectarian India, Brauner tried to attract Anna Kashfi, or the former Miss Austria, Nadja Tiller. Since "The Pearl of Love" had been an obvious dry run, one might suppose that Lang would persist with his idea of a native Indian for his female star. Wrong: Brauner preferred someone who might boost the box office in Germany, and Lang settled on Debra Paget, a sultry, Colorado-born actress with a Hollywood vogue. Lang himself described her once as "an actress who is seen [in the United States] as someone who can't carry a film on her own." Yet she would be paid 200,000 marks (roughly, $45,000, or nearly twice the director's salary).

Walter Reyer was signed to play Chandra, the Maharaja of Eschnapur. Chandra is locked into a rivalry with his brother Prince Ramigani—who becomes infatuated with Seetha. The other significant parts were taken by German actors, with only minor roles filled by Americans. Lang in the end had few mutual relationships with Hollywood actors, nor any open channels to the studios and talent agencies.

Now, in Europe, Lang once again gave interviews stressing his thorough and fanatical preparation. So thorough was he that not a single frame of footage had been shot by the end of June, though CCC had booked the first half of the Indian spectacular to open in theaters by Christmas. The friction between Lang and Brauner began, typically, over the long preproduction rigamarole

---

*Wagner was "disappointed," according to Lotte Eisner, and Lang's old friend "accepted a job on an indifferent film that was being shot in Geiselgasteig near Munich, and fell to his death in the course of shooting." Wagner's death did come in 1958, according to Ephraim Katz's *Film Encyclopedia*, but resulting from a car crash.

even before the onset of principal photography. The site of the first scenes, Lang delighted in telling interviewers, would be in the renovated factory in Spandau, where the director filmed explosions for *Das Testament des Dr. Mabuse*, twenty-five years earlier. "And so the circle closes . . ."

Brauner had appointed Eberhard Meichsner as his production manager to keep a wary eye on the director. When Lang returned to Berlin in June, Meichsner pressed Lang to roll the cameras. But the director refused to be hurried, and the shooting didn't begin until late July, by which time he and Meichsner were already dueling with memos.

From the first day Lang insisted he would not be able "to fulfill, even partially, the allotted amount of work" that Meichsner had estimated for daily progress. Meichsner had broken everything down according to camera setups and scene length; the schedule seemed generous and feasible. But the director himself was a master of memo minutiae, and wise to the basic powerlessness of the "producer surrogate."

Lang pointed out that according to Meichsner's projections, Seetha would have to be made up and costumed three times in a single day. The entire company would have to be moved from one studio to another, which would take half an hour. "According to our schedule for twenty scenes, that leaves about twenty-five minutes per scene," wrote Lang. "These twenty-five minutes per scene are not really twenty-five minutes, because on the first day of shooting absolutely nobody is used to working together . . ."

Memo to Lang from Meichsner, Berlin, August 7, 1958: "A one-hundred-percent perfectionism cannot but affect the budget (it does not stem from inability or lack of cooperation) . . . Dear Mr. Lang, you know as well as I do that production costs do not just depend upon the length of filming, but are also influenced to a great extent by the many minor details of decor and by trying to obtain a perfect end result . . ."

Memo to Lang from Meichsner, Berlin, August 13: "It will certainly interest you to learn something about how much work we are getting done, as compared to our schedule. We are one day behind schedule; actually two days behind—because we started late . . .

"Perhaps the proportion of takes to prints can be cut down if you could start the scene while the camera is running—i.e., to keep the interval before you turn on the camera as short as possible. The same applies to the end of a scene. It would be a good idea to stop the scene right after the cut you are planning."

Memo to Meichsner from Lang, Berlin, August 15: "I hope you have written to the other departments in this regard. Because otherwise I have to assume that this letter has only been written so that the production can cover up and that someone is trying to put the blame on the director for any delays . . .

"Because the hard work I am doing requires my complete concentration, I hoped not to be forced to have to keep records of every delay and to submit daily reports to you, and above all I thought that we would be working as a team.

"I would like to add that I would really like to request you to refrain from using those well-known sentences that begin with the words, 'Dear Mr. Lang, we are in Germany—etcetera etcetera.' I have made many films of world-wide reputation . . . and there can be no doubt about my affection for the German people (with the exception of Hitler supporters)—otherwise I wouldn't have taken on Mr. Brauner's proposal. But I don't want to feel too tempted to have to tell you what people in the rest of the world think and say about all the things that happened in Germany."

Memo to Lang from Meichsner, August 18. "You should not interpret remarks made about German practices and how we do things in Germany (for example in response to your remark, "that's a lot of nonsense")—whether they came from a conscious or an unconscious mistrust or from hard feelings—in any other way than how I intended them to be understood. 'In Germany,' or 'for us here,' or 'at the CCC' or 'at the Gloria,' et cetera 'usually' or 'we work this way' or 'this or that is possible or impossible in view of our budget."

"We simply have to make our films more cheaply and perhaps for that reason more crudely than, for example, in America, which has a larger market. Wanting to understand this any other way will cause dangerous misunderstandings. May I ask you, very politely, to trust me? With long films like this, under—Lord knows—rather trying conditions, people can only work together in a relationship based on mutual trust, or else the project is condemned right now to failure."

Arthur Brauner intervened, writing Lang on September 10, 1958: "Since I have given up any hope of finishing the film according to schedule—on the contrary—we are slowing down from day to day and we are using more and more material—I find it necessary, with all respect and affection for you, to remind you of the agreement we reached on our first day of shooting. I cannot permit any more infringements if they involve any financial costs at all.

"After looking at the most recent outline, I am convinced that many scenes could be done more efficiently and quicker than they have been done up to now. Particularly in the snake-dance scene, where there was an unprecedented waste of time and material. We filmed twenty-three times as much as what will appear in the film."

The director agreed to drop brief scenes and lop a little time off the production chart in Berlin. As for the rest, Lang held fast. According to director Robert Siodmak, Brauner couldn't stand it "if you get angry and yell at him. He hates arguments and usually gives in." The peacemaker was often Brauner's wife Maria, generally viewed as Brauner's chief ambassador—charming, also Polish, also Jewish and a survivor of the horrors of World War II. Lang couldn't help but like her.

"If he liked the people, if he had any connection with them, he was a really charming man," recalled Brauner. "Privately, he was a completely different individual, a Viennese man who brought flowers for my wife. We had a lot of photographs taken with him. We had a lot of private evenings together and then he was no longer the strong and 'dry' Fritz Lang. He was open, very open. He had a sense of humor, and a human feeling."

Brauner visited the set as often as possible, though he was gearing up to produce eighteen other motion pictures that year. On the producer's birthday, the film's director staged one of those calculated performances that he had perfected (for publicity benefit) in Hollywood. With star Debra Paget, in front of the entire cast and crew, Lang marched in and knelt down in front of

Maharaja Brauner, presented the delighted producer with a cake, and led a group singalong of "Happy Birthday."

Brauner was outfoxed. It was the producer who usually backed down. With the budget steadily rising, Brauner wrote Lang's agent that "Herr Lang is such a brilliant director and so decisive in every area that he is the only person who decides about lengthening and shortening the film, about spending more or spending less. We can only look on, powerless to control whether he films an angle once or ten times."

The premiere of *Das indische Grabmal* was postponed until January. The company finished in Berlin and left for India in mid-October, with exteriors planned south of Delhi, where Lang had already scouted locations for "The Pearl of Love." "India was also very expensive," remembered Brauner. "During the shooting we sent cables and telexes, and telexes and cables, because my production manager was desperate. Lang thought this was usual, normal."

The production manager was captive to the director's whims, and in India Lang felt even more freedom to disregard his memos. India made Lang ebullient. The government once again treated him as an honored guest of state. The filming was going well. Lang was enjoying himself again, and his vitality seemed to belie his years.

"I admired his unheard-of energy," said actor Paul Hubschmid. "He didn't always inspire love in his co-workers, and he didn't mince words when he was unhappy with someone. He could be merciless with someone who didn't understand his work. He took care of everything and everybody, so much so, as to show the makeup artist how to attach a beard, the architect how to build a reservoir, et cetera. He controlled each button of wardrobe, each thrust of a sword. He played the actors' roles for them, jumping on a horse to show them how he wanted it done; he was an expert in camerawork. In short, he could make a film all alone—if he had more than two legs, two arms, and a head.

"During the hours of filming, he had no other diversions," continued Hubschmid. "But when the sun set, he sat down, surrounded by his devotees, a drink in his hand (by the way, he knew how to prepare the best martinis in the world), on the terrace of his hosts in Udaipur, telling marvelous stories about the great era of film, and he himself representing that era, sitting before us in flesh and blood. I have to say that he never ceased to fascinate me."

Brauner had extracted a concession from Lang that the India scenes would be edited simultaneously with the earlier footage, while the director was absent from Berlin. In November, the formal end of shooting would be marked by Lang's triumphantly publicized return to Berlin and a gala reception for Germany's press. Behind the scenes there had been bitterness and mutual recriminations. The budget had soared to a reported 4.7 million marks. But the first half of the Indian epic would make its January opening after all, and Brauner proved gracious.

"It was not easy because he [Lang] knew everything better," said Brauner. "And I left him alone because I knew he was of a certain age, and after his experiences I had to give him the freedom more or less. He demanded the best, the highest quality, because he had to defend the name 'Fritz Lang,' and because his story was a monumental legend."

After the press fete, the director and others in the company attended the opening of the Sechstagerennen at the Sportpalast. Just like the old days: Lang wore "his celebrated monocle from the twenties in his eye," according to newspaper accounts. Sitting among the other Berliners, Fritz Lang was fully aware of the stir he was causing as, with reporters surrounding him and scribbling away, he watched cyclists compete from all over the world.

Der Tiger von Eschnapur ended up running 101 minutes, while *Das indische Grabmal* was edited to 102.

The first film involved the introduction of characters and place: the plot to overthrow Chandra, the romance between the architect Berger and the palace dancer Seetha, the flight of the lovers pursued by the jealous maharaja's soldiers. The second focused on the rebellion fostered by a coalition between the warlords and Ramigani, the maharaja's scheming brother. Seetha and Berger return to the palace, where Berger is jailed and Seetha is forced to undergo a deadly ritual. Chandra intervenes to save her, Berger escapes, and Ramigani and his conspirators attack the palace.

Sumptuous films, bursting with magic, danger, spectacle, and pageantry, the Indian epic showed the director luxuriating as never before in his romantic imagination.

Seetha is one of Lang's double-women: a Madonna and Mary Magdalene rolled into one. Her parentage is obscure; as in other Fritz Lang films, it takes a folk song to trigger for her a set of mysterious childhood memories. Debra Paget, while an improbable Indian, is well-costumed, photogenic, and seductive to watch; her writhing temple dance inspired a textbook example of the director's bravura mise en scène.

Berger is transparently a stand-in for the director; the script makes a point of mentioning that he has studied architecture in Vienna and Paris. Unfortunately, Paul Hubschmid's performance grows compelling only when the maharaja chooses to torture him—nearly starving his character to death and choking him in chains.

The maharaja is also Lang: the Meister of Metropolis, the hard-shelled, unloved man at the top. The maharaja may be demonic, but his unrequited love for the palace dancer is almost touching in the film's eyes. When he offers her a jeweled necklace, he bares his own vulnerability. "It is the gift of a lonely man who seeks the way to a woman's heart." A line that might have been volunteered by the director.

In Germany, especially, the judgment was harsh when *Der Tiger von Eschnapur* and *Das indische Grabmal* were released in early 1959.

"The almost unanimous panning of both films was directed mainly toward the director," wrote Claudia Dillmann-Kühn. "Some papers referred to his past in tones almost of denunciation, as if they had to settle a score with him because of his emigration, or his re-emigration, or because of both."

In Vienna, one critic referred to the two Indian films as an "orgy of trash and kitsch," noting, "It is understandable from a human point of view that the almost seventy-year-old man might want to win the hearts of the new bosses in the German film industry. But a time when he could claim to follow higher artistic goals seems to be finally over."

In France, where a special French-language version was issued, featuring French actors substituted into main roles, *Der Tiger von Eschnapur* and *Das indische Grabmal* fared somewhat better. Although only a minority of the French press praised the films, some—including a critic writing in *Cahiers du Cinéma*, a home base for the nouvelle vague—saw them as among the director's most accomplished work.

There would come to exist almost as many versions of the Indian films as there were variations of *Metropolis*, and almost as many divergent opinions. In America the two films were edited down, dubbed, and stitched into one feature, then released by American-International Pictures as *Journey to the Lost City*, ninety-two minutes long, in 1960. It is the only English-language version of Lang's Indian epic ever widely released in U.S. theaters. Eugene Archer of *The New York Times* gave the bastardized form of Lang's Indian films a magnanimous review, calling *Journey to the Lost City* "exhilarating nonsense," which "may or may not be art, but no one will deny that it is unusual."

American critic Jonathan Rosenbaum, an admitted Fritz Lang enthusiast, was unable to see the director's version of *Der Tiger von Eschnapur* and *Das indische Grabmal* until, in 1978, he attended a screening of English-subtitled 35-mm prints at the British Film Institute in London. His essay is one of the most thoughtful on the films.

"What are the signs of disintegration?" Rosenbaum asked in his piece, going ahead to list qualities that marked an aging director's poignant return to an outmoded context:

"1. A conscious naïveté that is sought and achieved, aimed at a child's sensibility.

"2. A naked artifice of props, actor-props, color schemes and schematic plots laid bare, so that even the wires holding up the fake snake in Debra Paget's religious dance inside a cave temple are visible.

"3. A displacement (or misplacement) of narrative interest shortly after the beginning . . .

"4. A series of structural arrows which wind up confounding all sense of continuity and direction . . . "

Concluding that *Der Tiger von Eschnapur* and *Das indische Grabmal* were "made by someone who knows more about the subject than most— and a game that is played honestly," Rosenbaum conceded that most "critics hung up on 'craft' and intentionality [would] never be able to see it as a dazzling achievement." But he himself believed "there is nothing in cinema like it. I'll go even further: It has the only cave in movies that's worthy of Plato's."

A film can reflect more than its surface attributes; it can also offer insights into a director's soul. Dedicated Langians, recognizing that the Indian films displayed all the hard-fought colors of the director's palette, could detect truth and beauty and subtlety others missed.

The director was crushed by the critical reception in Germany. Lang and Thea von Harbou had worked on *Das indische Grabmal* together when they first met and fell in love, returning to the formula had seemed a guarantee of success, and a kind of homecoming. Lang himself thought highly of the work he had done—especially on Part I, *Der Tiger von Eschnapur*. Now Lang complained bitterly about how Germany had the film critics such a nation deserved. The director swore never to return to the country.

Artur Brauner, however, was pleased. Throughout Europe, Lang's Indian films attracted huge crowds and ended up generating a "big profit," Brauner said. "I didn't care what the critics said—I liked the films." Brauner made the right consolation speech to Lang, quoting one of the director's own maxims back at him. "You are making films not for the critics," the producer told Lang, "you are making films for the audience."

The director listened, and was heartened. Brauner wanted Lang to consider another remake of a classic film. The producer suggested *Die Nibelungen*, even went so far as to mention that possibility in the press. Lang recoiled. The worst obstacle, he mused in later interviews, would have been the dialogue of the screenplay. "The first difficulty was: How to make the Nibelungs speak? You can't say, 'Hello, Kriemhild.' Neither can you say, 'O, noble knight.' And then, the film would have been too expensive. I wanted the press to know that I didn't want [to do the film], but the producer said, 'Let's do this nicely. You will say that I can't have Brando [in the cast], and under those circumstances, you can't do the film . . .' "

According to Lang, Brauner forwarded a number of other proposals, including a remake of *Metropolis*, and even a musical version of *Der müde Tod*. In each case the answer was no. Brauner then suggested an update of *The Cabinet of Dr. Caligari*; no, but Lang countered that he would consider tackling F. W. Murnau's 1926 film of *Faust*. "Except for a few cuts," the director explained in a later interview, "the film would have followed, word for word, the original. But it was too great a risk. My producer thought about it, felt some people out, but didn't find a favorable response."

The experience of the Indian epic may have done nothing for Lang's opinion of critics, but it did restore some faith in himself. He was now alive to future prospects. And once he had a writer on the hook, he didn't easily let him go. So it was that with Werner Jörg Lüddecke, who had co-written the Indian films, the director now went to work on a script called "Unter Ausschluss der Öffentlichkeit" ("Behind Closed Doors"), a contemporary-youth story of the type he had often mentioned in interviews. Their collaboration sparked items for the German press, but the full scenario would never be finished.

Almost two years would go by while Brauner floated other remake propositions.

Then the producer had his worst idea yet: resurrecting Dr. Mabuse, whom the director had made immortal in his 1922 two-parter and then killed off in the 1933 sequel. Brauner had obtained the story rights from the Norbert Jacques estate and wanted to introduce a new series based on the genius of crime who had so intrigued Brauner as a boy.

"No, the bastard is dead and buried," declared Lang.

But the director was growing anxious about money, and all too aware that his own vague ideas for films never made it across the finishing line. Too, he had to consider the likelihood that Brauner would go ahead and produce a Mabuse film with *or* without Fritz Lang, which would be almost as hurtful as being cut off from the remake of *M*. A writer named Jan Fethke had already submitted a new Mabuse story, and Heinz Oskar Wuttig, another onetime journalist who had turned to film, was at work on a screenplay. This weighed on Lang's decision. It didn't take him long to change his mind.

The director got to thinking: a modern Mabuse would be "a way of saying certain things about our time." Lang accepted the job, and flew to Berlin to collaborate with Wuttig.

He brought a few ideas with him: in one of those articles he liked to clip, Lang had read about rifles that shot tiny, almost invisible, pellets of poison. That provided the germ of an assassination sequence of the type that traditionally opened a Mabuse film. Lang also wanted to incorporate an allusion to Berlin's Hotel Adlon, which the Nazis had planned to set aside for foreign visitors and businessmen after the war, intending to bug its rooms and corridors with eavesdropping devices and surveillance equipment. Integrated into the storyline would be a contemporary luxury hotel with an underground wall of video screens monitored round-the-clock by the mysterious heir to Dr. Mabuse. The voyeuristic "video-eyes" would inspire the film's evocative title: *Die tausend Augen des Dr. Mabuse (The 1000 Eyes of Dr. Mabuse)*.

Screenwriter Wuttig, like Lüddecke before him, found Lang a severe taskmaster at the work sessions. "He fights like a lion for a comma," said Wuttig. But unlike before, with the Indian epic, the fighting lion had to plunge into filming almost immediately.

The cameraman Lang used, Karl Loeb, had worked with Fritz Arno Wagner on numerous films in the 1940s and 1950s. The art directors were Erich Kettelhut—the latter, the only member of the Ufa team of the Golden Decade to reunite with Lang after Hollywood—and Kettelhut's post-war partner Johannes Ott. More circles closing.

A British actress by the name of Dawn Addams, best-known for her leading role in Chaplin's 1957 *A King in New York*, would play Marion, a young woman first seen in the film teetering on a high ledge and threatening suicide. (She is being hypno-manipulated by Mabuse.) The handsome if inanimate leading man Peter Van Eyck—German-born but an American citizen—would play a businessman visiting Berlin to finalize purchase of an atomic plant. He falls in love with the mysterious Marion.

Mabuse, in the story, is rumored to be alive—no matter that he has expired in *Das Testament des Dr. Mabuse*. Wolfgang Preiss would portray the latest incarnation of the master of crime and disguise. Gert Fröbe, who later on gained some notoriety as the heavy in one of the James Bond pictures, *Goldfinger*, would play Commissioner Kraus, who, along with a secret agent (Werner Peters), is on the elusive Mabuse's trail.

The budget was smaller, the schedule tighter, and other restraints were more firmly worded in the director's contract, this second time around working with Artur Brauner.

* * *

The third Mabuse film ought to have been a psychopolitical tour of the new Germany. Curiously, though, it became less of an emotional canvas for Lang than the Indian epic. At least India held some novelty for the director. Berlin was an old friend he no longer recognized, no longer felt comfortable with.

"He expected to see 'our Berlin' again, the Berlin in which he was very happy and busy," said Howard Vernon, one of the *Die tausend Augen des Dr. Mabuse* cast. "He didn't find that at all."

It was not merely Berlin that had changed, of course. It was Lang himself. Undeniably he felt old, and revisiting former haunts only reminded him that he was part of a vanished time—an extinct species. It was reflected in one of the nicknames Lang began to adopt for himself: The Last Dinosaur. He pronounced it "Dee-No-Sore."

The director was infinitely saddened by the bombed-out ruins, the gleaming new buildings, and the evolution of streets such as Friedrichstrasse, where his own Fritz-Lang-Film GmbH used to be. "We used to walk up and down Friedrichstrasse," the director would sigh, "looking at the beautiful legs of young girls."

He was naturally unenthusiastic about the actors whom Brauner had rounded up. Two of them, Lotte Eisner said in her memoirs, behaved disrespectfully toward the director. Referring to Van Eyck and Fröbe as "the scum of the German film industry," Eisner wrote that on the set during breaks these "two would-be big shots" pushed their weight around in front of Lang. "Look, here, Herr Lang, look what I can do!" Fröbe would mock the director. "Poor Fritz," Eisner commented, "had to clap while Fröbe dished up his hackneyed old numbers in front of his drooling fans."

The German crew also showed the director too little respect. They would tease him, marching in step as they carried tree-trunk props, roaring out, "Achtung!" and "One, two, three!" The good humor Lang exhibited during the shooting of *Das indische Grabmal* all but evaporated. "Can't you do anything without marching!" Lang would scream at the crew. "Haven't you learned anything? It starts for fun and then you know how it ends . . ."

"He [Lang] didn't think that was very funny," wrote Lotte Eisner. "It just reminded him of everything he found most sickening about the Germans."

Lang's history of starting out well with a producer, then inevitably having a falling-out, was doomed to repeat itself on this second Artur Brauner production. It didn't take long for the director to decide that Brauner had delusions of grandeur and was trading on Fritz Lang's reputation. Their interaction turned cold and formal, and Brauner's every intrusion was seen as a capital offense, his every ingratiating move some kind of trick.

"Fritz had a little bit of a persecution complex, like many directors, toward producers," said Howard Vernon.

One of the few bright spots was Vernon, an actor who, like Dan Seymour, made a career of supporting roles. He was in Jean-Luc Godard's *Alphaville* and Woody Allen's *Sleeper*, among many appearances in a lengthy screen career. At this time Vernon's agent was Manfred Fürst, a former Max Reinhardt performer who had escaped to Hollywood during the Hitler era and then returned to set up shop in post-war Germany. Fürst took his client over to meet Lang one day, when filming on *Die tausend Augen des Dr. Mabuse* was close to starting.

They had one of those awkward first meetings that sometimes endeared people to Lang. Vernon remembered he couldn't help but stare at the celebrated filmmaker as if Lang were a stone monument.

"What's wrong with me?" asked the director gruffly. "Is my fly open?"

"No," replied Vernon. "Besides, I wouldn't dare look at Mr. Lang's fly."

Vernon had been erroneously introduced to the director as "an American actor from Paris." The actor had to straighten out his résumé: he had more than one citizenship, and spoke several languages, including fluent English, German, and French. Lang appreciated this complex lineage, but chastised Vernon for being so late with his approach. By now there were only a few small roles left to be cast in the film. "I couldn't come sooner," the actor replied sharply, "since I didn't know you were here."

Lang raised an eyebrow. "You're Jewish, aren't you?"

"No, should I be?" asked Vernon.

"No," said Lang, "but you have a Yiddish chutzpah."

"Yes," said Vernon. "Otherwise, you don't get on in life."

Lang agreed with that, sealing their friendship. And the director hired Vernon to play the minor but noticeable part of gang member Number 12, whose assassination attempt sets in motion the film's plot. Soon the director and Vernon began spending time together, on and off the set, and over time the actor would become one of the director's closest friends.

The friendship led to one of the uncommon instances were Lang acted decisively in another's best interests. While in Berlin, Vernon was also interviewed by Richard Widmark, who considered casting him for *The Secret Ways*, a picture the American actor was producing in Germany and other European locales. To help him make up his mind, Widmark wanted to view Vernon's scenes in Lang's film-in-progress, and one day Vernon mentioned this to the director. To Vernon's surprise, Lang began to disparage and ridicule Widmark, listing all the terrible things about Widmark that he could come up with. But Vernon didn't care; he still wanted his chance in the Widmark film.

The next day the director summoned his actor-friend into his office and informed him that he had telephoned Widmark, waking Widmark up at his hotel to give him a full report on Vernon. The report was this: Vernon was an awful actor, an unpleasant character; one lost a lot of time with him in a production, and the result was always bad. By the time Lang had finished his litany of what was wrong with Vernon, it dawned on Vernon that the director had actually done the *opposite*, but was too self-conscious to admit it. In fact, Lang did send over the required footage and then, putting on his very best manner, he had phoned Widmark and gone out of his way to recommend Vernon for the job. "He didn't want to admit how nice he could be," said Vernon. "It was pudeur—a French word. He wanted to hide his feelings."

On the set of the last motion picture that he would ever direct, after forty-five years in the profession, Fritz Lang seemed, to Vernon, almost matter-of-fact about the trouble and toil. "He worked like an electrician putting a new electric line into a building," recollected Vernon. One day, in fact, the director and his friend fell into a discussion about directing technique, and Vernon made the mistake of loosely throwing around the word "art."

"What is art?" flared Lang.

"That is as difficult to explain as what is love," answered Vernon.

"I am not an artist," declared the director. "I am a craftsman." Lang had switched to German to use the German word *Handwerker*—literally, "hand-worker."

"Art or craft? Both, it was both," reflected Vernon. "He [Lang] knew what he was, and who he was. He knew his worth, his value. But at the same time he was a very modest man. It was really a mixture of the two for him—artist and craftsman."

Released in Germany in the fall of 1960, *Die tausend Augen des Dr. Mabuse* proved both a rote exercise and a flight of the subconscious, a comic-book thriller that served as a mask for the director's submerged emotions. It said less about the Germany of "our time" than it did about a director stuck somewhat ambivalently in his own time.

The film is better than its reputation, however, and some have seen it as a curtain call of Lang's distinguishing themes and images. There is no stinting on the camerawork, with the Meister deploying the full arsenal of age and experience: extreme close-ups, slanting angles, moody lighting, fluid and illusory perspective.

Mabuse is alive and well—somehow—in the story. The police are on the case. As usual, their information-gathering tentacles rival those of Mabuse. Both sides have their paranoiac's quota of spies, informants, weird specialists, and prognosticators.

Lang liked to say in interviews that the 1933 Mabuse was a symbolic Hitler. Here, playing the considerate returned exile, the director declined the chance to make any explicit mention of the Führer. The only political thesis is the vague threat of international terror that had bubbled beneath the surface of many Fritz Lang films. German audiences could watch without being offended in the slightest.

Marion (Dawn Addams) was one of Lang's unhappily married ladies, made twice as sexy by the camera's lingering gaze. One of the most erotically charged moments in the director's oeuvre comes when Marion steps out of a bath, slips on her bra, and stares into a mirror, applying her lipstick. Watching from behind the two-way mirror is Travers (Peter Van Eyck); he has denounced the spying device, put in place by an over-zealous detective, but can't bring himself to avert his eyes, nor repress his arousal.

Travers is the Lang of the past, of *Die Spinnen* days, a hero rushing about frantically trying to solve a conspiracy and save the world. Phones are filled with nitroglycerin, rooms trap and slay their victims, strange gadgetry crops up at the slightest excuse. The final car chase is vintage Lang, ending with another Mabuse shooting off to a bang-up death.

Travers has his hands full throughout the story. Women cannot hope to compete with the adventure that fills his life. "No one has ever interested me," Travers declares. "No one." Until Marion. After the evil is conquered,

Travers and Marion will pledge their troth. The film cannot quite believe in their future happiness—but to Fritz Lang love, like politics, often amounted to no more than sublime foolishness.

The German critics detested *Die tausend Augen des Dr. Mabuse* ("full of stale thriller gags and muddled riddles," opined the *Frankfurter Allgemeine Zeitung*), but the film made money at home and proved a *succès d'estime* once again in England and France, where the cognoscenti gave it a warm reaction.

The director had gone back in time in other ways—back to the pre-1924 days when his German reputation was meaningless in the American marketplace. Lang's last film would never be released nationwide in the United States. It took six years for a badly dubbed version to sneak into a Forty-second Street theater. A Lang aficionado, Roger Greenspun, contributed a piece to *Film Comment* extolling *Die tausend Augend des Dr. Mabuse* as a "superb" work, "dense, complex, exuberant, mysterious," which deserved a fate better than the "ignorant indifference" it met in the director's adopted country.

Against the bitter disappointment of the Indian and Mabuse films, Fritz Lang could console himself with the certainty that his life's work was being preserved and rediscovered by artists, intellectuals, young filmmakers, and students all over the world.

The canonization started in Paris. The hard-charging young critics of *Cahiers du Cinéma* and *Positif* had begun to celebrate the director in the early 1950s, finding hidden virtues and meaning in his culminating American films. Truffaut, Rohmer, Chabrol, Rivette, Godard, and Georges Franju were among the nouvelle vague exponents who extolled Lang. (Rivette would show scenes from *Metropolis* in his *Paris Nous Appartient* [*Paris Belongs to Us*], "in effect, a homage to Lang," in Richard Roud's words.)

When the director passed through Paris—first promoting the Indian epic, later the third Mabuse—French critics favored him with in-depth interviews, solemnly probing Lang on the subjects of Expressionism, symbolism, the social critique of his scenarios, and the like. In such formal colloquies he was often asked about the themes of individual films, and the overall interpretation of his body of work. He had spent nearly forty years refining his rapport with journalists, and had grown accustomed to giving pat answers while evading personal issues. Lang preferred to stress social and philosophical implications within his films, and allow people to fill in some of the blanks with their own ideas.

Cineasts were, if anything, more deferential than journalists, although they would venture at times to disagree with his definitive statements, saying that the significance of certain scenes, certain films, seemed as much personal as sociological in his career. Lang would scoff—but later he would think back and reconsider. Sometimes such interviews revealed things to Fritz Lang that he had never realized about himself—about his films, and his inner nature—that he could only now bring himself to admit.

His French canonization was made official by Lotte Eisner and the Cinémathèque Française in Paris, which had collected a batch of Lang's scripts and professional papers, and made a mission of sealing his legend. On June

11–26, 1959, Henri Langlois's festival of twenty-two films drew Lang to the city that had succored him at critical junctures in his life. The rapt attention of young people devoted to his life's work moved him. The director had thought himself a "perpetual exile," he admitted in a letter to Langlois. Now he saw that Paris would always offer a symbolic home for him. "You showed me that it [the festival] was fruitful for the young," the director wrote to Eisner. "Maybe my attitude was 'I don't care,' but Mary [Mary Meerson, Langlois's companion] and Langlois cured me of that. And for that, I am deeply in their debt."

A Hollywood fixture for twenty years, the director had left the American continent only once, on behalf of 20th Century–Fox. Now, with his last production behind him, it seemed his bags were always packed, and Lang was zipping around the globe at will. Increasingly, beginning with a retrospective of his films at the National Film Theatre in London in 1962, his destination was the latest film festival, the newest retrospective where he was a guest of honor.

Wherever he went, his paths crossed with Berliners from long ago. He often stuck out his hand and made a point of saying, "I am more mellow nowadays." And it was true. Conrad von Molo, living in Munich, met up with Fritz Lang again, and tried to set differences aside; to his surprise, he discovered that he liked the director as much as before. Rudolph Joseph, an assistant to G. W. Pabst who had known Lang only glancingly in the Berlin years, found himself on a panel with the director at a film festival in Latin America. He had never liked Lang, and now found himself astonished to be enjoying his company. Joseph sat down and wrote a postcard to his brother, "Age is wonderful . . . Now I'm on a first-name basis with this famous son of a bitch."

As long as someone provided a first-class ticket and hotel, as well as expenses for a traveling companion, Lang was available. The honorarium was also welcome. His escort was often Lily Latté, who continued to live in Lang's house, functioning as his assistant, secretary, and domestic manager. She was also, in Lang's words, his "moral support." Especially if the itinerary passed through England or Germany, Latté went along for the ride, stopping off to see her own circle of friends.

Her longtime lover Peter Heiman, who had returned to California, was once again briefly integrated into Latté's life. Once again Heiman made a threesome for dinners or events. Heiman liked Lang, liked arguing with him, considered him a friend—although he admitted to himself it was a friendship based on an unusual affair à trois.

When Heiman tried one more time to convince Latté to leave the director, however, things ended badly. In the early 1960s, Lang needed a companion on one of his European jaunts and asked Latté to come along with him. Heiman argued that Lang didn't really need her; there would be plenty of acolytes on the other end of the trip to guide him. Finally, Heiman issued an ultimatum. "You must choose—him or me." Latté chose Lang—as she always had—and went away to Europe. Her thirty-year love affair with Peter Heiman was over. Heiman never saw either Latté or Fritz Lang again.

The old pattern resumed: the director began encouraging friends to become sexually involved with Latté. One who did was Rudolph Joseph's brother, Albrecht, the former secretary to Franz Werfel who was married to the sculptress Anna Mahler, daughter of Alma and Gustav Mahler. Lang had seen Albrecht Joseph's documentary about his wife at a UCLA screening, and liked it so much that he sought Joseph out, nurturing a friendship. The director then facilitated Joseph's affair with Latté in the 1960s by making it clear to him that Latté was unattached and available. "Lang liked the idea of Lily having another lover," recalled Rudolph Joseph. "He assured my brother he had never had an affair with her, which nobody, including my brother, believed."

Yet the relationship between the director and the woman who had helped him leave Nazi Germany was as close—and quarrelsome—as ever. And when all was said and done, Lily Latté must have understood Fritz Lang better than anyone. "We all know he's difficult [Latté wrote in a 1961 letter to Paul Erich Marcus]. He always was and becomes more so in his old age. He never could deal with people properly except when it came to hypnotizing women. He is aggressive, impatient in discussions, and a know-it-all.

"But he is increasingly obsessed with the idea that his career has been completely misguided. He never again achieved what he did with *M* and that wounds him deeply. He is a complete pleasure-killer; toward himself, too. He knows exactly how old he is and how sick, and that he really isn't provided for in his old age. If he needs money to live on, he has to earn it.

"He has absolutely no knowledge of human nature and for that reason he experiences lots of disappointments. He longs for friends and fritters away his time on affairs with women to somehow confirm to himself that he is successful after all. He is a very unhappy person, since, even for a normal life, he's too much—if you know what I mean.

"We like him very much. Each for his own reasons. And you could count any other people who like him on one hand.

"After thirty years it wouldn't be quite right for me to talk about love," Latté added. "Hitler threw us together. I held on to him, because he was a lot more colorful than anyone else I happened to meet. Now it's a habit and a feeling that one belongs somewhere, at least a little. And it's too late to start another life.

"There is also too much common ground in lots of daily things, be it language, symbols, memories, reactions, that I would miss very much. And you like him too. There must be a reason for that. He must give us something that we can't define but which makes us feel affection for him. For us it's certainly not [a case of] a legendary figure from the twenties. I don't want to ask you to feel pity for him. Try to understand him."

As time went by, Lang came to prefer the "moral support" of Howard Vernon or Pierre Rissient on his film-festival trips. Having a man along made it easier for him to indulge his need for female companionship. He kept an eye out for women while on the road, and at home in Beverly Hills liked his afternoon assignations—when he could play the Viennese charmer, with flowers and chocolates and romantic ballads on the turntable. Prostitutes remained a once-or even twice-weekly habit, friends say. Even at home, though Lang still claimed appointments off the premises whenever he had a rendezvous, to keep Lily Latté guessing.

"I'd drive him around town," recalled David Bradley. "He'd say, 'Take me to such and such a bakery.' I'd ask, 'Should I come in?' 'No, wait in the car for me.' He would load up with long French bread, meats, mustards and sauces, and all sorts of things. I'd say, 'Where would you like to go next?' He'd say, 'Go here . . . go there . . . ' I'd say, 'Why don't you come up and let me make you a lunch?' 'No, you ask too many questions.' That was one of his stock responses.

"So we would go very close to where I live, on the flats before Sunset Boulevard, and he would say, 'Pull up here.' I didn't know what it was about at first. He would trundle out with all that stuff and ring a bell. He'd say, 'I see you later.' It was a whorehouse. Now and then there were such women."

More respectable relationships also spiced up his life. It appears Lang was juggling more than one girlfriend in the early 1960s, fortuitously on separate continents. The friendship of Paul Erich Marcus in England was quite useful. Not only could Marcus be enlisted to run out and get Lang his favorite pipe tobacco (Dunhill's #965: "my mixture"), but more than once the director wrote to his friend to send some embossed stationery from a posh London hotel, so Lang could send notes to a skeptical lady friend in support of some elaborate cover story. When Lang's affairs overlapped, his alibis were byzantine.

His relationship with the Washington, D.C., lady tapered off after the director went to work on *Das indische Grabmal*. But Lang kept in touch, and their romance would be rekindled intermittently over the years. His Washington paramour was determined to live her own life independently in the nation's capital, and that suited Lang.

On one of his first return trips to Germany, the director met a red-haired actress, much younger than himself, whom he awarded a small part in *Die tausend Augen des Dr. Mabuse*. For a time his ardor for this actress supplanted any other, and "The Fox"—his nickname for her—became Lang's consort whenever he traveled in Europe.

Apparently, the Fox had a taste for older men in the film business, for when Lang mentioned her name to Conrad von Molo one day, von Molo flinched—he, too, had engaged in a fling with her. Her youthfulness sometimes bothered the director, who was over seventy during the time of their affair. "How could she love, actually physically love, an old man like me?" Lang asked actor Howard Vernon in Paris one day.

"Well, maybe she has an Oedipal complex, the other way around," answered his friend.

"What?"

"She may be one of those girls that has a relationship with her father, like some boys have with their mother."

"Oh, that's possible!" said Lang. "I never thought about that."

Probably he hadn't. He didn't often reflect upon the psychological aspects of his own world.

Perhaps Fritz Lang's most faithful company on airplanes and in foreign hotels was Peter, the pet monkey. Kokoschka had a life-sized doll to remind him of his former beloved, Alma Mahler. Lang also guarded his cherished memento of love lost.

Nobody in Hollywood remembers laying eyes on Peter before the late 1950s.

Now Peter seemed indispensable, a part of every trip. The most important key in the massive collection of keys that Lang carried around—many of their locks long in disuse—was the key to the little trunk where Peter was curled up for transportation. Peter the monkey was there with Lang at film festivals, in hotel rooms (where he was the first thing out of the luggage), at dinners and meetings with ersatz producers. The D.C. lady had given Peter a little knitted sweater, and he had other outfits appropriate for any occasion.

Peter was the director's best friend, his only child, his irreproachable sounding board. Lang would tuck Peter in bed at night, wake him up in the morning. Lang would mix two martinis: one for himself, one for Peter. He gauged other people by their reactions to Peter. When someone approached him about a possible film project, the director always listened cordially, before invariably turning to Peter and asking, "What do you think?"

After finishing his last film, *Die tausend Augen des Dr. Mabuse* in 1960, Lang had turned seventy. The well-wishers included the mayor of Vienna. Lang couldn't have cared less. "Thank God they didn't make me into an honorary citizen," grumbled the director to a friend. But it did bother Lang that he had not yet been invited as an honored guest to Berlin for the city's annual Festspiéle. He imagined that the film festival director carried a grudge against his work, and that city officials resented his U.S. citizenship. When birthday greetings came from all over the world, but not, officially, from his once-beloved Berlin, Lang would feel let down. "Berlin kept mum," he'd sigh to friends.

If not critically acclaimed, Lang's third Mabuse film had proved tremendously popular with German audiences, prompting Artur Brauner to go ahead and churn out five more, including, in 1962, a remake of the one Goebbels had banned, *Das Testament des Dr. Mabuse.* That was the last straw. Brauner, Lang decided, had turned out just like all the others. It became his constant refrain that the producer had fallen behind in paying his profit residuals.

On his part, Brauner thought Lang's bitterness was not really over money. It was over Berlin and Germany, and what the German critics had said about the Indian films and *Die tausend Augen des Dr. Mabuse*—his final work. "He [Lang] was so disappointed, so terribly disappointed, you cannot imagine," said Brauner. "I think he died because he was so disappointed."

Most of all Lang was disappointed in himself. He had fastened on the idea that *M* was his only masterpiece. He had fastened on the idea that he had made nothing but mistakes in his career. Personal—political—professional mistakes. Now, at screenings and film festivals he attended, he sought out the humanism in other director's works, which showed compassion for people and their hardships; he himself had focused too much on the architecture and style of film. In doing so he had unnecessarily alienated himself from people, damaged his work, and robbed his soul.

Film upon Fritz Lang film replayed itself in his mind, reminding him of his mistakes. It was only human—it was the nature of directors—to wish for one more chance. One more film. A handful of directors from his generation were still active. Others—Ford, Hawks, Hitchcock—would repeat themselves in their autumnal years with variations of earlier themes. Similarly, many of the film projects Lang envisioned in retirement were virtual remakes of his most famous works. Their technology could be updated, obtrusive mistakes corrected, scenes perfected at last. It was as if Fritz Lang longed to do penance.

One of the projects the director worked on fitfully was "The Legend of the Last Vienna Fiaker," a scenario he claimed to have begun back in 1933. He talked about it with Conrad von Molo in Munich, reminding his former assistant editor of his hopes for the subject before his life was upended by Hitler. Von Molo urged him to write up the scenario; von Molo would produce, Lang would direct. But the story Lang wrote in the form of a synopsis would, like so many others, never become a script.

Although Lang was perturbed when Seymour Nebenzahl or Artur Brauner encroached on the territory of one of his classic titles, he continued to dream about refilming one of his own sentimental favorites—*Die Frau im Mond.* Public fascination with the space race between the United States and the Soviet Union would provide a publicity blast-off. This idea was inevitably mentioned to producers who inquired about his plans, and Lang could regale them with anecdotes about the lavishness and authenticity of his 1929 silent film. With the right financing, Lang would assure producers, he could make the updated version even more true to the future of space travel.

With Heinz Oskar Wuttig, his co-writer on the third Mabuse film, Lang spent several months in Munich from 1961 to 1962 collaborating on a screenplay called ". . . Und morgen: Mord!" (". . . and Tomorrow: Murder!") which was announced as a story about a "seemingly respectable bourgeois" whose repressive adolescence caused him to commit obsessive sexual crimes. "When he is discovered, he commits suicide," according to one synopsis. "Only the police commissioner, with some few others, know the reality behind the dead man's laudatory obituary."

"Und morgen: Mord!" sounds as though it might have harbored elements of a veiled autobiography; it might, also, have finally amounted to Fritz Lang's remake of *M.* ". . . Und morgen: Mord!" was even mentioned in the German trade papers as "upcoming." But this too was premature publicity, and nothing came of the project.

It was poignant how often this aging director would tell interviewers he hoped to make a film about the problems of "modern youth" in today's society. Young people had always stimulated Lang. Back in Ufa days, he had been one of the first to cultivate college audiences with lecture appearances. Now Lang was back in touch with young people on the film-festival and college-lecture circuit, and often expressed the hope that their concerns would be reflected in whatever he might attempt to do next.

In Rome, from 1961 to 1962, Lang worked on some attractive prospects— including another epic set in India.

Lang took on the India project for a Rome-based production company, agreeing to live in Rome on and off for several months. He helped develop a script for "Kali Yung and Moon of Dassemra," a film that would focus on the nineteenth-century mass killings perpetrated by a secret cult, the Brotherhood of Thugs.* The hero of the screen story was a young cholera doctor, falsely accused of cult involvement, trying to clear his name by eradicating the conspiratorial society.

Mingling with the international film community in Rome, which in those days included many people moonlighting from Hollywood, Lang struck up a modest friendship with fellow U.S. director Nicholas Ray, and for the first time met *The Big Heat* novelist William P. McGivern. McGivern later recounted his dinner engagement with Lang one evening, sketching a portrait of the lion not altogether mellowed in winter.

Lang, McGivern wrote, was "stocky, powerful, and impeccable in blazer and gray flannels." His white hair flew from under a beret. Meeting McGivern in a hotel lobby, the director swore in German, Italian, and English, angry about hotel inconveniences. At dinner, "though I was the host, Lang picked the restaurant, the menu, the wines and the conversation." At one point the director was choosing "a gourmet's selection of cheeses as his last course," when Lang turned away briefly to say something, and the waiter prematurely whisked the tray away. "Lang swung around," reported McGivern, "slapped him across the shoulder with full force, and said, 'I'm not finished yet!'" Concluded McGivern: "It was like the stunning and privileged action of a nobleman of fifteenth-century France."

Later Lang and McGivern went to a private party at the home of a unit manager for *Two Weeks in Another Town*, the Vincente Minnelli picture being shot in Rome. Lang was seated in a corner trying to answer MacGivern's questions about *The Big Heat* when above the noise of the party, from the other side of the room, an upraised, distinctly American voice could be heard to proclaim, "The one thing you've got to learn in this business is not to pay any attention to directors . . ." The director did a "double-take," according to McGivern, and turned to stare at rugged Hollywood actor Guy Madison lecturing "a big football-player-turned-actor." Roaring, Lang leaped to his feet, "his voice so huge and angry it stopped every other sound in the room, and what he shouted was: '*Boy! Shut up!*'

"Madison looked stunned and Lang strode toward him, shaking his fist and saying again, 'Boy, shut up, I tell you! A *director* doesn't *speak* to you unless he sees something in your performance he can *improve*. The director knows what he *wants*. Don't tell this new actor dumb and stupid things based on your own impressions. *I think they are ignorant!*' Guy Madison was speechless, near tears even . . ."

Lang and McGivern left shortly after to continue the partying at Nick Ray's villa.

But it was one thing to cut a commanding figure at a film festival—or private party. It was one thing to accept a directing job, and another thing to follow it through to completion. By stages, in Rome, a heavy-hearted Fritz Lang realized he was through. The director had an experience on the "Kali Yung" project that drove home what he already knew, in his heart, to be the

---

*This notorious cult appears in both *Gunga Din* and *Indiana Jones and the Temple of Doom*. Lang's project was eventually filmed by Italian director Mario Camerini in 1963 as *Kali Yug— La Dea della Vendetta*.

true problem: the willpower, the energy, the fighting spirit necessary to direct a film—they were things he no longer possessed.

The "Kali Yung" project went so far as scouting locations in India. As had happened with "The Pearl of Love," Lang took a trip with the appointed producer; one trip, and his participation collapsed. Lang decided he didn't really like the script, nor could he trust the other producer, nor did he have the stamina or zest. This time the journey to India, visiting sites and interviewing personnel in unbearably hot weather, he found "very stressful." The man who had once prized India in his imagination decided he now hated the reality of the place, and would never return under any conditions.

Now the director talked events over with Lily Latté, and agreed with her assessment: it would be better for him to take a second mortgage on the house than it would be to embark on grueling adventures that might undermine his health.

The phone call from Jean-Luc Godard came at a propitious moment.

Godard was the Bertolt Brecht of the nouvelle vague: an impossible, mercurial man, a piercing critic-filmmaker whose writings and films were increasingly marked by an uncompromising raised fist of chic aesthetic and political radicalism.

A Sorbonne-educated intellectual, Godard had lived a checkered life, working as an odd-job laborer and one-man band in order to support his love of the cinema. He was one of the zealots who had formed cliques around the dogmatic French film journals. (As a critic, he had started out using a Teutonic pseudonym—Hans Lucas.) With his first feature film, 1959's *A Bout de Souffel (Breathless)*, he had leaped to the front ranks of nouvelle vague experimenters, and with subsequent films he became the movement's enfant terrible—increasingly trenchant, cold as dry ice, confrontational.

The filmmaker was in the process of adapting an Italian best-seller by Alberto Moravia, *A Ghost at Noon*, for which producers Carlo Ponti and Joseph Levine had pledged Godard's first multimillion-dollar budget. The story was about an Italian couple, a scriptwriter and his wife, whose relationship is strained. The writer has embarked on a version of Homer's *Odyssey*. The producer expects a costume spectacular. The director prefers a Freudian interpretation. When the producer propositions the writer's wife, the writer meekly accepts the situation—finally wrecking his marriage. The story ends in a freakish automobile accident.

The adaptation would be called *Le Mépris (Contempt)*. In Godard's version, the two main characters would become a French couple, the producer a vulgar American, and the director—well, Godard sought someone of international distinction whose real-life identity would force audiences to think about an artist forced to prostitute himself. Godard asked Jean Cocteau, but Cocteau declined (in ill health, he would die in 1963). Then Godard thought of Lang— though, ironically, in Moravia's novel, the director is a German by way of Hollywood described as "not in the same class as the Pabsts and Langs."

Godard's reverence for Fritz Lang was explicit. Among Godard's writings was an essay where he had listed Lang above D. W. Griffith, von Stroheim, Abel Gance, even Eisenstein, as someone whose greatness was demonstrated by his facile transition to sound—and by his ability to play the Hollywood game, according to Godard, "without cheating."

Everything about the offer—the prestige associated with a Godard film, the featured billing, his actor's salary—sounded good. Lang, who had never really acted professionally, readily accepted, and flew to Italy. During the spring and summer of 1963, he worked on location with a group that included Michel Piccoli as the writer reworking the *Odyssey*; Brigitte Bardot as his wife; and Jack Palance as the American producer.

It was a thoroughly agreeable, familial experience. Lang felt comfortable with Piccoli and Bardot, chatting endlessly with the latter about animals and pets. Surprisingly, the director also felt at ease with the unorthodox Godard, and vice versa.

A novelist couldn't have invented more incomparable filmmakers than these two, whose careers bookended the history of cinema. Godard used his scripts merely as springboards for improvisation. His lighting was undramatic. He was interested in "effects, not action," and sought a Brechtian detachment from the material. His actors were encouraged to act with sangfroid.

"More amused than baffled by Godard's unconventional methods, Lang shares with his younger colleague only the cigar habit and an unbounded love for the motion picture," reported *The New York Times*. "In fact, Lang's working methods are diametrically opposed; the seventy-three-year-old veteran, who recently completed *The 1,000 Eyes of Dr. Mabuse* in Germany and who returns to direction with his upcoming . . . 'And Tomorrow Murder,' is strictly a desk-bound creator, who only rarely makes a script change during shooting . . ."

Godard himself would portray an assistant director in a couple of scenes, positioning himself as Lang's disciple. "I think," Lang was quoted as saying about the innovative filmmaker, "he's trying to continue what we were all like at the beginning—the day when we started to make our first films, only his approach is different." For his part, giving a location interview, Godard described the seventy-three-year-old director as "an old Indian chief, tranquil and serene, who had meditated at length and finally understood the world, and who has given up the warpath to younger and more turbulent poets."

In the film Lang would wear his monocle and a blue pinstripe double-breasted suit. Encouraged to come up with his own dialogue, the director wrote some of his lines as the camera rolled—speaking off the cuff, the way he had always done his best writing.

The nouvelle vague was fond of film-buff inside jokes, and some of Lang's scenes were intentionally ironic. The character he plays, who is called Fritz Lang in the scenario, favors pretentious photography of statuary, while the producer demands nudity and blood. (Godard's own producers were pressing him for more nude footage of Brigitte Bardot.) Lang is allowed to quote Dante and Hölderlin, holding forth on the eternal fight of the individual against fate and the gods. He makes a reference to Cinemascope (and, indirectly, to *Moonfleet*) as not "meant for human beings. Just for snakes . . . and funerals." His oft-told anecdote about Eddie Mannix and *Fury*—how his direction elevated that script beyond the ability of MGM's front office to recognize it—is recycled into a diatribe by the *Odyssey*'s producer, making the same complaint about Lang.

At one point Michel Piccoli's character remarks to Lang how much he and his wife enjoyed watching *Rancho Notorious* with Marlene Dietrich on the television one night. The director forthrightly replies that he himself prefers *M*. This was also Godard's joke on himself. Not only did the *Cahiers du Cinéma* crowd champion his Hollywood films above the Berlin ones, but Godard had actually written that *M* was "the least good film of Lang's."

"This [film] is an anti-*Cahiers* position on Lang's own career," wrote Andrew Sarris when *Contempt* was released, "and Lang's description of Cinemascope as a process suitable for photographing snakes and funerals is aesthetically reactionary enough to make [French film theorist] André Bazin roll over in his grave. Lang's kind words for [producer] Sam Goldwyn are the final confirmation that Godard has allowed Lang to speak for himself, rather than as a mouthpiece for Godard."

One of *Contempt*'s scenes showed Brigitte Bardot sitting in her bath, while perusing Luc Moullet's 1963 book *Fritz Lang*, one of the first published about the director's career. This is accompanied by a voice-over, a citation from the book, in which Lang mused on the subject of murder, as he liked to do in interviews and conversations:

"The crime of passion is pointless. I am in love with a woman . . . she is unfaithful to me . . . I kill her . . . well now, what do I have? I have lost my loved one, since she is dead. Or, if I kill her lover, she detests me . . . And I lose her just the same. Killing can never solve anything."

The scene provided a noteworthy publicity still of Bardot in the bathtub with Lang's name slyly advertised on the book's cover. The meaning of some of the scenes, including the ending, eluded Lang—and endings were important, after all. Lang had a talk with the director, trying to puzzle it out. In the final shot, the writer's wife and the producer are glimpsed lying dead in a sports car on the highway. No people are around them and traffic is passing by. Lang didn't understand that. "Have they had an accident?" Lang wondered. "In which case, why no people? Are they dead, sleeping, or what?"

Apart from spells of Brigitte Bardot preening in the nude, many film critics found *Contempt* boring—a studied and abstruse film. Younger critics generally felt otherwise, seeing in Godard's work, among other things, a heartfelt tribute to one of his idols. The world of cinema will be forever indebted to Godard for this Fritz Lang swan song. One elegiac image—just a few moments really, sans dialogue—spoke volumes: The director is seen lighting up a cigarette, after others have exited a scene; the camera tracks beside the elder statesman of film as he walks slowly along a street, alone, apparently lost in thought. Godard's camera watches him contemplatively while, in the background, Georges Delerue's eloquent score rises on a gorgeous note.

Several critics on New York's *Village Voice* (among them the intellectual essayist Susan Sontag and Lang's old friend Herman Weinberg) listed Godard's film among the year's Top Ten. "What is so moving about *Contempt*?" wrote Andrew Sarris in his *Village Voice* column "Simply the spectacle of Fritz Lang completing a mediocre film with a noble vision in his mind and at the edge of his fingertips. Godard appears in the film as Lang's assistant, and he presents Lang's instructions to the camera crew, as if in the bulky figure of this curious man who has always known how far to compromise in order to endure is hidden the real Homeric parable of *Contempt.* Where Mastroianni in Fellini's *8 ½* is an artist who just happens to be a movie director, Lang in *Contempt* is a movie director who just happens to be an artist."

Contempt was a fitting capstone to a magnificent career.

Other projects would arise, of course, always to be revealed as mirages.* Lang was feeling his age, and felt wary of the demands directing a film would place on him. Pierre Rissient recalled a time when he was traveling with Lang on an Air France flight, after one of the film festivals. "Maybe I should not say it because it concerns me," said Rissient. "But he had received an offer to do a film, and I had made two short films that he liked, especially the composition and framing. He said, one night, that as he didn't have a son, he would like to take me as his assistant because I could help him with his eyes. I could help him to frame. It would be as if he was giving his knowledge to a son."

There was one final possibility the director took seriously: "Death of a Career Girl." This scenario was intended as a starring vehicle for his German girlfriend, "the Fox," last of the "virgin stars." Written in sections on the road in Mannheim, Frankfurt, and Paris between 1964 and 1965, it was only a treatment, never a fully-fledged screenplay. By now the director was usually working alone, in longhand on a yellow legal pad. Lang wrote a German and English version of the story, while Howard Vernon cooperated with a version translated into French.

In an article in *Sight and Sound,* David Overbey summarized the Langian scenario. It started with a Parisian *Rahmenhandlung,* "a beautiful and financially successful businesswoman," moving, "drink in hand, through her luxury apartment," as she ponders suicide and reviews the events of her life.

An intricate back story reveals that, in 1943, the woman, then sixteen, slept with a Nazi officer "in order to solicit information that will save the life of an RAF pilot, all the time biting a small gold cross hanging round her neck in order not to cry." Afterward she was "raped by twenty of her drunken comrades in the resistance."

A year later in Capri, she sleeps with the pilot "perhaps because of compassion, or loneliness, or weariness . . . or simply because she cannot stand hearing any longer that he 'loves' her." She steals half his money, but finds herself, months later in Rome, pregnant but too poor to arrange an abortion. "A boy is born. She first attempts to smother him, changes her mind, places the gold cross about his neck and leaves him before a convent door. She is almost run over by a carload of wealthy Italian youths and their well-dressed laughing whores, whose gay life she envies bitterly."

Later, back in Paris, she takes menial jobs before becoming a "try-on" girl in a fashion house, where "in order to keep her job, she moves from bed to bed, although she is now totally indifferent to sex." Fate throws her into the company of famous artist Richard Feling, twenty years older than her and "a painter of great talent and integrity," for whom she becomes a model. "He teaches her all he knows of the social graces, and assists her in educating herself generally. They become friends; later, lovers."

But Feling's snobbish circle treat her badly, and she leaves him to pursue her own ambitions. She marries a rich industrialist, "and uses his wealth to gain entrance to the power centers of society and big business." She takes a lover, Raoul, a rival social figure, and her husband grows to hate her. "She then plots to make it appear that her husband has tried to kill her. The plot succeeds and the husband kills himself."

Now Raoul's mistress, she "learns the secrets of his business empire," but encounters the artist Feling at an exhibition of his work. His arthritis has stopped his creativity. "They speak intimately and Feling, still in love with her, warns her that she is in mortal danger of losing her soul. Their meeting changes nothing, for she uses her relationship with Raoul to take over his empire, thus destroying him."

She takes Raoul's place at the pinnacle of society and "holds court in Paris for all the successful in all areas of human endeavor. Her apartment is fully equipped with hidden recording devices which monitor conversations at her parties, through which she consolidates her position and gains even more power. She decides to produce an heir, and seduces a somewhat unwilling Feling. During her pregnancy, the opportunity to take control of an international cartel by adding one small company to her holdings presents itself, but she will need all her considerable sex appeal to triumph."

She decides to have an abortion. "The newspapers announce the death of Feling. While there is speculation that it was suicide, she knows: he simply could no longer live. She is racked with something like guilt, and her frenzied attempts to forget lead her from city to city in a round of drugs, drink, and indiscriminate sex. One evening in Rome, numbingly drunk, she goes to bed with a young Italian. Waking in the morning, she finds about the neck of her sleeping lover a chain with a small gold cross bearing her own teeth marks."

Returning to the present, the woman steps into her bath, ready to kill herself with a razor blade. "Her [servant] announces that the officers of her company have arrived. The razor blade drops slowly to the bottom of the tub. She declares the meeting open."

It is all too easy to see this ultimate scenario as a summation of all the familiar characters and situations that had gone before. And perhaps the director had been moved by the autobiographical strain of his appearance in *Contempt*.

For Lang himself was the nameless Career Girl, and the famous artist of integrity, *and* the hollow industrialist destroyed by love. He was the foundling of a convent who yearned for his mother, for her long-lost loving embrace. The Nazis screwed the career girl–director. Lang screwed them back. Sex, fame, and power couldn't atone for the emptiness, the guilt. Suicide loomed as the only solution. Death in a bathtub . . .

But not this time. Not for the Career Girl, nor for the director whose career was ebbing away as surely as blood in water. Destiny might be littered with falsehoods and compromises, but business must proceed as usual. This could be the only possible ending. The Career Girl remains resolute, optimistic, rising up from a failed suicide in the bath to meet with new officers of the company—Fritz Lang's own new producers?

Lang tried hard to stir up interest in "Death of a Career Girl," but "the Fox" was no box-office commodity. The scenario had to be set aside. As the hands of time moved came another flash of hope. Jeanne Moreau, the worldly actress who had shone in films by Louis Malle, Truffaut, Antonioni, and Buñuel, gave a published interview saying she admired Lang and would love to work under his tutelage. Moreau's star might be bright enough to ignite the project.

Pierre Rissient labored mightily to arrange a meeting between Lang and Jeanne Moreau. Howard Vernon set up a Paris hotel room for dinner and decorated it with flowers that Lang had specified for the occasion. The director was nervous, almost like a boy, walking into that room. Nobody but Lang knows what went on there.

Some of his friends liked to fantasize that he and Jeanne Moreau made love. Others, furious to this day, believe that the actress led Lang on, then disappointed him profoundly by stopping short of commitment. But what happened was likely very mundane. The two of them likely had a long dinner and discussion afterward, and Moreau could only have realized that the director was an old man who on a film set would no longer have the courage and vigor to be Fritz Lang.

On the heels of *Contempt,* in 1964, Fritz Lang was chosen as president of the seventeenth International Cannes Film Festival jury—the first American jury head in the festival's history, even if Lang spoke French and German as often and as well as English.

Because of his impaired eyesight, he could barely see the screen, but a companion—usually Pierre Rissient—would sit next to him and whisper about the films being screened. The French press accorded him respect, and at a press conference asked him a number of French-style questions, to which he duly gave French-style answers.

"When films are very long, do you leave before the end?"

"Never. It is a question of honor among thieves."

"What are you interested in, in life?"

"Life."

"Yes, but what particularly? Mankind, nature, reading, travel?"

"Everything. Light, a leaf that falls from a tree. For a director, nothing is ever lost. Even films without interest are interesting. One can see what they should not do."

"How do you work?"

"Like everyone, by trying to make a vague vision real. It is very difficult."

"Is there a project in the next few years that you plan on doing?"

"I work very hard toward my next mistake."

"Do you have a 'Langian' recipe for happiness to give us, after so many rich experiences and such a full life?"

"Live on the same rhythm as a loved soul."

Death, a constant specter in Fritz Lang films, began to shadow the director's life.

His brother Adolf Lang, had died, at the age of seventy-six, in 1961. Lang had not seen Dolf since the early 1930s. He had delegated all communications to Lily Latté. Letters from Dolf desperately pleading for financial help were met with recitations of the director's own burdens: medical expenses, property taxes, major repairs for the house, et cetera. According to Friedrich Steinbach, Dolf was more interested in reconciling with his brother than in the token packages he sent. But the director's grudge was permanent. Lang regarded his brother as a moocher. Dolf died in a public nursing home, his wife soon after.

The deaths of old friends grieved him more. Peter Lorre died of a stroke in March of 1964. Death claimed Gerda Maurus in Düsseldorf in 1968. Teodor Adorno died in Switzerland in 1969. Reading the newspaper, he and Lily Latté would make a point of keeping track of the obituaries of former Berliners. "With time," Lang wrote to a friend, "one is more and more alone."

Scientist Willy Ley, Lang's rocket-travel friend, also died in mid-1969, just weeks before the launching of Apollo 11 and man's first footsteps on the moon. Lang wrote an article for the *Los Angeles Times* lamenting the irony that Ley, who had become the curator of the National Air and Space Museum in the United States, had not lived to see the milestone.* Lang and Ley used to sit out on his terrace at night, the director wrote, and Lang would point up at the moon, jokingly calling it "my location set." When Lang wondered if men would ever walk on its surface, Ley, "perfectly certain and confident," always assured him, "We will be there!"

Lang missed Peter Lorre especially. He had never reached a sought-after intimacy with the actor associated with his biggest success. Shortly before Lorre's death, the two were reunited at a UCLA student showing of *M* as part of a series called "A Tribute: The American Film and its Creators." Lang joked publicly about his callous treatment of Lorre during the shooting of *M*, and after thirty years the actor was able to laugh it off.

---

*Ironically, Ley's co-consultant on Lang's *Die Frau im Mond*, Hermann Oberth, was invited to the Apollo 11 launch as a special guest of the National Aeronautics and Space Administration.

"I wish I could talk to Peter," Lang would say occasionally, after Lorre's death, overlooking the fact that he had rarely talked with the actor during his lifetime. Lang made do by staying in touch with Celia Lovsky, Lorre's ex-wife, to whom he had stayed faithful as a friend and whom he had cast in small parts. She is the woman who sells Anne Baxter a blue gardenia in Lang's film of the same name, as well as the matriarch featured in a painting on the wall of the ganglord's mansion in *The Big Heat*. The director acted benevolently toward Lorre's extended family, which generated endless Sturm und Drang for the Lang household. "Nobody should know about that," Lang told Dan Seymour, "because I am known as a no-good shit."

Taking the place of the scripts he no longer worked on feverishly was the daily journal he strictly maintained. No associate, no assistant, no secretary recalled the director's keeping such a daily log during the Hollywood years. Lang had kept a diary of activity and thoughts during World War I; then, for fifty years, he had been too busy.

Nowadays, he wrote mostly in English: recording his private thoughts, appointments and meals, everyone he spoke to or saw, every visitor, every phone call—everything. It was a chronicle of an old man's minutiae, complete with little Langian sketches and arrows and annotations. The call girls who serviced him were entered into the journal with observations and remarks—"even some exclamation points," in Pierre Rissient's words.

Friends were at first disconcerted when Lang interrogated them, asking them to remind him precisely when they had arrived at his house, what they said or ate, when they had left. The chronology had to be precise down to the minute. Nothing could be left out.

7:30 A.M.: I awake. 8:47 A.M.: I bathe and shave. 11 A.M.: So-and-so arrives. 12:15 P.M.: Lunch at such-and-such a place, with details of the food and size of servings. 2:53 P.M.: So-and-so goes home. 3:30 P.M.: The phone rings. Et cetera, et cetera.

"Why is it necessary to be so very precise?" Friends, overcome by curiosity, asked.

"If you have been interrogated by police for twenty-four hours," the director, would answer mysteriously, stabbing his finger at them, "then you would understand why." Those few who knew the story silently took this as a reference to the demise of Lisa Rosenthal.

Although the director was no longer actively involved in film projects, he continued to clip crime items and important newspaper stories. He kept abreast of political events. The articles about Nixon and Reagan piled up; he wasn't going to let another Hitler sneak up on him. He also kept folders of articles and observations on larger themes and philosophical concepts.

Lang maintained a folder labeled "Violence and Ethics," which he kept under the living room couch on which he liked to recline and read. "Violence and Ethics" was a subject that had always fascinated Lang, and with the world in a worse mess than ever, he believed, violent options had to be rejected and ethical values reaffirmed.

Other subjects presented themselves in the course of his daily life. One evening in Paris, Howard Vernon invited Lang to a dinner at his apartment. It was an unusual invitation—typically Lang went to restaurants—but he accepted, and Vernon went to some trouble to organize a suitable evening. He made arrangements for a female dinner guest to keep the director company, while he himself brought the young man who was currently his lover. The dinner for four was perfect. But Lang seemed a little uneasy. The director had never before realized that Vernon was a homosexual.

Lang approached the subject gingerly with Vernon, some time afterward. The director asked solicitously after Vernon's boyfriend—using a word in German that meant "lover." When Vernon said he was no longer involved with the young man, Lang registered surprise. "Oh . . . I'm sorry," the director said. "You must be very sad." Vernon said no; that was sometimes the nature of a homosexual relationship. Lang expressed curiosity about homosexuality, and proceeded to ask Vernon many questions on the subject.

After the director's death, Vernon, helping Lily Latté with the task of cleaning out the house, looked under the living room sofa and found the "Violence and Ethics" folder, and he was surprised to notice "—*and* Homosexuality" had been added in Lang's hand. "Homosexuality was a perfectly new and totally unexplored thing for Fritz," explained the actor. "Somehow it was interesting for his curious and searching mind."

The director knew there would be books written about him, and he had an ambivalent relationship with the people who were determined to write them. He had remained cordial with Siegfried Kracauer and Kurt Pinthus, who both ended up, after fleeing Hitler, in New York academic circles. He met with them on his trips there in the 1940s. When, however, Kracauer wrote his book *From Caligari to Hitler*, about the history and social significance of early German film, the director felt deceived. He hated Kracauer's book, with all of its anti-Lang insinuations.

He often complained that the history of German film had been falsified by Kracauer—"consciously or unconsciously, I'm not quite clear on that." Indirectly, he meant that the history of his own life had been distorted. Was it not a bitter experience to have been one of the geniuses of the cinema, then to be ignored in the United States and reviled in Germany? History needed to be set right by a new generation of scholars and historians.

The first two books about Lang were published in France in 1963, followed by another in 1964; the first in the English language was Peter Bogdanovich's, published in the United States and United Kingdom simultaneously, in 1969.* Lang was very much alive to read and critique these books, generally welcoming these and other authors who aspired to chronicle his career—until their books came out and disappointed him. Lotte Eisner, Paul Rotha, Alfred Eibel, and others were invited to his house and accorded hospitality. Lang even gave some of the writers, visiting from afar, phone numbers of local prostitutes from his private black book. Then Lang would actually *direct* them on how to behave with one of his referrals, admonishing them if they failed to add to

---

*The first full-length book about Lang written in Germany would not appear until 1976.

the expected fee a box of candy or a dozen roses. "For, never forget, above all a prostitute is a woman," Lang would say.

But the director had mixed feelings about such authors, who might also antagonize him if he decided they were trading off his name. Gero Gandert, from Berlin's Kinemathek archives, went to some lengths to meet up with Lang in Hamburg and Munich in the early 1960s. Gandert was studiously recreating the screenplay of *M*, for which there was no shooting script extant, to be published in a book. Because the topic was his favorite film, Lang was at first open to Gandert.

Gandert had blocked out dozens of characters for which there were no names in the story, and several scenes where more than one character spoke simultaneously. Lang had a remarkable memory for the characters' names and was able to supply the garbled dialogue. A couple of scenes were missing from available prints, and therefore unrepresented in Gandert's draft; these Lang was able to dictate by heart.

Every scene, every shot, every angle seemed lodged in his head; but he was fallible—sometimes the specifics were *only* in his head. Gandert recalled showing Lang the pages describing the scene where Hans Beckert retreats to the warehouse surrounded by the beggars' organization. Lang looked at what Gandert had written down, and frowned. "Stop, that's wrong!" he said. The director took out a sketchbook and made some drawings from memory. He remembered where all the cameras had been placed. When Lang had finished his sketching, he compared his refreshed notes to Gandert's reconstruction, and admitted, "No, you were right."

When Gandert tried to conduct a tape-recorded interview with him, then, Lang balked. Extemporaneous questions and answers, later to be transcribed, worried him. The director was usually at his most relaxed and eloquent in interviews, but later on, he knew, the transcript would betray his malapropisms and syntactical errors, not to mention remarks that ought to remain private. He preferred to review the transcript of his interviews, improving his rhetoric and correcting heated "misstatements."

It was extremely hot in Germany during that summer when they met. On the day of the appointed interview session, Gandert lugged his heavy tape recorder by tram to the hotel where Lang was staying. As soon as he asked his first questions, Lang blew up. "The questions are too stupid for me!" "At that moment," recounted Gandert, "I had to decided whether to say 'Kiss my ass, Mr. Lang' or meekly go back to work—for an honorarium less than the cheapest waitress could make." A dedicated archivist, Gandert decided in favor of film history.

Gandert came another time, lugging his tape recorder and bringing with him the questions in written form so that Lang could ponder and study them before framing his replies. Lang took so long pondering and studying them that there could be no possibility of turning on the tape recorder that day; instead Lang vowed to answer the questions by mail.

"When the answers came back," said Gandert, "the sentences were so long, the subject didn't meet the verb." Gandert made some corrections, and wrote a letter politely asking Lang's approval. Lang said okay. Later, the director would denounce the book, and tell people at film festivals in Europe that the script and information were all wrong—no matter that he had furnished much of it himself. The director would admit privately that what annoyed him most was that once again someone else was making money off *M.*

When Gretchen Berg, the daughter of his old friend, critic Herman Weinberg, interviewed him in 1965, the director also found fault. Berg had compiled a transcript of Lang's thoughts and memories after a long evening spent at his home with a handful of friends. Upon reviewing his own words, Lang decided the interview was "unauthorized." He feared that it might give an erroneous impression of him, or perhaps form the basis for an unexpurgated book. After all, Weinberg himself had written books about Josef von Sternberg and Ernst Lubitsch.

Lang's fears went so far that he decided to consult his lawyers. He itemized a four-page list of errors and wrongful impressions conveyed by his own words. Lily Latté tried to arbitrate, as she always did in such unfortunate cases, but when portions of the interview were published in *Cahiers du Cinéma*, Lang blew his temper. He refused to speak to Gretchen Berg, and even, for a long time, to her father, who took pains to intercede and make amends.*

One of the points in the Gretchen Berg interview that worried him the most was his unrehearsed recollection of the making of *Fury*. In a casual way Lang had made a number of negative assertions about Joseph L. Mankiewicz. When explaining to Lily Latté and others why he was so opposed to publication of the Gretchen Berg piece, he insisted that he was worried about a lawsuit from Mankiewicz; he didn't want to provoke Mankiewicz, though the idea that the producer of *Fury* would rise up and sue him over a remark about incidents that dated back thirty years was uniquely Langian.

When active as a director, Lang had been unusually proprietary about his personal publicity. Now, in retirement, even though he made a show of concern for film history, most of the interviews were purely about himself. "If you concentrated exclusively on him," said Charles Higham, "he was fine, but like so many people in his position, if you strayed an inch from the subject, he would get bored. General conversation bored him."

Higham and Joel Greenberg interviewed Lang for their 1969 book of interviews, *The Celluloid Muse: Hollywood Directors Speak.* Higham interviewed the director again for another project, "Time-Life History of the Movies." At one point Lang ventured to ask Higham what other members of the profession were going to be included in the line-up. "When I mentioned the names, his face went completely blank for lack of interest. He asked it only out of minimal politeness."

Peter Bogdanovich had a dismaying experience with Lang. In 1966, Bogdanovich, then a columnist for *Esquire*, ran into Josef von Sternberg at a Hollywood bookstore, and asked him for Fritz Lang's phone number—although the two Vienna-born directors were "the opposite of friendly," in Bogdanovich's words. Von Sternberg advised Bogdanovich to be discreet about

---

*Although their 30-year friendship temporarily suffered, Lang later demonstrated his character by writing a glowing introduction to Herman G. Weinberg's book *Saint Cinema: Selected Writings, 1929–1970,* which gave no evidence that there had ever been any falling-out.

where he had acquired the private listing. "I never heard Joe say anything against Fritz, but Fritz was very negative about Joe."

Bogdanovich proposed to Lang a series of interviews that would be fashioned into a monograph honoring the relatively unheralded Hollywood phase of the director's career. "In some cases," Bogdanovich felt that "the American films were some of his best films." Lang responded to that verdict with enthusiasm, and Bogdanovich, with his wife Polly Platt assisting him, interviewed the film director for several days.

At first warm and encouraging, Lang slowly turned against Bogdanovich. He seemed to hold Bogdanovich's youth and ambition against him. "I was, I think, not bad-looking, my whole life ahead of me," said Bogdanovich, "and maybe that irritated him." Bogdanovich and his wife used to refer to Lang as Iago, because he would behave pleasantly to Bogdanovich's face, then whisper conspiratorially against him in Polly Platt's ear. It seemed to irritate Lang that Bogdanovich had a beautiful wife, and that the couple appeared to be devoted. More than once Lang predicted a bad ending to the marriage. "Fritz was jealous of a good relationship," said Bogdanovich. "Though, prophetically he was correct, because the marriage did end."

When the Bogdanovich book was ready, the galleys were sent to Lang. The director scratched a few things out, concentrating on people and events that were particular thorns in his past. Lang polished up the version of how *Metropolis* was conceived, and once again took pencil to the whole *Fury* story, making sure he was comfortable with the precise wording of his reminiscences. He carefully reviewed his stated account of the collaboration between him and Brecht. He tried to edit out gratuitous remarks about his experiences with Gary Cooper and Marlene Dietrich.

Speaking of *Fury*, Lang had told Bogdanovich, "One of my greatest enemies in this matter was Mr. Spencer Tracy . . ." He crossed that out, though Bogdanovich left it in for publication. Apropos of Dietrich, he tried to cross out, "She is responsible for a lot of disagreeable things in my life . . ." Bogdanovich left that in as well. Maybe Lang held on to the galleys too long. Maybe he didn't even bother to send them in. But when he read his own words in cold type, his only desire was to block or disown the complimentary book.

The director tried to threaten publication with letters to the book's publisher. When publication went forward anyway, Lang went around town insisting that he never realized *Fritz Lang in America* was intended to be a book; that it was, he believed, only supposed to be a magazine article. "Which was bullshit," according to Bogdanovich.*

The director never confronted Bogdanovich personally; he simply cut off all communication between them. "He went around town and acted like I had stolen the book," recalled Bogdanovich. "I didn't get it. To this day, I don't get it."

---

*Shortly thereafter, Bogdanovich made his first feature film as a director—*Targets*, a Langian story with a climax involving a Vietnam veteran who goes berserk at a drive-in horror show. In his interviews with Lang, Bogdanovich had asked the director what he thought of the newly invented zoom lens. Lang replied that he didn't like it much, but thought it might have possibilities in showing the path of a bullet. Bogdanovich used that idea in one scene of *Targets*, the camera zeroing in as if shot from the barrel of a gun.

One thing Gero Gandert, Gretchen Berg, and Peter Bogdanovich had in common was that their intentions were flattering. Their articles and books were extremely favorable to Lang. But that didn't matter: The director's paranoid perfectionism only saw mistakes and devious motives. When one author wrote to Lang, submitting the manuscript of his forthcoming book about him, it didn't matter that the tone was judicious and the bulk of the text approving. Lang sent back a blistering letter, saying the book was swollen with inaccuracies; the director didn't want to aid the author in the slightest, and if the book was going to be issued anyway, the publisher must be an idiot.

The director tried to make certain amends whenever the occasion arose.

He made a point of asking Roddy McDowall to take him to the set of a television production starring Barbara Stanwyck. Stanwyck was on the director's short list of adored actors. "But Fritz felt guilty about something, I gather, in relation to what happened during *Clash by Night*," McDowall said. Stanwyck greeted the director graciously, and they retreated to her dressing room, where they spoke privately. Afterward the director seemed touched that Stanwyck could be so forgiving.

Lang was hurt when others chose to remember "the bad things better." He was dismayed at Henry Fonda's remarks, in published interviews, excoriating the director. He was similarly wounded when Edward G. Robinson's autobiography, *All My Yesterdays*, came out in 1973 without one mention of Fritz Lang; *Scarlet Street*, a film that meant the world to its director, was remembered by its star as a project he hastened to finish, "so monotonous was the story and the character I played."

The director pinned his hopes on Lotte Eisner. Eisner had been there; she could speak as a witness to events. She was a longtime friend. She was one hundred percent in his pocket.

Throughout the 1960s, Lang patiently answered Eisner's questions toward a book—questions asked in letters or in person, in Beverly Hills or, more often, in Paris, when he visited the Cinémathèque for events and screenings.

Eisner meant well, but she was often wrong, in Lang's view, and he was vigilant about her misinterpretations. Lang had come around to being a passionate defender of Thea von Harbou, for example, and time and again he had to stick up for von Harbou and her vital contribution to his career. For the sake of posterity, Lang preferred that Eisner play down his former wife's Nazism. Eisner had become too anti-German, Lang thought. The director reminded her over and over how much Berlin and Germany had meant to them both. He criticized passages she showed him in which Eisner's "loathing for Germany" came across undisguised.

"You at one time (just as I did) appreciated the German cultural milieu," Lang wrote to her in 1968, "stood up against German anti-Semitism . . . Can you abolish from your life Schiller, Kleist, Heine? I loved *Faust* from the bottom of my heart! . . . No, dear, dear Lotte, these are things which belong to us, which we cannot tear from our hearts."

Because she took so long with her book about Lang, Eisner exasperated the director. He, in turn, exasperated her with his infinite changes and emendations. To Lang, everything could be corrected, improved, perfected. Everything could be broken down, until it became a litany of infinite, numbing detail.

"We talked and wrote about every chapter of my book—that was a privilege that only a few authors have," recollected Eisner in her memoirs. "In his search for perfection, no detail remained unmentioned. There was no lapse that I was not rebuked for."

In a typical letter of December 29, 1971, Lang itemized his corrections:

Page 7, paragraph 2: Lang recommends writing "a piece of sugar" instead of a "Zuckerl." A Zuckerl is the wrong term, Lang noted, a candy from that Konditorei [i.e., pastry shop] at the edge of the Balkans that only ignorant people would call Vienna.

Page 7, paragraph 3: Eisner had written about a scuffle with a dog. "I don't think scuffle is quite right. You don't have a scuffle with a dog," the director explained.

Page 7, paragraph 4: Eisner had applied the word "kidnapping" to a stolen napkin. Lang thought "kidnapping" ought not apply to an object. "I think, dear Lotte, you should write this paragraph a little more clearly."

Page 7, paragraphs 7 and 8: "I would really advise you to leave these two paragraphs out completely."

Page 8, paragraph 2: Instead of the word "treasure," Lang suggested his own word—"fortune."

Page 8, paragraphs 3 and 4: "Transition between paragraphs unclear," Lang noted.

Page 8, paragraph 5: "I would advise you to describe the headquarters in *Die tausend Augen des Dr. Mabuse* in this paragraph, where four television screens report on everything that is happening in and in front of the Hotel Luxor."

Page 8, paragraph 6: "And, dear Lotte, Professor Jordan [the Mabusian character in the film] doesn't work a strange machine made of levers and pipes. It is a perfectly normal television *Umschaltgerät* that has been around every studio for years. You know so many people. Get someone to show one to you sometime."

Page 8, paragraph 7: "This is wrong! At the time of the Nazis there was no television. Just leave out the paragraph."

Page 8, paragraph 8: "Don't understand."

Page 8, paragraph 11: "Change in wording."

Page 9, paragraph 1: "Dear Lotte, come on . . ."

Page 9, paragraph 2: "Please leave out the whole paragraph and get off old dead Harbou's back. You should be above that kind of never-ending griping . . .

"Oh Lotte, I *hate* it when I *have* to be critical . . ."

Every paragraph, every line, sometimes every word.

Eisner suffered endlessly. She did worship Lang, and so wanted to please him. But Lang had a peculiar attitude about the people who worshiped him— the only people he permitted into his presence. He basked in their adoration, yet doubted their fawning opinions, which he made a point of ferreting out and rejecting. It was almost a crazy game with him.

Eisner was not the only one of his admirers whom he tortured. But she was one of the most vulnerable, and he would tease her most cruelly—address her as "Geliebte Eckersfrau" in his letters, alluding to Eckermann, Goethe's loyal and meticulous but mediocre personal secretary; or, worse, "Eckersau"—"sau" meaning "pig." He would call her ugly, and to others, out of her earshot, point up her physical flaws. ("She always claimed I took her to bed. A filthy idea. There's only one thing you should do with a hunchback—touch it for luck!") He would challenge her with deceptive questions: "What is your favorite Fritz Lang film, Lotte?" Then lance her with her own replies. "Dummkopf! That one is not any good at all! I just waited to see what you would say!"

More than once he reduced Lotte Eisner—in effect, the ghostwriter of the story of his life—to tears. Then Lang's friends would have to prop her up again with the reassurance that, deep down, the director really loved her. Or did he? Friends aren't sure. "My theory is that he suffered her because she was useful to him," said Kevin Thomas. "But she reminded him of his own age and that bothered him."

Her book was "pending" for nearly twenty years, because Lotte Eisner was really too much like Lang as a writer. She wrote and rewrote, criticized and edited herself, tore chapters up and started writing again; one finally had to rip pages out of her hand. And as sometimes happened with Lang, the writing didn't necessarily improve. Sometimes it became more tangled. And Eisner had been living so long as a polyglot that her book was sprinkled with three languages: German, French, and English—whose syntaxes and vernaculars often mingled confusingly.

"He [Lang] got disgusted with her at the end," said Dan Seymour, "because she was writing, writing, writing, but nothing ever showed up."

"I will read it in the hereafter," Lang would say to Eisner, with a heavy sigh. There was comfort in that Liliom-like belief, as there was comfort in the notion that this was a book he would never have to reject. Any such book was bound to be a definitive distortion. Any book that sealed his fate within its pages was a Fritz Lang nightmare.

In 1965, Lang was decorated with the Order of Letters and Arts from France. In 1966 he received the Commander's Cross, Order of Merit, from the Federal Republic of Germany. In 1972 the director accepted Yugoslavia's Order of the Yugoslav Flag.

Lang stayed in demand in Paris, where the Cinémathèque housed his collection and cineasts kept his name before the public. A mint print of *The Woman in the Window* was reissued there in 1969, and Nunnally Johnson buried the hatchet, writing an article saluting Lang. "Where is home for a man like me now who was born in Austria, lived in Germany, went to America, then back to Germany?" the director told a reporter for the *Los Angeles Times*. "Where is my chez lui? It must be where my children are—in the Cinémathèque Française."

In 1971, Lang yielded to long-standing invitations to return to Vienna. He flew there in the spring, was voted a Medal of Honor by the city council, and had a day set aside in his honor by Vienna Mayor Felix Slavik. The director stayed at the Hotel Sacher, and to Viennese filmmaker Peter Hajek he seemed a man at peace with himself. "He had an incredible amount of time for us," remembered Hajek. "In fact, he got really carried away and had loads and loads of time. And then [afterward] he went out on his own. He went for a walk somewhere. He did say his sight was very bad, but I didn't have the impression that he couldn't see . . . he just went off on his own."

The director visited a cigar store in the neighborhood where he grew up, and was pleased that someone there remembered the Lang family of yore. But when an actual emissary from the Lang family—Adolf Els, a cousin—tried to take the director for a visit to the cemetary where Dolf and his wife Eugenie were buried, reuniting the two brothers at least at gravesite, the director balked. "What is dead, is dead," Lang declared.

The two places where Lang felt most neglected were, ironically, Berlin and Hollywood. Berlin accorded him civic honors during the annual film festival in the summer of 1971, but by then it was late in his life and Lang found the bitterness hard to overcome. The red carpet was rolled out, a Mercedes placed at his disposal for a week of activities. All Lang could think about, as he went through the motions, was all the years he had been ignored, all the transgressions of the "idiotic" Kracauer book, and all the negative notices Germany's critics had heaped on his last films.

Lil Dagover ("God bless face-lifting!") and Gustav Fröhlich ("who I really could have gone without seeing") were invited to share the dais at the main ceremony. The mayor gave a speech honoring him, and Lang was "passed around like a lobster salad." The director noted the precise identities of people charged with squiring him around, and deduced that he had been invited by the city government and not by the film festival organizers. "Comment unnecessary."

Finally, there came a dress ball, and festival officials showed up, flocking around Lang, belatedly paying some attention to him. "Zum Kotzen!" was how Lang felt.*

"Maybe I sound ungrateful," Lang wrote to Paul Erich Marcus, "and maybe I really have become a blasé fool, but the honors I am accorded—*and don't write this down anywhere or tell it to anyone*—bore me to death. In my opinion, they have more to do with the eighty-odd years that I've been beautifying the planet than with my films. But still," added the director, "Berlin was always an old love of mine. The mayor's invitation meant a lot to me, in spite of everything that I've just written. As if this great love was finally, after such a long time, reciprocated after all."

In America Lang also became a star—at least, on the college and film-buff circuit, where he was kept busy making personal appearances at festivals and universities. Many of these requests were from California institutions (Claremont, Chico State, USC, or UCLA), but there were also quite a few invitations from out of state (Arizona, Chicago, and Oregon). Lang appreciated the college gigs; he appreciated the speaking fees, but he also found a genuine measure of enjoyment in interacting with young students.

With his black eyepatch he resembled an old pirate. Thick glasses usually supplanted the monocle, fitting over the patch. In spite of this elaborate getup, he didn't want people to realize his eyesight was terrible; Fritz Lang didn't want to be pitied—this director known for his visual mastery, who could no

---

*"It makes you want to puke!"

longer see to walk, or know where to turn his eyes. His eyesight had become a terrible handicap. He adjusted with courage and dignity. "Now that I have practically lost my sight," he told Frederick Ott, "I sometimes think I am able to see the past more clearly."

How blind he was seemed to vary according to the occasion, however. The director would be fumbling along with one of his helpers, then all of a sudden make an unexpected comment, startling the person at his side with some visual perception of the surroundings.

"He [Lang] just saw differently out of one eye than out of the other," wrote Curt Riess. "That is normal for old people. But for him, whose eyes were more important to him than anything else, it was awful. He simply couldn't get used to it."

"We had signals," recalled Dan Seymour. "I'd walk in [to a college lecture] with him. He never had a cane and people didn't realize he was blind. They'd seat us in the front. I'd steer him. He'd hold on to my arm or lean against my arm, and we'd move through the crowd pretty good. He'd say, 'How many people?' I'd look around and tell him. When they called him up, later on, he'd take his bow and mark where I was sitting. I gave him signals which way to turn so that he could call on questioners and answer questions. He gave the impression that he could see, although he could not see very well. He could only see outlines."

The Museum of Modern Art organized a festival of Lang's silent features in Manhattan in 1967. *Variety* covered the MOMA program; their report was filed by Paul Jensen, who later wrote the first English-language study of Lang's work. The festival-goers were probably the audience Lang had always catered to, Jensen observed, consisting "in unequal parts of New York City intellectuals, old German friends of Lang (including scientist Willy Ley), film buffs, and young would-be filmmakers." In a question-and-answer period, Lang earned applause with his oft-made statement that he would like to direct one more film, concentrating on the problems of modern youth.

The Los Angeles County Museum followed suit by organizing a retrospective of his work in 1969. Lang appreciated the retrospectives, but also enjoyed finding details to complain about. He didn't like the musical score the L.A. Museum used to accompany one of his silent films. "I don't like music with my films. They were made to be silent. They should stay silent. Anytime there is music, somebody obstructs my rhythms."*

While college and museum honors drifted his way, Lang stayed a forgotten man in Hollywood's film industry. A man with enemies at every studio and in every union, Lang had never been nominated as Best Director by the Directors Guild, never been nominated for an Academy Award. (Indeed, only a single one of his films had earned so much as one nomination—that for the original story of *Fury*.)

Lang felt overlooked. "Here was a man who should have been honored," said Dan Seymour. "He was honored in Europe but never here. That was his

---

*Of course, strictly speaking, none of his films were originally presented "silent."

greatest frustration. I know he was deeply hurt by it, though he would never say so."

He didn't feel bitter about Hollywood, only regretful and profoundly chastened. In spite of everything, Lang loved Hollywood—a sentiment that had never been reciprocated. Perhaps he had made mistakes, had misbehaved. Wasn't now the time for forgiveness and acceptance?

Lang didn't care to dwell on this unhappiness. He preferred the illusion that Fritz Lang was, and remained, a vital part of Hollywood. He wielded his name just as in the old days, using "director" as an honorific; picking up a phone to make a restaurant reservation, he would declare, "This is Director Lang, calling about a table . . ."

Once, going out to dinner with Howard Vernon, Lang asked his friend to make a reservation at one of their usual haunts. Vernon went to the phone and did so accordingly. Afterward, Lang asked him, "Did you tell them it was for Fritz Lang?" Howard Vernon said no, he hadn't. "Ah," said Lang, "you should have said the name. We'll take care of it when we get there, then we'll get a better table."

So they went, and naturally the director put on a huge display. "Lang is here!" The waiter behaved deferentially to him, escorting them to a well-placed table. Lang busied himself behind one of those enormous menu cards, bent over his magnifying glass. The headwaiter scurried over, whispering to Howard Vernon, "Mr. Lang . . . Mr. Lang . . . isn't he connected with the cartoons?" Vernon whispered back, "No, that is Walter Lantz. This is Fritz Lang, the *director*." "Because," said the headwaiter, "I really wanted to tell him how much I love the Woody Woodpeckers." "Oh," said Vernon, "don't tell him that."

Finally, in 1973, the Directors Guild of America offered a formal tribute to Lang. By then the director was over eighty, virtually blind, in altogether frail condition. But it meant a lot to him to be feted by the guild of his American colleagues. He wanted everything about the evening to be perfect.

Lang asked his friend, *Los Angeles Times* critic Kevin Thomas, who was on the panel of guests, to mention a recent U.S. newspaper article that had cited the artistic significance of the director's first Mabuse film. Thomas thought that was unnecessary, considering the Hollywood nature of the tribute, and left it out. After all, anyone who knew Lang's career didn't need to be reminded about the virtues of *Doktor Mabuse, der Spieler.*

Afterward, when he and Thomas went out for drinks at a Century City bar, Lang could barely contain himself. The first *Mabuse* was all but unknown to most people in Hollywood, Lang complained, and he was furious that Thomas hadn't mentioned it. To the end, he felt he had to educate America about the Fritz Lang of Germany. "What touched me," said Thomas, "was he actually thought it was important to mention a rave review of something that everybody knew and regarded as a classic in the first place."

It was there, at the Directors Guild tribute, that the Last Dinosaur made a remarkable statement about fate, and himself. It had been over forty years since his first film, and thirteen years since his last. He had been pondering fate, in his life and work, for a long time. Most critics thought Fritz Lang's films were about the fight *against* fate and destiny. The philosophy the aging director now articulated rejected much of this critical theory, and bespoke his thoughtful stoicism approaching death.

"All of my German films and the best of my American ones deal with fate," Lang said at the Directors Guild tribute. "I don't believe in fate anymore. Everyone makes fate for himself. You can accept it, you can reject it and go on. There is no mysterious something, no God who puts the fate on you. It is you who makes the fate yourself."

A director who had suffered more than his fair share at the hands of fate thus executed a complete turnaround at the end of his life. What had Fritz Lang finally admitted? That not everything is preordained? Not everything was someone else's fault? That life was more complicated than the through-line of the best scenario? Perhaps, that tragedy and mistakes flowed naturally from actions, and from a life completely lived?

For the last ten or fifteen years of his life, Fritz Lang may have been lonely, but he was not alone. He had a coterie of younger friends whom he adopted and who adopted him.

He was touched to hear how his protegés restored and collected 16-mm copies of his films as if they were paintings. He watched his silent films for the first time in decades with this circle of friends in small basement screening rooms, sometimes with other Berlin–era luminaries—including people he disliked, such as Josef von Sternberg—invited along for the chance to glimpse a rare curio from the past.

Lang's feelings were always mixed with trepidation on such occasions. "I remember listening to him talk to my dog Tor," said David Bradley, whose house was a mecca for such screenings. "Fritz was sitting in a big chair next to Tor, talking to him. 'Tor, I'm very unhappy. You haven't made any movies, so you can't possibly understand. I have made movies and I am very unhappy. I'm very on edge, sitting here, looking at this movie. How lucky you are to be a dog!'"

Lang was especially hurt that his American friends tended to focus on the German period (whereas, predictably, the Europeans gravitated to the Hollywood works). "Why don't you ever show my American films?" Lang would demand. "Why do you always show the German?" "Because," Bradley replied on more than one occasion, "they're better." Oh!—that was the last thing Lang wanted to hear.

He had little routines that he observed with each of his friends. The barbershop at the Century Plaza Hotel, where he liked to go with Dan Seymour to get his hair cut, followed by lunch at the Garden Room. (He liked to introduce Seymour to people stopping by the table as "my adopted bastard son.") A Saturday lunch with Cornelius Schnauber in Beverly Hills. He'd take Kevin Thomas to the Cafe Swiss on Rodeo Drive, and maybe Howard Vernon too if he was in town. ("Maybe I was the son he never had," said Howard Vernon.) The favored places were well-lit, the menu familiar—martinis and traditional dishes the director could count on to meet his expectations.

He had varying degrees of openness with his friends. Most had met him in the years of retirement, when he was still crusty but indeed mellowed. He was as cautious as he always had been with his secrets, especially with the jour-

nalists and writers among them. Even on the most carefree and intimate occasions, Lang steered away from certain painful subjects and cut off indiscreet
inquiries with a withering remark.

They themselves felt frustrated by the way he compartmentalized his
friends and turned nearly all of them into assistants and helpmates. They
realized they would always be closed off from knowing what was in Fritz Lang's
heart. "If he had been able to let go of some of his class-consciousness and
his reserve, he would have gone to his grave with more positive experiences
with other people," wrote Lotte Eisner in her memoirs.

They were his surrogate children, and he tried to raise them up in the world.
Lang asked Paul Erich Marcus in England to clip the London movie reviews
and send them to him, so he could read them out to Kevin Thomas as examples of proper English prose. "He tried very hard to make me a great critic,"
recalled Kevin Thomas. "When, at some point, I think he realized I was not
going to be a great critic, he cared for me anyway. He didn't hold it against
me."

They paid him back in various ways. Thomas made sure that Lang was
mentioned regularly in the *Los Angeles Times*: few other film directors had
their birthdays remembered in print, or had so much space devoted to their
old films when they cropped up at revival showings. On occasion Thomas even
served as a "ghostwriter" for Lang, the émigré who never stopped fretting over
his command of English. Once, the director even asked his friend up to the
house to help compose a birthday telegram for Asta Nielsen.

When the adoptive sons came to visit him from other cities or countries,
they were invited to stay over in the house, and when they did, Lang took
over their lives. The director had no future project, so they became a kind of
Fritz Lang production. His surrogate children would spend the day doing what
Lang himself was no longer able to do. He arranged their schedules, according
to a very precise script. He sent them to the planetariums, theme parks, and
tourist places he himself had always enjoyed.

Once, when Howard Vernon came from Paris, Lang insisted Vernon spend
the day at Marineland of the Pacific in Palos Verdes. Vernon replied that he
had seen enough of Marineland in newsreels. Lang said documentaries did not
do justice to the place. "You must go!" Then the director instructed Vernon
as to where *exactly* he should go inside the oceanic theme park: where to begin
his tour, where to pause and look at a particular sight, when to stop and watch
the penguins being fed, and so on.

"I went there because I didn't want to disappoint him," remembered Vernon. "But Marineland is a place where you go with children or even two or
three friends together, but a man alone? It was so silly."

Lang even advised his actor friend to take his camera and take photographs
of the wonderful sights. He told Vernon which shots to get and how to obtain
the best lighting and angles. Vernon didn't really want to take his camera
along, but to humor his friend he did so. When the actor came back from
Marineland and gave his report, Lang demanded to know how many photographs Vernon had taken. "How many? One roll?! That's not enough. And
they're probably not good photos besides."

"That was just like him," recalled Vernon. "I never would have dared to say that I don't like that sort of picture anyway, since it is sold on postcards for fifty cents."

Some of the director's friends jokingly referred to the Summit Ridge house as the Web, with all of the threadlike filaments manipulated by Fritz Lang, the Master Spider. Once drawn into the Web, there was no end to what the Master Spider might impose.

For example, Lang himself usually took long naps in the afternoons. David Overbey was visiting the director one day, and announced he was going to spend the afternoon at a bookstore during Lang's rest. The director was chagrined beyond reason. No, Overbey had better stay in the house that day. After all, the director had a magnificent library—Overbey could feel free to browse to his heart's content. "But I'll never have any books of my own unless I get to the bookstore," pleaded Overbey.

"Ah, I remember," Lang said. "What I actually want you to do today is watch *Che!* on television." Overbey replied that he really didn't want to watch *Che!* and especially not on television. But Lang simply would not take no for an answer. The director insisted Overbey had to see this film, that afternoon. "So I sat there while he slept and watched *Che!*, and you'd better pay attention because afterward he asks questions."

The surrogate sons made boon escorts to the latest screenings and excursions to Hollywood theaters. They knew the latest films and trends. They helped compensate for Lang's pitiful eyesight. Right up until he lost his health, the director prided himself on being up-to-date with the newest filmmakers and rapidly evolving technology.

The director retained a soft spot for the nouvelle vague. He stayed patient with increasingly abstract and pretentious directors such as Antonioni and Godard, even though, when he was at a film festival at Rio de Janeiro, he almost walked out on Godard's *One Plus One* (aka *Sympathy for the Devil*), a muddled Rolling Stones pseudo-documentary. The director tugged at Lotte Eisner's sleeve and said, "I can't stand it anymore. Let's go!" But she hissed back, "Fritz, if we leave now, all of Rio will know that we walked out of a film by Jean-Luc Godard." So Lang stayed.

He appreciated the intellectualism and the militancy of the new breed. If Lang had ever been asleep on the subject of the Nazis, if he had once acted the coward where anti-Communism in America was concerned, he had matured into a left-leaning regulation liberal no longer afraid to give voice to heretical political opinions. "I know I should be a Communist," he'd sigh, "but I'm too old."

Lang especially made a point of seeing the topically oriented films of the 1960s, those which tracked the gusting political winds. One of the last important films he saw, ironically, was *The Sorrow and the Pity*, Marcel Ophuls's documentary examining the Nazi occupation of France during World War II. Lang was eighty, the film was three and a half hours long, but he had read all about it, and insisted on going.

The director remained as opinionated as always, and had his adamant likes and dislikes. Lang could endure any horror film and find something positive to like about it. In the same sentence he might ridicule Orson Welles's *Citizen Kane* ("that scrapbook of Expressionism") while ticking off the merits of *Pretty*

Maids All in a Row, a sexy murder comedy directed by nouvelle vague film-maker Roger Vadim. (Maybe it was because Vadim would never be thought of in the same breath as Fritz Lang.)

A longtime opponent of the Production Code, Lang found himself mourn-ing its passing, and bemoaning the excesses of nudity and sex that took up increasing screen time in the early 1970s. At the same time Lang found it his professional obligation to keep up with the burgeoning field of pornographic films. He was over eighty when he expressed a desire to see *Deep Throat,* the X-rated hit starring Linda Lovelace that was so controversial. So one of his surrogate sons trooped with him down to one of the smut theaters on Santa Monica Boulevard. Lang sat up front, close to the screen, peering at the close-ups of fellatio with his outsized magnifying glass. "He wanted to see it because everybody was talking about it in this town and it was selling out," said Dan Seymour.

Afterward, the director pronounced *Deep Throat* disgusting. Not everyone in the Web knew that the Master Spider had gone to watch the hard-core film, so another time, another surrogate son was recruited to take the director back to the relevant theater. Once again Lang watched *Deep Throat*—up close, front row, magnifying glass—and once again Fritz Lang pronounced it dis-gusting.

Directing can be an isolated profession, and Lang had not developed close relationships with any colleagues in the field, neither in Hollywood nor else-where around the world.

When in 1968 the French government attempted to take over management of the Cinémathèque, Lang was among those who rallied to the support of Henri Langlois, recruiting others in Hollywood. He conferred with Pierre Ris-sient about a petition to be circulated among U.S. directors, and advised Ris-sient to obtain Josef von Sternberg's signature first, lest von Sternberg's status somehow be offended. Lang on the subject of von Sternberg's ego could hardly be trusted, however. And when the petition came back to Lang, with his imagined rival's name at the head of the column, the director simply reached up and scratched the signature of Fritz Lang on an imaginary line above von Sternberg's.

When the greatest directors from around the world visited Hollywood, one of the people they always wanted to meet was Fritz Lang. Lang's early works had made a powerful impression on Luis Buñuel, the iconoclastic director of *Los Olvidados, Viridiana, Diary of a Chambermaid,* and *Tristana.* Buñuel had praised *Metropolis* in print. Seeing *Der müde Tod* shortly thereafter—at its 1926 reissue at the Vieux-Colombier Cinéma in Paris, which specialized in foreign revivals—had influenced Buñuel's decision to devote himself to the medium.

Like Lang, the Spanish director had been exiled from his native land and spent much of his career as a globe-trotter, working in France, Mexico, and the United States. When asked who his favorite filmmakers were, Buñuel in-variably replied "the Germans," by which he meant especially G. W. Pabst, F. W. Murnau, and Lang.

Jean-Claude Carrière, Buñuel's assistant, tried to bring Buñuel and Lang together at the Venice Film Festival in 1967, where _Belle de Jour_ was in competition. Invited to have a drink with Jean-Paul Sartre, Carrière and Buñuel found themselves in a bar where Fritz Lang was nursing a martini. "Look, there's Lang," Carrière told Buñuel, "Would you like to meet him?" Buñuel was shy, almost like a college boy at the prospect. "You could see him fighting against the desire," said Carrière. Buñuel said, "This disgusting old man?"

Lotte Eisner also had tried to introduce them at the San Sebastian Film Festival. The two of them turned up at the same reception. By then (this was 1970), Lang could hardly see without his magnifying glass; as for Buñuel, his hearing was poor. Eisner recollected: "I said to Buñuel, 'Luis, I want to introduce you to Fritz Lang.' And to Fritz, I said, 'Look, there's Buñuel!' But Buñuel, who was almost deaf, didn't hear me, and Fritz Lang, who was almost blind, didn't see him. And so the two old veterans of the cinema walked past each other."

The first and only meeting of these two titans of the cinema would take place in the spring of 1973. Buñuel's visit to Hollywood that year, when _The Discrete Charm of the Bourgeoisie_ won the Oscar as Best Foreign Language Film, was celebrated with a party in his honor. Lang, eighty-two, came briefly, but felt too poorly to stay. The following day, at the Beverly Wilshire Hotel, where he was staying, Buñuel received a private invitation to visit Lang at his home. Carrière remembered Buñuel's nervousness. "He came to my room—I swear—to ask me if he should wear a tie: a normal tie or a bow tie. Like a young boy going to a first rendezvous."

"We talked to each other for an hour," recalled Buñuel in one interview, "so I had the chance to tell him what a decisive influence his films had had on the course of my life. Before I left I asked him, which is not something I usually do, for a signed photo from him. He was surprised but got one and signed it. It was a recent photo and I asked him if he still had one from the twenties, from the era of _Der müde Tod_ and _Metropolis_. He found one and wrote a wonderful dedication on it."[*]

Asked once which of his American colleagues he admired, Lang had replied: John Ford, George Cukor, Billy Wilder, and William Wyler—two of them American-born; one, like himself, from Vienna; and one Alsatian, with Teutonic antecedents. Lang was to have a noteworthy encounter with Ford and with another giant among directors, Jean Renoir, at the Montreal Film Festival in 1970, when his friend Pierre Rissient worked hard to corral all three.

Ford and Renoir probably did not feel the same way about Lang as he did about them. According to Lotte Eisner, although Renoir lived only a stone's throw away from Lang, he "didn't want to have anything to do with him, because he resented Lang's remakes of _La Chienne_ and _La Bête Humaine_." Over the years Eisner had paved the way for amity between them by patiently

---

[*]From Hollywood, Buñuel traveled to Mexico, where he was preparing his next production. According to Carrière, Buñuel was like Lang in another respect: always fighting his feelings. So when Arturo Ripstein, a young Mexican director, came by one day and asked about the inscribed photo, Buñuel told him, "Oh, it's nothing. If you want it, take it." And Ripstein took the Lang memento away.

explaining to Renoir that Lang's remakes were contract requirements—which, at least in the case of *Scarlet Street*, was not quite true.

Rissient brought the three film directors together over drinks. What was memorable about the occasion was that it was distinctly unmemorable. Here was a glorious chapter of film history: the three of them round a table, Lang with his martini, Ford with his whiskey, Renoir with his glass of wine. And these three directors, eloquent in their films, were in each other's presence quiet and polite, almost nondescript.

A steady stream of interviewers and film buffs continued to visit Lang's house till the end. Not since his last Hollywood production in 1956 had the director employed a full-time agent or publicist; now Lily Latté was also the last agent, the last publicist. "Once Fritz had armies to command," quipped someone in the circle; "now, only Lily." It was Latté who screened the visitors, assessing the letters and phone calls, she who provided guests with refreshments. It was she, when Lang's memory failed him, who would prompt him.

Latté was "Lang's best audience and living encyclopedia," wrote Axel Madsen in *Sight and Sound*, "when stories have to be authenticated or fleshed out with detail." Reported Madsen: " 'Mickey', he [Lang] will call out in her direction, 'Isn't it true Harry Cohn nearly didn't want me to direct *The Big Heat* because I showed up with glasses and he found me less authoritarian than when wearing my monocle?' "

Before his death, she was already taking over the archives—embellishing even the details of Lang's love life that might have personally bothered her. Someone might mention that they ran across a reference to an affair Lang supposedly had had with actress Wendy Barrie in 1941. "Wendy Barrie? Did I have a love affair with Wendy Barrie?" Lang would call out to Latté, who was usually well out of sight in the kitchen. "No," came the exasperated reply, "that was Virginia Gilmore." Ah yes, now Lang remembered . . .

Lotte Eisner had for a long time pushed Lang to "regularize" his household by marrying Latté. She was one of the faction that believed the two were truly in love, no matter how much Lang berated "the Latté." Eisner thought the director had an unrequited familial urge. "I think he would have liked to have had a family," wrote Eisner. "It seems very clear he regretted that, if you look at the pictures of Fritz with his monkey."

Others believed Lang felt yoked to Latté, treated her abominably as a consequence. If Latté coughed—and she was always coughing—he insisted that she was coughing purely to make noise that would cause him discomfort. If she rattled a pan in the kitchen, he would scream at her to let him have some peace and quiet.

As late as 1971, visiting Vienna, Lang pointedly denied rumors that he and Latté had married. He wrote an Austrian cousin who had inquired after his marriage: "Thank you very much for the greetings to my wife. Unfortunately, I must disappoint you, I am not in fact married, despite all the newspaper reports that I have wed."

Lang hinted, in private conversation, that there was mysterious bad blood between him and "the Latté," a secret historical episode that he would reveal to people the next time he saw them. This episode would expose her true, unpleasant nature. But always it was the next time, and somehow the director never got around to providing the specifics.

"He felt guilty about her toward the end of his life," said Kevin Thomas. "He'd say, 'You know I like Lily but I don't love her.' But I think he was talking about sex." On the other hand, Latté did love Lang, Thomas added. "Totally. No question about it. In the long haul, yes."

In the end they were bound by time, memory, convenience, and an intense love that almost seemed to verge on hate. Sometime in the early 1970s—as his eighty-fifth birthday approached—Lang realized it was time to make arrangements for the welfare of the woman who had dedicated herself to his well-being for nearly forty years. According to Kevin Thomas, Lang's attorney Martin Gang more or less commanded the director to marry Latté. She had to be protected financially, as his death loomed. She had been in unstable health for years, and needed the director's benefits and insurance.

One factor that influenced the director was his obsession that some distantly remote relative might come out of the woodwork to claim the name of Lang. On his trip to Vienna in 1971, he had met a young girl, a niece, and invited her to Hollywood. When she arrived, she disappointed him; her homeland flavor had disappeared, and she seemed to him just like everybody else, trying to use Fritz Lang to finagle a job in movies. There were relatives in Austria and others living in Belgium who also claimed family ties.

Marriage would be the final means of controlling his legacy. So Lang finally agreed to marry Latté, although it was a ceremony that nobody witnessed. Lang told Dan Seymour that he and Lily were quietly married in Palm Springs. He told Howard Vernon that the two of them had eloped to Las Vegas. And he told Cornelius Schnauber that a rabbi had been summoned up to the house to formalize their union.

At last, it seemed, Lily Latté had become the third Frau Lang. The Directors Guild was notified for pension purposes. A will was drawn up where she was cited as Fritz Lang's wife and legal heir, and when the obituaries were written, she would be so described.

And yet a search of all available records in California and Nevada reveals no certificate of the marriage. It appears to have been the last of the director's legends.

A clipping service, Argus in Switzerland, collected his notices and articles from periodicals around the world. His seventy-fifth and eightieth birthdays were occasions for stacks of neatly itemized clippings of birthday greetings from newspapers and magazines in Germany, Paris, London, Brazil, Spain, the Netherlands, Vienna, and Eastern Europe. The German headlines read "Poet des Stummfilms," "Der Pionier mit dem Monokel," "Der Regisseur der Regisseure."

A series of illnesses had begun to take a toll. Shortly before his eightieth birthday, Lang had suffered a gallbladder attack, for which he had to be hospitalized. His gallbladder had acted up throughout his life, but this attack was his most serious. The director was not able to get out of bed every day after that, and when he did, he was confined to the house. All but legally blind, he knew visitors by their voice, their footsteps, or their perfume.

His final years were dutifully recorded in his journal—sometimes, these days, in other people's handwriting. He kept track of the number of Seconal and Valium he was taking, as well as the quality of borscht and osso bucco. His wits were intact, as was his appetite. One lunch, set down in his final year, consisted of two eggs, three sausages, a slice of ham, chocolate cake, and a martini.

It fell to Lily Latté to arrange everything now—even the prostitutes who came to Summit Drive when Lang was no longer able to leave the house.

Lang stayed sexually active even in his declining years. He told Pierre Rissient that old age did not hamper him. "He told me this one day—up to age seventy-seven, it was fine," Rissient said. "After that, it was more difficult." Toward the end of his life, Lang told Kevin Thomas, a young college coed, a fan of his films, obliged him every now and then by coming around to give him a "wonderful head." But prostitutes were more reliable, and if Lang said it once, he said it a thousand times, "Let's face it, prostitutes can do it better."

A few faithful friends stayed in touch. One of the regular phone-callers was Joan Bennett. In the living room of her home in New York hung the portrait of her which the director had commissioned for *The Woman in the Window*. Once the actress made a tape recording of one of her college lecture appearances, answering questions from the audience by reminiscing fondly about the films she had made with Lang. The tape ended with her comment, "I hope my daughter goes back and tells Fritz how much I still love him." Her daughter did take the tape to Lang, who was moved by the declaration.

There were fewer interviews toward the end. Lang had less and less patience with the same old questions, and, one suspects, the same old answers. In the early 1970s, cinematographer William Fraker captured the aging master for William Friedkin, the director of *The French Connection*, for a planned documentary. But after a number of sessions, during which Lang recycled familiar anecdotes (*Metropolis*: "I was interested in the relationship of the working class to a kind of dictatorship"), his impatience at what he considered foolish questions showed, and Lang snapped at the interviewer like an old turtle.

Toward the end, he had stopped kidding himself. When people asked him if he was planning any future projects, he shook his head. "Too late!" he would murmur. "Too late!"

Lang celebrated his last birthday, his eighty-fifth, in a wheelchair. There were birthday articles feting his career from all over Germany. In honor of the date, a festival of his films was organized in Munich, and another retrospective was put on by the Moscow Film Institute, which proclaimed his birthday a milestone in the history of the cinema.

"Sometimes I wonder what kind of films I would make today if I were able," Lang told the *Los Angeles Times*, in the last birthday article cooked up by Kevin Thomas. "With the world the way it is, I think they would be very critical—very aggressive. I would want to show how television has robbed the young people of their imagination. But that would only be a small part of all I would have to say."

"It's easy to grow old," Lang would tell his friends, "It's hard to *be* old." He was as besieged by frailties and multiple illnesses as any of his victim-heroes. Fate was closing in on Fritz Lang. Sometimes he would plead, "Help me end it all . . ." But the director, unlike so many of his film's characters, would not end life a suicide.

The Christmas holiday season before he died, the Schnaubers went up to see him, close to the date of his birthday. They were shocked at his appearance. He had deteriorated physically. His clothes hung on him. He had a big male nurse who had to carry him into the living room to greet people.

Cornelius Schnauber recalled that Lang asked him, rather poignantly, if he would return a long-playing record the director had lent him—a Bing Crosby Christmas album featuring "White Christmas" and other standards. After getting it back, Lang put on this LP every day and lay in bed listening to it, Latté later told the USC professor.

He had become very sentimental about his childhood, and seemed drawn again to his Catholicism. One day Lang asked Latté to get him a copy of the "Our Father," whose words he had forgotten; then he asked for a priest to come and see him. It was shortly before he died. The director and the priest spoke privately. "Somehow he [Lang] was a religious man," said actor Howard Vernon. "He needed it. I don't know if it was a faith built on fear, or respect of God. But he did consider himself a Catholic, which I found amusing, and *not* Jewish. But he also felt himself Jewish. He felt both, maybe, according to the circumstances—a rabbi for marriage, a priest for dying."

On August 2, 1976, his suffering ended. Death came at 9:05 A.M., after a stroke. Lang was eighty-five.

Variety hailed him as "one of the leaders of the German expressionist school of filmmaking." The *Los Angeles Times* commented that his films had "set a world standard in suspense and visual composition." *The New York Times* noted that "The film world of Lang, whose innovative craftsmanship influenced hundreds of younger directors and put an indelible stamp on the art of cinema, was populated largely by psychopaths, master criminals, prostitutes, child murderers, sadists, and the insane."

As Fritz Lang lay dying, no doubt he thought of Liliom and wondered if it was true there was a heaven. Perhaps, it was true, he had made mistakes, had misbehaved from time to time. Wasn't death truly the moment of forgiveness and acceptance?

Wasn't he, unlike Liliom, redeemed by his films?

Fury, You Only Live Once, Man Hunt, The Woman in the Window, above all *Scarlet Street,* were among the best of his Hollywood years. But if some people preferred *Moonfleet* or responded to *Beyond a Reasonable Doubt,* it didn't matter. Lang had learned to accept those opinions gratefully, and was long last past worrying whether *M* had been his ultimate achievement.

The first two *Mabuse* films, *Die Nibelungen* and *Metropolis*: these were works of wonder that would awe and entertain people as long as the cinema was celebrated. *Der müde Tod* and *Spione* perhaps were more for German tastes, but they too had proved enduring works.

M showed the humanity of evil—and to his surprise, the more he thought about it, the humanity of Fritz Lang. So did *The Big Heat,* his last great film in Hollywood, almost as powerful and personal an achievement.

Wouldn't such work, lasting long beyond his mortal time, redeem Fritz Lang?

The director had not wanted a fancy burial ceremony. He had gone with Lily Latté to Forest Lawn cemetery to pick out a plot; it was important to him that it be near the roadway, so visitors would not have to walk far. His will stipulated that he be buried in the ground ("It is my wish to go back from whence I came: That is the earth") in an inexpensive wooden coffin. The marker would read, simply: "Fritz Lang. Born: 1890: Vienna. Died: 1976: Hollywood."

When Dan Seymour called Joan Bennett with news of the director's death, the actress sobbed into the phone for several minutes. The only mourners at the private funeral were Kevin Thomas, the Seymours, and Lily Latté. At Lang's request, Dan Seymour placed Peter the monkey inside Lang's casket before it was lowered into the soil.

Howard Vernon flew in from Paris to help Lily Latté with funeral arrangements, and was in the living room with her several days later when the telephone rang. Latté picked up the receiver, listened, then said sharply, "What? Mr. Lang has died. Several days ago! Didn't you know?" Bang!—she put the phone down, turned to Vernon, and hissed, "A whore!"

One of the chores she would no longer have to perform.

Fritz Lang's will was dated March 21, 1975, approximately a year before his death.

In the will, which was sealed by request, Lang declared for the record that he was married to Lily Latté. "We have known each other for more than forty years," Lang said in an unusual statement, "during which time we have faced many ups and downs together and not once has my wife ever deserted or disappointed me. We have a mutual, deep and heartfelt affection for each other (affection being a word I prefer to 'love' which latter word has been so terribly misused during these recent decades)."

Latté was designated as his inheritor and the executrix of the estate. But Dan Seymour was cited as substitute executor if Latté's health should fail. If his "wife" did not survive him after 180 days, Lang stipulated that three-quarters of the estate would go to the Seymours, with the remaining one-fourth set aside for Howard Vernon.

Lang's distrust of blood ties was borne to the grave. "I have, except as otherwise in this will specified, intentionally and with full knowledge omitted to provide for my heirs living at the time of my decease," his will stated. To anyone who claimed, contested, or sought to invalidate the will, Lang apportioned "the sum of one dollar only."

Lily Latté would outlive Fritz Lang by eight years—a feat no one could have predicted, since her health had always been worse than his. After his death, many of Lang's friends drifted away, and the flow of interviewers and buffs ceased. A lonely Latté became convinced that most of Lang's friends had never liked her anyway.

She, who had always kept the financial books, became more paranoid about the estate and income than Lang had ever been. The household and medical expenses had multiplied. From the day of the director's death, Latté worried incessantly, trying to pare costs—even on graveside flowers. In her desperation, she even contemplated giving public programs about Fritz Lang, lecturing about her husband the way Feuchtwanger's widow did about hers. But this idea went nowhere.

So did her proposition to Howard Vernon that they collaborate on a book telling the whole truth about Fritz Lang's life and career. She would take all the money, but, like Lang, needed a writer as collaborator. Vernon could keep the copyright for "pocket money." When Vernon declined, saying that his friend had always discouraged any biography, Latté was affronted. Vernon was one of several of the director's friends who finally decided that Latté was a cold, ambitious woman whose only goal had been to dominate Fritz Lang and assume his mantle.

"Finally, I didn't like that woman," stated Vernon. "She was grasping. To me, she was a negative person. She manipulated him so that he stayed her creature. She didn't do everything out of kindness and a good heart. To her, it was more of a means to keep him under her wing."

"We all thought Lily was a saint," agreed David Overbey, "until we found out differently. It was a matter of her becoming Mrs. Lang at the end of his life. She wanted it very much. It was a matter of the prestige involved."

A handful stayed attentive to Latté—especially the Seymours and Kevin Thomas. They paid her regular visits and provided a lifeline by phone. Inevitably, when it came to disposition of Lang's estate, they outflanked the others on controversial decisions.

Sometime in the early 1980s, Latté signed over all of Fritz Lang's film and script copyrights to Thomas Sessler Verlag, a long-entrenched theatrical publisher in Vienna. The details of this arrangement have never been made public, and establishing how many copyrights belong to Lang could involve litigation on the self-perpetuating level of Dickens's Jarndyce and Jarndyce. To this day Thomas Sessler Verlag has gone to court inconclusively trying to assert ownership and revenue rights.

Latté adopted Lang's concerns with other issues as well. In the final years of his life, Lang had written, in German, a 20- to 30-page short story called "The Wandering Jew." It was "a kind of fable about a Wandering Jew," according to Pierre Rissient. After Lang's death, Rissient asked Latté if he might arrange for its publication. "No," she replied, "because Fritz would want to be known as an atheist."

She went to the lengths of registering a treatment for another Fritz Lang script some five years after the director's death. A sketchy Western, called "An American Michael Kolhaas," the script became the last one to be filed under Lang's name. It was dated July 24, 1981, and duly noted as the property of Lily Latté, without any indication of when, during his final, enfeebled years, Lang wrote it.

Cornelius Schnauber was particularly concerned about the tangible mementos of Lang's career, which he wanted to bring to USC under the auspices of the Special Collections department. While the director was still alive, Lang had resisted USC blandishments, but Latté proved more open-minded on the subject (interested in the financial details as well as a commitment to honor Lang's legacy).

The Cinémathèque in Paris, which had done so much to promote and uphold the director's name, plunged into a period of disarray after Henri Langlois's death in 1977, shortly after Lang's. Partly for this reason the French repository was left behind in the maneuvering over Lang's estate; it, too, made the mistake of ignoring the widow.

With Latté's cooperation, Schnauber was able at one point to make a general inventory of the director's possessions. He made a list that included Lang's voluminous journals, slides, and private 8-mm films, script drafts and copies of Lang's American films, interview tapes, unproduced treatments and screenplays, memoranda and contracts, hundreds of private letters, a stack of favorite menus, a collection of Christmas decorations, another of Indian jewelry, art objects from various cultures, and the director's favorite German and American Christmas records.

Schnauber was especially alert to Lang's journals, and among them he was keenly interested in the diary the director had kept while lying in a hospital bed during World War I. There were six volumes of the World War I journal alone. Schnauber knew this for a fact, because he had persuaded Latté to let him peruse them at his home for several months from 1978 to 1979. His examination revealed that the journals disclosed "very personal relationships," story ideas, notes on the war, society, and the tenor of the times.

Schnauber intended to have the journals preserved and duplicated (their penciling was already faded). But in the summer of 1979, Schnauber had to leave on a trip, and Latté grew paranoid that the journals might be stolen in his absence, So she asked him to give them back to her for safekeeping. It was a fatal error; he would never see them again.

When he returned from his trip, Latté had grown even more defensive and told him that she was going to go through all the documents and possessions and remove anything to do with Lang's personal life, or certain problems he had encountered while directing his films. "She used the argument, and I can vouch for this, that Lang had often said, 'My life is nobody's business; if someone wants to judge me, let them do it from my films,' " Schnauber wrote later. The first possessions began to vanish. Others were crated up and marked, "To Be Destroyed."

She gave the letters between Lang and Theodor Adorno to British film historian Thomas Elsaesser. She sold a handful of significant documents, including Lang's passport and pieces of revealing correspondence, to the Stiftung Deutsche Kinemathek in Berlin. Lang's first editions and German books were auctioned off in Germany through Cornelius Schnauber. The University of Wyoming in Laramie acquired the remainder of his library, some files and folders, and the director's home movies.

The treasure trove of belongings that Lang had saved over the years was divided and scattered and some of it destroyed. The parties warring over the director's earthly goods after his death had competing financial, as well as personal, motives. Schnauber had German publishing agreements. Dan Seymour ran an antiques sideline, and in one of his subsequent books Schnauber would make the assertion that certain valuables, over which Seymour had maintained access, appeared in Hollywood shops after Latté's death.

According to Schnauber, Seymour's worst transgression was mishandling Lang's invaluable journals, particularly the World War I diary. Latté gave them to Seymour with the advice that he destroy any unsavory material. Nearly all of the early journal entries were in German, however; Schnauber wondered if Seymour understood enough German to review all of the pages. Schnauber proposed that everything be locked up for fifty years. Seymour told him it was his opinion that the journals were virtually worthless.

In the midst of this infighting, Latté made an important decision. The Motion Picture Home had offered her medical supervision and care for the rest of her life in exchange for ownership of the Lang house and belongings. But the Motion Picture Home wanted Latté to vacate immediately, rather than to pay for continuing medical costs and a full-time nurse on the premises. So Latté contacted USC instead and inquired if the college had resources to help her stay in the house, provided she bequeath the estate to USC. An annuity was arranged, Lang's will countermanded, and legal papers drawn up.

The agreement was signed on July 17, 1984. On September 14, Latté formally appointed Geoffrey Gilchrist of the University of Southern California as her executor. The will stipulated that the entire Fritz Lang estate be liquidated upon her death to benefit USC, in exchange for $160,000 for the house, payable to her in monthly installments.

The revised will repeated the "one-dollar-only" clause set aside for contestants of the will, identical to that which appeared in the original document. Howard Vernon was completely cut out of any inheritance. Latté listed a number of personal bequests, including the sum of five thousand dollars and "my late husband's ring with ruby-colored stones" to Dan Seymour. The latter was obliged to assist the USC executor in the sorting and disposition of personal effects.

Only two months later, on November 24, 1984, Lily Latté died in the hospital, at age eighty-four. It took a few days for word to spread among her handful of surviving friends, and for notices to begin to appear in the newspapers. Only the Seymours and Kevin Thomas were present at the gravesite when she was laid to rest alongside Fritz Lang.

The estate was appraised at approximately $210,000, including checking and savings accounts, shares, and proceeds from a Butterfield and Butterfield auction. Item number 12 of the inventoried appraisal—"Material connected with decedent's late husband's work, such as, but not limited to, scripts, articles, interviews, photos, et cetera"—was estimated at zero worth.

Before the house could be secured after her death, a number of prized possessions known to the inner circle disappeared. For example, Lily Latté's will expressly donated a pre-Columbian gold pendant and a "Swedish Orrefors large crystal flower vase with dancing nude figure" to her only surviving relatives, Clemens and Josette Auerbach. The Orrefors vase was never found among her effects.

Other Fritz Lang belongings found their way into friendly hands. Cornelius Schnauber kept the 1968–1973 letters between Lotte Eisner and Lang, for a future book he intends to write; his wife received the Lang-Latté collection of Christmas decorations ("among them a very artistically stylized set of reindeer in iron"), the Indian jewelry, and Christmas records. These personal bequests to friends ("that's what Fritz Lang wanted himself," according to Schnauber) are not listed in either will.

Nor are the monogrammed pill-case, cigarette case, and other Fritz Lang souvenirs shown to the author by Dan Seymour during an interview. Nor are the director's precious journals itemized anywhere. It is hard to say what happened to the journals, or how many there were, but fair to judge they would be appraised at far more than "zero worth" by film archives around the world. Indeed, to film scholars they would be priceless.

Dan Seymour insisted that the only journals lost were a few tossed out accidentally by a maid. But Kevin Thomas, one of those journalists cultivated by the director who had dedicated himself to Lang, admitted there was wholesale destruction.

"Lily felt it her mission to go through his files. The scholar, the historian, the cineast in me wanted to see everything preserved. Yet I knew I couldn't counter what Fritz would have wished. I knew I'd have wished to have those things destroyed. So, in all good conscience, I couldn't say, 'Lily, you've got to save these things for posterity.' "

At his home before his death, Seymour brought out for the author to examine several of the journals chronicling the director's last years: large black volumes with crabbed handwriting, mostly in English. Seymour said there were many more; he didn't know how many. He said he had the World War I journals in his garage or "somewhere." He would dig them up and be sure to have them available for inspection on the next visit. This was just a few months before his death in 1993, at age seventy-eight; when his widow was contacted, some months later, she said that she had been looking for the World War I journals—which contain the roots of Fritz Lang's cinema and the secret identity of his first wife—but could not find them anywhere.

Lang's home on Summit Ridge stayed on the market for several years, until its sale finally netted some $700,000-plus to benefit USC and the School of Cinema. This put the Lang estate at a worth of nearly one million dollars, in spite of all the suspense about finances, even without factoring in the "zero worth" of memorabilia.

The buyer for the house, incidentally, was Michael Nesmith, whose mother invented Liquid Paper, and who is best known in the United States as the tall, wry Texan who played lead guitar in the pop-rock group the Monkees.

In 1994, the Stiftung Deutsche Kinemathek in Berlin asked 324 film critics to name the one hundred best German films of all time.

M easily topped the list, with 306 votes. Second place went to *Das Kabinett des Dr. Caligari*, a film Lang had advised in preproduction, with 292 votes. *Metropolis* was number 8. Lang had four other films in the top thirty-five: *Dr. Mabuse, der Spieler* was number 17; *Die Nibelungen* was tied at the number 19 spot; *Der müde Tod* was number 21; *Das Testament des Dr. Mabuse* ranked number 35. The only director with as many films in the Top Hundred was G. W. Pabst.

Up in heaven, if there is a heaven for tyrannical screen artists, the director is reading this with a smile and a frown. The smile is for the perfect martini in his hand and the ideal producer he has met up with there. If only he could redo, remake, everything!

The frown is for Lotte Eisner's book, which, of course, as he foretold, Lang finally has been able to read in heaven. Eisner's book was published in 1976, shortly after Lang's death, and dedicated to "my old friend Fritz Lang, whom fate did not enable to hold this book in his hand." She bent over backward to honor that friendship. Lang was given credit for even the silliest things: the title of *The Return of Frank James*, with its "double meaning"; even the choice of name for Jesse James's brother Frank, "rightly named, upright, straightforward, naturally decent." No Fritz Lang film was less than worthy, even *American Guerrilla in the Philippines*. There, location photography was mandated by the director's "passion for documentary detail"; somehow Lang had transformed an episodic script into a "chanson de geste, reminiscent of Brecht's epic theater."

Her book would turn out to be "a saint's life," in the words of David Overbey, who assisted Eisner. In her memoirs, eight years later, Eisner admitted that the Lang book was "patchy" and "cursed." There were translation and other problems, but the real, emotional problem for Eisner was her closeness to her subject. She couldn't break free with her own thoughts. Knowing Lang for nearly fifty years had finally intimidated her.

Up in heaven, Lily Latté is off on an errand. Lotte Eisner, who died in 1983, is sitting to one side of the director, fearfully awaiting his remarks. Peter the monkey sits on the other side. Lang's monocle is clenched in his eye. He has filled pages and pages of a yellow pad with his criticisms and corrections. The director looks up at Peter, gives him a theatrical wink. "Are you ready . . . ?"

When Fritz Lang is finished with that book, he will start right in on this one.

Key: Sc: Screenwriter; Ph: Photography; Art dir: Art Direction.
Approximate running time in parentheses.
Cast listings are partial.

AS WRITER:

1917
Die Peitsche (The Whip)
Director: Adolf Gartner.
(Stuart Webbs–Film Co.)

Die Hochzeit im Exzentrikklub (The Wedding in the Eccentric Club)
Director: Joe May. Ph: Carl Hoffmann.
Cast: Harry Liedtke, Magda Magdaleine, Bruno Kastner,
Paul Westermeier, Kathe Haack.
(May-Film)

Hilde Warren und der Tod (Hilde Warren and Death)
Director: Joe May. Ph: Curt Courant.
Cast: Mia May, Hans Mierendorff, Bruno Kastner, Georg John.
(May-Film)

1918
Lilith und Ly
Director: Erich Kober.
Cast: Elga Beck, Hans Marschall.
(Fiat Film)

1919
Die Rache ist mein (Revenge Is Mine)
Director: Alwin Neuss.
Cast: Otto Paul, Alwin Neuss, Arnold Czempin, Helga Molander,
Marta Daghofer (Lil Dagover), Hanni Rheinwald.
(Decla)

Die Bettler–GmbH (Beggars Ltd.)
Director: Alwin Neuss. *Cast:* Ressel Orla, Fred Selva-Goebel, Fritz
Achterberg, Otto Paul, Marta Daghofer (Lil Dagover).
(Decla)

Wolkenbau und Flimmerstern (Castles in the Sky and Rhinestones)
As co-screenwriter (with Wolfgang Geiger).
Director: Unknown.
Cast: Margarete Frey, Karl Gebhard-Schröder, Albert Paul, Ressel Orla.
(Decla)

Die Frau mit den Orchideen (The Woman With Orchids)
Director: Otto Rippert. Ph: Carl Hoffmann.
Cast: Werner Krauss, Carl de Vogt, Gilda Langer.
(Decla)

Totentanz (Dance of Death)
Director: Otto Rippert. Ph: Willy Hameister.
Art dir: Hermann Warm.
Cast: Sascha Gura, Werner Krauss, Josef Roemer.
(Helios-Film)

Die Pest in Florenz (Plague in Florence)
Director: Otto Rippert. Ph: Willy Hameister. Cast: Theodor Becker, Marga
Kierska, Erich Bartels, Juliette Brandt, Erner Hübsch, Otto Mannstaedt.
(Decla)

1920
Die Herrin der Welt (Mistress of the World)
Part 8: Die Rache der Maud Ferguson (The Revenge of Maud Ferguson)
As co-screenwriter and assistant director.
Director: Joe May.
Cast: Mia May, Michael Bohnen.
(May-Film)

1921
Das indische Grabmal (The Hindu Tomb)
Part 1: Die Sendung des Yoghi; Part 2: Das indische Grabmal
As co-screenwriter (with Thea von Harbou).
Director: Joe May. Ph: Werner Brandes.

Cast: Mia May, Conrad Veidt, Lya de Putti, Olaf Fönss, Erna Morena,
Bernhard Goetzke, Paul Richter.
(May-Film)

AS DIRECTOR:

1919

Halbblut (The Half-Breed)
As screenwriter and director. Ph: Carl Hoffmann.
Cast: Ressel Orla, Carl de Vogt, Gilda Langer,
Carl Gebhard-Schröder, Paul Morgan.
(Decla-Bioscop)

*"The title Halbblut—literally half-blood, with racist connotations—was
always translated as 'The' (masculine) Foreigner,' or more often, 'The' (masc.)
Half-breed,' while it is clear that the film is about the 'destiny of woman.' The
best translation would be 'The (feminine) Cur . . . '*
Georges Sturm, *Fritz Lang—films/textes/références*

Der Herr der Liebe (Master of Love)
As director and producer. Sc: Leo Koffler. Ph: Emil Schünemann.
Art dir: Carl Ludwig Kirmse.
Cast: Carl de Vogt (Disescu), Gilda Langer (Yvette), Erika Unruh.
(Helios Film)

*"The second of Lang's films with no surviving print, Der Herr der Liebe is
another story of unhappy love in the mode of a society drama."*
E. Anne Kaplan, *Fritz Lang: A Guide to References and Resources*

Die Spinnen (The Spiders)
Part I: Der goldene See (The Golden Lake)
As screenwriter and director. Ph: Emil Schünemann. Art dir: Otto Hunte,
Carl Ludwig Kirmse, Hermann Warm, Heinrich Umlauff.
Cast: Carl de Vogt (Kay Hoog), Ressel Orla (Lio Sha), Lil Dagover (Sun
priestess), Paul Morgan (expert), Georg John (Dr. Telphas), Rudolf [Bruno]
Lettinger (Terry Landon), Edgar Pauly (Four-Finger John), Paul Biensfeldt,
Friedrich Kühne, Harry Frank.
(Decla-Bioscop, approx. 81 mins.)

*". . . impressively staged, combining location shooting with realistic studio
interiors designed by Otto Hunte. The decor was often exotic. Notable in this
regard was the sequence in the Inca City, a pastiche of temples and statues
amidst luxuriant tropical foliage."*
Frederick Ott, *The Films of Fritz Lang*

Harakiri (Madame Butterfly)
As director. Sc: Max Jungk, based on the play *Madame Butterfly* by John
Luther Long and David Belasco. Ph: Max Fassbender.
Art dir: Heinrich Umlauff.
Cast: Paul Biensfeldt (Daimyo Tokujawa), Lil Dagover (O-Take-San, his

daughter), Georg John (Buddhist monk), Meinhart Maur (Prince Matahari), Rudolf Lettinger (Karan), Erner Hübsch (Kin-Be-Araki), Käte Küster (Hanake, O-Take-San's servant), Niels [Nils] Prien (Olaf J. Anderson), Herta Hedén (Eva), Harry Frank, Joseph Roemer, Loni Nest (child). (Decla-Bioscop, approx. 108 mins.)
"An unimportant minor work . . ."
Michael Töteberg, *Fritz Lang mit Selbstzeugnissen und Bilddokumenten*

1920
Die Spinnen (The Spiders)
Part II: Das Brillantenschiff (The Diamond Ship)
As *screenwriter and director.* Ph: Karl Freund. Art dir: Otto Hunte, Carl Ludwig Kirmse, Hermann Warm, Heinrich Umlauff.
Cast: Carl de Vogt (Kay Hoog), Ressel Orla (Lio Sha), Georg John (the Master), Rudolf Lettinger (Terry Landon, diamond king), Thea Zander (Ellen, his daughter), Reiner-Steiner (Captain of the Diamond Ship), Friedrich Kühne (All-Hab-Mah, the Yogi), Edgar Pauly (Four-Finger John), Meinhard Maur (the Chinese man), Paul Morgan (the Jew), K. A. Römer, Gilda Langer, Paul Biensfeldt, Lil Dagover (Priestess of the Sun God). (Decla-Bioscop, approx. 95 mins.)
". . . a thoroughly entertaining cliff-hanger, The Spiders has all the ingredients of the pioneering American and French silent serials."
Kevin Thomas, *The Los Angeles Times*

Das wandernde Bild (The Wandering Image)
As *co-screenwriter (with Thea von Harbou) and director.*
Ph: Guido Seeber. Art dir: Otto Hunte, Erich Kettelhut.
Cast: Mia May (Irmgard Vanderheit), Hans Marr (Georg Vanderheit John, her brother), Rudolf Klein-Rohden [Klein-Rogge] (Will Brand), Harry Frank, Loni Nest. (May-Film GmbH, approx. 87 mins.)
"The action is said to be punctuated by an explosion, avalanches, cliff-hanger chases, a fall from a mountain, 'almost too many good things.'"
Lotte Eisner, *Fritz Lang*

1921
Kämpfende Herzen (aka Die Vier um die Frau)
(Fighting Hearts or Four Around a Woman)
As *co-screenwriter (with Thea von Harbou) and director.* Based on a piece by R. E. Vanloo. Ph: Otto Kanturek. Art dir: Ernst Meiwers, Hans Jacoby. Cast: Carola Toelle (Florence Yquem), Hermann Boettcher (her father), Ludwig Hartau (Harry Yquem), Anton Edthofer (Werner Krafft/William, his brother), Rudolf Klein-Rogge (Upton), Robert Forster-Larrinaga (Meunier), Lilli Lohrer (first maid), Harry Frank (Bobby), Leonhard Haskel/Paul Rehkopf (swindlers), Gottfried Huppertz (headwaiter), Hans Lüpschütz (hoodlum), Lisa von Marton (Margot), Erika Unruh (prostitute), Paul Morgan (hustler), Edgar Pauly (man), Gerhard Ritterband (newspaper boy). (Decla-Bioscop)

"*Outside the European retrospectives [it is] still more or less unknown in the United States...*"
Paolo Cherchi Usai and Lorenzo Codelli,
Before Caligari: German Cinema, 1895–1920

Der müde Tod (The Weary Death, aka Destiny)
As co-screenwriter (with Thea von Harbou) and director. Ph: Erich
Nitzschmann, Hermann Saalfrank (old German episodes), Fritz Arno
Wagner (Venetian, Oriental, and Chinese episodes).
Art dir: Robert Herlth (Chinese episode), Walter Röhrig (German episode),
Hermann Warm (Venetian and Oriental episode). Costumes: Umlauff
Museum, Hamburg. Lighting: Robert Hegerwald. Music: Peter Schirman.
Cast: Lil Dagover (young woman), Bernhard Goetzke (Death), Walter
Janssen (lover), Hans Sternberg (mayor), Carl Rückert (vicar), Max Adalbert
(lawyer), Erich Pabst (teacher), Paul Rehkopf (sexton), Hermann Picha
(tailor), Edgar Klitzsch (doctor), Georg John (beggar), Marie Wismar (old
woman), Aloisha Lehnert (mother).
Oriental episode: Lil Dagover (Zobeide), Walter Janssen (Frank), Bernhard
Goetzke (El Mot), Rudolf Klein-Rogge (dervish), Eduard von Winterstein
(caliph), Erika Unruh (Aisha).
Venetian episode: Lil Dagover (Fiametta), Rudolf Klein-Rogge (Girolamo),
Lewis Brody (Moor), Lothar Müthel [Mütel] (confidante), Lina Paulsen
(nurse), Walter Janssen (Giovanfrancesco).
Chinese episode: Lil Dagover (Tiaotsien), Walter Janssen (Liang), Bernhard
Goetzke (archer), Paul Biensfeldt (A Hi, magician), Karl Huszar (emperor),
Max Adalbert (treasurer), Paul Neumann (hangman).
(Decla-Bioscop, 122 mins.)
"*The film remains one of Lang's most brilliant cinematic achievements.*"
Roger Manvell and Heinrich Fraenkel, *The German Cinema*

1922
Doktor Mabuse, der Spieler (Dr. Mabuse, the Gambler)
Part I: Der grosse Spieler—ein Bild der Zeit
(The Great Gambler—A Picture of the Time)
Part II: Inferno: Ein Spiel von Menschen unserer Zeit
(Inferno: A Play About People of Our Times)
As co-screenwriter (with Thea von Harbou) and director. Based on the novel
by Norbert Jacques. Ph: Carl Hoffmann. Art dir: Carl Stahl-Urach, Otto
Hunte, Erich Kettelhut, Karl Vollbrecht. Costumes: Vally Reinecke.
Cast: Rudolf Klein-Rogge (Dr. Mabuse), Aud Egede Nissen (Cara Carozza,
the dancer), Gertrude Welcker (Countess Told), Alfred Abel (Count Told),
Bernhard Goetzke (Detective von Wenk), Paul Richter (Edgar Hull), Robert
Forster-Larrinaga (Dr. Mabuse's servant), Hans Adalbert Schlettow (Georg,
the chauffeur), Georg John (Pesche), Karl Huszar (Hawasch, manager of the
counterfeiting factory), Grete Berger (Fine, Mabuse's servant), Julius
Falkenstein (Karsten, Wenk's friend), Lydia Potechina (the Russian woman),
Julius E. Herrmann (Schramm, the proprietor), Karl Platen (Told's servant),

Anita Berber (dancer), Paul Biensfeldt (man with the pistol), Edgar Pauly (fat man), Lil Dagover, Julie Brandt, Auguste Prasch-Grevenberg, Adele Sandrock, Max Adalbert, Gustav Botz, Heinrich Gotho, Leonhard Haskel, Erner Hübsch, Gottfried Huppertz, Hans Junkermann, Adolf Klein, Erich Pabst, Hans Sternberg, Olaf Storm, Erich Walter, Willi Schmidt-Gentner. (Decla-Bioscop/Ufa *Der Grosse Speiler*, 120 mins.; *Inferno*, 93 mins.)
"Dr. Mabuse der Spieler *combined expressionist techniques, a* Fantômas *style of thriller, and the growing German fascination with the superman (in this case, the super-criminal)."*
David Robinson, *The History of World Cinema*

1924
Die Nibelungen (The Nibelungs)
Part I: Siegfried
Part II: Kriemhilds Rache (Kriemhild's Revenge)

As co-screenwriter *(with Thea von Harbou) and director. Based on* Das Nibelungenlied *and Norse sagas. Ph:* Carl Hoffman, Günther Rittau, and Walter Ruttman. *Art dir:* Otto Hunte, Erich Kettelhut, Karl Vollbrecht. Music: Gottfried Huppertz. Costumes: Paul Gerd Guderian, Aenne Willkomm, Heinrich Umlauff. *Makeup:* Otto Genath.
Cast: Paul Richter (Siegfried), Margarethe Schön (Kriemhild), Theodor Loos (King Gunther), Hanna Ralph (Brunhild), Georg John (Mime, the Smith, and Alberich in I, Blaodel in II), Gertrud Arnold (Queen Ute), Hans Carl Müller (Gerenot), Erwin Biswanger (Giselher), Bernhard Goetzke (Volker von Alzey), Hans Adalbert Schlettow (Hagen Tronje), Rudolf Rittner (Markgraf Rüdiger von Bechlarn), Hardy von François (Dankwart), Fritz Alberti (Dietrich von Bern), Georg August Koch (Hildebrand), Rudolf Klein-Rogge (King Etzel), Hubert Heinrich (Werbel), Grete Berger (Hun), Frieda Richard (lecturer), Georg Jurowski (priest), Iris Roberts (page), Rose Lichtenstein.
(Decla-Bioscop/Ufa *Siegfried*, 130 mins.; *Kriemhilds Rache*, 95 mins.)
"For sheer pictorial beauty of structural architecture,
Siegfried *has never been equalled."*
Paul Rotha, *The Film Till Now*

1927
Metropolis

As co-screenwriter *(with Thea von Harbou) and director. Ph:* Karl Freund, Günther Rittau, Eugen Schüfftan (special effects). Art dir: Otto Hunte, Erich Kettelhut, Karl Vollbrecht. Sculptures: Walter Schultze-Mittendorf. Costumes: Aenne Willkomm. Music: Gottfried Huppertz.
Cast: Brigitte Helm (Maria/ the mechanical Maria), Alfred Abel (Joh Fredersen), Gustav Fröhlich (Freder), Rudolf Klein-Rogge (Rotwang), Fritz Rasp (Slim), Theodor Loos (Josaphat), Heinrich George (Grot, the foreman), Olaf Storm (Jan), Hanns Leo Reich (Marinus), Heinrich Gotho (master of ceremonies), Margarete Lanner (woman in the car), Max Dietze Georg John/Walter Kühle/Arthur Reinhard/Erwin Vater (workers)/Grete Berger/Olly Böheim/Ellen Frey/Lisa Gray/Rose Lichtenstein/Helene Weigel

(female workers); Beatrice Gargal/Anny Hintze/Margarete Lanner/Helen von Münchhofen/Hilde Woitscheff (women in the eternal garden); Fritz Alberti (robot).
(Ufa, 150 mins.)

"One of the last examples of the imaginative—but often monstrous—grandeur of the Golden Period of the German film, Metropolis *is a spectacular example of Expressionist design (grouped human beings are used architecturally) with moments of almost incredible beauty and power (the visionary sequence about the Tower of Babel), absurd ineptitudes (the lovesick hero in his preposterous knickerbockers), and oddities that defy analysis (the robot vamp's bizarre, lewd wink). It's a wonderful, stupefying folly."*
Pauline Kael, 5001 Nights at the Movies

1928
Spione (Spies)
As co-screenwriter (with Thea von Harbou), director and producer.
Based on von Harbou's novel. Ph: Fritz Arno Wagner. Art dir: Otto Hunte, Karl Vollbrecht. Music: Werner R. Heymann.
Cast: Rudolf Klein-Rogge (Haghi), Gerda Maurus (Sonia), Lien Deyers (Kitty), Louis Ralph (Morrier), Craighall Sherry (Police Chief Jason), Willy Fritsch (No. 326), Paul Hörbiger (Franz, the chauffeur), Lupu Pick (Dr. Matsumoto), Fritz Rasp (colonel Jullusic), Hertha von Walther (Lady Leslane), Julius Falkenstein (hotel manager), Georg John (train conductor), Paul Rehkopf (hoodlum), Hermann Vallentin, Grete Berger.
(Fritz-Lang-Film GmbH/Ufa, 140 mins.)

"One of his major silent films. True, Dr. Mabuse *came first, but the under-rated* Spione *was far better made; aside from a superb sense of composition, an element missing from the earlier work, this imitation is technically more creative and fluid, with a faster pace and admirably controlled acting."*
Paul M. Jensen, *The Films of Fritz Lang*

1929
Die Frau im Mond (Woman in the Moon)
As director and producer. Sc: Thea von Harbou, based on her novel.
Ph: Curt Courant, Oskar Fischinger, Otto Kanturek. Special effects: Konstantin Tschetwerikoff. Art dir: Otto Hunte, Emil Hasler, Karl Vollbrecht. Backdrop photographs: Horst von Harbou. Music: Willi Schmidt-Gentner. Technical advisers: Dr. Gustav Wolff, Joseph Danilowatz, Prof. Herman Oberth, Willy Ley.
Cast: Klaus Pohl (Prof. George Manfeldt); Willy Fritsch (Wolf Helius); Gustav von Wangenheim (Hans Windegger); Gerda Maurus (Frieda Venten); Gustl Stark-Gstettenbauer (Gustav); Fritz Rasp (Walt Turner); Tilla Durieux/Hermann Vallentin/Max Zilzer/Mahmud Terja Bey/Borwin Walth (financiers); Margarete Kupfer (Mrs. Hippolt); Max Maximilian (Grotjan, Helius's chauffeur); Alexa von Porembsky (flower vendor); Gerhard Dammann (foreman); Heinrich Gotho, Karl Platen, Alfred Loretto, Edgar Pauly, Josephine (the Mouse).
(Fritz-Lang-Film GmbH/Ufa, 146 mins.)

"Its silly melodramatics aside, the film offers a stunning and remarkably prophetic depiction of a flight to the moon."
Gene Wright, *The Science Fiction Image*

1931
M

As *director*. Sc: Thea von Harbou. Ph: Fritz Arno Wagner. Camera operator: Karl Vass. Art dir: Karl Vollbrecht, Emil Hasler. Backdrop photographs: Horst von Harbou. Music: Excerpts from Grieg's *Peer Gynt*. Sound: Adolf Jansen. Editor: Paul Falkenberg.
Cast: Peter Lorre (Hans Beckert), Ellen Widmann (Frau Beckmann), Inge Landgut (Elsie, the child), Gustaf Gründgens (Schränker), Fritz Odemar (Cheater), Paul Kemp (pickpocket), Theo Lingen (confidence man), Ernst Stahl-Nachbaur (police chief), Franz Stein (minister), Otto Wernicke (Chief Inspector Lohmann), Theodor Loos (Commissioner Groeber), Georg John (blind peddler), Rudolf Blümner (attorney), Karl Platen (watchman), Gerhard Bienert (police secretary), Rosa Valetti (servant), Hertha von Walther (prostitute), Friedrich Gnass (burglar), Josef Almas, Carl Balhaus, Hans Behal, Josef Dahmen, Hugo Döblin, J. A. Eckhoff, Else Ehser, Karl Elzer, Erwin Faber, Ilse Fürstenberg, Heinrich Gotho, Heinrich Gretler, Günther Hadank, Robert Hartberg, Ernst Paul Hempel, Oskar Höcker, Albert Hörrmann, Albert Karchow, Werner Kepich, Hermann Krehan, Rose Lichtenstein, Lotte Löbinger, Sigurd Lohde, Alfred Loretto, Paul Mederow, Margarete Melzer, Trude Moos, Hadrian M. Netto, Maja Norden, Edgar Pauly, Klaus Pohl, Franz Polland, Paul Rehkopf, Hans Ritter, Max Sablotzki, Alexander Sascha, Leonard Steckel, Karl Heinz Stroux, Wolf Trutz, Otto Waldis, Borwin Walth, Rolf Wanka, Ernst Wulf, Bruno Ziener, Swinborne, Gelin Wannemann, Rhaden, and Agnes Schultz-Lichterfeld.
(Seymour Nebenzahl for Nero-Film A.G., 117 mins.)
"It was not only Lang's first talkie, but his first important film after the pretentious duds he had made during the stabilized period. M again reaches the level of his earlier films, Destiny *[aka* Der müde Tod*] and* Nibelungen, *and moreover surpasses them in virtuosity."*
Siegfried Kracauer, *From Caligari to Hitler*

1933
Das Testament des Dr. Mabuse *(The Last Will of Dr. Mabuse)*

As *co-screenwriter (with Thea von Harbou) and director*. Based on characters from the Norbert Jacques novel. Ph: Fritz Arno Wagner, Karl Vass. Art dir: Karl Vollbrecht, Emil Hasler. Music: Hans Erdmann.
Cast: Rudolf Klein-Rogge (Dr. Mabuse), Oskar Beregi (Dr. Baum), Karl Meixner (landlord), Theodor Loos (Dr. Kramm, assistant to Baum), Otto Wernicke (Detective Lohmann), Klaus Pohl (Lohmann's assistant, Müller), Wera Liessem (Lilli), Gustav Diessl (Thomas Kent), Camilla Spira (Jewel-Anna), Rudolf Schündler (Hardy), Theo Lingen (Hardy's friend), Paul Oskar Höcker (Bredow), Paul Henckels (lithographer), Georg John (Baum's servant), Ludwig Stössel (worker), Hadrian M. Netto (Nicolai Grigoriew), Paul Bernd (blackmailer), Henry Pless (Dunce), A. E. Licho (Dr. Hauser),

Karl Platen/Anna Goltz/Heinrich Gretler (sanitarium assistants), Gerhard Bienert/Paul Rehkopf/Franz Stein/Eduard Wesener/Bruno Ziener/Michael von Newlinski, Heinrich Gotho/Josef Dahmen.
(Seymour Nebenzahl for Nero-Film A.G., 122 mins.)

"Lang is the High Priest of the psychological film. From the megalomaniacal Dr. ("I am the State!") Mabuse in his early film, Mabuse, the Gambler; *through the coldly psychotic master-criminal Haghi, in* Spies; *the nymphomaniacal robot woman and her demented creator Rotwang, in* Metropolis; *the lust-murderer in* M; *the blood-lust of a mob in* Fury; *and now the paranoiac Professor Baum in* The Last Will of Dr. Mabuse, *Fritz Lang has dissected several of the most important aberrations that sometimes afflict the human mind."*
Herman G. Weinberg, *Saint Cinema*

1934
Liliom

As director. Sc: Robert Liebmann, with dialogue by Bernard Zimmer, based on the play by Ferenc [Franz] Molnár. Ph: Rudolph Maté, Louis Née. Art dir: Paul Colin, René Renoux. Music: Jean Lenoir, Franz Wachsmann (Franz Waxman). Assistant dir: Jacques Pierre Feydeau.
Cast: Charles Boyer (Liliom), Madeleine Ozeray (Julie), Florelle (Madame Muscat), Robert Arnoux (strong man), Roland Toutain (sailor), Alexandre Rignault (Hollinger), Henri Richaud (commissioner), Richard Barencey (purgatory policeman), Antonin Artaud (knife grinder), Raoul Marco (detective), Pierre Alcover (Alfred), Léon Arnel (clerk), René Stern (cashier), Maximilienne (Madame Menoux), Mimmi Funès (Marie), Viviane Romance (cigarette girl), Mila Parély (secretary in heaven); Rosa Valetti, Lily Latté.
(Erich Pommer for 20th–Fox Europa, 120 mins.)

"A film of real worth. It is based on Molnár's beautiful play about a poor but charming crook. With the exception of a well-handled village fair, it remains ordinary enough until Liliom dies and ascends to Heaven. Now the screen spread before us a light-hearted picture-postcard sort of Paris, with clouds and stars and noisy choirs of angels, cherubs escaped from some circus who look rather like mechanical rabbits, and bells, more and more bells ringing out during this vertiginous ascension as lovely as the best things in Melies."
Maurice Bardèche and Robert Brasillac, *The History of Motion Pictures*

1936
Fury

As co-screenwriter and director. Sc: Bartlett Cormack, based on the story "Mob Rule" by Norman Krasna. Ph: Joseph Ruttenberg. Art dir: Cedric Gibbons, William A. Horning, Edwin B. Willis. Costumes: Dolly Tree. Music: Franz Waxman. Editor: Frank Sullivan. Assistant dir: Horace Hough.
Cast: Spencer Tracy (Joe Wilson), Sylvia Sidney (Katherine Grant), Walter Abel (district attorney), Bruce Cabot (Kirby Dawson), Edward Ellis (sheriff), Walter Brennan (Bugs Meyers), Frank Albertson (Charlie), George Walcott (Tom), Arthur Stone (Durkin), Morgan Wallace (Fred Garrett), George Chandler (Milton Jackson), Roger Gray (Stranger), Edwin Maxwell

(Vickery), Howard Hickman (governor), Jonathan Hale (defense attorney),
Leila Bennett (Edna Hopper), Esther Dale (Mrs. Whipple), Helen Flint
(Franchette), Frank Sully (dynamiter).
(Joseph L. Mankiewicz for Metro-Goldwyn-Mayer, 94 mins.)
*"The same power to catch vividly the truthful detail makes the lynching
[scene] of almost unbearable horror. I am not trying to exaggerate, but the
brain does flinch at each recurring flick of truth in much the same way as at
the grind-grind of an electric road-drill: the horrible laughter and inflated
nobility of the good citizens, the youth leaping on a bar and shouting, 'Let's
have some fun,' the regiment of men and women marching down the road into
the face of the camera, arm in arm, laughing and excited like recruits on the
first day of a war, the boy singing out at the Sheriff, 'I'm Popeye the Sailor-
man,' at last the first stone, until the building is ablaze, the innocent man is
suffocating behind the bars, and a woman holds her baby up to see the fire.
Any other film this year is likely to be dwarfed by Herr Lang's
extraordinary achievement."*
Graham Greene, *Graham Greene on Film*

1937
You Only Live Once
As *director*. Sc: Gene Towne and Graham Baker, based on a story by Towne.
Ph: Leon Shamroy. Art dir: Alexander Toluboff. Music: Alfred Newman.
Song: "A Thousand Dreams of You" by Louis Alter and Paul Francis
Webster. *Editor*: Daniel Mandell. Assistant dir: Robert Lee.
Cast: Sylvia Sidney (Joan Graham), Henry Fonda (Eddie Taylor), Barton
MacLane (Stephen Whitney), Jean Dixon (Bonnie Graham), William
Gargan (Father Dolan), Warren Hymer (Buggsy), Charles "Chic" Sale
(Ethan), Margaret Hamilton (Hester), Guinn Williams (Rogers), Jerome
Cowan (Dr. Hill), John Wray (warden), Jonathan Hale (district attorney),
Ward Bond (guard), Wade Boteler (policeman), Henry Taylor (Kozderonas),
Jean Stoddard (stenographer), Ben Hall (messenger), Walter De Palma.
(Walter Wanger for United Artists, 86 mins.)
*"Visually striking, the composition and lighting, in their brooding, atmospheric
effects, sometimes recall those of expressionism. Though its plot is largely
melodramatic, the total effect of the film (much helped by the touching
warmth of Sylvia Sidney and Fonda) is very powerful."*
Georges Sadoul, *Dictionary of Films*

1938
You and Me
As *director and producer*. Sc: Virginia Van Upp, based on a story by Norman
Krasna. Ph: Charles Lang, Jr. Art dir: Hans Dreier, Ernst Fegté. Set
decoration: A. E. Freudeman. Music: Kurt Weill, Boris Morros. Songs: "The
Right Guy for Me" by Weill and Sam Coslow; "You and Me" by Ralph
Freed and Frederick Hollander. Musical adviser: Phil Boutelje.
Editor: Paul Weatherwax.
Cast: Sylvia Sidney (Helen Roberts), George Raft (Joe Dennis), Robert
Cummings (Jim), Barton MacLane (Mickey), Roscoe Karns (Cuffy), Harry

Carey (Mr. Morris), Warren Hymer (Gimpy), George E. Stone (Patsy),
Guinn Williams (cab driver), Vera Gordon (Mrs. Levine), Carol Paige (torch
singer) Bernadene Hayes (Nellie); Egon Brecher (Mr. Levine), Joyce
Compton (curly blonde), Cecil Cunningham (Mrs. Morris), Willard
Robertson (Dayton), Roger Gray (attendant), Adrian Morris (Knucks), (Red)
Harlan Briggs (McTavish), Paula de Cardo and Harriette Haddon (cigarette
girls), Matt McHugh (newcomer), Paul Newlan (bouncer), Margaret Randall
(clothes thief), Jack Pennick, Kit Guard, Fern Emmett, Max Barwyn, James
McNamara, Blanca Vischer, Herta Lynd, Jimmie Dundee, Terry Ray, Sheila
Darcy, Jack Mullhall [Mulhall], Sam Ash,
Ruth Rogers, Julia Faye, Arthur Hoyt.
(Fritz Lang for Paramount, 90 mins.)
*"Genuinely odd but likable film about an ex-con who falls in love with Sydney
and marries her, unaware that she's a former jailbird herself. Unusual mix of
gangsterism, sentiment, Damon Runyonesque comedy, and music (by Kurt
Weill!)—with even some rhythmic dialogue!"*
Leonard Maltin, *Leonard Maltin's TV Movies and Video Guide*

1940
The Return of Frank James
As director. Sc: Sam Hellman. Ph (Technicolor): George Barnes, William V.
Skall. Art dir: Richard Day, Wiard B. Ihnen. Set decoration: Thomas Little.
Costumes: Travis Banton. Sound: W. D. Flick, Roger Heman. Music: David
Buttolph. Technical dir: Natalie Kalmus. Editor: Walter Thompson.
Associate: Morgan Padelford.
Cast: Henry Fonda (Frank James), Gene Tierney (Eleanor Stone), Jackie
Cooper (Clem), Henry Hull (Major Rufus Todd), J. Edward Bromberg
(George Runyan), Donald Meek (McCoy), Eddie Collins (station agent),
John Carradine (Bob Ford), George Barbier (judge), Ernest Whitman
(Pinky), Charles Tannen (Charlie Ford), Lloyd Corrigan (Randolph Stone),
Russell Hicks (prosecutor), Victor Kilian (preacher), Edward McWade
(Colonel Jackson), George Chandler (Roy), Irving Bacon (bystander), Frank
Shannon (sheriff), Barbara Pepper (Nellie Blane), Stymie Beard (Mose),
William Pawley/Frank Sully (actors), Louis Mason (watchman), Davidson
Clark (officer).
(Darryl F. Zanuck and Kenneth Macgowan for 20th Century–Fox, 92 mins.)
*"It is thematically central to the works of Fritz Lang, directing his first
Western. In Lang, individuals are at the mercy of groups of people who
represent their particular environments—whether they are allowed to go free
depends not on justice but on the whims of the people. Not much action,
but Lang creates a flavorful Western milieu."*
Danny Peary, *Guide For the Film Fanatic*

1941
Western Union
As director. Sc: Robert Carson, based on a Zane Grey novel. Ph
(Technicolor): Edward Cronjager, Allen M. Davey. Art dir: Richard Day,
Albert Hugsett. Set decoration: Thomas Little. Costumes: Travis Banton.

Music: David Buttolph. Technical dir: Natalie Kalmus. Associate: Morgan
Padelford. Sound: Bernard Fredericks, Roger Heman. Editor: Robert
Bischoff.
Cast: Robert Young (Richard Blake), Randolph Scott (Vance Shaw), Dean
Jagger (Edward Creighton), Virginia Gilmore (Sue Creighton), John
Carradine (Doc Murdoch), Slim Summerville (Herman), Chill Wills
(Homer), Barton MacLane (Jack Slade), Russell Hicks (governor), Victor
Kilian (Charlie), Minor Watson (Pat Grogan), George Chandler (Herb),
Chief Big Tree/Chief Spotted Horse/Chief Thundercloud (Indian leaders),
Dick Rich (Porky), Harry Strang (henchman), Charles Middleton
(stagecoach rider), Addison Richards (Captain Harlow),
Irving Bacon (barber), J. Edward Bromberg.
(Harry Joe Brown for 20th Century–Fox, 95 mins.)
*"In [Lang's] Westerns, the mise-en-scène is simple, it suffices to serve the plot
... the discretion and the peculiarity of the camera movements, the sobriety of
the acting, American and classical, make for very austere works, even down to
the choice of landscapes, which are a little too bleak. In the living universe of
the Western they jar, almost annoyingly. It's true that this sobriety emphasizes
remarkably the moral dignity of the heroes, which is very well rendered by the
cold concentration the actors bring to the parts. This lyrical rigor reminds one
of Hawks,
minus the humor."*
Luc Moullet, *Fritz Lang*

Man Hunt

As director. Sc: Dudley Nichols, based on the novel *Rogue Male* by Geoffrey
Household. Ph: Arthur Miller. Art dir: Richard Day, Wiard B. Ihnen. Set
decoration: Thomas Little. Costumes: Travis Banton. Music: Alfred
Newman. Sound: Eugene Grossman, Roger Herman. Editor: Allen McNeil.
Cast: Walter Pidgeon (Captain Thorndike), Joan Bennett (Jerry), George
Sanders (Quive-Smith), John Carradine (Mr. Jones), Roddy McDowall
(Vaner), Ludwig Stössel (Doctor), Heather Thatcher (Lady Risborough),
Frederick Walcock (Lord Risborough), Roger Imhof (Captain Jensen), Egon
Brecher (Whiskers), Lester Matthews (major), Holmes Herbert
(Farnsworth), Eily Malyon (postmistress), Arno Frey (police lieutenant),
Fredrik Vogeding (ambassador), Lucien Prival (man with umbrella), Herbert
Evans (Reeves), Keith Hitchcock (Bobby).
(Kenneth Macgowan for 20th Century–Fox, 102 mins.)
"Much of Man Hunt *takes place in an improbable, chiaroscuro London,
redolent of Pabst's* Dreigroschenoper, *where shadows lurk down cobbled alleys,
and the most stolidly British face may suddenly twitch with Nazi fanaticism.
Lang builds the tension slowly and inexorably, tightening the trap of the hero's
isolation—his sole ally a Cockney prostitute, touchingly played by Joan
Bennett."*
Philip Kemp, *World Film Directors: Volume One, 1890–1945*

1943
Hangmen Also Die

As co-screenwriter and director. Sc: Bertolt Brecht and John Wexley, based on a story by Lang and Brecht. Ph: James Wong Howe. Art dir: William Darling. Costumes: Julie Heron. Music: Hanns Eisler. Song: "No Surrender," by Eisler and Sam Coslow. Sound: Fred Lau. Editor: Gene Fowler, Jr. *Assistant production* manager: Carley Harriman. Assistant dir: Walter Mayo, Fred Pressburger.

Cast: Brian Donlevy (Dr. Franz Svoboda), Walter Brennan (Prof. Novotny), Anna Lee (Mascha Novotny), Gene Lockhart (Emil Czaka), Dennis O'Keefe (Jan Horak), Alexander Granach (Alois Gruber), Margaret Wycherly (Ludmilla Novotny), Nana Bryant (Mrs. Novotny), Billy Roy (Beda Novotny), Hans von Twardowski (Reinhard Heydrich), Tonio Selwart (Haas, Gestapo chief), Jonathan Hale (Dedic), Lionel Stander (cabby), Byron Foulger (Bartos), Virginia Farmer (landlady), Louis Donath (Shumer), Sarah Padden (Miss Dvorak), Edmund MacDonald (Dr. Pillar), George Irving (Necval), James Bush (worker), Arno Frey (Itnut), Lester Sharpe (Rudy), Arthur Loft (General Vortruba), William Farnum (Viktorin), Reinhold Schünzel (Inspector Ritter), Philip Merivale.

(Arnold Pressburger, Fritz Lang and T. W. Baumfeld for United Artists, 140 mins.)

". . . it is rich with clever melodrama, over-maestro directional touches, and the sort of Querschnitt sophistication for detail which Lang always has. It's most interesting as a memory album. There's a heroine straight out of the Berlin of the middle twenties, and the Nazis are also archaic, nicely-presented types . . ."
James Agee, *Agee on Film*

1944
Ministry of Fear

As director. Sc: Seton I. Miller, based on the Graham Greene novel. Ph: Henry Sharp. Art dir: Hans T. Dreier, Hal Pereira. Music: Victor Young. Set decoration: Bert Granger. Editor: Archie Marshek. Assistant dir: George Templeton.

Cast: Ray Milland (Stephen Neale), Marjorie Reynolds (Carla Hilfe), Carl Esmond (Willi Hilfe)k, Dan Duryea (Travers), Hillary Brooke (second Mrs. Bellane), Percy Waram (Inspector Prentice), Erskine Sanford (Mr. Rennit), Thomas Louden (Mr. Newland), Alan Napier (Dr. Forrester), Helena Grant (Mrs. Merrick), Aminta Dyne (the first Mrs. Bellane), Mary Field (Miss Penteel), Byron Foulger (Newby), Lester Matthews (Dr. Morton), Eustace Wyatt (blind man).

(Seton I. Miller for Paramount, 84 mins.)

"Little to do with the novel, but a watchable, well-detailed little thriller on Hitchcock lines, once you forgive the usual phoney Hollywood England."
Leslie Halliwell, *Leslie Halliwell's Film Guide*

The Woman in the Window
As *director*. Sc: Nunnally Johnson, based on the novel *Once Off Guard*
by J. H. Wallis. Ph: Milton Krasner. Special effects: Vernon Walker. Art dir:
Duncan Cramer. Set decoration: Julia Heron. Costumes: Muriel King. Music:
Arthur Lange. Editor: Marjorie Johnson. Assistant dir: Richard Harlan.
Cast: Edward G. Robinson (Professor Wanley), Joan Bennett (Alice Reed),
Raymond Massey (Frank Lalor), Dan Duryea (Heidt), Edmond Breon (Dr.
Barkstone), Thomas E. Jackson (Inspector Jackson), Arthur Loft (Mazard),
Dorothy Peterson (Mrs. Wanley), Carol Cameron (Elsie), Bobby Blake
(Dickie), Frank Dawson.
(Nunnally Johnson for International Pictures/RKO, 99 mins.)
*"Lang was allowed to develop the world of his imagination: Night scenes
dominating an evocation of an urban environment, the light shining on a rain-
swept corner, the raincoated figures drifting by, the sodden reflections in shop
windows, the harsh revelations of character in subtle glances and intonations."*
Charles Higham, *The Art of the American film, 1900–1971*

1945
Scarlet Street
As *director*. Sc: Dudley Nichols, based on the novel and play *La Chienne* by
Georges de la Fouchardière (with Mouézy-Eon). Ph: Milton Krasner. Special
photographic effects: John P. Fulton. Art dir: Alexander Golitzen. Set
decoration: Russel A. Gausman, Carl Lawrence. Costumes: Travis Banton.
Paintings: John Decker. Music: Hans J. Salter. Editor: Arthur Hilton.
Assistant dir: Melville Shyer.
Cast: Edward G. Robinson (Christopher Cross), Joan Bennett (Kitty), Dan
Duryea (Johnny); Margaret Lindsay (Millie), Rosalind Ivan (Adèle), Samuel
S. Hinds (Charles Pringle), Jess Barker (Janeway), Arthur Loft (Dellarowe),
Vladimir Sokoloff (Pop Lejon), Charles Kemper (Patch-Eye), Russell Hicks
(Hogarth), Anita Bolster (Mrs. Michaels), Cyrus W. Kendell (Nick), Fred
Essler (Marchetti), Edgar Dearing/Tom Dillon (police officers), Chuck
Hamilton (chauffeur), Gus Glassmire/Howard Mitchell/Ralph Littlefield/
Sherry Hall/Jack Stratham (workers), Rodney Bell (Barney), Byron Foulger
(landlord), Will Wright (cashier).
(Walter Wanger for Diana Productions/Universal, 102 mins.)
*"I like almost all of Lang's movie: the slick New York streets, flashing black
and white night shadows and contrasts; the contemptible behavior of Kitty and
Johnny; and the meek, masochistic Chris. But the ending pales compared to
Renoir's treatment: there we see the character years later, a bum, but one at
peace with himself, watching rich people carry off a painting for which they've
paid an enormous sum, one of his. Simon manages to laugh at it all—the folly
of his life, the folly of everyone's life. It's no less mean an existence, he's
saying, but less bleak and self-pitying than Lang's disposition of Chris. 'La
Chienne' translates as 'the bitch,' who emerges here as a triumvirate: wife,
mistress, and life itself."*
Barry Gifford, *The Devil Thumbs a Ride*

1946
Cloak and Dagger

As *director*. Sc: Ring Lardner, Jr., and Albert Maltz, based on a story by
Boris Ingster and John Larkin, suggested by a book by Corey Ford and
Alastair MacBain. Ph: Sol Polito. Art dir: Max Parker. Set decoration: Walter
Hilford. Special effects: Harry Barndollar, Edwin DuPar. Music: Max Steiner.
Editor: Christian Nyby. Assistant dir: Russ Saunders. Technical adviser:
Michael Burke.
Cast: Gary Cooper (Prof. Alvah Jasper), Lilli Palmer (Gina), Robert Alda
(Pinkie), Vladimir Sokoloff (Dr. Polda), J. Edward Bromberg (Trenk),
Marjorie Hoshelle (Ann Dawson), Ludwig Stössel (the German), Helene
Thimig (Katherine Loder), Dan Seymour (Marsoli), Marc Lawrence (Luigi),
James Flavin (Col. Walsh), Pat O'Moore (the Englishman), Charles Marsh
(Enrich), Larry Olson (Tommy), Don Turner (Erich), Rosalind Lyons,
Connie Gilchrist.
(Milton Sperling for United States Pictures/Warner Bros., 106 mins.)
*"Lang's last movie about the Nazis has its moments of genuine excitement
and some of visual significance, but overall the film is uneven."*
Robert A. Armour, *Fritz Lang*

1948
Secret Beyond the Door

As *director and co-producer*. Sc: Silvia Richards, based on the story "The
Secret Beyond the Door" by Rufus King. Ph: Stanley Cortez. Set decoration:
Russell A. Gausman, John Austin. Production designer: Max Parker.
Music: Miklos Rosza.
Editor: Arthur Hilton. Assistant dir: William Holland.
Cast: Joan Bennett (Celia Lamphere), Barbara O'Neil (Miss Robey), Michael
Redgrave (Mark Lamphere), Anne Revere (Caroline Lamphere), Natalie
Schafer (Edith Potter), Paul Cavanagh
(Rick Barrett), Anabel Shaw (society girl), Rosa Rey (Paquita),
James Seay (Bob Dwight), Mark Dennis (David), Donna De Mario (gypsy),
David Cota (her lover), Celia Moore.
(Fritz Lang and Walter Wanger for Diana Productions/Universal, 99 mins.)
*"As labored as the story sounds, Lang envelops the film with
a rich, sharply etched visual quality . . ."*
Robert Ottoson, *A Reference Guide to the American Film Noir: 1940–1958*

1950
House by the River

As *director*. Sc: Mel Dinelli, based on a novel by A. P. Herbert. Ph: Edward
Cronjager. Art dir: Boris Leven. Set decoration: Charles Thompson, John
McCarthy, Jr. Special effects: Howard and Theodore Lydecker. Costumes:
Adele Palmer.
Music: George Antheil. Editor: Arthur D. Hilton. Production manager:
Joseph Dillpe. Assistant dir: John Grubbs. Associate producer: Robert Peters.
Cast: Louis Hayward (Stephen Byrne), Lee Bowman (John Byrne), Jane

Wyatt (Marjorie Byrne), Dorothy Patrick (Emily Gaunt), Ann Shoemaker (Mrs. Ambrose), Jody Gilbert (Flora Bantam), Peter Brocco (coroner), Howland Chamberlain (district attorney), Margaret Seddon (Mrs. Whittaker), Sarah Padden (Mrs. Beach), Kathleen Freeman (Effie Ferguson), Will Wright (Inspector Sarten), Leslie Kimmell (Mr. Gaunt), Effie Laird (Mrs. Gaunt).
(Howard Welsch for Fidelity Pictures/Republic, 88 mins.)
"A little-known work yet of capital importance in his oeuvre . . ."
Bertrand Tavernier and Jean Pierre-Coursodon, *50 ans de cinéma américain*

American Guerrilla in the Philippines

As director. Sc: Lamar Trotti, based on the Ira Wolfert novel. Ph: Harry Jackson; special photographic effects: Fred Sersen. Art dir: Lyle Wheeler, J. Russell Spencer. Set decoration: Thomas Little, Stuart Reiss. Costumes: Travilla. Music: Cyril Mockridge. Musical dir: Lionel Newman. Editor: Robert Simpson. Production manager: F. E. Johnson. *Second-unit dir*: Robert D. Webb.
Assistant dir: Horace Hough.
Cast: Tyrone Power (Chuck Palmer), Micheline Presle [Prelle] (Jeanne Martinez), Jack Elam (Spenser), Bob Patten (Lovejoy), Tom Ewell (Jim Mitchell), Tommy Cook (Miguel), Robert Barrat (Gen. Douglas MacArthur), Juan Torena (Juan Martinez), Miguel Anzures (Philippine traitor), Eddie Infante (Col. Dimalanta), Orlando Martin (Col. Benson), Carleton Young (Col. Phillips), Chris De Varga, Erlinda Cortez, Rosa del Rosario, Kathy Ruby.
(Lamar Trotti for 20th Century–Fox, 105 mins.)
"A conventional war story, but well mounted and paced by director Lang."
Tony Thomas and Aubrey Solomon, *The Films of 20th Century–Fox*

1952
Rancho Notorious

As director. Sc: Daniel Taradash, based on the story "Gunsight Whitman" by Silvia Richards. Ph: Hal Mohr. Art dir: Robert Priestly, Wiard B. Ihnen. Music: Emil Newman. Songs: "The Legend of Chuck-a-Luck," "Gypsy Davey" and "Get Away, Young Man" by Ken Darby. Editor: Otto Ludwig.
Assistant director: Emmett Emerson.
Cast: Marlene Dietrich (Altar Keane), Arthur Kennedy (Vern Haskell), Mel Ferrer (Frenchy Fairmont), Gloria Henry (Beth), William Frawley (Baldy Gunder), Lisa Ferraday (Maxine), John Raven (dealer), Jack Elam (Geary), Dan Seymour (Paul), George Reeves (Wilson), Rodric Redwing (Rio), Frank Ferguson (preacher), Charles Gonzales (Hevia), Francis MacDonald (Harbin), John Kellogg (salesman), Stan Jolley (Warren), Jose Dominguez (Gonzales), John Doucette (Whitey), Stuart Randall (Starr), Frank Graham (Ace Maguire), Fuzzy Knight (barber), Roger Anderson (Red), Felipe Turich (Sanchez), Lloyd Gough (Kinch), Russell Johnson (dealer).
(Howard Welsch for Fidelity Pictures RKO, 89 mins.)
"Rancho Notorious *shows Lang's ability to take the Western genre and strip*

*it of sham atmosphere, landscape and horses. It is a portrait of a man warped
by his own need for vengeance, the theme that Lang pursued so fruitfully for
forty years and which was the natural concern of an artist driven from his own
country by tyranny."*
David Thomson, A *Biographical Dictionary of Film*

Clash by Night
As *director*. Sc: Alfred Hayes, based on the Clifford Odets play.
Ph: Nicholas Musuraca. special photographic effects: Harold Wellman.
Art dir: Albert S. D'Agostino, Carroll Clark. Set decoration: Darrell Silvera,
Jack Mills. Music dir: C. Bakaleinikoff. Music: Roy Webb.
Song: "I Hear a Rhapsody" by Joe Gasparre, Jack Baker, and George Fragos.
Editor: George J. Amy. Executive producer: Jerry Wald.
Cast: Barbara Stanwyck (Mae Doyle), Paul Douglas (Jerry D'Amato), Robert
Ryan (Earl Pfeiffer),
Marilyn Monroe (Peggy), J. Carroll Naish (Uncle Vince),
Keith Andes (Joe Doyle), Silvio Minciotti (Papa d'Amato).
(Harriet Parsons for Wald-Krasna Productions/RKO, 105 mins.)
"A gripping story of lust and betrayal."
Scott & Barbara Siegel, *The Encyclopedia of Hollywood*

1953
The Blue Gardenia
As *director*. Sc: Charles Hoffmann, based on a story by Vera Caspary.
Ph: Nicholas Musuraca. Art dir: Daniel Hall. Special effects: Willis Cook. Music:
Raoul Kraushaar. Song: "Blue Gardenia," by Bob Russell and Lester Lee,
arranged by Nelson Riddle and sung by Nat "King" Cole. Editor:
Edward Mann.
Cast: Anne Baxter (Norah Larkin), Richard Conte (Casey Mayo), Ann Sothern
(Crystal Carpenter), Raymond Burr (Harry Prebble), Jeff Donnell (Sally Ellis),
Richard Erdman (Al), George Reeves (Capt. Haynes), Ruth Storey (Rose), Ray
Walker (Homer), Celia Lovsky (blind woman), Frank Ferguson (drunk), Alex
Gottlieb, Nat "King" Cole (himself).
(Alex Gottlieb for Gloria Films/Warner Bros., 90 mins.)
*"One must imagine that Lang made films that were, in some sense, at cross
purposes with his own intellectual views, as if in the hope that he might be
wrong, just as he probably operated with two diametrically opposed estimations
of his audience (respect/disdain). This is not an unfamiliar position within
cultural politics. In my opinion, it is this absolutely fundamental ambivalence,
running throughout the cinematic experience of this relatively 'light' films, that
makes* The Blue Gardenia *so disturbing."*
Janet Bergstrom, "The Mystery of *The Blue Gardenia*," *Shades of Noir*

The Big Heat
As *director*. Sc: Sidney Boehm, based on the William McGivern novel.
Ph: Charles Lang, Jr. Art dir: Robert Peterson. Set decoration: William
Kiernan. Music: Daniele Amfitheatrof. Editor: Charles Nelson. Assistant dir:
Milton Feldman.

Cast: Glenn Ford (Dave Bannion), Gloria Grahame (Debbie Marsh), Jocelyn Brando (Katie Bannion), Alexander Scourby (Mike Lagana), Lee Marvin (Vince Stone), Jeanette Nolan (Bertha Duncan), Peter Whitney (Tierney), Willis Bouchey (Lt. Wilkes), Robert Burton (Gus Burke), Adam Williams (Larry Gordon), Howard Wendell (Commissioner Higgins), Cris Alcaide (George Rose), Michael Granger (Hugo), Dorothy Green (Lucy Chapman), Carolyn Jones (Doris), Ric Roman (Baldy), Dan Seymour (Atkins), Edith Evanson (Selma Parker), Linda Bennett, Kathryn Eames, Rex Reason.
(Robert Arthur for Columbia Pictures, 90 mins.)
"A piece of art as philosophically penetrating and stylistically complex as any in the cinema."
Colin McArthur, *The Big Heat*

1954
Human Desire
As *director*. Sc: Alfred Hayes, based on *La Bête Humaine* by Emile Zola. Ph: Burnett Guffey. Art dir: Robert Peterson. Set decoration: William Kiernan. Music: Daniele Amfitheatrof. Editor: Aaron Stell. Assistant dir: Milton Feldman.
Cast: Glenn Ford (Jeff Warren), Gloria Grahame (Vicki Buckley), Broderick Crawford (Carl Buckley), Edgar Buchanan (Alec Simmons), Kathleen Case (Ellen Simmons), Peggy Maley (Jean), Diane DeLaire (Vera Simmons), Grandon Rhodes (John Owens), Dan Seymour (bartender), John Pickard (Matt Henley), Paul Brinegar (brakeman), Dan Riss (prosecutor), Victor Hugo Greene (Davidson), John Zaremba (Russell), Carl Lee (John Thurston), Olan Soule (Lewis).
(Lewis J. Rachmil and Jerry Wald for Columbia, 90 mins.)
"Where Renoir's The Human Beast is the tragedy of a doomed man caught up in the flow of life, Lang's remake, Human Desire is the nightmare of an innocent man enmeshed in the tangled strands of fate. What we remember in Renoir are the faces of [Jean] Gabin, [Simone] Simon and [Fernand] Ledoux. What we remember in Lang are the geometrical patterns of trains, tracks and fateful camera angles. If Renoir is humanism, Lang is determinism. If Renoir is concerned with the plight of his characters, Lang is obsessed with the structure of the trap."
Andrew Sarris, *The American Cinema*

1955
Moonfleet
As *director*. Sc: Jan Lustig and Margaret Fitts, based on the John Meade Falkner novel. Ph: Robert Planck. Art dir: Cedric Gibbons, Hans Peters. Set decoration: Edwin B. Willis, Richard Pefferle. Costumes: Walter Plunkett. Music: Miklos Rozsa. Flamenco music: Vincente Gomez. Editor: Albert Akst. Assistant director: Sid Sidman. Cast: Stewart Granger (Jeremy Fox), George Sanders (Lord Ashwood), Joan Greenwood (Lady Ashwood), Viveca Lindfors (Anne Minton), Jon Whiteley (John Mohune), Liliane Montevecchi (gypsy dancer), Sean McClory (Elzevir Block), Melville Cooper (Felix Ratsey), Alan Napier (Parson Glennie), John Hoyt (Magistrate Maskew),

Donna Corcoran (Grace), Jack Elam (Damen), Dan Seymour (Hull), Ian Wolfe (Tewkesbury), Lester Matthews (Major Hennishaw), Skelton Knaggs (Jacob), Richard Hale (Starkill), John Alderson (Greening), Ashley Cowan (Tomson), Frank Ferguson (coachman), Booth Colman (Captain Stanhope), Peggy Maley (tenant).

(John Houseman and for Metro-Goldwyn-Mayer, 87 mins.)

"What Fritz Lang's Moonfleet *shows me today that I didn't recognize as such in 1955 is the discontinuity of the separate decors, the isolated surreal landscapes stretching off at oblique angles to one another. Like the dark well in the movie that's weirdly and improbably 'lit' by a candle wedged into a recess halfway down, each of the characters seems to be isolated by the upholsteries of slightly different genres, no two viewpoints ever quite coinciding. They seem to inhabit a once-ordered universe whose father-god-director is drifting away from his children, lost in his own dreams, taking all the connective narrative tissue with him . . ."*

Jonathan Rosenbaum, *Moving Places: A Life at the Movies*

1956
While the City Sleeps

As *director.* Sc: Casey Robinson, based on the novel *The Bloody Spur* by Charles Einstein. Ph: Ernest Laszlo. Art dir: Carroll Clark. Set decoration: Jack Mills. Costumes: Norma. Music: Herschel Burke Gilbert. Editor: Gene Fowler, Jr. Sound Editor: Verna Fields. Assistant dir: Ronnie Rondell.

Cast: Dana Andrews (Edward Mobley), Rhonda Fleming (Dorothy Kyne), Sally Forrest (Nancy Liggett), Thomas Mitchell (Griffith), Vincent Price (Walter Kyne), Howard Duff (Lt. Kaufman), Ida Lupino (Mildred), George Sanders (Mark Loving), James Craig (Harry Kritzer), John Barrymore, Jr. (Robert Manners), Vladimir Sokoloff (George Palsky), Robert Warwick (Amos Kyne), Ralph Peters (Meade), Larry Blake (police sergeant), Edward Hinton (O'Leary), Mae Marsh (Mrs. Manners), Sandy White (Judith Fenton), Celia Lovsky (Miss Dodd), Pitt Herbert (bartender), Andrew Lupino.

(Bert E. Friedlob for Thor Productions/RKO 100 mins.)

"Top-notch Lang, despite what you might have read."
Michael Weldon, *The Psychotronic Encyclopedia of Film*

Beyond a Reasonable Doubt

As *director.* Sc: Douglas Morrow. Ph: William Snyder. Art dir: Carroll Clark. Set decoration: Darrell Silvera. Music: Herschel Burke Gilbert. Song: "Beyond a Reasonable Doubt" by H. G. Gilbert and Alfred Perry. Assistant dir: Maxwell Henry. Editor: Gene Fowler, Jr.

Cast: Dana Andrews (Tom Garrett), Joan Fontaine (Susan Spencer), Sidney Blackmer (Austin Spencer), Philip Bourneuf (Thompson), Barbara Nichols (Sally), Shepperd Strudwick (Wilson), Arthur Franz (Hale), Robin Raymond (Terry), Edward Binns (Lt. Kennedy), William Leicester (Charlie Miller), Dan Seymour (Greco), Rusty Lane (Judge), Joyce Taylor (Joan), Carleton Young (Kirk), Trudy Wroe (hat-check girl), Joe Kirk (clerk), Charles Evans (governor), Wendell Niles (announcer).

(Bert E. Friedlob for Thor Productions/Universal, 80 mins.)
"The critics were outraged by the plot, but it should not have been surprising from a man whom the world, Nazism, war, deportation, McCarthyism, et cetera, confirmed as a rebel. His rebellion had turned to disgust."
François Truffaut, *The Films In My Life*

1959

Der Tiger von Eschnapur (The Tiger of Bengal)
Das indische Grabmal (The Indian Tomb)
As co-screenwriter and director. Sc: Werner Jörg Lüddecke and Lang, based on the novel by Thea von Harbou and a script by von Harbou and Lang. Ph: Richard Angst. Art dir: Helmut Nentwig, Willy Schatz. Costumes: Claudia Herberg, Günther Brosda. Music: Michel Michelet (*Tiger*); Gerhard Becker (*Grabmal*). Choreography: Robby Gay, Billy Daniel. Editor: Walter Wischniewsky. Assistant dir: Frank Winterstein.
Cast: Debra Paget (Seetha), Paul Hubschmid [Henri Mercier in French version] (Harald Berger), Walter Reyer (Chandra, the Maharaja of Eschnapur), Claus Holm (Dr. Walter Rhode), Sabine Bethmann (Irene), Valery Inkijinoff (Yama), René Deltgen (Prince Ramigami), Jochen Brockmann (Padhu), Jochen Blume (Asagara), Luciana Paoluzzi (Bahrani), Guido Celano (General Dagh), Angela Portulari (peasant), Richard Lauffen (Bhowana), Helmut Hildebrand (Ramigani's servant), Panos Papadopoulos (messenger), Victor Francen.
(Eberhard Meichsner and Louise de Masure for Arthur Brauner/CCC Films, *Tiger*, 101 mins; *Grabmal*, 102 mins.)
"All that remained in the end was an unyielding tightness, a sharp focus with nothing left to focus on but the rote performances of zombie actors trapped in the screenplays of Beyond A Reasonable Doubt and The Tiger of Eschnapur. The world might change, but the camera—impersonal and soulless, the prisoner of its own mechanism—could finally say one thing. It told what a camera was."
Geoffrey O'Brien, *The Phantom Empire*

1960

Die tausend Augen des Dr. Mabuse (The Thousand Eyes of Dr. Mabuse)
As co-screenwriter and director. Sc: Heinz Oskar Wuttig and Lang, based on an idea by Jan Fethke and the character created by Norbert Jacques. Ph: Karl Loeb. Art dir: Erich Kettelhut, Johannes Ott. Costumes: Ina Stein. Music: Bert Grund. Editors: Walter and Waltraute Wischniewsky.
Cast: Dawn Addams (Marion Menil), Peter Van Eyck (Travers), Wolfgang Preiss (Jordan), Gert Fröbe (Commissioner Kras), Lupo Prezzo (Cornelius), Werner Peters (Hieronymous P. Mistelzweig), Andrew Checchi (Hotel Detective Berg), Reinhard Kolldehoff (clubfoot), Howard Vernon (No. 12), Nico Pepe (hotel manager), David Cameron (Parker), Jean-Jacques Delbo (servant), Marie Luise Nagel (blonde), Werner Buttler (No. 11), Linda Sini (Corinna), Rolf Moebius (police officer), Bruno W. Pantel (reporter), Albert Bessler (hotel engineer).
(Artur Brauner for CCC Filmkunst, 103 mins.)

"Lang's The Thousand Eyes of Dr. Mabuse *at first glance looks like a B-movie, full of stock figures, cheap special effects, and broad acting. West German critics failed to see any saving graces in the tale of a criminal madman with his vast information system, his 'thousand eyes.' The film does have subversive charms, however. In the guise of a pulp thriller, Lang created a self-reflective modernistic text concerned with the dynamics of the cinematic medium, its voyeuristic penchant and insatiable desire for spectacle. Teasing the spectator with disjunctive cross-cuts, elliptical leaps from one space to another which leave out information and explanations, Lang presented a world where the police keep tabs on people every bit as rapaciously as a sinister megalomaniac."*

Eric Rentschler, "Germany," World Cinema Since 1945

AS ACTOR

1963

Le Mépris (Contempt)

As an actor. Dir: Jean-Luc Godard. Sc: Godard, based on the novel *Il Disprezzo* [*A Ghost at Noon*] by Alberto Moravia. Ph: Raoul Coutard. Music: Georges Delerue. Editors: Agnes Guillemot, Lila Lakshmanan.

Cast: Brigitte Bardot (Camille Javal), Jack Palance (Jeremy Prokosck), Michel Piccoli (Paul Javal), Fritz Lang (Fritz Lang), Giorgia Moll (Francesca Vanini), Jean-Luc Godard (Lang's assistant director), Linda Veras (a siren).

(Joseph E. Levine, Georges de Beauregard and Carlo Ponti for Films Concocordia-Compagnia, 100 mins.)

Researching, interviewing, and reporting for *Fritz Lang: The Nature of the Beast* took me to Vienna, Berlin, Frankfurt, Munich, Paris, London, New York, Los Angeles, and (surprisingly!) Laramie, Wyoming. I investigated libraries and archives in most of these cities, and also ones in Connecticut, Illinois, Texas, and Wisconsin. My fax machine buzzed with messages from Belgundi in Belgaum, India. I was fortunate to see Fritz Lang films in theaters and museums, wherever I roamed. In Berlin I was able to watch several, rare pre-Ufa silent features at the Stiftung Deutsche Kinemathek; one night I was lucky to stumble across the East German archive print of *Metropolis* unspooling in an East Berlin loft, with "live" music from an avant-garde band. Passing through Rome, my itinerary coincided with a screening of the Italian print of *Die Nibelungen*, with piano accompaniment, at the Accademia Filarmonica Romana. In Paris I welcomed a chance to see *La Femme au gardénia* (*The Blue Gardenia*) reprised at a small Left Bank moviehouse. Even in Milwaukee, Wisconsin, where I live, opportunities arose, including *The Big Heat* shown on the big screen at the now-shuttered Paradise Theater—a revival occasion which renewed the film's impression on me as a work of profound and world-weary compassion.

From the outset I resolved to read everything extant about Fritz Lang, and to walk in the footsteps of those who had done important research and interviews before me, as well as to find my own path with fresh sources and discoveries. Among the discoveries were the director's home movies mysteriously set aside among his possessions in Wyoming (these home movies go unspecified, for example, in the recent *Fritz Lang: La mise en scéne*, a joint publication of the Cinémathéque Française, the Museo Nazionale del Cinema and the Filmoteca Generalitat Valenciana, which attempts to catalogue all of Lang's archival holdings worldwide). I don't think anyone else before me had passed through the barbed-wire gates of the Berlin Document Center to examine Allied interrogation records, relating to Lang and his second wife, Thea von Harbou. Versions of Lang's 1914 letter to a Parisian friend, which sheds vital illumination on his pre-World War I activities, exist in several archives; in London I managed to locate and read the original, still in the possession of the recipient's daughter. The director's love affairs were a constant subplot of his life story; Kay Francis's diaries at Wesleyan University were one "find" that helped me corroborate the gossip.

In Vienna I was fortunate enough to contact and have tea with a gentleman in his 90s, a Lang cousin, who had often visited the family residence where the director was raised as a boy. I located and spoke to the personal secretary who had worked for Lang and von Harbou in Berlin at the height of their creativity and fame. I took a train to Munich and spent a memorable afternoon with the man—an assistant editor on *M*—who probably introduced Lang to Lily Latté, and Thea von Harbou to her Indian lover Ayi Tendulkar, and who knew firsthand about Lang's fabled flight from Goebbels Germany in 1933. I was passed along as word spread of the book, and introduced to the aging representatives of the onetime Hollywood émigré community as well as the few privileged persons, generally much younger, who had formed the director's inner circle until his death.

To a certain extent I raced time to capture the memories of people from the long-ago Vienna, Berlin, and Paris phases of Lang's life—no less so from the director's tenure in Hollywood. Sometimes, visiting people, I felt uncomfortably like an angel of death. The ever-provocative Gottfried Reinhardt, the self-deprecating Joseph L. Mankiewicz, Dan Seymour and Howard Vernon—both of whom were extravagant with their courtesies—there were others whom I encountered that have passed away since this project was begun, four years ago. I am leaving some names off; listing them gives me no pleasure.

Everywhere I traveled I was reminded of the universality of the cinema and the permanent magic of the name of Fritz Lang. People responded promptly and warmly to my inquiries and solicitations. Film scholars who might be presumed to be rivalrous greeted me and exchanged information (sometimes vehemently disagreeing with my constantly-evolving opinions). Fellow authors and film historians made suggestions for research and interviews, opening up their own private files of unpublished transcripts.

Beyond a few trite phrases, I do not speak or read German; that was half of the risk and excitement in tackling this book. Nor could I claim, starting out, to be an expert on the career of Fritz Lang. Although I made a concerted effort to seek out many of the dinosaurs of the profession, when I worked for *The Boston Globe* from 1973–1976, Lang is one whom I was fated never to meet, or know. Now my research confirms that, truly, few did know him, in his heart. Getting to understand such a man was the other half of the job.

The facts of a person's life can be narrowed down considerably, although of course some will remain stubbornly elusive. The larger truths about someone are the more complicated challenge. I always go to work on a subject, optimistic about detecting the stubborn facts as well as clarifying larger truths. The friends of this book—and there were many—were tolerant of my optimism. If the result is at all satisfactory, then it is greatly owed to their trust and goodwill.

Sources and letters: Forrest Ackerman, Clemens Auerbach, Charles Bennett, Margaret Brenman-Gibson, Rock Brynner, Phil Gersh, Geoffrey Gilchrist, Dolly Haas, Niels von Harbou, Virginia Gay Hayden, Jane Kallir, Peter Knize, Paul Kuttner, Joseph Laitin, Joseph L. Mankiewicz, Margot Stevens Morrow,

Elfriede Nagel, Robert Parrish, Birgit V. Puttkamer, Maurice Rapf, Elizabeth Reisch, Leni Riefenstahl, Joyce Saydah, Curt Siodmak, Prof. Alexander Stephan, Georges Sturm, Mrs. Indumati Tendulkar.

Especially: John E. Pommer for his patience with my queries; and to Daniel Taradash, who corresponded voluminously with me, helping to fill in the blanks on *Rancho Notorious*, and then for accuracy's sake read parts of the book relating to that film.

Interviews: Peter Bogdanovich, Mrs. Curtis (Anne Maria) Bernhardt, David Bradley, Artur Brauner, Jeff Corey, Min Selvin Crutcher, Andre De Toth, Andries Dienum, Douglas Fairbanks Jr., Rudi Fehr, Rudi Feld, Gene Fowler, Jr., Gero Gandert, Vera Gilbert-Smith, Hilde Guttmann, Peter Heiman, Charles Higham, Erwin Hillier, Marlene and Volker Hucklenbroich, Sam Jaffe, Rudolph S. Joseph, Karen-Maria Kane, Ring Lardner Jr., Viveca Lindfors, Gilbert Mandelik, Roddy McDowall, Conrad (Kurt) von Molo, Ruth Albu Morgenroth, Harold Nebenzal, David Overbey, John Pommer, Gottfried Reinhardt, Silvia Richards, Pierre Rissient, Henry Rogers, Hilda Rolfe, Cornelius Schnauber, Dan Seymour, Sylvia Sidney, Dr. Friedrich Steinbach, Vinayak Tendulkar, Kevin Thomas, Viege Traub, Howard Vernon, Peter Viertel, John Wexley, Jane Wyatt, and Fred Zinnemann.

Especially: Thanks to Sid Selzer in San Diego, for going to lengths to bring me into contact with Peter Heiman. In Los Angeles, Nat Segaloff interviewed Sam Jaffe on my behalf. In London, Clare Beresford asked questions of Hilde Guttmann for this book, and also in Vienna, she interviewed Dr. Friedrich Steinbach a second time, after he had already been interviewed there by the author. (Dr. Steinbach also cooperated with the loan of photographs and correspondence clarifying points of information for this book.) The interview with John Wexley, who died in 1985, dates back to my session with him from 1983.

Advice and Assistance: Other authors, journalists, and colleagues in the field of film study were gracious with their cooperation. I owe a debt of gratitude to Steven Bach, John Baxter, Matthew Bernstein, Kevin Brownlow, Paul Buhle, Mark Burman, Bill Cappello, Michel Ciment, Prof. Ronald L. Davis, Lizzie Francke, David Goodrich, Ann Harris, Charles Higham, Richard Lamparski, Kevin Macdonald, Todd McCarthy, James L. Neibaur, James Robert Parish, Richard Schickel, David Stenn, Brian Thomsen, David Thomson, and Betty D. Ulius.

Especially: Alan Dein, who supplied photographs and a wealth of background information about Hilde Guttman. Selden West, working on a book about Spencer Tracy, answered my Tracy-related questions and made suggestions on the *Fury* chapter. Matthew Bernstein was wonderfully supportive; not only was his book *Walter Wanger: Hollywood Independent* a vital source, but Bernstein offered further leads and research out of his experience. He also read and critiqued the sections of the book relating to Wanger and Lang.

Hospitality and friendship: Diane Shooman and Heiner Meyer in Vienna; John Baxter and Bertrand Tavernier in Paris; Dr. Jürgen Bretschneider and Dr. Harald Fisher of Henschel Verlag in Berlin; Ulrike Seeberger in Frankfurt; William B. Winburn and Regula Ehrlich in New York City; and last but never least, Ken Mate in Los Angeles.

Extracurricular activity: For giving me the occasional newspaper or magazine assignment to help keep me solvent, I am indebted to Barry Gewen of *The New York Times* Sunday book review department; David Mehegan, Book Editor of *The Boston Globe*; Richard Jameson of *Film Comment*; and Thomasine Lewis of *Live!* magazine.

Films: Not all of Fritz Lang's films are easily available in video, or are presented that often on television. Few crop up in U.S. repertory movie theaters. I was aided in finding several titles by the remarkably resourceful Dave Martin in San Francisco; John Baxter sent me unexpurgated versions of *Der Tiger von Eschnapur* and *Das indische Grabmal*; A Million and One World-Wide Videos, Orchard Hill, Georgia, scoured the earth for a few films; and the hard-working folks at Video Visions, Milwaukee, did the rest.

In Austria: Elisabeth Streit and Prof. Walter Fritz, Austrian Film Archives; Dr. Wolfgang Kuderna, Austrian Military Archives; Xaver Challupner, Austrian Theater Museum; Peter Hajek; Mrs. Rudolf Leopold; Lower Austrian archives (Anton Lang file); National Library; Dr. Michaela Laichmann and Dr. Peter Csendes, Rathaus (City Hall), Vienna; Willibald Rosner; Stephan Schwarz; Satyr-Filmwelt Books; Heinz Vogel, Society for Blinded War Veterans; Prof. Wolfdieter Bihl, University of Vienna; and Annie Weich.

In Germany: David G. Marwell, Director, Berlin Document Center; Hans-Michael Bock; Astrid Dostert, CCC Filmkunst GmbH; Dieter Ostermayr; Georges Sturm; and *Der Tagespiegel*.

Especially: Wolfgang Jacobsen, Gero Gandert and, above all, Werner Sudendorf of the Stiftung Deutsche Kinemathek in Berlin, who bemusedly accepted me into their domain. Sudendorf squired me around on my visits and after I was gone acceded to many long-distance requests. I am thankful for his erudition as well as his generosity of spirit. He wisely dispenses his secrets—some, not all. "We must save some for future generations," Sudendorf told me.

In Paris: Michel Ciment, Eve-Marine Dauvergne, Bernard Eisenschitz, and especially Dominique (Brun) Dardayrol, who opened the doors of the Cinémathèque Française to me, even on days when the library was supposed to be officially closed.

Archives and organizations in the U.S.: Barbara Hall, Margaret Herrick Library, Academy of Motion Picture Arts and Sciences, Beverly Hills; Rick Ewig, American Heritage Center, University of Wyoming, Laramie; Karen Mix, Special Collections, Mugar Memorial Library, Boston University; Ronald J. Grele, Oral History Research Office, Columbia University; J. Kevin O'Brien, Privacy Acts Section, Federal Bureau of Investigation; Ron Magliozzi, Film Study Center, Museum of Modern Art; Diane S. Nixon, Regional Director, National Archives—Pacific Southwest Region; Kay Bost, DeGolyer Library, Southern Methodist University; Lorrayne R. Jurist, Twentieth Century–Fox; Brigitte Kueppers, Special Collections, University Research Library, University of California at Los Angeles; Nancy Romero, Rare Book Room, University of Illinois, Urbana; David O. Selznick Collection, University of Texas, Austin; Chris Baruth, American Geographical Society Collection, Golda Meir Library, University of Wisconsin, Milwaukee; Jeanine Basinger and Leith G. Johnson, Wesleyan Cinema Archives, Wesleyan University; and Maxine Fleckner Ducey and Ruta Abolins of the Wisconsin Center for Film and Theatre Research, State Historical Society, Madison, Wisconsin.

Especially: The Cinema-Television Library and Archives of the Performing Arts at the University of Southern California, Los Angeles, keeper of Fritz Lang's large bequest of personal and professional papers (and many other disparate collections). Although film scholars are notoriously sectarian, the USC archivist, Ned Comstock, is one topic on which they can unite in agreement. He is one of the most pleasant, organized, knowledgeable about his job. On the home front, also, I feel it necessary to mention that I couldn't sustain my work without the reference tools and impressive holdings of the Milwaukee Public Library.

Brenda Heintz, Heike Siebert, Christiane Schroeter, and Andrew Kreiss aided with remedial translation of German letters and articles. Charla Reetz spent hours in the local libraries making xeroxes of clippings. Hayley Buchbinder took on the task of reading actress Kay Francis's 1939–1940 journals at Wesleyan University. Wendy Daniell did copious amounts of French translation, quickly and at an economical rate.

Ryta Kroeger in Connecticut read the long first draft of the book and endeavored to correct my English. Ulrike Seeberger in Nuremberg, who translated my Jack Nicholson book for the German market, also read the *Fritz Lang* draft and endeavored to police my foreign-language mistakes. Larry Green of Vancouver, who has written to me after every one of my books has been published, correcting film facts, read a draft with an eye to making sure nothing—or at least not too much—of that sort would happen again.

John Baxter (Paris), Joel Greenberg (Sydney), Charles Higham (Los Angeles) and David Thomson (San Francisco) proved their selfless friendship by reading the manuscript and barraging me with criticisms. The book was no doubt improved in the process, and of course any failings that persist should not be held against any of them.

Every book has unsung saints and heroes, and chief among them in this case was Clare Beresford, who amazingly enough replied to my plea for an assistant scribbled on a 3 × 5 piece of paper torn out from a notebook and posted on a University of Vienna bulletin board. A graduate student native to Canada, she took up the chore—after my first visit to Vienna—of investigating the Viennese roots of Fritz Lang's life and career. After acquitting herself admirably in Vienna, she accompanied me on trips to London and Berlin (twice), where she collaborated further on research and interviews. Once I figured out she was receptive to impossible demands, I only worked her harder. All the German text translations are by Ms. Beresford, unless otherwise noted. She proved a boon companion, interpreter, detective, and collaborative thinker who, from initial progress right through to final form, constructively influenced the shape and ideas of the book.

Fritz Lang: The Nature of the Beast, finally, owes more than a nod and a wink to Tom McCormack, the recently retired Editorial Director of St. Martin's Press, who circled Fritz Lang's name off a list of potential biography subjects. Tom, who also green-lighted my Robert Altman and George Cukor books, always treated me better than my sales might warrant. I will be consoled in his absence by Calvert Morgan, Jr., the editor he bestowed on me one or two books ago, who can be as tough as he is supportive and understanding.

Gloria Loomis, my agent, not only supervises my contracts, but watches over me in other regards. For this book, she even loaned me money, when the advance ran out! My wife and three boys—Tina, Clancy, Bowie and Sky—accept the fact that the money always does run out when their Daddy—husband—is immersed in another book. God love them.

SOURCE NOTES

So many good articles and books have been written about Fritz Lang, and about Fritz Lang's films, that an entire reference volume exists which itemizes and indexes them. That is E. Ann Kaplan's *Fritz Lang: A Guide to References and Resources* (Boston: G.K. Hall, 1981). The earth will be spared a couple of trees if I refer interested readers to Kaplan's comprehensive book, while listing below only the most important sources specific to my work.

Another valuable reference is the French book *Fritz Lang: films/textes/ références* by Georges Sturm (Nancy, France: Presses Universitaires de Nancy, 1990), which takes a chronological—as well as film-by-film—approach to the director's life and his work. In the same category of general-reference merit is *Trois Lumiéres* by Alfred Eibel (Paris, Flammarion, 1988), the first Fritz Lang book and still a key one—including Eibel's original 1963 text as well as sidebar contributions from many of the director's collaborators.

One of the books to which I referred again and again was Lotte Eisner's influential *Fritz Lang* (London: Secker & Warburg, 1976) as well as her autobiography *Ich hatte einst ein schönes Vaterland—Memoiren* (with Martje Grohmann) (Heidelberg: Wunderhorn, 1984)—published only in Germany. I also consulted Eisner's more general history of the Golden Age of German Cinema, *The Haunted Screen* (Berkeley: University of California Press, 1969) and a related study, Siegfried Kracauer's oft-quoted *From Caligari to Hitler: A Psychological History of the German Film* (Princeton, N.J.: Princeton University Press, 1947).

Peter Bogdanovich's *Fritz Lang in America* (New York: Praeger, 1969) is a model work of its kind that is mentioned—and quoted from—repeatedly in this book.

Underrated but extremely worthwhile was Frederick Ott's *The Films of Fritz Lang* (Secaucus, N.J.: Citadel Press, 1979) as well as Ott's companion volume *The Great German Films: From Before World War I to the Present* (Secaucus, N.J.: Citadel Press, 1986).

Especially useful because it is a collection of extracts, interviews, and reviews from the 1920s to the early 1930s, pertaining to Lang and his silent films, was Fred Gehler and Ulrich Kasten's *Fritz Lang: Die Stimme von Metropolis* (Berlin: Henschel, 1990).

Several of Curt Riess's books proved a treasure-trove of Lang-related anecdotes and Berlin-era show business information: especially *Das gab's nur einmal* (Munich: Molden, 1977), *Das war ein Leben. Erinnerungen* (Munich:

Langen Müller, 1986) and *Meine berühmten Freunde. Erinnerungen* (Freiburg im Breisgau: Herder, 1987).

For German screen facts and historical background, I consulted *Filmkünstler: wir über uns selbst*, edited by Hermann Treuner (Berlin: Sibyllen, 1928); Gerhard Lamprecht's *Deutsche Stummfilme* (Berlin: Deutsche Kinemathek, 1967–1970); Michael Hanisch and Joachim Reichow's *Filmschauspieler A–Z* (Berlin: Henschel, 1980); and Hans-Michael Bock's *Cinegraph: Lexikon zum deutschsprachigen Film* (Hamburg: 1984). *The International Dictionary of Films and Filmmakers* edited by Nicholas Thomas (Detroit, Washington D.C., London: St. James Press, 1993) was another well-thumbed source.

Transcribed Fritz Lang interviews are cited often in the text. These include Charles Higham and Joel Greenberg's interview with the director in *The Celluloid Muse* (New York: Henry Regnery, 1969); Bernard Rosenberg and Harry Silverstein's interview with Lang in *The Real Tinsel* (New York: Macmillan, 1970); the "Fritz Lang Seminar" from the American Film Institute's *Dialogue on Film*, April 1975; and "Fritz Lang Remembers," an interview by Gene D. Phillips, *Focus on Film*, Spring, 1975, which was excerpted in the *Village Voice* as "Fritz Lang's Last Interview" on August 16, 1976.

Of unique value was a series of carefully formulated replies that Lang made, sometime in the mid-1960s, to questions about his youth in Vienna and Paris. This text, which was apparently intended for use in an historical book by a French author, was found in Lang's USC files. It runs several single-spaced pages and is referred to below as "Answers to Questions." Likewise in the USC files, the raw transcript of the Gretchen Berg interview—which formed the basis of a two-part 1965–1966 interview with the director in *Cahiers du Cinéma*, as well as a piece in Canada's *Take One* about Lang and *Contempt*—offered many hitherto unpublished nuggets and insights.

Just when this book was almost done, Todd McCarthy invited me to a private screening of rare interview footage of Lang from an unfinished, early-1970s documentary photographed by William Fraker and directed by William Friedkin. Not only was I able to hear new versions of the director's familiar anecdotes, but I had a chance on the spot to compare recollections with Pierre Rissient, also present for the screening, who had first heard most of the stories from Lang in other contexts.

Judging by his Wyoming, USC, and Cinémathèque archives, Lang's personal correspondence—as opposed to writing of a professional nature—was limited. But his and Lily Latté's letters to Paul Erich Marcus (PEM), as well as Lang's letters to Julius Singer—most of these represented in the Kinemathek files—were crucial for opening a window into his psychology, offering tidbits of information, and forming a chronology of events.

VIENNA

Chapter One: 1890–1911

Georges Sturm provided an early reading copy of his fascinating "Essai Biographique sure les Parents de Fritz Lang." I investigated many of the same sources as Sturm, sometimes coming up with different conclusions as to Lang's genealogical roots and influences, but his research stimulated my own. His letters and faxes to me generally helped inform the pre-Hollywood chapters.

I also drew heavily from "Answers to Questions" in the USC files, an abundant source of information and perspective about Lang's childhood and time in Vienna.

The Wiener Centralbad is described in "Das Dampfbad aus 1001 Nacht" by Gunther Martin in *Wien Aktuell*, no. 6, 1976.

"Who worked the land himself . . ." is from "Entretien avec Fritz Lang" in *Cinémagazine*, April 10, 1925, as cited by Sturm in *Fritz Lang: films/textes/référénces*.

"Which isn't justified in the continuity . . ." is from Sturm's "Essai Biographique."

"A big leather mannequin . . ." is from Lang's script "Scandal in Vienna."

"Their faces are fresh . . ." is from Lang's script "Scandal in Vienna."

"My parents went twice a month . . ." is from *Fritz Lang in America*.

"I like folk songs, but . . ." is from "Answers to Questions."

"Having a musical background for a love scene . . ." is from "Fritz Lang Remembers."

"That this very good-looking girl . . ." is from the Gretchen Berg transcript.

Lang bragged about reading "ze pulp" in "Whither the Film Industry?" by Maxine Garrison in the June 10, 1945 *Pittsburgh Press*.

"I thought the James Boys were . . ." is from the "Henry Fonda Seminar" in the American Film Institute's *Dialogue on Film*, November, 1973.

"There were the most lovely things there . . ." is from "Answers to Questions."

"I have lost a long list of things . . ." is from "Answers to Questions."

"I went about my business in those days . . ." is from "Answers to Questions."

"I loved my mother very much . . ." is from Lang's Feb. 12, 1972, letter to PEM, which contains a number of interesting statements about his childhood and parents.

Details of Lang's early education were obtained from Vienna's Jahresberichte der K. und K. Staatsrealschule Neustiftgasse (1901–1902—1909–1910), especially Bericht for 1907–1908, which lists information pertaining to Lang's graduating class and final exam.

"A secret selection of censured books . . ." is from "Answers to Questions."

"While his parents thought he was asleep . . ." is from the profile of Lang in *Mein Film*, March, 1926.

Peter the "wonder of nature" is described in the Dec. 7, 1908, edition of *Wiener Sonn-und Montagszeitung*.

"Karl Kraus never forgave me for that . . ." is from "Answers to Questions."

"Viennese women were the most beautiful . . ." is from "Answers to Questions."

"Spittelberg was not a Berg . . ." is from "Answers to Questions."

"He pretended to be studying . . ." is Curt Riess from *Meine berühmten Freunde*.

"About halfway through every month . . ." is from *Die literarische Welt*, Oct. 21, 1927, as cited in Gehler and Kasten's *Fritz Lang*.

The Todesfall-Aufnahme, or will and itemization of possessions taken at the time of Paula Lang's death, is available among public court records at the Lower Austrian Archives.

Chapter Two: 1911–1918

"Then I fell in love . . ." is from *The Real Tinsel*.

The "blue martini" anecdote is from Charlotte Chandler's book *The Ultimate Seduction* (Garden City, New York: Doubleday, 1984).

"Fritz Lang never told me how . . ." is Curt Riess from *Meine berühmten Freunde*.

"A public exhibition of his work . . ." is from *The Films of Fritz Lang*. The supposed exhibit is also mentioned in *Fritz Lang in America* and other Lang articles and books.

Much of the background and detail relevant to Lang's stay in Paris come from his August 29, 1914, letter to Julius Singer. The story of how this letter came to light is curious. Apparently, Lang wrote to Singer in 1965, wishing to obtain a copy of the original correspondence to boost his memory for "Answers to Questions." Singer dispatched the letter from London, Lang copied it by hand and returned the original. The versions on deposit at both the Kinemathek in Berlin and USC in California are evidently replicas. The original resides with Julius Singer's daughter, Vera Gilbert-Smith, in London; I visited her there to read the original, which differs slightly in content and wording from the copied forms. But it is true of all versions that after several pages the letter breaks off abruptly, without any closing salutation or signature, so that it appears the final page is missing. Singer's post–1965 correspondence with Lang suggests that this page had long been missing. "So the rest will have to be left up to your imagination," Singer wrote the director.

One find: There is also, in the USC archives, a postcard from Lang at 42 rue de maistre, Paris, addressed to his parents in Gars am Kamp. It is dated July 6—either 1913 or 1914—before the outbreak of the war, and though otherwise an inconsequential communication, confirms he was still in close touch with his parents.

"We did think of war occasionally . . ." is Stefan Zweig quoted from *The World of Yesterday* (New York: Viking, 1943).

"I looked at these things with great pleasure . . ." is from *Fritz Lang in America*.

"Wandered around the new medium . . ." is from "Answers to Questions."

"The Viennese women and girls . . ." is from "Answers to Questions."

"Made it look like war . . ." is from "Answers to Questions."

"Instead of enjoying myself . . ." is from *The Real Tinsel*.

"My social and political thinking first began . . ." is from "Answers to Questions."

Lang's and other civil registration records are at the Rathaus in Vienna. His military records, including the "Kopfzettel der Gemusterten," are in regimental files at the Austrian Military Archives, also in Vienna.

Books that provided a requisite frame of reference for Lang's military career include *Lutsk: der russische Durchbruch im Juni, 1916* by Maximilian Schönovsky-Schönwies (Vienna: Braumüller, 1919); Edmund von Glaise-Horstenau, *Österreich-Ungarns letzter Krieg, 1914–1918* (Vienna: Militärwissenschaftlichen Mitteilungen, 1930); *The Army of Francis Joseph*, Gunther E. Rothenburg (Purdue U. Press, Lafayette, Indiana, 1976).

Jure Mikuz's significant article, "Une contribution aux sources de la formation artistique de Fritz Lang," appeared in *Positif*, November, 1984; and Neva Skapin Slibar's complementary article, "Visuelle Verführungskünste: Die vergessenen Blumenständer des *Dr. Mabuse*" was published in *Parnass* (Vienna), no. 1, 1989. See also Jure Mikuz's book, *Fritz Lang* (Ljublana: Moderna galerija, Revija, Ekran, 1985).

"With the death of the old Kaiser . . ." is from "Answers to Questions."

"As it turned out . . ." is from *Fritz Lang in America*.

"In spite of my relations with women . . ." is from "Answers to Questions."

"Life stripped to its rawest . . ." is from *The Films of Fritz Lang*.

"The first shock of my professional life . . ." is from "Answers to Questions."

"The owner of the theater must have thought . . ." is from *Fritz Lang in America*.

Lang's account of meeting Peter Ostermayr has many published versions, but this one is principally drawn from "Answers to Questions." I also had input from Peter Ostermayr's nephew, Dieter Ostermayr in Munich, and referred to the book *Munich Portraits: Peter Ostermayr* (Munich: Verlag Günter Olzog, 1957).

"With the best will and the best coach . . ." is from *The Real Tinsel*.

"Something which only happens in fairy tales . . ." is from *The Real Tinsel*.

"Every member had to . . ." is from "Answers to Questions."

"Der Hias" is reviewed in the *Wiener Allgemeine Zeitung* of May 4, 1918.

Erich Pommer's version of meeting Lang was assembled from various sources. Wolfgang Jacobsen's book *Erich Pommer, ein Produzent macht Filmgeschichte* (Berlin: Argon, 1989) is a definitive-to-date study of Pommer's career that also chronicles the making of *Dr. Caligari*, Lang's first visit with Pommer to America, the *Metropolis* saga and other crucial events. I also perused the Pommer material in *Trois Lumiéres* and Herbert G. Luft's enlightening two-part article in *Films in Review* ("Erich Pommer," October and November issues, 1959). Lang wrote extensively about his relationship with Pommer in his June 10, 1964 letter to PEM. And finally, John Pommer, the producer's son, refined for me the anecdote of their first encounter, working off his father's original notes. Indeed, he assisted me with all issues related to his father's career.

Lilith und Ly is covered in "Der Vampyr in Fernsehstudio: *Lilith und Ly* ein vergessener Film von Fritz Lang" by Walter Fritz in *Aktion*, April 1969. See also Walter Fritz's *Kino in Österreich 1896–1930* (Vienna: Österreichischer Bundesverlag, 1981).

BERLIN

Chapter Three: 1918–1921

As much as possible, the view of post-War history throughout this chapter is out of Lang's own mouth, culled from diverse interviews and especially from "TV Flashbacks," a February 2, 1955 transcript between interviewer Paul Coates and the director, commenting on this period, a copy of which exists in his USC files.

Of constant reassurance, when trying to sort out the multiple studios and filming sites of 1920s Berlin, was Wolfgang Jaccobsen's book *Babelsberg. Ein Filmstudio 1912–1992* (Berlin: Argon, 1992), especially the Jacobsen, Karl Prümm, and Werner Sudendorf articles. Also: Jacobsen's *Geschichte des Films* (Stuttgart: JB Metzler, 1993). The early years of German cinema were illuminated by *Before Caligari: German Cinema, 1895–1920*, ed. Paolo Cherchi Usai and Lorenzo Codelli (Madison: University of Wisconsin Press, 1990). Edifying background on Joe May came from Hans-Michael Bock and Claudia Lenssen's *Joe May—Regisseur und Produzent* (München: Edition text+kritik, 1991). And Klaus Kreimeier's *The Ufa Story: A History of Germany's Greatest Film Company, 1918–1945* (New York: Hill and Wang, 1996) provided essential history and context for understanding the workings of the Ufa firm.

Herman G. Weinberg is quoted from *The Lubitsch Touch* (New York: Dutton, 1968).

"In order to earn a few more marks . . ." is from "Answers to Questions."

"They came in carriages and rented cars . . ." is from Michael Hanisch's generally expert *Auf den Spuren der Filmgeschichte. Berliner Schauplätze* (Berlin: Henschel, 1991).

"Respected him as an artist . . ." is quoted in *The Films of Fritz Lang*.

"My car was repeatedly stopped . . ." is from Eisner's *Fritz Lang*.

"Do you think it can be good? . . ." is from *Fritz Lang in America*.

Lil Dagover is quoted from her memoirs *Ich war die Dame* (Munich: Schneekluth, 1979).

The *Dr. Caligari* sequence of events is covered in a letter written by Lang that was published in *Caligari and Caligarismus*, Walter Kaul, ed. (Berlin: Kinemathek, 1970). Siegfried Kracauer's introduction to the script of *The Cabinet of Dr. Caligari* (London: Lorrimer, 1972) was also consulted, and the subject is amply reviewed in Mike Budd's *The Cabinet of Dr. Caligari: Texts, Contexts, Histories* (New Brunswick, N.J.: Rutgers University Press, 1990).

All biographical accounts of Thea von Harbou must start with Reinhold Keiner's first-rate *Thea von Harbou: und der deutsche Film bis 1933* (Hildesheim, Zürich, New York: Olms, 1991), which apart from its film history merits, also contains appendices by von Harbou's cousin Dr. Anne-Marie Durand-Wever and writer-director Arthur Maria Rabenalt, as well as transcribed interviews with former Berlin film and theater critic Hans Feld, writer Felix Lützkendorf, von Harbou's final secretary Elfriede Nagel and (especially) Conrad (Kurt) von Molo (the latter, dating from 1981). These I supplemented with correspondence with Elfriede Nagel, my own fruiful 1993 interview with von Molo in Munich, and letters and interviews with several of von Harbou's nephews and nieces—Niels von Harbou (the son of Horst, the Ufa still photographer), Brigitte K. Puttkamer (Thea's niece, who as a child had a tiny part in *M*) and especially Karen-Maria Kane in Munich (another niece, who among surviving family members professed to have known von Harbou best).

"Several days after that . . ." is from Hans Feld's 1980 interview in *Thea von Harbou.*

Erich Kettelhut's remarkable unpublished memoirs, quoted extensively in the Berlin chapters of this book, are on deposit at the Kinemathek in Berlin. So is Gero Gandert's wide-ranging tape-recorded interview with Alfred Zeisler.

"It was a lie . . ." is from Georges Sadoul's "Fritz Lang" essay in *Histoire générale du cinéma*, vol. 3 (Paris: Denoel, 1953).

Lang comments on his mother's will in his February 12, 1972 letter to PEM.

The early "lost and restored" Fritz Lang films are reported and reviewed by Jürgen Kasten in "Melodramatik, Aktion und Verwirrung—Drei frühe Filme von Fritz Lang im Zürcher Filmpodium" in the January 9, 1992 edition of Zurich's *Neue Zürcher Zeitung.*

Chapter Four: 1921–1922

"The childhood dream which most influenced . . ." is from the January 1, 1927 *Berliner Tageblatt*, as cited in Eisner's *Fritz Lang.*

"I shall never forget . . ." is Robert Herlth quoted in Eisner's *Fritz Lang.*

"For the fire in the old people's home . . ." is from Eisner's *Fritz Lang.*

"When my writer, architect, cameraman . . ." is from "Answers to Questions."

Lisa Rosenthal's death was reconstructed from numerous second-hand and even third-hand sources—especially Charles Higham (who related his unpublished conversations with Karl Freund on the incident), Hans Feld (from Lotte Eisner's memoirs, principally), Alfred Zeisler (reinforcing the Freund account), and Fritz Arno Wagner (via Gero Gandert). Cornelius Schnauber, Pierre Rissient and especially Howard Vernon (related their private exchanges with Lang on the subject). As the text makes clear, there is no proof positive of the death, marriage to Fritz Lang, or even existence of the director's first wife. The reputable French film scholar Bernard Eisenschitz told me he was half-inclined to believe it was all a clever fiction Lang had managed to concoct to dramatize his otherwise humdrum life.

Jean Renoir's comment ("Sodom and Gommorah were reborn there . . .") is from his autobiography *My Life and My Films* (New York: Atheneum, 1974). Klaus Mann is quoted from his and Erika Mann's *Escape to Life* (Boston: Houghton-Mifflin, 1939). Stefan Zweig's "the Babylon of the world . . ." is from *The World of Yesterday.*

"A small bright spot, Mabuse's face gleams . . ." is Kracauer from *From Caligari to Hitler.*

"A symptom of a Europe that was falling apart . . ." is Klein-Rogge from Ufa publicity, 1924, as cited in Sturm's *Fritz Lang: films/textes/référénces.*

"Dr. Mabuse was a Superman . . ." is from Gero Gandert's "Fritz Lang über

M: Ein Interview" in M, Gandert and Ulrich Gregor, eds. (Hamburg: Marion von Schroder, 1963).

"I had in mind a monster . . ." is from *Meine berühmten Freunde*.

Chapter Five: 1923–1924

On the subject of German-American film business relations during the 1920s, I consulted Thomas J. Saunders's meticulously researched *Hollywood in Berlin: American Cinema and Weimar Germany* (Berkeley: University of California Press, 1994).

"Naturally, having much more money . . ." is from "Fritz Lang Remembers."

Lang's Berlin residence was described in "Sammler Wohnungen—Fritz Lang, Berlin" in the August, 1924 *Innendekoration*. See also the December 1932 *Die Dame*. The footnoted Goethe translation is from Bernard Taylor and the 1932 Oxford University Press edition of *Faust*.

Hilde Guttmann was interviewed twice, once by phone, and a second time in person in London. In addition, Alan Dein supplied a transcript of one of Guttmann's public speeches where she talked about Fritz Lang and Thea von Harbou, along with photographs from his collection featuring Guttmann, Lang, von Harbou and Ayi Tendulkar.

Carl Hoffmann "knows the secret of photographing a woman . . ." is from Ufa publicity, as cited in *The Haunted Screen*.

"This 'drawing together,' this mysterious communication . . ." is from *The Ufa Story*.

The decor and design of *Die Nibelungen* is intriguingly analyzed in Sabina Hake's "Architectural Hilstories: Fritz Lang and the Nibelungs" in *Wide Angle*, July, 1990.

My account of the filming of *Die Nibelungen* draws on numerous sources, including two articles in the *New York Times*: "How Siegfried Was Produced" from the September 6, 1925, issue, and T. R. Ybarra's " 'Die Nibelungen' Meets Disaster in Berlin" from April 29, 1924.

"When the second reel was being shown . . ." is from Peter Bogdanovich's interview with Edgar G. Ulmer in *Kings of the Bs*, edited by Todd McCarthy and Charles Flynn (New York: Dutton, 1975).

"By making the Siegfried legend into a film . . ." is part of "Fritz Lang Gives His Last Interview."

Lang's first U.S.-Hollywood trip is reported in "German Director, Fritz Lang, Here" in the October 14, 1924 *New York Telegraph*; and "German Director Tells of Visit to Hollywood" in the November 30, 1924 *New York Times*. It is also chronicled in Jacobsen's *Erich Pommer* and Ott's *The Films of Fritz Lang*.

"I saw a street lit as if in full daylight . . ." is from *The Films of Fritz Lang*.

"I remarked to Pommer . . ." is from the Gretchen Berg transcript.

"The sensational landscape intoxicated me . . ." is from Carl Zuckmayer's *A Part of Myself* (New York: Harcourt Brace Jovanovich, 1966); and "Arizona and Texas remind you . . ." is from *Bertolt Brecht Journals 1934–1955*, as translated by Hugh Rorrison and edited by John Willett (New York: Routledge, 1993).

Lang writes about his first American adventure in "Zwischen Bohrtürmen und Palmen: ein kalifornischer Reisebericht" in the January, 1925 *Filmland*.

Chapter Six: 1925–1927

Apart from Lang's various reminiscences, chief among the sources which helped recreate the making of *Metropolis* were Gustav Fröhlich's autobiography *Waren das Zeiten: Mein Film-Heldenleben* (Munich: Herbig, 1982), the Gretchen Berg transcript and Erich Kettelhut's memoirs. Gustav Fröhlich also reminisces in *Trois Lumiéres*. Heide Schönemann's book *Filmbilder—Vorbilder* (Berlin: Edition Hentrich, 1992) proved illumination about the architecture and design of the film. Citations from Thea von Harbou's novel are from the 1963 Ace edition, which made a point of following the text of the first, 1927 English-language version. Many English-language sources, for example, refer to the Master of Metropolis as "John Fredersen," which was in fact one of the dubious changes from "Joh Fredersen" of the German version. Von Harbou's novel and this book therefore refer to the character as Joh.

Lang's 1924 visit to Vienna is reported in the *Film-Kurier* of May 19, 1924, as cited in Gehler and Kasten's *Fritz Lang*.

The Lien Deyers and Gerda Maurus vignettes are drawn from a transcript between Lang and interviewer Carol Hellman in the director's USC collection, as well as various Ufa publicity. The Gerda Maurus file at the Berlin Document Center also contained biographical information and career background about the actress.

A small item mentioning the Lang-von Harbou summer vacation of 1924, pinpointing the genesis of *Metropolis*, occurs under "Film-Ertrablatt" in the July 4, 1924, *Illustrierte Wiener Extrablatt*.

"Full of turning, twisting, circling light . . ." is from "Was ich in Amerika sah" in the December 11, 1924, *Film-Kurier*, as cited in Gehler and Kasten's *Fritz Lang*. See also *Fritz Lang—Metropolis* (Munich: Münchner Filmmuseum and Münchner Filmzentrume. V., 1988).

"The cameraman told the technicians . . ." is from the Gretchen Berg transcript.

Brigitte Helm's story of discovery and casting comes from the Gretchen Berg transcript, an interview with Lang in the March 3, 1927 *Mein Film*, and *Brigitte Helm: From Metropolis to Gold, Portrait of a Goddess* by Peter Herzog and Gene Vazzana (New York: Corvin, 1994).

"With his megaphone, he encouraged us . . ." is Theodore Loos quoted in *The Films of Fritz Lang*.

Karl Freund is quoted from "Meine Arbeit an *Metropolis*—Ein Gespräch mit Karl Freund" in the January 7, 1927, *B.Z. am Mittag*.

"Rearranged the scenes . . ." is from Eisner's *Fritz Lang*. See also Marie Seton's biography *Sergei M. Eisenstein* (New York: Grove Press, 1960).

Thea von Harbou's on-the-set reportage "Thea v. Harbou: Bis eine Szene so weit ist . . ." is quoted from the *Ufa Magazin*, January 14–20, 1927 (translation by Heike Siebert and Christiane Schroeter).

The subject of Lang and kitsch is notably developed in Lang's essay "Kitsch—Sensation—Kultur und Film" in E. Beyfuss and A. Kossowsky, *Das Kulturfilmbuch* (Berlin: Carl P. Chryselins'scher Verlag, 1924).

"I have often said that I didn't like *Metropolis* . . ." is from "La nuit viennoise—Une confession de Fritz Lang" by Gretchen Berg as published in *Cahiers du Cinéma*, nos. 169 and 179, August 1965 and June 1966.

"I was not so politically minded . . ." is from *Fritz Lang in America*.

"I didn't think in those days a social question . . ." is from *The Films of Fritz Lang*.

H. G. Wells's essay about *Metropolis* was published as "Mr. Wells Reviews A Current Film: He Takes Issue With This German Conception of What the City of One Hundred Years Hence Will Be Like" in the April 17, 1927, *New York Times*; also cited are "An Impression of the German Film 'Metropolis' " by Herman G. Scheffauer in the March 6, 1927, *New York Times*, and " 'Metropolis' Film Seen in the January 11, 1927 *New York Times*.

Luis Buñuel's original appraisal of *Metropolis* was republished in *Luis Buñuel: A Critical Biography* by Francisco Aranda (London: Secker & Warburg, 1975).

Channing Pollock writes about his tinkering with *Metropolis* in *Harvest of My Years* (Indianapolis/New York: Bobbs-Merrill, 1943.) Also cited is "German Film Revision Upheld as Needed Here" by Randolph Bartlett in the March 13, 1927 *New York Times*.

David L. Parker wrote about the American reediting of *Metropolis* in The Library of Congress Newsletter No. 12.

Chapter Seven: 1928–1929

"More patriotic than a German junker . . ." is from Willy Fritsch's . . . *das kommt nicht wieder* (Stuttgart: Classen, 1963).

"Luckily, the two artists are used . . ." is from "Thea von Harbou und Fritz Lang in Wien" in *Mein Film*, February 24 and March 3, 1927.

"Fritz Lang is staying in Germany! . . ." is from the June 29, 1927, *Film-Kurier*.

"As soon as possible . . ." is quoted from *The Ufa Story*.

"Only a small film compared to *Metropolis* . . ." is quoted from Eisner's *Fritz Lang*.

"This was done no less than 23 times . . ." is from Paul Hörbiger's *Ich habe für Euch gespielt* (Munich, Berlin: Herbig, 1979).

Anecdotes about Gerda Maurus under Lang's tutelage are drawn especially from Curt Riess's books.

"The soft movement back and forth . . ." is from *The Films of Fritz Lang*. Ott makes a point of stating that this train trip came on the back end of one of Lang's vacations to Istanbul. If so, perhaps the publicity stop-over in Vienna was part of the itinerary.

The *Spione* publicity trip, with both Thea von Harbou and Gerda Maurus accompanying Lang to Vienna, is reported in the *Österreichische Kino Journal* of April 21, 1928.

The tidbit about Lang paying half the costs of Oberth's rocket experiments comes from Hans Barth's *Hermann Oberth: Vater der Raumfahrt* (Esslingen:

Bechtle, 1991). Oberth's experiments were also reported in "Moon Rockets Lure Germany's Savants" by Guido Enderis in the September 22, 1929, *New York Times*.

"Thinking back, I realized to my own surprise . . ." is from Willy Ley's *Rockets, Missiles and Men in Space* (New York: Viking, 1968).

"That was the happiest time of my life . . ." is from the Gretchen Berg transcript.

"I was disgusted . . ." is from *The Real Tinsel*.

Lang and von Harbou's *Die Frau im Mond* publicity trip to Vienna is reported in "Fritz Langs und Thea von Harbous Besuch in Wien" in the December 5, 1929, *Mein Film*.

Chapter Eight: 1930–1931

Published accounts differ about aspects of Peter Lorre's life story. I have done my best to reconcile the discrepancies by comparing reputable books and articles, including, but not limited to, "Reluctant Menace" by Quentin Reynolds in the January 18, 1936 *Collier's*; "Peter Lorre" by Herbert G. Luft in the May, 1960 *Films in Review*; *The Films of Peter Lorre* by Stephen D. Youngkin, James Bigwood and Raymond G. Cabana Jr. (Secaucus, N.J.: The Citadel Press, 1982); and *Peter Lorre. Seine Filme—sein Leben* by Friedmann Beyer (Munich: Heyne, 1988).

Lorre himself recounts his discovery by Lang at a dress rehearsal for *Frühlings Erwachen* in the March 17, 1933 *Mein Film*.

Gottfried Reinhardt wrote about Lorre's relationship with Lang in his German-language memoir *Der Apfel fiel von Stamm* (Munich: Langen Müller, 1992); and Curt Riess writes about the actor, the director and filming of *M* in *Das gab's nur einmal* as well as his book *Gustaf Gründgens* (Hamburg: Hoffmann und Campe, 1965).

"I started to become interested in human beings . . ." is from "Film—Die Kunst unserer Zeit" by Erwin Leiser in *Film und Fernsehen*, no. 8, 1983, as cited by Sturm.

The *M* questionnairre addressed to Alan S. Downer at Princeton, which is dated c. March 16, 1948, is on deposit in Lang's USC files.

"I took no credit for it . . ." is from Henry Hart's interview with Lang, "Fritz Lang Today Gently Deprecates Some of His Past," in the June-July, 1956 *Films in Review*.

"Without realizing it, I had grabbed him . . ." is from Leiser in *Film und Fernsehen*, as cited by Sturm.

"We worked faster than usual that day . . ." is from the Gretchen Berg transcript.

"I am a musical moron . . ." is from "Fritz Lang Remembers."

"Mr. and Mrs. Lang, this film shows . . ." is from *The Great German Films*.

All quotations from Goebbels's diaries are from *Die Tagebücher von Joseph Goebbels: Sämtliche Fragmente*, ed. Else Fröhlich, Vol. 1, 1924–1941 (Munich: Saur, 1987).

Helpful to my appreciation of *M* was Roger Manvell's introduction to *Masterworks of the German Cinema*, which includes the *M* script (New York: Harper & Row, 1973).

Crucial to fleshing out the life story of Lily Latté were a series of letters from her cousin Clemens Auerbach to the author.

Chapter Nine: 1932–1933

"Thefts of explosives and mysterious thefts..." is from Fritz Lang's September 26, 1930, letter to Norbert Jacques, published in *Zensur: Verbotene deutsche Filme 1933–1945*, Kraft Wetzel and Peter Hagemann (Berlin: Stiftung Deutsche Kinemathek, 1978), as cited by Sturm.

Fritz Arno Wagner is quoted from a 1933 interview in *Trois Lumiéres*.

The Lotte Eisner reportage from the *Mabuse* set ("a fantastical kind of reality, etc....") was published first in *Film-Kurier* in 1933, then in a French periodical, and then recycled with variations in two of her books, *Fritz Lang* and *Ich hatte einst ein schönes Vaterland—Memoiren*. This version is translated from her memoirs.

"Although Jewish, Lang possesses all the qualities..." is from the December 19, 1929, *Cinemonde*, as cited by Sturm.

On the subject of Goebbels and the cinema, I consulted Ralf George Reuth's *Goebbels* (Munich: Piper, 1990), Helmut Heiber's *Goebbels* (New York: Hawthorn Books, 1972), Roger Manvill and Heinrich Fraenkel's *Doctor Goebbels: His Life and Death* (London: Heinemann, 1960), and Curt Riess's *Goebbels* (Baden-Baden: Dreieckverlag, 1950).

Gösta Werner's article "Fritz Lang and Goebbels: Myth and Facts" from the Spring, 1990 *Film Quarterly* was a tremendous help in clarifying Lang's actions and movements in 1933, and I myself examined the director's passport and travel documents on deposit at the Kinemathek in Berlin.

Goebbels's address to German filmmakers is reported by Dr. Gerd Albrecht in his book *Nationalsozialistische Filmpolitik* (Stuttgart: Enke Verlag, 1969). I also consulted the informative *Film in the Third Reich: Art and Propaganda in Nazi Germany* by David Stewart Hull (New York: Touchstone, 1969).

Lang's reputed membership in a Nazi organization is noted in Hans-Michael Bock's *Cinegraph*.

Curtis Bernhardt is quoted from *Curtis Bernhardt*, a Directors Guild of America Oral History by Mary Kiersch (Metuchen, N.J.: DGA and Scarecrow Press, 1986).

Paul Erich Marcus (PEM) is quoted from *Strangers Everywhere* (London: John Lane, The Bodley Head, 1939).

"His producer, who happened to be Jewish..." is Curt from Riess's *Meine berühmten Freunde*.

I have collated many different versions and variations of the Goebbels story, including: "Fritz Lang Puts on Film the Nazi Mind He Fled From" from the *New York World-Telegram* of June 11, 1941; "Speaking of Movies" by John T. McManus, *PM*, March 18, 1943; "May Mann's Going Hollywood," published September 4, 1943, in the *Ogden Standard-Examiner* (noted, in Lang's USC files, as having been arranged by Dave Epstein, the director's publicist); "Skylines of New York" by Lawrence Perry in the *Dayton Daily News* of March 21, 1943 (also syndicated by the North American Newspaper Alliance); an advance copy of Joseph Addison's article about Fritz Lang as slated to appear in *Screen Stars*, July 1945; "The Nine Lives of Doctor Mabuse" by John Russell

Taylor in *Sight and Sound*, Winter, 1961–1962; "Fritz Lang Talks About Dr. Mabuse" by Mark Shivas from *Movie*, November 1962; and "A Master with Graph Paper and Monocle" in *The German Tribune* of December 25, 1965.

The numerous book versions include *Meine berühmten Freunde, The Celluloid Muse, The Real Tinsel* and the Lang interview in Andrew Sarris's *Interviews With Film Directors* (New York: Bobbs-Merrill, 1967). In addition, I tape-recorded—and make frequent reference in my book to—Lang's version of events as proffered to director William Friedkin for his filmed documentary interview dating from the early 1970s.

Billy Wilder's hand-me-down version of events appears in Hellmuth Karasek's *Billy Wilder* (Hamburg: Hoffmann und Campe, 1992).

German film historian Eric Rentschler is quoted from "Nazi Cinema: Goebbels's Aryan Hollywood, 1933–1945" in *Film Comment*, November–December, 1994.

The Lang-von Harbou divorce records are on deposit at the Kinemathek in Berlin.

The Austrian article about Lang heading to Paris to work with Pommer, "Fritz Lang wieder bei Pommer," appeared in the August 18–24, 1933 *Mein Film*.

Lang mentions a "midnight inquisition" with Goebbels in an undated transcript (c. 1942) of an interview conducted by Jimmy Starr, part of the publicity file for *Hangmen Also Die* in the director's USC files. "The Monster of Hollywood," an interview with Lang by Mary Morris—which is included in *Trois Lumiéres*—also clearly quotes the director as saying his meeting with Goebbels took place "one night." "The Monster of Hollywood" is also undated (c. 1945).

Willi Winkler wrote about "Ein Schlafwandler bei Goebbels" in *Der Spiegel*, Nov. 26, 1990.

"It was a case of two characters growing apart . . ." is from "The Monster of Hollywood."

"Our separation was amicable . . ." is from *The Films of Fritz Lang*.

Andrew Marton is quoted from *Andrew Marton*, a Directors Guild of America Oral History by Joanne D'Antonio (Metuchen, N.J.: DGA and Scarecrow Press, 1991).

Arthur Maria Rabenalt is quoted on the subject of Thea von Harbou and the fate of *A Child, a Dog, a Vagabond* from his book *Goebbels und der "Grossdeutsche" Film* (Munich: Herbig, 1985). Rabenalt makes similar remarks in Reinhold Keiner's *Thea von Harbou: und der deutsche Film bis 1933*.

Howard Rodman's novel *Destiny Express* (New York: Atheneum, 1990)— capturing Fritz Lang's final days in Hitler's Germany—pretends little in the way of facts; but it is a perceptive as well as pleasureable fiction, and is recommended for further reading.

PARIS

Chapter Ten: 1933–1934

"Die Legende" is included in *Der Berg des Aberglaubens und andere Geschichten*, edited by Cornelius Schnauber (Vienna: Europaverlag, 1988),

Charlotte Chandler's plot synopsis is from her book *The Ultimate Seduction*.

Janet Flanner (Genêt) is quoted from *Paris Was Yesterday: 1925–1939* (New York: Viking, 1972). Her Paris column was datelined April 19, 1933.

"So much turbulent political water . . ." is cited in *The Films of Fritz Lang*.

Lang arriving in Paris, interviewed by Curt Riess, is from *Meine berühmten Freunde.*

"In my mind it was a double error . . ." is from *Spiel im Dassein* (Paris: Robert Laffont, 1963) See also *Max Ophüls* by Claude Beylie (Paris: Seghers, 1963).

Apart from my own interview with Gilbert Mandelik, I have drawn on Frederick Ott's as quoted in *The Films of Fritz Lang.*

Franz Waxman is quoted on the subject of *Liliom* in *Trois Lumiéres*, drawn from a letter to Herbert G. Luft, originally incorporated in his "Erich Pommer" articles for *Films in Review*.

Bernard Zimmer is quoted from *Trois Lumiéres*.

The Charles Boyer anecdote comes from "Fonda on Ford" by Rui Nogueira in *Sight and Sound*, (Spring, 1973).

"*Liliom* I always liked very much . . ." is from "Fritz Lang Seminar."

Background on the David O. Selznick trip to Paris is drawn from David Thomson's book *Showman: The Life of David O. Selznick* (New York: Knopf, 1992), and also from "Mr. Selznick's Fruitful Trip" in the *New York Times* of June 17, 1934.

"Fritz Lang could have been a diplomat . . ." is George Cukor as quoted in *The Films of Fritz Lang.*

HOLLYWOOD

Chapter Eleven: 1934–1936

I was greatly aided in tracing the provenance of Egon Schiele's artworks by Jane Kallir.

Most of Lang's American publicity releases are preserved in his USC files, but some of those which are cited in the text appear in overlapping archives—especially the Paramount collection at the Margaret Herrick Library of the Academy of Motion Picture Arts and Sciences, the 20th Century–Fox material in Special Collections at UCLA, and the Jerry Wald collection at the USC Cinema-Television Library.

All quotes from Peter Bogdanovich are from *Fritz Lang in America*, except in Chapter Twenty-One, where they are drawn from my interview with Bogdanovich.

Lang's files on "Tomorrow," "The Man Behind You," "Hell Afloat,"

"Passport to Hell" *Fury* and most of his subsequent, U.S. productions—realized or not—are among the voluminous USC deposits, containing contract information, filming and budget schedules, script drafts, memoranda, publicity, notes, photographs, and other production-related records. When possible, I cross-referenced these production papers with similar files under Lang's name at the Cinémathéque in Paris.

Salka Viertel is quoted from her memoirs *The Kindness of Strangers* (New York: Holt, Rinehart and Winston, 1969).

Helpful to depicting the European émigré community in Hollywood were several books: Klaus and Erika Mann's book *Escape to Life; The Hollywood Exiles* by John Baxter (London: Macdonald and Jane's, 1976); *Strangers in Paradise: The Hollywood Émigrés, 1933–1950* by John Russell Taylor (New York: Holt, Rinehart and Winston, 1983); and *Exiled in Paradise: German Refugee Artists and Intellectuals in America From the 1930s to the Present* by Anthony Heilbut (New York: Viking, 1983).

Frederick Hollander (née Friedrich Holländer) is quoted from his book *Those Torn From Earth* (New York: Liveright, 1941). Vladimir Pozner is quoted from "bb" in *Brecht: As They Knew Him*, edited by Hubert Witt (New York: International Publishers, 1974).

John Huston is quoted on the subject of Salka Viertel from his autobiography, *An Open Book* (New York: Knopf, 1980).

A compelling true-life book about the lynching incident that inspired *Fury* is Harry Farrell's *Swift Justice: Murder and Vengeance in a California Town* (New York: St. Martin's Press, 1992).

"I wonder sometimes if it serves any purpose . . ." is from "Fritz Lang Remembers."

"You must have worked with producers . . ." is from "Fritz Lang Seminar."

My footnote about Lang's claims re: his activist role in the founding of the Directors Guild is backed up by the DGA pamphlet "The First 48 Years"; the "Directors Organize!" article in the January 17, 1936 *Daily Variety*; and the "Directors Form Guild" account in the rival *Hollywood Reporter* of the same date. *The New York Times* reported on the Guild's birth pangs in "A Guild for Directors" of January 26, 1936. The complete listing of attendees of the first general meeting is in the *Hollywood Reporter* of January 23, 1936; and all of the principal founders are listed by David Robb in his definitive article "Directors Guild Born Out of Fear 50 Years Ago" in the *Daily Variety* of October 29, 1985.

"I had some trouble . . ." is from *Fritz Lang in America*.

For Joseph L. Mankiewicz's side of the complicated behind-the-scenes story of *Fury*, I am indebted to Michel Ciment's interview with Joseph Mankiewicz in *Passeport pour Hollywood* (Paris: Seuil, 1987); and to Richard Schickel, who kindly provided an unpublished transcript of his own interview with Mankiewicz. I also consulted *Pictures Will Talk: The Life and Films of Joseph L. Mankiewicz* by Kenneth L. Geist (New York: Scribner's, 1978). Mankiewicz's seven-page letter to me about Lang and *Fury*, full of anecdotes and humorous asides, was dated January 29, 1993, and signed by his assistant Stefan Petrucha. It arrived in the mail one day after Mankiewicz's February 5, 1993, death was reported in the news.

Footnote: "As shoeshine people . . ." is Lang quoting L. B. Mayer in *Fritz Lang in America*. Lang makes similar remarks in *The Celluloid Muse*.

Apart from my interview with Sylvia Sidney for this book, I also interviewed her on the subject of Lang when I was working for *The Boston Globe*. "There was always someone who was his patsy . . ." is from my profile of her entitled "Sylvia Sidney has her 'Summer Wishes' " from the July 7, 1974, *Boston Globe*.

Joseph Ruttenberg is quoted from several sources: including *Five American Cinematographers: Interviews with Karl Struss, Joseph Ruttenberg, James Wong Howe, Linwood Dunn and William H. Clothier* by Scott Eyman (Metuchen, N. J. and London: Scarecrow Press, 1987); *Hollywood Cameramen* by Charles Higham (Bloomington, Indiana: Indiana University Press, 1970); and *Trois Lumiéres*, where Ruttenberg is one of the people who contributed reminiscences.

Curt Riess's anecdote about Lang's face-to-face showdown with L. B. Mayer is from *Meine berühmten Freunde*, with just a hint that the story might have come from Lily Latté.

"A stupid thing . . ." is from "Fritz Lang Remembers."

Graham Greene's film criticism is collected in *Graham Greene on Film: Collected Film Criticism 1935–1940*, edited by John Russell Taylor (New York: Simon and Schuster, 1972).

Fury's popularity among New York film critics is reported in a January 5, 1937 *New York Times* article. See also B. R. Crisler's January 31, 1937 "Film Gossip of the Week" column in *The New York Times*.

Fritz Lang's March 28, 1937 telegram to Marlene Dietrich is in the Dietrich collection at the Kinemathek in Berlin.

Two outstanding books about Marlene Dietrich do not disagree about her relationship with Lang. I have cited both *Marlene Dietrich: Life and Legend* by Steven Bach (New York: Morrow, 1992), and Maria Riva's *Marlene Dietrich* (New York: Knopf, 1993). See also *Blue Angel* by Donald Spoto (New York: Doubleday, 1992).

Douglas Fairbanks, Jr., who was also interviewed, wrote an engaging book, *The Salad Days: An Autobiography* (New York: Doubleday, 1988), that I referred to for its mention of his friendship with the director and his appreciation for the private side of Lang.

Chapter Twelve: 1936–1938

Ben Hecht on Walter Wanger is quoted from *A Child of the Century* (New York: Ballantine, 1970).

Sylvia Sidney's notion of the genesis of *You Only Live Once* is drawn from "Sylvia Sidney" by Jeff Laffel in the September–October 1994 *Films in Review*.

The portrait of Gene Towne and Graham Baker is drawn from Matthew Bernstein's *Walter Wanger: Hollywood Independent* (Berkeley, University of California Press, 1994).

The San Quentin musical program and jailhouse sketch I stumbled across while examining boxes of unitemized material from the Fritz Lang estate at the American Heritage Center in Laramie, Wyoming.

Leon Shamroy is quoted from *Hollywood Cameramen*.

Some of Henry Fonda's remarks in this chapter ("Lang took a whole day to shoot . . .") are from "Fonda on Ford." The rest ("It just doesn't occur to him . . .") are from "Reflections on Forty Years of Make-Believe, An Interview with Henry Fonda" by Curtis Lee Hanson in *Cinema* of December, 1966.

"What he [Lang] would do . . ." is from Sylvia Sidney's interview in the September–October, 1994 *Films in Review*.

The frog anecdote appears in "A frog defies Hollywood" by Lang, substituting for columnist Virginia Wright, in the *Hollywood Citizen-News* of August 15, 1947.

There is one provocative school of critical theory that holds that Eddie Taylor (Henry Fonda) may be in fact guilty of the bank robbery in *You Only Live Once*, and that Lang left the issue deliberately vague in the film. See *"You Only Live Once: The Doubled Feature"* by George Wilson in *Sight and Sound*, Autumn, 1977.

"To interpret the cowboy in the light . . ." is from Lang's publicity essay, "Was This the Real West?" See also "Westerns for Adults"—apparently timed to promote *Western Union*—both in the director's USC files.

All Kurt Weill quotations are from *Speak Low (When You Speak Love): The Letters of Kurt Weill and Lotte Lenya*, edited and translated by Lys Symonette and Kim H. Kowalke (Berkeley: University of California Press, 1996). For the relationship between Weill and Lang, see also *The Days Grow Short: The Life and Music of Kurt Weill* by Ronald Sanders (Hollywood: Silman-James Press, 1991).

Sam Coslow is quoted from his autobiography *Cocktails for Two: The Many Lives of Giant Songwriter Sam Coslow* (New Rochelle, N. H.: Arlington House, 1977).

For production background and information on Lang's two Paramount films—*You and Me* and *Ministry of Fear*—I read script drafts and production memoranda in the studio's collection at the Margaret Herrick Library. It is interesting that the Paramount publicity release (dated March 8, 1938) which is quoted in the text ("He kept her rehearsing . . .") also makes a point of referring to Lang as an Austrian. Copies of many of these studio documents also turn up in Lang's USC files and at the Cinémathèque in Paris.

The early formation of the Hollywood Anti-Nazi League and related political organizations is extensively covered in Marta Mierendorff's *William Dieterle: Der Plutarch von Hollywood* (Berlin: Henschel Verlag, 1993). My personal bibles on the history of Hollywood left-wing activity, leading to the blacklist, are *The Inquisition in Eden: Politics in the Film Community, 1930–1960* by Larry Ceplair and Steven Englund (Garden City, New York: Anchor, 1980); Victor S. Navasky's *Naming Names* (New York: Viking, 1980); and Nancy Lynn Schwartz's *The Hollywood Writers' Wars* (New York: Alfred A. Knopf, 1982). I tirelessly recommend them to people interested in the subject.

Paul Kohner is quoted from his October 29, 1937, letter to Luis Trenker included in "The Trenker-Kohner Correspondence," *Filmexil* no. 1 (Berlin: Stiftung Deutsche Kinemathek, 1992).

Chapter Thirteen: 1939–1941

In addition to Nat Segaloff's interview with Sam Jaffe for this book, I consulted the Sam Jaffe "oral history" on deposit at the Margaret Herrick Library.

I obtained Lang and Lily Latté's citizenship and immigration records from the National Archives—Pacific Southwest Region after formally requesting them from the U.S. Department of Immigration and Naturalization Services. See also "Footnote on a Patriotic Occasion" by Theodore Strauss in the August 11, 1940 *New York Times*.

Records and documents pertaining to disposition of the Lang family estate in Austria came from municipal and court files in Vienna and Gars am Kamp. Partly because of the Nazification of Austria, there had to be follow-up reports on the proceedings, which dragged on for years; in fact, the most recent update in Austrian Department of Agriculture files, which may have been precipitated by inquiries from Lily Latté or family members, is dated September 19, 1977, only a year after Lang's death in the U.S.

I examined production records and memoranda for the three Fritz Lang/ 20th Century–Fox films producer Kenneth MacGowan was associated with— *The Return of Frank James*, *Western Union* and *Man Hunt*—among his papers in the Manuscripts Room at UCLA. These three films, plus Lang's abortive participations in *Confirm and Deny* and *Moontide*, were covered more substantially in production records in the 20th Century–Fox studio collection, also at UCLA in Special Collections. Again, duplicates of some of this material can be found at USC and at the Cinémathèque.

"He knew how I felt . . ." is Henry Fonda from *Cinema*.

"As an example, let's say it is night . . ." is from *Fritz Lang in America*.

"Not only was it a wrong picture . . ." is Henry Fonda from *Cinema*.

"I saw Henry Fonda with . . ." is Jackie Cooper from his Southern Methodist University "oral history."

Gene Tierney is quoted from *Self-Portrait* (New York: Wyden, 1979).

Carl Zuckmayer is quoted from *A Part of Myself*.

Lang's "romantic publicity," including the Kay Francis items, are neatly clipped among his USC files. Leith G. Johnson was extremely helpful in pinpointing the director's name in entries of the actress's diaries held at the Wesleyan Cinema Archives.

Rock Brynner is quoted on the subject of his mother, Virginia Gilmore, from *Yul: The Man Who Would Be King: A Memoir of Father and Son* (Simon and Schuster, New York, 1989).

The first, pre-World War II wave of anti-Red hearings in Hollywood is reported in "Hollywood Names Cited in Red Inquiry" in the *Los Angeles Times* of August 15, 1940; and "Red Plot to Grab Studios Charged" in the *Los Angeles Examiner* of August 15, 1940. Lang is prominent in both accounts. Lang's correspondence with his publicity representative, Henry Rogers, is at USC, along with the director's drafted statement—signed by him—which was reprinted in its entirety in the *Los Angeles Times* of August 16, 1940. The anti-Red investigation was then followed up in other articles in the Los Angeles newspapers before the story petered out after several days.

Jean Renoir writes about Dudley Nichols in *My Life and My Films*.

"He gave a very characteristic answer . . ." is from *Fritz Lang in America*.

Gene Fowler, Jr., interviewed for this book, was cross-referenced in two other "oral histories": the one done for Southern Methodist University and one on deposit at the Margaret Herrick Library. I have quoted from all three interviews. I did not interview his wife, editor Marjorie Johnson Fowler, but she was also interviewed both for SMU and the Academy of Motion Picture Arts and Sciences: I compared and drew from both transcripts.

Sam Fuller is quoted from *Trois Lumiéres*.

Generally informative about Lang's 20th Century–Fox stint was Nick Smedley's "Fritz Lang Outfoxed: The German Genius as Contract Employee" in the January–February, 1991 *Sinema*.

Chapter Fourteen: 1941–1945

"Had decided that Lang..." is from John T. McManus's "Speaking of Movies" in the March, 18, 1943, *PM*, touting the joint release of *Hangmen Also Die* and *Das Testament des Dr. Mabuse*.

"The first moment in which..." is from "Noted Director's Main Concern is 'Stop Hitler' " in *The Daily Worker*, April 25, 1943.

"Was made as an allegory..." is from Lang's new prologue to the 1943 American release of *Das Testament des Dr. Mabuse*, as quoted in Kracauer's *From Caligari to Hitler*.

"Made the picture as an anti-Hitler picture..." is from Lang's interview with Eileen Creelman under "Picture Plays and Players: Fritz Lang Discusses Two of His Films, 'Hangmen Also Die' and a Very Old One" in the March 20, 1943 *New York Sun*.

"To expose the masked Nazi theory..." is from John T. McManus's "Speaking of Movies in PM."

Martha Feuchtwanger's "oral history" is on deposit at UCLA.

Helpful to my understanding of the Brecht-Lang collaboration was James K. Lyon's well-considered *Bertolt Brecht in America* (Princeton, N.J.: Princeton University Press, 1980). Generally applicable to my portrait of Brecht was *Brecht: As They Knew Him*.

"It was only because of an impassioned plea..." is from Axel Madsen's "Lang," an interview with the director in *Sight and Sound*, Summer, 1967. This is an unusually candid interview with Lang about *Hangmen Also Die*. Madsen may have caught the director off-guard, since Lang's associates told me that after it was published he professed to be furious about the piece.

Anna Lee is quoted from her Southern Methodist University "oral history."

Hangmen Also Die's performance in the annual "Best Film" balloting is chronicled in "Watch on Rhine' Voted Best Film" from the December 19, 1943, *New York Times*.

Pete Martin's close-up of Nunnally Johnson, included in *Pete Martin Calls On* ... (New York: Simon and Schuster, 1962), aided my portrait of the writer-producer. I have also depended on Tom Stempel's definitive work on Johnson's career: including Stempel's "oral history" with Johnson done for the American Film Institute, and his book *Screenwriter: the Life and Times of Nunnally Johnson* (San Diego, New York, London: A. S. Barnes–The Tantivy Press, 1980). See also *Flashback: Nora Johnson on Nunnally Johnson* (New York: Doubleday & Co., 1979) and *The Letters of Nunnally Johnson* edited by Dorris Johnson and Ellen Leventhal (New York: Knopf, 1981).

"Fritz was a manipulator..." is Marjorie Fowler from the "oral history" at the Margaret Herrick Library.

"We started out, of course, with the advantage . . ." is from David Overbey's "Interview: Edward G. Robinson" in *Take One* (May 1978), and so is Lang's response, "How the hell would he know . . . ?"

"I think the book was better than the picture . . ." is from "Picture Plays and Players: Fritz Lang Talks of Forming His Own Company and of His Next Drama, 'Scarlet Street' " by Eileen Creelman in the *New York Sun* of April 17, 1945.

"It had to be a happy ending . . ."is Marjorie Fowler from her "oral history" at the Margaret Herrick Library.

"He snapped his fingers . . ." is Marjorie Fowler from the "oral history" at the Margaret Herrick Library.

"He was part of everything . . ." is from "Interview: Edward G. Robinson."

"Made a difference of one million dollars . . ." is from "Fritz Lang Gets Hep to Box Office" by Philip K. Scheuer in the *Los Angeles Times* of Oct. 21, 1945.

Lang's 1944–1945 professional flirtation with David O. Selznick is courtesy of Matthew Bernstein's research at the DOS archives.

Chapter Fifteen: 1945–1946

"Rearranging the folds . . ." is from "Interview: Edward G. Robinson."

"Toward the end, where Bennett . . ." is from Marjorie Fowler's "oral history" at the Margaret Herrick Library.

Walter Wanger, Dudley Nichols, and other Diana Productions memos and correspondence are cited from Matthew Bernstein's *Walter Wanger: Hollywood Independent*, my own research in the Wanger papers at the Wisconsin Center for Film and Theater Research, and cross-referenced production material in Lang's USC files.

Dudley Nichols's March 2, 1945, letter to Lang, on RKO stationery, is in the director's USC files.

The Ludwig Bemelmans memos and transcripts are in Lang's USC files.

Gene Fowler (Sr.) is quoted on the subject of John Decker from *Minutes of the Last Meeting* (New York: Viking Press, 1954).

Dan Duryea is quoted from *Trois Lumiéres.*

Hans Salter is quoted from his "oral history" at the Margaret Herrick Library.

Dudley Nichols is quoted from an undated, three-page letter to Walter Wanger in Lang's USC files.

Relevant to *Scarlet Street's* censorship battle, Matthew Bernstein supplied a copy of his exhaustive article "A Tale of Three Cities: The Banning of *Scarlet Street*," in advance of its publication in a film periodical. Contemporary accounts of the censorship fight include "Calling Attention to Sin" by Bosley Crowther in *The New York Times* of Feb. 17, 1946; and "Film Censors Ban 'Scarlet Street' " from *The New York Times* of Jan. 5, 1946.

"I could not rejoice on V-E day . . ." is from Maxine Garrison's "Whither the Film Industry?"

Lang makes his criticism of *The Seventh Cross* in "The Monster of Hollywood."

A remake of *Die Frau im Mond* was bandied about in the *Hollywood*

Reporter of May 11, 1944; and also in "Rocket Guns From Press Agent's Idea," by Frederick C. Othman in the *Hollywood Citizen-News* of June 5, 1944.

Much of Thea von Harbou's story, post-1933, comes from Berlin Document Center material, supplemented with interviews with her niece Karen-Maria Kane, who was in close contact with von Harbou during the post-War years, and with Vinayak Tendulkar and Mrs. Indumati Tendulkar, both of whom lived with Lang's ex-wife in Berlin for brief periods of time.

Helpful to illuminating von Harbou's contribution to Nazi filmmaking during the Third Reich was Erwin Leiser's *Nazi Cinema* (London: Secker and Warburg, 1974).

"I can still see how she came . . ." is from "My Cousin Thea" by Dr. Anne-Marie Durand-Wever, as quoted in Keiner's *Thea von Harbou: und der deutsche Film bis 1933*.

Milton Sperling is characterized partly with the help of his daughter's biography of him and members of the Warner family, *Hollywood Be Thy Name: The Warner Brothers Story* by Cass Warner Sperling and Cork Millner with Jack Warner, Jr. (Rocklin, Ca.: Prima, 1994).

Michael Burke is quoted from his memoirs *Outrageous Good Fortune* (Boston: Little, Brown and Co., 1984). Burke's variegated career was also chronicled by Arthur Daley in "Cloak and Dagger Man" in the Sept. 28, 1966 *New York Times*.

Lilli Palmer is quoted from *Change Lobsters and Dance* (New York: Macmillan, 1975).

Marc Lawrence is quoted from *Long Time No See: Confessions of a Hollywood Gangster* (Palm Springs, Ca.: Ursus Press, 1991).

Albert Maltz is quoted from his "oral history" at UCLA.

Chapter Sixteen: 1946–1947

Architect-designer Paul László is profiled in the August 18, 1952 *Time*.

Lang made a public pledge to support Wallace according to "Wallace Carries Campaign to Beverly Hills Elite" in the May 17, 1948 *Los Angeles Times*.

Apart from my own interview with Silvia Richards, I am grateful to Matthew Bernstein for letting me review and incorporate the transcript of his exchange with the scenarist for his Walter Wanger book.

Apart from my own interview with Hilda Rolfe, I read and enjoyed "The Perfectionist," about Fritz Lang, which Rolfe authored for *Film Comment* in its November–December 1992 issue. Rolfe also kindly perused portions of the manuscript corresponding with the years of her Diana Productions employ, making corrections and criticisms.

"As publicity-conscious as an actress . . ." is from the Associated Press's story "He Scares Actors," carried over the wires in mid-September of 1946.

Michael Redgrave is quoted from *In My Mind's I* (New York: Viking Press, 1983).

"Fritz was a real Jekyll-and-Hyde character . . ." is Joan Bennett quoted from *The Bennett Playbill* by Joan Bennett and Lois Kibbee (New York: Holt, Rinehart and Winston, 1970).

The taped-straws anecdote is from "A frog defies Hollywood."

Production manager M. A. Slater's memo to Walter Wanger, complaining about Lang, is dated March 4, 1947. The producer's memo to Lang is dated March 5, 1947, and prompted Lang's March 10, 1947 three-page rebuttal to Wanger. All are Inter-Department Communications on Diana Productions stationery, in Lang's USC files.

Min Selvin's memo to Walter Wanger, concerning Lang's ideas for *Secret Beyond the Door* publicity, is dated April 18, 1947, and is also in the director's USC files.

"It was a disaster . . ." is quoted from "Joan Bennett" by Ronald Bowers in the June–July, 1977, *Films in Review*. Interestingly, the actress did not make this statement for the record until after Lang's death.

Chapter Seventeen: 1948–1952

The chronology of Lang's reaction to the American remake of *M* is a little jumbled. The director appears to have begun complaining privately to friends in the press when he first caught wind of the project. The first grumbling mention of it in German newspapers appears to be in Bert Reisfeld's "Filmgespräche mit Fritz Lang" for the June 28, 1952 *Frankfurter Neue Presse*. I was supplied by Harold Nebenzal with an (undated, c. 1951–1952) Ezra Goodman column from Los Angeles newspapers which makes reference to already-published reports of a Lang-Seymour Nebenzahl rift. Goodman's column aired Lang's side along with Nebenzahl's vehement response.

Early script drafts and story conference notes for *American Guerrilla in the Philippines* are on deposit in the Rare Book Room of the University of Illinois-Urbana. For production background, see also "Film Campaign on Luzon" by Harold Mendelsohn in *The New York Times* of April 2, 1950.

Joseph Losey's point of view on the *M* remake is culled from several sources: including David Caute's *Joseph Losey: A Revenge on Life* (London: Faber and Faber, 1994); Losey's remarks as cited in *Conversations With Losey* by Michel Ciment (London: Methuen, 1985); and Losey's contribution to *Trois Lumiéres*.

For my account of the Directors Guild meeting, I have drawn on Robert Parrish's recollections in *Growing Up in Hollywood* (New York: Harcourt Brace Jovanovich, 1976). In a letter to the author shortly before his death in December of 1995, Parrish was unable to expand on his account of the meeting with regard to Lang's specific political allegiances.

All Federal Bureau of Investigation files were obtained under Freedom of Information Act (FOIA) auspices, and these include some sixty to seventy pages of FBI, Department of Justice, Navy, or Immigration and Naturalization Service reports.

My source on Martin Gang is Victor Navasky's *Naming Names*.

Chapter Eighteen: 1952–1953

Daniel Taradash worked hard to help me recreate the story behind *Rancho Notorious*. His letters to me included copies of May 7 and June 21, 1951 telegrams from Lang to Taradash; a lengthy May 31, 1951 letter from Lang to Taradash; and a June 23, 1963 letter from Taradash to Alfred Eibel responding to questions similar to my own. In addition Taradash supplied copies of production material from his own archival deposits at the American Heritage Center in Laramie, Wyoming.

Marlene Dietrich is quoted from her memoirs *Marlene* (New York: Weidenfeld & Nicolson, 1989).

"We didn't know it that he . . ." is from "Fritz Lang Seminar."

Philip Dunne is quoted about Wald on the subject of Jerry Wald from his memoirs *Take Two: A Life in Movies and Politics* (San Francisco: McGraw-Hill, 1980). Jean Negulesco is quoted about Wald from his memoirs *Things I Did and Things I Think I Did* (New York: Linden Press, 1984).

The Jerry Wald collection at USC provided script drafts and memoranda relevant to backgrounding the Fritz Lang films Wald produced—*Clash by Night*, *The Big Heat*, and *Human Desire*.

My characterization of Alfred Hayes is partly drawn from his portrait in *Wobblies, Pile Butts, and Other Heroes* by Archie Green (Urbana: University of Illinois Press, 1993).

"A very interesting man . . ." is from *Fritz Lang in America*.

"Poor Marilyn was a scared girl . . ." is from *The Celluloid Muse*.

I also consulted *Marilyn Monroe* by Donald Spoto (New York: Harper-Collins, 1993).

"Barbara, may I speak very frankly? . . ." is from *Starring Barbara Stanwyck* by Ella Smith (New York: Crown, 1974).

Lang's troubles with the blacklist were drawn from various sources, including Cornelius Schauber's *Fritz Lang in Hollywood* (Vienna: Europaverlag, 1986), which makes use of Lang correspondence not generally available in USC files. Lang's agent, Nat Goldstone, is a genuine mystery; there are those on the Hollywood left who say he was apolitical and fundamentally good-hearted, and others who believe that at times Goldstone acted as a middle-man brokering deals like Lang's that expunged left-tinged pasts.

Helpful on detailing the interaction of Jerry Wald, Harry Cohn, and Lang during the making of the director's two Columbia productions—*The Big Heat* and *Human Desire*—was Bernard Dick's *The Merchant Prince of Poverty Row: Harry Cohn of Columbia* (Lexington, Ky.: The University Press of Kentucky, 1993). Dick's book explores the relatively unplumbed Columbia Pictures collection at the American Heritage Center in Laramie, Wyoming.

Janet Bergstrom writes about "The Mystery of The Blue Gardenia" in *Shades of Noir*, edited by Joan Copjec (London: Verso, 1993).

Chapter Nineteen: 1953–1956

Lang's late 1940s–early 1950s publicity grab-bag includes: "Opinion With Accent: Foreign Actresses Act," circulated by the Associated Press in 1947, a variation of which was published (July 13, 1947) in the *Chicago Sunday Times*; "The more the audience is absorbed . . . ," which is from "Screen Has Reached Its Maturity, Fritz Lang Says" in the July 22, 1947 *Hollywood Citizen-News* (the copy in Lang's file has "written by Dave Epstein" scribbled on it); "I have to work fast . . . ," which is from Philip K. Scheuer's "Lang Does His Best to Give 'em Misery" in the *Los Angeles Times* of Sept. 20, 1953; and Lang on women and glamour from "Director Fritz Lang Lists Dislikes and Likes of

U.S. Girls" by Lydia Lane in the *Los Angeles Times* of June 20, 1954. "Perfectionist De-Luxe" by Gertrude Shanklin is also cited from the December 1945 issue of *Movieland*. The rather lengthy Rhonda Fleming press release, noted in the text, also contains an account of Lang's education and early career, as well as his fateful meeting with Goebbels. It is bylined "By Fritz Lang, Noted Motion Picture Director" and appears in various drafts on Bernie Williams-Kay Mulvey Press Release stationery. All of these drafts and articles, and numerous others, are in Lang's USC files.

Colin McArthur's monograph on *The Big Heat* was published as part of the BFI Film Classics series (London: BFI Publishing, 1992).

"Whose front page was . . ." is from a biography of Broadway columnist Dorothy Kilgallen, *Kilgallen* by Lee Israel (New York: Dell, 1979). Sydney Boehm broke Kilgallen into the newspaper profession on the city desk of the *New York Evening Journal*.

"Lang said he had liked all the characters . . ." and all other William P. McGivern quotes are from McGivern's "Flashback: Roman Holiday" in the October, 1983 *American Film*.

Silvia Richards was glimpsed on the front page of the March 26, 1953, *Los Angeles Times* ("Secret Red School Near L.A. Revealed to House Probers") and also on the jump page of the lead story of *The Los Angeles Examiner* ("Former Party Worker Tells Fund Raising Parties Here") of the same date. *Daily Variety*, sans photo, also covered the story of her testimony ("Communist 'Blacklist' of Anti-Red Writers Gets House Probe Airing") on that day.

"The French consider this . . ." is from the Gretchen Berg transcript.

John Houseman is quoted from *Front and Center* (New York: Simon and Schuster, 1979).

Viveca Lindfors is quoted from my interview with her and also from her Southern Methodist University "oral history."

Stewart Granger is quoted from *Sparks Fly Upward* (New York: G. P. Putnam's, 1981).

For background on *Moonfleet*, see also "Views on the Screen Directed by Fritz Lang" by M. A. Schmidt in *The New York Times* of September 3, 1954.

"Why, in Paris, they adore this film . . ." is from the Gretchen Berg transcript.

"A crime out of despair . . ." is from "Fritz Lang Seminar."

Gilbert Adair's *Flickers: An Illustrated Celebration of 100 Years of Cinema* was published by Faber and Faber (London: 1995). Stephen Jenkins is quoted from *Fritz Lang: The Image and The Look* (London: British Film Institute, 1981).

Joan Fontaine is quoted from her Southern Methodist University "oral history."

"Owing to my agent's negligence . . ." is from *The Celluloid Muse*.

"Dark Spring" is discussed in "Lang, director of *M*, Seeks to Escape Net" by Don Ross for the *New York Herald-Tribune* of May 20, 1956.

"The Pearl of Love" treatment is on deposit at the American Heritage Center.

Lang's German "homecoming" was reported in many articles, including "Europa ist immer noch unbequem" by Karena Niehoff in Berlin's *Tagesspiegel*, October 21, 1956.

On the subject of Lang, Henri Langlois, and the Cinémathéque in Paris, I consulted A *Passion for Films: Henri Langlois and the Cinémathéque Française* by Richard Roud (New York: Viking, 1983) and *Henri Langlois: First Citizen of Cinema* by Glenn Myrent and Georges P. Langlois (New York: Twayne, 1994).

"Everyone looks for love . . ." is from "The Monster of Hollywood."

Chapter Twenty: 1957–1964

Artur Brauner is quoted from my interview with him, his autobiography *Mich gibt's nur einmal: Rückblende eines Lebens* (Munich–Berlin: Herbig, 1976), and—especially all citations of correspondence and production memoranda—Claudia Dillman-Kühn's comprehensive *Artur Brauner und die CCC* (Frankfurt am Main: Deutsches Filmmuseum, 1990). See also Brauner's letter to Hamburg's *Die Zeit* of October 21, 1966 ("Fritz Lang war nicht zu bändigen").

Robert Siodmak is quoted from *Zwischen Berlin und Hollywood*, edited by Hans C. Blumenberg (Munich: Herbig, 1980).

One of the key "German comeback" articles was "Fritz Lang bleibt in Deutschland" by Ludwig Maibohm which appeared in *Frankfurter Neue Freie Presse* of February 28, 1958.

Werner Jörg Lüddecke, Volcker Schlöndorff, Paul Hubschmid and Heinz Oskar Wuttig are all quoted from *Trois Lumiéres*.

Jonathan Rosenbaum is quoted from *Placing Movies: The Practice of Film Criticism* (Berkeley, Los Angeles, London: University of California Press, 1995).

"The first difficulty was . . ." and "Except for a few cuts . . ." are from *Trois Lumiéres*.

Roger Greenspun wrote about Lang's third Mabuse film in the March, 1973 *Film Comment*.

"We all know he's difficult . . ." is from Lily Latté's March 12, 1961, letter to PEM.

Most of Lang's unproduced treatments and scenarios are in his USC files. Several of them are reproduced with commentary in Schnauber's *Der Berg der Aberglaubers und andere Geschichten* and in Vol. 2, *Der Tod eines Karrieregirls und andere Gesichten*, also edited with commentary by Schnauber (Vienna: Europaverlag, 1987).

Lang is depicted in Rome in "Flashback: Roman Holiday."

Lang's quotes on Godard and *Contempt* are drawn from "Godard's 'Ghost,' Roman-Style" by Robert F. Hawkins, which appeared in *The New York Times*, June 16, 1964; and "Fritz Lang: 'Contempt' " by Gretchen Berg, from *Take One*, November–December 1968. See also the interview book *Godard on Godard* (London: Secker & Warburg, 1972).

Andrew Sarris's "Films" column about Lang, Godard, and *Contempt* appeared in *The Village Voice* of January 28, 1965, spilling over to the *Voice's* February 4, 1965 issue.

"Fritz Lang's Career Girl" was synopsized and analyzed by David Overbey in *Sight and Sound* of Autumn, 1975.

Lang's remarks at Cannes are translated from *Trois Lumiéres*.

Chapter Twenty-One: 1965–1976

Schnauber's *Fritz Lang in Hollywood* offers a good deal of sympathetic information and observations about Lang's twilight years, treating, in addition, the dispersal of the estate.

"Sci-Fi Filmmaker's Debt to Rocket Man Willy Ley" by Lang appeared in the *Los Angeles Times* of July 27, 1969.

Edward G. Robinson is quoted from his autobiography *All My Yesterdays* (New York: Hawthorn, 1973).

The Lang-Eisner correspondence is quoted from Schnauber's *Fritz Lang in Hollywood* and from Eisner's *Ich hatte einst ein schönes Vaterland—Memoiren*. The director's itemized list of corrections to the *Fritz Lang* manuscript also comes from Eisner's autobiography.

"Where is home for a man like me . . ." is from "Fritz Lang Still a Film Perfectionist" by Mary Blume in the May 2, 1969, *Los Angeles Times*.

"He had an incredible amount of time . . ." is Peter Hajek quoted from an interview with Clare Beresford.

Lang revealed his hurt feelings about Berlin in his July 21, 1971 letter to PEM.

Paul Jensen's report, "Fritz Lang's 'Act' A Hit With Buffs" appeared in the December 27, 1967, issue of *Variety*. Later, Jensen wrote one of the first English-language books about Lang's work, the satisfactory *The Films of Fritz Lang* (London: Zwemmer, 1969).

"Now that I have practically . . ." is from *The Films of Fritz Lang*.

"All of my German films . . ." is from *The Films of Fritz Lang*.

Lang's relationship with Luis Buñuel comes from Eisner's autobiography as well as John Baxter's biography *Buñuel* (London: Fourth Estate, 1994). I am also grateful to the ever-erudite and obliging Baxter for supplying me with a copy of his transcribed interview with Jean-Claude Carriére, commenting on Lang's meeting with Buñuel.

"Lang's best audience and living encylopedia . . ." is from Axel Madsen's "Lang."

"Thank you very much for the greetings . . ." is from Karin Obholzer's "Fritz Lang, der berühmte Verwandter."

The Joan Bennett tape-recording is among Lang's USC deposits.

"Sometimes I wonder . . ." is from "Director Fritz Lang Turns 85" by Kevin Thomas in the *Los Angeles Times*, December 5, 1975. See also "Fritz Lang to Mark Birthday" by Thomas in *Los Angeles Times*, December 5, 1970.

Copies of the "Last Will and Testament of Fritz Lang" (dated March 21, 1975) and "Last Will and Testament of Lily Latté" (dated September 14, 1984) were supplied to the author by Geoffrey Gilchrist, the USC-appointed executor of the Lang–Latté estate.